AF776126

ACCOUNTABILITY FOR HUMAN RIGHTS VIOLATIONS BY INTERNATIONAL ORGANISATIONS

Jan Wouters
Eva Brems
Stefaan Smis
Pierre Schmitt
(eds.)

intersentia
Antwerp – Cambridge – Portland

Distribution for the UK:
Hart Publishing Ltd.
16C Worcester Place
Oxford OX1 2JW
UK
Tel.: +44 1865 51 75 30
Email: mail@hartpub.co.uk

Distribution for the USA and Canada:
International Specialized Book Services
920 NE 58th Ave. Suite 300
Portland, OR 97213
USA
Tel.: +1 800 944 6190 (toll free)
Tel.: +1 503 287 3093
Email: info@isbs.com

Distribution for Austria:
Neuer Wissenschaftlicher Verlag
Argentinierstraße 42/6
1040 Wien
Austria
Tel.: +43 1 535 61 03 24
Email: office@nwv.at

Distribution for other countries:
Intersentia Publishers
Groenstraat 31
2640 Mortsel
Belgium
Tel.: +32 3 680 15 50
Email: mail@intersentia.be

Accountability for Human Rights Violations by International Organisations
Jan Wouters, Eva Brems, Stefaan Smis and Pierre Schmitt (eds.)

© 2010 Intersentia, the editors and the authors
Antwerp – Cambridge – Portland
www.intersentia.com

ISBN 978-1-78068-066-8
NUR 828

No part of this book may be reproduced in any form, by print, photoprint, microfilm or any other means, without written permission from the publisher.

SUMMARY OF CONTENTS

CONTENTS

PART III. INTERNATIONAL CIVIL ADMINISTRATION

PART IV. ECONOMIC GOVERNANCE

ABBREVIATIONS

ADB	Asian Development Bank
ADL	Anti-Discrimination Law
AMIS	African Union Mission in Sudan
AMISOM	African Union Mission in Somalia
ARV	Antiretroviral Drug
ASR	Articles on State Responsibility
ATCA	Alien Tort Claims Act
BverfG	Bundesverfassungsgericht
CCA	Common Country Assessment
CEDAW	Convention on the Elimination of All Forms of Discrimination against Women
CERD	Convention on the Elimination of All Forms of Racial Discrimination
CESCR	Committee on Economic, Social and Cultural Rights
CIL	Coal India Limited
CIVPOL	Civilian Police
CoE	Council of Europe
CONOPS	Concepts of Operations
CPT	European Committee for the Prevention of Torture and Inhuman or Degrading Treatment or Punishment
CRC	United Nations Convention on the Rights of the Child
DRC	Democratic Republic of Congo
DSU	Dispute Settlement Understanding
EAP	Environmental Action Plan
EC	European Community
ECHR	European Convention for the Protection of Human Rights and Fundamental Freedoms
ECJ	European Court of Justice
ECommHR	European Commission on Human Rights
ECtHR	European Court of Human Rights
ELDO	European Launcher Development Organization
EPZ	Export Processing Zone
ERRC	European Roma Rights Centre
EU	European Union
EULEX	European Union Rule of Law Mission in Kosovo

FAO	Food and Agriculture Organization of the United Nations
FIAN	Food First Information and Action Network
GATT	General Agreement on Tariffs and Trade
GSP	General System of Preferences
HPCC	Housing and Property Claims Commission
HPD	Housing and Property Directorate
HRC	Human Rights Committee
IACHR	Inter-American Commission on Human Rights
IACtHR	Inter-American Court of Human Rights
IAT	International Administrative Tribunal
IBRD	International Bank for Reconstruction and Development
ICC	International Criminal Court
ICCPR	International Covenant on Civil and Political Rights
ICESCR	International Covenant on Economic, Social and Cultural Rights
ICFTU	International Confederation of Free Trade Unions
ICJ	International Court of Justice
ICRC	International Committee of the Red Cross
ICTR	International Criminal Tribunal for Rwanda
ICTY	International Criminal Tribunal for the Former Yugoslavia
IDA	International Development Association
IFC	International Finance Corporation
IFI	International Financial Institution
IHL	International Humanitarian Law
ILA	International Law Association
ILC	International Law Commission
ILO	International Labour Organization
IMF	International Monetary Fund
IMP	Independent Monitoring Panel
INBAR	International Network for Bamboo and Rattan
INTERFET	International Force in East Timor
IP	Intellectual Property
IPR	Intellectual Property Right
IPTF	International Police Task Force
ISAF	International Security Assistance Force
ITA	International Territorial Administration
KFOR	Kosovo Force
KPS	Kosovo Police Service
LDC	Least Developed Country
LNT	Administrative Tribunal of the League of Nations
LOAC	Law of Armed Conflict
LSMS	Legal System Monitoring Section

MDB	Multilateral Development Bank
MFN	Most Favoured Nation
MINUSTAH	United Nations Stabilisation Mission in Haiti
MONUC	United Nations Organization Mission in the Democratic Republic of the Congo
MoU	Memorandum of understanding
MSU	Multinational Specialised Units
NAFTA	North American Free Trade Agreement
NATO	North Atlantic Treaty Organization
NFTC	National Foreign Trade Council
NHRC	National Human Rights Commission
OAS	Organization of American States
OCTA	US Omnibus Trade and Competitiveness Act
OECD	Organization for Economic Co-operation and Development
OHR	Office of the High Representative
OIK	Ombudsperson Institution for Kosovo
OIOS	Office of International Oversight Services
OPCW	Organisation for the Prohibition of Chemical Weapons
OPLAN	NATO Operation Plan
OSCE	Organization for Security and Co-operation in Europe
OTCA	Omnibus Trade and Competitiveness Act
PAP	Project-affected person
PIC	Peace Implementation Council
PIFWC	Person Indicted For War Crimes
PIK	Police Inspectorate of Kosovo
PISG	Provisional Institutions for Self Government
PRDSS	Property with Designated Special Status
R&R	Resettlement and Rehabilitation
ROE	Rules of Engagement
SC-SL	Special Court for Sierra Leone
S&DT	Special and Differential Treatment
SEZ	Special Economic Zone
SOFA	Status of Forces Agreement
SOMA	Status of Mission Agreement
SOP	Standing Operating Procedure
SRSG	Special Representative of the Secretary General
STANAG	Standardization Agreement
TEC	Treaty establishing the European Community
TEU	Treaty on European Union
TFEU	Treaty on the Functioning of the European Union
TPRM	Trade Policy Review Mechanism
TRIPs	Agreement on Trade-Related Aspects of Intellectual Property

UDHR	Universal Declaration of Human Rights
UN	United Nations
UNAMA	United Nations Assistance Mission in Afghanistan
UNAMET	United Nations Assistance Mission in East Timor
UNAMI	United Nations Assistance Mission for Iraq
UNAMID	United Nations – African Union Mission in Darfur
UNAT	United Nations Administrative Tribunal
UNDAF	United Nations Development Assistance Framework
UNDP	United Nations Development Programme
UNEF	United Nations Emergency Force
UNESCO	United Nations Educational, Scientific and Cultural Organization
UNFICYP	United Nations Peacekeeping Force in Cyprus
UNHCR	United Nations High Commissioner for Refugees
UNICEF	United Nations Children's Fund
UNIFIL	United Nations Interim Force in Lebanon
UNOMIG	United Nations Observer Mission in Georgia
UNMIBH	United Nations Mission in Bosnia and Herzegovina
UNMIK	United Nations Interim Administration Mission in Kosovo
UNMIS	United Nations Mission in Sudan
UNOSOM	United Nations Operation in Somalia
UNPROFOR	United Nations Protection Force
UNTAET	United Nations Transitional Administration in East Timor
UNTAG	United Nations Transition Assistance Group
WBAT	World Bank Administrative Tribunal
WHO	World Health Organization
WTO	World Trade Organization

ACCOUNTABILITY FOR HUMAN RIGHTS VIOLATIONS BY INTERNATIONAL ORGANISATIONS: INTRODUCTORY REMARKS

Jan WOUTERS, Eva BREMS, Stefaan SMIS and Pierre SCHMITT

I. BACKGROUND

On 16–17 March 2007, an international conference on the theme of the present volume was organised in Brussels to mark the first issue of the journal *Human Rights & International Legal Discourse*. A selection of contributions presented at the conference has been published in the journal[1], while other papers including the keynotes have been adapted and are included in the present book, in addition to new contributions. The further conceptualisation of this book, the painstaking editing process, the collection of additional contributions, the updating of many chapters in liaison with the authors and the writing of a number of additional chapters, including the present editorial introduction, took place as part of an ongoing inter-university project between the Universities of Leuven (Katholieke Universiteit Leuven), Brussels (Vrije Universiteit Brussel) and Ghent (Universiteit Gent) funded by the Fonds Wetenschappelijk Onderzoek – Vlaanderen. We are grateful to the Fonds Wetenschappelijk Onderzoek – Vlaanderen, the Vlaamse Interuniversitaire Raad – University Development Cooperation, the Cabinet of the Minister of Foreign Affairs of Belgium, the Royal Flemish Academy of Belgium for Sciences and Arts, the Minister of External Relations of the Brussels Capital Region, and our universities for their support.

II. AIM OF THE BOOK

The present book is designed to explore the mechanisms through which accountability can be realised for violations of human rights committed by, or attributable to, international organisations and their staff. The subject is at the

[1] See 1 *Human Rights & International Legal Discourse* 2 (2007) pp. 211–441.

intersection between human rights law, public international law and the law of international organisations. It profoundly affects some of the basic tenets and doctrines of the latter legal arena.

Some may consider the theme of the book far-fetched. How could one imagine international organisations violating human rights? Have they not been set up by their Member States with the purpose of contributing to the provision of global or regional public goods and does this not imply that they generally protect and promote, rather than violate, human rights? Some international organisations and bodies have even specifically been established to protect and promote human rights. One may think of regional human rights courts with great achievements, such as the European Court of Human Rights and the Inter-American Court of Human Rights, and of the plurality of bodies, committees and offices set up in the framework of the United Nations (UN), from the UN Human Rights Council to the treaty bodies that monitor the respect for the global human rights treaties and the Office of the High Commissioner for Human Rights. The UN itself is a prominent example of an international organisation which, from its inception in 1945, not only 'reaffirm[ed] faith in fundamental human rights'[2] but has as one of its primary objectives 'promoting and encouraging respect for human rights and for fundamental freedoms for all'[3], including promoting such respect and observance of human rights at a universal level.[4] Many other international organisations, particularly also regional ones (e.g. the European Union (EU), the African Union (AU) and the Organization of American States (OAS)), include human rights protection among their primary or accessory goals.

One should note that international organisations have proliferated enormously (currently their number is well over 500)[5] and over the years they have unfolded an unprecedented scope and intensity of activities in a wide range of policy fields. This expansion may be explained by the need for collective action to face global and regional problems: international organisations provide a means to institutionalise inter-State cooperation.[6] International organisations are frequently intervening in peace-keeping operations and military action. They sometimes even exercise administrative powers over territories. Many of them are heavily involved in international policy-making and/or standard-setting. Together

2 Third recital of the preamble of the Charter of the United Nations (UN Charter).

3 Art. 1(3) UN Charter; see also Art. 13(1)(a) (General Assembly), Art. 62(2) (ECOSOC), Art. 76(c) (trusteeship system).

4 Art. 55(c) UN Charter.

5 C.F. Amerasinghe, *Principles of the Institutional Law of International Organizations*, 2nd edn. (Cambridge, Cambridge University Press 1996) p. 6.

6 J.-M. Coicaud, 'International organisations, the evolution of international politics, and legitimacy', in J.-M. Coicaud and V. Heiskanen, eds., *The Legitimacy of International Organisations* (Tokyo/New York/Paris, United Nations University Press 2001) p. 545.

with an increasing impact of the activities of international organisations on the lives of people around the world, inevitably situations multiply in which human rights (political, civil, but also economic, cultural and social) may be threatened or violated through the actions, operations or policies of such organisations.

Since international organisations exercise important aspects of public authority and even act as substitute for States in some instances, an efficient accountability system has to be created in order to review the decisions made and to sanction any misconduct, similarly to the checks and balances established to control democratic governments. As observed by Thomas Hammarberg, the Council of Europe's Commissioner for Human Rights, 'an international accountability deficit is no good for anyone, least of all the local population. No one, especially an international organisation, is above the law.'[7]

The theme of responsibility of international organisations has progressively gained the attention of legal scholars[8] and international bodies in the past two decades. Especially the work of the International Law Commission (ILC) and of the International Law Association (ILA) should be mentioned in this respect.

The ILC decided to include the topic in its work programme in 2000.[9] Two years later, it established a Working Group and appointed a Special Rapporteur,

---

7 T. Hammarberg, Council of Europe Commissioner for Human Rights, 'International Organisations acting as quasi-governments should be held accountable', 8 June 2009, also available at the Commissioner's website at www.commissioner.coe.int.

8 See *inter alia,* H.G. Schermers, 'Liability of International organisations', *Leiden Journal of International Law* (1988) pp. 3–14; P. Klein, *La responsabilité des organisations internationales dans les ordres juridiques internes et en droit des gens* (Bruxelles, Bruylant 1998); R. Higgins, 'The Responsibility of States Members for the Defaults of International Organizations: Continuing the Dialogue', in S. Schlemmer-Schulte and K.-Y. Tunk, eds., *Liber Amicorum I.F.I. Shihata. International Finance and Development Law* (The Hague/London/Boston/New York, Kluwer Law International 2001) pp. 441–448; A. Reinisch, 'Governance without Accountability?', *German Yearbook of International Law* (2001) pp. 270–306; A. Reinisch, 'Securing the Accountability of International Organisations', 7 *Global Governance* (2001) pp. 131–149; I. Seidl-Hohenveldern, 'Liability of Member States for Acts or Omissions of an International Organization', in S. Schlemmer Schulte and K.-Y. Tunk, eds., op. cit. in this note, pp. 727–739; K. Wellens, *Remedies against International Organisations* (Cambridge, Cambridge University Press 2002); K. Wellens, 'Accountability of International organisations: Some Salient Features', 97 *American Society of International Law Proceedings* (2003) pp. 241–245; K. Wellens, W.E. Holder and G. Hafner, 'Can International organisations be controlled? Accountability and Responsibility', 97 *American Society of International Law Proceedings* (2003) pp. 236–240; K. Wellens, 'Fragmentation of International Law and Establishing an Accountability Regime for International organisations: The Role of the Judiciary in Closing The Gap', 25(4) *Michigan Journal of International Law* (2004) pp. 1159–1181; S. Yee, 'The Responsibility of States Member of an International Organisation for its Conduct as a Result of Membership or Their Normal Conduct Associated with Membership', in M. Ragazzi, ed., *International Responsibility Today. Essays in Memory of Oscar Schachter* (Leiden/Boston, Martinus Nijhoff Publishers 2005) pp. 436–454.

9 ILC, *Report of its fifty-second session, 1 May to 9 June and 10 July to 18 August 2000*, UN Doc. A/55/10, pp. 135 *et seq.*

Professor Giorgio Gaja.[10] From its fifty-fifth (2003) to its sixty-first (2009) sessions, the ILC has received seven reports[11] from the Special Rapporteur and provisionally adopted draft articles 1 to 66.[12] According to draft article 3, '[e]very internationally wrongful act of an international organization entails the international responsibility of the international organization.' Draft article 4 provides that '[t]here is an internationally wrongful act of an international organization when conduct consisting of an action or omission: (*a*) [i]s attributable to the international organization under international law; and (*b*) [c]onstitutes a breach of an international obligation of that international organization.' The ongoing process of ILC work has permitted one to take into consideration the comments made by States and international organisations on the draft articles provisionally adopted by the ILC and to consequently make amendments thereto. For instance, in the 2006 report, draft article 28(1) went as follows: '[a] State member of an international organisation incurs international responsibility if it circumvents one of its international obligations by providing the organization with competence in relation to that obligation, and the organization commits an act that, if committed by that State, would have constituted a breach of that obligation.'[13] In 2009, the ILC substantially modified the provision and proposed draft article 60(1), which no longer links State responsibility to the conferral of powers to an international organisation:

> 'A State member of an international organization incurs international responsibility if it seeks to avoid complying with one of its own international obligations by taking advantage of the fact that the organization has competence in relation to the subject matter of that obligation, thereby prompting the organization to commit an act that, if committed by the State, would have constituted a breach of the obligation.'[14]

Partly prior to and parallel with the work of the ILC on the responsibility of international organisations, another important attempt in this area was made by the ILA. It established a specific Committee in 1996 to study the accountability of international organisations. The ILA Committee took a broader approach than the one taken by the ILC. Whereas the ILC only focuses on the responsibility towards Member and Non-Member States[15], the 'recommended rules and practices' of the

---

10 ILC, *Report of its fifty-fourth session, 29 April to 7 June and 22 July to 16 August 2002*, UN Doc. A/57/10, pp. 228 *et seq.*

11 See http://untreaty.un.org/ilc/guide/9_11.htm.

12 ILC, *Report of the sixty-first session 4 May to 5 June and 6 July to 7 August 2009*, UN Doc. A/64/10, chapter IV, paras. 31–51.

13 See, with commentary, ILC, *Report of the Fifty-eighth session, 1 May to 9 June and 3 July to 11 August 2006*, UN Doc. A/61/10, p. 283.

14 ILC, *Report of the sixty-first session, 4 May to 5 June and 6 July to 7 August 2009*, UN Doc. A/64/10, p. 38.

15 ILC, *Report of its fifty-fourth session, 29 April to 7 June and 22 July to 16 August 2002*, UN Doc. A/57/10, p. 229.

ILA Committee cover the accountability of an international organisation towards their members and third parties[16], i.e. 'victims or wrongdoers who are not members of the [international organisation] concerned: states, other [international organisation]s, individuals or legal persons, including private entities'.[17] Moreover, the ILA Committee focused on the 'accountability of international organisations', which is a broader concept than their responsibility. According to the final report of the ILA Committee published in 2004, '[a]ccountability of [international organisation]s is a multifaceted phenomenon. The form under which accountability will arise will be determined by the particular circumstances surrounding the acts or omissions of an [international organisation], its member States or third parties. These forms may be legal, political, administrative or financial. A combination of the four forms provides the best chances of achieving the necessary degree of accountability.'[18] The concept of accountability is thoroughly analysed by Ige F. Dekker in Chapter 2 of this book.

III. CONTENTIOUS LEGAL ISSUES

A. ARE INTERNATIONAL ORGANISATIONS BOUND BY INTERNATIONAL HUMAN RIGHTS NORMS?

As a preliminary to the analysis of the accountability of an international organisation for human rights violations, the binding character of international human rights law has to be assessed in regard to international organisations, which – with one exception for the EU[19] – are not bound as signatories by any human rights treaty.[20]

---

16 ILA, *Report of the seventy-first conference, Berlin 2004* (London, International Law Association 2004), p. 4.

17 *Ibid.*, p. 20.

18 ILA, *Report of the seventy-first conference, Berlin 2004* (London, International Law Association 2004), p. 5. Footnotes omitted.

19 Reference is made to the UN Convention on the rights of persons with disabilities, to which the EU (prior to the entry into force of the Treaty of Lisbon: the EC) is a signatory. It should also be noted that the Treaty of Lisbon (Treaty of Lisbon amending the Treaty on European Union and the Treaty establishing the European Community, Lisbon, 13 December 2007, *O.J. C* 306 (17 December 2007); consolidated versions of the Treaty on European Union (TEU) and the Treaty on the Functioning of the European Union (TFEU) as they are amended by the Lisbon Treaty are published in *O.J. C* 85 (30 March 2010)) empowers the EU to accede to the European Convention for the Protection of Human Rights and Fundamental Freedoms: Art. 6(2) Treaty on European Union. Accession by the EU has become possible from the point of view of the Council of Europe now that Protocol No 14 (Protocol No. 14 to the Convention for the Protection of Human Rights and Fundamental Freedoms, amending the control system of the Convention, done at Strasbourg 14 May 2004 (CETS No. 194, entered into force on 1 June 2010) inserts Art. 59(2) into the Convention, enabling the EU to accede to the latter.

20 A. Reinisch, 'Developing Human Rights and Humanitarian Law Accountability of the Security Council for the Imposition of Economic Sanctions', 95(4) *American Journal of*

Indeed, the international human rights legal framework is generally designed for States. But does this mean that international organisations are not bound by any international human rights norms? This question necessitates, in the first place, a query into the international legal personality of the international organisation at hand[21] and the legal consequences flowing from its status as a subject of international law.[22] If their independent personality is recognised, international organisations will be held internationally responsible for their acts in case of a violation of an applicable international norm.[23]

The aforementioned question also begs another fundamental issue, namely the extent to which international human rights norms not only belong to established rules of treaty law, but also form part of customary international law and/or general principles of international law.[24] Although there seems to be a convergence of views on the obligation of international organisations to respect at least *some* human rights[25], controversies persist, notably as to the identification of sources of this obligation and its scope. For several authors, this obligation rests on the customary status of international human rights. The massive adoption and continuous affirmation of the fundamental human rights listed in the Universal Declaration of Human Rights (UDHR)[26] have, so it is submitted, transformed these rules – or at least some of them – into customary international law.[27] As

International Law (2001) p. 854; A. Clapham, *Human Rights Obligations of Non-State Actors* (Oxford, Oxford University Press 2006) p. 91.

21 ICJ, *Reparation for Injuries Suffered in the Service of the United Nations*, Advisory Opinion, *ICJ Rep.* (1949) pp. 173–219. The international legal personality of international organisations has given rise to heated debates among scholars. See notably J. Klabbers, *An Introduction to International Institutional Law* (Cambridge, Cambridge University Press 2009) pp. 46–52; N.D. White, *The law of international organisations*, 2nd edn. (Manchester, Manchester University Press 2005), pp. 30–70. Nigel D. White notably examines international organisations which have no international legal personality, such as the Organization for Security and Co-operation in Europe (OSCE).

22 ICJ, *Interpretation of the Agreement of 25 March 1991 between the WHO and Egypt*, Advisory Opinion, *ICJ Rep.* (1980) p. 73.

23 Apart from the ongoing work of the ILC in this area and the final report published by the ILA in 2004, op. cit. n. 16, see the references mentioned *supra* in footnote 8.

24 See O. De Schutter, Chapter 4.

25 T. Meron, *Human Rights and Humanitarian Norms as Customary Law* (Oxford, Clarendon Press 1989) pp. 94–96; H. Hannum, 'The Status of the Universal Declaration of Human Rights in National and International Law', 25 *Georgia Journal of International and Comparative Law* (1995–1996) pp. 287–395; C. Tomuschat, *Human Rights: Between Idealism and Realism Actors* (Oxford, Oxford University Press 2003) p. 4; T. Ahmed and I. de Jesús Butler, 'The European Union and Human Rights: an International Legal Perspective', 17(4) *European Journal of International Law* (2006) pp. 771–801; J. Wouters and C. Ryngaert, 'Impact on the Process of the Formation of Customary International Law', in M.T. Kamminga and M. Scheinin, eds., *The Impact of Human Rights Law on General International Law* (Oxford, Oxford University Press 2008) pp. 111–131.

26 UN General Assembly, Resolution A/217 (III), *Universal Declaration of Human Rights*, UN Doc. A/RES/3/217 A, 10 December 1948.

27 See notably H. Hannun, loc. cit. n. 25, at p. 322; C. Tomuschat, op. cit. n. 25, at p. 4.

customary international law applies to all subjects of international law, it is clear that such customary human rights norms are also binding upon international organisations.[28] Other authors consider that human rights have become general principles of international law through the medium of the 'general principles of law recognized by civilized nations' mentioned in Article 38(1)(c) of the Statute of the International Court of Justice.[29] Such general principles would not require State practice bur rather result from 'a variety of ways in which moral and humanitarian considerations find a more direct and spontaneous "expression in legal form".'[30] Moreover, some provisions of human rights law – such as the prohibition of racial discrimination – are considered as norms of *jus cogens*.[31] It is generally admitted that peremptory rules bind international organisations.[32]

Nevertheless, if obligations there are, their scope and content need to be clarified. In addition to the obligation to respect human rights, the question must be raised whether international organisations with no specific mandate in the area of human rights bear an obligation to protect, report on or monitor human rights. This question has been fiercely debated in relation to international development actors, such as the international financial institutions (IFIs) or the United Nations Development Program (UNDP). Let us take a closer look at these bodies in order to better gauge the debate and its sensitivities.

Human Rights are not mentioned in the Articles of Agreement of the International Monetary Fund (IMF), of the International Bank for Reconstruction and Development (IBRD) and the International Development Association (IDA). At the IMF, this has been interpreted as indicating that the organisation has no mandate to promote human rights.[33] At the World Bank, former General

28 H.G. Schermers, 'The Legal Bases of International Organization Action', in R.-J. Dupuy, ed., *Manuel sur les organisations internationales – A Handbook on International Organizations* (Dordrecht/Boston/London, Martinus Nijhoff Publishers 1998) p. 402; C. Tomuschat, 'International Law: Ensuring the Survival of Mankind on the Eve of a New Century: General Course on Public International Law', 281 *Recueil des Cours de l'Académie de Droit International* (2001) pp. 134–135

29 See B. Simma and P. Alston, 'The Sources of Human Rights Law: Custom, Jus Cogens, and General Principles', 12 *Australian Yearbook of International Law* (1988–1989) p. 82, at pp. 102–108.

30 *Ibid.*, at p. 105.

31 B. Kondoch, 'Human Rights Law and UN Peace Operations in Post-Conflict Situations', in N.D. White and D. Klaasen, eds., *The UN, Human Rights and Post-Conflict Situations*, (Manchester, Manchester University Press 2005) p. 36.

32 H.G. Schermers, loc. cit. n. 28, at p. 402.

33 G.B. Taplin, 'Speaking Points: Globalization and its Impacts on the Full Enjoyment of Human Rights', Speech to Sub-Commission on the Promotion and Protection of Human Rights, 8 August 2001, available at www.unhchr.ch/huricane/huricane.nsf/view01/7A33AABB095C5 1F3C1256AA300282C86; see also G. Capdevila, 'IMF Not Taking into Account Human Rights Issues', 13 August 2001, available at www.globalpolicy.org/component/content/article/209/42944.html. Internet pages last visited on 3 March 2010.

Counsel R. Dañino acknowledged that 'human rights and international human rights law have become increasingly relevant to helping the Bank achieve its mission and fulfil its purposes' and that 'it is now evident that human rights are an intrinsic part of the Bank's mission.' Yet, he added that the role of the Bank (and by extension, the Fund) 'is not that of an enforcer of human rights obligations.' Indeed, enforcement 'is primarily the responsibility of member countries and of other, non-financial entities, such as the United Nations treaty monitoring bodies and regional human rights organizations.'[34]

The relationship between IFIs and human rights has been discussed at length by scholars.[35] Some authors suggest that international financial institutions should have with respect to human rights generally a 'duty of vigilance' to ensure that their actions have no negative effects on the human rights situation in their borrowing members.[36] Others go further and consider that the IFIs' substantial influence over borrowing countries make it 'increasingly untenable that the IFIs should function without human rights responsibilities within their spheres of influence, and without accountability for the impact of their economic decisions on the exercise of human rights.'[37]

34 R. Dañino, 'Legal Opinion on Human Rights and the Work of the World Bank by the Senior Vice-President and General Counsel', 27 January 2006, available at www.ifiwatchnet.org/sites/ifiwatchnet.org/files/DaninoLegalOpinion0106.pdf.

35 See *inter alia* D.D. Bradlow, 'The World Bank, the IMF, and human rights', *Transnational Law & Contemporary Problems* (1996) pp. 47–90; J.A. Fox and C.D. Brown, eds., *The Struggle for Accountability, The World Bank, NGOs and Grassroots Movements* (Cambridge, MIT Press 1998); D.L. Clark, 'The World Bank and Human Rights: The Need for Greater Accountability', *15 Harvard Human Rights Journal* (2002) pp. 205–226; S.I. Skogly, *The Human Rights Obligations of the World Bank and the International Monetary Fund* (London, Cavendish 2001); M. Darrow, *Between Light and Shadow: the World Bank, the International Monetary Fund and International Human Rights Law* (Oxford, Hart Publishing 2003); W. van Genugten, P. Hunt and S. Mathews, eds., *World Bank, IMF and Human Rights* (Nijmegen, Wolf Legal Publishers 2003); B. Carin and A. Wood, eds., *Accountability of the International Monetary Fund* (Ottawa, Ashgate and the International Development Research Centre 2005); B. Ghazi, *The IMF, the World Bank Group and the Question of Human Rights* (Ardsley, Transnational 2005); K. De Feyter, 'The International Financial Institutions and Human Rights: Law and Practice', in F. Gómez and K. De Feyter, eds., *International Protection of Human Rights: Achievements and Challenges* (Bilbao, University of Deusto 2006) pp. 561–592; R. Dañino, 'The Legal Aspects of the World Bank's Work on Human Rights: Some Preliminary Thoughts', in A. Palacio, C. Sage and S. Woolcock, eds., *The World Bank Legal Review: Law, Equity and Development,* vol. 2 (Leiden/Boston, Martinus Nijhoff Publishers 2006) pp. 295–324; D. Kinley, 'Human Rights and the World Bank: Practice, Politics and Law', in A. Palacio, C. Sage and S. Woolcock, eds., *The World Bank Legal Review: Law, Equity and Development,* vol. 2 (Leiden/Boston, Martinus Nijhoff Publishers 2006) pp. 353–383; L. Boisson de Chazournes, 'The Bretton Woods Institutions and Human Rights: Converging Tendencies', in W. Benedek, K. De Feyter and F. Marella, eds., *Economic Globalisation and Human Rights* (Cambridge, Cambridge University Press 2007) pp. 210–263.

36 P. Klein, 'La responsabilité des organisations financières internationales et les droits de la personne', *Revue Belge de Droit International* (1999) p. 97.

37 M.E. Salomon, 'International Economic Governance and Human rights Accountability', in M.E. Salomon, A. Tostensen and W. Vandenhole, eds., *Casting the Net Wider: Human rights, Development and New Duty-Bearers* (Antwerp, Intersentia 2007) p. 27.

In a recent study on the impact of structural adjustment programmes on human rights in 131 developing countries between 1981 and 2003, R. Abouharb and D. Cingranelli concluded that 'equitable economic development efforts would be more efficient and many of the negative impacts of World Bank and IMF loans and grants would be mitigated or eliminated if the IFIs pursued a human-rights based strategy of development assistance.'[38] Despite this external pressure, the IFIs maintain their suspicion towards human rights and show reluctance to integrate them in their operations.[39]

Another important development actor is the UNDP, which works with 166 countries in order to achieve progress in development. At the UN World Summit of 2005, heads of government recognised that peace and security, development and human rights are the three interlinked and mutually reinforcing pillars of the UN system.[40] Despite this consensus, the relationship between human rights and development has been subject to disagreement between UN Member States. Indeed, both within the General Assembly Triennial Comprehensive Policy Review (TCPR) process and the General Assembly's System-wide Coherence (SWC) process, Member States diverged on the place of human rights in UN development activities. The G-77 and China expressed their concern about the inordinate emphasis given to human rights in UN development activities. The Group feared a discrimination against developing countries if human rights were to be considered as UN development objectives. Human rights 'could be misused to introduce new conditionalities on international development assistance. This is not acceptable to the developing countries.'[41] Similar arguments were raised within the UNDP Executive Board discussions on the UNDP strategic plan 2008–2011. The final strategic plan states that 'while UNDP should uphold universal United

---

38 R. Abouharb and D. Cingranelli, *Human Rights and Structural Adjustment* (Cambridge, Cambridge University Press 2008) p. 13.

39 G.A. Sarfaty considers that human rights are a marginal issue at the World Bank because of the organisational culture of the latter. 'Human rights are a particularly difficult set of norms to incorporate into an economic institution because doing so forces employees into a struggle between principles and pragmatism – that is, it creates a tension between normative, intangible values and goals, and practical ways to solve problems (which may make it necessary to reconcile competing principles). In an environment like the Bank where most issues are subject to cost-benefit analysis, employees may be ambivalent about principles that appear to be non-negotiable or subject to trade-offs. They may perceive potential costs in trying to render seemingly incommensurable values commensurate.' G.A. Sarfaty, 'Why Culture Matters in International Institutions: The Marginality of Human Rights at the World Bank', 103 *American Journal of International Law* (2009) pp. 647–683.

40 UN General Assembly, '2005 World Summit Outcome', UN Doc. A/Res. 60/1 (2005), paras 9 and 72; see also UN General Assembly, 'Human Rights Council', UN Doc. A/Res. 60/251 (2006), sixth recital; UN General Assembly, 'The Role of the United Nations in Promoting a New Global Human Order', UN Doc. A/Res. 62/213 (2008), second recital.

41 M. Akram, Statement on behalf of the Group of 77 and China at the operational activities segment of the 2007 substantive session of the ECOSOC, 12 July 2007, available at www.g77.org/statement/getstatement.php?id=070712.

Nations norms and standards, including those related to human rights, UNDP does not have any normative or monitoring role with regard to human rights.'[42] Yet, the terms 'normative' or 'monitoring role' have not been defined in the plan.[43]

B. ACCOUNTABILITY OF MEMBER STATES OF INTERNATIONAL ORGANISATIONS

Next to the accountability of international organisations themselves, the question arises whether Member States are or remain accountable for violations of human rights attributed to the international organisation of which they are a member. If one recognises that international organisations are bound by international human rights norms, the accountability for acts of the international organisation relies exclusively on the international organisation itself, and not on its Member States. However, it can be argued that a 'piercing of the veil' is or should be possible[44], since it would prevent Member States from evading their obligations in acting through the international organisation.[45] Such piercing of the veil would permit either holding top officials and/or collaborators of the organisations personally liable for human rights violations, and/or reaching (some of) the Member States that are behind the decisions in question that result in human rights violations.

The evasion by Member States of their obligations by acting (in one way or another) through international organisations constitutes an abuse of the legal personality of an international organisation. Moreover, situations can and do occur where Member States take advantage of their prerogatives as laid down in the constitutional act of the international organisation. If violations of human rights result from such behaviour of a Member State (or a number of Member States) that – based on its (or their) prerogatives in the decision-making process of the international organisation at hand (for example the veto right within the Security Council) – forces through a decision, should there not at least be the possibility for a concurrent accountability of this (these) Member State(s)?[46]

42 Executive Board of the UNDP and the United Nations Population Fund, ' UNDP Strategic Plan 2008–2011, Accelerating Global Progress on Human Development', UN Doc. DP/2007/43/Rev.1, 22 May 2008.

43 For a comprehensive analysis of the relation between human rights and UNDP, see M. Darrow and L. Arbour, 'The Pillar of Glass: Human Rights in the Development Operations of the United Nations', 103 *American Journal of International Law* (2009) pp. 446–501.

44 C. Brölmann, *The Institutional Veil in Public International Law. International Organisations and the Law of Treaties* (Amsterdam, Oxford, Hart Publishing 2007) pp. 262–267.

45 M. Hirsch, *The Responsibility of International Organizations Toward Third Parties: Some Basic Principles* (Dordrecht-Boston-London, Martinus Nijhoff Publishers 1995) p. 170.

46 See J. d'Aspremont, 'The Limits of the exclusive responsibility of international organizations', 1(2) *Human Rights & International Legal Discourse* (2007) pp. 217–229; J. d'Aspremont, 'Abuse of the Legal Personality of International organisations and the Responsibility of Member States', *International Organisations Law Review* (2007) pp. 91–119.

A way of ensuring that Member States do not evade their obligations by acting through international organisations would be to consider that international organisations are bound by the treaties that bind their Member States. Frederik Naert thoroughly analyses this question in chapter 5 of this book.[47] Moreover, the ILC has integrated the topic of Member States seeking to avoid compliance in its draft article 60, provisionally adopted in 2009 and mentioned *supra*, II.[48]

C. OBSTACLES TO ACCOUNTABILITY OF INTERNATIONAL ORGANISATIONS

Even if recognised in principle, accountability of international organisations for human rights violations faces difficult obstacles in practice. There is no international court that generally has jurisdiction over international organisations. Moreover, national courts may not adjudicate claims against international organisations because of the immunity traditionally granted to them.[49] As a consequence, one is almost completely dependent on the goodwill of an international organisation to submit itself to an accountability mechanism. This being said, recent years have seen an evolution in international and national case-law grounded on the human rights principle of access to courts to waive immunity and offer individuals a mechanism to challenge acts of international organisations.[50] In the parallel cases *Waite and Kennedy v Germany* (1999) and *Beer and Regan v Germany* (1999), the European Court of Human Rights ruled that immunity of jurisdiction of international organisations was permissible insofar as 'the applicants had available to them reasonable alternative means to

---

47 F. Naert, Chapter 5.

48 ILC, *Report of the sixty-first session, 4 May to 5 June and 6 July to 7 August 2009*, UN Doc. A/64/10, p. 38. See the text corresponding to footnote 14.

49 A. Reinisch, *International Organisations before National Courts* (Cambridge, Cambridge University Press 2000). For certain international organisations, constitutive documents provide for a limited immunity, as for instance Article VII (3) of the IBRD Articles of Agreement: 'Actions may be brought against the Bank only in a court of competent jurisdiction in the territories of a member in which the Bank has an office, has appointed an agent for the purpose of accepting service or notice of process, or has issued or guaranteed securities. No actions shall, however, be brought by members or persons acting for or deriving claims from members. The property and assets of the Bank shall, wheresoever located and by whomsoever held, be immune from all forms of seizure, attachment or execution before the delivery of final judgment against the Bank.'

50 See for instance Brussels Labour Court of Appeals, Belgium, *Siedler v. Western European Union*, 17 September 2003, *Journal des Tribunaux* (2004) p. 617; Case Note by E. David, 'L'immunité de juridiction des organisations internationales', *Journal des Tribunaux* (2004) p. 619; Cour de Cassation (soc.), France, *African Development Bank v. Haas*, 25 January 2005, *Journal des Tribunaux* (2005) p. 454; Case Note by E. David, 'Observations', *Journal des Tribunaux* (2005) p. 454; A. Reinisch, 'The Immunity of International Organizations and the Jurisdiction of their Administrative Tribunals', 7 *Chinese Journal of International Law* (2008) pp. 285–306; P. Sands and P. Klein, *Bowett's Law of International Institutions*, 6th edn. (London, Sweet & Maxell 2009) p. 498.

protect effectively their rights under the Convention'.[51] While this case-law attempts to reconcile individual rights with the rights of the organisation, it also raises fundamental questions on the role of national courts. It requires national courts to assess the complaint mechanisms established by the international organisations. The question is whether national courts have the required expertise to decide on such cases and whether they constitute an appropriate forum to assess the specificities of the dispute settlement mechanisms set up by international organisations. Moreover, the rejection of immunity by national courts may open the door to divided decisions of the courts of different Member States of international organisations and lead to uncertainty and tensions.[52] Furthermore, interference by the national judiciary may threaten the independence of an international organisation in the discharge of its mission.[53] Finally, even in the case of a victim obtaining a judgment convicting an international organisation, the question arises how this person can enforce the national decision.

These legal issues have direct and concrete implications for victims. In 2007, a group called the 'Mothers of Srebrenica' asked a Dutch court – The Hague District Court – to indict the UN for its failure to prevent the Srebrenica massacre and asked for financial compensation. In July 2008, the court ruled that it had no jurisdiction as the UN enjoys full immunity from actions by national courts.[54] This decision was upheld on 30 March 2010 by the Court of Appeal in The Hague. The Court of Appeal considered that because of the UN's 'special position' in providing peacekeeping and ensuring peace and security around the world, 'it is very important that the UN has the broadest immunity possible allowing for as little discussion as possible' in order to permit the UN to undertake its duties.[55] The 'Mothers of Srebrenica' had also requested the Court

---

51 ECtHR, *Beer and Regan v. Germany*, Application No. 28934/95, 33 *EHHR* (2001) p. 3; ECtHR, *Waite and Kennedy v. Germany*, Application No. 26083/94, 30 *EHHR* (1999) p. 261.

52 The D.C. Court of Appeals noted in *Broadbent v. Organization of American States* (1980) that '[a]n attempt by the courts of one nation to adjudicate the personnel claims of international civil servants would entangle those courts in the internal administration of those organizations. Denial of immunity opens the door to divided decisions of the courts of different member states passing judgment on the rules, regulations, and decisions of the international bodies. Undercutting uniformity in the application of staff rules or regulations would undermine the ability of the organization to function effectively.' *Marvin R. Broadbent et al. v. Organization of American States et al.*, US Court of Appeals, DC Cir, 8 January 1980, 628 F.2d 27, 30–35 (DC Cir 1980).

53 F. Mégret, 'The Vicarious Responsibility of the United Nations for "Unintended Consequences of Peace Operations"', in C. Aoi, C. de Cooning and R. Thakur, eds., *The 'Unintended' Consequences of Peace Operations* (Tokyo, United Nations University Press 2007).

54 District Court in The Hague, The Netherlands, *The Association of Citizens Mothers of Srebrenica v. The Netherlands and the UN (Incidental Proceedings)*, 295247/HA ZA 07–2973, 10 July 2008.

55 Court of Appeal in The Hague, The Netherlands, *The Association of Citizens Mothers of Srebrenica v. The Netherlands and the UN (Appeal)*, 200.022.151/01, 30 March 2010.

of Appeal to submit the question whether the UN enjoys absolute immunity or not to the European Court of Justice. They argued that fundamental human rights enshrined in the legal order of the European Union were threatened by this immunity. This request was rejected by the Court of Appeal. As to the argument on their right of access to courts raised by the plaintiffs, the Court of Appeal held that this right is not limited by the immunity of jurisdiction of the UN since the victims can sue the perpetrators of the genocide and the State. Srebrenica survivors and victims' families used the latter possibility in the past and filed a claim for compensation against the Dutch government, arguing that Dutch troops failed to take effective action to prevent the massacre. Yet, on 10 September 2008, the Hague District Court rejected the claim for compensation and ruled that the Dutch government could not be held responsible since the Dutch battalion was under UN command. Consequently, the Dutch State had transferred its powers in the area of security and freedom to the UN and could not be held liable for any violation committed during UN operations.[56] As a follow-up to the decision of 30 March 2010 by the Court of Appeal in The Hague, lawyers for the families have declared that they may bring the case to the Dutch Supreme Court and once again request that the question be submitted to the European Court of Justice.[57]

D. THE NEED TO CREATE MECHANISMS TO ENSURE ACCOUNTABILITY

This example illustrates the urgent need to create mechanisms to ensure accountability of international organisations. Various mechanisms may be envisaged.[58] Some have already been established, such as the Inspection Panel at the World Bank[59], or the European Ombudsman[60], who deals with complaints from citizens about maladministration by EU institutions. Certain mechanisms have been established by the UN, such as specific procedures for third-party claims with a private law character in peace support operations. Most of these

---

56 District Court in The Hague, The Netherlands, *Individual Claimants v. The Netherlands*, 265618/HA ZA 06–1672, 10 September 2008.

57 Law Firm Van Diepen Van der Kroef, Press Release, 'Issue of UN immunity surprisingly not submitted to European Court of Justice by Court of Appeals in The Hague', 30 April 2010, available at www.vandiepen.com/upload/file/srebrenica/srebrenica-press-20100330.pdf.

58 See for instance S. Kuyama and M.R. Fowler, eds., *Envisioning Reform. Enhancing UN Accountability in the Twenty-First Century* (New York, United Nations University Press 2009).

59 International Bank for Reconstruction and Development, International Development Association, Resolution No. IBRD 93–10, Resolution No. IDA 93–6, 'The World Bank Inspection Panel', available at http://siteresources.worldbank.org/EXTINSPECTIONPANEL/Resources/ResolutionMarch2005.pdf.

60 Article 228 of the Treaty on the Functioning of the European Union.

claims were settled by a local claims review board composed of UN officials and specifically established for a peacekeeping mission.[61] Another important example of internal mechanisms set up by the UN are the UN Dispute Tribunal and the UN Appeals Tribunal[62], which replaced the UN Administrative Tribunal as of 31 December 2009.[63] They have jurisdiction to adjudicate applications alleging non-observance of contracts of employment of staff members of the UN Secretariat or of their terms of appointment. Similar to the UN, the European Union has set up a European Union Civil Service Tribunal to deal with staff disputes.[64] These mechanisms constitute very elaborate examples of an internal justice system established by international organisations. Other mechanisms remain at the level of theoretical suggestions, such as the creation of an independent human rights court or panel.[65] It is noticeable that each of these mechanisms is specifically established to ensure the accountability of one single international organisation. One may be tempted to imagine a general mechanism to ensure accountability, applicable to all international organisations that accept its competence, such as the establishment by the UN Human Rights Council of a working group with the mandate of receiving complaints about the effects on the human rights situation of intergovernmental organisations' operations.[66] However, will the specificity of each international organisation not run counter to the establishment of a general system? Would tailor-made instruments corresponding to the specific mission and nature of the international organisation concerned not be preferable in order to optimise accountability?

---

61 UN Secretary-General Report, 'Financing of the United Nations Protection Force, the United Nations Confidence Restoration Operation in Croatia, the United Nations Preventive Deployment Force and the United Nations Peace Forces headquarters Administrative and budgetary aspects of the financing of the United Nations peacekeeping operations: financing of the United Nations peacekeeping operations', UN Doc. A/51/389 (1996) paras. 20–33; UN Secretary-General Report, Administrative and budgetary aspects of the financing of the United Nations peacekeeping operations', UN Doc. A/51/903 (1997) paras. 7–11; K. Schmalenbach, *Die Haftung Internationaler Organisationen im Rahmen von friedenssichernden Maßnahmen und Territorialverwaltungen* (Frankfurt am Main, Peter Lang 2004).

62 UN General Assembly, 'Administration of justice at the United Nations', A/Res/62/228, 6 February 2008.

63 UN Secretary-General, 'Transitional measures related to the introduction of the new system of administration of justice – Secretary-General Bulletin', SGB/2009/11, 24 June 2009.

64 Decision 2004/752/EC, Euratom of the Council of 2 November 2004 establishing the European Union Civil Service Tribunal, OJ L 333/7, 9 November 2004.

65 T. Hammarberg, loc. cit. n. 7.

66 Cf. the proposal of S.I. Skogly, op. cit. n. 35 at p. 188.

IV. STRUCTURE OF THE BOOK

A. GENERAL CONCEPTS

The first part of the book focuses on a number of general concepts and fundamental problems. This pertains in the first place to the notion of 'accountability'. This book's title uses the term 'accountability', and not 'liability' or 'responsibility', for human rights violations of international organisations. **Ige F. Dekker** analyses these different concepts in his contribution and critically assesses the work of the International Law Commission on this topic.

Even though many international organisations have an international legal personality which is to be distinguished from their Member States, **Niels M. Blokker** examines whether international organisations are really independent actors and whether such independence corresponds to a functional necessity.

The question arises whether there remains also a form of responsibility for the Member States of the organisation. The interrelation between international organisations and their Member States is addressed by **Olivier De Schutter**, who suggests a logic of sliding scales in the law of international responsibility: 'the more the organisation itself complies with human rights, and establishes mechanisms, whether internal or external, relying either on international monitoring bodies or on national courts, in order to ensure such compliance, the less there will be reasons to suspect that, by transferring powers to the organisation, the Member States have somehow 'circumvented' their human rights obligations.'[67]

Frederik Naert discusses two aspects of the responsibility of Member States in the context of international organisations. In a first part, he analyses whether international organisations are bound by treaties binding their Member States, because that might be one way of ensuring that Member States do not evade their obligations when they act through international organisations. The second part of Frederik Naert's contribution reflects on the responsibility of Member States for their own actions in the framework of international organisations. **Matteo Tondini** describes the possibility of suing before national and international judicial/supervisory bodies States that belong to international organisations.[68]

---

67 O. De Schutter, at p. 128.

68 See also C.F. Amerasinghe, 'Liability to Third Parties of Member States of International organizations: Practice, Principle and Judicial Precedent', 85(2) *American Journal of International Law* (1991) p. 275; A. Reinisch, op. cit. n. 49.

B. PEACE AND HUMANITARIAN OPERATIONS

The risk of violations of human rights by international organisations is especially high when they exercise direct operational command and/or power, such as in the case of peacekeeping and humanitarian operations.[69] This is the focus of the second part of the book. As explained by **Ulf Häußler** in his contribution on accountability for possible human rights violations by international organisations in the course of peace missions, '[t]oday's peace missions differ considerably from classical Blue Helmet peacekeeping (…) many of these peace missions have become increasingly embedded in receiving states' power balances, and some are expected to remain in that position for significant periods.'[70] **Peter R. Baehr** focuses his analysis on the accountability of the United Nations in the case of Srebrenica, while **Kristin Bergtora Sandvik** investigates the role of procedural accountability in the organisation of humanitarian projects, especially on refugee resettlement. She postulates notably that '[a]ccountability measures are governance tools with complex effects. Devised as *means* to achieve greater legitimacy for bureaucratic interventions – by way of installing institutional cultures of human rights and administrative justice – these measures may themselves be transformed into instrumental ends through everyday practice.'[71]

C. INTERNATIONAL CIVIL ADMINISTRATION

Furthermore, one notices a significant expansion of the traditional peacekeeping missions, which have evolved toward complex operations and have even sometimes been entrusted with international territorial administration.[72] In the third part of this book, the analysis of the accountability for human rights violations of international organisations concentrates on such cases of international territorial administration. **Ralph Wilde** focuses on the normative identity of the UN and explains the general denial of the legitimacy of international trusteeship as a way of understanding why the accountability

---

69 F. Mégret and F. Hoffmann, 'The United Nations as Human Rights Violator? Some Reflections on the United Nations Changing Human Rights Responsibilities', 25 *Human Rights Quarterly* (2003) pp. 314–342; A. Faite, J. and L. Grenier, eds., *Expert Meeting on Multinational Peace Operations: Applicability of International Humanitarian Law and International Human Rights Law to UN Mandated Forces*, 80 Geneva, ICRC, October 2004; N.D. White and D. Klaasen, eds., op. cit. n. 31; M. Zwanenburg, *Accountability of Peace Support Operations* (Leiden/Boston, Martinus Nijhoff Publishers 2005); H. Langholtz, B. Kondoch and A. Wells, eds., 10 *International Peacekeeping: The Yearbook of International Peace Operations* (2006).

70 U. Häußler, at p. 215.

71 K. Sandvik, at p. 289.

72 H. Krieger, *The Kosovo Conflict and International Law: An Analytical Documentation* (Cambridge, Cambridge University Press 2001); R. Kolb, G. Porretto and S. Vité, *L'application du droit international humanitaire et des droits de l'homme aux organisations internationales: forces de paix et administrations civiles transitoires* (Brussels, Bruylant 2005).

structures operating in relation to international territorial administration have been inadequate. **Eric De Brabandere** examines the issues of international territorial administration and accountability in concentrating on the UN Transitional Authority in East Timor, while **Remzije Istrefi** analyses the case of the UN Mission in Kosovo.[73] In the latter case, the United Nations Interim Administration (UNMIK) has set up a non-judicial mechanism to address human rights abuses by the surrogate State (UNMIK), namely the Ombudsperson Institution. **Gjylbehare Bella Murati** addresses the role of the Ombudsperson in Kosovo, focusing in particular on the analysis of violations concerning the right to property, the right to liberty and security of an individual and the right to freedom of expression.

D. ECONOMIC GOVERNANCE

Rather than being directly and operationally involved, many international organisations operate mainly through policies in the areas of their specific mission, from development financing to the promotion of culture, health, justice, labour standards, monetary stability or trade. That is what the fourth part of the book focuses on. The organisations' particular focus on their own specialised mission may bring them to inadvertently or even consciously neglect or prejudice human rights protection in specific areas. Especially in the realms of international economic governance such policies have attracted increasing attention in terms of their human rights implications. Throughout the years human rights problems arising from the policies of the Bretton Woods institutions, i.e. the International Monetary Fund and the World Bank Group have received considerable academic attention.[74] **Rekha Oleschak-Pilai**'s contribution analyses the World Bank's Inspection Panel, while **Pierre Schmitt** focuses on the International Monetary Fund's accountability for human rights violations. Moreover, the other pillar of the international economic order – the World Trade Organization (WTO) – offers an intriguing example of the complexities of the relationship between an international organisation and its Members as far as the responsibility for respecting human rights is concerned. WTO Members are in an awkward position as WTO rules and disciplines are legally binding upon them and oblige them to implement such rules and disciplines in their national policies and legal systems, thereby often compelling them to prioritise trade over other societal values, including certain human rights. **Jeroen Denkers** and **Nicola Jägers** ask

[73] See also J. Cerone, 'Minding the gap: outlining KFOR accountability in post-conflict Kosovo', *12 European Journal of International Law* (2001) pp. 469–488; E. Abraham, 'The Sins of the Saviour: Holding the United Nations Accountable to International Human Rights Standards for Executive Order Detentions in its Mission in Kosovo', 52(5) *American University Law Review* (2003) p. 1291.

[74] See the references mentioned *supra* n. 35.

whether the WTO forms an obstacle to enforcing human rights obligations. **Stefaan Smis, Stephen Sevidzem Kingah** and **Christine Janssens** focus on the relationship between one particular WTO agreement, the TRIPs Agreement (trade-related aspects of intellectual property rights), and human rights, notably the issue of access to cheaper AIDS medicines. The authors find that, although international trade can enhance human rights in some situations, the TRIPs Agreement has a negative impact on the right of access to cheaper HIV/AIDS medicines. Intellectual property and the right to health need not be friends or foes and a proper balance may be found. Finally, **Gauthier de Beco** analyses the possibility of using human rights indicators to improve the accountability of development agencies for their human rights obligations.

E. STAFF OF INTERNATIONAL ORGANISATIONS

Last but not least, the book's fifth part concerns human rights related problems affecting the staff of international organisations. In the employment relationship with their own staff, international organisations are in a position of direct authority in which infringements of human rights can take place. In 2003, some 110 000 to 130 000 people were working as international public servants.[75] **Chittharanjan Felix Amerasinghe** examines the accountability of international organisations for violations of the human rights of staff, with an emphasis on the recourse to judicial machinery for staff. **Sarah Hunt** focuses her analysis on the UN and the difficulties faced by litigants within the UN internal legal system. **Osmat Azzam Jefferson** analyses how workplace equality is understood, applied, and valued through practice in international organisations. She evaluates why such equality is an illusory concept and notes that it is in the international organisations' best interest to 'redesign and implement effective equality-based rules and to examine rules-based governance structures.' As a distinguished international legal practitioner, **Edward Kwakwa** examines human rights obligations of international organisations in general and as applied to staff relations in particular from an international organisation's point of view, namely the World Intellectual Property Organization.

---

75 H.G. Schermers and N.M. Blokker, *International Institutional Law. Unity within Diversity*, 4th ed. (Boston/Leiden, Martinus Nijhoff Publishers 2003) para. 496.

PART I

GENERAL CONCEPTS

ACCOUNTABILITY OF INTERNATIONAL ORGANISATIONS: AN EVOLVING LEGAL CONCEPT?

Ige F. DEKKER*

I. INTRODUCTION

The purpose of this contribution is to discuss and review the question whether the concept of 'accountability' is or should be an element in the law of international organisations. In international legal discourse the term 'accountability' still seems to be most frequently used as a synonym for the traditional international legal concepts of responsibility and/or liability. In this sense 'accountability' is based on the so-called responsibility-for-wrongfulness doctrine and thus limited to situations in which the conduct of an international organisation constitutes a breach of an applicable international obligation. This approach to the constraints of the use by international organisations of their powers is and will be of continuing importance and deserves continued attention as, for instance, is reflected in the reports and draft articles of the International Law Commission on the responsibility of international organisations.[1]

However, at the same time the view is held that the traditional concepts of responsibility and liability to control the activities of international organisations are too formal and limited, as already appears from the fact that they are rarely applied in practice.[2] It is asserted that international organisations should

---

* Professor of International Institutional Law, School of Law, Utrecht University, The Netherlands. This contribution is based on an earlier publication by the author: 'Making Sense of Accountability in International Institutional Law. An analysis of the Final Report of the ILA Committee on Accountability of International Organisations from a conceptual legal perspective', 36 *Netherlands Yearbook of International Law* (2005) pp. 83–118.

1 As matters stand at present, see ILC, *Report of the Sixty-first Session*, UN Doc. A/64/10 (2009), chapter IV, paras 31–51. The Special Rapporteur of the International Law Commission, Professor Giorgio Gaja, has hitherto presented seven reports on the topic. See http://untreaty.un.org/ilc/guide/9_11.htm.

2 See ILC, *Report of the Fifty-ninth session*, UN Doc. A/62/10 (2007) Chapter VIII p. 179. See more in general, D.M. Curtin and A. Nollkaemper, 'Conceptualizing Accountability in International and European Law', 36 *Netherlands Yearbook of International Law* (2005) pp. 3–20 at pp. 5–7. I.F. Dekker and R.A. Wessel, 'De aangeproken lidstaat. De internationale

'account' for their performance in a much broader way than only on the basis of clear violations of their obligations established under international law. International organisations – in the sense of international *governmental* organisations – have increasingly expanded their powers and activities and they often operate on the basis of ambiguous institutional and substantive principles and rules. In addition, the complex governance structures of international organisations have resulted in a wide range of 'stakeholders' which ask for different kinds of formal and informal mechanisms and processes to protect their legitimate interests. In other words, it is contended that the formal and limited models of controlling international organisations underlying the notions of responsibility and liability should be replaced by the less formal and more open model of what is called the 'accountability' of international organisations.

The notion of 'accountability' first entered international institutional law in relation to some specific international organisations such as the World Trade Organization,[3] the International Monetary Fund,[4] the World Bank,[5] the United Nations,[6] and, quite prominently, the European Union.[7] More recently, 'accountability' was also introduced in a more general way as notion applicable to all international organisations.[8] Previously, the most important attempt in these respects was made by the 'Final Report of the International Committee on the Accountability of International Organisations', which was adopted by the International Law Association in 2004.[9] According to this Final Report,

aansprakelijkheid en verantwoordelijkheid van de staat als lid van een internationale organisatie', Preadvies voor de Staatsrechtconferentie, Universiteit Utrecht, 11 December 2009, in L.F.M. Besselink and R. Nehmelman, eds., *De aangesproken staat: verantwoordelijkheid, aansprakelijkheid en immuniteit van de overheid* (Nijmegen, Wolf Legal Publishers 2010), forthcoming.

3 C. Bellmann and R. Gerster, 'Accountability in the World Trade Organization', 30 *Journal of World Trade* (1996) pp. 31–74.

4 W.E. Holder, 'International Organizations: Accountability and responsibility', *American Society of International Law Proceedings* (2003) pp. 231–236.

5 I.F.I Shihata, *The World Bank Inspection Panel: In Practice*, 2nd ed. (Oxford, Oxford University Press 2000) pp. 237–240.

6 C. Ku and H. Jacobson, *Democratic Accountability and the Use of Force in International Law* (Cambridge, Cambridge University Press 2002).

7 C. Harlow, *Accountability in the European Union* (Oxford, Oxford University Press 2002); A. Arnull and D. Wincott, *Accountability and Legitimacy in the European Union* (Oxford, Oxford University Press 2002); D.M. Curtin, 'European Legal Integration: Paradise Lost?', in D.M. Curtin, et al., eds., *European Integration and Law* (Antwerpen, Intersentia 2006) pp. 1–54.

8 See N.D. White, *The Law of International Organisations*, 2nd ed. (Manchester, Manchester University Press 2005), Chapter 7 'Accountability', pp. 189–229; G. Hafner, 'Accountability of International Organizations', *American Society of International Law Proceedings* (2003) pp. 236–240; G. Hafner, 'Accountability of International Organizations – A Critical View', in R. St.J. Macdonald and D.M. Johnston, eds., *Towards World Constitutionalism. Issues in the Legal Ordering of the World Community* (Leiden, Martinus Nijhoff Publishers 2005) pp. 585–630; V.P. Nanda, 'Accountability of International Organizations: Some Observations', 33 *Denver Journal of International Law and Policy* (2004) pp. 379–388.

9 ILA, *Report of the Seventy-first Conference, Berlin 2004* (London, International Law Association 2004) pp. 164–234.

'accountability' of international organisations has to be conceived in terms of legal and non-legal forms and mechanisms, without *per se* considering the issue of the traditional legal concepts of liability and responsibility of these organisations for damaged caused and/or breaches of international law. In other words, 'accountability' is presented in this report as a notion encompassing legal, political, administrative and financial forms of internal and external scrutiny and monitoring of activities and omissions of international organisations, of which liability and responsibility are important but separate components.

The question remains whether it is possible and useful to conceptualise 'accountability' as an actual or potential component of the legal system of international organisations. Before trying to answer this question, I shall first give a short overview of the different approaches to the concept of 'accountability' in international political and legal doctrine and summarise the main findings of the International Law Association Committee on the Accountability of International Organisations. It will be submitted that the rather traditional approach to international (institutional) law underlying this study makes it difficult to conceptualise an unequivocal legal concept of the 'accountability' of international organisations. This contribution aims to demonstrate that on the basis of a more modern and realistic view of the plurality of legal phenomena in present day legal systems, a coherent legal concept of the 'accountability' of international organisations can be developed.

II. CONCEPTS OF ACCOUNTABILITY

A. APPROACHES TO ACCOUNTABILITY

Within international political and legal studies, the term 'accountability' was introduced quite recently[10] but it has gained, in relatively short time, great popularity. As is often the case with other new, attractive catchwords, the notion of 'accountability', as one author noted, 'crops up everywhere performing all manner of analytical and rhetorical tasks and carrying most of the burdens of democratic "governance".'[11] However, there are enough political and legal academic studies that take the notion of 'accountability' serious.

Notwithstanding the fact that the notion is frequently used in books, journal articles and academic conferences, it has *not* acquired a clearly defined meaning.

10 For the origin of the term 'accountability' see C. Harlow, op. cit. n. 7, p. 1; G. Hafner, 'Accountability of International Organizations – A Critical View', loc. cit. n. 8, at pp. 588–590.

11 R. Mulgan, '"Accountability": an Ever-Expanding Concept?', 78 *Public Administration* (2000) pp. 555–574, at p. 555.

Given the many different understandings and definitions, two broad lines seem to emerge in the literature: the 'evaluative' and the 'analytical' approach.[12] According to the former, 'accountability' is seen as a broad value covering other values and goals, such as good governance, democracy, participation, transparency, equity, efficiency, integrity and responsibility. Although such an all-embracing approach can be useful for certain purposes – for example for a comparative analysis of the performance of international organisations[13] – it is of little use for the development of a concept as part of the legal system of international organisations (or any other legal system, for that matter).

If one does not want to exclude the latter possibility, one has to approach the concept in a more confined, analytical way. In this sense, 'accountability' can be described 'as involving the justification of an actor's performance *vis-à-vis* others, the assessment or judgment of that performance against certain standards, and the possible imposition of consequences if the actor fails to live up to applicable standards.'[14] Such a conceptualisation of 'accountability' as a social relationship has been developed in the disciplines of international relations and public administration. But is has also started to trickle into the study of the law of international organisations, in particular that of the European Union in particular. According to such an analytical approach, the 'accountability of an international organisation' can be understood as a relationship between an international organisation and a certain forum – a political or judicial entity – in which (1) the international organisation has to justify its conduct, (2) the forum has the right to assess this conduct on the basis of prior established principles and rules, and to pass judgment, and (3) the international organisation may face certain consequences, such as formal or informal sanctions.[15] Although this approach to accountability is described as a narrow one in political science, from the perspective of international (institutional) law it is certainly broad. It widens

---

12 See M. Bovens, 'Analysing and Assessing Public Accountability. A Conceptual Framework', *European Governance Papers* no. C-06-01, EUROGOV, 2006, pp. 6–7, available at www.connex-network.org/eurogov/; J.L. Mashaw, 'Accountability and Institutional Design: Some Thoughts on the Grammar of Governance', in M. Dowdle, ed., *Public Accountability: Designs, Dilemmas and Experiences* (Cambridge, Cambridge University Press 2006) pp. 115–156.

13 See R. Lloyd, J. Oatham and M. Hammer, *The 2007 Global Accountability Report* (London, One World Trust 2007). This report assesses 'the capability of 30 of the world's most powerful intergovernmental organisations, international non-governmental organisations, and transnational corporations to be accountable to civil society, affected communities, and the wider public" on the basis of four dimensions of accountability: transparency, participation, evaluation, and complaint and response mechanisms. See also L.Verhey, Ph. Kiiver, S. Loeffen, eds. *Political Accountability and European Integration* (Groningen, Europa Law Publishing 2009).

14 D.M. Curtin and A. Nollkaemper, loc. cit. n. 2, at p. 4. In the same sense: R.W. Grant and R.O. Keohane, 'Accountability and Abuses of Power in World Politics', 99 *American Political Science Review* (2005) pp. 29–43, at pp. 29–30.

15 See M. Bovens, loc. cit. n. 12.

the scope of the traditional understanding of international legal accountability, potentially far beyond the limitations of the established international legal principles of responsibility and liability.

B. THE ILA CONCEPT OF ACCOUNTABILITY

The aforementioned Final Report of the ILA Committee on the Accountability of International Organisations,[16] clearly aims to present accountability as an existing or evolving concept of the law of international organisations. The ILA Committee introduces the notion as a quite normal fact of international legal life: there is no reason at all, as a matter of principle, why international organisations could or should not be held accountable for disadvantages and repercussions resulting from their acts or omissions. As is the case with other subjects of international law, the power of international organisations entails their accountability.[17] For this reason, the ILA Committee felt that a precise definition of accountability was not needed, although it made an attempt to approach the notion in a descriptive way. According to the Committee, the multifaceted phenomenon of 'accountability' is mainly reflected in its different *forms* and *levels*. The Committee distinguishes four different *forms* under which 'accountability' may arise – legal, political, administrative and financial – and assumes that a combination of these four forms provides the best chances of achieving the necessary degree of accountability.[18]

More crucial in the approach of the ILA Committee are the three *levels* of accountability of international organisations, which also form the basis of the structure of the Final Report and thus, as may be expected, determine the content of the notion. The three 'interrelated and mutually supportive' levels of accountability of international organisations are defined in the Final Report as follows:

'– [First level] the extent to which international organisations, in the fulfilment of their functions as established in their constituent instruments, are and should be subject to, or should exercise, forms of internal and external scrutiny and monitoring, irrespective of potential and subsequent liability and/or responsibility;
– [Second level] tortious liability for injurious consequences arising out of acts or omissions not involving a breach of any rule of international law and/or institutional law (e.g. environmental damage as a result of lawful nuclear or space activities);

16 ILA, *Report of the Seventy-first Conference, Berlin 2004* (London, International Law Association 2004) pp. 164–234 (referred to below as the Final Report).
17 Final Report, p. 168.
18 *Ibid.*

- [Third level] responsibility arising out of acts or omissions which do constitute a breach of a rule of international law and/or institutional law (e.g. violations of human rights or humanitarian law, breach of contract, gross negligence, or as far as institutional law is concerned acts of organs which are *ultra vires* or violate the law of employment relations).'[19]

The first level covers, according to the ILA Committee, essentially the availability and proper functioning of mechanisms to monitor the conduct of international organisations by Member States and third parties. The main mechanisms of accountability at this first level are as mentioned: the submission of reports, the collection and dissemination of information and the carrying out of inspections. This kind of monitoring takes place on an everyday basis and aims at bringing about normal accountability of international organisations without the functioning of international organisations would be impossible. Careful monitoring may cause international organisations either to maintain or to adjust their course of conduct, without entailing any further consequences at all. But these processes may also bring to the surface acts or omissions which in turn may give rise to liability and/or responsibility of international organisations. Liability for injurious consequences may also result from the normal course of conduct of international organisations and become operational by invoking pre-existing arrangements to that end or by any *ad hoc* legal, political and financial settlement. Again, in the view of the ILA Committee the processes of accountability may end here or may be upgraded to the third level when acts or omissions of international organisations do constitute a breach of international (institutional) law. In that case the accountability of international organisations is carried forward all the way ending up in full scale international legal responsibility.

The main part of the Final Report consists of a wide range of what is named 'recommended rules and practices' which are related to the three levels of accountability and – as a separate aspect – to the remedies against international organisations. They cover rules and practices for both the institutional and operational activities of international organisations, and are accompanied by clear explanatory notes.[20] It is stressed by the ILA Committee that this format was explicitly chosen so as not to prejudge whether any recommended rule or practice should be seen as a recommendation for sound internal practice or whether it was operative on a legal level, and in the latter case whether it was *de lege lata* or *de lege ferenda*. This, however, does not exclude, according to the Final Report, that 'many of the recommended rules and practices reflect existing rules of international law'

---

19 Final Report, p. 169.

20 Final Report, pp. 164–166, 169, 171.

although the ILA Committee underlines that its mandate 'did not preclude it from formulating rules constituting, to a reasonable extent, progressive development.'[21]

As to the first level of accountability forty-eight recommendations are formulated which, it is asserted, are based on upon principles, objectives and concepts common to all international organisations and are to be seen as standards or yardsticks by which the performance of international organisations should be evaluated in order to render the notion of accountability operational.[22] They include rules and practices with regard to transparency, participation in decision-making, access to information, sound financial management, reporting and evaluation, good faith, constitutionality and institutional balance, stating reasons for decision, procedural regularity, objectivity and impartiality, and due diligence.

With regard to the second and third levels of accountability, the Final Report formulates 'primary' as well as 'secondary' rules and practices.[23] The first are concerned with identifying the applicable law to the acts, activities and omissions of international organisations, and special attention is given to the obligations of international organisations in the field of environmental protection, human rights and humanitarian law. The 'secondary' rules and practices on the liability and responsibility of international organisations are concerned with the attribution and consequences of breaches of international obligations. As a principle of existing customary international law, it is stated that international organisations themselves may be held responsible for their wrongful acts but this does not exclude the joint or several responsibility of the Member States for the non-fulfilment by their international organisation of its obligations towards third parties.[24] The guiding policy concern for elaborating the rules and practices is to maintain the balance between preserving the necessary autonomy in the decision-making of international organisations and guaranteeing that such international organisations will not be able to avoid accountability.[25] In line with the general international rules on the attribution of wrongful acts,[26] the basic question is who has the authority to exercise 'effective control' over the activities concerned.

---

21 Final Report, pp. 170–171.

22 Final Report, pp. 172–183.

23 Final Report, pp. 185–205.

24 With regard to the issue of the *responsibility* of international organisations, the ILA Committee seems to take a somewhat broader approach to the subject than the International Law Commission is doing. The 'recommended rules and practices' of the ILA Committee cover all kinds of responsibility to be assumed by international organisations and not only those towards Member States and other States, which seem to be the main focus of the International Law Commission.

25 See Final Report, pp. 168, 198–199.

26 See most recently, ICJ, *Case Concerning the Application of the Convention on the Prevention and Punishment of the Crime of Genocide*, 26 February 2007, available at www.icj-cij.org, paras. 394–400.

The recommended rules and practices on the remedies against international organisations deal with the appropriate procedures and it's functioning for all three levels of accountability.[27] Available remedies on the first level generally will have a non-judicial nature – such as procedures involving ombudsmen, inspection panels and commissions of inquiry – whereas on the second and third levels judicial remedies – adjudication and arbitration – play an important role. According to the ILA Committee, the importance of less formal remedies to control international organisations can hardly be overestimated, not only because of its preventive potential but also because of the of the procedural obstacles facing in particular non-state actors to bring international organisations before international and domestic courts.

C. CRITICAL ASSESSMENT

The elaboration of the first level of accountability by the ILA Committee – the most innovative part of its conceptualisation of the accountability of international organisations – appears to halt between two opinions about the subject. On the one hand, accountability functions as a general value encompassing other important values like good governance, democracy, openness, and integrity. This approach is very much disclosed by majority of the recommended rules and practices formulated under the first level of accountability, which are primarily concerned with standards for good behaviour of international organisations. In addition, accountability in the opinion of the ILA Committee seems to function not only as a retrospective mechanism but also as a proactive instrument for controlling international organisations' conduct. For, as the ILA Committee expressly states, international organisations should be subject to and should exercise the indicated forms of scrutiny and monitoring.

On the other hand, the ILA Committee appears to have a narrower concept of accountability in mind where it underlines that all component entities of the international community in principle are entitled to raise the accountability of international organisations provided 'their interests or rights have been or may be affected by acts, actions or activities of international organisations.'[28] Also the importance attached in the Final Report to the appropriate remedies for all three levels of accountability indicates that accountability is to be seen as a relationship between an international organisation and another party, which has or may have

---

27 Final Report, pp. 205–230. This part of the Final Report is largely based on K. Wellens, *Remedies against International Organisations* (Cambridge, Cambridge University Press 2002). See also K. Wellens, 'Fragmentation of International Law and Establishing an Accountability Regime for International Organizations: the Role of the Judiciary in Closing the Gap', 25 *Michigan Journal of International Law* (2003–2004) pp. 1159–1181.

28 Final Report, p. 169.

an interest in a decision or other act already taken by the international organisation. This analytical approach to the issue seems to be very much inspired by the basic form of the second and third levels of accountability – the liability and responsibility of international organisations – which both concern a violation of an international legal obligation by an international organisation *vis-à-vis* another actor.[29] However, the ILA Committee stresses at the same time the differences between the legal and non-legal aspects of accountability. So it distinguishes between legal and non-legal *forms* of accountability, between legal and non-legal *interests* and between legal and non-legal *remedies*, as well as, with regard to the 'recommended rules and practices', between recommendations which operate at a legal level, be it *de lege lata* or *de lege ferenda*, and recommendations reflecting only sound internal practices of international organisations. In addition, the distinction between the levels of accountability, at least partly, is characterised by the fact that the *legal* forms, interests, remedies and norms dominate the second and third levels of accountability and the *non-legal* forms, interests, remedies and norms the first one. It is stated that the 'diversity of forms of accountability clearly rules out, from the start, any requirement that only legal interests may trigger accountability',[30] implying that the impairment by an international organisation of those other, non-legal, interests only triggers the accountability of the organisations under the first level of accountability.

The question centres upon what assumptions these distinctions between legal and non-legal phenomena are made. It is probably not too far-fetched to say that the overall analysis by the ILA Committee of the concept of accountability is predominantly governed by a rather traditional approach to what is legal and not, confining a legal system to a set of duty-imposing rules of conduct and competence-conferring rules. The recommended rules and practices listed under the second and third levels of accountability satisfy these criteria and reflect a system for the accountability of international organisations which consists of a set of mandatory rules of conduct and competences to deal with breaches of those rules. However, also the recommendations on the first level of accountability, although according to the ILA Committee not necessarily reflecting existing legal obligations, focus primarily on standards of behaviour

29 It is asserted here that on a conceptual level there is no fundamental difference between concepts of liability and responsibility. Even in a situation in which the ILA Committee holds that the liability of an international organisation arises, a breach of international legal obligation must have occurred, for instance one derived from the precautionary principle. See I. Brownlie, *Principles of Public International Law*, 4th ed. (Oxford, Clarendon Press, 1990) pp. 433–444; A. Boyle, 'State Responsibility and Liability for Injurious Consequences of Acts not Prohibited by International Law: A Necessary Distinction?', 39 *International and Comparative Law Quarterly* (1990) p. 1.

30 Final Report, p. 169. See also First Report, p. 603.

and thus reaffirm more than less the traditional approach to what counts as law and what not.

As explained in more detail elsewhere, this kind of approach to international law is widely held, also in scholarly works on international institutional law, although in most instances in an implicit way.[31] With regard to decisions of international organisations it is generally accepted that those decisions which are legally binding are legally valid and thus do exist as independent elements of the international legal system. The implication of this line of reasoning is that decisions of international organisations which are *not* legally binding are *not* legally valid and thus do *not* exist as independent elements of the international legal system. However, this logical conclusion is hardly ever drawn. On the contrary, there is a general acknowledgement in the literature and international case law of the legal importance of non-binding decisions of international organisations. But this prominent understanding has strangely enough not altered principally the assumption traditionally underlying the legal analysis of equating the legal *validity* of a rule with its *binding* character. For, it is held that the legal significance of the normative effects of such non-legally binding decisions still lay in the function they have in relation to mandatory rules of international law.

For sure, the recognition by the ILA Committee of the fact that the exercise of legal powers by international organisations leading to breaches of non-legally binding rules and practices – purposes, principles, inducements, declarations – may incur also forms of accountability is, as such, an important and innovating insight. The ILA Committee, however, fails to draw the line till the end. It accepts that international organisations have to account for more than violations of legally binding rules of conduct resulting in its responsibility but leaves undecided what the nature is of those other forms of accountability. On the one hand, it stresses the non-legal character of this accountability – not only with regard to the interests but also with regard to its forms and remedies – but at the same time it is relating these forms of accountability to standards that in its opinion at least partly reflect existing international law. The result is an ambiguous concept of accountability, not only reflecting an evaluative and functional character but, more importantly, also encompassing essentially different phenomena, namely legal and non-legal realities. Such an approach, at least at the conceptual level, will hardly contribute to a better understanding of how to deal with the complex legal and social realities of international organisations.

---

31 D.M. Curtin and I.F. Dekker, 'The EU as a 'Layered" International Organisation: Institutional Unity in Disguise', in P. Craig and G. de Búrca, eds., *The Evolution of EU Law* (Oxford, Oxford University Press 1999) pp. 83–136; I.F. Dekker and R.A. Wessel, 'Governance by International Organizations: Rethinking the Normative Force of International Decisions', in I.F. Dekker and W.G. Werner, eds., *Governance and International Legal Theory* (Leiden, Martinus Nijhoff Publishers 2004) pp. 215–236.

III. AN INSTITUTIONAL CONCEPT OF ACCOUNTABILITY

A. AN INSTITUTIONAL APPROACH

The traditional approach to the law of international organisations has proven to be unsatisfactory. It fails to explain and account for the existence of numerous factors in international institutional law, as well as their effects, by their systematic and *a priori* exclusion as independent elements from the legal system of international organisations. The least one can say is that the assumptions of the traditional approach to international institutional law in contemporary society are debatable, both on theoretical and empirical grounds. From a theoretical point of view, there is no reason whatsoever to reduce in advance all possible elements of the legal system to rules of conduct. Since one has no *a priori* access to the 'true' nature and function of law, it is advisable to approach the legal system of international organisations without prejudicing its possible content. From the empirical perspective, it is generally admitted that significant parts of the law of international organisations consist of rules constituting all kinds of legally relevant regimes – or of rules empowering organisations or organs to create such regimes – which are certainly not be seen as separate, legally binding rules of conduct. For example, it is uncontested that resolutions of international organisations formulating certain goals to be achieved or expressing an opinion on a certain situation, or non-binding advisory opinions declaring certain general principles of law, have become increasingly important elements of the legal system of international organisations.

From this perspective there is no reason to leave undecided, as the ILA Committee does, whether the many recommended rules and practices of (mainly) the first level of accountability belong to the *legal* systems of international organisations. As is stated in the Final Report, these rules and practices are derived from common principles, objectives and notions related to the accountability of international organisations and reflect considerable practice.[32] On that basis there seems to be no obstacle to consider those recommendations as reflecting legally *valid* rules and practices of the legal system of international organisations. The fact that these rules and practices may not have a legally *binding* character is, as such, not a convincing reason to exclude them from the legal system. As independent elements of the legal system they may have their own legal effects, for instance the legitimisation of conduct of the different actors involved in the accountability of international organisations. An analysis from such a point of view will make it possible to conceptualise the existing or potential *legal* regime of accountability of international organisations in all its legal shades.

32 Final Report, p. 172.

This line of thought is, in theoretical terms particularly developed under the heading of the so-called 'institutional legal theory'.[33] In order to account for the plurality of legal phenomena, the institutional legal theory conceives of the legal system as a system of so-called 'legal institutions' which, as systems of institutional rules, make it possible to create legal facts. 'Legal institutions' in this sense can be characterised as distinct legal systems governing specific forms of social conduct within an overall legal system for the purpose of effecting a social practice that can be interpreted as resting on a common belief in their existence.[34] Thus, every legal institution has its counterparts in social reality, the 'real' institutions, which reveal themselves in the form of recurrent and enduring legal and other practices. Legal institutions – or legal institutional concepts – in this sense must have, at least in their basic form, a *unitary* character. This requirement of unity has, in the first place, the purpose of indicating that the legal institution can be dealt with as a more or less autonomous phenomenon within the legal system of which it is an element, and that it, in a meaningful way, can be distinguished from other legal institutions or concepts. Secondly, unity means that the legal institution has to be coherent, meaning that the different parts of the legal regime of the institution are connected by some fundamental common legal rules or principles. If the concept of accountability of international organisations can be conceived of as a legal institution the question would be which kind of 'human linguistic activity' could obtain validity as part of the legal regime of that institution, and which facts, therefore, have to be taken seriously by the relevant legal community. Besides legal obligations to follow a certain course of action, there are other elements of a legal regime – such as principles, inducements and purposes – which are institutional legal realities too and for that reason give rise to different expectations and different patterns of legitimising conduct.

B. ACCOUNTABILITY AS A LEGAL INSTITUTION

As previously stated, from the perspective of the institutional legal theory there is no reason to exclude *a priori* any interests from the legal framework of international organisations. Then the question arises whether the accountability of international organisations for breaches of legally binding rules of conduct, on the one hand, and the accountability of international organisations for breaches of other rules, on the other, is so different that, at least on a conceptual level, the notions of responsibility or liability and 'other' forms of accountability should be kept apart. The proposition here is that, once one accepts no *a priori* restrictions on which organisational acts or omissions can count as *legal* acts, there is no

---

33 See for a general enunciation and references I.F. Dekker and R.A. Wessel, loc. cit. n. 31, at pp. 215–236.

34 See D.W.P Ruiter, *Legal Institutions* (Dordrecht, Kluwer International 2001) pp. 71–99.

logically binding reason to distinguish between different levels of accountability on the basis of the non-legal or legal character of these levels.

At all levels of legal accountability: *first*, an act or omission of an organ of an international organisation, actually or potentially, affects an interest of one or more other entities, including other organs and staff of the organisation, Member States, and third parties such as non-Member States, other international organisations, private legal persons and individuals; *second*, the international organisation which, actually or potentially, affects the legal interests of other entities has a duty to explain and a right to justify its behaviour on the basis of valid international norms; *third*, the affected party has a right to an adequate, effective and enforceable remedy; *fourth*, the parties can opt to resolve the issue inter se or can accept the judgment of a forum such as another political organ of the organisation or an independent judicial or quasi-judicial body; *fifth*, the Member States can bear *indirect* accountability for the act or omission of the organisation and a Member State can bear *direct* accountability if the act or omission of the organisation or its implementation can be attributed to that Member State; *sixth*, the rules for implementation of international accountability relating to, for instance, proof of damage, causality and modes of satisfaction, will apply when relevant.

According to this line of thought it is possible to conceptualise the accountability of international organisations as legal institution – or institutional legal concept – in a legally unambiguous way. The fundamental principles underlying this concept, as formulated above, are the same irrespective of the level of accountability. In other words, the situations in which the accountability of international organisations may arise concern always situations in which an international organisation allegedly does not comply with a legally valid – but not necessarily also legally binding – rule or principle of international law. Within this unambiguous legal framework many different legal forms of accountability may arise, depending on the legal effect of the infringed rule concerned. A situation of non-compliance by an international organisation with a general principle of good governance regarding, for instance, potential critical reactions by affected parties, will differ from a situation in which an international organisation breaches a specific rule of conduct laid down in a treaty provision. On this basis different levels and forms of legal accountability could be distinguished. Of course, it would be advisable to reserve, also within this framework, the term 'legal responsibility' for the forms of legal accountability in which an international organisation breaches an international legal obligation. However, one should be careful in legal analyses with distinctions between 'legal' forms of accountability, on the one hand, and 'political', 'administrative' and 'financial' forms of accountability, on the other. In so far as the latter forms are part of the legal system governing international organisations, they are all *legal* forms too. In the same sense all legitimate remedies available under the legal framework of an international organisation will have a *legal* character and not only the (quasi-)judicial remedies.

C. ACCOUNTABILITY AND THE INSTITUTIONAL CHARACTER OF INTERNATIONAL ORGANISATIONS

It goes without saying that an international legal concept of 'accountability' is only applicable to those international organisations that possess 'international legal personality'. Holding otherwise would be problematic because international organisations without such a status do not legally exist as a separate entity in the international legal system and cannot, as such, be accountable for their activities or omissions.[35] Historically, this would have excluded a lot of entities that call themselves international organisations because their international legal status was rarely regulated in their constitutive documents and an implicit recognition of this status was for a long time a very controversial subject. However, nowadays the *presumption* of international legal personality seems to be in theory and practice generally accepted for every entity which is established by States (or other international legal subjects) under international law and is entrusted with legal powers of its own.[36] The presumption of international legal personality relates to the legal validity – and hence the existence – of an international organisation which aims to be accepted not only by the members of the organisation but also by other legal subjects.

However, the recognition of the international legal personality of international organisations has not diminished their inherently complex structure as a legal institution.[37] International organisations are traditionally based on an 'alliance', which can be described as an enduring (multilateral) contractual legal relationship between States (or other international legal subjects), in most cases laid down in a treaty, that serves to achieve common objectives by a set of legitimate expectations about their reciprocal behaviour. At the same time an international organisation has the institutional form of a legal person, i.e. an entity that has the capacity, through collective decision-making, to act, both internally and externally. The original (multilateral) contractual relationship between the State parties is *supplemented* by a set of (constitutional) relationships of each of the Member States with the international organisation. In other words, with the creation of an international organisation the alliance between the

35 See R.A. Wessel, 'Revisiting the International Legal Status of the EU', 5 *European Foreign Affairs Review* (2000) p. 507.

36 See J. Klabbers, *An Introduction to International Institutional Law* (Cambridge, Cambridge University Press 2002) pp. 42–69; N.D. White, op. cit. n. 8, at pp. 30–69.

37 See D.W.P Ruiter, op. cit. n. 34, at pp. 102–115.

Member States is not replaced by the international organisation as a legal person but *both* legal institutional forms exist legally side-by-side.

A significant amount of controversial legal views and issues discussed in international institutional law can be traced back to this dual character, including the powers and accountability of international organisations. Powers are the central element of the internal legal regime of international organisations, along with other kinds of legal rule such as rules of conduct, principles, inducements and purposes. Through the power-conferring rules an international organisation is able to develop is own legal regime through the creation and interpretation of its rules and review of the implementation of its rules as well as to promote that its legal existence is also socially taken into account as a factual situation. Power-conferring rules make it possible that an international organisation is a living entity both in the legal world as well as in social reality. For this reason alone, the discussion about the foundation of the legal powers of an international organisation is a crucial one but, of course, it is also central to the issue of its legal accountability. According to one school of thought international organisations derive their powers exclusively from the Member States – also labelled the subjective approach – while another one maintains that the powers are inherently vested in international organisations themselves – the objective approach. In general these two approaches are presented as mutually exclusive. However, neither logical argument nor empirical evidence makes such a presentation necessary. On the contrary, the dual structure of international organisations indicates that a legally more realistic approach would be based on the idea that both foundations of the powers of international organisations are not mutually exclusive but are complementary. Also with regard to power-conferring rules there is no reason to reduce *a priori* the possible foundations of such rules other than that they themselves must be based on a rule of the legal regime of the organisation or a rule of the international legal system of which it forms a part.

This fundamental dual character of international organisations and their powers has, of course, far-reaching repercussions on the legal regime of accountability of international organisations too. A complete replacement of the alliance between the Member States by the international organisation as a legal person would have made the legal picture quite unequivocal. In that case, the international organisation alone would be accountable to third parties for the acts and omissions attributable to the organisation. That is not to say that the question of the attributability of acts or omissions to an international organisation is an easy one.[38] However, the dual character of international organisations brings in the controversial question of the residuary or separate accountability of Member States for the acts and omissions of their organisations. For that reason the ILA

[38] See Final Report, pp. 200–205.

Committee underlines that, although international organisations should be seen as autonomous entities, its recommendations 'contain references to member states, since international organisations are ultimately composed of member states and decisions of international organisations are, in most cases, taken as a result of initiatives and proposals of individual member states.'[39] Again, one is confronted here with the competing claims of the autonomy of the international organisation, on the one hand, and the legislative sovereignty of the Member States, on the other.[40] As long as neither in theory nor in practice the choice is made for lifting the dual character of international organisations, the problems connected to the indirect or direct accountability of Member States for the acts or omissions of their international organisations will remain an inherent part of the legal regime of the accountability of international organisations.

IV. CONCLUDING OBSERVATION

From the foregoing analysis it may be concluded that the accountability of international organisations can be seen as a coherent legal concept of existing international institutional law, albeit in a different way as conceptualised in the thought provoking Final Report of the ILA Committee on this subject. It is asserted that such a legal concept is only possible on the basis of accepting a different theoretical approach to international law than traditionally held. Making use of the insights of the so-called institutional legal theory, an alternative concept of accountability is presented covering in principle all situations of claims of non-compliance by international organisations with legally valid – but not necessarily also legally binding – rules and principles of international law. Such a concept is governed by a set of basic principles but within this legal regime a lot of different forms of accountability are possible, depending on the legal effect of the infringed rule concerned. Such a concept of accountability seems to reflect in a more adequate way than the traditional notions of responsibility and liability the character, development and needs of the complex legal systems of international organisations. Most importantly, it may improve the protection of the international rule of law and the compensation and satisfaction of victims of violations of these rules and principles, whether they are States, international organisations, people, private entities or individuals.

---

39 Final Report, p. 171.

40 See also Resolution II of the *Institut de Droit International*, 'The Legal Consequences for Member States of the Non-Fulfilment by International Organisations of their Obligations toward Third Parties', 66-II *Annuaire de l'Institut de Droit International* (1996) p. 445.

INTERNATIONAL ORGANISATIONS AS INDEPENDENT ACTORS: SWEET MEMORY OR FUNCTIONALLY NECESSARY?

Niels M. Blokker*

I. INTRODUCTION

The question of whether international organisations are independent actors is a question that has to be addressed in a book devoted to 'accountability for human rights violations by international organisations.' If international organisations would not be independent actors, there would be no need for them to be accountable. This very same starting point was also chosen by the International Law Commission when in 2003 it engaged in extensive discussions over the definition of international organisations, in the context of its work on the responsibility of international organisations. Article 2(a) of the Draft Articles adopted in first reading defines an international organisation as 'an organization established by a treaty or other instrument governed by international law and possessing its own international legal personality.'[1] If an organisation would not have its own legal personality, it can by definition have no obligations of its own, and therefore it cannot be *itself* responsible for a violation of obligations. No responsibility without personality.

International organisations *are* independent actors. And precisely because they are independent, it is realistic to assume that international organisations, as such, may violate human rights. In some cases, UN peacekeepers have been involved in 'sexual exploitation and abuse'. In 2005, a thorough UN study concluded that with regard to MONUC, the UN's operation in the DRC, 'sexual exploitation and

---

* Professor of International Institutional Law (Schermers Chair), Leiden University, and deputy head of the international law division at the Netherlands Ministry of Foreign Affairs. The views expressed in this contribution are those of the author, not necessarily those of the Dutch Government. This is the text of an oral presentation for the conference 'Accountability for human rights violations by international organisations' that took place in Brussels, 16–17 March 2007; it has only slightly been revised and updated.

1 International Law Commission, *Report of the Sixty-first session (4 May to 5 June and 6 July to 7 August 2009)*, UN Doc. A/64/10, p. 20.

abuse was widespread, involving both civilian and uniformed personnel'.[2] This study made a number of recommendations. As a follow up, a draft convention on the criminal accountability of UN officials and experts on mission has been proposed. One of the elements of this draft convention is that the UN should give priority to facilitate the exercise of jurisdiction by the host State, by waiving the immunity of the persons concerned. Another example pertains to financial sanctions imposed by the UN and EU upon individuals who are believed to be involved in terrorism. It has been questioned whether these sanctions are in accordance with human rights such as property rights, the right to be heard, and the right to effective judicial review.

Questions such as these have already been raised now for some time. And for an equally long period of time has it been difficult to give answer to these questions. Because international organisations *are* established as independent actors, there may be all kinds of legal barriers in addressing alleged human rights violations. In most cases, in order to guarantee their independence, international organisations enjoy immunity from jurisdiction in their Member States. As a result, it may be difficult for national courts to deal with complaints about human rights violations by international organisations that are brought before them. This has always been the case, not only in recent years. But as a result of the increased dynamism of international organisations, in particular since the end of the Cold War, these questions have now been asked more frequently and in a more fundamental manner than before.

So there is every reason to ask ourselves the question why international organisations need to be independent, if this may lead to human rights violations and if this may make it so difficult to address such violations before national courts. Therefore this contribution discusses the rationale of creating international organisations as independent actors. Is this 'independence' a characteristic that had to be given to international organisations in particular in earlier days, when they would otherwise not be able to act in a world in which States were more sovereign than they are today? Should academics and practitioners in the world of international organisations consider this as a 'sweet memory'? Or do international organisations today still need to be independent to perform their functions? I submit that we can only find proper ways and means to deal with human rights violations by international organisations if we fully understand why international organisations are independent actors. Without such awareness, ways and means may be suggested that will either be ineffective or will throw away the baby (the international organisation) with the bathwater (the violation of human rights).

---

2 UN General Assembly, 'Comprehensive Review of the Whole Question of Peacekeeping Operations in All Their Aspects', UN Doc A/59/710 (2005) p. 9.

More concretely, three issues will now be analysed, all relating to the theme of international organisations as independent actors. First, the attribution of powers; second, the issue of legal personality; third, the theory and practice of the independence of secretariats of international organisations.

II. ATTRIBUTION OF POWERS

The first issue is very basic and may be explained as follows: suppose that Belgium, China, Congo, France, Ghana, Indonesia, Italy, Panama, Peru, Qatar, Russia, Slovakia, South Africa, the UK and the US would decide to meet and discuss how to deal with one of the major issues now on the international agenda, for example the Middle East or the situation in Iraq. One would agree that such a meeting could issue recommendations, statements etc. But there would be a fundamental difference if the same 15 States – as members of the UN Security Council – would meet as the Security Council. It would be of a fundamental difference if the decisions taken would not be decisions of these 15 States sitting together, but decisions of an organ called the UN Security Council. Why is this so different? This is of course for two reasons. First, because States have agreed in the UN Charter to attribute substantial powers to the Security Council. As stated in Article 24, paragraph 1, the Security Council acts 'on their behalf'. On the basis of the powers vested in it, the Security Council has the authority to do things that 15 States meeting on an ad hoc basis cannot do. Second, as laid down in Article 25 of the Charter, States have agreed 'to accept and carry out the decisions of the Security Council'. Most fundamental is the first element, the attribution of powers, which could be characterised in general terms as follows. It is the powerful idea of giving powers to a collective body:

- that represents membership as a whole
- that takes decisions in accordance with agreed decision-making rules
- that has to respond to developments in practice, and therefore has to use these powers to pursue the aims of the organisation.

This may be illustrated through another example. Very often the example of the Security Council is given in these discussions, but it works the same way in other organisations, including organisations that most of us have probably never heard of. For example, the International Network for Bamboo and Rattan (INBAR). This organisation was created 13 years ago. It is based in Beijing. As the Preamble of the constitution of this organisation indicates:

> 'Believing that greater benefits would accrue to all institutions and individuals involved in bamboo and rattan production and development if an international

> organisation were established for the promotion and coordination of bamboo and rattan research and development, training and information exchange [...].'[3]

This organisation has three organs: the Council as the plenary organ, the Board of Trustees, made up of not less than 8 and not more than 16 Trustees who serve in their personal capacity, and the Secretariat headed by a Director General. The Council and the Board have a number of specified powers and functions. For example, the Board has to approve the Network's programmes and operational plans. The Council has the more general task to give guidance to the work of the Board. It is these organs that further develop cooperation between the members, through powers that have been attributed to them.

No matter whether it is the UN Security Council, the organs of the International Network for Bamboo and Rattan, or organs of other international organisations to which members have attributed powers: it is this idea of power attribution to a new collectivity that gives strength and added value to cooperation between States. It is this idea that makes the difference between regular, *ad hoc* meetings of States on the one hand, and meetings of international organs on the other. It is an elaboration of the idea of '*Eendracht maakt macht*' ['Union is strength'] which was until some 200 years ago the device of the Netherlands, and which has been taken over by Belgium as its motto since it became independent, known in French as '*l'Union fait la force*'. This is part of the answer to the question why and how an international organisation is more than the sum of its members.

In this context it is interesting to look at the International Law Commission's Draft Articles on Responsibility of International Organizations. A few years ago, draft Article 28, paragraph 1, went as follows:

> 'A State member of an international organisation incurs international responsibility if it circumvents one of its international obligations by providing the organisation with competence in relation to that obligation, and the organisation commits an act that, if committed by that State, would have constituted a breach of that obligation.'[4]

It has been recognised in doctrine and in the case law of the European Court of Human Rights that it is not excluded that under certain conditions State responsibility may arise when States attribute competences to international organisations. However, the general rule as originally proposed by the ILC is quite another thing. This provision was too broad. For example, if applied to the

3 Agreement on the Establishment of the International Network for Bamboo and Rattan, available at http://r0.unctad.org/commodities/agreements/Inbaren.pdf. Internet pages last visited in July 2009.

4 See, with commentary, International Law Commission, *Report of the Fifty-eighth session (1 May to 9 June and 3 July to 11 August 2006)*, UN Doc. A/61/10, p. 283.

UN, members could be responsible for having conferred general and far-reaching powers on the Security Council. Using these powers, it is not excluded that the Security Council may act in such a way that, if States would have done the same, these acts would be considered wrongful acts for which they would have been responsible. Yet subsequently, if UN members could be held responsible for such an action because they had conferred certain powers on the Security Council in 1945, this would encroach too much upon the independence of the UN as well as the need for the Security Council to be able to take far reaching action to maintain international peace and security. Thus, the ILC's original provision could have easily frustrated the functioning of the Council, as its members may want to avoid any risk of being held responsible for actions undertaken on the basis of powers given to it long ago.

Moreover, in general such a State responsibility could hamper the creation of new organisations or the attribution of the necessary powers to such organisations, since members may in the future be held responsible for acts of the organisation that are considered necessary for the performance of its functions. In particular, the proposed Article 28 disregarded the importance of implied powers of international organisations.

One should not misunderstand this criticism. I do not favour giving *carte blanche* to organisations to use their powers freely and perhaps disregard human rights. But in my view draft Article 28 was not the right solution in this search for accountability. By focusing on the responsibility of the members for bestowing powers on international organisations, the proposed draft overlooked a key feature of international organisations: powers are given to the organisation. It is impossible to ensure that this attribution of powers will *always* be accompanied by all international obligations by which *each* of the members of the organisation is bound. There is no practice supporting the broad scope of draft Article 28, and this proposal could have negatively affected the dynamism that is requested from international organisations. It is to be welcomed that in its sixty-first session the ILC substantially modified the provision in question. The newly proposed draft Article 60, para. 1, does not link State responsibility anymore to the conferral of powers to an international organisation:

> 'A State member of an international organization incurs international responsibility if it seeks to avoid complying with one of its own international obligations by taking advantage of the fact that the organization has competence in relation to the subject matter of that obligation, thereby prompting the organization to commit an act that, if committed by the State, would have constituted a breach of the obligation.'[5]

5 International Law Commission, *Report of the Sixty-first session (4 May to 5 June and 6 July to 7 August 2009)*, UN Doc. A/64/10, p. 38.

This first issue relating to the attribution of powers is about substance. The subject matter in relation to which powers have been given to a new collectivity is an international, cross-border issue. States can no longer fully control such issues that have outgrown the national level. I do not need to refer to terms such as 'interdependence' or 'globalisation'. There is a common interest among the States concerned to control external influences on what previously was exclusively in the national *domaine réservé* or, as it is sometimes put, to 'pool sovereignty'. States may of course decide not to be involved in decision-making on cross-border issues at a higher level, but the problem is that sooner or later they will be affected by decisions taken at this higher level in which they are not involved. As former Foreign Secretary Hurd of the UK once said about the Treaty on European Union:

> 'It is against our fundamental interests to isolate ourselves from the continent of Europe [so] that policies are organised there which deeply affect our security or our prosperity but in which we have no important say. If that were to happen we could keep our sovereignty as a slogan but its substance would have gone.'

But this first issue about substance is only part of the story of international organisations as independent actors. In addition, there is another crucial issue involved, that is of an institutional nature. Certain powers can be transferred to a higher decision-making level, but this higher level must be defined. Powers cannot simply be launched in the air, or in a vacuum. It is crucial that in practice these powers are used by something that is separate, or, as the ICJ said in 1949, 'in detachment from' the members. As is often said, this 'something' must have a *volonté distincte*. This is what a constitution must give to an international organisation. Otherwise there will not be a constitution creating a separate institution, but a treaty laying down rights and obligations of the parties. Such a treaty would be only '*la rencontre de* [...] *volontés qui suivent chacune leur idée*' (Renard); there would be no newly created *volonté distincte*. Powers therefore have to be given to a collectivity that has a certain status. This status is created by giving the organisation legal personality. As stated by the ICJ in 1996, the object of constituent instruments of international organisations is 'to create new subjects of law endowed with a certain autonomy, to which the parties entrust the task of realizing common goals.'[6] Legal personality is the second issue discussed in this contribution.

6 ICJ, *Legality of the Use by a State of Nuclear Weapons in Armed Conflict*, Advisory Opinion, *ICJ Rep.* (1996) pp. 97–100.

III. INTERNATIONAL LEGAL PERSONALITY

Why are international organisations usually legal persons? As we all know, the founders of the UN did not want to say explicitly in the Charter that the UN had international legal personality. But it did not take long before practice showed that the UN could not perform its functions without such status, when the UN needed to present claims to Israel after its mediator Count Bernadotte was killed. Such a status was necessary for two main reasons. First of all, for reasons of principle. To be able to do their work as independent actors, international organisations must be in the position to make claims *themselves*; to conclude treaties *themselves*; to send and receive delegations *themselves;* as well as to protect their staff and agents *themselves*. With regard to this last point of staff protection, the ICJ stated in its 1949 Advisory Opinion on *Reparation for Injuries Suffered in the Service of the United Nations* – and later repeated this in its 1999 *Cumaraswamy* Opinion:

> 'In order that the agent may perform his duties satisfactorily, he must feel that this protection is assured to him by the Organisation, and that he may count on it. To ensure the independence of the agent, and, consequently, the independent action of the Organisation itself, it is essential that in performing his duties he need not have to rely on any other protection than that of the Organisation.'[7]

Apart from this first reason why international legal personality is needed, there is a very practical second main reason. If the organisation would not be in the position to act, the only alternative would be for the members collectively to act. If the UN would not have the capacity to bring a claim after the killing of one of its agents, the members would have to do this together. But this would be very impractical and time consuming. As the ICJ said in 1949: 'The functions of the Organisation could not be effectively discharged if they involved the concurrent action, on the international plane, of fifty-eight or more Foreign Offices [...]'.[8]

Since then it has in practice been accepted that international legal personality does not have to be given explicitly to international organisations. Such personality may also be implied, and this is indeed how this issue usually has been dealt with during the past few decades. This has become a classic part of textbooks on the law of international organisations. Nevertheless, even though considerable practice has developed, the question why international organisations have to be legal persons re-emerged in the 1990s. Since the 1990s there seem to be two different

---

7 ICJ, *Reparation for Injuries Suffered in the Service of the United Nations*, Advisory opinion, *ICJ Rep.* (1949) pp. 173–219; ICJ, *Difference Relating to Immunity from Legal Process of a Special Rapporteur of the Commission on Human Rights*, Advisory opinion, *ICJ Rep.* (1999) pp. 62 and following.

8 ICJ, *Reparation for Injuries Suffered in the Service of the United Nations*, Advisory opinion, *ICJ Rep.* (1949) pp. 173–219.

developments regarding the issue of international legal personality. On the one hand it has become quite normal – and not as exceptional as before – to include a provision in constitutions of international organisations, in which *explicitly* international legal personality is given to the newly created collectivity. Apparently the founders are sufficiently convinced that their creation needs this status. Apparently they do not feel the traditional reluctance to say so explicitly. Examples are not only well known organisations such as the International Criminal Court, but also organisations such as the Bamboo and Rattan Network mentioned before. The agreement establishing this Network explicitly states (Article 1.2): 'The Network shall enjoy full juridical personality in international law.'[9]

However, on the other hand, since the 1990s there has also been a reluctance to grant international legal personality in certain cases. In at least two cases States had extensive discussions on this and concluded that their creation should not operate as an international legal person. The first case is that of the European Union. At the time of its creation, in 1992, this was not yet a real issue. There was no explicit provision on international legal personality of the Union in the Maastricht Treaty. But when the Union started to operate, practice demonstrated, as in the case of the UN, that this was an issue. It was therefore extensively discussed during the negotiations for the 1997 Amsterdam Treaty. In June 1997, it was one of the top issues on the agenda of the European Council. At this high political level, the proposal was rejected to include in the Amsterdam Treaty an explicit provision on international legal personality of the EU. The day after the Amsterdam Summit meeting, Tony Blair proudly declared before the House of Commons: 'others wanted to give the EU explicit legal personality across all pillars. At our insistence, this was removed'. However, as is so often the case, practice proved to be more powerful than politics. In practice it became soon clear that the Union could not operate its own policies, in particular in the second pillar, the Common Foreign and Security Policy. In 2001 the EU for the first time became a party to a treaty, in its own name, apparently implying that it had the capacity to do so. Since then, the EU has concluded a rapidly increasing number of treaties. What the ICJ stated in 1949 for the UN was as much true 50 years later for the EU: to achieve its ends 'the attribution of international legal personality is indispensable.'[10] The Treaty of Lisbon, which entered into force on 1 December 2009, has put an end to this discussion by spelling out in Article 47 EU Treaty that '[t]he Union shall have legal personality.'

The second case in which States had extensive discussions on the issue of legal personality, and concluded that their creation should not operate as an international legal person is that of the Organization for Security and

9 *Supra* n. 2.

10 ICJ, *Reparation for Injuries Suffered in the Service of the United Nations*, Advisory opinion, *ICJ Rep.* (1949) p. 178.

Co-operation in Europe (OSCE). This organisation started to function in 1975 as a conference, the CSCE. Therefore it was only normal that it was not a legal person. However, in practice after 1975 semi-permanent institutional structures have been created, as was recognised when the CSCE was renamed into OSCE in 1994. But no international legal personality was given to this new organisation. Not in the 1990s, not in another round of negotiations in 2000–2001. Only in 2006, the negotiations have resumed in an attempt to reach consensus in a near future.

Why is the absence of international legal personality a problem for the OSCE? It is true that in practice *ad hoc* solutions are found. In the absence of treaty-making capacity, non-legally binding MoUs are made. Host countries for OSCE Institutions have adopted national legislation dealing with the status, privileges and immunities of these institutions – for example, in 2002 the Netherlands adopted a law to give the necessary status, privileges and immunities to the High Commissioner on National Minorities. However, these *ad hoc* solutions are second or third best stopgap measures. Many practical problems continue to take place. To mention just a few: the OSCE cannot conclude seat agreements with its host States. It is not recognised as an official international organisation by a number of other international organisations. In many countries the OSCE does not have the necessary privileges and immunities; for example, the organisation and its staff are often not exempted from customs duties and taxation. Often the OSCE cannot conclude contracts. In addition, taxation will often result in inequality between local staff in different missions, and places the OSCE at a disadvantage if compared to other organisations. OSCE Missions sometimes did not have international personnel for considerable time, because of difficulties with accreditation and acceptance of personnel. In some cases national customs and police authorities have seized OSCE vehicles or documentation or have entered OSCE premises. So: what solution should be found to deal with these problems?

The key answer is that the OSCE participating States should give international legal personality to the organisation. What the International Court of Justice stated in 1949 for the UN is as much true now for the OSCE: to achieve its ends 'the attribution of international personality is indispensable.' The OSCE needs international legal personality in order to perform its functions. This will give it the necessary status in its relations with States and other international organisations. It will give it the capacity to conclude treaties within the scope of operation of the organisations. It will make it possible to give the necessary legal status, privileges and immunities to staff of the organisation. The OSCE Ministerial Council has therefore rightly decided in December 2006, that a new attempt should be made to reach consensus. An informal working group has been created to finalise work on a draft convention on legal personality, if possible in 2007.[11] The main hurdle is not any more that States do not want to give OSCE international legal personality. The main problem is that the Russian Federation wants *much more* than only a convention on legal personality, privileges and immunities. Annexed to the Decision of December 2006 is an interpretative statement by the Russian Federation, in which it stressed that it would only agree to this if a Charter or Statute would be drawn up, as a founding OSCE document. This document would need to contain OSCE 'basic goals and principles along with reference to existing commitments and the structure of its main decision-making bodies'. '[T]he entry into force of a convention on privileges and immunities, if and when there is agreement on a draft, will be possible only in conjunction with the entry into force of a statute or charter of the OSCE.'[12] This is likely to become a difficult issue, as almost all the other 55 participating States of the OSCE do not seem to share the Russian ambition to prepare a fully fledged constitution for the OSCE. In October 2007, the Working Group achieved consensus on the text of a draft convention, although three footnotes referring to an OSCE Charter were attached. However, at the political level no agreement could be reached and the draft Convention was not adopted by the 2007 Madrid Ministerial Council.[13]

The conclusion that may be drawn from this is that practice has demonstrated that international organisations need international legal personality in order to be able to perform their functions as independent actors. At times States may find it difficult to accept this, for political reasons (the examples of UN, EU and OSCE). But time and again it becomes clear that this is also something they can no longer control, something more powerful than themselves.

IV. THE THEORY AND PRACTICE OF THE INDEPENDENCE OF INTERNATIONAL SECRETARIATS

Therefore, international organisations are usually international legal persons. I will now look inside these legal persons, to examine more closely a very

11 Organisation for Security and Co-operation in Europe, Ministerial Council, Decision No. 16/06 on the Legal Status and Privileges and Immunities of OSCE (2006) available at www.osce.org/documents/mcs/2006/12/22611_en.pdf.

12 *Ibid.*

13 For an overview until Spring 2009, see S. Brander, 'Making a Credible Case for a Legal Personality for the OSCE', *OSCE Magazine* (March-April 2009) pp. 18–22, available at www.osce.org/publications/sg/2009/02/36302_1421_en.pdf; H. Tichy and U. Köhler, 'Legal Personality or not – The Recent Attempts to Improve the Status of the OSCE', in I. Buffard, J. Crawford, A. Pellet and S. Wittich, eds., *International Law between Universalism and Fragmentation. Festschrift in Honour of Gerhard Hafner*, 455–478 (2008).

important type of organ, the Secretariat. Secretariats are very important components of the institutional structure of international organisations. They are often perceived as 'the face' of an international organisation. We need to look at these components in particular if we want to know more about international organisations as independent actors. This is the third and final issue I would like to mention here.

It has taken some time before the status of international secretariats and the status of the people working there was well defined. Originally staff members working for international organisations were seen as a special kind of diplomats. To the extent they needed privileges and immunities, diplomatic privileges and immunities were applied. This is perhaps understandable. But after a while it became clear, in doctrine and in practice, that international civil servants are different from diplomats. It is their task to serve membership as a whole, not only a sending State as in the case of diplomats. The founding fathers of the League of Nations and the ILO did not lay down a well defined and generally agreed status for staff members in the constitutions of these organisations. It has been in particular the practice of these organisations that has defined in more detail their status. The drafters of the UN Charter benefited from this experience. Article 100 of the Charter spells out two well known key obligations. First: the obligation for the Secretary-General and staff not to seek or receive instructions from governments or other external bodies. Furthermore, they have to refrain from any action which might reflect on their position as international officials responsible only to the UN. This first main obligation is of course immediately followed by a counterpart obligation for the members of the UN not to influence these international officials. More precisely: to respect the exclusively international character of the responsibilities of the Secretary-General and its staff.

These twin obligations have become the standard rule when new international secretariats are created. If you look at the constitutions of organisations established in recent years, for example the Organisation for the Prohibition of Chemical Weapons or the International Coffee Organization, you will often find provisions similar to Article 100 of the UN Charter. Thus, such twin obligations seem generally accepted and well established. However, this is one of those fields within the law of international organisations that suffers from discrepancies between rules and practice. Practice is fraught with examples of cases where States considered international staff essentially as their nationals and did not respect their independent status. The title of a book published some years ago is telling in this regard; 'The international civil servant: an endangered species' by Jacques Lemoine.[14]

14 J. Lemoine, *The International Civil Servant: An Endangered Species* (Dordrecht, Kluwer Academic Publishers 1995).

The tension between rules and practice can be seen in particular with regard to the heads of international secretariats. Traditionally, these heads are generally appointed for a particular term, and usually constitutions do not give organs of the organisation the power to dismiss the person concerned. This is an important safeguard for their independence, in the interest of all members. Under the traditional system, if members were no longer satisfied with his or her performance, the person concerned was simply not reappointed. For example, Boutros-Ghali was not reappointed as Secretary-General of the UN when the US vetoed this proposal in the Security Council. Such practices are certainly open to criticism, as was the case with Boutros-Ghali, of which he attests to in his autobiography, *Unvanquished*.[15] But this is how the system works, and how a balance is found between independence and accountability.

This balance is disturbed when a Secretary-General could be dismissed *during* his or her term. Such a possibility would make it necessary for the Secretary-General to seek the agreement of membership for all kinds of decisions he or she would have to take. This could easily paralyse the Secretariat. Nevertheless, this is what happened when the Organisation for the Prohibition of Chemical Weapons (OPCW) in 2002 decided to remove from office former Director-General Bustani, less than two years after he was reappointed for a second term. The danger involved in this was well perceived by the Administrative Tribunal of the ILO, where Mr. Bustani brought a complaint against his dismissal. The Tribunal set aside the decision to dismiss Bustani, and considered the following:

> '[...] the independence of international civil servants is an essential guarantee, not only for the civil servants themselves, but also for the proper functioning of international organisations. In the case of the heads of organisations, that independence is protected, *inter alia*, by the fact that they are appointed for a limited term of office. To concede that the authority in which the power of appointment is vested – in this case the Conference of the States Parties of the Organisation – may terminate that appointment in its unfettered discretion, would constitute an unacceptable violation of the principles on which international organisations' activities are founded [...], by rendering officials vulnerable to pressures and to political change.'[16]

This is very much true, and the Tribunal has clearly shown its independence in this judgment. Nevertheless, States do not always share this view about the balance between independence and accountability. It is perhaps surprising to see that a few constitutions drawn up in recent years – for example, the constitution of the Bamboo and Rattan Network – provide for the possibility to dismiss the head of the Secretariat.

---

15 B. Boutros-Ghali, *Unvanquished: A US-UN Saga*, (London, New York, I.B. Tauris 1999).

16 ILOAT, Judgment No. 2232, 16 July 2003, available at www.ilo.org/public/english/tribunal/fulltext/2232.htm.

V. CONCLUDING REMARKS

International organisations need a sufficient amount of independence to be able to perform their functions. I have briefly discussed three important elements that enable international organisations to operate as independent actors: the attribution of powers, international legal personality, and the independence of the modern international secretariat.

This is the era of accountability. International criminal tribunals and the International Criminal Court have been created to put an end to impunity for the perpetrators of the most serious international crimes. There must be criminal accountability of persons in UN operations who are involved in sexual exploitation and abuse. Leaders in business and government have to be accountable for many things. It is becoming less acceptable that States abuse the notion of sovereignty and refuse to account for what they do or not do. It is therefore not surprising that similar demands for accountability are made with regard to international organisations. International organisations do not operate in a vacuum; if this is indeed an era of accountability, it also affects international organisations. It is no coincidence that within the International Law Association a Committee on accountability of international organisations was created, which in 2004 presented its report in which a number of recommended rules and practices are proposed. It is also of no coincidence that the International Law Commission is presently drafting rules on the responsibility of international organisations.

In principle, these efforts to improve the accountability of international organisations are to be welcomed. First of all, because, as independent actors, international organisations have certainly in recent years carried out a wide variety of activities for which they have to be accountable, in particular when things go wrong. Secondly, because *only* if adequate accountability mechanisms are in place, there will be the necessary confidence to enable international organisations to perform their functions as independent actors; to attribute powers to them when necessary, to give them international legal personality; and to allow international secretariats to function independently, both in theory and in practice.

But next to these advantages there is one danger involved in the quest for accountability of international organisations. This is the danger that this quest for accountability will disturb the delicate balance between independence of the organisation and control by its members. Claims that an international organisation has to be more accountable may easily result in more control by members over the organisation and a corresponding decrease of independence. Perhaps, on a slightly cynical note, there is even the danger of abuse of accountability: if today States would like to influence the work of international organisations to their advantage, an effective strategy would probably be to claim that such influence is necessary to deal with an accountability gap. In short: accountability claims as disguised attempts to undue control by members over the organisation.

My conclusion is therefore threefold:

- international organisations are independent actors; even though States may sometimes find this difficult to accept, in practice they often do not have a choice, it is something beyond their control;
- being independent actors, they need adequate accountability mechanisms;
- these mechanisms must respect the need for international organisations to operate sufficiently independently, in sufficient detachment from the members.

HUMAN RIGHTS AND THE RISE OF INTERNATIONAL ORGANISATIONS: THE LOGIC OF SLIDING SCALES IN THE LAW OF INTERNATIONAL RESPONSIBILITY

Olivier De Schutter*

The proliferation of international agencies is a result of the interdependency of States as well as of a growing recognition that, without collective action, global problems cannot be solved effectively. Collective action is needed, if we want to combat growing inequalities between countries.[1] It is needed if we want to control private actors, particularly transnational corporations who thrive on the recent wave of globalisation. And it is needed, if we want to make progress towards a world governed by an international rule of law.[2] International

* Professor of Human Rights Law at the University of Louvain (Belgium) and at the College of Europe (Natolin); Visiting Professor, Columbia University. A preliminary draft had been commented upon by Pierre d'Argent, Pierre Klein, and Hélène Ruiz Fabri, whom I thank for their insightful remarks. Any errors which remain are mine.

1 See the United National Millenium Declaration, adopted by the UN General Assembly on 8 September 2000 (A/55/L.2); and the 'road-map' for implementing goals, including Millennium Development Goals (MDGs) and Millennium Human Rights Goals, related to the Declaration, presented by the UN Secretary-General (A/RES/56/95). The 'road-map' contains a list of goals for each chapter of the Declaration, including eight Millennium Development Goals and six Millennium Human Rights Goals. On the relevance of human rights to the achievement of the Millenium Development Goals, see *The Millenium Development Goals and Economic, Social and Cultural Rights. A Joint Statement by the UN Committee on Economic, Social and Cultural Rights and the UN Commission on Human Rights' Special Rapporteurs on Economic, Social and Cultural Rights* (29 November 2002); and P. Alston, 'Ships Passing in the Night: The Current State of the Human Rights and Development Debate Seen Through the Lens of the Millennium Development Goals', 27 *Human Rights Quarterly* (2005) pp. 755–829.

2 See, on these different arguments in favour of international cooperation and the establishment of international agencies, J.-M. Coicaud, 'International organizations, the evolution of international politics, and legitimacy', in J.-M. Coicaud and V. Heiskanen, eds., *The Legitimacy of International Organizations* (Tokyo-New York-Paris, United Nations University Press 2001) pp. 545–6. On the role of international organisations as fora for the development of international law, see also J.E. Alvarez, *International Organizations as Law-Makers* (Oxford, Oxford University Press 2005) pp. 601–608 (suggesting that, due to the large representation within modern international organisations of both States and non-State actors, treaties may

organisations are established as a means to institutionalise such forms of inter-State cooperation.[3] Many of them fulfil a crucial function in contributing to the promotion and protection of human rights, which have become a shared responsibility of the international community.

At the same time, the development of international organisations brings about its own problems. The problem most discussed is the lack of accountability for human rights violations. With few exceptions, only States are bound under international human rights treaties, while the exercise of powers by international organisations risks going unchecked and therefore, we face the classical problem of the transfer of powers unmatched by corresponding responsibilities.[4] However, while the problems over accountability are indeed real, the almost exclusive focus on such issues risks obfuscating other potential difficulties that can emerge once we seek to make the requirement of accountability operational. For once we turn to the institutional implications of requiring accountability, we encounter the following dilemma: on the one hand, the need to ensure accountability when measures are adopted by international organisations that threaten human rights, may lead to affirm the international responsibility of their Member States for such measures.

---

be negotiated within that framework which are 'intended to codify, but that also progressively develop, the fundamental constitutive rules of the international system – such as the rules governing treaties, the way states ought to conduct their diplomatic relations, or those governing the global commons', such legislative treaties in addition having the capacity to influence the formation of general customary rules).

3 In this contribution, the notion of 'international organisations' is understood as under Article 2(1)(i) of the Vienna Convention on the Law of Treaties, 1155 *UNTS* (1969) p. 331) or under Article 2(1)(i) of the Vienna Convention on the Law of Treaties between States and International Organizations or between International Organizations of 20 March 1986, UN Doc. A/CONF.129/15, as organisations set up by States in order to favour intergovernmental cooperation. In principle, the members of such international organisations are States, who conclude among themselves a treaty in order to establish the organisation. While these characteristics are not necessarily inherent to all international organisations, they are sufficiently common for us to build an approach to the problems of international responsibility which presumes that such characteristics are present. This has also been approach to the work of the International Law Commission on responsibility of international organizations: see ILC, *First report on responsibility of international organizations*, by Mr. G. Gaja, Special Rapporteur, UN Doc. A/CN.4/532, 26 March 2003, paras. 12–14. Article 2 of the Draft Articles on responsibility of international organizations defines the term 'international organization' for the purpose of the Articles as referring to 'an organization which includes States among its members insofar it exercises in its own capacity certain governmental functions'.

4 See generally on this question I. Brownlie, 'The Responsibility of States for the Acts of International Organizations', in M. Raggazi, ed., *International Responsibility Today. Essays in memory of Oscar Schachter* (Leiden/Boston, Martinus Nijhoff Publishers 2005) p. 355; A. Reinisch, 'Securing the Accountability of International Organizations', 7 *Global Governance* (2001) pp. 131–149; A. Reinisch, 'Governance without Accountability', *German Yearbook of International Law* (2001) pp. 270–306; H.G. Schermers, 'Liability of International Organizations', 1 *Leiden Journal of International Law* (1988) pp. 3–14; W.E. Holder, 'Can International Organizations be Controlled? Accountability and Responsibility', 97 *American Society of International Law Proceedings* (2003) pp. 231–240.

But such an insistence on Member States' responsibility could jeopardise the ability of international organisations to fulfil their functions effectively, since such a development may lead States to tighten their control on the decision-making of the international organisation, or to reserve the right not to comply with its decisions. If, however, we seek to impose upon international organisations that they comply directly with human rights obligations, we run another risk: such organisations may be tempted to act beyond their attributed powers in order to promote and protect human rights, in conditions which may be neither legitimate nor compatible with the instrument setting them up in the first place.

In the face of this dilemma, Dan Sarooshi has proposed establishing a clear distinction between *delegations of powers* to international organisations and *transfers of powers*. According to this distinction, the former case enables States to retain the right to exercise powers on a unilateral basis; they are not bound to comply with any measure adopted by the organisation on the basis of the delegation of powers; and, in principle, they may put an end to the conferral of powers. In the latter case, by contrast, States are bound to comply with obligations flowing from the exercise by the organisation of the powers which have been transferred to it.[5] Hence, Sarooshi suggests that a possible way to avoid that the transfer of powers will result in a conflict between different international obligations is 'for the negotiating States to decide to 'delegate' and not 'transfer' their powers to an organization so that they will not be bound to comply with decisions taken by the organization when exercising conferred powers'.[6] This would ensure that no attribution of powers to international organisations will result in States circumventing their international obligations. But the price we pay is high: it disables the international organisation, by providing an easy 'exit' to States unwilling to comply with certain measures it may adopt. There is no pooling of sovereignty here: rather, a simple *à la carte* form of inter-State cooperation.[7]

In order to address the dilemma effectively, however, we need to take seriously both horns. We have to ensure that the transfer of powers does not become a vehicle for its members avoiding their international obligations. But we must also do so without depriving the organisation from the power to oblige its members,

5 See D. Sarooshi, *International Organizations and their exercise of sovereign powers* (Oxford, Oxford University Press 2005) chapter 5, sect. II pp. 58–64.

6 *Ibid.*, at p. 103. For instance, 'the World Health Organization, the Universal Postal Union, and the International Civil Aviation Organization are given powers such that an organ of the organization can adopt binding regulations by majority decision, but in such cases the Member States have an express right to contract out of, or make reservations to, the application of a specific regulation to them, usually before it enters into force' (p. 59; reference is made for these examples to A. Chayes and A. Chayes, *The New Sovereignty: Compliance with International Regulatory Agreements* (Cambridge, Mass, Harvard University Press 1995) pp. 226–7).

7 In the remainder of this contribution, I will not distinguish between the two expressions.

and not run the risk of the organisation moving beyond its mandate, even when under the pretext of better complying with human rights obligations. This contribution seeks to address the question of human rights accountability in the activities of international organisations by exploring solutions that overcome this dilemma. In exploring this question, a distinction has to be made between the content of the human rights obligations of international organisations and the question of accountability *per se*. Part I addresses the question of whether or not international organisations are bound, under international law, to respect human rights. It examines whether such obligations can be derived from the pre-existing human rights obligations of the Member States establishing or acceding to the international organisation or, conversely, whether such organisations should be grounded upon customary international law or on the general principles of law. The conclusion of this inquiry is that, while it would be possible to build a theory deriving the obligations of the international organisation from the pre-existing obligations of its Member States – particularly those imposed under the human rights treaties to which these States are parties – this line of reasoning ultimately fails on practical grounds, as it results in excessive obstacles being imposed upon international co-operation. In contrast, grounding the human rights obligations of international organisations on general public international law, independently of any commitments of their Member States under human rights treaties, appears both feasible and compatible with the requirements of international co-operation.

However, accountability requires not only that certain human rights obligations are recognised to exist. It also requires mechanisms to be established that provide remedies to potential victims, whether before national or international courts. Parts II and III turn to that separate question of accountability. Part II explores the international responsibility of the Member States of an international organisation, where measures adopted by the latter result in a violation of human rights. This initial focus on State responsibility is justified by two reasons. First, since they are grounded in general international law rather than in human rights treaties, the human rights obligations imposed on international organisations are less far-reaching than those imposed on the States to which they owe their existence. Second, only in a limited range of situations will it be possible for a victim to file a claim directly against the international organisation for an act resulting in a violation of human rights since, in general, no international court will have jurisdiction over the issue, whereas national courts typically will be barred from adjudicating such claims, because of the immunity of jurisdiction enjoyed by international organisations. In order to evaluate the emerging regime of State responsibility for the acts of international organisations of whom it is a member, Part II considers the three moments which characterise such membership: it distinguishes (1) the initial attribution of competences to the international organisation; (2) the participation in the decision-making procedures within the organisation; and (3) the implementation, by its Member States, of any acts adopted within the international organisation. The following thesis is put forward: while the international law of State responsibility has offered answers concerning whether a responsibility may exist at each of these moments, it has failed to consider their interrelationship. This segmented approach to State responsibility constitutes the main source of its insufficiencies. As an alternative, a 'sliding scales' theory of State responsibility is presented. Accordingly, the role of the State at any of the three junctures distinguished above is evaluated by taking into account its role at the other junctures: in particular, the more a State retains influence on the decision-making process within the international organisation, or the more it may obstruct implementation of the decisions of the organisation, the easier it will be to justify the delegation of extensive powers to the international organisation, even in circumstances where such a transfer of powers could result in the adoption by the international organisation of measures that infringe upon human rights.

Part III then examines the mechanisms that allow for international organisations to be held accountable for any violations of human rights to which they contribute or which they commit. Three such mechanisms are discussed in turn: self-regulation, accession of the international organisation to treaty-based international regimes, and judicial control exercised by national courts. The respective strengths and weaknesses of each of these mechanisms are highlighted. On the basis of this review, the logic of sliding scales for the evaluation of State responsibility is expanded further to include the emergence of those mechanisms. It is argued that the standards used for evaluating the responsibility of the Member States of international organisations for the acts of the latter should take into account whether or not accountability mechanisms have been set up ensuring that the organisation will comply with any human rights standards equivalent to those imposed on the Member States. This results in a reverse principle of proportionality: the more the international organisation is subject to monitoring mechanisms, whether internal or external, the more it would be acceptable for States to transfer large competences to the organisation and to renounce controlling the organisation from within or blocking the implementation of any decisions adopted by the organisation.

I. THE HUMAN RIGHTS OBLIGATIONS OF INTERNATIONAL ORGANISATIONS

This Part examines whether or not international organisations are bound by human rights obligations under international law. This inquiry should not be confused with the broader question of accountability in cases of human rights violations committed by international organisations. The former is more precise, as well as logically prior to the question of 'accountability' – which connotes whether or not victims of human rights violations may seek remedies before international or national instances, as well as hold either the international organisation itself or its Member States to account for the said violations. Accordingly, these two questions deserve distinct treatment. Indeed, the imposition of human rights obligations directly upon international organisations is neither a necessary nor a sufficient condition for accountability to exist. It is not necessary, due to the potential existence of a forum before which victims of human rights violations by the organisation may seek a remedy against one or more of the Member States of the organisation, where the organisation itself cannot be targeted. And it is insufficient, because even if we agree that international organisations have certain human rights obligations, this does not ensure that there will exist such a forum before which victims may file claims. Part III of this contribution examines the mechanisms through which international organisations can be held accountable for human rights violations. In this Part, we focus only on the question of the normative bases for imposing human rights obligations on international organisations.

The principle is of course that, as subjects of international law, international organisations are 'bound by any obligations incumbent upon them under general rules of international law, under their constitutions or under international agreements to which they are parties'.[8] For the moment, we leave aside the specific case where an international organisation has acceded to an international human rights treaty.[9] Instead, we examine the classical situation where the international organisation is not a party to any such treaty, and where we therefore must identify elsewhere the source of any human rights obligation it may be imposed. In any case, since most human rights treaties are not open to the participation of international organisations, it is in principle only by identifying sources of human rights obligations in general international law that we can hope to impose on them such obligations. Happily, this task is far from insuperable. While it seems difficult to argue that international organisations should be considered to inherit the human rights obligations imposed on their Member States (1.), there is indeed a growing consensus in legal doctrine that most, if not all, of the rights enumerated in the Universal Declaration on Human Rights have acquired the status of legally binding norms (2.). The debate has now shifted, from the question of whether or not these rights have such status, to the question of the foundations for recognising them their status.

---

8 ICJ, *Interpretation of the Agreement of 25 March 1991 between the WHO and Egypt*, Advisory Opinion, *ICJ Rep.* (1980) pp. 89–90, at para. 37.

9 See Part III, B.

A. THE INTERNATIONAL ORGANISATION 'SUCCEEDING' TO THE HUMAN RIGHTS OBLIGATIONS OF ITS MEMBER STATES

It has sometimes been argued that, when States transfer certain competences to an international organisation – seeking to establish a further means in pursuing international cooperation – the organisation 'succeeds' to the international obligations of its Member States, as stipulated in the treaties in force *vis-à-vis* those States.[10] Both the term and the doctrine are misleading. Since international organisations are not sovereign entities, they do not 'succeed' to their Member States as happens in situations of succession of States.[11] International

[10] The discussion in this section is restricted to human rights obligations imposed under international *treaties* concluded by the Member States of an international organisation. In theory, the question of the impact of such preexisting obligations of Member States is also posed as regards obligations imposed under customary international law or general principles of law, since not all such obligations imposed on States will *ipso facto* be obligatory for an international organisation: subjects of international law may differ, even under general international law, as regards the scope and content of their rights and duties (ICJ, *Reparation for Injuries Suffered in the Service of the United Nations*, Advisory Opinion, *ICJ Rep.* (1949) p. 174, at 178: 'The subjects of law in any legal system are not necessarily identical in their nature or in the extent of their rights, and their nature depends upon the needs of the community'). But deriving obligations of the international organisation from the preexisting obligations of its Member States is less relevant as regards these other sources of international obligations, since the principle of the relative effect of treaties (which are *res inter alios acta* for third parties, thus also for any international organisation not a party to treaties concluded by States) would not apply. On the contrary, as detailed in the next section, international organisations are in principle bound by human rights obligations under general international law, whether through customary international law or through the general principles of law.

[11] See the Vienna Convention on Succession of States in respect of Treaties, UN doc. A/CONF.80/31 of 22 August 1978, as corrected by A/CONF.80/31/Corr.2 of 27 October 1978. As is well known, the Human Rights Committee has taken the view under the International Covenant on Civil and Political Rights that 'once the people are accorded the protection of the rights under the Covenant, such protection devolves with territory and continues to belong to them, notwithstanding change in government of the State party, including dismemberment in more than one State or State succession or any subsequent action of the State party designed to divest them of the rights guaranteed by the Covenant'. It follows, according to the Committee, that 'international law does not permit a State which has ratified or acceded or succeeded to the Covenant to denounce it or withdraw from it' (Human Rights Committee, *General Comment No. 26. Continuity of obligations*, UN doc. CCPR/C/21/Rev.1/Add.8/Rev.1, 8 December 1997, paras. 4–5). The view adopted by the Committee on the question of State succession to the ICCPR is not in conformity with general public international law (comp., for example, American Law Institute, *Restatement (Third) of the Foreign Relations Law of the United States* (1987) (St. Paul, Minn., American Law Institute Publishers 1987), §210(3), Reporters' Note 4; I. Brownlie, *Principles of Public International Law*, 5th edn. (Oxford, Oxford University Press 1998) p. 663; A. Cassese, *International Law*, 2nd edn. (Oxford, Oxford University Press 2005) p. 78; M. Shaw, *International Law*, 5th edn. (Cambridge, Cambridge University Press 2003) p. 875). It is clearly based on the idea that international human rights treaties are specific, and that questions such as the denunciation by States parties of the ICCPR or of State succession should take this specificity into consideration (see M. Kamminga, 'State Succession in Respect of Human Rights Treaties', 7

organisations do not become parties to international human rights treaties binding upon their Member States simply because they have been attributed certain powers that could be exercised in violation of the rights recognised under those treaties. The question of succession, in this context, is of a limited nature. It is whether international organisations are bound by the pre-existing substantive international obligations of their Member States (apart from the participation in the human rights regime), or whether, since they are separate subjects of international law, they may in principle disregard any such pre-existing obligations.

We should not confuse the question of 'succession' thus circumscribed with the inquiry of whether or not an international organisation should ensure that it will not impose obstacles to the fulfillment, by its Member States, of their obligations, even when such international organisations have been attributed certain exclusive competences and must exercise those competences in order for the Member States to comply with their international obligations.[12] It is axiomatic that States may not escape pre-existing treaty-based commitments by the conclusion, with other parties, of another treaty covering the same subject, whose provisions would in some way conflict with the earlier treaty: the posterior treaty could not be invoked against the parties to the earlier treaty, for whom it is a *res inter alios acta*.[13] This rule, which is directly derived from the principle of

European Journal of International Law (1996) p. 469, at pp. 482–483; R. Higgins, 'The International Court of Justice and Human Rights', in K. Wellens, ed., *International Law: Theory and Practice. Essays in Honour of Eric Suy* (The Hague, Martinus Nijhoff Publishers 1998) p. 691, at pp. 696–697). A member of the Committee, Mr Nisuke Ando, expressed doubts about this doctrine (see his individual opinion appended to Human Rights Committee, *Kuok Koi v. Portugal*, Communication No. 925/2000, final views of 22 October 2001, UN doc. CCPR/C/73/D/925/2000). Whether or not the position of the Human Rights Committee is correct as a matter or international law, this position seems difficult to transpose to international organisations 'succeeding' to States parties to international human rights treaties when competences are transferred to international organisations, since participation of the latter in the Covenant's monitoring system is not envisaged by the text of the Covenant. At most, this position amounts to stating that States parties to the ICCPR may not divest the population under their jurisdiction from the rights they enjoy under the Covenant, by transferring powers to an international organisation not offering a similar protection. This is also the position adopted in this contribution.

12 One way to read to interesting attempt of Tawhida Ahmed and Israel de Jesús Butler to locate the human rights obligations of the European Union in general public international law, is to see this as an attempt to use a theory of 'succession', as derived from Article 307 TEC (now Article 351 TFEU) (referred to hereunder, see text corresponding to n. 13–24) as implying that, *as a matter of general public international law*, the European Union would somewhat 'inherit' the human rights obligations of its Member States. I would resist reliance on that specific argument, although I share their view that there are other grounds to impose human rights obligations on the EU. See T. Ahmed and I. de Jesús Butler, 'The European Union and Human Rights: an International Law Perspective', 17 *European Journal of International Law* (2006) pp. 771-801.

13 See Art. 30 of the Vienna Convention on the Law of Treaties of 23 May 1969 (1155 *UNTS* 331), entitled 'Application of successive treaties relating to the same subject-matter' (see, specifically,

the obligatory character of international treaties (*pacta sunt servanda*), applies also to treaties concluded by States in order to establish international organisations to which certain powers are delegated, to the extent such delegations of power may have an impact on the ability of the Member States to comply with their pre-existing obligations. Therefore, the rule may lead the international organisation to provide that its Member States will not be imposed obligations, as members of the organisation and as a result of the internal decision-making process within that organisation, which would lead them to have to disregard such prior commitments.

Until the Kadi judgment delivered on appeal by the European Court of Justice (ECJ)[14], Article 307 TEC used to provide a perfect example of such a practice.[15] By stipulating that the rights and obligations arising from agreements concluded with third States by the Member States before the date of their accession of the European Union 'shall not be affected' by the obligations imposed on the

---

Article 30 §4, b)). As explained by Special Rapporteur Fitzmaurice: 'Since anything that some of the parties to a treaty do *inter se* under another treaty is clearly *res inter alios acta*, it cannot in law result in any formal diminution of the obligation of these parties under the earlier treaty, or affect juridically the rights or position of the other parties, which remain legally intact and subsisting' (G. Fitzmaurice, 'Third Report', *ILC Yearbook* (1958), vol. II, p. 43). For further discussions of the rule, see in particular Ch. Rousseau, 'De la compatibilité des normes juridiques contradictoires dans l'ordre international', 39 *Revue générale de droit international public* (1932) pp. 133–192; E.W. Vierdag, 'The Time of the Conclusion of a Multilateral Treaty: Article 30 of the Vienna Conveniotn on the Law of Treaties and Related Provisions', 59 *British Yearbook of International Law* (1988) pp. 92–111; W. Czaplinski and G.M. Danilenko, 'Conflict of Norms in International Law', 21 *Netherlands International Law Review* (1990) pp. 12–28; J. B. Mus, 'Conflicts Between Treaties in International Law', 29 *Netherlands International Law Review* (1998) pp. 208–232.

14 ECJ, Joined Cases C-402/05P & C-415/05P, *Yassin Abdullah Kadi and Al Barakaat International Foundation v. Council of the European Union and Commission of the European Communities* [2008] ECR I-6351 (hereafter ECJ, *Kadi*).

15 With the entry into force of the Lisbon Treaty on 1 December 2009 (Treaty of Lisbon amending the Treaty on European Union and the Treaty establishing the European Community, Lisbon, 13 December 2007, *O.J. C* 306 (17 December 2007); consolidated versions of the Treaty on European Union (TEU) and the Treaty on the Functioning of the European Union (TFEU) as they are amended by the Lisbon Treaty are published in *O.J. C* 85 (30 March 2010)), this provision has been replaced by Article 351 TFEU, according to which: 'The rights and obligations arising from agreements concluded before 1 January 1958 or, for acceding States, before the date of their accession, between one or more Member States on the one hand, and one or more third countries on the other, shall not be affected by the provisions of this Treaty. To the extent that such agreements are not compatible with this Treaty, the Member State or States concerned shall take all appropriate steps to eliminate the incompatibilities established. Member States shall, where necessary, assist each other to this end and shall, where appropriate, adopt a common attitude. In applying the agreements referred to in the first paragraph, Member States shall take into account the fact that the advantages accorded under this Treaty by each Member State form an integral part of the establishment of the Community and are thereby inseparably linked with the creation of common institutions, the conferring of powers upon them and the granting of the same advantages by all the other Member States.'

Member States under EU law, this provision sought to 'lay down, in accordance with the principles of international law, that the application of the Treaty does not affect the duty of the Member State concerned to respect the rights of non-member countries under a prior agreement and to perform its obligations thereunder'.[16] As has been noted by the European Court of Justice in the *Burgoa* case, while Article 307 TEC refers only to the obligations the Member States owe to third countries, 'it would not achieve its purpose if it did not imply a duty on the part of the institutions of the Community not to impede the performance of the obligations of Member States which stem from a prior agreement'.[17] Therefore, the useful effect of the rule requires that the institutions of the EU do not seek to impose on the EU Member States that they comply with obligations under EU law that would run counter to their other, pre-existing, international undertakings. However, the Court emphasised that 'that duty of the Community institutions is directed only to permitting the Member State concerned to perform its obligations under the prior agreement *and does not bind the Community as regards the non-member country in question*'.[18] This has been reaffirmed in more recent cases, particularly in the *Kadi* and *Yusuf* judgments delivered by the Court of First Instance of the European Communities (CFI) on 21 September 2005.[19] In those cases, the question was raised whether certain measures[20] adopted by the European Community (now the European Union) in order to put into effect certain restrictive measures against Usama bin Laden, members of the Al-Qaeda network and the Taliban and other associated individuals, groups, undertakings and entities, in accordance with Security

16 ECJ, Case 10/61, *Commission v. Italy*, [1962] ECR 1.

17 ECJ, Case 812/79, *Attorney General v. Burgoa*, [1980] ECR 2787, at para. 9. See also CFI, Case T-315/01, *Kadi v. Council and Commission*, [2005] ECR II-3649, at para. 197 (hereafter CFI, *Kadi*); CFI, Case T-306/01, *Ali Yusuf and Al Barakaat International Foundation v. Council and Commission*, [2005] ECR II-3533, at para. 247 (hereafter CFI, *Ali Yusuf*).

18 ECJ, Case 812/79, *Attorney General v. Burgoa*, [1980] ECR 2787, at para. 9 (emphasis added). See also, for a reaffirmation of this statement, CFI, Case T-184/95, *Dorsch Consult v. Council and Commission* [1998] ECR II-667, at para. 74. For other examples where Article 307 TEC was invoked, see ECJ, Case C-324/93, *Evans Medical and Macfarlan Smith* [1995] ECR I-563, at para. 27; Case 10/61, *Commission v. Italy* [1962] ECR 1; Case C-158/91, *Levy* [1993] ECR I-4287; and Case C-124/95, *Centro-Com* [1997] ECR I-81, at para. 56.

19 CFI, *Kadi*, at para. 192; CFI, *Ali Yusuf*, at para. 242. In these two companion cases, the applicants sought the annulment of Council Regulation (EC) No 881/2002 of 27 May 2002 imposing certain specific restrictive measures directed against certain persones and entities associated with Usama bin Laden, the Al-Quaida network and the Taliban. The Court of First Instance had to address the question whether the EU was bound to contribute to the implementation of the sanctions decided by the UN Security Council.

20 Council Regulation (EC) No 881/2002 of 27 May 2002 imposing certain specific restrictive measures directed against certain persones and entities associated with Usama bin Laden, the Al-Quaida network and the Taliban and repealing Council Regulation (EC) No 467/2001 prohibiting the export of certain goods and services to Afghanistan, strenghtening the flight ban and extending the freeze of funds and other financial resources in respect of the Taliban of Afghanistan, *OJ* 2002 L 139/9.

Council Resolutions 1267 (1999), 1333 (2000) and 1390 (2002), were compatible with the fundamental rights protected in the EU legal order. In order to address the question, the Court of First Instance first had to ask itself whether the EU is bound by the UN Security Council resolutions. It answered:

> '... unlike its Member States, the Community as such is not directly bound by the Charter of the United Nations and that it is not therefore required, as an obligation of general public international law, to accept and carry out the decisions of the Security Council in accordance with Article 25 of that Charter. The reason is that the Community is not a member of the United Nations, or an addressee of the resolutions of the Security Council, or the successor to the rights and obligations of the Member States for the purposes of public international law.'[21]

In other terms, it is one thing to impose on an international organisation that it does not create obstacles to the compliance by its Member States with pre-existing international obligations which they remain bound by, and which they may not derogate from simply by joining the international organisation; it would be quite another for the international organisation as such to be bound vis-à-vis third parties, in the international legal order. The cases of *Kadi* and *Ali Yusuf* emphasise this very distinction. In these cases, the Council of the EU and the European Commission had defended the view that it followed from Article 103 of the Charter of the United Nations (UN Charter) that 'the Community, like the Member States of the United Nations, is bound by international law to give effect, within its spheres of competence, to resolutions of the Security Council, especially those adopted under Chapter VII of the Charter of the United Nations'.[22] The CFI concludes that the argument is valid, 'subject to this reservation that it *is not under general international law*, as those parties would have it, *but by virtue of the EC Treaty itself*, that the Community was required to give effect to the Security Council resolutions concerned, within the sphere of its powers'.[23] The CFI does consider in these cases that 'in so far as the powers necessary for the performance of the Member States' obligations under the UN Charter have been transferred to the Community, the Member States have undertaken, pursuant to public international law, to ensure that the Community itself should exercise those powers to that end'.[24] But this public international law obligation is imposed on the EU Member States, not on the European Community itself. It is only by virtue of EC law that the Community has an obligation to contribute to the fulfilment, by the EU Member States, of their obligations under the UN Charter.

---

21 CFI, *Kadi*, at para. 192; CFI, *Ali Yusuf*, at para. 242.
22 CFI, *Kadi*, at para. 153; CFI, *Ali Yusuf*, at para. 206.
23 CFI, *Kadi*, at para. 207; CFI, *Ali Yusuf*, at para. 257 (emphasis added).
24 CFI, *Kadi*, at para. 198; CFI, *Ali Yusuf*, at para. 248.

It is precisely this distinction which is missed by Pierre Pescatore, when he writes that '[b]y transferring certain powers and responsibilities to the Community, the Member States could not free themselves from the observation of standards agreed to in relation with third States; respect for the stability of international agreements and good faith in international relations make it essential therefore to admit that the transfer of powers has *ipso jure* entailed a succession to certain treaty rights and obligations in relation to third States'.[25] But the second sentence does not follow from the first. Contrary to what is asserted, the transfer of powers from the EU Member States to the EU may be ignored by the third States, parties to prior international agreements binding on the EU Member States. For these third States, the EU treaties are a *res inter alios acta*: unless they agree to the substitution of the EU to its Member States for the fulfilment of the latter's obligations towards them, such 'succession' cannot take place, and it certainly does not constitute the automatic result of the transfer of powers. The position of P. Pescatore may be contrasted with that adopted by the Court of First Instance in the *Kadi* and *Yusuf* cases, where it found that, 'first, the Community may not infringe the obligations imposed on its Member States by the Charter of the United Nations or impede their performance and, second, that in the exercise of its powers it is bound, by the very Treaty by which it was established, to adopt all the measures necessary to enable its Member States to fulfil those obligations'.[26] Stating that, *under the EC Treaty*, the Community is bound to exercise its powers so as to enable its Member States to fulfil their international obligations, is not equivalent to stating that, *as a matter of general public international law*, the Community itself is bound to comply with those international obligations.

This is not to say, of course, that the pre-existing obligations of the Member States, as defined in the human rights treaties to which those States are parties, have no impact on the obligations of the international organisation in the international legal order; it means, simply, that the obligations of the international organisation do not derive from the mere prohibition imposed on the Member States to set aside their pre-existing obligations by setting up, or acceding to, an international organisation. A distinct, but potentially more powerful, argument in favour of a link between the two sets of obligations is that no subject of international law may transfer to another subject more powers than those which it possesses: *nemo plus juris transferre potest quam ipse habet*.[27] In that sense, *as*

---

25 P. Pescatore, 'External relations in the case-law of the Court of justice of the European Communities', *Common Market Law Review* (1979) pp. 615–645, at pp. 637–638.

26 CFI, *Kadi*, at para. 204; CFI, *Ali Yusuf*, at para. 254.

27 M.H. Arsanjani, 'Claims against international organizations: *quis custodiet ipsos custodes*', *Yale Studies in World Public Order* (1981) pp. 131–176, at p. 132; F. Morgenstern, *Legal Problems of International Organizations* (Cambridge, Grotius 1986) p. 32; and other authors cited by P. Klein, *La responsabilité des organisations internationales dans les ordres juridiques internes et en droit des gens* (Bruylant, Bruxelles 1998) p. 341. In his dissenting opinion to the

a matter of international law, the international organisation would not be allowed to act in violation of the pre-existing obligations of its Member States, not precisely because it would be bound by the same obligations, but rather because it would thereby be acting beyond its powers, so that any acts violating those obligations should be considered void. This argument has been put forward by Henry Schermers:

> 'As no one can transfer more powers than he has, the Member States were not competent to transfer any powers conflicting with these [treaties they were parties to prior to their accession to the EC] to the Communities when they were established. [...] All government power was restricted in the sense that it could not go beyond the lines drawn in the [European] Convention [on Human Rights]. [...] In transferring power to a newly established Community, the Member States could not grant the Community any possibility to infringe the rights guaranteed by the Convention. Any rules made by the Community contrary to the Convention are therefore void.'[28]

It is crucial to note that this prohibition imposed on the international organisation does not depend on the organisation having been attributed any specific powers to *implement* the said pre-existing obligations of its Member States. Such a capacity would be required, of course, if the organisation were to substitute itself to its Member States for the execution of those obligations – a substitution which, again as exemplified by European Community law, may be allowed under specific circumstances, so narrowly defined however that this would in any event remain exceptional.[29] But, insofar as the obligation of the

---

Advisory Opinion of the International Court of Justice on *Legal Consequences for States of the Continued Presence of South Africa in Namibia (South West Africa) notwithstanding Security Council Resolution 276 (1970)*, delivered on 21 June 1971, Judge Fitzmaurice thus mentioned that '[i]n so far as [...] the United Nations could legitimately exercise any supervisory powers [on South Africa in respect of its mandate on South West Africa], these were perforce *derived* powers – powers inherited or taken over from the League Council. They could not therefore exceed those of the Council, – for *derived* powers cannot be other or greater than those they derive from. There could not have been transferred or passed on from the League what the League itself did not have, – for *nemo dare potest quod ipse non habet*, or (the corollary) *nemo accipere potest id quod ipse donator nunquam habuit*' (at para. 65). In the *Kadi* case referred to above, the Court of First Instance refers to this principle, and cites in that respect, 'by analogy', its 1972 judgment delivered in the International Fruit Cases (see n. 29 hereunder): see CFI, *Kadi*, at para. 196.

28 H.G. Schermers, 'The European Communities bound by Fundamental Human Rights', 27 *Common Market Law Review* (1990) p. 249, at pp. 251–252.

29 See ECJ, Joined cases 21 to 24/72, *International Fruit Company and others v. Produktschap voor Groenten en Fruit*, [1972] ECR 1219. The Court concludes in that judgment that the European Economic Community is bound by the General Agreement on Tariffs and Trade (GATT), since (a) 'at the time when they concluded the Treaty establishing the [EEC] the Member States were bound by the obligations of the [GATT]'; (b) 'the Community has assumed the functions inherent in the tariff and trade policy'; (c) 'by conferring those powers on the Community, the Member States showed their wish to bind it by the obligations entered into under the [GATT]'; (d) the transfer of powers to the Community 'has been put into concrete form in different ways within the framework of the [GATT] and has been recognised

international organisation is simply defined as a *prohibition* to take measures which, if they were adopted by its Member States, would constitute a violation of the international obligations of the latter, there is no need for the organisation to have been delegated powers in the domain considered: rather, the prohibition applies to the exercise by the organisation of the powers it has been attributed, however broadly or narrowly such powers have been defined.[30]

Grounding the international obligations of the organisation on the rule according to which '*derived* powers cannot be other or greater than those they derive from' – to borrow from the formulation of judge Fitzmaurice[31] – also has an impact on the identification of the obligations concerned. In principle, such obligations should correspond to any international obligation of *any* Member State of the organisation, without it being necessary that *all* the Member States are bound by the said obligation.[32] In other terms, when they establish an international organisation, the Member States set it up with an implicit understanding that the organisation is not attributed any power beyond those possessed by the Member States at the time it is established, and that such powers as have been transferred shall not be exercised in violation of the obligations of the Member States, including those which are not common to all the Member States concerned.

The problem is that this doctrine, defensible as it is in theory, is unworkable in practice as regards multilateral organisations with an evolving membership, i.e., to which new Member States may accede after the entry into force of the treaty establishing the organisation. Indeed, its consequence would be – if taken literally – that, by agreeing to any supplementary State acceding to the organisation, all the other Member States would be accepting that the competences of the organisation will be implicitly limited to whichever measures it may take without violating the international obligations of that new Member State. It is precisely in order to avoid a situation in which the institutions of the European Union would thus become straightjacketed by the combination of all the human rights commitments of the Member States of the EU that the European Court of Justice

by the other Contracting Parties' (paras. 10–18). This example is not unique, but it remains quite exceptional, even for a supranational organisation such as the European Community. See also ECJ, Case 38/75, *Douaneagent der NV Nederlandse Spoorwegen*, [1975] ECR 1439 (as regards the EC substituting itself to its Member States for the implementation of the Convention on the Nomenclature of Goods in Customs Tariffs, 347 UNTS 127); and ECJ, Joined Cases 3, 4, and 6/76, *Kramer*, [1976] ECR 1279 (as regards the EC substituting itself to its Member States for the implementation of the North-East Atlantic Fisheries Convention, 486 UNTS 157). For further references and a discussion, P. Klein, op. cit. n. 27, at pp. 332–340; and T. Ahmed and I. de Jesús Butler, loc. cit. n. 12, at pp. 783–792.

30 I return to this distinction further. See text corresponding to n. 191–195.

31 See *supra*, n. 27.

32 In this respect also, the doctrine functions in a remarkably different fashion than the doctrine of substitution, as exemplified by the *International Fruit* cases referred to *supra*, n. 29.

has declined to include among the general principles of law it upholds human rights instruments which have not been ratified by all the Member States, or which impose only *à la carte* obligations on the Member States.[33] Indeed, this too may explain the original insertion of Article 234 in the EEC Treaty (Article 307 TEC, now Article 351 TFEU), as well as the interpretation by the European Court of Justice of its implications: whereas, in accordance with general public international law, it was agreed that the EEC Treaty should not impose on the Member States of the Community that they violate pre-existing international obligations, it was at the same time *not* assumed that those obligations would be shifted on the European Community itself, since this could have resulted in endangering the deepening of European integration.[34] That provision was a

33 The Court considers that, apart from the European Convention on Human Rights – which Article 6 §2 of the Treaty on the EU in any case refers to explicitly –, whose 'special significance' in EU law it recognises and which it applies as if it were binding on the EU, the International Covenant on Civil and Political Rights should be complied with (ECJ, Case 374/87, *Orkem v. Commission* [1989] ECR 3283, at para. 31; ECJ, Joined Cases C-297/88 and C-197/89, *Dzodzi* [1990] ECR I-3763, at para. 68), and that '[t]his also true of the Convention on the Rights of the Child [of 20 November 1989] *which, like the Covenant, binds each of the Member States*' (emphasis added) (ECJ, Case C-540/03, *European Parliament v. Council* [2006] ECR I-5769). This statement was made in a judgment rejecting as ill-founded the action of the European Parliament for the annulment of certain provisions of the Family Reunification Directive (Council Directive 2003/86/EC of 22 September 2003 on the right to family reunification (OJ 2003 L 251, p. 12)), which, in the view of the Parliament, violated a number of international human rights instruments as well as the EU Charter of Fundamental Rights. In contrast to the European Convention on Human Rights and the International Covenant on Civil and Political Rights, the Court notes about the Council of Europe Social Charter that: 'So far as concerns the Member States bound by these instruments, it is also to be remembered that the Directive provides, in Article 3(4), that it is without prejudice to more favourable provisions of the European Social Charter of 18 October 1961, the amended European Social Charter of 3 May 1987 [*sic*; while the Court here reproduces a mistake of the European legislator itself, the actual name and date of this instrument is the Revised European Social Charter of 3 May 1996], the European Convention on the legal status of migrant workers of 24 November 1977 and bilateral and multilateral agreements between the Community or the Community and the Member States, on the one hand, and third countries, on the other' (para. 107). However, since it, too, has been accepted by all the EU Member States, the European Social Charter in more recent cases was recognised to constitute a source of inspiration for the development of the fundamental rights included by the European Court of Justice among the general principles of law (see, as regards the right to take collective action, ECJ, Case C 438/05, *International Transport Workers' Federation, Finnish Seamen's Union, v. Viking Line ABP, OÜ Viking Line Eesti* [2007] ECR I-10779, para. 43; and ECJ, Case C-341/05, *Laval un Partneri Ltd v. Svenska Byggnadsarbetareförbundet, Svenska Byggnadsarbetareförbundets avd. 1, Byggettan, Svenska Elektrikerförbundet* [2007] ECR I-11767, para. 90). Admittedly, the Court refers here to the fundamental rights it considers included among the general principles of law which it ensures respect for, without implying that there would exist an international law obligation imposed on the EU or the EC to comply with the said instruments. But the practical concerns would be the same, whatever the status of the obligation and its normative foundation: it would be imposing excessive constraints on the international organisation, to require from it that it complies with the preexisting obligations of each and every member State.

34 Quite to the contrary, in situations of conflict betwen one member State's international obligations and the requirements of EC law, the member State is obliged to put an end to the conflict, if necessary, be denouncing the preexisting treaty: see Article 307, second paragraph,

compromise provision, aimed of course at avoiding the imposition on the Member States of conflicting international obligations, but also and at the same time at facilitating the pursuit of intergovernmental cooperation. This is well illustrated by the reference made to that provision by the European Court of Human Rights, which cites Article 307 TEC as an illustration of the fact that States have 'recognised the growing importance of international co-operation and of the consequent need to secure the proper functioning of international organisations'.[35] It is precisely the possibility of further international co-operation and the proper functioning of international organisations which would be put in jeopardy if, following the principle *nemo plus juris transferre potest quam ipse habet*, we were led to conclude that the international organisation, insofar as it is transferred certain powers, is also imposed the full set of international obligations imposed on the States having made such a transfer. We must therefore look elsewhere for the source of human rights obligations imposed on international organisations under international law.

The significance of the obligation imposed under Article 307 TEC to respect pre-existing international obligations of the EU Member States has been narrowed down by the judgment delivered by the ECJ on 3 September 2008 in *Kadi and Al Barakaat* on appeal from the CFI, which thoroughly revisited the relationship between European Community law and international law.[36] The ECJ asserted the constitutional hegemony of the EU, explaining that an international agreement cannot affect the allocation of powers fixed by the Treaties or, consequently, the autonomy of the Community legal system.[37] An international agreement cannot have the effect of prejudicing the constitutional principles of the EC Treaty.[38] The Court placed the emphasis on the need for implementation of UNSC Resolutions to be in accordance with the EC legal order. Indeed, the Court stated that 'the review by the Court of the validity of any Community measure in the light of fundamental rights must be considered to be the expression, in a community

TEC, quoted *supra* n.15, and in the case-law, see ECJ, Case C-324/93, *Evans Medical and Macfarlan Smith* [1995] ECR I-563, at para. 27; ECJ, Case C-158/91, *Levy* [1993] ECR I-4287; and ECJ, Case C-124/95, *Centro-Com* [1997] ECR I-81, at para. 56.

35 ECtHR, *Bosphorus Hava Yolları Turizm ve Ticaret Anonim Şirketi v. Ireland*, Application No. 45036/98, 42 *EHRR* (2006) p.1, at para. 150.

36 ECJ, *Kadi*, see *supra* n. 14. For comments, see D. Halberstam and E. Stein, 'The United Nations, the European Union, and the King of Sweden: Economic Sanctions and Individual Rights in a Plural World Order', 46(1) *Common Market Law Review* (2009) pp. 13–72; P. d'Argent, 'Arrêt "Kadi": le droit communautaire come droit interne', *Journal de droit européen* (2008) p. 265; T. Tridimas and J.A. Gutiérrez-Fons, *EU Law, International Law and Economic Sanctions against Terrorism: The Judiciary in Distress?*, Research Papers in law, n°3/2008, College of Europe, available at www.coleurope.eu; G. de Búrca, 'The EU, the European Court of Justice and the International Legal Order after Kadi', 51 *Harvard International Law Journal* (2009) pp. 1–49.

37 ECJ, *Kadi*, at para. 282.

38 *Ibid.*, at para. 285.

based on the rule of law, of a constitutional guarantee stemming from the EC Treaty as an autonomous legal system which is not to be prejudiced by an international agreement. The question of the Court's jurisdiction arises in the context of the internal and autonomous legal order of the Community […].'[39] The Court recognised that 'the powers provided for in Articles 60 EC[40] and 301 EC[41] may be exercised only in pursuance of the adoption of a common position or joint action by virtue of the provisions of the EC Treaty relating to the CFSP which provides for action by the Community. Although, because of the adoption of such an act, the Community is bound to take, under the EC Treaty, the measures necessitated by that act, that obligation means, when the object is to implement a resolution of the Security Council adopted under Chapter VII of the Charter of the United Nations, that in drawing up such measures the Community is to take due account of the terms and objectives of the resolution concerned and of the relevant obligations under the Charter of the United Nations relating such implementation.'[42] The Court noted that the UN Charter does not impose the choice of a particular model for the implementation of resolutions.[43] The ECJ stated that 'it is not a consequence of the principles governing the international legal order under the United Nations that any judicial review of the internal lawfulness of the contested Regulation in the light of fundamental freedoms is excluded by virtue of the fact that that measure is intended to give effect to a resolution of the Security Council adopted under Chapter VII of the Charter of the United Nations.'[44] Moreover, the obligation imposed on the institutions of the EU to respect pre-existing international obligations of the Member States shall not take precedence over fundamental rights, the protection of which the ECJ ensures in fulfilling its function under Article 220 TEC.[45] 'Article 307 EC may in no circumstances permit any challenge to the principles that form part of the very foundations of the Community legal order, one of which is the protection of fundamental rights, including the review by the Community judicature of the lawfulness of Community measures as regards their consistency with those fundamental rights.'[46]

The ECJ concluded that, if the UN Charter and the Security Council Resolutions *were to be classified as part of the hierarchy of norms within the Community legal order*, they would rank higher than secondary law but lower than primary law, in

39 *Ibid.*, at paras. 316–317.
40 The Lisbon Treaty has moved this provision to Article 75 TFEU.
41 With the Lisbon Treaty this provision has been replaced by Article 215 TFEU.
42 ECJ, *Kadi*, at paras. 295–296.
43 *Ibid.*, at para. 298.
44 *Ibid.*, at para. 299.
45 With the Lisbon Treaty this provision has been repealed and replaced, in substance, by Article 19 TEU.
46 ECJ, *Kadi*, at para. 304.

particular to the general principles of which fundamental principles form part.[47] Given that the Court found the contested measures to be in breach of the right to a hearing, the right to judicial protection and the right to property, it annulled Regulation No 881/2002.

While the CFI had showed that the European Community was bound by the UN Charter, the ECJ did not pronounce itself on this issue. The latter avoided ruling on this question since it established the primacy of primary law, in particular the general principles of which fundamental rights form part on the UN Charter. Its implications concern, rather, the question of implementing decisions of international organisations, which will be analysed in point II C of this contribution.

B. HUMAN RIGHTS AS PART OF GENERAL PUBLIC INTERNATIONAL LAW

Some have alleged that human rights, at least those which are recognised universally, have acquired a customary status in international law.[48] In this section, I examine this claim. I conclude that a more promising normative source of human rights in general public international law – allowing to impose on international organisations certain human rights obligations – is in the general principles of law, also mentioned in Article 38(1) of the Statute of the International Court of Justice among the sources of international law.

1° Human rights as customary international law

Custom requires establishing both consistent identifiable state practice, and evidence of a belief that this practice is rendered obligatory by the existence of a rule of law requiring it (*opinio juris sive necessitatis*).[49] Yet, it has been argued that, in the field of human rights, evidence of custom could be based on the

47 *Ibid.*, at paras. 305–308.

48 See, in particular, L.B. Sohn, 'The Human Rights Law of the Charter', 12 *Texas International Law Journal* (1977) pp. 129–140 at pp. 132–134; T. Meron, *Human Rights and Humanitarian Norms as Customary Law* (Oxford, Clarendon Press 1989); N.S. Rodley, 'Human Rights and Humanitarian Intervention: The Case Law of the World Court', 38 *International and Comparative Law Quarterly* (1989) p. 321, at p. 333; L. Henkin, *The Age of Rights* (New York, Columbia University 1990) p. 19; H. Hannum, 'The Status of the Universal Declaration of Human Rights in National and International Law', 25 *Georgia Journal of International and Comparative Law* (1995–1996) pp. 287–395.

49 ICJ, *North Sea Continental Shelf Cases (Federal Republic of Germany v. Denmark and Federal Republic of Germany v. the Netherlands)*, Judgment, *ICJ Rep.* (1969) p. 44, at para. 77. 'Not only must the acts concerned amount to settled practice, but they must also be such or be carried out in such a way, as to be evidence of a belief that this practice is rendered obligatory by the existence of a rule of law requiring it. The need for such a belief, i.e. the existence of a subjective element, is implicit in the very notion of the opinio juris sive necessitatis. The states

resolutions of the General Assembly of the United Nations and other international organisations, demonstrating a clear commitment of the international community towards certain values,[50] while inconsistent State practice would not be an obstacle in identifying such custom.[51] Alternatively, it has been suggested that State 'practice', for the purposes of custom determination in the field of human rights, is composed of official declarations[52] and participation in the negotiation of human rights instruments, as well as of incorporation of human rights within the national legal orders. At least three arguments have been put forward in favour of this position. First, it may be in any case artificial to dissociate, within the evidence of the emergence of a rule of customary international law, the 'practice' from the '*opinio juris*', since the State practice which matters is one which is legally significant (as it testifies to the emergence of the rule), and since the *opinio juris* can only be identified from State practice itself.[53] This, for instance, is the attitude adopted by the 1987 *Restatement (Third) of the Foreign Relations Law of the United States*, which finds State 'practice' to result from support by States for declarations or resolutions invoking human rights, or from condemnation of violations committed by other

concerned must therefore feel that they are conforming to what amounts to their legal obligation. The frequency or even habitual character of the acts is not in itself enough'.

50 In the case ICJ, *Military and Paramilitary Activities in and against Nicaragua (Nicaragua v. United States)*, Order, *ICJ Rep.* (1991) p. 47, the International Court of Justice seeks to determine the legal status of the obligation imposed on States to refrain in their international relations from the threat or use of force against the territorial integrity or political independence of any State, or in any other manner inconsistent with the purposes of the United Nations. It attaches an important weight in this regard to U.N. General Assembly resolutions: 'The Court has [...] to be satisfied that there exists in customary international law an opinio juris as to the binding character of such abstention [...] This opinio juris may, though with all due caution, be deduced from, inter alia, the attitude of the Parties and the attitude of States towards certain General Assembly resolutions... The effect of consent to the text of such resolutions cannot be understood as merely that of a reiteration or elucidation of the treaty commitment undertaken in the Charter. On the contrary, *it may be understood as an acceptance of the validity of the rule or set of rules declared by the resolution by themselves*' (at para. 188). The reasoning of the Court on this point, however, may be explained by the need to establish a rule on the basis of State practice which consists in an abstention (to rely on the use of force). In that context, statements, such as UN General Assembly resolutions, necessarily must play a role, in order for the abstention to be interpreted as stemming from a sense of obligation. I thank Hélène Ruiz Fabri for drawing my attention to this point.

51 T. Meron, op. cit. n. 48, at pp. 106–114.

52 A particularly important statement in that regard is the Proclamation of Teheran, Final Act of the International Conference on Human Rights, Teheran, 22 April to 13 May 1968, UN Doc. A/CONF. 32/41 at 3 (1968), where it was stated unanimously that the Declaration 'states a common understanding of the peoples of the world concerning the inalienable and inviolable rights of all members of the human family and constitutes an obligation for all members of the international community' (para. 2).

53 See P.-M. Dupuy, 'L'unité de l'ordre juridique international. Cours général de droit international public', *Recueil des cours*, t. 297 (2002) p. 166 ('La coutume est l'expression d'une opinio juris manifestée dans et par une pratique. Elle ne résulte pas de l'adjonction des deux éléments mais de la révélation de l'un par l'autre').

States.[54] But, in addition, since they concern the relationship between a State and its own citizens, human rights violations are difficult to document. They trigger fewer reactions from other States than might violations of international law which infringe upon the interests of the latter States, so that 'custom' in the field of human rights would emerge only with difficulty.[55]

Thus, a 'modern' view of custom has gained some acceptance in the field of human rights.[56] This view presents itself as a substitute to the classical view as reflected in Article 38(1) of the Statute of the International Court of Justice. In the 'modern' approach, State 'practice' in the usual sense of 'behaviour' is less determinative than authoritative statements made by governments or intergovernmental bodies. In general, this turn (favoured in part by a general identity crisis of custom as a source of international law) has been encouraged by well-intentioned authors, eager to provide human rights law with a standing in customary law which would compensate for what was perceived in the 1970s and 1980s as the lack of enthusiasm of States in the ratification of human rights treaties. However, this 'modern' view results in distorting the classical notion of custom in such a way that the notion is barely even recognisable under its new disguise. It is also ideologically biased towards the recognition of certain particular human rights as forming part of customary international law. The result of the 'new' approach emphasises deducing from statements rather than proceeding by induction from State behaviour. In practice, the result has been that those civil and political rights which are recognised in United States constitutional law and which the United States invokes against other States are included, while other rights, equally essential and whose status is identical within the international bill of rights, are excluded.[57]

A certain dissatisfaction has therefore emerged with the substitution of a 'modern' view of custom to the 'traditional' view. This in turn has led to two reactions. One part of the doctrine has sought to accommodate the competing claims of the 'traditional' and the 'modern' views of custom. For instance, Frederic Kirgis has put the requirements of State practice and *opinio juris*, which compete for influencing the emergence of custom, on a sliding scale: whereas, on

54 American Law Institute, op. cit. n. 11, §701, n. 2. For the background, see O. Schachter, 'International Law in Theory and Practice: General Course in Public International Law', *Recueil des cours* vol. 178 (1982-V) p. 2 at pp. 333–342. For a quite similar view of human rights as forming part of customary international law, see T. Meron, op. cit. n. 48.

55 C. Tomuschat, *Human Rights Between Idealism and Realism* (Oxford, Oxford University Press 2003) p. 34; and O. Schachter, 'International Law in Theory and Practice', op. cit. n. 52 at p. 334.

56 For a useful discussion, see M. Akehurst, 'Custom as a Source of International Law', *British Yearbook of International Law* (1974–5) p. 1; L. Henkin, 'Human Rights and State 'Sovereignty'', 25 *Georgia Journal of International Law* 37 (1995–1996).

57 See B. Simma and P. Alston, 'The Sources of Human Rights Law: Custom, Jus Cogens, and General Principles', 12 *Australian Yearbook of International Law* 82 (1988–1989) pp. 94–95.

one end of the scale, highly consistent State practice should suffice to establish the existence of *opinio juris*, conversely and at the other end, strong indications that there exists a consensus among States about the unacceptability of certain forms of behaviour may establish custom, even if State practice is inconsistent.[58] But, alternatively, we may turn to other arguments in order to ground human rights law in general international law. The most provising avenue in this direction is to identify human rights as general principles of law, which may be derived from the national legal systems.

2° *Human rights as general principles of law*

This means of recognising the Universal Declaration of Human Rights as a source of legal obligations is encouraged by the approach adopted by the International Court of Justice itself. The Court has refrained from stating that the Declaration as such, in the totality of its articles, should be considered as customary international law. But it did refer to the Declaration on a number of occasions, albeit always with respect to a specific right and without always clarifying the source of the authority of the Declaration. For instance, alluding to the prohibition of arbitrary arrest or detention stipulated in Article 9 of the Universal Declaration of Human Rights, it stated in the *Hostages* case that '[w]rongfully to deprive human beings of their freedom and to subject them to physical constraint in conditions of hardship is in itself manifestly incompatible with the principles of the Charter of the United Nations, as well as with the fundamental principles enunciated in the Universal Declaration of Human Rights'.[59] The language referring to such 'fundamental principles' is not new. Already in the *Corfu Channel* Case, the Court mentioned 'obligations [...] based [...] on certain general and well-recognized principles', among which it mentioned what it labelled 'elementary considerations of humanity'.[60] In the Advisory Opinion it delivered on the issue of *Reservations to the Convention on the Prevention and Punishment of the Crime of Genocide*, it referred to 'the principles underlying the Convention' as 'principles which are recognized by civilized nations as binding on States, even without any conventional obligation'.[61] Almost identical language may be found in later cases. In its Advisory Opinion on the *Legality of threat or use of nuclear weapons*, referring to

58 F. Kirgis, 'Custom on a Sliding Scale', 81 *American Journal of International Law* (1987) p. 146. This proposal has been built upon, in particular by J. Tasioulas, 'In Defence of Relative Normativity: Communitarian Values and the Nicaragua Case', 16 *Oxford Journal of Legal Studies* (1996) p. 85 and by A.E. Roberts, 'Traditional and Modern Approaches to Customary International Law: A Reconciliation', 95 *American Journal of International Law* (2001) p. 757.

59 ICJ, *United States Diplomatic and Consular Staff in Tehran (United States of America v. Iran)*, Judgment, *ICJ Rep.* (1980) p. 7, at 42.

60 ICJ, *Corfu Channel*, Judgment, *ICJ Rep.* (1949) pp. 4 and following, at p. 22.

61 ICJ, *Reservations to the Convention on the Prevention and Punishment of the Crime of Genocide*, Advisory Opinion, *ICJ Rep.* (1951) p. 19.

the *Corfu Channel* dictum, the Court stated that 'it is undoubtedly because a great many rules of humanitarian law applicable in armed conflict are so fundamental to the respect of the human person and 'elementary considerations of humanity' [...], that the Hague and Geneva Conventions have enjoyed a broad accession. Further these fundamental rules are to be observed by all States whether or not they have ratified the conventions that contain them, because they constitute intransgressible principles of international customary law'.[62] Similarly, in the *Nicaragua v. United States* Case, the Court had mentioned the 'fundamental general principles of humanitarian law' as the source of obligations for the defendant State.[63] The Case *Concerning East Timor* similarly referred to the 'principle' of self-determination as 'one of the essential principles of contemporary international law'.[64]

These statements should be taken with a degree of caution. They refer alternatively to general principles of international law which may be derived both from custom and from treaties, or which are so fundamental to the international legal order that they are, in the view of the World Court, axiomatic; or to general principles of law, common to all the main legal traditions.[65] But it is at least arguable that these statements qualify human rights among the 'general principles of law recognized by civilized nations' mentioned by Article 38(1)(c) of the Statute of the International Court of Justice.[66] Indeed, enthusiastic as they are about the grounding of international human rights law in customary international law, the reporters of the *Restatement (Third) of the Foreign Relations of the United States* note that 'there is a willingness to conclude that prohibitions [against human rights violations] common to the constitutions or laws of many states are general principles that have been absorbed into international law'.[67] This conclusion also may be seen to follow from the fact that the Universal Declaration of Human Rights has been implemented, or even sometimes almost literally reproduced, in a large number of bills of rights in the world.[68]

We may conclude that international organisations, as subjects of international law, must comply with general public international law in the exercise of their

---

62 ICJ, *Legality of the Threat or Use of Nuclear Weapons*, Advisory Opinion, *ICJ Rep.* (1996) p. 226, at p. 257 (para. 79).

63 ICJ, *Military and Paramilitary Activities in and against Nicaragua (Nicaragua v. United States of America)*, Judgment, *ICJ Rep.* (1986) p. 14, at pp. 113–114.

64 ICJ, *Concerning East Timor (Portugal v. Australia)*, Judgment, *ICJ Rep.* (1995) p. 90, at p. 102 (para. 29).

65 I owe this remark to Pierre d'Argent.

66 See B. Simma and P. Alston, loc. cit. n. 57, at pp. 102–108; H. Hannum, 'The Status of the Universal Declaration of Human Rights in National and International Law', op. cit. n. 48, at pp. 351–352; T. Meron, op. cit. n. 48, at p. 88.

67 American Law Institute, *Restatement (Third) of the Foreign Relations Law of the United States*, op. cit. n. 11, at §701, n. 1, at p. 154.

68 For a sample, see the appendix to H. Hannum, 'The Status of the Universal Declaration of Human Rights in National and International Law', op. cit. n. 48.

activities, and that this includes a requirement to comply with the Universal Declaration on Human Rights as general principles of law. But it is here that we encounter the problem of accountability, as defined above[69]: if indeed international organisations are bound to comply with human rights obligations, before which instances may remedies be exercised by victims of their activities? And whether or not international organisations as such are bound by human rights obligations, are not their Member States internationally responsible for any of their acts which lead to human rights violations, under the international human rights treaties to which the States themselves are parties or under other, non conventional mechanisms? I turn now to such problems of accountability.

II. THE PROBLEM OF ACCOUNTABILITY – ONE: STATE RESPONSIBILITY

The problem may be stated fairly concisely. States are bound by human rights obligations under international law, which are imposed on them by treaties to which they are parties, or under general international law. If they transfer certain powers to international organisations which are authorised to exercise these powers by adopting binding decisions, or by developing certain activities which impact negatively upon human rights, which entity will be found internationally responsible? The State may legitimately assert that, since the international organisation has a distinct legal personality,[70] the State should not be imputed the acts that the organisation itself adopts unless exceptional circumstances prevail: in principle, the veil of the organisation should not be lifted. But the international organisation may consider that, precisely because it is a separate

69 See the introduction to part I of this contribution.

70 Not any international agreement, even endowed with an institutional structure for its implementation, shall be recognised an international legal personality. But the existence of a certain autonomy of will of the international organisation – a will distinct from that of its Member States – shall in principle be deemed sufficient for there to exist such separate legal personality. It has been acknowledged that international legal personality results from the capacity of the subject to hold rights or to be imposed duties under international law, and to exercise those rights or be held accountable to such duties in the international legal process. This was the position of the International Court of Justice in the *Reparation for Injuries Suffered in the Service of the United Nations* case, where it ruled that the United Nations is a 'subject of international law and capable of possessing international rights and duties, and that it has the capacity to maintain its rights by bringing international claims'. This conclusion that the United Nations have an international legal personality was based on the finding that 'the Organization was intended to exercise and enjoy, and is in fact exercising and enjoying, functions and rights which can only be explained on the basis of the possession of a large measure of international personality and the capacity to operate upon an international plane.' ICJ, *Reparation for Injuries Suffered in the Service of the United Nations*, Advisory Opinion, *ICJ Rep.* (1949) p. 179. Problems of accountability resulting from inter-State cooperation in situations other than those that lead to the establishment of an international organization fall outside the scope of this contribution and shall not be discussed here.

legal person, it is not bound by the international obligations of the States to which it owes its coming into existence. We may seek to assert that the international organisation nevertheless may not adopt measures which would violate the human rights its Member States were bound to respect according to their pre-existing international obligations, and that the international organisation in any case should comply with human rights as these are part of the general principles of international law.[71] But these answers are only partially satisfactory. While the first answer is far from consensual, the second answer remains inadequate, since the human rights included among those principles may not correspond to the full list of human rights binding upon the Member States of the organisation (most of these rights will be stipulated in human rights treaties to which those States are parties, rather than have a pedigree under general public international law). In addition, whereas, by acceding to human rights treaties, States often have agreed to submit to certain dispute settlement mechanisms, some of which are of a jurisdictional or quasi-jurisdictional nature, similar fora typically do not exist before which the individual aggrieved by the acts adopted by an international organisation can bring forward his or her claim.

A first solution to this predicament has been to assert the responsibility of States for the acts of international organisations. As illustrated by the hesitations of the International Law Commission when it prepared its Articles on the Responsibility of States for internationally wrongful acts,[72] the circumstances in which such responsibility may arise are still the subject of an intense debate within mainstream legal scholarship. Yet, a consensus seems to be emerging on six situations where such a responsibility might occur. Presented in the order in which these hypotheses appear in the International Law Commission's 2001 Articles on Responsibility of States for internationally wrongful acts and in the draft Articles on responsibility of international organizations provisionally adopted by the International Law Commission,[73] there are in particular a

71 See, for a discussion of the affirmations above, Part I, A and B respectively, where I express doubts about the first proposition, while supporting the second.

72 See ILC, *Articles on State responsibility for internationally wrongful acts*, adopted in 2001 by the ILC (UN Doc A/56/10 2001) and taken note of by the UN General Assembly (Res 56/83). The ILC ended up agreeing simply on a 'non-prejudice' clause. Under the slightly misleading title of 'Responsibility of an international organization', Article 57 of the draft Articles reads: 'These articles [listed in the text adopted by the ILC in August 2001] are without prejudice to any question of the responsibility under international law of an international organization, or of any State for the conduct of an international organization' (*Official Records of the General Assembly, Fifty-sixth Session, Supplement No. 10* and corrigendum (A/56/10 and Corr.1), chap. IV, sect. E.1, para. 76).

73 ILC, *Report of the Fifty-eighth session (1 May to 9 June and 3 July to 11 August 2006)*, UN Doc. A/61/10, chapter VII, paras. 77–91. Hereinafter, the draft articles on responsibility of international organizations provisionally adopted by the International Law Commission, in the state in which they were presented to the sixty-first session of the UN General Assembly,

number of classical instances, already similar to situations where State responsibility is alleged in situations in which they enter into relationships with other States. These circumstances whereby a State may be responsible for wrongful acts adopted by an international organisation are: (1) where a State puts its organs at the disposal of the organisation, but retains effective control over these organs, which commit a violation of human rights[74]; (2) where a State is complicit of a violation of human rights committed directly by the international organisation by providing aid and assistance to the organisation in the commission of the violation[75]; (3) where a State directs and controls an international organisation in the commission of an internationally wrongful act by the latter[76]; (4) where a State coerces the commission of a wrongful act by the international organisation[77]; or (5) where a State accepts international responsibility for an act directly attributable to the international organisation.[78] In addition – and this has been the most controversial provision to be included

will be referred to as the 'ILC draft articles on responsibility of international organizations (2006)'. Although structured along largely similar lines, the ILC Articles on Responsibility of States for internationally wrongful acts and the ILC draft Articles on responsibility of international organizations focus, respectively, on the responsibility of States (including in their relationships with other States: see chapter IV) and the responsibility of international organizations. In principle, the provisions related to the responsibility of States in their relationship to international organisations (whether or not they are members of those international organisations) should be dealt with exclusively in the former set of articles. However, due to the hesitations of the ILC when it worked on that topic, this gap had to be covered in certain provisions of the ILC draft Articles on Responsibility of international organizations. Thus, articles 25 to 27 of this text largely correspond to articles 16 to 18 of the Articles on the Responsibility of States for internationally wrongful acts, but they focus on the relationships between a State and an international organisation; and articles 28 and 29 are specific to this topic, without corresponding to any equivalent in the Articles on State responsibility for internationally wrongful acts. See ILC, *Report on the work of its Fifty-eighth session (1 May to 9 June and 3 July to 11 August 2006)*, mentioned *supra*, at para. 86. The draft Articles on responsibility of international organizations have been modified after the finalisation of this contribution. For the most recent version of these Articles, see ILC, *Report of the Sixty-first session (4 May to 5 June and 6 July to 7 August 2009)*, UN Doc. A/64/10, chapter IV, paras. 31–51 (hereinafter referred to as 'ILC draft articles on responsibility of international organizations (2009)').

74 ILC draft articles on responsibility of international organizations (2006), art. 5; ILC draft articles on responsibility of international organizations (2009), art. 6.

75 ILC draft articles on responsibility of international organizations (2006), art. 25; ILC draft articles on responsibility of international organizations (2009), art. 57.

76 ILC draft articles on responsibility of international organizations (2006), art. 26; ILC draft articles on responsibility of international organizations (2009), art. 58.

77 ILC draft articles on responsibility of international organizations (2006), art. 27; ILC draft articles on responsibility of international organizations (2009), art. 59.

78 ILC draft articles on responsibility of international organizations (2006), art. 29; ILC draft articles on responsibility of international organizations (2009), art. 61. While this provision (former article 29) is presented by G. Gaja, the Special Rapporteur of the International Law Commission on the question of the responsibility of international organizations, as an original provision having no equivalent in the 2001 articles on the Responsibility of States for internationally wrongful acts, it is in fact modelled closely on Article 11 of the ILC Articles on Responsibility of States for internationally wrongful acts.

in the draft Articles on responsibility of international organizations – it was provided by article 28 of the draft Articles in their 2006 version, that the Member States of an international organisation may be responsible (6) where a Member State circumvents one of its international obligations by providing the organisation with a competence in relation to that obligation, which the organisation exercises in a way which results in a human rights violation which, if it had been directly attributable to the State, would have constituted a violation of its international obligations.[79]

Is this sufficient? Whether or not this regime of State responsibility (as now expanded upon by the discussions on State responsibility which took place in the context of the debate on the responsibility of international organisations for internationally wrongful acts) ensures that victims of human rights violations committed by international organisations will have an effective remedy at their disposal depends, of course, on which remedies are available to victims against the international organisation itself, where the act is directly attributable to the organisation.[80] However, for the reasons detailed in part III of this contribution, only in highly exceptional cases, or within certain regional organisations, will it be possible for a victim to file a claim directly against the international organisation for an act resulting in a violation of human rights. The problem is not only that, since they are grounded in general international law rather than in human rights treaties,[81] the human rights obligations imposed on international organisations are less far-reaching than those imposed on the States to which they owe their existence. The problem is also of a jurisdictional nature. In general, no international court will have jurisdiction over the issue. And national

---

79 This provision has been replaced by Article 60 of the ILC draft articles on responsibility of international organizations (2009), pursuant to which '[a] State member of an international organization incurs international responsibility if it seeks to avoid complying with one of its own international obligations by taking advantage of the fact that the organization has competence in relation to the subject matter of that obligation, thereby prompting the organization to commit an act that, if committed by the State, would have constituted a breach of the obligation. Paragraph 1 applies whether or not the act in question is internationally wrongful for the international organization.'

80 This is the reason why grounding the discussion of State responsibility for the internationally wrongful acts of the international organisation on the specific example of the responsibility of the EU Member States under the European Convention on Human Rights, as adjudicated by the European Court of Human Rights, brings about a serious distortion in perspective. The EU has developed sophisticated internal mechanisms of accountability, including through judicial review, which go far beyond those usually found within international organisations (see *infra*, text corresponding to n. 164–170). In addition, the European Court of Human Rights has taken into account the existence of such mechanisms in developing its approach to the responsibility of the EU Member States under the European Convention on Human Rights. On the difficulty of generalising from this specific case, see also hereafter, text corresponding to n. 93–97.

81 On the possible normative foundations for imposing human rights obligations on international organisations, see *supra*, part I.

courts typically will be barred from adjudicating such claims, because of the immunity of jurisdiction enjoyed by international organisations.[82] Therefore, we may be justified in taking as our departure point that any regime of State responsibility for internationally wrongful acts which may result in allowing the State to evade certain obligations imposed on it under the human rights treaties to which it is a party should be considered in principle as insufficiently protective.

In order to evaluate the emerging regime of State responsibility for the acts of international organisations of which it is a member, we might consider three moments that characterise such membership. First, there is the moment of attributing competences to the international organisation, when it is set up by the adoption of an intergovernmental agreement. Second, there is the participation in the decision-making procedures within the organisation: the State may, or may not, have the capacity to exercise a decisive influence on such decision-making. Third, comes the moment of implementation of any acts adopted within the international organisation: in general, the organisation is dependent upon its Member States for such implementation, since it does not have at its disposal the necessary means to ensure implementation of its decisions without the assistance of the Member States. My thesis is that, while the international law of State responsibility has offered answers concerning whether a responsibility may exist at each of these moments, it has failed to consider their interrelationship, and that this is the main source of its insufficiencies.[83]

A. THE ESTABLISHMENT OF THE INTERNATIONAL ORGANISATION AND THE INITIAL TRANSFER OF POWERS

Consider first the moment at which an international organisation is set up, and certain powers are transferred to it by its Member States in order to allow it to fulfil its objectives. Under the title 'International responsibility in case of provision of competence to an international organization', Article 28 of the draft articles on responsibility of international organizations provisionally adopted by the International Law Commission in 2006 states:

> '1. A State member of an international organization incurs international responsibility if it circumvents one of its international obligations by providing the organization

82 See *Infra*, part III, C.

83 This idea was initially put forward in O. De Schutter and O. Lhoest, 'La Cour européenne des droits de l'homme juge du droit communautaire: Gibraltar, l'Union européenne et la Convention européenne des droits de l'homme', *Cahiers de droit européen* (2000) pp. 141–214.

> with competence in relation to that obligation, and the organization commits an act that, if committed by that State, would have constituted a breach of that obligation.
> 2. Paragraph 1 applies whether or not the act in question is internationally wrongful for the international organization.'[84]

Despite its perhaps ambiguous use of the concept of 'circumvention', this provision does not limit the responsibility of States to the situation where there exists a proven specific *intention* to circumvent the international obligation by attributing certain powers to an international organisation, or where the Member State may be said to be abusing its rights by setting up the international organisation. Conversely, the use of this concept 'is meant to exclude that international responsibility arises when the act of the international organization, which would constitute a breach of an international obligation if taken by the State, has to be regarded as an unwitting result of providing the international organization with competence'.[85] In other words, while excluding that a State may escape its pre-existing international obligations by setting up an organisation to which powers are attributed which the organisation will be authorised to exercise in a way which results in a violation of those obligations,[86] this provision allows for the transfer of powers if precautions have been taken to ensure that these powers will be exercised in compliance with those obligations. While this does not necessarily require that the international organisation be imposed the same international obligation as that imposed on the Member State, imposing such an obligation on the organisation is of course the most efficient means to ensure that it will exercise its powers in accordance with the international obligations of its Member States, i.e., that the Member States will not be accused of 'circumventing' their international obligations by setting up the organisation. 'Circumvention is more likely to occur when the international organization is not bound by the international obligation'; however, 'the sheer existence of an international obligation for the organization does not necessarily exempt the State from international responsibility'.[87]

The rule contained in draft Article 28 is directly borrowed from the case-law of the European Court of Human Rights. This case-law developed when questions were raised about the compatibility with the requirements of the European Convention on Human Rights of transfers of powers to the European Union.

---

84 ILC draft articles on responsibility of international organizations (2006), art. 28.

85 ILC, *Report of the Fifty-eighth session (1 May to 9 June and 3 July to 11 August 2006)*, op. cit. n. 73, chapter VII, pp. 283–284.

86 To the extent the obligations of the State have their source in international treaties to which it is a party, Article 28 is a mere application of the *pacta sunt servanda* rule, one implication of which is that a State may not escape obligations imposed under one treaty by the conclusion, with other parties, of another international agreement: see *supra* n. 12.

87 ILC, *Report of the Fifty-eighth session (1 May to 9 June and 3 July to 11 August 2006)*, op. cit. n. 73, chapter VII, p. 286.

The European Court of Human Rights has emphasised in this context that the Convention 'does not exclude the transfer of competences to international organisations provided that Convention rights continue to be 'secured'. Member States' responsibility therefore continues even after such a transfer'.[88] However, the Court at the same time has sought not to discourage the development in the future of intergovernmental cooperation, and to offer a reading of the Convention, to the fullest extent possible, in the light of any relevant rules and principles of international law applicable in relations between the Contracting Parties.[89] In its recent case-law, it therefore concluded that it would presume the compatibility with the European Convention on Human Rights of acts adopted by States in fulfilment of the obligations imposed upon them as members of an international organisation, to the extent that these acts may be adequately reviewed for their compatibility with fundamental rights in the system set up within that organisation itself. It stated in the *'Bosphorus Airways'* case[90] that:

> 'State action taken in compliance with such legal obligations [deriving from commitments of a State party to the Convention under a treaty concluded subsequently to their accession to the Convention] is justified as long as the relevant organisation [set up by such subsequent treaty] is considered to protect fundamental rights, as regards both the substantive guarantees offered and the mechanisms controlling their observance, in a manner which can be considered at least equivalent to that for which the Convention provides [...]. By 'equivalent' the Court means

---

88 ECtHR, *Matthews v. the United Kingdom*, Application No. 24833/94, 28 *EHRR* (1999) p. 364, at para. 32.

89 In conformity with Article 31 §3 (c) of the Vienna Convention on the Law of Treaties of 23 May 1969 and as according to the well-established case-law of the Court: see ECtHR, *Al-Adsani v. the United* Kingdom, Application No. 35763/97, 34 *EHRR* (2002) p. 11, at para. 55.

90 ECtHR, *Bosphorus Hava Yolları Turizm ve Ticaret Anonim Şirketi v. Ireland*, Application No. 45036/98, 42 *EHRR* (2006) p. 1. The case concerned the impounding on an aircraft, which was the property of the Yugoslav Airlines (JAT), the national airline of the former Yugoslavia, and had been leased by the applicant Turkish company. The impounding was decided in implementation of UN Security Council Resolution 820 (1993) of 17 April 1993, which provided that States should impound, *inter alia*, all aircraft in their territories 'in which a majority or controlling interest is held by a person or undertaking in or operating' from the FRY. That Resolution had been implemented by EC Regulation 990/93 which entered into force on 28 April 1993 (OJ L 102/14 (1993)), and implemented in turn in Ireland by the European Communities (Prohibition of Trade with the Federal Republic of Yugoslavia (Serbia and Montenegro)) Regulations 1993 (SI 144 of 1993). In a judgment of 30 July 1996 delivered in answer to a referral from the Irish Supreme Court, the European Court of Justice had confirmed that Article 8 of EC Regulation 990/93 applied to the aircraft concerned and that the impounding did not violate the fundamental rights of the applicant company: the restriction to the right to property of the company, in particular, was proportionate to the fulfilment of 'an objective of general interest (...) fundamental for the international community, which consists in putting an end to the state of war in the region and to the massive violations of human rights and humanitarian international law in the Republic of Bosnia-Herzegovina' (ECJ, Case C-84/95, *Bosphorus v. Minister for Transport, Energy and Communications and others*, [1996] ECR I-3953, at para. 26).

> 'comparable': any requirement that the organisation's protection be 'identical' could run counter to the interest of international co-operation pursued.'[91]

Such State action implementing obligations imposed under treaties entered into by States parties to the Convention after their accession to this latter instrument will be presumed compatible with the Convention: 'If such equivalent protection is considered to be provided by the organisation, the presumption will be that a State has not departed from the requirements of the Convention when it does no more than implement legal obligations flowing from its membership of the organisation'[92] – that is, when the State is deprived of any margin of appreciation in the implementation of those obligations. Such a presumption may not be absolute, however. The Court reiterates its view according to which 'absolving Contracting States completely from their Convention responsibility in the areas covered by such a transfer would be incompatible with the purpose and object of the Convention: the guarantees of the Convention could be limited or excluded at will thereby depriving it of its peremptory character and undermining the practical and effective nature of its safeguards'. It follows not only that the State 'is considered to retain Convention liability in respect of treaty commitments subsequent to the entry into force of the Convention',[93] but also that the presumption of compatibility with the Convention of acts adopted by States parties by which they implement obligations resulting from their membership of international organisations where fundamental rights are recognised a protection equivalent to that provided under the European Convention on Human Rights 'can be rebutted if, in the circumstances of a particular case, it is considered that the protection of Convention rights was manifestly deficient. In such cases, the interest of international co-operation would be outweighed by the Convention's role as a 'constitutional instrument of European public order' in the field of human rights'.[94]

The due diligence obligation imposed on the Member States of an international organisation when setting up the organisation and transferring to it certain powers thus emerged in a highly specific context: one in which a number of States parties bound by the European Convention on Human Rights decided to establish a supranational organisation – the European Community, now succeeded by the European Union – within which a judicial control of compliance with fundamental rights has emerged since the late 1960s.[95] The position of the

91 ECtHR, *Bosphorus Hava Yolları Turizm ve Ticaret Anonim Şirketi v. Ireland*, Application No. 45036/98, 42 *EHRR* (2006) p. 1, at para. 155.

92 *Ibid.*, para. 156.

93 *Ibid.*, para. 154.

94 *Ibid.*, para.156.

95 ECJ, Case 29/69, *Stauder v. City of Ulm* [1969] ECR 419; ECJ, Case 11/70, *Internationale Handelsgesellschaft v. Einfuhr- und Vorratsstelle Getreide* [1970] ECR 1125. The Court

European Court of Human Rights clearly was inspired by the attitude of the German Federal Constitutional Court (*Bundesverfassungsgericht*) towards European Community law. Only after it surmounted its initial hesitations and was convinced that fundamental rights are adequately protected in the legal order of the Community did the German Federal Constitutional Court agree to recognise the supremacy of European Community law, without a scrutiny of its compatibility with the fundamental rights protected under the German Basic Law (*Grundgesetz*).[96] It is already that attitude of the German courts which had led the European Commission of Human Rights, in 1990, to develop the doctrine of an 'equivalent protection', according to which the monitoring bodies set up by the European Convention on Human Rights should not control acts adopted by States parties as Member States of the European Community in fulfilment of their Community obligations insofar as the legal order of the Community provided for its own system of protection of fundamental rights which could be considered to be generally satisfactory.[97] That doctrine has been relied upon in later cases by the European Court of Human Rights, even before its spectacular reaffirmation in *Bosphorus Airways*. Most notably, it appears at least implicitly in

---

recognises not only that the EU institutions are bound to comply with fundamental rights, but in addition that the EU Member States may invoke the need to protect fundamental rights as general principles of law even where this may lead them to derogate from their obligations under EU Law (see, e.g., ECJ, Case C-368/95, *Familiapress*, [1997] ECR I-3689, at para. 24; ECJ, Case C-112/00, *Schmidberger*, [2003] ECR I-5659, at para. 81). This is crucial, since it renders unlikely, if not impossible, a situation where a State might have to forego its human rights obligations in order to comply with its obligations under EU law.

96 This case-law has been developing in different phases, to which judgments adopted respectively in 1974 ('Solange I') (BverfGE 37, 271 (280)), 1987 ('Solange II')(BverfGE 73, 339 (379)), 1993 (the 'Maastricht' decision) (BverfGE 89, 155 (174)) and 2000 (the 'Bananas' decision)(2 BvL 1/97, EuGRZ 2000, p. 328 (333)) correspond. The development of this case-law has been abundantly commented upon; I will therefore be excused for not describing it in detail. The main lesson is that, having been reassured by the development of a case-law of the European Court of Justice ensuring that fundamental rights will be protected within the legal order of the European Community at a level substantially equivalent to that provided by the German Basic Law – this case law being itself an answer to the doubts raised by certain national constitutional courts about the compatibility of the doctrine of supremacy of EC Law with the protection of fundamental rights under national constitutions –, the *Bundesverfassungsgericht* now applies a presumption of compatibility with the requirements of fundamental rights of EC Law. It will therefore agree to review the compatibility of EC/EU law with those requirements only in situations where the applicant brings forward elements tending to demonstrate that the level of protection of fundamental rights has not been maintained at the level at which it was found by the *Bundesverfassungsgericht* to be satisfactory in its 'Solange II' decision of 22 April 1987. See on these developments, *inter alia*, J. Limbach, 'La coopération des juridictions dans la future architecture européenne des droits fondamentaux. Contribution à la redéfinition des rapports entre la Cour constitutionnelle fédérale allemande, la Cour de justice des Communautés européennes et la Cour européenne des droits de l'homme', 12 *Revue universelle des droits de l'homme* (2000) pp. 369–372.

97 EComHR, *M. & Co v. Germany*, Application No. 13258/87, decision of 9 February 1990, *DR* 64, p. 138; EComHR, *Heinz v. the Contracting Parties also parties to the European Patent Convention* (Appl. No. 21090/92), decision of 10 January 1994, *DR* 76-A, p. 125.

two judgments the Court delivered on 18 February 1999 where it considered that the application by the German courts of the rule on immunity of jurisdiction of the European Space Agency does not constitute a violation of Article 6 §1 of the Convention, which guarantees in principle a right of access to court. Indeed, the Court considered there that, insofar as it corresponds to a long-standing practice established in the interest of the good working of international organisations and fits within a 'trend towards extending and strengthening international cooperation in all domains of modern society',[98] applying a rule on immunity of jurisdiction of international organisations is permissible under the Convention, insofar as 'the applicants had available to them reasonable alternative means to protect effectively their rights under the Convention'.[99] It thus recognised that the setting up of remedies within the internal structures of the European Space Agency could ensure compatibility with the requirements of Article 6 §1 of the Convention, although the immunity of jurisdiction of the ESA implied that it could not by sued before the domestic courts of Germany.

The case-law of the European Court of Human Rights leading to the *Bosphorus Airways* judgment seeks to ensure that the Convention will not constitute an obstacle to further European integration by the creation among the Member States of the Union of a supranational organisation – a development which, as the representatives of the European Commission argued in their submissions to the Court in that case, would be seriously impeded if the Member States were to verify the compatibility with the European Convention on Human Rights of the acts of Union law before agreeing to apply them, even in situations where they have no margin of appreciation to exercise. But the Court stops short of stating that, as the Member States have transferred certain powers to a supranational organisation, the European Union, their international responsibility could not be engaged for situations resulting directly from the application of European Community acts. The Convention remains applicable to such situations, and the States parties remain fully answerable to the supervisory bodies it sets up. It is only the level of scrutiny exercised by the European Court of Human Rights which is influenced by the circumstance that the alleged violation has its source in the application of an act adopted within the European Union. The Court considers that, insofar as the legal order of the European Union ensures an adequate level of protection of fundamental rights, and unless it is confronted with a 'dysfunction of the mechanisms of control of

---

98 ECtHR, *Beer and Regan v. Germany*, Application No. 28934/95, 33 *EHRR* (1999) p. 3, at para. 53; ECtHR, *Waite and Kennedy v. Germany*, Application No. 26083/94, 30 *EHRR* (1999) p. 261, at para. 63. Both judgments were decided by a unanimous Court.

99 ECtHR, *Beer and Regan v. Germany*, op. cit. n. 98, at para. 58; ECtHR, *Waite and Kennedy v. Germany*, op. cit. n. 98, at para. 73.

the observance of Convention rights' or with a 'manifest deficiency',[100] it may be allowed to presume that, by complying with the legal obligations under this legal order, the EU Member States are not violating their obligations under the ECHR.

But this creates two problems. First, it will be noted that the Court considers that a protection may be 'equivalent' to that provided by the European Convention on Human Rights although it remains *internal* to the international organisation concerned. But, however adequate the remedies available to individuals within the European Union legal order when they complain about violations of their fundamental rights, 'it remains the case that the Union has not yet acceded to the European Convention on Human Rights and that full protection does not yet exist at European level'[101]: therefore, by asserting that the EU Member States were in effect ensuring an 'equivalent protection' of the fundamental rights of the individual within the EU legal order, since the European Court of Justice protects these rights within the scope of its jurisdiction, the European Court of Human Rights in effect obliterates the added value that a form of judicial control *external* to the legal order concerned might represent. One concern is that this doctrine may lead, in the future, to allow for similar presumptions to apply as regards States parties to the European Convention on Human Rights which ensure effective judicial remedies against national measures and apply directly the European Convention on Human Rights.[102] But another problem is that its assimilation of both forms of monitoring, respectively internal and external to the legal order concerned, may not be justified. Indeed, it is doubtful whether this approach is compatible with the general international law of human rights,

100 ECtHR, *Bosphorus Hava Yolları Turizm ve Ticaret Anonim Şirketi v. Ireland*, Application No. 45036/98, 42 *EHRR* (2006) p. 1, at para. 166.

101 See the joint concurring opinion of Judges Rozakis, Tulkens, Traja, Botoucharova, Zagrebalsky, and Garlicki, to the *Bosphorus Hava* judgment of 30 June 2005. These six members of the Court, while agreeing with the operative provisions of the judgment, expressed a strong disagreement with the reasoning behind the *Bosphorus Hava* judgment, focused on the conditions under which a 'presumption' such as the one benefiting measures adopted by the EU could be justified.

102 The doctrine of 'equivalent protection' may indeed be extended further, to any situations where, at national level, such 'equivalent' protection is provided. This 'contamination' of the doctrine would clearly manifest the principle of subsidiarity in the system of the European Convention on Human Rights – i.e., the principle according to which the protection of the rights and freedoms of the Convention must primarily take place at national level, the intervention of the European Court of Human Rights being only justified where those internal mechanisms have failed to prevent violations from occuring or, if they do occur, from being remedied. Some might see this as a welcome development, in a context where the European Court of Human Rights manifestly cannot manage its increasing case-load, and where even the solutions offered by Protocol No. 14 to the Convention for the Protection of Human Rights and Fundamental Freedoms, amending the control system of the Convention, done at Strasbourg 14 May 2004 (CETS No. 194, entered into force on 1 June 2010) will have a limited impact on that situation.

where it is traditionally emphasised that the object and purpose of international human rights treaties is not only to impose substantive obligations on the States parties, but also to submit them to monitoring mechanisms ensuring a collective enforcement of these obligations.[103]

A second problem is that the doctrine developed by the European Court of Human Rights in *Bosphorus Airways*, and which inspired the formulation of draft Article 28 of the articles on responsibility of international organizations by the International Law Commission, allows for the possibility that a Member State of an international organisation will not be considered responsible for a violation of its international obligations, even where that State has transferred powers to an international organisation which the organisation then exercises by adopting measures which would constitute a violation of the international obligations if they had been adopted by the Member State itself. It will be sufficient for a State, in order to avoid being found internationally liable, to show that it has been taken by surprise: if the said violation could not have been reasonably anticipated, the mere fact that competences have been attributed to the international organisation in a domain in which the State was under certain international obligations cannot by itself trigger the international responsibility of that State. In other words, the obligation to ensure, when an international organisation is established, that it will not exercise its competences in a way which results in violations of the international obligations of States if the measures adopted were attributable to them, is not an obligation of ends: it is a mere obligation of means. And, for a State to escape international responsibility, it is enough that it has sought to ensure that the international organisation will not exercise its powers in violation with the international obligations of that State, even if it later appears that, in fact, the precautions taken were not sufficient. Of crucial importance, the liability of the State will thus be limited whether or not the State has reserved the right to veto the decision within the internal decision-making procedures of the organisation, or to block the implementation of the decision.

Is this satisfactory? The *Bosphorus Airways* doctrine was articulated by the European Court of Human Rights only following a long and searching examination of the level of protection of human rights achieved within the legal

---

[103] For instance, the Human Rights Committee states that the object and purpose of the International Covenant on Civil and Political Rights is not only to 'create legally binding standards for human rights by defining certain civil and political rights and placing them in a framework of obligations which are legally binding for those States which ratify', but also 'to provide an efficacious supervisory machinery for the obligations undertaken' (Human Rights Committee, General Comment No. 24: Issues relating to reservations made upon ratification or accession to the Covenant or the Optional Protocols thereto, or in relation to declarations under article 41 of the Covenant, 4 November 1994 (CCPR/C/21/Rev.1/Add.6)).

order of the European Union. Indeed, the Court distinguishes the *Bosphorus Airways* situation from *Pellegrini v. Italy* – where Italy was found to have violated the right to a fair trial guaranteed in Article 6 §1 of the Convention for having enforced a judgment delivered by the Vatican courts in violation of the rights of defence of the applicant[104] – on the basis that 'enforcement of a judgment not of a Contracting Party to the Convention [[105]] [...] is not comparable to compliance with a legal obligation emanating from an international organisation to which Contracting Parties have transferred part of their sovereignty'.[106] The implied suggestion is that, when States parties to the European Convention on Human Rights co-operate with one another, or implement decisions of international organisations offering an equivalent level of protection of human rights, they may subject the acts of the other States or emanating from such international organisations to only minimal review; instead, where they cooperate with States not parties to the European Convention on Human Rights, or when they implement secondary legislation adopted within international organisations not offering a protection of human rights at a level similar to that guaranteed by the European Convention on Human Rights, there could be no presumption that the measures adopted in the framework of such co-operation comply with the requirements of the Convention, and a strict scrutiny of such compliance therefore would be required. But the formulation of draft Article 28 of the articles on responsibility of international organizations makes no reference to such a verification. Instead of allowing a presumption of compatibility to be established in the presence of an 'equivalent protection' being ensured within the international organisation to which certain competences are being attributed, such presumption becomes the rule, and the presumption is reversed: only when such transfer of competences constitutes a 'circumvention' of a State's obligations shall it be treated as suspect. Admittedly, the International Law Commission's articles on responsibility of international organizations are not focused on the human rights obligations of States. Instead, they are wider in scope, and they intend to be applicable to any international obligations of States, whatever their nature. But this alone should not justify transforming into a rule (that a State cannot be held responsible for having transferred certain powers to an international organisation, which this organisation then exercises by the adoption of measures which, if these had been adopted by that State, would constitute a violation of its obligation) what was, in *Bosphorus Airways*, an exception (applying only to the case of an international organisation ensuring a protection of fundamental rights deemed equivalent to that offered by the European

104 ECtHR, *Pellegrini v. Italy*, Application No. 30882/96, 35 *EHRR* (2002) p. 44, at para. 40.
105 The Holy See is not a Contracting Party to the European Convention on Human Rights.
106 ECtHR, *Bosphorus Hava Yolları Turizm ve Ticaret Anonim Şirketi v. Ireland*, Application No. 45036/98, 42 *EHRR* (2006) p. 1, para. 157.

Convention on Human Rights). This is especially so since the State's responsibility which might result from the transfer of certain competences to the organisation is tailored neither on the degree of control it may exercise on the internal decision-making procedures of the organisation, nor on the ability of the State to obstruct the implementation of the decision after its adoption.

B. THE DECISION-MAKING PROCESS WITHIN THE ORGANISATION

The ILC's draft articles on responsibility of international organizations contain provisions closely inspired by the equivalent clauses of the articles on Responsibility of States for internationally wrongful acts, which relate to complicity (aid or assistance provided by a State in the commission of an internationally wrongful act by an international organisation: Article 25)[107]; to direction and control by a State over the commission of an internationally wrongful act by an international organisation (Article 26)[108]; or to coercion (Article 27).[109] However, these instances of State responsibility do not refer to the situation where, by participating in the decision-making process within the organisation, a State would be contributing to the adoption of a measure which, if that measure had been adopted by that State, might constitute a violation of its international obligations. Except in very exceptional circumstances, they will therefore be useless as regards the risk that a State uses the form of the international organisation in order to have measures adopted which would constitute human rights violations if such measures were adopted directly by that State.

More precisely, the draft provisions cited above suffer from two limitations. First, for the State to be internationally responsible, we must be in presence of an act which is an internationally wrongful act *of the international organisation itself*, or (under Article 27) which 'but for the coercion', would constitute an internationally wrongful act or the organisation.[110] Therefore, where the

---

107 ILC, Draft articles on responsibility of international organizations (2009), art. 57.

108 *Ibid.*, art. 58.

109 *Ibid.*, art. 59. This notion refers to a form of behaviour which may be deemed abusive, for instance the threat of withholding financial contributions in order to force the organisation to commit an internationally wrongful act: see J. d'Aspremont, 'Abuse of the Legal Personality of International Organizations and the Responsibility of Member States', *International Organizations Law Review* (2007) pp. 91–119 at p. 100.

110 According to Article 27 of the draft articles on responsibility of international organizations 2006 (Coercion of an international organisation by a State): 'A State which coerces an international organization to commit an act is internationally responsible for that act if: (a) The act would, but for the coercion, be an internationally wrongful act of that international organization; and (b) That State does so with knowledge of the circumstances of the act.'

organisation is not imposed international obligations identical to those of its Member States – in particular, where only the States are parties to international human rights treaties – no State responsibility will result from any 'coercion' being exercised on the international organisation, or from the complicity of the State with the act of the international organisation or the direction and control it has exercised on the commission of that act. Of course, this is based on an *a contrario* reading of the ILC draft articles, which postulates that, where the responsibility of the Member States for the acts of the organisation cannot be engaged under those articles, it shall not exist. Whether this is a fair reading of the intentions of the ILC is debatable. But there is hardly any doubt that the ILC articles, if adopted in their current form, will be used in this very way: to seek to exempt the Member States of an organisation when the acts of the latter are not in violation of its own obligations under international law, even if the same acts would have been in violation of the obligations of the Member States if they, rather than the organisation itself, had adopted such acts.[111]

Second, as regards Member States of the organisation, mere 'participation in the decision-making process of the organization according to the pertinent rules of the organization' shall not *per se* constitute complicity, direction and control, or coercion, unless an additional element is present. However, this latter rule may be delicate to apply. On the one hand, the legality of the participation of the State in the decision-making process of the international organisation does not necessarily exclude that such participation may amount to a form of complicity, direction and control, or coercion. On the other hand, mere participation in such decision-making process is not sufficient: 'The factual context such as the size or membership and the nature of the involvement will probably be decisive'.[112] In sum, the degree of influence a State is exercising in fact on the international organisation may lead to the conclusion that it is aiding or assisting the organisation in the commission of an internationally wrongful act[113]; that it is directing or controlling the organisation in the commission of such act; or that it is coercing the organisation to commit such act. However, the mere circumstance that a State is a member of an international organisation and has certain voting rights within the organisation does not entail that it will be internationally responsible, even if the organisation (whether aided or not by its vote) adopts an

---

111 I am indebted to Pierre d'Argent for drawing my attention to this point.

112 ILC, *Report of the Fifty-eighth session (1 May to 9 June and 3 July to 11 August 2006)*, op. cit. n. 73, p. 279 (commentary to article 25 of the draft articles on responsibility of international organizations, to which the commentaries to articles 26 and 27 refer).

113 It has sometimes been stated that the exercise of voting rights, while not in itself a violation by the State of its international obligations, could result in that State being an accomplice in the commission by the international organisation of an internationally wrongful act, at least where the State concerned knows or should have known that the adoption of the act was a violation of international law. See P. Klein, op. cit. n. 27, at pp. 468–470.

act which would be internationally wrongful if that act were attributable to the State.

This approach is significantly less requiring on States than the approach adopted by certain human rights treaty bodies, in particular the UN Committee on Economic, Social and Cultural Rights. Already in its 1990 General Comment on Article 22 of the International Covenant on Economic, Social and Cultural Rights, which relates to international technical assistance measures, this committee noted that 'States parties to the Covenant, as well as the relevant United Nations agencies, should [...] *make a particular effort to ensure* that [the protection of the most basic economic, social and cultural rights] is, to the maximum extent possible, built-in to programmes and policies designed to promote adjustment'.[114] This implied that States parties to the Covenant had obligations, *as Member States* of the international financial institutions in general and of the International Monetary Fund in particular, insofar as such institutions impose on indebted States certain austerity programmes as a condition for access to the international financial markets. In the General Comment on the right to the highest attainable standard of health, which it adopted in 2000,[115] the Committee on Economic, Social and Cultural Rights adopted an even stronger formulation, moving from the affirmation of an obligation of means to an obligation of result. It noted that 'States parties have an *obligation to ensure* that their actions as members of international organisations take due account of the right to health. Accordingly, States parties which are members of international financial institutions, notably the International Monetary Fund, the World Bank, and regional development banks, should pay greater attention to the protection of the right to health in influencing the lending policies, credit agreements and international measures of these institutions'.[116] A very similar formulation appears in the General Comment on the right to water.[117]

114 UN Committee on Economic, Social and Cultural Rights, General Comment No. 2 (1990), 'International technical assistance measures (Art. 22)', UN doc. E/1990/23), at para. 9.

115 UN Committee on Economic, Social and Cultural Rights, General Comment No. 14 (2000), 'The right to the highest attainable standard of health (article 12 of the International Covenant on Economic, Social and Cultural Rights)', UN Doc. E/C.12/2000/4 (2000), para. 39 ('In relation to the conclusion of other international agreements, States parties should take steps to ensure that these instruments do not adversely impact upon the right to health').

116 UN Committee on Economic, Social and Cultural Rights, General Comment No. 14 (2000), 'The right to the highest attainable standard of health (article 12 of the International Covenant on Economic, Social and Cultural Rights)', UN Doc. E/C.12/2000/4 (2000), para. 39.

117 See UN Committee on Economic, Social and Cultural Rights, General Comment No. 15 (2002), 'The right to water (arts. 11 and 12 of the International Covenant on Economic, Social and Cultural Rights)', UN Doc. E/C.12/2002/11, 26 November 2002, para. 36: 'States parties should ensure that their actions as members of international organisations take due account of the right to water. Accordingly, States parties that are members of international financial institutions, notably the International Monetary Fund, the World Bank, and regional

We may convey a better idea of the specific regime of international responsibility of States for the acts of international organisations of which they are members by contrasting this with a recent contribution to the debate on the issue of the 'abuse' by States of the international legal personality of the organisation. In this context, the expression of 'abuse' refers to the tendency of States to shield themselves behind the separate legal personality of the organisation in order to avoid international responsibility whereas in fact (just like the parent company behind its subsidiary) they dominate the organisation which is a mere instrument in their hands. In such circumstances, should not the acts of the organisation be attributed to its master – the State exercising a decisive influence on the organisation? Or, apart from any question of attribution, should we not consider that the States should be held internationally responsible for the acts by which they commit the abuse?

This was the question Moshe Hirsch had in mind, in his discussion of the situations where the 'veil' of the international organisation should be lifted – and its Member States be held internationally responsible for the wrongful act of the organisation.[118] His approach was a cautious one. Hirsch did consider that direct actions against the members of the organisation should be open in cases of 'abuse of the separate personality of the international organization for illegal acts or in order to evade some legal obligations'.[119] But he was hesitant about transposing per analogy the doctrines allowing the piercing of the veil of corporations in order to reach directly the shareholders, since this would lead to a too broad understanding of the responsibility of the Member States of an international organisation. Rather, his proposal was that we limit the doctrine to 'cases in which a single Member State has in fact complete, or almost complete, control over the activities of the organization. Considerable influence on the activities of the organization will not be sufficient to justify ignoring the legal personality of an international organization. Only where the degree of control exercised by a single member has led to a situation in which the organization is functionally identical with that member would it be justified to see the controlling state and the organization as one'.[120] Because Hirsch seemed to require a specific intention for such an abuse to exist, this hypothesis seems more narrowly defined than the 'circumvention' criterion proposed by professor G. Gaja, the Special Rapporteur

development banks, should take steps to ensure that the right to water is taken into account in their lending policies, credit agreements and other international measures'.

118 See M. Hirsch, *The Responsibility of International Organizations Toward Third Parties: Some Basic Principles* (Dordrecht-Boston-London, Martinus Nijhoff Publishers 1995) pp. 169–172.

119 *Ibid.*, at p. 170.

120 *Ibid.*, at pp. 171–172.

of the International Law Commission on international responsibility of international organizations.[121]

More recently, Jean d'Aspremont has put forward the view that 'when Member States effectively and overwhelmingly control the decision-making process of an international organization, [...] the legal personality of that organization can no longer constitute a shield behind which Member States can evade a responsibility that they would have incurred if they had themselves committed the contested action'. Such abuse over the decision-making process, we are told, exists 'when one or a few Member States overrule(s) the whole process, thereby stifling any adverse opinion that could be expressed'.[122] The separate international legal personality of the organisation in other terms becomes a mere fiction, an instrument in the hands of States exercising 'overwhelming control' on the organisation: such abuse should give rise to an international responsibility of the States which commit it.

While it presents itself as a significant expansion of the circumstances in which State responsibility may arise for participation in an international organisation – a claim I beg to be sceptical about[123] – the proposal in fact is not sufficiently protective of the interests corresponding to the international obligations of the Member States of an international organisation. It is indeed noteworthy that such 'overwhelming control' as would give rise to the 'abuse' of the international legal personality of the organisation, requires in d'Aspremont's view 'resort to types of pressure that are not expressly provided for by the constitutive treaty of the organization concerned. In other words, if a Member State overrules the decision-making process of an organization thanks to the procedural rights that

---

121 On the notion of 'circumvention' in the ILC's draft articles on responsibility of international organizations, see *supra*, text corresponding to n. 84–87.

122 J. d'Aspremont, 'Abuse of the Legal Personality of International Organizations and the Responsibility of Member States', op. cit. n. 109, at p. 109.

123 It is in fact doubtful whether this proposal goes beyond what is envisaged by the draft articles on responsibility of international organizations of the International Law Commission. Commenting on article 28 of the draft articles on responsibility of international organizations, J. d'Aspremont writes that this provision is, 'eventually, unsatisfactory as it only embodies situations of the provision of competence to the organization with the aim of circumventing international obligations binding the Member States. It boils down to a very narrow understanding of the abuse of the legal personality at the level of the creation of the organization. It fails to embody cases where Member States abuse the legal personality of international organizations at the decision-making level when exerting overwhelming control over the decision-making process of the organization' (op. cit. n. 109, at p. 100). In fact, on this precise point, the commentary to draft article 28 refers back to the distinction made under the commentaries to articles 25 to 27 between mere 'participation in the decision-making process of the organization according to the pertinent rules of the organization', and decisive influence being exercised within the organisation by one or more Member States. Although they relate to complicity, to direction and control, or to coercion, this distinction may also be invoked in the context of decision-making within the organisation.

it has been granted under the constitutive treaty of the organization, this cannot be considered overwhelming control. [...] For instance, if a permanent member of the Security Council persistently blocks the lifting of sanctions that have proved to infringe on some basic human rights, it cannot be deemed to be abusing the legal personality of the organization in the sense used in this Article and cannot accordingly be held jointly or concurrently responsible of the persistent violations of human rights'.[124]

This last example is particularly illustrative. When, in 1997, it adopted its General Comment on the relationship between economic sanctions and respect for economic, social and cultural rights,[125] the Committee on Economic, Social and Cultural Rights took the view that States imposing sanctions should not, in doing so, jeopardise the economic, social and cultural rights of the population in the targeted State, since this would constitute a violation of their obligations under the International Covenant on Economic, Social and Cultural Rights and, indeed, since the Universal Declaration on Human Rights may be considered as binding under general international law, whether or not they have ratified the Covenant. The Committee stated the following:

> 'While this obligation of every State is derived from the commitment in the UN Charter to promote respect for all human rights, it should also be recalled that every permanent member of the Security Council has signed the Covenant, although two (China and the United States) have yet to ratify it [[126]]. Most of the non-permanent members at any given time are parties. Each of these States has undertaken, in conformity with article 2, paragraph 1, of the Covenant to 'take steps, individually and through international assistance and cooperation, especially economic and technical, to the maximum of its available resources, with a view to achieving progressively the full realization of the rights recognized in the present Covenant by all appropriate means...'. When the affected State is also a State party, it is doubly incumbent upon other States to respect and take account of the relevant obligations. To the extent that sanctions are imposed on States which are not parties to the Covenant, the same principles would in any event apply given the status of the economic, social and cultural rights of vulnerable groups as part of general international law, as evidenced, for example, by the near-universal ratification of the Convention on the Rights of the Child and the status of the Universal Declaration of Human Rights.'[127]

---

124 J. d'Aspremont, op. cit. n. 109, at p. 110.

125 UN Committee on Economic, Social and Cultural Rights, General Comment No. 8 (1997), 'The relationship between economic sanctions and respect for economic, social and cultural rights', UN doc. E/1998/22.

126 China ratified the International Covenant on Economic, Social and Cultural Rights in 2001, after the date at which this General Comment was adopted.

127 UN Committee on Economic, Social and Cultural Rights, General Comment No. 8 (1997), 'The relationship between economic sanctions and respect for economic, social and cultural rights', UN doc. E/1998/22, at para. 51.

This passage is of course highly ambiguous, for it does not identify clearly the normative basis of the obligation of States adopting economic sanctions, particularly under Chapter VII of the UN Charter. The notion that an obligation would be 'doubly' incumbent upon a State, in particular, may be a source of confusion. At face value, the use of this expression would seem to betray a certain hesitation among the members of the Committee about whether the obligations of the States adopting sanctions have their source in the international undertakings of those States, or instead in the rights recognised to the population in the targeted State. The reality however, is that it can be both, and both at the same time. Of course, all that matters, where sanctions adopted by one State have an impact on the population of another State, are the obligations of the first State under international law, which may or may not include the obligation not to violate the rights of populations outside its borders. And the General Comment clearly implies not only that a State party to the International Covenant on Economic, Social and Cultural Rights is under an obligation not to violate the rights stipulated in the Covenant in other countries, but also that such an obligation could be violated by that State voting in favour of adopting or upholding economic sanctions which have a severe impact on the realisation of economic and social rights in the targeted country. But this does not mean that the obligations of the targeted State towards its own population are irrelevant to the determination of the question whether or not the State adopting sanctions has violated its own obligations. For, *in addition*, States parties to the International Covenant on Economic, Social and Cultural Rights may be violating their international obligations by coercing other States into violating their own obligations under either the Covenant or under other rules of international law.[128]

As illustrated by the example of the responsibility of UN Security Council members for the adoption of economic sanctions under Chapter VII of the UN Charter, there is a significant gap between the regime of State responsibility for the acts of international organisations of which a State is a member as it is currently emerging under general international law, and the way this same question is treated under certain human rights treaties.[129] The two approaches

128 This is of course the hypothesis envisaged under Article 18 of the International Law Commission's 2001 articles on Responsibility of States for internationally wrongful acts (op. cit. n. 70), under the heading 'Coercion of another State': 'A State which coerces another State to commit an act is internationally responsible for that act if: (a) The act would, but for the coercion, be an internationally wrongful act of the coerced State; and (b) The coercing State does so with knowledge of the circumstances of the act'.

129 It is not suggested here that the approach of human rights bodies has been consistent in the past, nor that they are all aligned on the position of the UN Committee on Economic, Social and Cultural Rights. Comp. the position adopted by the UN Committee on Economic, Social and Cultural Rights on economic sanctions with, e.g., EComHR, *Ilse Hess v. the United Kingdom*, Application No. 6231/73), 2 *DR* 73; 18 *Yearbook of the ECHR* 174 (1975). In this early

also create very different incentives for the States concerned. In a system in which States cannot be held internationally liable for the use they make of their voting powers within an international organisation, unless their influence on the decision-making process is decisive due to the weight of their vote,[130] they may be tempted to attribute to the organisation wide areas of competence without retaining a power to veto the decisions adopted within the organisation, knowing that the organisation can ignore their own international obligations. Instead, in a system where a State's international responsibility may result both from the delegation of powers to an international organisation and from the exercise by that State of its voting powers within the organisation once it is established, the States concerned will take care not to attribute to the international organisation competences without reserving for themselves the power to control the exercise by the international organisation of the powers it has been attributed. Perhaps because of the impact of international agencies such as the international financial institutions on the enjoyment and realisation of economic and social rights – an impact which is widely recognised as decisive – it is this latter regime that the UN Committee on Economic, Social and Cultural Rights that seeks to establish in the specific context of the International Covenant on Economic, Social and

case, the European Commission of Human Rights noted that, while the United Kingdom could in principle be held responsible for the situation of the Spandau prison, located in the British sector of West Berlin, and which the four allied powers controlled jointly, the application nevertheless was inadmissible *ratione personae*, as the United Kingdom alone could not, without the consent of the other three allied powers, modify the regime applied in the prison. Thus, the fact that the UK could not exercise decisive influence on the management of the prison of Spandau was the crucial factor in excluding its international responsibility under the European Convention on Human Rights. It should be added however that – although this is not alluded to in the decision of the Commission – the fact that the arrangement between the Allied Powers predated the signature and entry into force of the European Convention on Human Rights might have played a role in this outcome. The position of the UN Committee on Economic, Social and Cultural Rights also seems to contrast with that of the Human Rights Committee under the International Covenant on Civil and Political Rights, as illustrated by the case of *H. v.d.P. v. The Netherlands*, Communication No. 217/1986, views of 8 April 1987, UN Doc. Supp. No. 40 (A/42/40) at 185 (1987). In this case, the Human Rights Committee found a communication by a civil servant of the European Patent Office (Munich) to be inadmissible: the Committee, it stated, '…can only receive and consider communications in respect of claims that come under the jurisdiction of a State party to the Covenant. The author's grievances, however, concern the recruitment policies of an international organisation, which cannot, in any way, be construed as coming within the jurisdiction of the Netherlands or of any other State party to the International Covenant on Civil and Political Rights and the Optional Protocol thereto. Accordingly, the author has no claim under the Optional Protocol'. Here again however, it is unclear whether this is in straightforward opposition to the UN Committee on Economic, Social and Cultural Rights: recruitment policies are decided by the international organisation without any role in the decision-making process for the Member States of the organisation; the outcome might have been different if the contested measure had been adopted thanks to the votes of the Member States, parties to the International Covenant on Civil and Political Rights.

130 See *supra*, text corresponding to n. 112–113.

Cultural Rights. This regime may be 'self-contained', in the sense that it may not correspond to the emerging orthodoxy of general public international law; it may still be best suited to obligations imposed under international human rights treaties. In particular this pertains to where competences are transferred to international organisations which they may exercise by the adoption of measures which will take their Member States by 'surprise', with the result that any breaches of the international obligations of the States resulting from the adoption of such measures will be seen as the 'unwitting result' of the transfer of competences to the international organisation.

C. THE IMPLEMENTATION OF DECISIONS ADOPTED BY INTERNATIONAL ORGANISATIONS

Turning now to the third moment which characterises the contribution of States to the activities of international organisations, we are confronted with the question whether a State may be internationally responsible for complying with decisions adopted by the organisation in compliance with its internal rules of procedure, by implementing those decisions insofar as they are addressed to the State or by putting its organs at the service of such implementation – for example, by executing any judicial decision adopted within the organisation, or by adopting laws which implement decisions obligatory for the members of the organisation.

As confirmed by the work of the International Law Commission's articles on responsibility of international organizations which relates to the responsibility of States cooperating with international organisations, a State (whether or not a member of the organisation) may be internationally liable if it has put its organs at the disposal of the organisation, and these organs commit an internationally wrongful act, in situations where the organs remain controlled by the State. But the decisive question in such situations in relation to attribution of a given conduct is not who controls the organs, but rather 'who had effective control over the conduct in question'.[131] While this rule may be particularly relevant for UN peace-keeping operations to which Member States of the UN voluntarily commit troops, it could also be extended to situations where States put their Executive powers at the disposal of an international organisation in order to ensure that its decisions are effectively implemented. This would include, for instance, the execution of decisions of the international organisation which are addressed to individuals, whose rights may be violated as a result. However, when a State is obliged under the rules of the organisation to execute certain decisions – i.e., the

131 Second report on responsibility of international organizations, by Giorgio Gaja, Special Rapporteur to the International Law Commission, A/CN.4/541, 2 April 2004, at para. 40.

State would be internationally responsible if its organs did not comply with those decisions and did not faithfully implement them – it is doubtful whether its responsibility could be engaged under general international law even where the acts of the organisation would constitute a violation of its international obligations if they had been adopted by that State. Indeed, in such situations, it seems clear that the organisation exercises 'effective control' over the conduct of the organ, in the meaning attached to that expression by the draft articles on responsibility of international organizations, even though the organ remains that of the State and not that of the organisation itself.[132]

Again however, this regime does not correspond to what seems required under international human rights law. Unless it can be demonstrated that the measures adopted by the international organisation fully comply with the requirements imposed on its Member States under any human rights obligations imposed on them, these States should refuse to implement such measures, since they would engage their international responsibility by not doing so. This is clearly affirmed in the case-law of the European Court of Human Rights, certainly since the 1996 case of *Cantoni v. France*.[133] As already noted, in the 2005 *Bosphorus Airways* case, the Court reiterates its view according to which 'absolving Contracting States completely from their Convention responsibility in the areas covered by [the transfer of powers to an international organisation] would be incompatible with the purpose and object of the Convention: the guarantees of the Convention could be limited or excluded at will thereby depriving it of its peremptory character and undermining the practical and effective nature of its safeguards'. Therefore, said the Court, the State 'is considered to retain Convention liability

132 Article 5 of the draft articles on responsibility of international organizations (2006) (Conduct of organs placed at the disposal of an international organization by a State or another international organization) states: 'The conduct of an organ of a State or an international organization that is placed at the disposal of another international organization for the exercise of one of that organization's functions shall be considered under international law an act of the latter organization to the extent that the organization exercises effective control over the conduct of the organ.' See Second report on responsibility of international organizations, by G. Gaja, Special Rapporteur to the International Law Commission, A/CN.4/541, 2 April 2004, at para. 50.

133 In this case, the applicant, a retailer who had been facing proceedings for unlawfully selling pharmaceutical products, complained that the statutory definition of 'medicinal product' lacked sufficient clarity and precision to satisfy the requirements of Article 7 para. 1 of the Convention, which embodies the principle that only the law can define a crime and prescribe a penalty (nullum crimen, nulla poena sine lege), and from which it follows that an offence must be clearly defined in the law. The provision of the French Public Health Code under which the applicant had been prosecuted, however, was reproduced almost literally from an EC Directive. The Court considered this to be irrelevant: 'The fact [...] that Article L. 511 of the Public Health Code is based almost word for word on [Community Directive of 26 January 1965 (Directive EEC 65/65, OJ no. L. 369 of 9 February 1965), as amended on several occasions] does not remove it from the ambit of Article 7 of the Convention.' ECtHR, *Cantoni v. France*, Application No. 17862/91, *Reports* (1996) V, at para. 30).

in respect of treaty commitments subsequent to the entry into force of the Convention'.[134] Even in situations where a State does no more than faithfully implement decisions adopted by the organisation (and binding on that State), it may therefore be internationally responsible under the European Convention on Human Rights: it is irrelevant at this stage whether or not the State has any discretion in the adoption of such implementation measures.[135]

Of course, we could achieve the same result – in effect, affirming the primacy of human rights obligations of States over the obligations they are imposed as members of international organisations – through other means. Human rights, we might say, occupy a hierarchically superior position among the norms of international law.[136] First, since one of the purposes of international economic and social cooperation under the UN Charter is to promote 'universal respect for, and observance of, human rights and fundamental freedoms for all without distinction as to race, sex, language, or religion' (Article 55 c)), and since Article 56 of the UN Charter clearly imposes obligations both on the organisation itself and on its Member States to contribute to the fulfilment of this objective, it would follow from Article 103 of the UN Charter[137] that any international obligation conflicting with the obligation to promote and protect human rights should be set aside, in order for this latter objective to be given priority. Second, *jus cogens* norms are hierarchically superior to any other rules of international law – including, but not limited to, international treaties.[138] A number of prohibitions formulated in international human rights law have already been recognised as

134 ECtHR, *Bosphorus Hava Yolları Turizm ve Ticaret Anonim Şirketi v. Ireland*, Application No. 45036/98, 42 *EHRR* (2006) p. 1, at para. 154.

135 In the case-law of the European Court of Human Rights, whether or not the implementing State has a margin of discretion only becomes relevant when determining the degree of scrutiny to be exercised on the measures adopted by the State: where the international organisation guarantees a protection of human rights deemed 'equivalent' to that of the European Convention on Human Rights, and the State has no discretion in the adoption of implementation measures of decisions adopted within the organisation, the European Court of Human Rights will exercise a less demanding level of scrutiny. See *supra*, text corresponding to n. 90–94.

136 See generally I. Seiderman, *Hierarchy in International Law. The Human Rights Dimension* (Antwerpen-Groningen-Oxford, Intersentia-Hart 2001).

137 Article 103 of the UN Charter provides that '[i]n the event of a conflict between the obligations of the Members of the United Nations under the present Charter and their obligations under any other international agreement, their obligations under the present Charter shall prevail'.

138 In the context of the law of treaties, the Vienna Convention on the Law of Treaties (op. cit. n. 13) states that any treaty which, at the time of its conclusion, is in violation of a peremptory norm of general international law, is to be considered void. A peremptory norm of general international law is defined as 'a norm accepted and recognized by the international community of States as a whole as a norm from which no derogation is permitted and which can be modified only by a subsequent norm of general international law having the same character' (article 53). Article 64 of the Vienna Convention on the Law of Treaties adds that 'If a new peremptory norm of general international law emerges, any existing treaty which is in conflict with that norm becomes void and terminates'.

having the character of *jus cogens*.[139] These include at a minimum the prohibition of slavery and the slave trade, genocide,[140] racial discrimination, apartheid and torture,[141] as well as basic rules of international humanitarian law applicable in armed conflict, and the right to self-determination.[142] Other candidates for future recognition as peremptory norms of international human rights law are the application of the death penalty to juveniles (if not the precise age of majority for purposes of capital punishment)[143] and the prohibition of *refoulement*, i.e., of returning a person to a territory where she runs a risk of torture or of being ill-treated.[144]

These doctrines imply that, when confronted with a choice between two conflicting international obligations – one imposed under international human rights law, the other resulting from a decision adopted by an international organisation to which the State has transferred certain powers which this organisation may exercise by adopting decisions binding on its Member States – a State is not only allowed to set aside the latter obligation in order to comply with the former: it is obliged, under international law, to recognise such primacy of human rights obligations. Although, in theory, the sanctions attached to the

---

139 For an extensive discussion, see I. Seiderman, op. cit. n. 136, at pp. 66–105.

140 ICJ, *Armed Activities on the Territory of the Congo (New Application: 2002) (Democratic Republic of the Congo v. Rwanda)*, Judgment (Jurisdiction of the Court and Admissibility of the Application), at para. 64.

141 *Siderman De Blake v. Republic of Argentina*, 965 F.2d at 717 (9th Cir. 1992), *cert. denied*, 507 U.S. 1017 (1993); *In re Estate of Ferdinand E. Marcos Litigation (Trajano v. Marcos)*, 978 F.2d 493, 500 (9th Cir. 1992), *cert. denied, Marcos Manto v. Thajane*, 508 U.S. 972 (1993); *In re Estate of Ferdinand Marcos Human Rights Litigation (Marcos v. Hilao)*, 25 F.3d 1467, 1475 (9th Cir. 1994), *cert. denied*, 115 S.Ct. 934 (1995). These precedents in turn prompted the International Criminal Tribunal for former Yugoslavia to characterise torture as a *jus cogens* prohibition (see *infra*).

142 ICJ, *Concerning East Timor (Portugal v. Australia)*, Judgment, *ICJ Rep.* (1995) p. 90, at p. 102 (para. 29); and *Official Records of the General Assembly, Fifty-sixth Session, Supplement 10* (A/56/10), commentary to article 40 of the draft articles on State Responsibility, paras. (4)-(6) (also reproduced in J. Crawford, ed., *The International Law Commission's Articles on State Responsibility. Introduction, Text and Commentaries* (Cambridge, Cambridge University Press 2002) at p. 188). See also the consequences the International Court of Justice attaches to this characterisation of the right to self-determination in its Advisory Opinion of 9 July 2004, *Legal Consequences of the Construction of a Wall in the Occupied Palestinian Territory*, Advisory Opinion, *ICJ Rep.* (2004) p. 136, at p. 172 (para. 88).

143 See Inter-American Commission on Human Rights, Res. No. 3/87, Case 9647, [1987] *Inter-American Yearbook on Human Rights* 260. See the comments by I. Seiderman, op. cit. n. 136, at pp. 89–92.

144 It is, indeed, well established that even where an extradition treaty would in principle allow for, or prescribe, the extradition of a person to another State, the extraditing State is prohibited from doing so in the presence of such a risk. The Institute of International Law noted that 'extradition treaties should not be enforced if enforcement would violate a human rights norm external to the treaty. This argument, premised on the notion that there are certain higher norms in the field of human rights which take precedence over extradition treaties owes its origin to the notion of *jus cogens* (...)' (60 *Yearbook of the Institute of International Law* 214 (1983), at pp. 223–4). See I. Seiderman, op. cit. n. 136, at pp. 101–105.

hierarchical principle will differ according to whether it is based on Article 103 of the UN Charter or on the nature of the superior norms recognised as *jus cogens*,[145] in the situation envisaged here, the result will be the same: if an organisation adopts a decision in violation of a *jus cogens* norm, the treaty establishing the organisation will not be considered void, but such decision will be considered illegal and disapplied.[146] Indeed, the power of *jus cogens* is such that, should there be a conflict between the primacy asserted by Article 103 of the UN Charter – which extends to the decisions adopted by the Security Council acting under the UN Charter[147] – and *jus cogens* norms,[148] they should be resolved in favour of the

145 Whereas a treaty found to be in violation of a *jus cogens* norm is void and must be considered to have never existed, a treaty incompatible with obligations flowing from membership in the United Nations does not disappear; however, as a result of Article 103 of the UN Charter, it shall not be applied to the extent of such an incompatibility: see P.-M. Dupuy, 'L'unité de l'ordre juridique international. Cours général de droit international public', loc. cit. n. 53, at p. 305; and see also the Report of the Study Group of the International Law Commission (chaired by M. Koskenniemi), *Fragmentation of international law: difficulties arising from the diversification and expansion of international law*, UN Doc. A/CN.4/L.702, 18 July 2006 (also reproduced in the *Report of the Fifty-eighth session (1 May to 9 June and 3 July to 11 August 2006)* of the ILC to the UN General Assembly, op. cit. n. 73, chapter XII), para. 41: '(*a*) A rule conflicting with a norm of *jus cogens* becomes thereby *ipso facto* void; (*b*) A rule conflicting with Article 103 of the United Nations Charter becomes inapplicable as a result of such conflict and to the extent of such conflict'. Comp. J. Combacau, 'Logique de la validité contre logique d'opposabilité dans la Convention de Vienne sur le droit des traités', in *Mélanges M. Virally* (Paris, Pedone 1991) pp. 195–203.

146 See in this respect the position adopted by the International Law Commission in the course of the discussion of the Draft Articles on State Responsibility, in *Official Records of the General Assembly, Fifty-sixth Session, Supplement 10* (A/56/10), commentary to article 40 of the draft articles on State Responsibility, para. (3) (also reproduced in J. Crawford, ed., op. cit. n. 142, at p. 187) ('...one might envisage a conflict arising on a subsequent occasion between a treaty obligation, apparently lawful on its face and innocent in its purpose, and a peremptory norm. If such a case were to arise it would be too much to invalidate the treaty as a whole merely because its application in the given case was not foreseen').

147 ICJ, *Questions of Interpretation and Application of the 1971 Montreal Convention arising from the Aerial Incident at Lockerbie (Libyan Arab Jamahiriya v. United States of America)*, Order (provisional measures), *ICJ Rep.* (1992) p. 16, at para. 42, and ICJ, *Questions of Interpretation and Application of the 1971 Montreal Convention arising from the Aerial Incident at Lockerbie (Libyan Arab Jamahiriya v. United Kingdom)*, Order (provisional measures), *ICJ Rep.* (1992) p. 113, at para. 39.

148 It has been stated that such a conflict was 'difficult to contemplate': see the Report of the Study Group of the International Law Commission (chaired by M. Koskenniemi), *Fragmentation of international law: difficulties arising from the diversification and expansion of international law*, UN Doc. A/CN.4/L.702, 18 July 2006, at p. 24, para. (40) of the conclusions: 'The United Nations Charter has been universally accepted by States and thus a conflict between *jus cogens* norms and Charter obligations is difficult to contemplate. In any case, according to Article 24 (2) of the Charter, the Security Council shall act in accordance with the Purposes and Principles of the United Nations which include norms that have been subsequently treated as *jus cogens*'. Even at the time when those conclusions were written, this was a far too optimistic view for times such as ours when the UN Security Council may use its powers in ways which may lead to violations of internationally recognised human rights, as illustrated by the *Kadi* litigation referred to in the following footnote. See also, on the need to impose human rights obligations on the UN in order to take into account the new role of the UN as an organisation

primacy of *jus cogens* even over the UN Charter or measures adopted in accordance with the UN Charter. Article 103 of the UN Charter, after all, has the status of a provision included in a treaty establishing an international organisation, whatever the unique character of this organisation: it should thus be disapplied, as any other treaty rule, if it conflicts with *jus cogens* norms.[149]

In a way, therefore, Article 103 of the UN Charter and the characterisation of human rights norms as forming part of *jus cogens* may be seen to act as safeguard clauses: even where a State has inadvertently attributed certain powers to an international organisation in domains which may present a danger to human rights (and which domain, after all, doesn't present such a danger?), and where the organisation exercises these powers in ways which may lead to human rights violations, the State should always be justified in refusing to comply with any decisions adopted by the international organisation which result in such a consequence. But there are at least two problems with this.

First, both doctrines are fragile. Scholars have sometimes questioned whether Articles 55 and 56 of the UN Charter, which refer to human rights as an aim of the organisation and impose on the Member States that they contribute to the achievement of that aim,[150] in fact impose legal obligations, or whether instead, since they are drafted in such general terms, they merely define a programme of action for the organisation.[151] These views often seem to be confusing the question whether the UN Charter's provisions are self-executing, with the question whether they are legally binding; and they are premised on the

---

entrusted with tasks of global governance and the administration of territories through quasi-sovereign powers F. Mégret and F. Hoffmann, 'The UN as a Human Rights Violator? Some Reflections on the United Nations Changing Human Rights Responsibilities', 25 *Human Rights Quarterly* (2003) pp. 314–342. See also, in the same vein, S. Ratner, 'Foreign Occupation and International Territorial Administration: The Challenges of Convergence', *European Journal of International Law* (2005) pp. 695–719.

149 See, e.g., the separate opinion of judge *ad hoc* Elihu Lauterpacht to the Order of 8 April 1993 of the International Court of Justice on the Request for the Indication of Provisional Measures in the Case of the *Application of the Convention on the Prevention and Punishment of the Crime of Genocide (Bosnia and Herzegovina v. Serbia and Montenegro)*, Order, *ICJ Rep.* (1993) p. 440, para. 100; or the reasoning followed by the Court of First Instance of the European Communities in Kadi mentionned supra, n. 17, at paras. 226 and following.

150 Article 55 of the Charter imposes on the United Nations a duty to promote 'universal respect for, and observance of, human rights and fundamental freedoms for all without distinction as to race, sex, language or religion'; under Article 56, all Members of the United Nations 'pledge themselves to take joint and separate action in cooperation with the Organization for the achievement of the purposes set forth in Article 55'.

151 See, e.g., M.O. Hudson, 'Integrity of International Instruments', 42 *American Journal of International Law* (1948) pp. 105–108; H. Kelsen, *The Law of the United Nations* (The London Institute of World Affairs, London 1950) pp. 29–32. In favour of seeing in these provisions of the UN Charter the source of legal obligations, see in particular H. Lauterpacht, *International Law and Human Rights*, (New York, Frederick Praeger Inc. 1950) pp. 147–149.

indeterminate character of the content of the 'human rights and fundamental freedoms' referred to in the UN Charter, which the adoption in 1948 of the Universal Declaration of Human Rights precisely sought to make explicit.[152] In addition, the International Court of Justice seems to have definitively put an end to the controversy when it delivered its Advisory Opinion on the *Legal Consequences for States of the Continued Presence of South Africa in Namibia (South West Africa), notwithstanding Security Council Resolution 276 (1970)*, where it stated that 'to establish [...], and to enforce, distinctions, exclusions, restrictions and limitations exclusively based on grounds of race, colour, descent or national or ethnic origin which constitute a denial of fundamental human rights is a flagrant violation of the purposes and principles of the Charter'.[153] The views sceptical about the usefulness of Articles 55 and 56 of the UN Charter – and, hence, of using Article 103 of the UN Charter as an argument for the recognition of the primacy of human rights – nevertheless remain influential. As to the reliance on the doctrine of *jus cogens*, it is impeded by the persistent controversies surrounding both the precise contours of norms belonging to this category – controversies which statements by the International Court of Justice fed rather than put an end to – and the consequences resulting from the recognition of certain norms as having such character.

Second, even if both doctrines were successful at seeking to achieve the recognition of the primacy of human rights obligations of States over any of their other obligations – and we know that there have been noted instances of failure in this regard[154] – this would still only concern a relatively limited range of

152 UN General Assembly, Res. 217, *UN GAOR*, 3d sess., UN Doc. A/810 (1948) (adopted by 48 votes to none, with 8 abstentions).

153 ICJ, *Legal Consequences for States of the Continued Presence of South Africa in Namibia (South West Africa), notwithstanding Security Council Resolution 276 (1970)*, *ICJ Rep.* (1971) p. 16. While the statement was made in relation to the obligations of South Africa as a Mandatory power in South West Africa, it would seem to follow from the Opinion that the UN Charter imposes on all States that they comply, at a minimum, with a core set of human rights, which the Charter refers to without listing them exhaustively: see E. Schwelb, 'The International Court of Justice and the Human Rights Clauses of the Charter', 66 *American Journal of International Law* (1972) pp. 337–351, esp. pp. 348–349.

154 See in particular ECtHR, *Al-Adsani v. the United Kingdom*, Application No. 35763/97, judgment of 21 November 2001, at para. 61 ('Notwithstanding the special character of the prohibition of torture in international law, the Court is unable to discern in the international instruments, judicial authorities or other materials before it any firm basis for concluding that, as a matter of international law, a State no longer enjoys immunity from civil suit in the courts of another State where acts of torture are alleged'). In a joint dissenting opinion to this judgment, six members of the Court stated that this was in violation of the principle according to which: 'In the event of a conflict between a *jus cogens* rule and any other rule of international law, the former prevails. The consequence of such prevalence is that the conflicting rule is null and void, or, in any event, does not produce legal effects which are in contradiction with the content of the peremptory rule'. However, it could be argued that, in *Al-Adsani*, the conflict was not between the prohibition of torture, on the one hand,

human rights – those which are universally recognised, in contrast to those which are stipulated in specific treaties in force as regards the Member State concerned. Moreover, even more importantly, we should bear in mind the difference between a decision adopted by an international organisation which is in direct conflict with any human rights obligations of its Member States, and such a decision which merely impedes the realisation of human rights by the Member States concerned. Direct, 'open' conflicts will not occur frequently. Much more frequent will be the situations where the law-making or dispute-settlement activities of the international organisation will restrict the policy space available to its Member States, which they need in order to realise a number of human rights under their jurisdiction – for instance, to improve the affordability of education, to provide a decent work to all members of its active population, or to make medicine more accessible. This is, for instance, why international financial institutions, or the law of the World Trade Organization, are seen by a rapidly expanding literature as a threat to human rights: the concern is not that rules contained in the Articles of Agreement of the IFIs or in the WTO agreements are in conflict with the requirements of human rights, in the sense that they cannot be reconciled with one another; it is that the policies pursued by the IFIs, or the clarification of the WTO rules through adjudication, are making it more difficult for States to achieve certain objectives which correspond to what the full realisation of human rights, especially economic and social rights, would require.

In its Kadi judgment[155], the European Court of Justice opened a new breach into the obligation of Member States to implement an international organisation's decision. Indeed, though the Court recognised that the Community must respect international law and attach 'special importance'[156] to United Nations Security Council Resolutions, there is no special status to be granted to Community measures implementing these resolutions when submitted to judicial review. The

and the immunity of foreign States from civil proceedings, on the other; it was rather between the right of access to a court – whose status a *jus cogens* is quite unclear – and that immunity.

155 ECJ, *Kadi*.

156 *Ibid.*, at paras. 293–294, the Court states that '[o]bservance of the undertakings given in the context of the United Nations is required just as much in the sphere of the maintenance of international peace and security when the Community gives effect, by means of the adoption of Community measures taken on the basis of Article 60 EC and 301 EC, to resolutions adopted by the Security Council under Chapter VII of the Charter of the United Nations. In the exercise of that latter power it is necessary for the Community to attach special importance to the fact that, in accordance with Article 24 of the Charter of the United Nations, the adoption by the Security Council of resolutions under Chapter VII of the Charter constitutes the exercise of the primary responsibility with which that international body is invested for the maintenance of peace and security at the global level, a responsibility which, under Chapter VII, includes the power to determine what and who poses a threat to international peace and security and to take the measures necessary to maintain or restore them.'

Court of Justice ruled that the EC legal order is an autonomous order from that of international law.[157] It placed the emphasis on the need for implementing Security Council Resolutions in accordance with the EC legal order. No provision of the Treaty abrogates the application of fundamental rights and Article 307 EC (now Art. 351 TFEU) may not take precedence over fundamental rights. The European Court of Justice recalled that effective judicial protection is a general principle within Community law enshrined in constitutional traditions of Member States and established in Articles 6 and 13 of the European Convention on Human Rights.[158] This protection notably requires the communication to the persons concerned of the grounds for their names being included on the sanctions lists.[159] Moreover, these persons have a right of defence and a right to be heard.[160] Given that the ECJ found the contested regulations in breach of the right to be heard, the right to judicial protection and the right to property, it annulled Regulation No 881/2002 insofar as it concerned Yassin Abdullah Kadi and the Al Barakaat International Foundation.

At the same time, the Court ordered the effects of Regulation 881/2002 to be maintained for a period of maximum three months in order to allow the possibility to remedy the infringements found. Following this judgment, the Commission communicated the narrative summaries of reasons provided by the UN Al-Qaida and Taliban Sanctions Committee to Mr Kadi and to the Foundation and gave them the possibility to comment on these grounds. It received comments, examined them and considered that the listing was justified. Therefore, a new Regulation was adopted on 28 November 2008.[161]

D. THE LOGIC OF SLIDING SCALES IN EXAMINING QUESTIONS OF STATE RESPONSIBILITY

As long as we remain within the orthodox understanding of the conditions of State responsibility, as embodied by the provisions of the International Law Commission's draft articles on responsibility of international organizations which relate to the responsibility of States cooperating with international organisations (2006), a State may escape international responsibility if it transfers certain powers to an international organisation, not realising at that time that

157 ECJ, *Kadi*, at paras. 316–317.
158 *Ibid.*, at para. 335.
159 *Ibid.*, at para. 336.
160 *Ibid.*, at paras. 337–338.
161 Commission Regulation (EC) No 1190/2008 of 28 November 2008 amending for the 101st time Council Regulation (EC) No 881/2002 imposing certain specific restrictive measures directed against certain persons and entities associated with Usama bin Laden, the Al-Quaida network and the Taliban, *OJ* 2008 L 322/25.

such powers could be exercised in violation of the human rights obligations of that State; if it then participates in the decision-making process within the organisation, while remaining unable to decisively influence the outcome of that process; and if it then faithfully implements any measures adopted by that international organisation, even though such measures could make it more difficult for the State concerned to comply with those human rights obligations. The problem, it seems, is that we adopt a segmented view of the State's international responsibility. We reason as if such responsibility must have its origin *either* in the initial transfer of powers, *or* in the participation in the decision-making process, *or* in the contribution a State makes to the life of the international organisation by implementing its decisions. Instead, a holistic view might be more appropriate, according to which these three moments could be considered together, and evaluated as a whole – as a sequence of events, the *combined effect* of which alone results in a violation of human rights. Under this competing logic, the transfer of powers to an international organisation would be acceptable, even if it results in a risk that the organisation will adopt certain measures conflicting with the international obligations of its Member States, to the extent that the Member States retain a power to veto such measures, or to influence their content to a decisive extent; or at least, failing that, to the extent that they can refuse to comply with such measures when asked to take measures of implementation, without engaging their responsibility under the law of the organisation. The precise formula according to which the responsibility of a State resulting from the acts of the international organisation of which it is a member cannot be detailed here. The basic idea, however, can be stated quite easily: instead of examining *separately* what a State may or may not do when transferring competences to an international organisation, whether or not it may be internationally responsible for how it exercises its voting powers within the organisation, or whether such responsibility may follow from the implementation of the decisions adopted by the organisation, we should consider these acts *together*, as both mutually reinforcing and mutually dependent upon one another. The logic of portioning should give way to the logic of sliding scales: the more a State takes risks at one segment of the chain, for instance by transferring large powers to the organisation and by renouncing any veto power on the decisions it may take in exercising them, the more that State should reserve its right not to implement such decisions if they violate its human rights obligations.

However, such logic should not be limited to evaluating State responsibility. It should include in the equation of State responsibility any other mechanisms through which human rights are taken into account in the activity of international organisations. It is to these mechanisms that we now turn.

III. THE PROBLEM OF ACCOUNTABILITY – TWO: THE RESPONSIBILITY OF INTERNATIONAL ORGANISATIONS

As we have seen, it is increasingly recognised that, since they are part of general public international law, universally recognised human rights are binding upon international organisations as on any other subject of international law. However, a separate question is that of the mechanisms which would allow to hold international organisations accountable for any violations of human rights which they commit, or which they contribute to. In this Part, I distinguish three such mechanisms: self-regulation, accession of the international organisation to international regimes (in particular treaty-based regimes), and judicial control exercised by national courts. I discuss each of these mechanisms in turn, highlighting their respective strengths and weaknesses.

A. SELF-REGULATION

In recent years, we have seen a proliferation of initiatives through which international organisations voluntarily choose to develop procedures which aim to ensure that they will comply with human rights, or at least, with certain standards related to human rights but which are better adapted to their specific areas of activity. The examples are many, and they are striking in their diversity. Certain mechanisms are purely voluntary, without any reference to external forms of control or pre-existing standards. Thus, the World Bank[162] and the International Monetary Fund have developed a set of operational policies, rather comparable to internal codes of conduct regulating their activities, which integrate human rights considerations. In addition, institutional mechanisms have been set up for monitoring compliance. Both the World Bank and the IMF have set up 'independent'[163] internal evaluation units to enhance accountability and improve the effectiveness of the strategies of these institutions: these are the Independent Evaluation Group (IEG) for the of IBRD/IDA, IFC and MIGA; and the Independent Evaluation Office (IEO) for the Fund. In addition, alleged

162 This term refers to the institutions of the World Bank group, including not only the International Bank for Reconstruction and Development (IBRD) set up in 1944 at the Bretton Woods conference in New Hampshire, but also the International Development Association (IDA) (established in 1960), the International Finance Corporation (IFC) (established in 1956), the Multilateral Investment Guarantee Agency (MIGA) (established in 1985), and the International Centre for the Settlement of Investment Disputes (ICSID) (established in 1966).

163 The units are independent in the sense that they are not part of the administrative hierarchy of the institutions concerned, and they report directly back to the Board of Executive Directors of of IBRD/IDA, IFC and MIGA. The independency of these evaluations has been improved by the merger in November 2005, under the authority of the Director-General, Evaluation (DGE), of all independent evaluation work performed in these institutions.

breaches of the aforementioned operational policies may be examined by the World Bank's Inspection Panel (for IBRD and IDA operations) or Compliance and Accountability Ombudsman (CAO) (for the IFC and MIGA). These are promising developments.[164] However, these mechanisms remain internal to the operations of the international financial institutions. And human rights considerations, if relevant at all to the evaluation of the operations of the international financial institutions, are so only indirectly – not because of a recognition that they would constitute binding obligations on these institutions, but because they are integrated in their operational policies or in the terms of reference of the evaluation mechanisms which have been set up. A number of authors have rightly described these as important limitations to the potential effectiveness of such mechanisms.[165]

In other cases, international agencies have chosen to submit to existing monitoring mechanisms, although they were not originally a party to the intergovernmental agreements establishing these mechanisms. Thus, sect. 2 of Regulation 1999/1 adopted by the United Nations Interim Administration Mission in Kosovo (UNMIK) provides that in the discharge of its functions, UNMIK shall comply with international human rights standards.[166] On 23 August 2004, the UNMIK and the Council of Europe concluded an Agreement whereby UNMIK accepted not only to comply with the substantive provisions of the Council of Europe Framework Convention for the Protection of National

---

164 The literature is overwhelming. On the internal evaluation units, see P.G. Grasso, S.S. Wasty, R.V. Weaving, *World Bank Operations Evaluation Department – The First 30 Years*, The International Bank for Reconstruction and Development/The World Bank (2003). More generally on the human rights dimension of the activities of the World Bank and the IMF, see in particular, L. Boisson de Chazournes, 'The Bretton Woods Institutions and Human Rights: Converging Tendencies', in W. Benedek, K. De Feyter, and F. Marrella, eds., *Economic Globalization and Human Rights* (Cambridge, Cambridge University Press 2007) pp. 210–242; D. Bradlow, 'The World Bank, the IMF and Human Rights', 6 *Transnational Law and Contemporary Problems* (1996) p. 63; R. Dañino, 'The Legal Aspects of the World Bank's Work on Human Rights', in P. Alston and M. Robinson, eds., *Human Rights and Development. Towards Mutual Reinforcement* (Oxford, Oxford University Press 2005) p. 509; M. Darrow, *Between Light and Shadow: The World Bank, the International Monetary Fund and International Human Rights Law* (Oxford, Hart Publishing 2003); S.I. Skogly, *The Human Rights Obligations of the World Bank and the International Monetary Fund* (London, Cavendish 2001). On the International Monetary Fund in particular, see D. Bradlow, 'Operational Policies and Procedures and an Ombudsman', in B. Carin and A. Woods, eds., *Accountability of the International Monetary Fund* (Ottawa, etc, Ashgate and the International Development Research Centre 2005) p. 89.

165 D.L. Clark, 'The World Bank and Human Rights: The Need for Greater Accountability', 15 *Harvard Human Rights Journal* (2002) pp. 205–226.

166 This provision states that 'In exercising their functions, all persons undertaking public duties or holding public office in Kosovo shall observe internationally recognized human rights standards and shall not discriminate against any person on any ground such as sex, race, color, language religion, political or other opinion, national, ethnic or social origin, association with a national community, property, birth or other status'.

Minorities, but also to be bound by the provisions on the monitoring of the implementation of the FCNM by UNMIK in Kosovo.[167] A similar agreement was concluded between the UNMIK and the Council of Europe on technical arrangements related to the 1987 European Convention for the Prevention of Torture and Inhuman or Degrading Treatment or Punishment, allowing the European Committee for the Prevention of Torture and Inhuman or Degrading Treatment or Punishment (CPT), by means of visits, to examine the treatment of persons deprived of their liberty in Kosovo with a view to ensure their protection and to prevent risks of torture or ill-treatment. While emphasising 'that the present Agreement does not make UNMIK a Party to the Convention and that it is without prejudice to the future status of Kosovo to be determined in accordance with Security Council resolution 1244 (1999)', the agreement provides that UNMIK shall permit visits by the CPT to any place in Kosovo where persons are deprived of their liberty by an authority of UNMIK. In 2006, an exchange of letters was concluded between the Secretaries General of the Council of Europe and the North Atlantic Treaty Organization (NATO), allowing the CPT to exercise its monitoring functions also as regards detention facilities managed by the NATO troops under K-FOR. As a result of the 2004 Agreement and the 2006 exchange of letters, a delegation of the CPT made its first visit to Kosovo from 21 to 29 March 2007.

By far the most developed mechanism of self-regulation – so sophisticated, in fact, that we tend to forget its voluntary nature – is that developed within the European Union since the late 1960s, when the European Court of Justice delivered its first judgments including fundamental rights among the general principles of law it ensures respect.[168] Much has been achieved since those leading cases, of course. Since 1992, the case-law of the European Court of Justice has been confirmed in the Treaty on the European Union.[169] Since 2000, it has been codified in a Charter of Fundamental Rights, the legally binding character of which has been affirmed in Article 6(1) TEU, as inserted by the Lisbon Treaty.[170] In addition, measures have been adopted to ensure a prevention of

---

167 On this Agreement see R. Hofmann, 'Protecting Minority Rights in Kosovo', in K. Dicke et al., eds., *Weltinnenrecht, Liber amicorum Jost Delbrück*, (Berlin, Duncker & Humblot 2005) p. 347. In accordance with the agreement, UNMIK submitted its Report on 2 June 2005 and, subsequent to a visit to Kosovo in October 2005, the Advisory Committee adopted an opinion on 25 November 2006. After this opinion had been introduced to the GR-H on 21 February 2006, UNMIK decided to make the opinion publicly accessible on 2 March 2006. On 21 June 2006, the Committee of Ministers adopted a Resolution on the basis of the opinion of the Advisory Committee.

168 See *supra*, n. 95. The development of general principles of law by the European Court of Justice has been based on Article 220 TEC, repealed and replaced in substance by Article 19 TEU under the Lisbon Treaty.

169 See currently Article 6(3) TEU.

170 The Charter was solemnly proclaimed by the Presidents of the European Parliament, the Council and the Commission on 7 December 2000 (OJ C 364, 18.12.2000, p. 1). It has been

human rights violations within the EU law- and policy-making. In April 2005, the Commission adopted a Communication[171] by which it seeks to improve the compliance of its legislative proposals with the requirements of the Charter. On 15 June 2005, it has adopted a new set of guidelines for the preparation of impact assessments,[172] which now pay a much greater attention to the potential impact of different policy options on the rights, freedoms and principles listed in the EU Charter of Fundamental Rights.[173] Remarkable as they are, these developments nevertheless remain of a voluntary kind. They do not imply an acceptance by the European Communities – or, now, by the European Union – that they are bound to comply with the requirements of international human rights law.[174] The inclusion of fundamental rights among the general principles of law was, rather, a means to reassure the national courts of the EU Member States that the supremacy of European Community law would not oblige these national courts to set aside human rights guarantees set out in the national constitutions.[175] The search for legitimacy was predominant; not any sense of the European institutions that they were bound to act in conformity with human rights.

Apart from the obvious need for international organisations to build their legitimacy,[176] the extraordinary proliferation of self-regulatory mechanisms may be explained by two factors. First, such mechanisms may be seen as an alternative

proclaimed, in a revised form, on 13 December 2007, in order to be referred to by the TEU as amended by the Treaty of Lisbon as having the same legal force as the treaties (*OJ* C 303 of 14.12.2007, p. 1).

171 Communication from the Commission, Compliance with the Charter of Fundamental Rights in Commission legislative proposals. Methodology for systematic and rigorous monitoring, COM(2005) 172 final of 27 April 2005.

172 SEC(2005)791, 15.6.2005.

173 Indeed, a specific report was commissioned by the European Commission (DG Justice, Freedom and Security) to EPEC (European Policy Evaluation Consortium), in order to ensure the adaptation of the guidelines on impact assessment to human rights requirements: see EPEC, *The Consideration of Fundamental Rights in Impact Assessment. Final Report*, December 2004, 61 pages.

174 For an attempt to show the limitations resulting from this situation and to ground the human rights obligations of the European Union in international law, see T. Ahmed and I. de Jesús Butler, loc. cit. n. 12. In part I of this contribution, I have expressed my doubts about the attempt to build a theory of 'succession' of the EU to its Member States on the existing case-law of the European Court of Justice (see *supra*, text corresponding to n. 10–26); and I have indicated the limitations resulting from taking as a departure point either customary international law, as Ahmed and Butler do, or – perhaps more plausibly – the general principles of law (see *supra*, text corresponding to n. 46–67). However successful these efforts may prove to be in the future, for now at least, it is clear that the system of human rights protection established within the legal order of the European Union remains internal to the EU, which has not recognised that it was bound to comply with international human rights under general public international law.

175 See op. cit. n. 96.

176 See T.M. Franck, 'Legitimacy in the International System', 82 *American Journal of International Law* (1988) pp. 705–759; A. Buchanan and R.O. Keohane, 'The Legitimacy of Global Governance Institutions', 20 *Ethics and International Affairs* (2006) pp. 405–437.

to the reliance on the responsibility of Member States for the acts of international organisations. A distinct advantage of self-regulation is that, in contrast to the alternative of Member State responsibility, this solution will not provide a pretext for the Member States of the organisation to insist on better controlling decision-making within the organisation, for instance by being allowed to veto certain decisions or refuse to cooperate in the process of implementation. Second, self-regulation may be preferred to subordination to an international regime or to submission to the jurisdiction of national courts – two avenues I briefly explore below – either because these latter solutions are much more threatening to the international organisation – representing a more serious limitation to their freedom to choose how to exercise the powers they have been attributed – or because, when they do not represent such a threat, they are ineffective – facing obstacles such as the impossibility for international organisations to accede to treaties devised for the participation of States only or immunity of jurisdiction before national courts. In other words, self-regulation seems to ensure that the activity of the international organisation will be perceived as legitimate and as operating in conformity with the shared values of human rights, without putting in jeopardy in any way its ability to perform the functions it has been set up for: with self-regulation, we would have, as it were, the best of two apparently irreconcilable worlds.

Of course, by their very definition, these self-regulatory mechanisms have not been imposed on the international organisation 'from above' or from the outside: they result, instead, from a choice of the organisation; and they remain internal to the organisation. But we should not equate the voluntary character of such mechanisms with any inherent weakness they would present as per definition. As the example of the European Union shows, certain of these mechanisms, for instance when they include judicial procedures and a reference to external standards,[177] are extremely robust, and probably more effective in the protection of human rights they ensure than any available alternative.

---

[177] It may be recalled that, within the EU, the fundamental rights which are considered to belong to the general principles of law which the European Court of Justice ensures respect for, are developed by the Court on the basis of the international human rights treaties the EU Member States have ratified. The European Convention on Human Rights has been recognised a 'special significance' in this context: it is applied by the ECJ as if it were obligatory for the EU institutions, and it is read in accordance with the case-law of the European Court of Human Rights, despite the absence of any formal link between the legal order of the European Union and the system of the European Convention on Human Rights. See ECJ, Case C-249/96, *Grant,* [1998] ECR I-621; ECJ, Case C-185/95, *Baustahlgewebe*, [1998] ECR I-8417; ECJ, Case C-274/99, *Connolly*, [2001] ECR I-1611, and ECJ, Case C-71/02, *Karner*, [2004] ECR I-3025. For a further elaboration, see O. De Schutter, 'L'influence de la Cour européenne des droits de l'homme sur la Cour de justice des Communautés européennes', in G. Cohen-Jonathan and J.-Fr. Flauss, eds., *Le rayonnement international de la jurisprudence de la Cour européenne des droits de l'homme* (Bruxelles, Bruylant-Nemesis 2005) pp. 189–242. However, the European Court of Justice appears to be willing to seek inspiration, in developing the general principles

There are also more positive reasons to think of self-regulation as the ideal mechanism through which the accountability of international organisations can be improved. The voluntary adoption by the organisation of certain standards guiding its conduct or those of its officials allows it to choose standards sufficiently detailed, tailored to the specific context in which the organisation operates, and whose definition can go significantly beyond the minimum obligations flowing, under general public international law, from its constitution, the agreements to which it is a party, customary international law or general principles of law. The mechanisms through which such standards are monitored, moreover, exhibit a diversity which can go far beyond the classical 'normative-judicial' approach consisting in defining standards and setting up a body, judicial or quasi-judicial, to ensure compliance: they can comprise, for instance, impact assessments, participatory mechanisms, inspection panels or ombuds institutions. Such mechanisms may demonstrate a shift away from a stockholders approach to the legitimacy of international organisations – according to which the interests that matter are those, primarily or exclusively, of its Member States – to a shareholders approach under which all interests potentially affected by the activities of the organisation are considered relevant to the definition of its rule and policy-making. In that sense, because of their flexibility and their adaptability to new contexts, self-regulatory mechanisms introduced by international organisations may be better suited to accommodate the emergence of new interests in the international legal process, as represented by a variety of non-governmental organisations.[178] The more such mechanisms develop, the more their participatory dimension is emphasised, and the more international organisations will build their legitimacy on the non-governmental organisations and grassroots movements they interact with and consult.[179] This can be in

of law it ensures respect for, only from the international human rights treaties binding on all the EU Member States: for further developments see *supra*, n. 33.

178 On the emergence of international civil society and of NGOs as participants in the international legal process, see, e.g., presented in alphabetical order: L. Boisson de Chazournes, 'The World Bank Inspection Panel: About Public Participation and Dispute Settlement', in T. Treves et al., eds., *Civil Society, International Courts and Compliance Bodies* (The Hague, TMC Asser Press 2005) pp. 187–203; H. Cullen and K. Morrow, 'International civil society in international law: The growth of NGO participation', 1 *Non-State Actors and International Law* (2001) pp. 7–39; M. Edwards, *Future Positive. International Cooperation in the 21st Century* (London, Earthscan 1999); M. Edwards and S. Zadek, 'Governing the Provision of Global Public Goods: The Role and Legitimacy of Nonstate Actors', in I. Kaul, P. Conceiçãio, K. Le Goulven, and R.U. Mendoza, eds., *Providing Gobal Public Goods. Managing Globalization* (New York and Oxford, UNDP and Oxford University Press 2003) pp. 200–224; R. Falk, *On Humane Governance: Toward a New Global Politics* (Cambridge, Polity 1995); M. Kamminga, 'The Evolving Status of NGOs under International Law: A Threat to the Inter-State System?', in P. Alston, ed., *Non-State Actors and Human Rights* (Oxford, Oxford University Press 2005) pp. 93–112, M. Shaw, *Global Society and International Relations*, (Cambridge, Polity 1995).

179 As noted by J. Alvarez: 'The legitimacy of NGOs and [international organizations] are often intertwined. NGOs have arguably enhanced the political legitimacy of some [international

addition to their main source of legitimacy, which stems from the mandate they have been given by the States to which they owe their existence. But it can also move them further away from this mandate, and become an alternative and competing source of legitimacy, as international organisations may be tempted to conspire with those new actors against narrowly defined governmental interests.[180]

B. ACCESSION TO INTERNATIONAL HUMAN RIGHTS TREATIES

International human rights treaties have traditionally been open to accession and ratification by States only. This may, however change rapidly in the years to come. Both the expansion of the competences transferred to international organisations by States and the voluntary acceptance by these organisations of certain human rights obligations to the extent that they activities may impact on human rights, make such a route at once more plausible and perhaps more desirable than a few years ago.

---

organizations] by providing forms of accountability not otherwise available, but NGOs' participation has also benefited some NGOs by enhancing their own international stature or legitimacy' (J.E. Alvarez, op. cit. n. 2 at p. 612). See also on what Alvarez labels a 'symbiotic relationship' between NGOs and international organizations S. Charnovitz, 'Two Centuries of Participation: NGOs and International Governance', 18 *Michigan Journal of International Law* (1997) p. 183, at pp. 274–275. Coicaud has noted that, although it can gain from interacting more systematically with non-State actors, the challenges faced by international organisations in order to improve their legitimacy and 'address the weak sense of international community that exists' are not to be underestimated. In the process, international organisations will have to 'revisit their relations of cooperation with the actors that are both their partners and competitors, especially states, regional arrangements, private actors, non-governmental organizations, and individuals. [However,] improving the relations of collaboration with these actors is destined to be a complex task, particularly because each tends to have an agenda that does not necessarily coincide entirely with those of the others. [...] States [in particular] will have to become less protective of their sovereign powers: more willing, for instance, to share power with international organizations and non-governmental organizations, and more open to claims about individuals' (J.-M. Coicaud, loc. cit. n. 2 at p. 547).

180 This development has been documented, for instance, as regards the World Bank: see J.A. Fox and C.D. Brown, eds., *The Struggle for Accountability: The World Bank, NGOs and Grassroots Movements*, (Cambridge, MIT Press 1998). It is particularly visible in the instrumentalisation by the European Union of civil society organisations, and the shaping, by the EU, of a 'European civil society' whose agenda the EU institutions have actively determined: see O. De Schutter, 'Europe in Search of Its Civil Society', 8 *European Law Journal* (2002) pp. 198–217; and R. Sanchez Delgado, *Comment l'Europe construit la société civile* (Paris, Dalloz 2007). The debate on the participation of NGOs in dispute settlement within the WTO is equally illustrative of this emerging conflict between two competing legitimacies: see, e.g., St. Charnovitz, 'Opening the WTO to Non-Governmental Interests', 24 *Fordham International Law Journal* (2001) pp. 173–216; and R. Howse, 'Membership and its Privileges: the WTO, Civil Society, and the Amicus Brief Controversy', 9 *European Law Journal* (2003) pp. 496–510.

The recent practice of the EU may be announcing future developments in this direction. The first steps towards the EU acceding to human rights treaties have been in the framework of the Council of Europe. In 1997, the Convention on Human Rights and Biomedicine was the first human rights instrument adopted within the framework of the Council of Europe providing for the accession of the European Community.[181] In 1999, the Committee of Ministers of the Council of Europe adopted a set of Amendments to the Council of Europe Convention for the Protection of Individuals with regard to Automatic Processing of Personal Data,[182] in order to allow for the accession to the Convention of the European Communities. The Amendments also adapt the provisions of the Convention related to the voting rights of the Parties, in order to take account the possibility that the European Communities will exercise the voting rights of its Member States in matters for which it has been transferred competences.[183] This development followed the adoption by the European Community of Directive 95/46/EC of the European Parliament and of the Council of 24 October 1995 on the protection of individuals with regard to the processing of personal data and on the free movement of such data,[184] which, it was considered, empowered the EC to conclude international agreements in the areas covered by the said directive. And the 2007 Treaty of Lisbon amending the EU Treaty now provides for the possibility of the EU acceding to the European Convention on Human Rights.[185]

Can this be generalised? In 2003, the European Commission, representing the European Community, was authorised to negotiate the UN Convention on the Rights of Persons with Disabilities, alongside the EU Member States. This followed a request of the Commission,[186] which it justified by the adoption of a EC legislative instrument on the question of discrimination in work and

---

181 Convention for the protection of Human Rights and dignity of the human being with regard to the application of biology and medicine: Convention on Human Rights and Biomedicine (CETS No. 164, opened for signature in Oviedo, on 4 April 1997), Article 33(1). The European Community, however, has not signed the Convention.

182 CETS No. 108, opened for signature on 28 January 1981 in Strasbourg.

183 A new para. 3 is to be inserted in Article 20 of the Convention: 'Every Party has a right to vote. Each State which is a Party to the Convention shall have one vote. Concerning questions within their competence, the European Communities exercise their right to vote and cast a number of votes equal to the number of Member States that are Parties to the Convention and have transferred their competencies to the European Communities in the field concerned. In this case, those Member States of the Communities do not vote, and the other Member States may vote. The European Communities do not vote when a question which does not fall within their competence is concerned'

184 *OJ* L 281 of 23.11.1995 p. 31.

185 See Article 6(2) TEU, as modified by the Lisbon Treaty.

186 Communication of the Commission to the Council and the European Parliament, 'Towards a United Nations legally binding instrument to promote and protect the rights and dignity of persons with disabilities', COM(2003) 16 final of 24 January 2003.

employment.[187] The Convention was adopted after three years of discussions by the United Nations General Assembly on 13 December 2006, and opened for signature on 30 March 2007. As a result of the involvement of the European Community in the negotiations, the Convention contains a provision (Article 44) on 'Regional integration organisations', providing the conditions under which such organisations may accede to this new instrument.[188] The Convention defines a 'regional integration organisation' as 'an organisation constituted by sovereign States of a given region, to which its Member States have transferred competence in respect of matters governed by this Convention'. Upon acceding to the Convention, such organisations 'shall declare, [...] the extent of their competence with respect to matters governed by this Convention. Subsequently, they shall inform the depositary of any substantial modification in the extent of their competence'.[189] The exercise of voting rights in the framework of the Convention is regulated as under the Amendments to the Council of Europe Convention for the Protection of Individuals with regard to Automatic Processing of Personal Data.[190]

Were it not for the stipulations of human rights treaties, which traditionally are open to accession only of States, these precedents could be imitated in other areas in which the European Union has taken legislative action, thereby exercising competences it has been attributed by its Member States. Of course, in the absence of a general power of the Community or the Union in the field of fundamental rights,[191] the limits imposed on the exercise of the international powers of the Community or the Union are a serious obstacle to their accession

187 Council Directive 2000/78/EC of 27 November 2000 establishing a general framework for equal treatment in employment and occupation, *OJ* L 303 of 2.12.2000, p. 16.

188 See also Article 12 of the Optional Protocol, providing the Committee on the Rights of Persons with Disabilities, the expert body set up under the Convention, with the competence to receive individual communications.

189 Article 44(1) of the Convention.

190 According to Article 44(4) of the Convention: 'Regional integration organizations, in matters within their competence, may exercise their right to vote in the Conference of States Parties, with a number of votes equal to the number of their Member States that are Parties to this Convention. Such an organization shall not exercise its right to vote if any of its Member States exercises its right, and vice versa'.

191 See on this the opinion delivered on 28 March 1996 by the European Court of Justice: Opinion 2/94, *Accession of the European Community to the European Convention for the Protection of Human Rights and Fundamental Freedoms*, [1996] ECR I-1759, para. 20. The Court stated in that opinion that the Community institutions do not have at their disposal a 'general power to enact rules on human rights or to conclude international conventions in this field', although it did not question that respect for human rights constituted a 'condition of lawfulness of Community acts': see paras. 27 and 34 of the opinion. On this opinion, see, inter alia, O. De Schutter and Y. Lejeune, 'L'adhésion de la Communauté européenne à la Convention européenne des droits de l'homme. A propos de l'avis 2/94 de la Cour de justice des Communautés européennes', *Cahiers de droit européen* (1996) p. 555; G. Gaja, 'Opinion 2/94', 33 *Common Market Law Review* (1996) p. 973.

to international instruments for the protection of human rights. However, even under the present definition of the external powers of the Union, the accession to a number of international instruments in the field of human rights protection may be envisaged.[192] Just as the achievements of the European Community in the field of data protection have been deemed sufficient to envisage the accession of the Community to the convention concluded on this question in the framework of the Council of Europe, similarly the acquis of EC Law in the field of equal treatment between women and men and in the field of non-discrimination on grounds of race or ethnic origin would appear sufficient to identify a power of the Community to accede to the United Nations Conventions on the Elimination of All Forms of Discrimination against Women (CEDAW)[193] and on the Elimination of All Forms of Racial Discrimination (CERD).[194] It has also been argued that the EU should accede to the 1996 Revised European Social Charter, adopted within the Council of Europe as a complement, in the field of economic and social rights, to the 1950 European Convention on Human Rights[195]; or to the Geneva Convention on the status of refugees of 28 July 1951.[196]

Indeed, the time perhaps has come to question the classical approach to the question of the competence of international organisations to accede to international agreements, when the concerned agreements concern the promotion and protection of human rights. It is well established that the competence of international organisations is a limited one: they may only act under the condition that, and insofar as, they have been attributed the power to do so by the Member States to which they owe their existence.[197] We may ask

192 *Report on the situation of fundamental rights in the European Union in 2003*, prepared for the EU Network of Independent Experts on Fundamental Rights, January 2004, pp. 19–20. Report available on http://ec.europa.eu/justice_home/cfr_cdf/index_en.htm#. Internet pages last visited in February 2009. For the sake of transparency, it should be disclosed that I was the main author of this report.

193 1249 UNTS 20378, adopted by UN Gen. Ass. Res. 34/180 of 18 December 1979. All the 27 Member States of the EU have ratified this instrument.

194 660 UNTS 9464, adopted by UN Gen. Ass. Res. 2106 A(XX) of 21 December 1965, and opened for signature at New York on 7 March 1966. All the 27 Member States of the EU have ratified this instrument.

195 The Revised European Social Charter of 3 May 1996 (ETS, n° 163) improves upon the original European Social Charter of 18 October 1961, by extending the list of rights protected. On the question of the accession of the European Union to the Council of Europe Social Charter, see O. De Schutter, 'Anchoring the European Union to the European Social Charter: The Case for Accession', in G. de Búrca and B. de Witte, eds., *Social Rights in Europe* (Oxford, Oxford University Press 2005) pp. 111–152; and, for a more technical discussion, O. De Schutter, *L'adhésion de l'Union européenne à la Charte sociale européenne*, EUI Working Paper LAW No. 2004/11, 42 pages.

196 149 UNTS 2545.

197 In its advisory opinion on *Legality of the use by a State of nuclear weapons in armed conflict*, the International Court of Justice stated that: '[…] international organizations […] do not, unlike States, possess a general competence. International organizations are governed by the

however, which implications follow from the accession of international organisations to human rights treaties? By acceding to such instruments, the Parties undertake to respect certain minimal standards for the benefit of the persons under their jurisdiction, which implies in the first place that they will not adopt any measures which derogate from these standards. Insofar as the undertaking is purely negative (formulated as an obligation to abstain from), it is irrelevant whether or not the Party has the competence to take measures which implement the given standard. It is only where the undertaking is also to adopt certain measures – to fulfil positive obligations (to act) – that the question of competences may play a role.

If we agree to take this distinction between negative and positive obligations as a departure point, two views may be defended as to the impact, on the exercise by the international organisation of its competences, of its accession to an international human rights treaty. Both views acknowledge that, by agreeing to be bound by an international agreement for the promotion and protection of human rights, an international organisation – however limited its competences in the subject-matter covered by the said treaty – would be committing itself to comply with the prescriptions of the agreement insofar as it remains within its attributed competences. Under a first view, this would imply two sets of obligations: first, in exercising its competences, the international organisation would be duty-bound to respect the rights stipulated in the concerned instrument; second, it would undertake to exercise the competences it has been attributed to the extent required in order to protect and fulfil those rights, insofar as required by that instrument. In other terms, whereas the organisation may be obliged to adopt certain measures, to the extent that human rights treaties impose certain positive obligations, it would only have to do so to the extent that this does not lead the organisation to go beyond the principle of specialty.

This view was clearly put forward in the current discussions on the accession of the European Union to the European Convention on Human Rights.[198] When it examined this question during the 'European Convention' which prepared the ground for the Inter-governmental conference of 2003–2004, the Working Group established in order to study the twin questions of the incorporation of the EU Charter of Fundamental Rights in the new Treaty and

'principle of specialty', that is to say, they are invested by the States which create them with powers, the limits of which are a function of the common interests whose promotion those States entrust to them' (*ICJ Rep.* (1996) pp. 66, at p. 78 (para. 25)).

198 See further O. De Schutter, 'L'adhésion de l'Union européenne à la Convention européenne des droits de l'homme comme élément du débat sur l'avenir de l'Union', in M. Dony et E. Bribosia, eds., *L'avenir du système juridictionnel de l'Union européenne* (Bruxelles, éd. de l'ULB 2002) pp. 205–256.

of the accession of the Union to the European Convention on Human Rights noted:

> 'The Group agrees on the central importance of the fact that accession by the Union to the ECHR [...] will in no way modify the allocation of competences between the Union and the Member States. According to the Group's common understanding, the legal 'scope' of the Union's accession to the ECHR would be limited to issues in respect of which the Union has competence; it would thus not lead to any extension of the Union's competences, let alone to the establishment of a general competence of the Union on fundamental rights. Accordingly, 'positive' obligations of the Union to take action to comply with the ECHR would arise only to the extent to which competences of the Union permitting such action exist under the Treaty.'[199]

Thus, according to this view, while accession to an international human rights agreement would not result in a transfer of supplementary powers to the acceding international organisation, it might affect the exercise of any powers it has been attributed, to the extent that positive obligations to protect and fulfil human rights are imposed under the said treaty. It has been put forward in legal doctrine, in particular, that this should be the consequence of the EU taking seriously its commitment to international human rights.[200] However, another view may be defended, according to which, because of the constraints imposed by the principle of specialty (also expressed, in the context of the EU, as the principle of conferral), their accession to international human rights treaties should be seen as imposing only negative obligations on the acceding international organisations: not only should it not lead to the transfer of supplementary powers to the international organisation, but in addition it should not influence the purposes for which the organisation should exercise the powers it has been attributed. According to this alternative view, the principle of specialty not only

---

199 European Convention, Final report of Working Group II, doc. CONV 354/02 (22 October 2002), p. 13 (footnote omitted).

200 See O. De Schutter, 'The Implementation of Fundamental Rights through the Open Method of Coordination', in O. De Schutter and S. Deakin, eds., *Social Rights and Market Forces. Is the open coordination of employment and social policies the future of Social Europe?* (Bruxelles, Bruylant 2005) pp. 279–343, at pp. 301–334 (arguing, at p. 308, that 'a positive obligation [should be imposed on the EU to legislate in order to implement human rights] where, in the absence of action at the level of the Union, we may witness a 'race to the bottom' by Member States tempted to diminish the level of protection of fundamental rights within their jurisdiction'); and T. Ahmed and I. de Jesús Butler, loc. cit. n. 12, at p. 800 (arguing that 'in those areas where the EC and EU have competence, not only are their institutions under an obligation to refrain from actively violating human rights, but that they are also under the obligation to protect and fulfil human rights in those areas'). For a discussion of the thesis put forward in the first of these two contributions, see M. Lindfelt, *Fundamental Rights in the European Union – Towards Higher Law of the Land? A Study of the Status of Fundamental Rights in a Broader Constitutional Setting* (Åbo, Åbo Akademi University Press 2007) pp. 306–314.

implies that the international organisation may not exercise powers which it has not been attributed, but also that it should only use such powers for the fulfilment of the aims for which they have been attributed – so that adding the objective of protecting and fulfilling human rights to the aims of the organisation, would be bringing about a fundamental change in its mandate, and disrupting the division of competences between the organisation and its Member States.[201]

Each of these views takes a different position on the implications, for the principle of specialty of international organisations, of imposing that such organisations comply with human rights as defined in international human rights instruments and as expounded by the monitoring bodies set up under those instruments. What both these views have in common, however, is that they treat accession of an international organisation to an international agreement in the field of human rights and attribution of competences to an international organisation as two entirely separable questions. Since, in order to accede to a human rights treaty, an international organisation does not need to have competences in the 'domain covered' by the said treaty – insofar as the treaty merely imposes on the organisation that it exercises its competences, whatever these may be, in accordance with its requirements – accession to such a treaty may be envisaged for any organisation whatsoever, whichever the competences it has been attributed. And since any 'positive' obligations flowing from the treaty will be imposed on the international organisation only insofar as it has received the competences required to comply with such obligations, such accession should not, in principle, affect the constraints imposed on the organisation by the principle of specialty.

A distinct but related question is that which the European Court of Justice refers to as the principle of 'autonomy' of the international organisation. In the specific context of the EU, this principle is derived from the rule according to which the European Court of Justice ensures observance of the law in the interpretation and application of Union law[202] as well as from the undertaking of the Member States not to submit a disagreement on the interpretation or application of the EU Treaties to any other mode of settlement than those provided for by the EU Treaties.[203] The European Court of Justice saw in those provisions the expression of a general principle, according to which that Court itself must remain the

201 See A. von Bogdandy, 'The European Union as a human rights organization? Human rights and the core of the European Union', 37 *Common Market Law Review* (2000) pp. 1307–1338 (arguing, against proposals that the EU should develop a proactive fundamental rights policy, that this would have a powerful centralizing effect, and that such a prospect 'might upset the constitutional balance within the Union, infringe the subsidiarity principle and encroach on the guarantee of constitutional autonomy as part of national identity' (p. 1317)).

202 Article 220 EC (former Article 164 of the EC Treaty).

203 Article 292 EC (former Article 219 of the EC Treaty).

ultimate interpreter of the law of the Union, and more particularly of the rules in the EU Treaties establishing the division of competences between the Union and its Member States. The principle of autonomy of the Union's legal order consequently rules out that the Court of Justice can be bound by the interpretation which another court of law may give of Union law. Situated according to Opinion 1/91 of 14 December 1991 'at the foundations of the Community', this principle thus requires that questions of interpretation and application of Union law cannot be settled according to procedures outside the European Union, but only according to the rules of settlement which the Union itself has instituted.[204]

For our purposes, the principle of autonomy thus described is relevant to the extent that it has sometimes been asked whether it would be compatible with this principle to allow a jurisdiction other than the European Court of Justice to make authoritative decisions about the division of competences between the EU and its Member States, in the process of adjudicating on the international responsibility of the EU in the framework of international agreements to which it is a party.[205] It should be noted, however, that even in the context of EU law, the said principle does not exclude all forms of international commitment of the European Union that are placed under the control of an international court outside the European Union's legal order: as long as an external jurisdiction does not authoritatively interpret EU law, leaving this to be decided by the European Court of Justice itself, it may pass judgment on the question whether or not the EU has complied with its international obligations.[206] In addition, mechanisms are available which would allow the determination of the respective competences of the EU Member States and the European Union to be made within the legal order of the EU, under the supervision of the European Court of Justice, even in situations where a jurisdiction external to the legal order of the EU – such as the European Court of Human Rights, in the event of the accession of the EU to the European Convention on Human Rights – would be allowed to decide that the EU and/or its Member States are in violation of their international obligations.

---

204 See Opinion 1/91 of 14 December 1991, Draft agreement between the Community, on the one hand, and the countries of the European Free Trade Association, on the other, relating to the creation of the European Economic Area, [1991] ECR I-6079 ('First EEA opinion'); Opinion 1/92 of 10 April 1992, [1992] ECR I-2821 ('Second EEA opinion').

205 Indeed, this question was central to the debate which resulted in requesting an opinion from the European Court of Justice about the accession of the European Community to the European Convention on Human Rights. The Court delivered its opinion in 1996 (op. cit. n. 191), but without providing an answer to that question.

206 Opinion 1/91, op. cit. n. 204, at para. 40 ('The Community's competence in the area of international relations and its authority to enter into international agreements necessarily entails the possibility of submitting to the decisions of a court of law that has been set up or designated by virtue of such agreements for the interpretation and application of their provisions').

Essentially, such a mechanism would consist in identifying a joint responsibility of both the EU and its Member States, and it would be left for the EU and its Member States themselves to decide – in accordance with the EU treaties – which entity should take action in order to put an end to the violation.[207]

We may ask, finally, whether the principle of autonomy – despite the apparent specificities of the EU legal order and the role of the European Court of Justice – is not a mere platitude, and the product of a simple misunderstanding about the task of the international adjudicator. Where an international organisation accedes to an international treaty and submits to a monitoring mechanism established under that treaty, it is unavoidable that this mechanism will have to 'interpret' the measures adopted by that organisation, in order to decide whether the said measures are compatible with its international obligations. Exceptionally, it may even have to 'interpret', for similar reasons, the agreement through which the organisation is established, for instance in order to decide whether the organisation's agents have acted *ultra vires* in certain cases.[208] But such 'interpretations' have no pretence to being authoritative, i.e., to impose any particular normative reading of these instruments: for the international adjudicator, the measures adopted by the international organisation and the treaty establishing that organisation are mere 'facts'; they are not the 'law' which the adjudicator takes as the basis of her legal reasoning. The circumstances which led the European Court of Justice to identify a 'principle of autonomy' at the basis of the EU legal order were highly specific:[209] we should avoid extrapolating from the situation it was then presented with what is, upon closer examination, a rather artificial – if not totally imaginary – obstacle to the accession of international organisations to international agreements, probably based on a misunderstanding about the status of the 'interpretation' under such agreements of the measures adopted by the international organisation.

In sum, while there is still no example yet of an international organisation having acceded to an international human rights treaty, it is clearly in this direction that

207 On this question, see O. De Schutter, loc. cit. n. 198. Article 44(1) of the UN Convention on the rights of persons with disabilities also complies with the principle of autonomy, since it is for the regional integration organisation itself (acting in according with the internal rules of the organisation and its constitutive treaty) to declare which are the areas for which it has been attributed competences in the fields covered by the treaty.

208 On the question of the attribution of *ultra vires* conduct to international organisations, see Second report on responsibility of international organizations, by G. Gaja, Special Rapporteur to the International Law Commission, A/CN.4/541, 2 April 2004, paras. 23–27.

209 A separate court, but in which certain judges of the European Court of Justice were to be sitting, was to interpret within the Agreement establishing the European Economic Area provisions worded exactly like provisions from EC law: the result was that the interpretation of such provisions in this setting would inevitably have an impact on the interpretation of EC law by the European Court of Justice itself.

the EU is moving. The example of the EU may be inspiring other regional integration organisations, or even other international organisations, to follow suit. If we take into account the specific nature of the obligations imposed under human rights treaties, the question of whether such organisations possess the required competence to accede to such treaties may be easier to answer than is traditionally thought. Nor would this be incompatible with the principle of specialty under which international organisations operate, since, in accordance with their specific status among the subjects of international law, international organisations would only be required to take action in order to comply with any positive obligations imposed upon them to the extent that they have been attributed the competence to do so. Finally, we should not fear that the interpretation, by human rights bodies, of any measures adopted by the international organisation or of its constitutive treaty, may take the Member States by surprise – for example, by imputing to the international organisation a failure to act, whereas it has no competence to adopt the measure required: regrettable as it is, such an erroneous reading of the 'facts' by the human rights body concerned should not affect the existing division of competences between the organisation and its Member States.

C. THE ROLE OF NATIONAL COURTS

Finally, where self-regulation has failed, and whether or not there exist remedies at international level against human rights violations by international organisations, one possible option is to seek to file claims against such organisations before national courts. After all, if international organisations are bound to respect customary international law and the general principles of law – including internationally recognised human rights, as we have seen[210] – could not national courts impose on them that they comply with those norms? Doesn't international human rights law begin at the level of the national authorities?

The main obstacle this avenue will be facing resides in the immunity of jurisdiction generally recognised to international organisations before domestic courts.[211] The importance of this argument has been confirmed by August Reinish in his empirical study of the practice of national courts when facing suits

210 See *supra*, part I, B of this contribution.

211 The literature on the subject is rapidly expanding. The most influential writings, listed by chronological order, are J.-F. Lalive, 'L'immunité de juridiction des Etats et des organisations internationales', *Recueil des cours de l'Académie de droit international*, vol. 84 (1953-III) pp. 205–396; A.S. Muller, *International Organizations and Their Host States: Aspects of Their Legal Relationship* (The Hague/London/Boston, Kluwer Law International 1995), esp. chap. 5 on immunity of jurisdiction; M. Singer, 'Jurisdictional Immunity of International Organizations: Human Rights and Functional Necessity Concerns', 36 *Virginia Journal of International Law* (1995) pp. 53–163; E. Gaillard and I. Pingel-Lenuzza, 'International Organizations and

against international organisations.[212] Yet, this obstacle is not necessarily insuperable. Certain international organisations have renounced benefiting from such immunity in their constitutive instruments. This is the case, in particular, for two member organisations of the World Bank Group (the International Bank for Reconstruction and Development (IBRD) and the International Development Agency (IDA)), which provide for the possibility of legal action being brought against the institution 'only in a court of competent jurisdiction in the territories of a member' in which the Bank has offices.[213] Although the resulting waiver of immunity has sometimes been interpreted very restrictively in order to ensure that it will remain compatible with the fulfilment by the IBRD of its functions, a suit based on alleged violations of human rights universally recognised should not be treated as having a disruptive effect on its activities such as to justify upholding the immunity rule.[214] National courts have also considered that immunity of jurisdiction should only be granted when it is expressly invoked by

Immunity from Jurisdiction: to Restrict or to Bypass', 51 *International & Comparative Law Quarterly* (2002), pp. 1–15.

212 Whether it is based on domestic law, on treaty law, or on customary international law – although it is debatable whether there exists in fact such a customary norm, and whether therefore immunity of jurisdiction should be recognised to the international organisation in the absence of any specification in the agreement with the host State (see the position of the Belgian Court of Cassation: Cass., 12 March 2001 *(Ligue des Etats arabes v. T.), Revue critique de jurisprudence belge* (2002) p. 377, casenote J. Verhoeven) –, this argument appears to be the 'avoidance technique' most frequently resorted to by national courts for declining jurisdiction in claims filed against international organisations. See A. Reinisch, *International Organizations before National Courts* (Cambridge, Cambridge University Press 2000) p. 127 and ff. The other avoidance techniques documented by Reinisch are the lack of recognition of the legal personality of international organisations; the refusal to attribute a particular act to the organisation, in particular because it has been adopted *ultra vires*; doctrines of act of state, political questions, or other doctrines of non-justiciability; lack of jurisdiction of the forum court; absence of case or controversy; or abuse of right by the plaintiff.

213 Article VII, section 3 of the Articles of Agreement of the IBRD; and Article VIII, section 3 of the IDA Agreement. In contrast, the International Monetary Fund claims full immunity from 'all forms of judicial process except to the extent that it expressly waives its immunity for the purpose of any proceedings or by the terms of any contract' (Article IX, section 3 of the IMF Agreement).

214 See *Mendaro v. World Bank* 717 F.2d 610, 614–15 (D.C. Cir. 1983), where the US Court of Appeal for the District Court of Columbia Circuit held that the justification for granting immunity to international organisations was to enable them to pursue their functions more effectively, in particular, to operate freely from unilateral control by a member state over their activities within its territory. This led the Court to offer a very restrictive interpretation of the waiver of immunity contained in the Agreement establishing the IBRD in the context of a sexual harassment suit based on Title VII of the 1964 Civil Rights Act against the IBRD by a former employee. The Court of Appeals observed that 'such a waiver would expose the Bank to disruptive interference with its employment practices by requiring the Bank to adopt the local employment policies of each of its member countries, which would imply devastating administrative costs'. See the comment by M. Leigh, 'Mendaro v The World Bank', 78(1) *American Journal of International Law* (1984) pp. 221–223.

the defendant international organisation – that, in other terms, the waiver could be implicit.[215]

Even beyond the rather exceptional case where, explicitly or tacitly, the international organisation concerned waives its right to immunity of jurisdiction, it should be asked whether the blanket invocation of its immunity by the international organisation may be reconciled with the requirements of the right of access to a court, as recognised in international human rights law.[216] As we have seen,[217] the European Court of Human Rights has adopted the view that the application by national courts of the doctrine on immunity of jurisdiction of an international organisation does not constitute a violation of Article 6 §1 of the European Convention on Human Rights,[218] to the extent that 'the applicants had available to them reasonable alternative means to protect effectively their rights under the Convention'.[219] The Court considered that 'bearing in mind the legitimate aim of immunities of international organisations [...], the test of proportionality cannot be applied in such a way as to compel an international organisation to submit itself to national litigation in relation to employment conditions prescribed under national labour law. To read Article 6 §1 of the Convention and its guarantee of access to court as necessarily requiring the application of national legislation in such matters would [...] thwart the proper functioning of international organisations and run counter to the current trend towards extending and strengthening international cooperation'.[220]

This reasoning, while perfectly defensible for a specialised human rights jurisdiction whose role it is to apply a human rights treaty, cannot be simply reproduced in other fora. The European Court of Human Rights is established in order to ensure the observance of the engagements undertaken by the Parties in the European Convention on Human Rights.[221] Any other international undertakings of the States parties to the Convention, including those – such as agreements providing for immunities – which are potentially conflicting with

---

215 See, e.g., the position of the Brussels Court of Appeals: Bruxelles (9ème ch.), 19 November 1996 (*Eurocontrol v. PSRC*), *Pasicrisie*, II, p. 119.

216 See M. Singer, loc. cit. n. 211, at pp. 53–165 (arguing, at pp. 91–95, that the international responsibility of a member State of the international organisation could be engaged for granting immunity to the international organisation in the absence of an adequate alternative remedy). See also K. Wellens, *Remedies against international organizations* (Cambridge, Cambridge University Press 2002) p. 214.

217 See *supra*, text corresponding to n. 98–99.

218 Article 6§1 secures to everyone the right to have any claim relating to his civil rights and obligations brought before a court (see the *Golder v. the United Kingdom* judgment of 21 February 1975, Series Application No. 18, pp. 13–18, at paras. 28–36).

219 ECtHR, *Beer and Regan v. Germany*, op. cit. n. 98, at para. 58; ECtHR, *Waite and Kennedy v. Germany*, op. cit. n. 98, p. 261, at para. 95.

220 ECtHR, *Beer and Regan v. Germany*, op. cit. n. 98, at para. 62.

221 See Article 19 of the European Convention on Human Rights.

the requirements of the Convention – such as its requirement that a right of access to a court be guaranteed for the determination of civil rights and obligations – cannot bind the European Court of Human Rights. Their status is similar to that of the internal law of the States parties: far from being bound by such competing international agreements, the Court is to evaluate their compatibility with the European Convention on Human Rights, for instance, where such agreements are invoked in order to justify restrictions to the rights and freedoms guaranteed in the Convention, in order to decide whether such restrictions respect the principle of proportionality. In this respect, non-specialised international tribunals or national courts are in a markedly different position: in principle, the different international agreements concluded by a State all have the same normative weight, since they are not hierarchically ordered, and the problem then becomes one of reconciling conflicting international obligations with one another.

Therefore, the reasoning adopted by the European Court of Human Rights in cases where States or international organisations were recognised a jurisdictional immunity before the national courts of the States parties only can inspire solutions before other courts if we posit that human rights treaties, to the extent that they guarantee a right of access to a court, should be seen as in some way hierarchically superior to other international agreements concluded by the State concerned, or to other sources of international law providing for such immunity of jurisdiction. Again, we would need to ground the assertion of a primacy of human rights treaties on Article 103 of the UN Charter or on the specific position of human rights norms recognised as *jus cogens* which, due to this specific status, should be allowed to override any other rule which does not have the same status, including rules on immunity of jurisdiction.[222]

---

222 See *supra*, n. 154, the joint dissenting opinion filed by six members of the European Court of Human Rights to the judgment delivered on 21 November 2001 by the Grand Chamber of the Court in the case of *Al-Adsani v. the United Kingdom* (Appl. No. 35763/97). See also para. 28 of the dissenting opinion of Ms Van den Wyngaert, judge *ad hoc*, to the judgment of 14 February 2002 delivered by the International Court of Justice in the Case concerning the *Arrest Warrant of 11 April 2000 (Democratic Republic of Congo v. Belgium), ICJ Rep.* (2002). While there are both dissenting opinions, it is notable that the opinions of the majority which they oppose did not take a position on the question of whether the rules regarding immunity (of foreign States, in the case of *Al-Adsani*; of Foreign Affairs Ministers, in the case concerning the *Arrest Warrant of 11 April 2000*) may be invoked as an obstacle to the application of rules imposing obligations which have the nature of *jus cogens* norms. This silence may be explained by the fact that, in both cases, the majority saw the conflict not between a) a *jus cogens* norm on the one hand and b) immunity on the other hand, but as between a) the right of access to a court in order to seek reparation from a violation of jus cogens (*Al-Adsani*) or the exercise of universal jurisdiction in order to ensure prosecution for such violation (the *Arrest Warrant* case) on the one hand, and b) immunity on the other.

The potential, but also the weaknesses, of these arguments have been explored above,[223] and we need not revisit them here. It should be noted however that, while it may narrow the range of situations where jurisdictional immunity will be denied, a reference of universally recognised human rights – as would be required in any case in order to justify asserting the primacy of human rights obligations over claims to immunity of jurisdiction by the international organisation, on the basis of Article 103 of the UN Charter or of the *jus cogens* status of human rights norms – presents one significant advantage, from a policy point of view. It is well known that the main argument in favour of recognising jurisdictional immunities to international organisations is that such immunities allow them to function properly, without having to take into account, in each of the countries in which they operate, the locally applicable legislation, which – for example in their staff policies – would otherwise create important operational difficulties.[224] But human rights claims filed against international organisations, again, are specific in this respect. Precisely because they are universally recognised, human rights can be imposed on international organisations wherever they operate. The removal of immunities in human rights claims would not create the disruptive effects which, in contrast, the imposition on international organisations of the *lex fori* might cause. This is one more reason for allowing claims against international organisations to proceed, when such claims allege that the defendant organisation has violated human rights: where this is indeed the argument invoked by the plaintiff, it would seem difficult for the organisation to allege that it cannot reconcile compliance with human rights with the smooth conduct of its operations.

D. THE LOGIC OF SLIDING SCALES EXPANDED

In the previous sections of this later analysis, I have reviewed briefly three mechanisms through which international organisations could be made accountable for human rights violations they commit or for which they share responsibility. These mechanisms are self-regulation – the voluntary integration, within the organisation's internal decision-making processes, of a concern for human rights; accession to international human rights treaties; and supervision by national courts. Far from being mutually exclusive, these mechanisms may be, instead, complementary. Until now, self-regulation has constituted the preferred and most frequently met mechanism of accountability. But, while we should not underrate the potential effectiveness of this mechanism, this tendency has been developing essentially by default: it is because of the obstacles, both

223 See *supra*, n. 150–154.
224 See the argument of the United States Court of Appeal in *Mendaro v. World Bank* 717 F.2d 610, 614–15 (D.C. Cir. 1983).

technical and political, to the accession of international organisations to international human rights treaties or to such organisations submitting to the jurisdiction of national courts, that self-regulation has been the rule.

The logic of sliding scales referred to above can be further expanded, in order to take into account the existence of these mechanisms, or the lack thereof. In part II of this contribution, we examined whether the Member States of an international organisation could be considered internationally responsible in situations where that organisation violates human rights. We identified as one potential problem in constructing a satisfactory regime of international responsibility, the adoption of a segmented approach to State responsibility – one which considers separately the role of the State in setting up the organisation, its role in the decision-making process of the organisation, and finally its role in contributing to the implementation of any decisions adopted within the organisation. Instead, it was then suggested, a holistic approach might be preferred, which would follow the logic of sliding scales. According to this logic, the role of the State at any of these junctures should be evaluated by taking into account its role at the other junctures: for instance, the more a State retains influence on the decision-making process within the international organisation, or the more it may obstruct implementation of the decisions of the organisation, the easier it will be to justify the delegation of extensive powers to the international organisation, although such a transfer of powers may result in the adoption by the international organisation of measures which infringe upon human rights.

By the same logic, the standards used for evaluating the responsibility of the Member States of international organisations for the acts of the latter should take into account whether or not accountability mechanisms have been set up ensuring that the organisation will comply with any human rights standards equivalent to those imposed on the Member States. This results in a reverse principle of proportionality: the more the international organisation is subject to monitoring mechanisms, whether internal or external, the more it would be acceptable for States to transfer large competences to the organisation and to renounce controlling the organisation from within or blocking the implementation of any decisions adopted within the organisation. Such a reverse proportionality constitutes the underlying philosophy of the 'equivalent protection' doctrine put forward by the European Court of Human Rights in the *Bosphorus Airways* case.[225] The more robust the protection of human rights in the activities of the organisation, in other terms, the more we should accept that, for the sake of international cooperation, the Member States take the risk of transferring powers to the organisation without preserving the ability to influence how such powers will be exercised. From this point of view, self-

225 See *supra*, text corresponding to n. 90–94.

regulation, the accession of the international organisation to international human rights treaties, and the submission to the jurisdiction of national courts, are of course not necessarily equivalent: each mechanism, and any of the many variations which exist in each category, presents distinct strengths and weaknesses, and we should be sceptical of any attempt to offer too broad generalisations in this regard. The main point, however, is a simple one: before concluding whether a State has 'circumvented' its international obligations by transferring powers to an international organisation, we should ask, not only which influence it has retained on the decision-making process of the organisation or in the implementation of its decisions, but also whether the organisation itself is subject to certain forms of accountability, how effective these are, and whether they may be seen as an adequate substitute for the responsibility of the Member States themselves.

IV. CONCLUSION

International law is still in a state of flux as regards the division of responsibilities between international organisations and their Member States where the acts of the former, apart from potentially engaging the responsibility of the organisation itself, are alleged to also potentially engage the responsibility of the latter. States have divested themselves of a number of sovereign powers. They have transferred these powers to international organisations which, insofar as they are autonomous from the Member States and are not merely an instrument of inter-State cooperation without a will of their own, are recognised an international legal personality distinct from that of their Member States. Therefore, international organisations are potentially internationally responsible in situations, and for acts, for which their Member States cannot be held responsible. But – with the notable exception of the European Union – these international organisations have only recently become aware of their human rights responsibilities. They have sought to take such responsibilities into account by setting up various mechanisms of self-regulation, on a voluntary basis. Only rarely have they agreed to submit to the jurisdiction of national courts. And only one of them – the European Union, again – has sought to formally accede to human rights conventions, allowing for an external supervision of their activities.

A regime of international responsibility of States and international organisations which takes into account the interrelationship between both responsibilities should define the scope of the Member States' responsibility by evaluating whether, and through which mechanisms, the international organisation to which they have delegated certain powers seeks to ensure that it exercises these powers in compliance with human rights. Insisting on the responsibility of the

Member States is entirely justified until such mechanisms are set up which ensure that the international organisation itself will be accountable for any human rights violations it commits. While the accession of the international organisation to the same human rights instruments already binding on its Member States may be the most effective of such mechanisms, both because the substantive standards will be identical to those imposed on the Member States and because, in general, such accession will place the international organisation under some form of external supervision, this is by no means the only possibility. As illustrated in the case-law of the European Court of Human Rights, an 'equivalent' protection of human rights may be achieved by self-regulation, if it is sufficiently robust institutionally and if the normative standards are at least comparable to those imposed on the Member States of the organisation. The logic of sliding scales proposed in this contribution suggests that we tailor the obligations imposed on the Member States of the international organisation – in particular their obligation not to 'circumvent' their international obligations by establishing such organisations or transferring them powers – to the effectiveness of any such mechanisms which ensure (more or less adequately) the accountability of international organisations.

Although it is still in flux, the general direction of the relevant international legal practice is clear. In order to ensure that the development of inter-State cooperation through the setting up of international organisations with a distinct legal personality will not lead the Member States of international organisations to evade their international obligations, we tend to insist on a prohibition to thus 'circumvent' such obligations. The risk is not only that this will impose further obstacles on international cooperation (although, arguably, for entirely legitimate reasons). As illustrated by the proposal of Dan Sarooshi,[226] it is also that the Member States could invoke their potential international responsibility for the internationally wrongful acts of the organisation in order to reassert their control over the organisation, thus putting in jeopardy the independence of the organisation, however crucial such independence may be for the satisfactory fulfilment of the organisation's aims – it is, after all, not despite, but on the contrary because of, their independence *vis-à-vis* their Member States, that we think of international organisations as essential actors in today's interdependent world.

But the alternative – insisting on the setting up of mechanisms ensuring the direct accountability of the international organisations – also is fraught with dangers. By insisting on the human rights responsibilities of international organisations, are we not asking them in effect to betray the mandate for which they were originally established, and which should, in principle, guide the

[226] See *supra*, text corresponding to n. 5–6.

exercise by these organisations of the competences they have been attributed? This is not an imaginary concern. The natural tendency has always been to interpret extensively the constituting charters of international organisations, thus expanding the organisational powers and scope of operations of many such organisations.[227] The concern is illustrated by the extensive debates on the compatibility with the mandate of the World Bank and the International Monetary Fund of the inclusion of human rights considerations in their operations.[228] Nor is the concern limited to the international financial institutions, whose Articles of Agreement, it has been considered until recently, may be read to prohibit the inclusion of non-economic considerations in their decision-making. After the European Union was called upon to mainstream human rights in its activities and to develop a more 'proactive' policy in this area,[229] it has been argued that this was not in conformity with the 'core mandate' of the Union.[230] With the exception of the United Nations, the Council of Europe, or other organisations whose mandates already refer explicitly to the promotion of human rights, it may be a thin line between insisting on compliance with human rights and requesting that the aims of the organisation be redefined so that it, too, transforms itself into a 'human rights organisation' – bound to exercise its competences in order to contribute to the protection and promotion of human rights.

There is no simple or immediate way out of this dilemma. However, in discussing the mechanisms through which the human rights accountability of international organisations could be improved, this contribution has emphasised the need to

---

227 See chapter 2 of J.E. Alvarez, op. cit. n. 2, at pp. 65–108.

228 See L. Boisson de Chazournes, loc. cit. n. 164, at pp. 212–223; P. Klein, 'Les institutions financières internationales et les droits de la personne', *Revue belge de droit international* (1999) pp. 97–114 (both examining the implications, for the ability of the Bretton Woods institutions to take human rights into account, of the prohibition imposed on them to make decisions on the basis of non-economic considerations). Article IV, section 10 of the Articles of Agreement of the International Bank for Reconstruction and Development states, under the heading 'Political Activity Prohibited': 'The Bank and its officers shall not interfere in the political affairs of any member; nor shall they be influenced in their decisions by the political character of the member or members concerned. Only economic considerations shall be relevant to their decisions, and these considerations shall be weighed impartially in order to achieve the purposes stated in Article 1'. While the Articles of Agreement of the IMF do not include a similar clause, the requirement to take only economic considerations into account has been seen as also applicable to the Fund. See also the other sources mentions *supra*, n. 164.

229 See P. Alston and J.H.H. Weiler, 'An "ever closer union" in need of a human rights policy', in P. Alston, ed., *The EU and Human Rights* (Oxford, Oxford University Press 1999) p. 3. See also O. De Schutter, 'Mainstreaming Human Rights in the European Union', in P. Alston and O. De Schutter, eds., *Monitoring Fundamental Rights in the EU. The Contribution of the Fundamental Rights Agency* (Oxford, Hart Publishing 2005) pp. 37–72.

230 See A. von Bogdandy, op. cit. n. 201 (arguing that 'The Union as an organization focused on progressive human rights policy would easily endanger the European constitutional set-up between the Union and the Member States without any real need for protecting human rights […]' (p. 1337)).

distinguish between the negative obligations (to abstain from violations) and the positive obligations (to protect and fulfil human rights) which are traditionally imposed on the parties to international human rights treaties.[231] Whereas, in order to be fulfilled, positive obligations require that the addressee possess the required competences to do so, negative obligations merely impose limits on how existing competences may be exercised. The implication is that, by requiring from an international organisation that it complies with human rights in the course of its activities, we are not asking it to expand its powers beyond those which it has been attributed by its Member States. We are not even necessarily asking that it exercise the powers it has been attributed with a view to ensuring the protection and promotion of human rights. We ask, rather, that when it takes action, and insofar as it takes action, it should ensure that it will not negatively impact upon human rights. In that sense, the danger of 'creeping competences' usually associated with the imposition of human rights responsibilities on international organisations should not be exaggerated: while such a danger cannot be ignored, neither should it be considered an unavoidable consequence.

The logic of sliding scales proposed in this contribution conveys a simple message to States setting up international organisations: the more the organisation itself complies with human rights, and establishes mechanisms, whether internal or external, relying either on international monitoring bodies or on national courts, in order to ensure such compliance, the less there will be reasons to suspect that, by transferring powers to the organisation, the Member States have somehow 'circumvented' their human rights obligations. In that sense, the approach to international responsibility advocated here seeks not simply to be more realistic about the twin dangers of threatening the independence of international organisations and risking that they transform themselves, whether wilfully or inadvertently, into 'human rights organisations': it also seeks to cut a path away from a vicious cycle, in which States seek to negate or undermine the independence of international organisations by arguing that they need to ensure that these organisations comply with human rights, while at the same time refusing that the international organisations establish mechanisms in order to improve such compliance, because of a fear that they would thereby betray their mandate.

---

[231] See *supra*, text corresponding to n. 197–201.

BINDING INTERNATIONAL ORGANISATIONS TO MEMBER STATE TREATIES OR RESPONSIBILITY OF MEMBER STATES FOR THEIR OWN ACTIONS IN THE FRAMEWORK OF INTERNATIONAL ORGANISATIONS

Frederik NAERT*

INTRODUCTION

This contribution briefly discusses two aspects of the responsibility of Member States in the context of international organisations. In the first part, the question is analysed whether international organisations are bound by treaties which bind their Member States because such a binding might be one way of ensuring that Member States do not evade their obligations by acting, in one way or another, through international organisations. Under this heading, attention will be paid to (1) general considerations; (2) the European Union (EU) and the General Agreement on Tariffs and Trade (GATT) as well as Customs Agreements; (3) the EU[1] and the European Convention on Human Rights (ECHR); (4) the EU and other Member State Treaties, including the United Nations (UN) Charter; and

* Member of the Legal Service of the Council of the European Union affiliated to the University of Leuven as Associate Fellow, Leuven Centre for Global Governance Studies and substitute lecturer, Institute for International Law, Faculty of Law. The views expressed in this contribution are solely those of the author and do not bind the Council or its Legal Service. This contribution is based on two sections from Chapter 7 of the author's Ph.D. Thesis (*International Law Aspects of the EU's Security and Defence Policy, with a Particular Focus on the Law of Armed Conflict and Human Rights*, KU Leuven, 2008), of which an updated version was published by Intersentia in December 2009.

1 Given that the former European Communities (EC) have now been succeeded by the EU, I will attempt to only specifically mention the EC where this is still somewhow relevant. Similarly, as a rule, I will refer to the consolidated versions of the Treaty on European Union (TEU) and the Treaty on the Functioning of the European Union (TFEU) as they are amended by the Lisbon Treaty (Treaty of Lisbon amending the Treaty on European Union and the Treaty establishing the European Community, Lisbon, 13 December 2007, *O.J. C* 306 (17 December 2007), which entered into force on 1 December 2009) and published in *O.J. C*

(5) other international organisations. In the second part, some reflections are offered on the responsibility of Member States for their own actions in the framework of international organisations – i.e. *linked to a Member State's own conduct*, in particular (1) responsibility for the actions of an international organisation resulting from the establishment of an international organisation and (2) responsibility of a Member State for its own subsequent conduct in the framework of an international organisation. This is by no means an exhaustive treatment of all aspects related to this topic. For instance, the question of Member State responsibility for acts of international organisations as such will not be addressed in this contribution.

I. ARE INTERNATIONAL ORGANISATIONS BOUND BY TREATIES CONCLUDED BY THEIR MEMBER STATES?

A. GENERAL CONSIDERATIONS

Much has been written, especially in the framework of the EU,[2] on whether international organisations are bound by some of the international agreements concluded by their Member States. The primary underlying reason why it is often attempted to achieve such a binding seems to be a concern that Member States could otherwise evade their obligations by transferring powers to an international organisation without the obligations attached to the exercise of such powers.[3]

However, a binding as such seems contrary to the relative nature of treaties[4] – see also the discussion of the reverse question whether Member States are bound

85 (30 March 2010). Where relevant, I will refer to the pre-Lisbon TEU and ex-TEC (Treaty establishing the European Community).

2 See e.g. the references in O. Elias, 'General International Law in the European Court of Justice: from Hypothesis to Reality?', 31 *Netherlands Yearbook on International Law* (2000) p. 4, n. 1 and R. Lawson, *Het EVRM en de Europese Gemeenschappen: bouwstenen voor een aansprakelijkheidsregime voor het optreden van internationale organisaties* (Deventer, Kluwer 1999) pp. 138–143.

3 E.g. M. Hirsch, *The Responsibility of International Organizations Towards Third Parties: Some Basic Principles* (Dordrecht, Martinus Nijhoff Publishers 1995) pp. 53–54 and P. Klein, *La Responsabilité des organisations internationales dans les ordres juridiques internes et en droit des gens* (Brussels, Bruylant 1998) pp. 338–342. On obligations related to powers transferred to an international organisation, see generally M. Hirsch, op. cit. this note, pp. 38–60.

4 Although P. Klein, op. cit. n. 3, at pp. 343–344 is right in stating that the Vienna Convention on the Law of Treaties between States and International Organizations or between International Organizations of 21 March 1986 (not yet entered into force; hereinafter '1986 VCLT') does not cover the effect for international organisations of treaties concluded only between States (and that neither does the Vienna Convention on the Law of Treaties of 23 May 1969; hereinafter '1969 VCLT') as this convention only covers agreements to which at least one international organisation is a party. However, it is unlikely that a different conclusion

by agreements concluded by an international organisation[5] – and is by no means obvious. Moreover, as I will demonstrate below, there seem to be very few cases

than the relativity of treaties would exist according to whether or not an agreement counts an international organisation among its parties, all the more so since this rule is also contained in the 1969 VCLT and arguably reflects a basic principle of not binding third parties without their consent.

5 This issue was controversial during the preparation and negotiations of the 1986 VCLT and a provision on the matter in the ILC draft convention (article 36*bis*, see *Yearbook of the International Law Commission* (1982-II) Part 2, pp. 43–47) was rejected and not included in that convention (for a discussion, see e.g. C. Brölmann, *The Institutional Veil in Public International Law. International Organizations and the Law of Treaties* (Amsterdam, University of Amsterdam, Faculty of Law (thesis) 2005) pp. 273–290 and P. Manin, 'The European Communities and the Vienna Convention on the Law of Treaties between States and International Organizations or between International Organizations', 24 *Common Market Law Review* (1987) pp. 468–471). It may also be noted that in 1973 the Institut de Droit International left open this issue in article V of its resolution of 14 September 1973 on The Application of the Rules of the General International Law of Treaties to International Agreements Concluded by International Organizations (available at www.idi-iil.org/idiE/resolutionsE/1973_rome_01_en.pdf). Within the EU the Member States are bound by agreements concluded by the EU pursuant to article 216(2) TFEU (ex-300(7) TEC) but only under EU law and not at the international level, i.e. they are not parties to the agreement, although the ECJ has not been somewhat ambiguous with regard to the scope of this provision, by holding in its judgment of 26 October 1982 in Case 104/81 (*Hauptzollamt Mainz v C.A. Kupferberg & Cie KG a.A.*, [1982] ECR 3641, para. 13) that '[i]n ensuring respect for commitments arising from an agreement concluded by the Community institutions the member States fulfil an obligation *not only in relation to the non-member* but also and above all in relation to the Community which has assumed responsibility for the due performance of the agreement' (emphasis added). This has given rise to some debate over the nature of this obligation of Member States. However, the practice of mixed agreements implies that article 216(2) does not make the Member States formal parties to agreements concluded by the EU only and suggests that this provision only binds the Member States vis-à-vis the EU. This solution is also most in line with the separate legal personality of international organisations with treaty-making capacity and the relativity of treaties, even if Member States may in fact not entirely be strangers to such agreements. Indeed, the combination of articles 2(1)h and 34–35 of the 1986 VCLT arguably confirms this view despite the stipulation in its article 74(3) that its provisions 'shall not prejudge any question that may arise in regard to the establishment of obligations and rights for States members of an international organisation under a treaty to which that organisation is a party'. Article 2(1)(h) defines 'third State' and 'third organisation' respectively as '(i) a State, or (ii) an international organisation, not a party to the treaty'; Article 34 reads 'A treaty does not create either obligations or rights for a third State or a third organisation without the consent of that State or that organisation' and Article 35 stipulates that '[a]n obligation arises for a third State or a third organisation from a provision of a treaty if the parties to the treaty intend the provision to be the means of establishing the obligation and the third State or the third organisation expressly accepts that obligation in writing [...]'. This implies that Member States, if they are not formally a party to an agreement concluded by an international organisation, are third parties in respect of that agreement and are, in principle, not bound by it. Thus, whether Member States of an international organisation are bound by an agreement concluded by an international organisation is up to the rules of the organisation and is an internal matter. At best, it may be argued that, absent a specific rule confirming such binding effect in a given organisation, membership implies a good faith duty not to hinder the organisation to give effect to agreements it has lawfully entered into (in this sense H.G. Schermers and N.M. Blokker, *International Institutional Law*, 4th edn. (Boston/Leiden, Martinus Nijhoff Publishers 2003) p.1143, at para. 1787).

in which such a binding has been accepted: to my knowledge only the EU in relation to GATT and two customs agreements and under strict conditions that are rarely met in other cases.[6] Obviously, when Member States conclude an agreement *on behalf of* an organisation, this is a different matter and in such a case the organisation will be bound.[7] Likewise, where an international organisation concludes an international agreement in its own name, it will clearly be bound.

One of the bases invoked in doctrine for binding an international organisation to Member State treaties is an analogy of the rules of State succession with respect to treaties.[8] However, this is hardly a convincing thesis. First, only in some cases is there a real transfer rather than the creation of new and distinct powers.[9] Second, even where there is a real transfer of powers to an international organisation, this does not, at least not always or not fully, fit within the definition of State succession, even when applied by analogy. For instance, Article 1(2)b of the Vienna Convention on Succession of States in Respect of Treaties of 23 August 1978 (hereinafter '1978 VCSST') defines 'succession of States' as 'the replacement of one State by another in the responsibility for the international relations of territory', whereas it is clear that international organisations hardly ever, not even in the case of the EU, entirely replace their Member States in the responsibility for their international relations.[10] It may also be noted that the

6 P. Klein, op. cit. n. 3, at pp. 339–340 also mentions Article 3(a)ii of the INTELSAT operating agreement of 20 August 1971 (Washington DC, 1220 *UNTS* (1981) p. 149), which expressly provides for a succession/substitution but relating to a specific transit phase (limited to obligations incurred under a provisional agreement). Moreover, one might wonder whether this provision would have automatic effect towards third parties.

7 On this mechanism, see P. Klein, op. cit. n. 3, at pp. 326–330. This should be distinguished from cases in which Member States are authorised to conclude an agreement in the interest of an organisation but not formally on its behalf, see in respect of the EU, ECJ *Opinion 2/91* [1993] ECR I-1061, para. 5 of the Court's reasoning ('although, under the ILO Constitution, the Community cannot itself conclude Convention No 170, its external competence may, if necessary, be exercised through the medium of the Member States acting jointly in the Community's interest') and Council Decision of 2 March 2004 authorising the Member States to sign, ratify or accede to, in the interest of the European Community, the Protocol of 2003 to the International Convention on the Establishment of an International Fund for Compensation for Oil Pollution Damage, 1992, and authorising Austria and Luxembourg, in the interest of the European Community, to accede to the underlying instruments (2004/246/EC), *O.J. L* 78, 16 March 2004, p. 22.

8 See the discussion in P. Klein, op. cit. n. 3, pp. 334–335; R. Lawson, op. cit. n. 2, at pp. 85–98; K. Osteneck, 'Die völkerrechtliche Verplichtung der EG zur Umsetzung von UN-Sanktionen', 1 *Zeitschrift für europarechtliche Studien* (1998) pp. 113–115 and H.F. van Panhuys, 'Conflicts between the Law of the European Communities and Other Rules of International Law', 3 *Common Market Law Review* (1965–1966) p. 447 (the latter author submits that a transfer of obligations is not too readily to be assumed).

9 Similarly P. Klein, op. cit. n. 3, p. 342.

10 Similarly, K. Osteneck, loc. cit. n. 8, pp. 113–115. Compare P. Klein, op. cit. n. 3, pp. 334–335 and the references there, noting that at best it is only a partial succession. Interestingly, R. Lawson, op. cit. n. 2, at pp. 87–88, and H.G. Schermers, 'Community Law and International

rules of State succession do not appear to be applied to succession between international organisations.[11] Third, though this is not a conclusive argument, the customary status of the rules on State succession is notoriously unclear[12] and their application by analogy is a difficult and problematic undertaking.[13]

Several other theories that have been considered relate, in one way or another, to the transfer of powers, either on itself or in combination with the maxim *nemo plus juris transferre potest quam ipse habet.*[14] However, binding international

---

Law', 12 *Common Market Law Review* (1975) pp. 87–88, note that a proposal to include specific rules on succession of treaty obligations to international organisations in the work of the ILC and UN was rejected, although Lawson does not seem to see this as decisive. Schermers himself seems to qualify the substitution theory as a kind of succession (*id.*). The 2006 ILA Report on *Aspects of the Law of State Succession* (available online at www.ila-hq.org) explicitly states that '[i]t is clear that the creation of a supranational international organization, e.g. the European Community/European Union, does not amount to a situation of unification of States' and does not include this under another form of succession either (§9, p. 12, see also §21, p. 15).

11 Rather, such succession will normally be governed by specific arrangements either agreed by the organisations and/or imposed by its Member States. J.F. Weiss, 'Succession of States in Respect of Treaties Concluded by the European Communities', 42 *Tijdschrift voor Europees en Economisch Recht* (1994) p. 668, submits that 'there are no general legal rules on … succession between international organizations'. Compare A. Bleckmann, 'Zur Verbindlichkeit des allgemeinen Völkerrechts für internationale Organizationen', 37 *Zeitschrift für ausländisches öffentliches Recht und Völkerrecht* (1977) pp. 107–108, submitting that succession of international organisations is subject to distinct rules from State succession to the extent that proper rules have been formed in this respect. P. Klein, op. cit. n. 3, p. 371, mentions that some scholars have applied by analogy the rules on succession in respect of treaties in the 1978 VCSST. However, given the uncertain status of these rules (the convention only entered into force in 1996 and counts a mere 22 parties; see more generally on the lack of agreed rules on succession J.F. Weiss, loc. cit. this note, pp. 669–670), this is not obvious. Also, one may wonder to which case of State succession the succession of an international organisation should be assimilated (similarly, concerning State succession rules, Member State treaties and international organisations, W. Wormuth, *Die Bedeutung des Europarechts für die Entwicklung des Völkerrechts* (Frankfurt am Main, Peter Lang 2004) pp. 175–177).

12 See *supra* previous note; the 2002 ILA Report on *Aspects of the Law of State Succession* (available online at www.ila-hq.org), p. 2; R. Lawson, op. cit. n. 2, at pp. 88–89 (noting that the ICJ left the question open in respect of Article 34 of the 1978 VCSST in its Judgment of 25 September 1997 in the *Case concerning the Gabcíkovo-Nagymaros Project* (Hungary/Slovakia), at para. 123) and M. Hartwig, *Die Haftung der Mitgliedstaaten für Internationale Organisationen* (Berlin, Springer 1993) pp. 83–91 and p. 337.

13 Presumably, this kind of succession would be closest to that of a Union of States, see K. Meessen, 'The Application of Rules of Public International Law within Community Law', 13 *Common Market Law Review* (1976) p. 489 and K. Osteneck, loc. cit. n. 8, p. 114. But see the ILA's view op. cit. n. 10. Compare R. Lawson, op. cit. n. 2, at pp. 89–95, who argues in favour of an application of the continuity principle to human rights treaties but seems to consider that in practice what is applied for States is rather a simplified continuity (or succession).

14 See e.g. P. Klein, op. cit. n. 3, pp. 341–342 and especially pp. 344–349 (who seems, however, to mix this argument to some extent with the one that international organisations are, as a subject of international law, bound by general international law (at pp. 346–347); the latter argument may well be valid but cannot simply be extended to conventions) and H.G. Schermers, 'The Legal Bases of International Organization Action', in R.-J. Dupuy, ed., *Manuel sur les organisations internationales/A Handbook on International Organizations*, 2nd edn. (Dordrecht, Martinus Nijhoff Publishers 1998) pp. 403–404. A variant is the

organisations to agreements concluded by their Member States on this basis poses various difficulties, regardless of whether it is seen as a case of succession, transfer of or granting of powers. For instance, it is doubtful whether it can be applied where there is a creation of new powers rather than the transfer of existing powers, which is often the case with international organisations. Furthermore, such theories depend upon the timing of the transfer of power and would only cover a State's obligations existing before such a transfer and exclude agreements concluded after such a transfer.[15] Moreover, it would lead to an untenable situation. In particular, it entails binding an organisation to every obligation in force for any of its Member States (at the time of the transfer), at least where it is relevant to the activities of the organisation.[16] This is clearly not accepted in practice[17] and potentially leads to either incompatible obligations[18] or the splitting

'Hypothektheorie', according to which any powers transferred to an international organisation are transferred with the corresponding obligations, see e.g. A. von Arnauld, 'UN-Sanktionen und gemeinschaftsrechtlicher Grundrechtsschutz. Die "Soweit-Rechtsprechung" des Europäischen Gerichts Erster Instanz', 44 *Archiv des Völkerrechts* (2006) p. 206 and the discussion and references in A. Leenen, *Gemeenschapsrecht en volkenrecht* (Deventer/'s-Gravenhage, Kluwer/TMC Asser Institute 1984) p. 214 (deeming this theory inapplicable in respect of external relations); K. Osteneck, loc. cit. n. 8, p. 115 (who rejects this theory herself); C. Tomuschat, annotation in 43 *Common Market Law Review* (2006) pp. 542–543 (noting that this theory has now been rejected in German scholarship) and R. Uerpmann, *International Law as an Element of European Constitutional Law: International Supplementary Constitutions*, Jean Monnet Working Paper 9/03, available at www.jeanmonnetprogram.org/papers/03/030901-02.pdf, pp. 34–35 (who translates *Hypothek* as a servitude and notes that it is problematic from a time perspective and from the point of view that (some) international organisations exercise a proper jurisdiction and 'not a bunch of Member State jurisdictions').

15 This problem is recognised by H.G. Schermers, loc. cit. n. 14, pp. 403–404, who nevertheless tries to develop some arguments in favour of binding international organisations at least under some circumstances to agreements concluded by Member States after a transfer of powers.

16 This is recognised by E. Lagrange, *La représentation institutionnelle dans l'ordre international: une contribution à la théorie de la personnalité morale des organisations internationales* (The Hague, Kluwer Law International 2002) p. 428 and H.F. van Panhuys, loc. cit. n. 8, p. 447, who sates that 'the logical implication of this view would be that no institution could perform any act the effects of which would be incompatible with duties binding under international law upon any Member State vis-à-vis a third State prior to the coming into force of the relevant treaty and still in force' and submits that this cannot be assumed. H.G. Schermers, loc. cit. n. 14, p. 403 proposes some differentiation according to the nature of the agreements concerned.

17 For instance, NATO Member States not party to the 1997 Protocol Additional to the Geneva Conventions of 12 August 1949, and Relating to the Protection of Victims of International Armed Conflicts (Protocol I) will not accept that NATO is bound by this Protocol (a number of Member States that have acceded to NATO more recently were parties to this Protocol before this accession, e.g. Hungary, Latvia and Estonia to name but a few). Likewise, the UN does not feel bound by the ECHR even though this treaty was already in force for Switzerland when this country became a member of the UN. Even within the EU, when the ECJ applies parts of treaty provisions as general principles, especially concerning human rights, it requires at least a significant commonality. H.F. van Panhuys, loc. cit. n. 8, p. 447 submitted, in relation to the EC, that '[s]uch a far-reaching limitation [i.e. respect for all prior Member State treaty obligations] on the jurisdiction of the [EC] is hardly to be assumed', although he accepted broad participation in a treaty by Member States as presumptive evidence against EC powers that would infringe that treaty.

18 See also E. Lagrange, op. cit. n. 16, p. 428.

up of the organisation's exercise of powers and corresponding obligations according to which Member States would, absent the transfer to the organisation, have exercised jurisdiction over a person or entity, which would be impossible to apply in practice. An alternative to such a scenario is to take into account agreements to which all (or most) Member States are a party.[19] However, to do so is to make the binding mechanism less effective for organisations with a large membership[20] and, moreover, is at odds with the basis and underlying reason invoked for binding an organisation: Member States could perfectly escape their obligations and transfer more rights than they have (by not concurrently transferring obligations) as long as they are not shared by all Member States. Thus this theory is unworkable when applied in full, while its selective application considerably departs from its original intention and is not a convincing alternative.

In addition, Article 351 TFEU (ex-307 TEC), which allows an EU Member State to act contrary to EU law where this is required to comply with obligations it has towards third States under agreements entered into before its entry into the EU,[21]

---

19 In this sense P. Klein, op. cit. n. 3, pp. 344–349. H.G. Schermers, loc. cit. n. 14, p. 403, takes this into account but argues in favour of a presumption that an organisation is bound even where only some of its Member States are bound to a treaty. Compare M. Hirsch, op. cit. n. 3, at pp. 55–59, who suggests that where a majority of Member States are bound, the international organisation will be bound if the Member States that are not bound do not object and there are no other inconsistent obligations. If there is to be a compromise, this may be a workable and acceptable one.

20 See also P. Klein, op. cit. n. 3, at p. 342.

21 This provision has given rise to some discussion and has been clarified to a considerable extent in case law, see generally V. Constantinesco *et al.*, *Traité instituant la CEE: commentaire article par article* (Paris, Economica 1992) pp. 1497–1508; P. Eeckhout, *External Relations of the European Union. Legal and Constitutional Foundations* (Oxford, Oxford University Press 2004) pp. 333–342; C. Kaddous, *Le droit des relations extérieures dans la jurisprudence de la Cour de justice des Communautés européennes* (Brussels/Basel, Bruylant/Helbing & Lichtenhahn 1998) pp. 272–300; E.-U. Petersmann and C. Spennemann, 'Artikel 307', in H. von der Groeben and J. Schwarze, eds., *Kommentar zum Vertrag über die Europäische Union und zur Gründung der Europäischen Gemeinschaft*, 6th edn. (Baden-Baden, Nomos 2003) pp. 1643–1665; K. Schmalenbach, 'Art. 307', in C. Calliess and M. Ruffert, eds., *Kommentar des Vertrages über die Europäische Union und des Vertrages zur Gründung der Europäischen Gemeinschaft* (Zurich, Schulthess/Luchterhand 1999) pp. 2180–2186 and J. Vanhamme, *Volkenrechtelijke beginselen in het Europees recht* (Groningen, Europa Law Publishing 2001) pp. 260–265 and the jurisprudence cited there. Compare R. Voss, 'Die Bindung der Europäischen Gemeinschaft and vorgemeinschaftliche Verträge ihrer Mitgliedstaaten', 35 *Schweizerische Zeitschrift für internationales und europäisches Recht* (1996) pp. 166–167, who regards this provision as a manifestation of a constitutional principle of international law conform integration. The applicability of ex-Article 307 TEC to treaties concluded by Member States that acceded after the founding members was consistently included in accession treaties and has now been incorporated in Article 351 TFEU (and already in ex-Article 307 TEC) (see P. Eeckhout, op. cit. this note, p. 334). However, Article 351 TFEU remains problematic in that the evolution of EU powers may mean that a Member State can lawfully conclude an agreement with a third State in an area that later becomes an (exclusive) Union competence and that Member State can, at least in a strict reading of this provision, not invoke compliance

does not entail that the EU is bound by such agreements but only allows the Member State(s) concerned to invoke them, although it does oblige the EU not to impede that Member State from complying with its obligations.[22] This provision would be superfluous if the EU were automatically bound by earlier agreements binding its Member States.[23]

However, the jurisprudence of the European Court of Justice (ECJ) in relation to the ECHR shows that there may be indirect ways of binding an international organisation to at least some rules laid down in Member State treaties. Moreover, it must be noted that binding international organisations to agreements concluded by their Member States is not the only way to ensure that Member States do not evade their obligations. Continuing to hold Member States responsible for any violations of their own obligations even in respect of powers transferred to an international organisation may be an alternative way to achieve this aim. The latter possibility, (which, admittedly, is not without difficulties itself) will be discussed in Part II of this contribution.

B. THE EU, GATT AND CUSTOMS AGREEMENTS

To my knowledge, the only cases where an international organisation has succeeded or substituted its Member States in respect of treaties concluded by the latter are those of the EU in relation to the GATT and a few customs agreements (and the aborted European Defence Community). The former cases, especially that of the GATT, are well known[24] and I will only briefly mention their key features.

As the EU had been granted exclusive competences in the field of external trade relations,[25] the question soon arose whether the EU itself was bound by the

with such an agreement to refuse the application of later EU law: see e.g. J. Boulois, 'Le droit des Communautés européennes dans ses rapports avec le droit international général', 235 *Rec. Cours* (1992-IV) p. 68 and K. Meessen, loc. cit. n. 13, pp. 489–491. See also more generally J. Klabbers, *Treaty Conflict and the European Union* (Cambridge, Cambridge University Press 2008).

22 See ECJ, Case 812/79, *Attorney General v Juan C. Burgoa* [1980] ECR 2787, paras. 8–9; J. Boulois, loc. cit. n. 21, p. 69; J.-C. Gautron and L. Grard, 'Rapport général: Le droit international dans la construction européenne', in J.-C. Gautron and L. Grard, eds., *Droit international et droit communautaire: perspectives actuelles. Société française pour le Droit international. Colloque de Bordeaux* (Paris, Pedone 2000) pp. 88–92 and A. Leenen, op. cit. n. 14, pp. 208–211. See also P. Klein, op. cit. n. 3, p. 332, writing that this provision makes these treaty rules opposable to but not binding upon the EU.

23 In this sense also K. Meessen, loc. cit. n. 13, p. 489.

24 See e.g. the references *infra* n. 27; C. Kaddous, op. cit. n. 21, pp. 276–281 and R. Lawson, op. cit. n. 2, at pp. 80–82.

25 See especially the former Article 133 (ex 113) TEC.

GATT, even though it was not formally the EU but only the Member States that were parties to this treaty. In the celebrated *International Fruit Company* case, the ECJ held that the EU had taken the place of its Member States in relation to this agreement.[26] The Court based this conclusion mainly on the following considerations:

> '10. ... at the time when they concluded the [EEC Treaty] the member States were bound by the obligations of the [GATT].
> 11. By concluding a treaty between them they could not withdraw from their obligations to third countries.
> 12. On the contrary, their desire to observe the [GATT undertakings] follows as much from the very provisions of the EEC Treaty as from the declarations made by the member States on the presentation of the Treaty to the [GATT Contracting Parties] ...
> 13. That intention was made clear in particular by article 110 of the EEC Treaty,.., as well as by [article 234 §1].
> 14. The Community has assumed the functions inherent in the tariff and trade policy, ..., by virtue of articles 111 and 113 of the Treaty.
> 15 By conferring those powers on the Community, the member States showed their wish to bind it by the obligations entered into under the [GATT].
> 16. Since the entry into force of the EEC Treaty and more particularly, since the setting up of the common external tariff, the transfer of powers which has occurred in the relations between member States and the Community has been put into concrete form in different ways within the framework of the [GATT] and has been recognised by the other Contracting Parties.
> 17. In particular, since that time, the Community, acting through its own institutions, has appeared as a partner in the tariff negotiations and as a party to the agreements ... concluded within the framework [of the GATT], in accordance with ... article 114 ... EEC Treaty ...
> 18. It therefore appears that, in so far as under the EEC Treaty the Community has assumed the powers previously exercised by member States in the area governed by the [GATT], the provisions of that agreement have the effect of binding the Community.'

This has been interpreted as requiring the following elements for such a 'substitution' to take place: all Member States are a party to the agreement, (exclusive and/or exercised) competences in respect of the agreement have been transferred to the EU, the Member States and the EU have intended that the EU substitute them and the third parties to the agreement have accepted this.[27]

---

26 ECJ, Joined Cases 21–24/72, *International Fruit Company NV and others v Produktschap voor Groenten en Fruit* [1972] ECR 1219, especially paras. 10–18.

27 Similarly P. Klein, op. cit. n. 3, pp. 335–336; A. Leenen, op. cit. n. 14, pp. 211–215 and pp. 224–230; K. Schmalenbach, loc. cit. n. 21, p. 2185 and J. Vanhamme, op. cit. n. 21, pp. 107–108. Compare K. Meessen, loc. cit. n. 13, pp. 489–490, who stresses the consent of all parties concerned and K. Osteneck, loc. cit. n. 8, pp. 118–122 (who seems to focus on an external

Although some authors initially saw room for a broader application of this theory,[28] most scholars now agree that although it has a potential for extension to other treaties, its conditions will rarely be met.[29] Indeed, the ECJ has only applied the theory to two other (customs) conventions.[30]

C. THE EU AND THE ECHR

It is well known that the ECJ has in fact incorporated the ECHR in the EU legal order by way of general principles of EU law. Nevertheless, despite its virtual application of the ECHR as such and the reference to the ECHR in Article 6 TEU, it has not held that the EU is bound by the ECHR as such nor that it is a party thereto.[31] Although some have argued that the substitution theory set out by the ECJ in respect of the GATT could also be applied to the ECHR,[32] this has clearly not been the case.

---

manifestation of the taking over of powers (rather than the will of the Member States) and elaborates on the acceptance of third parties).

28 See e.g. P. Pescatore, 'External Relations in the Case-Law of the Court of Justice of the European Communities', 16 *Common Market Law Review* (1979) pp. 637–638 and the references in P. Klein, op. cit. n. 3, p. 336.

29 E.g. M. Bothe, 'Die Stellung der Europäischen Gemeinschaften im Völkerrecht', 37 *Zeitschrift für ausländisches öffentliches Recht und Völkerrecht* (1977) p. 126; G. Cahin, *La coutume internationale et les organisations internationales: l'incidence de la dimension institutionnelle sur le processus coutumier* (Paris, Pedone 2001) p. 522; J. Boulois, loc. cit. n. 21, p. 69; P. Klein, op. cit. n. 3, pp. 335–340 (though questioning whether this would not be desirable) and K. Meessen, loc. cit. n. 13, pp. 489–490 (seeing some room for application to other treaties but accepting that for most treaties the criteria will not be met).

30 ECJ, Case 38/75 *Douaneagent der NV Nederlandse Spoorwegen v Inspecteur der invoerrechten en accijnzen* [1975] ECR 1439, para. 21. See e.g. A. Leenen, op. cit. n. 14, p. 217.

31 E.g. C. Kaddous, op. cit. n. 21, p. 305 and A. Toth, 'Human Rights as General Principles of Law, in the Past and in the Future', in U. Bernitz and J. Nergelius, eds., *General Principles of European Community Law: Reports from a Conference in Malmö, 27–28 August 1999, Organized by the Swedish Network for European Legal Studies and the Faculty of Law, University of Lund* (The Hague, Kluwer Law International 2000) p. 82. R. Uerpmann, loc. cit. n. 14, p. 39 points out that the Court of First Instance has explicitly held that 'the ECHR is not itself part of Community law' in Case (T-347/94 *Mayr-Melnhof Kartongesellschaft mbH v. Commission of the European Communities* [1998] ECR II-1751, para. 311) and that 'the [ECHR] as such is not part of Community law' in Case T-112/98 (*Mannesmannröhren-Werke AG v. Commission of the European Communities* [2001] ECR II-729, para. 59).

32 The European Commission suggested this might already have been the case in its 1979 memorandum on EC accession to the ECHR: see *Bull. EC*, supplement 2/79, also referred to in P. Klein, op. cit. n. 3, p. 336. See also the references in C. Kaddous, op. cit. n. 21, pp. 305–306, especially note 1329. W. Ganshof van der Meersch, 'L'ordre juridique des Communautés européennes et le droit international', 148 *Recueil des cours de l'Académie de droit international de La Haye* (1975) Volume V, p. 194, argued that the EC was bound by the ECHR but it is not clear whether he bases this on the substitution theory. *Contra*: J. Boulois, loc. cit. n. 21, p. 69 and R. Lawson, op. cit. n. 2, at pp. 82–85. Compare A. Berramdane, 'La Cour européenne des droits de l'homme juge du droit de l'Union européenne', *Revue du droit de l'Union européenne* (2006) pp. 253–254, who on the one seems to argue that the European

The European Court of Human Rights too has never ruled that the EU is bound by the ECHR and has always declined jurisdiction to hear applications brought against the EU as such.[33] However, it has occasionally left open the possibility that the EU Member States might, at least in some circumstances, be responsible for violations of the ECHR by measures adopted in the EU sphere. This will be addressed below in Part II of this contribution.

The Lisbon Treaty envisages, in addition to the incorporation of the Charter of Fundamental Rights (by way of reference), that the EU will accede to the ECHR,[34] which will require an amendment of or protocol to the ECHR.[35]

D. THE EU AND OTHER MEMBER STATE TREATIES, INCLUDING THE UN CHARTER

1° General

Where the conditions for substitution are not met and there is no acceptance or incorporation in one way or another, whether imposed upon or adopted by the organisation, practice and the arguments set out above imply that an international organisation is not bound by an international agreement. Indeed, in practice most international organisations do not consider themselves bound by agreements to which they have not consented in one way or another.[36]

Court of Human Rights in fact applies the substitution theory to the EC in respect of the ECHR but on the other hand notes that the Court has not accepted complaints against the EC, while the author himself rejects substitution in this case.

33 See, after an elaborate analysis, R. Lawson, op. cit. n. 2, at pp. 39–51 and p. 518.

34 See (post-Lisbon) article 6(2) EU Treaty: 'The Union shall accede to the European Convention for the Protection of Human Rights and Fundamental Freedoms. Such accession shall not affect the Union's competences as defined in the Treaties'. See also Protocol No. 5 concerning the modalities of that accession. In March 2010, the Commission submitted draft negotiating directives to the Council for this accession, see 17 March 2010 Commission press release, http://ec.europa.eu/commission_2010–2014/reding/pdf/echr_background.pdf and the information at http://europa.eu/rapid/pressReleasesAction.do?reference=MEMO/10/84&format=HTML&aged=0&language=EN&guiLanguage=en. Compare Article I-9(2) Treaty establishing a Constitution for Europe (Rome, 29 October 2004, *O.J. C* 310 (16 December 2004); not entered into force; hereinafter 'EU Constitution').

35 See Article 17 of Protocol No. 14 to the ECHR, Strasbourg, 13 May 2004, *C.E.T.S.* No. 194, which inserts a new paragraph in Article 59 ECHR stipulating that '[t]he European Union may accede to this Convention'. This Protocol entered into force on 1 June 2010. The Council of the EU adopted negotiating directives for the EU's accession to the ECHR on 4 June 2010 and the negotiations started on 7 July 2010. See www.coe.int/t/der/brusselsoffice/Articles/RestArticles/Jagland_Reding_070710_en.asp.

36 See P. Klein, op. cit. n. 3, p. 343. At p. 375 the author admits that his own view to the contrary is not supported by practice neither by the views of most international organisations.

This is also the case for the EU, as is clear from the ECJ's limited application of the substitution theory, its position towards the ECHR and its interpretation of Article 351 TFEU (ex-307 TEC) (see the preceding subsections).

2° *The UN Charter*

For the purpose of this contribution, it is necessary to consider the position of the UN Charter and of decisions adopted pursuant thereto, especially by the UN Security Council.[37] Two aspects are relevant: on the one hand, does the special position of the UN Charter make it binding on international organisations generally and, on the other hand, does the EU legal order accord a special status to the UN Charter. Besides, the EU is bound to any rules of UN law that also reflect customary international law.[38]

Concerning the special position of the UN Charter, reflected especially in its article 103, it must be said first of all that this provision itself does not bind

---

37 See generally N. Angelet, 'La mise en oeuvre des mesures coercitives économiques des Nations Unies dans la Communauté européenne', 26 *Revue belge de droit international* (1993) pp. 500–533; S. Bohr, 'Sanctions by the United Nations Security Council and the European Community', 4 *European Journal of International Law* (1993) pp. 256–268; I. Canor, '"Can Two Walk Together, Except They Be Agreed?" The Relationship between International Law and European Law: the Incorporation of United Nations Sanctions against Yugoslavia into European Community Law Through the Perspective of the European Court of Justice', 35 *Common Market Law Review* (1998) pp. 137–187; W. Devroe and J. Wouters, *De Europese Unie. Het verdrag van Maastricht en zijn uitvoering: analyse en perspectieven* (Peeters, Leuven 1996) pp. 625–628; P. Eeckhout, op. cit. n. 21, pp. 424–444; C.D. Ehlermann, 'Communautés européennes et sanctions internationales: une réponse à J. Verhoeven', 18 *Revue belge de droit international* (1984–1985) pp. 96–110; O. Elias, loc. cit. n. 2, at pp. 26–24; P. Kapteyn, 'The Role of the ECJ in Implementing Security Council Resolutions', in E. de Wet and A. Nollkaemper, eds., *Review of the Security Council by Member States* (Antwerp, Intersentia 2003) pp. 57–62; P.-J. Kuijper, 'Implementation of binding Security Council resolutions by the EU/EC', in E. de Wet and A. Nollkaemper, eds., op. cit. in this note, pp. 39–55; N. Lavranos, *Legal Interaction between Decisions of International Organizations and European Law* (Groningen, Europa Law Publishing 2004) pp. 94–100; K. Lenaerts and E. de Smijter, 'The United Nations and the European Union: Living Apart Together', in K. Wellens, ed., *International Law: Theory and Practice: Essays in Honour of Eric Suy* (The Hague, Martinus Nijhoff Publishers 1998) pp. 447–453; K. Osteneck, loc. cit. n. 8, pp. 103–132; K. Osteneck, *Die Umsetzung von UN-Wirtschaftssanktionen durch die Europäische Gemeinschaft: völker- und europarechtliche Rahmenbedingungen für ein Tätigwerden der Europäischen Gemeinschaft im Bereich von UN-Wirtschaftssanktionsregimen unter besonderer Berücksichtigung der Umsetzungspraxis der EG-Organe* (Berlin, Springer 2004); R. Pavoni, 'UN Sanctions in EU and National Law: the Centro-Com Case', 48 *International & Comparative Law Quarterly* (1999) pp. 582–612; M. Vaucher, 'L'évolution récente de la pratique des sanctions communautaires à l'encontre des Etats tiers', 29 *Revue trimestrielle de droit européen* (1993) pp. 39–59 and J. Verhoeven, 'Communautés européennes et sanctions interntionales', 18 *Revue belge de droit international* (1984–1985) pp. 79–95.

38 This argument is developed extensively in Chapter 7 of the Ph.D. thesis on which this contribution is based (*supra*, author's affiliation note).

international organisations as such, since they are not a party to the Charter.[39] Article 2(6) of the UN Charter offers no solution either, since it only refers to the conduct of third *States*.[40] Also, pursuant to article 25 of the Charter, only members are obliged to accept and carry out UN Security Council decisions. Second, none of the provisions in the Charter contain a provision binding international organisations. In fact, one of the most relevant provisions, namely article 48(2), provides that decisions of the Security Council for the maintenance of international peace and security 'shall be carried out *by the [UN Members] directly and through their action in* the appropriate international agencies of which they are members' (emphasis added). Thus no obligation is imposed upon the organisations themselves but rather upon the UN Member States acting within these organisations.[41] Consequently, the Security Council also does not have a legal basis in the Charter for directly obliging international organisations to implement its decisions, though it may obviously call upon them to do so.[42]

Second, the effect of recognising the supremacy of the UN Charter in the 1969 and 1986 VCLT needs to be considered.[43] The safeguarding of the UN Charter

39 See also I. Pernice, 'Völkerrechtliche Verträge internationaler Organisationen', 48 *Zeitschrift für ausländisches öffentliches Recht und Völkerrecht* (1988) pp. 239–241 and R.A. Wessel, 'De Europese Unie in de internationale rechtsorde', in NVIR, ed., *De plaats van de Europese Unie in het veranderende bestel van de volkenrechtelijke organisatie. Preadvies* (123 Mededelingen van de NVIR) (The Hague, TMC Asser Press 2001) pp. 43–44.

40 It reads: 'The Organization shall ensure that *states* which are not [UN Members] act in accordance with these Principles so far as may be necessary for the maintenance of international peace and security' (emphasis added). W. Graf Vitzthum, 'Article 2(6)', in B. Simma, ed., *The Charter of the United Nations. A Commentary*, 2nd edn. (Oxford, Oxford University Press 2002) pp. 140–148, does not even address a possible applicability of article 2(6) with regard to international organisations. Compare K. Osteneck, loc. cit. n. 8, pp. 129–130, who seems to consider that this provision might apply to international organisations but argues that on the basis of the prohibition to impose obligations on third parties, it can only create a politically binding effect. But see P. Gilsdorf, 'Les reserves de sécurité du Traité CEE à la lumière du Traité sur l'Union Européenne', No. 473 *Revue du Marché Commun et de l'Union Européenne* (1994) p. 21, n. 24 who does seem to argue that article 2(6) UN Charter may be a basis for binding the EU.

41 See A. Reinisch & B.-O. Bryde, 'Article 48', in B. Simma, ed., *The Charter of the United Nations. A Commentary*, 2nd edn. (Oxford, Oxford University Press 2002), pp. 778–779 (noting that to try to achieve a more direct binding effect, the UN has included some provisions in its relationship agreements with a number of international organisations); K. Osteneck, loc. cit. n. 8, p. 129 and R. Lawson, op. cit. n. 2, at pp. 151–152.

42 Compare N. Lavranos, op. cit. n. 37, pp. 94–95, who seems to consider that this has not prevented the Security Council from imposing obligations on international organisations in practice. However, in hardly any of the resolutions which he cites there really is an *obligation*: rather, the organisations are urged, authorised, encouraged or called upon (the latter probably comes the closest to an obligation) to do something.

43 This is the one case in which a rule of general international law might exist that binds international organisations to decisions of another international organisation irrespective of whether specific provisions so stipulate. According to the rule laid down in article 30(6) 1986 VCLT, the rules pertaining to successive treaties 'are without prejudice to the fact that, in the event of a conflict between obligations under the Charter of the United Nations and obligations

supremacy in article 30(1) of the 1969 VCLT means that at least constituent treaties of international organisations concluded between States only must yield to UN obligations in case of conflict. However, where such a treaty would nevertheless contain a provision conflicting with a UN obligation (in a manner that cannot be resolved by interpretation in accordance with the latter obligation), it is doubtful whether *the organisation* established by that treaty could override this conflicting constituent treaty provision. Rather, it would seem that the Member States would incur international responsibility for not respecting their UN obligation when the conditions for Member State responsibility are met.

The post-Lisbon EU Treaties contain several references to the UN and the UN Charter, in particular:

- Article 3(5) TEU: 'In its relations with the wider world, the Union shall ... contribute to ... the strict observance and the development of international law, including respect for the principles of the United Nations Charter'.
- Article 21 TEU (which expands upon ex-11(1) TEU): 'The Union's action on the international scene shall be guided by ... respect for the principles of the United Nations Charter ... It shall promote multilateral solutions to common problems, in particular in the framework of the United Nations ... The Union shall ... preserve peace, prevent conflicts and strengthen international security, in accordance with the purposes and principles of the United Nations Charter ...'.
- Article 34 TEU (ex-19 TEU): 'Member States which are also members of the United Nations Security Council will concert and keep the other Member States and the High Representative fully informed. Member States which are

under a treaty, the obligations under the Charter shall prevail'. However, not only is this only a priority rule imposing only an indirect binding effect at best, but it is also textually not conclusive in that it only sets out a priority rule in the event of a conflict with obligations under the Charter but does not say whether the latter obligations exist for international organisations: see I. Pernice, loc. cit. n. 39, pp. 240. In fact, in the drafting of this provision there was a discussion within the ILC on whether article 103 UN Charter applied to international organisations and the ILC was unable to agree and chose a language which left the matter open (see *Yearbook of the International Law Commission* 1982-II, Part 2, pp. 40–41). Nevertheless, the very open ILC language was amended during the later negotiations and in the final text and it would seem to have been the intention to bind international organisations to article 103: see E. Lagrange, op. cit. n. 16, pp. 514–517 and especially R. Lawson, op. cit. n. 2, at pp. 154–157 (arguing in favour of the interpretation binding international organisations to article 103 but not to the entire UN Charter) but compare M. Kotzur, *infra* n. 64, p. 24 (rejecting a binding of international organisations to the (entire) UN Charter via article 103 of the Charter). Nevertheless, since the 1986 VCLT has not yet entered into force and this specific rule does not appear to be adhered to in practice (this argument is developed somewhat in Chapter 7 of the Ph.D. thesis on which this contribution is based), it does not appear to be part of general international law binding international organisations: see E. Lagrange, op. cit. n. 16, pp. 514–517; but see A. Toublanc, 'L'article 103 et la valeur juridique de la Charte des Nations Unies', 108 *Revue Générale de Droit International Public* (2004) p. 459.

members of the Security Council will, in the execution of their functions, defend the positions and the interests of the Union, without prejudice to their responsibilities under the provisions of the United Nations Charter. When the Union has defined a position on a subject which is on the United Nations Security Council agenda, those Member States which sit on the Security Council shall request that the High Representative be invited to present the Union's position.'

- Article 42(1) TEU (ex-17 TEU): 'The common security and defence policy shall ... provide the Union with an operational capacity drawing on civilian and military assets. The Union may use them on missions outside the Union for peace-keeping, conflict prevention and strengthening international security in accordance with the principles of the United Nations Charter'.
- Article 42(7) TEU: 'If a Member State is the victim of armed aggression on its territory, the other Member States shall have towards it an obligation of aid and assistance by all the means in their power, in accordance with Article 51 of the United Nations Charter'.
- The seventh consideration of the preamble of the TFEU: 'Intending to confirm the solidarity which binds Europe and the overseas countries and desiring to ensure the development of their prosperity, in accordance with the principles of the Charter of the United Nations'.
- Article 208(2) TFEU (ex-177(3) TEC): in the sphere of the EU's development cooperation 'The Union and the Member States shall comply with the commitments and take account of the objectives they have approved in the context of the United Nations and other competent international organisations'.
- Article 214(7) TFEU: 'The Union shall ensure that its humanitarian aid operations are coordinated and consistent with those of international organisations and bodies, in particular those forming part of the United Nations system'.
- Article 220(1) TFEU (ex-302–304 TEC): 'The Union shall establish all appropriate forms of cooperation with the organs of the United Nations and its specialised agencies, ...'
- Declaration (No. 13) concerning the common foreign and security policy: '... the EU and its Member States will remain bound by the provisions of the Charter of the United Nations and, in particular, by the primary responsibility of the Security Council and of its Members for the maintenance of international peace and security'.

This goes significantly beyond the pre-Lisbon EU Treaties. Under the TEC, in addition to cooperation with the UN, there was essentially only a general reference to a desire to act in accordance with the principles of the UN Charter in the preamble. That might have been sufficient to interpret EC law as far as possible in accordance with UN obligations,[44] but hardly seemed adequate to bind the EC as such.[45] Moreover, it was doubtful whether the substitution theory could be extended to UN obligations (despite two decisions of the Court of First Instance in that sense, see *infra*). Only in the area of development cooperation did the more specific provision of article 177(3) TEC possibly provide an obligation to comply with commitments undertaken by the EC and its member States within the UN.[46] Nevertheless, the ECJ stated that:

> 'Observance of the undertakings given in the context of the United Nations is required just as much in the sphere of the maintenance of international peace and security when the Community gives effect, by means of the adoption of Community measures taken on the basis of Articles 60 EC and 301 EC, to resolutions adopted by the Security Council under Chapter VII of the Charter of the United Nations.'[47]

However, the Court went on to say that:

> '295 Next, it is to be noted that the powers provided for in Articles 60 EC and 301 EC may be exercised only in pursuance of the adoption of a common position or joint action by virtue of the provisions of the EC Treaty relating to the CFSP [Common Foreign and Security Policy] which provides for action by the Community.
> 296 Although, because of the adoption of such an act, the Community is bound to take, under the EC Treaty, the measures necessitated by that act, that obligation means, when the object is to implement a resolution of the Security Council adopted under Chapter VII of the Charter of the United Nations, that in drawing up those measures the Community *is to take due account of* the terms and objectives of the resolution concerned and of the relevant obligations under the Charter of the United Nations relating to such implementation.'[48]

---

44 See ECJ, Cases C-84/95, *Bosphorus Hava Yollari Turizm ve Ticaret AS v Minister for Transport, Energy and Communications and others*, [1996] ECR I-3953, paras. 11–18 and C-177/95, *Ebony Maritime SA and Loten Navigation Co. Ltd v Prefetto della Provincia di Brindisi and others*, [1997] ECR I-01111, paras. 20–21, 24 and 31; O. Elias, loc. cit. n. 2, at pp. 27–28 and K. Osteneck, loc. cit. n. 8, p. 126. However, I. Canor, loc. cit. n. 37, p. 186 considers that the scope of this interpretation in conformity with UN obligations is not yet clear. On interpretation of EU law in conformity with international agreements, including the ECHR, see also A. Peters, 'The Position of International Law Within the European Community Legal Order', 40 *German Yearbook of International Law* (1997) pp. 71–73.

45 Similarly O. Elias, loc. cit. n. 2, at p. 26; R. Lawson, op. cit. n. 2, at p. 159 and A. Leenen, op. cit. n. 14, p. 230. Compare K. Osteneck, loc. cit. n. 8, pp. 103–132, who, in 1998, arrived at the conclusion that the EC had no obligation to implement UN sanctions decision under *international* law.

46 See also ECJ, Joined Cases C-402/05 P and C-415/05 P, *Yassin Abdullah Kadi and Al Barakaat International Foundation v. Council of the European Union and Commission of the European Communities*, 3 September 2008, at para. 292. However, even here, there may be questions as to the extent to which the *EU* might have to comply with commitments made by the *Member States* (does this provision mean that the EU and the Member States each should comply with their own commitments only or also that the EU must comply with the Member States' commitments – and in the latter case, only by those made by all Member States?).

47 *Ibid.*, at para. 293.

48 *Ibid.*, at paras. 295–296 (emphasis added).

By using the expression "*take due account of*", the Court did not seem to say that the EC was bound as such.

In any event, since, for nearly all EU Member States the UN Charter was in force before they entered the EU,[49] their obligations under the Charter towards third States may thus be opposed to the EU under article 351 TFEU (ex-307 TEC).[50] In addition, article 347 TFEU (ex-297 TEC) allows Member States to take measures affecting the common market 'in the event of...war, serious international tension constituting a threat of war, or in order to carry out obligations it has accepted for the purpose of maintaining peace and international security'.[51] Thus, it may be argued that those Member States could, under EU law, violate EU law when this is necessary to comply with their UN obligations.[52] Obviously, where the EU has taken adequate collective action, as is usually the case,[53] a Member State may no longer adopt unilateral measures.[54]

The EU also has a particular system for implementing UN sanctions. When they relate to external economic relations, sanctions normally come within the exclusive competences of the EU and therefore need to be adopted by the EU. However, the present system of implementing UN (and other) sanctions in the EU is that the Council first adopts a Union position, i.e. a CFSP instrument, under article 29 TEU (previously a common position under article 15 TEU) and that the EU (formerly EC) subsequently implements this on the basis of articles 215 TFEU (ex-301 TEC) and 75 TFEU (ex-60 TEC), if necessary combined with

49 Germany is an exception in this regard.

50 This provision is also cited by O. Elias, loc. cit. n. 2, at p. 26 and J. Vanhamme, op. cit. n. 21, pp. 27–28.

51 This provision is also cited by O. Elias, loc. cit. n. 2, at p. 26 and is discussed by J. Vanhamme, op. cit. n. 21, pp. 280–286.

52 The ECJ has stressed that there must be an obligation and not a mere permission, see e.g. Case C-124/95, *The Queen, ex parte Centro-Com Srl v HM Treasury and Bank of England*, [1997] ECR I-81246, para. 60 ('when an international agreement allows, but does not require, a Member State to adopt a measure which appears to be contrary to Community law, the Member State must refrain from adopting such a measure'). See also C. Kaddous, op. cit. n. 21, pp. 297 and 299.

53 Initially, the EC Member States implemented UN sanctions, see e.g. P.-J. Kuijper, loc. cit. n. 37, pp. 39–42. It may be noted that the EC and its Member States initially did not always implement UN sanctions swiftly, notably in the case of Rhodesia, see e.g. R. Lawson, op. cit. n. 2, at p. 153.

54 E.g. ECJ, Case C-124/95 (op. cit. n. 52, paras. 46–53) and O. Elias, loc. cit. n. 2, at p. 28.

article 352 TFEU (ex-308 TEC).[55] Thus, UN sanctions are normally incorporated and transformed in EU law.[56]

With respect to the pre-Lisbon *EU*, in addition to ex-article 19 on the EU role in the Security Council, which did not impose obligations upon the EU, we had an obligation to act in accordance with the principles of the UN Charter in the two cases specified in the CFSP. While the two cases were those in which respect for the UN Charter was probably most relevant, one may wonder why this respect was not stipulated in a more general manner for the entire CFSP. In any event, this is now the case under Articles 3(5) and 21 TEU.[57]

These references to the *(purposes and) principles* of the UN Charter give rise to the question what is covered by these principles. Article 2 of the Charter lists as principles that apply to the Member States the sovereign equality of the UN members; fulfilling in good faith the obligations assumed by members under the Charter; peaceful settlement of disputes; refraining in their international relations from the threat or use of force against the territorial integrity or political independence of any state or in any other manner inconsistent with the purposes of the UN; giving the UN every assistance in any action it takes in accordance with the Charter and refraining from giving assistance to any state against which the UN is taking preventive or enforcement action.[58] This does seem to cover the core principles and the main one that could be said to be missing, i.e. respect for human rights,[59] is already binding for the EU in other ways (see *supra*). Therefore, although one might ask the question whether the

55 Article 75 TFEU differs in some respects from ex-article 60 TEC. Ex-article 60 TEC allowed a Member State under certain conditions to already adopt provisional measures pending EU action. This provision also left open some questions, including whether it permitted Member State action until the Council had adopted measures or only until it had discussed the matter even where it decided not to adopt measures. See J. Bröhmer, 'Art. 60', in C. Calliess and M. Ruffert, eds., op. cit. n. 21, pp. 761–762. Likewise, the question arose whether Member State actions were permissible between the adoption of CFSP EU measures but pending their EC implementation. J.-M. Hauptmann, 'Article 73G C.E.', in V. Constantinesco, ed., *Traité sur l'union européenne (signé à Maastricht le 7 février 1992): commentaire article par article* (Paris, Economica 1995) p. 196 submited that the scope of what had become ex-article 60 TEC was limited to that of ex-article 301 TEC. I have not examined to what extent these questions remain the same under article 75 TFEU.

56 This application as EU law is stressed by O. Elias, loc. cit. n. 2, at p. 29. For an extensive discussion of the process of reception and transformation of international law in the EU legal order more generally (and through this medium also in the EU Member States), see N. Lavranos, op. cit. n. 37, who names this process 'communitarization' (*inter alia* at pp. 110–111 and 247) – a term also used by A. Peters, loc. cit. n. 44, pp. 34–35 and 76. See also J. Wouters, A. Nollkaemper & E. De Wet, eds., *The Europeanisation of International Law: the Status of International Law in the EU and its Member States* (The Hague, T.M.C. Asser Press 2008).

57 Compare articles 3(4) and III-292(1) and (2)c EU Constitution.

58 Compare R.A. Wessel, loc. cit. n. 39, p. 43, who seems to go further and to equate principles to provisions.

59 Rather, it is listed as a purpose in article 1(3) UN Charter.

obligations go any further,[60] this seems of little practical value here. Also, inasmuch as these principles reflect rules of customary international law, they would bind the EU via that source.[61] However, one of these principles deserves some further study: namely giving the UN every assistance in any action it takes in accordance with the Charter. In particular, through this obligation one could argue that the EU is, at least to some extent, also bound by decisions adopted by the UN Security Council. This may be a plausible argument, but it is uncertain whether the Member States intended this provision to have such a meaning.[62]

A further question is whether this is an obligation only in the internal legal order of the EU or also in the general international legal order. This is open to interpretation: on the one hand, it is part of the EU Treaty with a primarily internal focus, but on the other hand it is included in the provisions on external relations and may have been intended in part to affirm the EU's respect for the UN Charter also to the rest of the world. It may be noted that the EU has confirmed that its Common (previously European) Security and Defence Policy, which is part of the CFSP, will be developed in accordance with the principles of the UN Charter[63] and has more generally adopted a positive attitude towards the UN. Moreover, Declaration (No. 13) is remarkable because of the binding of the *EU* (albeit by the Member States) to the *provisions* of the Charter. While perhaps not intended to be a unilateral act, its precise language and public nature in the context of the Lisbon Treaty, combined with the other provisions regarding the UN Charter, may mean that it amounts to just that.

In addition, this Declaration arguably reinforces the above-mentioned TEU and TFEU provisions that require respect for the (principles of the) UN Charter and may assist in their interpretation, though it remains to be seen to what extent it will do so.

60 One could make the comparison with the debate on the scope of the spirit and principles of international humanitarian law with regard to UN forces.

61 This argument is developed extensively in Chapter 7 of the Ph.D. Thesis and book on which this contribution is based (*supra* author's affiliation note).

62 Compare K. Osteneck, loc. cit. n. 8, at p. 131, who, in the context of a discussion of whether UN sanctions can bind the EU via general principles of EU law (through the Member States), submits that the sanctions are too specific to qualify as principles. However, this need not be an obstacle for a binding effect on the basis of a principle that imposes respect for resolutions in general. Yet the question remains whether the reference to the principles was not intended to be limited to substantive principles and did not exclude this cooperative principle which is closely linked to membership.

63 See para. 2 of the 1999 Cologne Presidency Report: 'The European Union is committed to preserve peace and strengthen international security in accordance with the principles of the UN Charter… as provided for in Article 11 of the [EU Treaty]' and para. 26 of the Helsinki European Council Presidency Conclusions, 10–11 December 1999: 'The Union will contribute to international peace and security in accordance with the principles of the United Nations Charter. The Union recognises the primary responsibility of the United Nations Security Council for the maintenance of international peace and security'.

3° *The Yusuf and Kadi Judgments*

The legal force of the Charter in respect of the EU was addressed by the ECJ's Court of First Instance in two cases concerning EU anti-terrorism measures: *Yusuf* and *Kadi*.[64] The essence of these cases concerned the questions of the EC's competence to adopt sanctions against individuals (in respect of which the Court made an interesting though questionable link between EC competences under articles 60, 301 and 308 TEC and EU objectives to promote international peace and security[65]) and to what extent the Court could review the legality of EC measures and, directly or indirectly, UN Security Council measures, especially in the light of human rights. However, the point that is relevant for the purpose of this contribution is to what extent the Court held the EC to be bound by UN obligations. With respect to this question, the Court ruled that the EC was not directly bound by the UN Charter and Security Council decisions:

> '... unlike its Member States, the Community as such is not directly bound by the Charter of the United Nations and that it is not therefore required, as an obligation of general public international law, to accept and carry out the decisions of the Security Council in accordance with Article 25 of that Charter. The reason is that the Community is *not* a member of the United Nations, or an addressee of the resolutions of the Security Council, *or the successor to the rights and obligations of the Member States for the purposes of public international law*' (emphasis added).[66]

64 CFI, Cases T-306/01 *Yusuf and Al Barakaat International Foundation v. Council and Commission* and T-315/01 *Kadi v. Council and Commission*, Judgments of 21 September 2005. The Court of First Instance upheld EC anti-terrorism measures that were based on UN Security Council resolutions, ruling that the latter were binding upon the EC and its Member States and that it could not review their legality except under *ius cogens*. For a discussion, see e.g. R. Brown, 'Kadi v Council of the European Union and Commission of the European Communities: Executive Power and Judicial Supervision at European Level', 11 *European Human Rights Law Review* (2006) pp. 456–469; M. Kotzur, 'Eine Bewährungsprobe für die Europäische Grundrechtsgemeinschaft: zur Entscheidung des EuG in der Rs. Yusuf u.a. gegen Rat, EuGRZ 2005, S. 592 ff', 33 *Europäische Grundrechtezeitschrift* (2006) pp. 19–26; S. Steinbarth, 'Individualrechtsschutz gegen Maßnahmen der EG zur Bekämpfung des internationalen Terrorismus. Die Entscheidungen des EuG in den Rs. "Yusuf u.a." sowie "Kadi"', 9 *Zeitschrift für europarechtliche Studien* (2006) pp. 269–286; C. Tomuschat, loc. cit. n. 14, pp. 537–551; A. von Arnauld, loc. cit. n. 14, pp. 201–216; R. van Ooik & R. Wessel, 'De Yusuf en Kadi-uitspraken in perspectief: nieuwe verhoudingen in de interne en externe bevoegdheden van de Europese Unie', 54 *Tijdschrift voor Europees en Economisch Recht* (2006) pp. 230–241; R.A. Wessel, 'The Invasion by International Organizations. De toenemende samenhang tussen de mondiale, Europese en nationale rechtsorde', Inaugural Lecture, University of Twente (12 January 2006) (available at www.bbt.utwente.nl/legs/news/oratie_wessel_web.pdf), pp. 5–13 and R.A. Wessel, 'Editorial: the UN, the EU and *Jus Cogens*', 3 *International Organizations Law Review* (2006) pp. 1–6.

65 CFI, Case T-306/01 *Yusuf*, op. cit. n. 64, paras. 158–170 and CFI, Case T-315/01 *Kadi*, op. cit. n. 64, paras. 122–135. See also M. Kotzur, loc. cit. n. 64, p. 21. This linkage was interesting from the perspective of consistency between the EC and EU legal order.

66 CFI, Case T-306/01 *Yusuf*, op. cit. n. 64, para. 242 and CFI, Case T-315/01 *Kadi*, op. cit. n. 64, para. 192.

Thus the Court appears to reject a succession theory. However, it went on to say that the EC was bound to UN obligations by virtue of the EC Treaty. In particular, the Court argued that:

> '... at the time when they concluded the [EC Treaty] the Member States were bound by their obligations under the [UN Charter].
> By concluding a treaty between them they could not transfer to the Community more powers than they possessed or withdraw from their obligations to third countries under that Charter (...).
> On the contrary, their desire to fulfil their obligations under that Charter follows from the very provisions of the [EC Treaty] and is made clear in particular by Article 224 and the first paragraph of Article 234 (...).
> Although that latter provision makes mention only of the obligations of the Member States, it implies a duty on the part of the institutions of the Community not to impede the performance of the obligations of Member States which stem from that Charter (...).
> It is also to be observed that, in so far as the powers necessary for the performance of the Member States' obligations under the Charter of the United Nations have been transferred to the Community, the Member States have undertaken, pursuant to public international law, to ensure that the Community itself should exercise those powers to that end.
> In this context it is to be borne in mind, first, that in accordance with Article 48(2) of the [UN Charter], the decisions of the Security Council 'shall be carried out by the Members of the United Nations directly and through their action in the appropriate international agencies of which they are members' and, second, that according to the case-law (...), the Community must respect international law in the exercise of its powers and, consequently, Community law must be interpreted, and its scope limited, in the light of the relevant rules of international law.
> By conferring those powers on the Community, the Member States demonstrated their will to bind it by the obligations entered into by them under the [UN Charter] (...).
> Since the entry into force of the Treaty establishing the European Economic Community, the transfer of powers which has occurred in the relations between Member States and the Community has been put into concrete form in different ways within the framework of the performance of their obligations under the [UN Charter] (...).
> Thus it is, in particular, that Article 228a of the EC Treaty (now Article 301 EC) was added to the [EU Treaty] in order to provide a specific basis for the economic sanctions that the Community, which has exclusive competence in the sphere of the common commercial policy, may need to impose in respect of third countries for political reasons defined by its Member States in connection with the CFSP, most commonly pursuant to a resolution of the Security Council requiring the adoption of such sanctions.
> It therefore appears that, in so far as under the EC Treaty the Community has assumed powers previously exercised by Member States in the area governed by the [UN Charter], the provisions of that Charter have the effect of binding the Community (...).

> Following that reasoning, it must be held, first, that the Community may not infringe the obligations imposed on its Member States by the [UN Charter] or impede their performance and, second, that in the exercise of its powers it is bound, by the very Treaty by which it was established, to adopt all the measures necessary to enable its Member States to fulfil those obligations.'[67]

The Court repeatedly referred to the *International Fruit Company* cases (five times, the references are omitted in the quote above) and seemed to extend the substitution theory to the UN Charter in respect of sanctions ('in so far as under the EC Treaty the Community has assumed powers previously exercised by Member States in the area governed by the [UN Charter], the provisions of that Charter have the effect of binding the Community'), albeit possibly only under EC law.[68]

On this point, the judgments seemed to depart from the ECJ's established restrictive application of the substitution theory discussed above. A first difference is that most, but not all EC Member States were UN members before their accession to the EC. Germany is an exception in this instance. However, this exception is explained by the fact that Germany was a UN Member State at the time of the unambiguous transfer of sanctions competences to the EC and arguably poses no major problem. As to the other elements, there clearly has been a transfer of some competences to the EC.[69] The Court's view that 'by conferring those powers on the Community, the Member States demonstrated their will to bind it by the obligations entered into by them under the [UN Charter]' is, however, less convincing.[70] First, article 301 TEC

67 CFI, Case T-306/01 *Yusuf*, op. cit. n. 64, paras. 243–254 and CFI, Case T-315/01 *Kadi*, op. cit. n. 64, paras. 193–204.

68 Compare P. Klein, op. cit. n. 3, pp. 356–357, who notes that Greece invoked this substitution in ECJ, Case 204/86, *Hellenic Republic v. Council of the European Communities*, [1988] ECR VI-5323, para. 13. In this case, the ECJ (Judgment of 27 September 1988, paras. 27–28) dismissed the resolution invoked as being 'completely extraneous to relations between the Community and Turkey in the context of the Association'. Klein's argument (on pp. 357–358) that the Council has accepted that the Community is bound via its Member States to UN obligations is not convincing in that the Council only used the argument negatively (i.e. in the absence of an obligation for the Member States, the EC consequently has no obligation) and would not necessarily endorse the inverse position. While the Council seems to come closer to admitting that the EC might be bound by stating that EC organs are not bound by decisions of UN organs where the EC has not assumed powers previously exercised by the EC Member States, thus possibly implying that where this is the case, the EC would be bound ([1988] ECR VI-5334–5335), it is unsure whether it would go this far. Compare K. Osteneck, loc. cit. n. 8, p. 127, who argues that no conclusions can be drawn from this case.

69 But see I. Pernice, loc. cit. n. 39, pp. 240–241, who does not seem to consider that there was (in 1988) a transfer of competences to the EC.

70 Compare, e.g., K. Osteneck, loc. cit. n. 8, pp. 122–128, who, in 1998, arrived at the conclusion that the conditions of the substitution theory had not been met in respect of UN sanctions; as did C. Kaddous, op. cit. n. 21, p. 423–424; K. Lenaerts & P. Van Nuffel, *Constitutional Law of the European Union*, 2nd edn. (London, Sweet & Maxwell 2005) p. 756 note 463 and R. Lawson,

did not even mention the UN and only imposed an obligation on the EC to implement sanctions if required by a CFSP decision, irrespective of whether the latter is taken on the basis of a UN Security Council resolution. Two arguments can be made in favour of taking an interpretative stance with regards to this provision that leads to an obligation to implement UN Security Council resolutions. The first is that, as argued above, such an obligation may exist if the references in articles (5) and 21 TEU to 'the principles of the United Nations Charter', read together with Declaration No. 13, include the principle of giving the UN every assistance in any action it takes and is construed as requiring implementation of decisions adopted by the UN Security Council. An alternative argument is that the obligation for the EU under article 351 TFEU (ex-307 TEC) not to impede the Member States from fulfilling their obligations under the UN Charter includes an obligation to cooperate in implementing UN sanctions.[71] However, in both respects one may question whether it was the Member States' intention to so bind the EU also vis-à-vis third parties.[72] Second, and more importantly, the powers transferred to the EU in relation to the UN are only of a limited nature: not only do they cover only a fraction of the UN's field of activity but they are also limited to the *implementation* of decisions adopted by UN organs in which only the Member States have voting rights.[73] While the former may not pose an obstacle to an application of the substitution theory, which could be applied partially,[74] the latter does not sit well with the ECJ's limited acceptance of substitution. Admittedly, it may be argued that there is *some* recognition by the UN of the role of the EU, including in *implementing* UN sanctions and other measures.[75] Nevertheless, it is doubtful whether the UN

op. cit. n. 2, at p. 160 (who regards article 297 as essential in this respect). But see P.-J. Kuijper, loc. cit. n. 37, pp. 41–42, who, in 2003, argued that 'it may perhaps be possible' to make the analogy with the ECJ's substitution theory.

71 See A. von Arnauld, loc. cit. n. 14, pp. 206–207 and compare op. cit. n. 22 and accompanying text. For a similar argument in relation to the ECHR, see R. Uerpmann, loc. cit. n. 14, pp. 37–38.

72 K. Lenaerts & E. de Smijter, loc. cit. n. 37, p. 448 were of the view that the EC was not bound under international law but 'only' under EC law. M. Kotzur, loc. cit. n. 64, p. 24 also seems to take this view. Compare also R. Uerpmann, loc. cit. n. 14, pp. 37–38, who, in relation to a similar argument concerning the ECHR, saw this as a binding under EC law only.

73 Compare P.J.G. Kapteyn, loc. cit. n. 37, pp. 42–43, seeing some room for the application of the substitution theory but questioning its use in such a limited case because he perceived it as leading only to a binding of the EC by sanctions decisions to the extent that they had been implemented by the EC.

74 K. Osteneck, loc. cit. n. 8, pp. 103–132. But see R. Lawson, op. cit. n. 2, at pp. 83–84, who doubts whether a partial substitution is possible.

75 See P.-J. Kuijper, loc. cit. n. 37, pp. 42 and 51–52. For instance, in its efforts to combat terrorism, including through the use of sanctions, the Security Council has recognised the important role of international and (sub)regional organisations (see e.g. UN Security Council Resolution 1631 of 17 October 2005; the Declarations annexed to UN Security Council Resolutions 1377 of 12 November 2001 and 1456 of 20 January 2003 and five special meetings with such organisations discussed at www.un.org/sc/ctc/cooperation.html) and the EU has reported to the Security Council's Counter-Terrorism Committee on the measures that it has taken to implement relevant Security Council resolutions (see J. Wouters & F. Naert, 'The European Union and "September 11"', 13 *Indiana International & Comparative Law*

feels it can bind the EU as such.[76] Therefore, the argument that all conditions for substitution are met is plausible but not quite convincing, even when regarded as a matter of EU law only. In any event, if substitution can be this 'partial' and relate to non exclusive competences[77] and the mere implementation of certain specific international obligations, it would apply to numerous international obligations in force for the Member States which require EU implementing measures, including, arguably, the ECHR.

If the ECJ would have followed this line of argument, it would have been a positive development from the perspective of better integrating international law and EU law. In its appeals judgment in these cases, in which the ECJ set aside the Court of First Instance's judgments,[78] it did not really address this

Review (2002–2003) p. 755 note 211 and www.un.org/sc/ctc/countryreports/Creports.shtml). Nevertheless, it is clear that this is only a limited recognition.

76 Compare K. Osteneck, loc. cit. n. 8, p. 128, who, in 1998, felt that the UN did not perceive its decisions as binding the EC.

77 R. Lawson, op. cit. n. 2, at p. 160, regards article 297 as essential in rejecting the application of the substitution theory to the UN Charter. The EU's sanctions power does not appear to be comprehensive: for instance, it does not appear to extend to UN sanctions against Member States (K. Osteneck, loc. cit. n. 8, pp. 111–113) and, as set out above, leaves some room for Member State measures. P.-J. Kuijper, loc. cit. n. 37, pp. 45 and 47, submitted that for arms embargoes no EC act was required or even possible (in light of ex-article 296 TEC) but only a CFSP act and that Member State measures were useful and necessary concerning penal sanctions (though noting that the EC was not entirely without competences in the area of penal law, a point made clear by the ECJ in Case C-176/03 *Commission of the European Communities v. Council of the European Union*, [2005] ECR I-7879, paras. 38–53). One might add that, unless one accepts that a CFSP act may have direct effect in the Member States' legal orders, national implementing acts would also be necessary. See also R. Pavoni, loc. cit. n. 37, pp. 601–612 on what competences with regard to UN sanctions were still held by the Member States.

78 ECJ, Joined Cases C-402/05 P and C-415/05 P, *Yassin Abdullah Kadi and Al Barakaat International Foundation v. Council of the European Union and Commission of the European Communities*, 3 September 2008. For annotations, see e.g. CEDIN, ed., 'Actes du colloque sur la rencontre des droits (international, communautaire et interne)', No. 524 *Revue du Marché Commun et de l'Union Européenne* (2009) pp. 352–418; P.J. Cardwell, D. French & N. White, 'European Court of Justice, Yassin Abdullah Kadi and Al Barakaat International Foundation v Council and Commission (joined Cases C-402/05 P and C-415/05 P) Judgment of 3 September 2008', 58 *International & Comparative Law Quarterly* (2009) pp. 229–240; D. Curtin & C. Eckes, 'The Kadi Case: Mapping the Boundaries Between the Executive and the Judiciary in Europe', 5 *International Organizations Law Review* (2008) pp. 365–369; A. Cuyvers, 'Tussen Scyllii en Charybdii: terrorisme, rechtsbescherming en de verhouding tussen rechtsordes in Kadi', 58 *Ars aequi* (2009) pp. 155–164; P. d'Argent, 'Arrêt «*Kadi*»: le droit communautaire comme droit interne', *Journal de droit européen* (2008) pp. 265–268; J. d'Aspremont & F. Dopagne, 'Kadi: the ECJ's Reminder of the Elementary Divide between Legal Orders', 5 *International Organizations Law Review* (2008) pp. 371–379; G. de Búrca, *The European Court of Justice and the International Legal Order after Kadi*, Jean Monnet Working Paper 01/09 (2009), available at www.jeanmonnetprogram.org/papers/09/090101.pdf; E. de Wet, 'The Role of European Courts in Reviewing Conflicting Obligations under International Law', 5 *International Organizations Law Review* (2008) pp. 359–364; A. Gattini, 'Joined Cases C-402/05 P and C-415/05 P, *Yassin Abdullah Kadi and Al Barakaat International Foundation v Council and Commission*, Judgment of the Grand Chamber of 3 September 2008, nyr.', 46

point.[79] However, in two other recent judgments, the ECJ has confirmed its restrictive interpretation of the substitution theory.[80] Hence there is no broader acceptance of this theory.

As to the binding nature of *ius cogens*, the Court of First Instance held that rules of this nature are binding upon international organisations, including the UN Security Council:

Common Market Law Review 2009, pp. 213–239; S. Griller, 'International Law, Human Rights and the European Community's Autonomous Legal Order: Notes on the European Court of Justice Decision in Kadi', 4 *European Constitutional Law Review* (2008) pp. 528–553; L.M. Hinojosa Martínez, 'Bad Law for Good Reasons: the Contradictions of the Kadi Judgment', 5 *International Organizations Law Review* (2008) pp. 339–357 (addressing the substitution question at pp. 339–341); C. Janssens, 'Het Kadi-arrest van het Hof van Justitie inzake terrorismelijsten: de beslechting van enkele hete hangijzers met betrekking tot interne en externe bevoegdheidsafbakening en rechtsbescherming', 72 *Rechtskundig Weekblad* (2009) pp. 1410–1426; J.A. Kämmerer, 'Das Urteil des Europäischen Gerichtshofs im Fall "Kadi": ein Triumph der Rechtsstaatlichkeit?', 44 *Europarecht* (2009) pp. 114–130; M. Kotzur, 'Kooperativer Grundrechtsschutz in der Völkergemeinschaft: zur Rechtmittelentscheidung des EuGH (Große Kammer) vom 3. September 2008 in den verb. Rsn. Kadi u. a.', 35 *Europäische Grundrechtezeitschrift* (2008) pp. 673–680; N. Lavranos, 'Joined Cases C-402/05 P and C-415/05 *P, Yassin Abdullah Kadi and Al Barakaat International Foundation v. Council of the European Union and Commission of the European Communities* Judgment of the European Court of Justice (Grand Chamber) 3 September 2008, Not Yet Published', 36 *Legal Issues of Economic Integration* (2009) pp. 157–185; S. Menz & T.B. Scholz, 'The Kadi-case or the Legal Protection of Persons Included in the European Union "Anti-terror List"', 17 *European Journal of Crime Criminal Law and Criminal Justice* (2009) pp. 61–68; J.-M. Thouvenin, 'Le choc du droit communautaire et du droit international, encore l'arrêt Kadi', No. 524 *Revue du Marché Commun et de l'Union Européenne* (2009) pp. 30–31; T. Tridimas, 'Terrorism and the ECJ: Empowerment and Democracy in the EC Legal Order', 34 *European Law Review* (2009) pp. 103–126 (also available at www.carterruck.com/Documents// Terrorism_and_the_ECJ.pdf); L. van den Herik & N. Schrijver, 'Eroding the Primacy of the UN System of Collective Security: the Judgment of the European Court of Justice in the Cases of Kadi and Al Barakaat', 5 *International Organizations Law Review* (2008) pp. 329–338; N. Graf Vitzthum, 'Les compétences législatives et juridictionnelles de la Communauté européenne dans la lutte contre le terrorisme – l'affaire "Kadi"', 11 *Zeitschrift für Europarechtliche Studien* (2008) pp. 375–429; R.A. Wessel, 'The Kadi Case: Towards a More Substantive Hierarchy in International Law?', 5 *International Organizations Law Review* (2008) pp. 323–327.

79 E.g., in para. 307 the Court says 'supposing [article 300 EC Treaty] to be applicable to the Charter of the United Nations …'. Advocate-General Maduro, in his opinions in *Kadi* of 16 January 2008 and in *Al Barakaat* of 23 January 2008 also disagreed with the CFI on various points but did not really address the substitution argument either.

80 See ECJ, Case C-308/06, *International Association of Independent Tanker Owners (Intertanko) and Others*, 3 June 2008, at paras. 48–49 ('it does not appear that the Community has assumed, under the EC Treaty, the powers previously exercised by the Member States in the field to which Marpol 73/78 applies, nor that, consequently, its provisions have the effect of binding the Community (Case C-379/92 Peralta [1994] ECR I-3453, paragraph 16)') and Case C-188/07, *Commune de Mesquer*, 24 June 2008, at para. 85 ('the Community is not bound by the Liability Convention or the Fund Convention … it cannot be regarded as having taken the place of its Member States, if only because not all of them are parties to those conventions …').

> 'None the less, the Court is empowered to check, indirectly, the lawfulness of the resolutions of the Security Council in question with regard to *jus cogens*, understood as a body of higher rules of public international law binding on all subjects of international law, including the bodies of the United Nations, and from which no derogation is possible. ... International law thus permits the inference that there exists one limit to the principle that resolutions of the Security Council have binding effect: namely, that they must observe the fundamental peremptory provisions of *jus cogens*. If they fail to do so, however improbable that may be, they would bind neither the Member States of the United Nations nor, in consequence, the Community.'[81]

E. OTHER INTERNATIONAL ORGANISATIONS

I have no knowledge of any international organisation that has considered itself to be formally bound by treaties concluded by its Member States absent specific provisions to that effect. Similarly, Cahin submits that only very exceptionally international organisations are bound by Member State treaties.[82] Morgenstern writes that international organisations are reluctant to accept being bound by treaties to which they are not a party.[83] For instance, the IMF has rejected the argument that it would be bound by certain human rights treaties despite their broad ratification by its Member States.[84]

The same can be said in respect of decisions of other international organisations. Even within the UN family, specialised organisations do not generally feel bound by decisions adopted by UN organs absent specific provisions binding them, e.g. in their relationship agreement.[85] The World Bank, e.g., only has to 'have due

81 CFI, Case T-306/01 *Yusuf*, op. cit. n. 64, paras. 277–281 and CFI, Case T-315/01 *Kadi*, op. cit. n. 64, paras. 226–230.

82 G. Cahin, op. cit. n. 29, p. 522.

83 F. Morgenstern, *Legal problems of International Organizations* (Cambridge, Grotius 1986) pp. 33–34, noting that the ILO has felt morally bound to take into account ILO standards but that the applicability of these standards to the UN was rejected by a UN legal opinion.

84 This view was reportedly taken by the IMF's General Counsel in a legal brief dated 30 May 2001, see A. Clapham, *Human Rights Obligations of Non-State Actors* (Oxford, Oxford University Press 2006) pp. 145–149, especially pp. 146–147. See also François Gianviti, *Economic, Social and Cultural Rights and the International Monetary Fund*, Paper presented at the IMF Seminar on Current Developments in Monetary and Financial Law, Washington D.C., 7–17 May 2002, available at www.imf.org/external/np/leg/sem/2002/cdmfl/eng/gianv3.pdf, pp. 4–5 ('in the event that some or all members of an international organization adhere to a treaty containing such other objectives or values, this in itself does not result in these objectives or values becoming part of the organization's mandate unless and until agreement is reached to amend the organization's charter') and pp. 10–31; also cited by E. Denters, *The International Monetary Fund*, in J. Wouters, ed., *International Encyclopaedia of Laws. Intergovernmental Organizations* (The Hague, Kluwer Law International 2006) paras. 155–156.

85 See also A. Reinisch & B.-O. Bryde, loc. cit. n. 41, pp. 778–780. Compare P. Klein, op. cit. n. 3, pp. 350–359, who, as with treaties (see *supra* this section), argues that in some cases an obligation arises via the obligations of Member States.

regard for' Security Council decisions under articles 41 and 42 UN Charter[86] and has refused in some cases to apply UN General Assembly resolutions.[87] Practice to the contrary appears to be limited to an UNIDO legal opinion.[88] The inclusion of provisions in the relationship agreements, and the fact that some of them do not impose the binding force of Security Council resolutions, is significant and suggests that absent such provisions an international organisation is not bound as such by such decisions.[89]

II. SOME REFLECTIONS ON RESPONSIBILITY OF MEMBER STATES FOR THEIR OWN ACTIONS IN THE FRAMEWORK OF INTERNATIONAL ORGANISATIONS

As has been noted in the preceding section, most of the arguments put forward in favour of binding international organisations to treaties concluded by its Member States (or Member States' obligations more generally) are based on the consideration that a State should not be able to evade its international obligations by transferring powers to an international organisation. However, binding the organisation to Member State (treaty) obligations is not the only way to achieve this desired result. An alternative that has been discussed in the literature,[90] seems to be endorsed by the ILA[91] and the ILC[92] and enjoys some support in jurisprudence (see *infra*), is the view that Member States are to some extent responsible for acts of international organisations. It is not my intention to deal with the responsibility of international organisations themselves (currently under

86 See article VI of the UN-IBRD relationship agreement (15 August 1947, approved by the UN on 15 November 1947 and by the IBRD on 16 September 1947, 16 *UNTS* (1948) p. 346).

87 See e.g. A. Reinisch & B.-O. Bryde, loc. cit. n. 41, pp. 779–780; F. Morgenstern, op. cit. n. 83, pp. 28–30 and P. Klein, op. cit. n. 3, pp. 353–354.

88 Cited in E. Lagrange, op. cit. n. 16, pp. 514–515 (seeing it as apparently isolated) and P. Klein, op. cit. n. 3, p. 358.

89 Similarly, R. Lawson, op. cit. n. 2, at pp. 151–154, especially n. 68.

90 See especially the extensive analysis by R. Lawson, op. cit. n. 2, at pp. 189–199 and pp. 345–492. See also A. Clapham, op. cit. n. 84, p. 135 and Wessel in NVIR, ed., *De plaats van de Europese Unie in het veranderende bestel van de volkenrechtelijke organizaties* (124 Mededelingen van de NVIR) (The Hague, TMC Asser Press 2002) p. 40. Compare the rather critical view of A. Berramdane, loc. cit. n. 32, pp. 247–251, especially p. 248.

91 See the ILA's 2004 *Final Report on the Accountability of International Organisations* (available online at www.ila-hq.org), *inter alia* pp. 18–19, arguing, among others, that 'Membership of an IO can [...] not be considered to imply a corresponding reduction of state responsibility, although an authorisation granted by an IO to one or more Members, could in certain circumstances, prevent the breach of an international obligation by such Members' and that '[a] transfer of powers to an IO cannot ... exclude the responsibility of the States who transferred powers to an IO'. While this seems to be a legal argument this need not necessarily be the case given the ILA's meta-legal approach in this document (see pp. 5–6).

92 The ILC's view on this issue will be addressed in some detail below.

consideration by the ILC) nor with that of Member States for the acts of international organisations generally (also addressed in that context by the ILC) but only to discuss the basic elements of the responsibility of Member States for acts in the framework of international organisations that are contrary to international obligations *of a Member State*.[93] It may be noted that this did not *appear* to be addressed in the ILC's Draft Articles on *State* Responsibility since article 57 thereof stated that '[t]hese articles are without prejudice to any question of the responsibility under international law of an international organisation, or of any State for the conduct of an international organization' (but see *infra*, II.2).[94]

Member State responsibility in this sense may be argued to arise out of a number of different grounds. First, the responsibility of a Member State may result from the very fact of establishing an international organisation without binding it to the Member State's obligations and thereby enabling it to act contrary to an international obligation of that Member State. Second, the responsibility of a Member State may be based on its own conduct in the framework of an international organisation once it has been established. In this case, a further distinction may be made between a Member State's role in decision-making and its role in implementing a decision. Third, further grounds such as complicity and control over an international organisation by a State should also be mentioned but will not be discussed here.[95]

A. RESPONSIBILITY FOR THE ACTIONS OF AN INTERNATIONAL ORGANISATION RESULTING FROM ITS ESTABLISHMENT

The argument can be made that if States set up an international organisation that will exercise certain powers normally exercised by them or exercised to their advantage, without assuring that this organisation respects the obligations of these States in the exercise of such powers from which these States cannot derogate among them,[96] the States lay the basis for violations of their obligations and should be responsible themselves when an international organisation acts in a manner contrary to the Member States' obligations.[97] Although some see this

93 This key distinction is also made by R. Lawson, op. cit. n. 2, especially at pp. 280–287.

94 ILC, *Draft Articles on Responsibility of States for Internationally Wrongful Acts*, adopted on 31 May and 3 August 2001, *Report of the International Law Commission. Fifty-third session*, UN Doc. A/56/10, pp. 360–363.

95 See provisional draft articles 25–27 of the ILC's work on the responsibility of international organizations, UN Doc. A/61/10 (2006), pp. 277–282 and their successors in the 2009 draft articles.

96 E.g. because they include obligations towards a third State or because derogation was excluded.

97 See the discussion in M. Hartwig, op. cit. n. 12, pp. 285–287.

as a piercing of the separate international legal personality of the international organisation,[98] this need not necessarily be the case if one argues that the Member States are not simply responsible for the acts of the organisation, but rather incur responsibility by virtue of their own initial act of not binding an organisation to their own international obligations.

At the domestic level, a State will remain responsible if it transfers governmental powers to an agency even when that agency is independent: Article 5 of the ILC's Draft Articles on State responsibility[99] stipulates that '[t]he conduct of a person or entity which is not an organ of the State [...] but which is empowered by the law of that State to exercise elements of the governmental authority shall be considered an act of the State under international law, provided the person or entity is acting in that capacity in the particular instance'. The commentary to this article does not mention international organisations at all and presumably they are not intended to be covered by this article.[100] Nevertheless, it has been argued that they can fall within the terms of this provision,[101] a view which the text itself certainly permits.

Until recently, the work of the ILC on the responsibility of international organizations seemed to endorse this solution, albeit without reference to the State responsibility rules. In particular, draft Article 28(1), as provisionally adopted in 2006, stipulated that '[a] State member of an international organization incurs international responsibility if it circumvents one of its international obligations by providing the organization with competence in relation to that obligation, and the organization commits an act that, if committed by that State, would have constituted a breach of that obligation'.[102] The commentary made clear that no specific intent was required but seemed to leave open an exception where the 'circumvention' was 'an unwitting result of providing the international organization with competence'.[103] The latter consideration indicates that, in contrast with a domestic agency, the ILC appeared to view the case of international organisations as less absolute.

98 E.g. R. Uerpmann, loc. cit. n. 14, pp. 35–36.

99 *Supra* n. 94.

100 See, with respect to a similar provision in an earlier version, R. Lawson, op. cit. n. 2, at p. 272.

101 See, with respect to a similar provision in an earlier version, V. Lowe, 'Can the European Community Bind the Member States on Questions of Customary International Law?', in M. Koskenniemi, ed., *International Law Aspects of the European Union* (The Hague, Kluwer Law International 1998) pp. 163–164. The analogy of international organisations with 'indirect state administration' is also mentioned by R. Uerpmann, loc. cit. n. 14, p. 36, with further references.

102 UN Doc. A/61/10 (2006), p. 283. See also the Special Rapporteur's proposal that contained the same essence but slightly different wording: UN Doc. A/CN.4/564/Add.1 (2006), pp. 6–11.

103 Comment 2 to article 28, UN Doc. A/61/10 (2006), pp. 283–284.

There is also some support for this position in the jurisprudence of the European Court of Human Rights, which is also cited by the ILC and which has arguably developed two arguments that soften an otherwise absolute application of Member State responsibility. One is to take into account the importance and needs of international cooperation in determining whether a particular right has been violated or not, especially through the assessment of proportionality.[104] The other is to accept that where an international organisation is endowed with an equivalent level of human rights protection, the Court will, in principle, accept this as adequate.[105] The latter approach was articulated very clearly in *Bosphorus*, where the Court said that:

> '[s]tate action taken in compliance with [legal obligations flowing from its membership of an international organisation to which it has transferred part of its sovereignty] is justified as long as the relevant organisation is considered to protect fundamental rights, as regards both the substantive guarantees offered and the mechanisms controlling their observance, in a manner which can be considered at least equivalent to that for which the Convention provides [...] However, any such finding of equivalence could not be final and would be susceptible to review in the light of any relevant change in fundamental rights' protection.'[106]

However, in its later judgment in *Boivin*, the Court appears to have rejected responsibility on the sole basis of establishment by requiring a direct or indirect intervention of the respondent State:

> '... la décision litigieuse a été prise par un tribunal international échappant à la juridiction des Etats défendeurs, dans le cadre d'un conflit du travail qui s'inscrit entièrement dans l'ordre juridique interne d'Eurocontrol, organisation internationale possédant une personnalité juridique distincte de celle de ses Etats membres... à aucun moment la France ou la Belgique ne sont intervenues, directement ou indirectement, dans ce litige, et ne relève en l'espèce aucune action ou omission de ces Etats ou de leurs autorités qui serait de nature à engager leur responsabilité au regard de la Convention. ... Contrairement à la situation dans [d'autres] affaires, qui impliquaient toutes une intervention directe ou indirecte de l'Etat ou des Etats mis en

104 See e.g. ECtHR, *Waite and Kennedy v. Germany*, Application No. 26083/94, 30 *EHRR* (1999) p. 261, at paras. 54–63. See also ECtHR, *Beer and Regan v. Germany*, Application No. 28934/95, 33 *EHRR* (1999) p. 3, at paras. 64–73. See also, specifically regarding the EU, R. Lawson, op. cit. n. 2, at pp. 477–479 and A. Berramdane, loc. cit. n. 32, pp. 263–266.

105 For an extensive and critical discussion, see generally R. Lawson, op. cit. n. 2, at pp. 345–492.

106 ECtHR, *Bosphorus Hava Yolları Turizm ve Ticaret Anonim Şirketi v. Ireland*, Application No. 45036/98, 42 *EHRR* (2006) p. 1, at para. 155. See also ECtHR, *Naletilic v. Croatia*, Application No. 51891/99, Admissibility Decision of 4 May 2000, in which the Court ruled that the ICTY 'in view of the content of its Statute and Rules of Procedure, offers all the necessary guarantees' (para. 1.b).

> cause, on ne saurait dire que le requérant en l'espèce relève de la « juridiction » des Etats défendeurs au sens de l'article 1 de la Convention.'[107]

The ILC's draft Article 60(1) on the responsibility of international organizations as provisionally adopted in 2009, which replaces draft Article 28 as adopted in 2006 (see above), also appears to move away from responsibility for the establishment as such. Draft Article 60(1) now stipulates that '[a] State member of an international organization incurs international responsibility if it seeks to avoid complying with one of its own international obligations by *taking advantage of the fact that the organization has competence* in relation to the subject matter of that obligation, *thereby prompting the organization to commit an act that,* if committed by the State, would have constituted a breach of the obligation'.[108] The commentary still states that no specific intention of circumvention is required but now adds that the text means to exclude responsibility where an act of the organisation is an 'an unwitting result *of prompting a competent international organization to commit an act*'.[109] It further clarifies that in addition to competence of the organisation and an act of the organisation that would have constituted a breach if committed by the Member State (both of which were already included in 2006), there is a third requirement (not included in 2006), namely a 'significant link between the conduct of the member State seeking to avoid compliance and that of the international organization. The act of the international organization has to be prompted by the member State. An assessment of a specific intent on the part of the member State of circumventing an international obligation is not required. Circumvention may reasonably be inferred from the circumstances'.[110] This appears to require that the organisation be prompted to perform the specific act concerned by the Member State but without that Member State necessarily intending to circumvent its obligation. That suggests the mere establishment is not enough.

Despite these most recent developments, the principle of Member State responsibility by virtue of establishment seems sound at first sight as Member States should not be able to evade their international obligations. However, an unmitigated theory of Member State responsibility would mean that in order to avoid its responsibility from being engaged, each Member State would have to ensure that an international organisation respect all of its international obligations, at least towards those third parties that would have been entitled to the corresponding rights. This would be very difficult to apply: while it might

---

107 ECtHR, *Boivin v. 34 Members of the Council of Europe*, Application No. 73250/01, Admissibility Decision of 9 September 2008, pp. 7–8.

108 ILC, *Report of the Sixty-first session (4 May to 5 June and 6 July to 7 August 2009)*, UN Doc. A/64/10, p. 38 (emphasis added).

109 Comment 2 to Article 60, *ibid.*, p. 165 (emphasis added).

110 Comments 5 to 7 to Article 60, *ibid.*, pp. 165–166.

perhaps be conceivable at the European level (or any regional level more generally), it is difficult to see how it could function at the global level because it would impose regional standards on worldwide international organisations. Moreover, while in theory it might be possible to require respect only in relation to the beneficiary of the Member State's obligations, this would be very difficult to apply in practice.[111] It is therefore submitted that a mitigated theory is indeed necessary. It may also be noted that one may draw a parallel with the human rights protection in some EU Member States in which national constitutional Courts have accepted that the human rights protection offered in the framework of international organisations needs to be adequate but not necessarily entirely identical to that on the national level.[112] Another point of comparison is the European Court of Human Rights' jurisprudence on extradition, in which the Court does not impose full respect of the entire ECHR as a condition for extradition.[113]

The question then is what mitigation should there be. The European Court of Human Rights seems to have adopted a fairly adequate way of accommodating the different interests involved. The general equivalent protection test should guarantee a generally adequate protection and encourage Member States to impose such a protection on international organisations. This test is particularly appropriate if one regards the basis for Member State responsibility as relating to Member States' actions when establishing an international organisation (or when amending its constituent instruments).

---

111 One can hardly imagine the EU granting more protection to nationals or residents of one Member State than to those of other Member States. Similarly, it is hard to image the UN applying different standards in peacekeeping operations according to where such operations take place, although here a regional differentiation might not be unthinkable (albeit difficult from a sending State perspective where military contingents are concerned). In relation to obligations towards third States rather than individuals, this may be less difficult, although there respect for conflicting Member State obligations might entail an impossible position for an organisation.

112 E.g. in Germany, see J. Schwarze, 'Das allgemeine Völkerrecht in den innergemeinschaftlichen Rechtsbeziehungen', 18 *Europarecht* (1983) p. 2. The comparison between these two levels/ situations is also made by R. Uerpmann, loc. cit. n. 14, p. 33. See also T. Kingreen, 'Art. 6', in C. Calliess & M. Ruffert, eds., op. cit. n. 21, pp. 80–84.

113 Under the ECHR extradition/surrender is clearly prohibited when there is a real risk of torture or inhuman or degrading treatment (ECtHR, *Soering v. UK*, Application No. 14038/88, 11 *EHRR* (1989) p. 439). The situation for other rights is less clear. E.g., it would appear that a (real threat of a) violation of the right to a fair trial will not normally entail an obligation to refuse extradition/surrender but only exceptionally 'in circumstances where the fugitive has suffered or risks suffering a flagrant denial of justice in the requesting country' (ECtHR, *Einhorn v. France*, Application No. 71555/01, Decision of 16 October 2001 as to the admissibility, para. 32). See also ECtHR, *Drozd and Janousek v. France and Spain*, Application No. 12747/87, Judgment of 26 June 1992, para. 110: 'The Contracting States are, however, obliged to refuse their co-operation if it emerges that the conviction is the result of a flagrant denial of justice'. Obviously, this is not an ideal solution as it can lead to extradition/surrender in cases where 'lesser' violations are likely. However, any other solution could potentially make extradition/surrender almost impossible between many States. On balance, it may therefore be the best solution. Compare R. Lawson, op. cit. n. 2, at pp. 244–247.

The question that arises, however, is how to deal with individual violations despite generally equivalent protection. Several options present themselves. A first possibility is to regard the equal protection merely as entailing a presumption of compliance that may be rebutted in any given case for any violation of an obligation. In this case, maximum respect for Member State obligations would be ensured but Member States would be forced to set up a water tight system of respect for their obligations by international organisations. A second option would be to rely on proportionality as a means of limiting Member State responsibility in case of violations despite equal protection: in this case only serious violations would outweigh the interests of international cooperation. This option would combine the two above-mentioned tracks in the European Court of Human Right's jurisprudence and would seem preferable to the first one. It appears to be the option endorsed by the Court in *Bosphorus*.[114] A third option consists of rejecting Member State responsibility *on the basis of the establishment* in case of individual violations despite generally equivalent protection. At first sight, this seems difficult to accept in that it leads to a lack of responsibility for certain violations. However, it would least affect the separate legal personality. Moreover, the scope of this gap in protection might be significantly limited if Member States would incur responsibility for implementing decisions of international organisations that are contrary to their international obligations (see the following subsection). In that case, the gap in protection would be limited to situations entirely effected by an international organisation, which could possibly be covered by the ILC's *unwitting result* exception in its 2006 conception.

Yet even assuming that one of the above solutions might offer an adequate approach, a number of other difficulties have to be overcome. In particular, while the equal protection may work fairly well in respect of human rights and related areas of law, it is less obvious to assure equal protection in respect of other very varied and more inter-State obligations.[115] More importantly, it is doubtful whether the equivalent protection can be applied at all to more traditional inter-State obligations: whereas some balancing of interests seems acceptable between two 'common interest regimes' that mostly serve the interests of the international (or European) community and its citizens (e.g. human rights and close European integration), there appears to be little basis for allowing some States to partially

114 ECtHR, *Bosphorus*, op. cit. n. 106, para. 156: 'If such equivalent protection is considered to be provided by the organisation, the presumption will be that a State has not departed from the requirements of the Convention when it does no more than implement legal obligations flowing from its membership of the organisation. However, any such presumption can be rebutted if, in the circumstances of a particular case, it is considered that the protection of Convention rights was *manifestly* deficient. In such cases, the interest of international co-operation would be outweighed by the Convention's role as a "constitutional instrument of European public order" in the field of human rights' (emphasis added). A. Berramdane, loc. cit. n. 32, pp. 261–262 seems to be rather critical of this solution.

115 A provision such as article 351 TFEU might to some extent solve this problem.

sacrifice their obligations towards a third Party purely for their own interests. It is therefore submitted that these two situations must be distinguished, although it may be difficult to draw the line between the two.

Finally, from a practical perspective, determining what the ILC qualifies as an act that, if committed by that State, would have constituted a breach of that obligation, may not always be easy and *inter alia* gives rise to the question in what circumstances Member States would incur individual and/or joint responsibility.[116] For instance, if treatment by an international organisation of its staff is contrary to human rights obligations of some of its Member States, would all the Member States bound by the obligations concerned be responsible, or only the State in the territory of whom the violation occurs (if it is among those States)?[117] In case of responsibility by virtue of the *establishment*, the better view would seem to be that since the staff is employed by an organisation set up by all the Member States, all those Member States that are bound by the obligation will incur responsibility.

B. RESPONSIBILITY OF A MEMBER STATE FOR ITS OWN SUBSEQUENT CONDUCT IN THE FRAMEWORK OF AN INTERNATIONAL ORGANISATION

Apart from the question whether Member States may be held liable for the conduct of an international organisation due to their initial role in establishing it, there is also the question to what extent they can be held responsible for their own conduct in the framework of an international organisation, both in adopting decisions and in implementing them.

The ILC deliberately omitted this aspect from its work on the responsibility of international organizations, apparently feeling that it was adequately addressed in its work on state responsibility,[118] although it has addressed it to a very limited

116 See on this e.g. M. Hartwig, op. cit. n. 12, pp. 288–289; R. Lawson, op. cit. n. 2, at pp. 194–198 and R. Uerpmann, loc. cit. n. 14, p. 37.

117 See also R. Lawson, op. cit. n. 2, at pp. 195 and 298–300.

118 The Draft Articles proposed up to 2006 that were relevant concern the attribution of conduct to international organisations and the circumstances under which a Member State may be responsible for conduct of an international organisation, but hardly the conduct of a Member State in the framework of an international organisation. In respect of the latter, it was stated in the Fourth Report of the special rapporteur (UN Doc. A/CN.4/564/Add.1, para. 54) that '[n]ot all the questions that may affect the responsibility of a State in connection with the conduct of an international organization should be examined in the present context. For instance, questions relating to attribution of conduct to a State have already been covered in the articles on State responsibility. It would clearly be preferable not to consider them here again. Thus, if an issue arises as to whether a certain conduct is to be attributed to a State or to an international organization or to both, the current articles will provide criteria only for settling the question as to whether that conduct is to be attributed to an international organization,

extent most recently (see below). This choice seemed to imply that any conduct that is attributable to State organs, even when occurring within the framework of an international organisation, may lead to the responsibility of that State. This meant that the savings clause in article 57 of the ILC's Draft Articles on State Responsibility,[119] which provides that '[t]hese articles are without prejudice to any question of the responsibility under international law of an international organization, or of any State for the conduct of an international organization', was to be interpreted restrictively.

While this may seem obvious at first sight, State responsibility for conduct within an international organisation has been debated by scholars, especially in relation to decision-making, because representatives of States,[120] especially of Governments, in decision-making organs of international organisations act in a dual capacity: they remain state organs but they are also part of an organ of the international organisation.[121] Obviously, this is not the case for truly international (e.g. executive or judicial) offices in respect of which the office holder may not take instructions from a State.[122] Also, the matter becomes more complex in the case of representatives of a State in parliamentary bodies, which represent their State but cannot be said to be subject to its instructions and control in the same way as Government representatives – at least in democracies.

It is, however, submitted that the individual conduct (e.g. a vote) of at least Government officials that represent States in decision-making bodies of

---

while the articles on State responsibility will say whether that same conduct is to be attributed or not to a State' (see also UN Doc. A/61/10, pp. 277–278). Also, in the commentaries to draft articles 25 and 26, which deal with respectively aid or assistance and direction and control by a State to/over the commission of an internationally wrongful act by an international organisation, simple 'participation in the decision-making process of the organization according to the pertinent rules of the organization' seems to be ruled out in principle as a ground for Member State responsibility under these provisions (UN Doc. A/61/10, pp. 279–281). While this is essentially the same in the 2009 version (see ILC, *Report of the Sixty-first session (4 May to 5 June and 6 July to 7 August 2009)*, UN Doc. A/64/10, introductory comment 2 on p. 159 and Draft Articles 57 and 58 and comment 2 to both, pp. 160–162), because of the changes in the 2009 draft article 60 compared to the 2006 draft article 28, the issue is now addressed to some extent in this provision, see below.

119 *Supra* n. 94.

120 For instance, I. Pernice, loc. cit. n. 39, pp. 240 note 44, writes that voting engages the Member State's responsibility but questions whether a vote is still an act of a Member State. The ILA's 2004 *Final Report on the Accountability of International Organisations* (op. cit. n. 91), p. 25 states that 'the continuing role of Member States qua members of an organ of an IO is neutral as regards Member States' liability if the Organization has "une volonté distincte". […] a Member State neither incurs special liability nor avoids existing liability according to whether it is or is not a member of a particular organ'.

121 For an extensive analysis of the status of State representatives in international organisations, see E. Lagrange, op. cit. n. 16, pp. 135–167. See also M. Hartwig, op. cit. n. 12, pp. 272–280 and R. Lawson, op. cit. n. 2, at pp. 463–471.

122 As is, e.g., the case for members of the European Commission or the UN Secretary-General.

international organisations is attributable to their State and must be distinguished from the collective conduct of an organ (e.g. a decision adopted), which is attributable to the organisation.[123] That the mere vote in itself does not entail any direct consequences, because it only takes effect when it is transformed into a collective decision also reflecting other votes, is not, in my view, a convincing counter-argument.[124] The real question is whether the vote can constitute a breach of an international obligation independently from any breach that might result from the decision adopted. It is submitted that this can be the case but that it will not always be so. In particular, responsibility would arise for a vote that violates a rule which includes an obligation to not tolerate/encourage/incite certain conduct[125] or an obligation to take all lawfull measures to prevent a certain conduct[126] or to ensure respect for certain rules.[127] Thus whether a vote may lead to international responsibility depends on the nature of the obligation at stake. Therefore, I argue that a State engages its international responsibility by voting in relation to a decision when the mere vote itself amounts to a violation of an international obligation of that State. This view has some support in the jurisprudence of the European Court of Human Rights, especially the *Matthews* case.[128] Opponents of this argument in part invoke the older decision of the

---

123 Compare R. Lawson, op. cit. n. 2, at pp. 463–471, who seems to be in favour of Member State responsibility for votes but notes divergent views in doctrine and the *C.F.D.T.* case to the contrary (see *infra* on the latter). On this distinction between the collective act imputed to the organ and the underlying votes as decisions of individual members of that organ, see also R. Wessel, loc. cit. n. 39, p. 21 (citing Ruiter) and R. Wessel, 'Lowering the corporate veil. Het recht der internationale organisaties vanuit de institutionele rechtstheorie', in M.A. Heldeweg, R.J.P. Schobben and W.G. Werner, eds., *De Regel Meester. Opstellen voor Dick W.P. Ruiter* (Enschede, Twente University Press 2001) pp. 11–14. M. Hartwig, op. cit. n. 12, pp. 272–280 seems hesitant to admit Member State responsibility for decision-making.

124 *Contra*: E. Lagrange, op. cit. n. 16, pp. 332–343.

125 E.g. the obligation for States to refrain from 'organising, instigating, assisting or participating in acts of civil strife or terrorist acts in another State or acquiescing in organised activities within its territory directed towards the commission of such acts, when the acts referred to ... involve a threat or use of force', see Declaration on Principles of International Law concerning Friendly Relations and Co-operation amongst States in accordance with the Charter of the United Nations (Annex to UN General Assembly Res. 2625(XXV), 24 October 1970), 1.I.9.

126 E.g. to prevent genocide, see Article 1 Convention on the Prevention and Punishment of the Crime of Genocide (New York, 9 December 1948, 78 *UNTS* 277): 'The Contracting Parties confirm that genocide, ..., is a crime under international law which they undertake to prevent and to punish'. In its judgment of 26 February 2007 in the *Case concerning the application of the Convention on the Prevention and Punishment of the Crime of Genocide (Bosnia and Herzegovina v. Serbia and Montenegro)*, the ICJ identified the obligation to prevent genocide as a distinct obligation (at paras. 155–165) and held that Serbia and Montenegro was responsible for violating this obligation (at paras. 425–438) but that it had not committed genocide or complicity thereto because of a lack of attribution (at paras. 379–424).

127 E.g. the obligation to 'respect and *to ensure respect* for' the 1949 Geneva Conventions and the 1977 Additional Protocol I thereto '*in all circumstances*' (emphasis added; see respectively common article 1 and article 1(1)).

128 ECtHR, *Matthews v. the United Kingdom*, Application No. 24833/94, 28 *EHRR* (1999) p. 364, at paras. 32–33, in which the UK was held responsible for an act of EU law to which it had agreed and which required unanimity. While the act (Act Concerning the Election of the

European Commission of Human Rights in *C.F.D.T.*, in which it was held the Member States did not exercise their jurisdiction in participating in an EU Council decision.[129] However, the specific element of this decision does not appear to have been repeated in later jurisprudence and the Court's view in *Matthews*, even though it concerned (quasi) primary EU law, suggests it may no longer be valid. Indeed, in a 2002 decision in the *SEGI* case, the Court clearly regards Member States as responsible for decisions they adopt in the area of the CFSP.[130] An exception may exist in respect of decisions concerning Chapter VII of the UN Charter.[131] A similar evolution may be found in the Human Rights Committee's

---

Representatives of the European Parliament by Direct Universal Suffrage of 20 September 1976, annexed to Council Decision 76/787) was not an ordinary decision of an EU organ, required adoption in accordance with the respective constitutional requirements and was, according to the Court, an international instrument 'freely entered into by the United Kingdom', the latter element suggests the same may be true of other decisions of international organisations, at least when adopted by unanimity. Compare M. Breuer, 'Offene Fragen im Verhältnis von EGMR und EuGH. Zur Entscheidung des EGMR im Fall Emesa Sugar', 32 *Europäische Grundrechtezeitschrift* (2005) pp. 229–234 (arguing that the ECtHR may have left open the possibility of reviewing EC secondary law even without Member State implementing acts in ECtHR, *Emesa Sugar NV v. the Netherlands*, Application No. 62023/00, Admissibility Decision of 13 January 2005) and R. Uerpmann, loc. cit. n. 14, pp. 36–37.

129 ECommHR, *C.F.D.T.* v. *the European Communities, alternatively their Member States*, Application No. 8030/77, para. 7: 'the Commission considers that an examination of the applicant's complaints is also outside its jurisdiction ratione personae since these States by taking part in the decision of the Council of the European Communities had not in the circumstances of the instant case exercised their "jurisdiction" within the meaning of Article 1 of the Convention'). See E. Lagrange, op. cit. n. 16, pp. 337–338. Compare the discussion of this case by R. Lawson, op. cit. n. 2, at pp. 363–372.

130 ECtHR, *SEGI e.a. & GESTORAS PRO-AMNISTIA and others. v. Germany and others*, Decision as to the admissibility, Applications No. 6422/02 and No. 9916/02. 'CFSP decisions are therefore intergovernmental in nature. By taking part in their preparation and adoption each State engages its responsibility. That responsibility is assumed jointly by the States when they adopt a CFSP decision'. An alternative explanation might be that the ECtHR did not consider that the EU, as opposed to the EC, had legal personality and therefore had no option but to attribute the conduct to the member States. The summary nature of the wording used by the Court does not offer any insight into the reasons supporting its view on this point.

131 The ECtHR stated in its decision of 31 May 2007 in joined cases *Behrami & Behrami v. France*, Application No. 71412/01, and *Saramati v. France, Germany and Norway*, Application No. 78166/01, 45 *EHRR* (SE10) (2007) p. 85, at para. 149 that '[s]ince operations established by UNSC Resolutions under Chapter VII of the UN Charter are fundamental to the mission of the UN to secure international peace and security ..., the Convention cannot be interpreted in a manner which would subject the acts and omissions of Contracting Parties which are covered by UNSC Resolutions and occur prior to or in the course of such missions, to the scrutiny of the Court... This reasoning equally applies to voluntary acts of the respondent States such as the vote of a permanent member of the UNSC in favour of the relevant Chapter VII Resolution and the contribution of troops to the security mission: such acts may not have amounted to obligations flowing from membership of the UN but they remained crucial to the effective fulfilment by the UNSC of its Chapter VII mandate and, consequently, by the UN of its imperative peace and security aim' (at para. 149). *A contrario*, in other cases such voluntary acts arguably are attributable to the State concerned. Also, it remains to be seen whether the Court will not abandon the reasoning in this decision in the light of the severe criticism it has rightly attracted.

views in this respect: whereas in 1987 it held that 'the recruitment policies of an international organization ... cannot, in any way, be construed as coming within the jurisdiction of the Netherlands or of any other State party to the [ICCPR] and the Optional Protocol thereto',[132] it more recently stated that Member States remain bound by their obligations under the ICCPR when they deploy their armed forces in the framework of international organisations,[133] although the latter concerns the implementation of a decision rather than its adoption.

In addition to responsibility arising from its role in adopting a decision, a Member State may also incur responsibility for implementing a decision of an international organisation that is contrary to the Member State's international obligations. Indeed, in most cases where the rights of third parties are affected, Member States will play a role in implementing decisions of international organisations. Although in some respects the question whether the Member State has any discretion or not in this implementation may be relevant,[134] from the perspective of a Member State's obligation towards third parties this seems irrelevant: if it breaches an obligation from which it could not derogate, the fact that it acts in the framework of an international organisation is no excuse since it has itself created (or joined) this organisation and enabled it to make the Member State violate its obligations.[135] There is case law under the ECHR to this effect,[136]

---

132 HRC, 8 April 1987, *H.v.d.P. v. Netherlands*, Doc. CCPR/C/29/D/217/1986, para. 3.2. See on this case D. McGoldrick, 'Extraterritorial Application of the International Covenant on Civil and Political Rights', in F. Coomans & T. Kamminga, eds., *Extraterritorial Application of Human Rights Treaties* (Antwerp, Intersentia 2004) pp. 53–54.

133 General Comment 31 (21 April 2004), CCPR/C/74/CRP.4/Rev.6), para. 10. ('a State party must respect and ensure the rights laid down in the Covenant to anyone within the power or effective control of that State Party, even if not situated within the territory of the State Party (...) This principle also applies to those within the power or effective control of the forces of a State Party acting outside its territory, regardless of the circumstances in which such power or effective control was obtained, such as forces constituting a national contingent of a State Party assigned to an international peace-keeping or peace-enforcement operation').

134 This may, e.g., be relevant under EU law for determining whether a Member State or a Union institution is responsible for a violation of higher rules of EU law. Compare the ECJ's view that damage suffered as a consequence of EU sanctions adopted pursuant to sanctions imposed by the UN Security Council would not be attributable to the EU but only to the UN, see CFI, Case T-184/95, *Dorsch Consult Ingenieurgesellschaft mbH v. Council of the European Union and Commission of the European Communities*, [1998] ECR II-667, paras. 73–74; the appeals judgment (ECJ, Case C-237/98, *Dorsch Consult Ingenieurgesellschaft mbH v. Council of the European Union and Commission of the European Communities*, [2000] ECR I-4549) did not address this point.

135 One may draw a parallel to *force majeure* as a circumstance precluding wrongfulness under the rules of State responsibility as laid down in article 23 of the ILC's Draft Articles on State Responsibility (op. cit. n. 94), which in such a case could not be invoked because there would be no material impossibility and even if there were, it would be due 'either alone or in combination with other factors, to the conduct of the State invoking it' and that State 'has assumed the risk of that situation occurring'. But see M. Hirsch, op. cit. n. 3, at pp. 82–88.

136 See e.g. ECtHR, *Cantoni v. France*, Application No. 17862/91, para. 30 ('The fact, pointed to by the Government, that Article L. 511 of the Public Health Code is based almost word for word

although it has been qualified in *Bosphorus*[137] and was held to be subject to an exception for Chapter VII of the UN Charter.[138] The qualification deals with the one circumstance in which it would be harsh to hold a Member State responsible, namely where the Member State had provided for respect of such obligations by the organisation but where this has turned out to be ineffective in a specific case. Given the likeness to responsibility resulting from establishment, one could argue for a similar solution (see above). On the other hand, the situation is different because here we have specific (implementing) action by the Member State, which is in a position to refuse execution and thereby uphold its obligations towards a third party, even if this may entail its responsibility towards the international organisation and/or its other Member States. It is submitted that this difference justifies broader Member State responsibility for implementing decisions of international organisations. However, for 'common interest regimes', mitigation via proportionality in those cases where the Member State had provided for equivalent protection and has no discretion to implement the decision in conformity with its obligations, seems acceptable. It is precisely such an exception that was recognised by the European Court of Human Rights in *Bosphorus*.[139]

The ILC's most recent work touches upon member States' own responsibility for their subsequent conduct to some extent. In particular, the 2009 draft Article 60 discussed above now deals with subsequent conduct, more specifically prompting an organisation to perform an act that would be a breach of a Member State's obligation if it would be commited by the Member State. However, there is no further explanation on what 'prompting' means. For instance, does it mean the Member State must have proposed or actively encouraged the act, or does it go further and also cover cases in which a Member State has merely voted in favour of the act, or does it depend on whether the vote of the Member State was

---

on Community Directive 65/65 ... does not remove it from the ambit of Article 7 [ECHR]') and European Commission of Human Rights, decisions of 9 February 1990 in *M. & Co v. Germany* ('Under Article 1 [ECHR] the Member States are responsible for all acts and omissions of their domestic organs allegedly violating the Convention regardless of whether the act or omission in question is a consequence of domestic law or regulations or of the necessity to comply with international obligations') and of 16 January 1995 in *Gestra v. Italy* ('la Commission doit...contrôler que les effets de l'application, par les organes internes des Parties contractantes, d'autres conventions internationales conclues par la suite, ne portent pas atteinte aux droits et libertés garantis par la Convention'); see also R. Lawson, op. cit. n. 2, at pp. 473–476; A. Berramdane, loc. cit. n. 32, pp. 258–261 and M. Breuer, op. cit. n. 128, pp. 231–232.

137 ECtHR, *Bosphorus*, op. cit. n. 106. It was an impoundment by the Irish authorities pursuant to an EC Regulation that was challenged, i.e. Member State implementation.

138 See ECtHR, *Behrami & Saramati*, op. cit. n. 131.

139 ECtHR, op. cit. n. 106. The ECtHR held that compliance with EC law entailed a presumption of conformity with the ECHR to the extent that the EC has an equivalent level of protection but that this may be rebutted if this protection is 'manifestly deficient' (paras. 148–165). See also A. Berramdane, loc. cit. n. 32, pp. 258–261.

necessary for the adoption of the act?[140] Nor does this work cover implementation.

I therefore argue that there are three bases for Member State responsibility (leaving aside complicity). First, a Member State incurs international responsibility for an act committed by an international organisation that, if committed by that State, would have constituted a breach of an international obligation of that Member State, except for 'common interest regimes' in respect of which the Member State has provided for equivalent protection, with the caveat that where despite such equivalent protection there is a manifest violation that outweighs the interests of international cooperation, the Member State will remain responsible. Second, a Member State also engages its international responsibility by voting in relation to a decision when the mere vote itself amounts to a violation of an international obligation of that State. Third, a Member State is internationally responsible for implementing a decision that violates its international obligations except where it had provided for equivalent protection in relation to a 'common interest regime' and has no discretion to implement the decision in conformity with its obligations and only to the extent that the violation of its obligations is proportionate with the importance of international cooperation.

CONCLUSION

I have argued that international law, including the law of international organisations, presently contains no general mechanism binding international organisations to treaty obligations of their Member States and that such a substitution or succession remains exceptional. The risk that Member States evade their international obligations by acting through international organisations may nevertheless be mitigated if Member States remain to some extent responsible for their own behaviour in the framework of international organisations, including concerning the latter's establishment. While the law is not clear on this point, it offers a number of elements that support this view.

140 This distinction would be very significant in the context of the EU, in particular given that in the vast majority of cases, EU legal acts can only be adopted on a proposal of the Commission. Moreover, in one of the two areas in which member States have a right of initiative, namely the Common Foreign and Security Policy, it is likely that proposals for legal acts will most often formally be presented by the High Representative of the Union for Foreign Affairs and Security Policy even when one or more member States are at the origin of the idea.

THE 'ITALIAN JOB': HOW TO MAKE INTERNATIONAL ORGANISATIONS COMPLIANT WITH HUMAN RIGHTS AND ACCOUNTABLE FOR THEIR VIOLATION BY TARGETING MEMBER STATES

Matteo TONDINI*

I. INTRODUCTION

There is a need to clarify that Member States don't leave their human rights obligations at home and don't eliminate them by acting through sub-contractors like the Organisation of American States or the UN
Todd Howland[1]

In late May 2008, the release of a new report[2] by the international NGO 'Save the Children', concerning sexual abuse against minors allegedly committed by

* Researcher, Vrije Universiteit Amsterdam, Faculty of Social Sciences, Department of Governance Studies. An early version of this essay was presented at the international conference 'Accountability for Human Rights Violations by International Organisations', held in Brussels on 16–17 March 2007. The author wishes to thank Brian Concannon Jr., Esq. (Director of the Institute for Justice & Democracy in Haiti – OR, USA), Mr. Andi Dobrushi (formerly, legal advisor at the European Roma Rights Centre – Budapest), Mr. Todd Howland (ex Director of the Robert F. Kennedy Memorial Center for Human Rights – New York) and Prof. Rick Lawson (Leiden University – NL) for their contribution in exchanging useful material and information. Other thanks to Prof. Michael Pugh (University of Bradford – UK) for his precious remarks. Very special thanks to Dr. Katarina Månsson (OHCHR, Kampala and Geneva) for commenting on a previous draft of this contribution and generally for her unfailing patience in submitting valuable ideas and information during the drafting process. Without her kind support probably this text would not have seen the light of day. Notes and comments at m.tondini@fsw.vu.nl. Internet pages last visited on 12 August 2009.

1 Former Director of the Robert F. Kennedy Memorial Center for Human Rights, New York (see *Selective Memory at the United Nations: Human Rights in Haiti*, 1 March 2006, www.ijdh.org/articles/article_recent_news_3-28-06.htm).

2 C. Csáky, *No One to Turn To: The under-reporting of child sexual exploitation and abuse by aid workers and peacekeepers* (London, Save the Children 2008) available at www.savethechildren.org.uk/en/54_5706.htm. More than half of the children interviewed by Save the Children in all three countries knew of cases of forced sex with aid staff or peacekeepers. However, Save the Children itself seems not immune from similar practices: 'There were 15

United Nations (UN) officers in Sudan, Ivory Coast and Haiti, is once again undermining the world public opinion's confidence in the UN's capacity to operate according to its founding principles and purposes of peace and justice. Earlier, in January 2007, another similar scandal involving UN personnel had broken out in Sudan. In the latter case, according to media information, despite the fact that an internal report compiled by the United Nations Children's Fund (UNICEF) in July 2005 gave details about the problem and specified that the first indications of sexual exploitations had emerged within months of the UN force's arrival, the organisation at first tried to cover or deny allegations and finally awaited the scandal to explode before trying to react. In addition, the media reported that a number of complaints about the behaviour of international officers in Sudan had been previously filed before the competent UN local offices, but claims had not been tracked down nor had there been any attempt by the UN or local officials to interview the claimants. After the story was published, the organisation's reaction merely consisted in launching an internal inquiry, also asking media for help in collecting investigative material.[3] On the one hand, this episode reveals the organisation's lack of will and capacity in effectively dealing with human rights violations perpetrated by its personnel during peace operations.[4] On the other hand, it also illustrates the dearth of effective remedies at the victims' avail.

Where cross-control among internal agencies/offices fails, as well as internal investigation and settlement claim organs do not represent an impartial and credible instrument to seek justice against human rights violations committed by personnel belonging to international organisations, only an external and independent judicial or supervisory body may constitute a solid barrier against the

---

allegations of misconduct towards children made against its staff in 2007, three of which were proven and led to dismissal. Oxfam reported 12 allegations of exploitation or abuse in 2007, leading to three staff being sacked' (M. Pflanz, 'Six-year-olds sexually abused by UN peacekeepers', Daily Telegraph (27 May 2008) available at www.telegraph.co.uk/news/worldnews/2032996/Six-year-olds-sexually-abused-by-UN-peacekeepers.html).

3 K. Holt and S. Hughes, 'UN staff accused of raping children in Sudan', Daily Telegraph (3 January 2007); M. Pflanz, 'UN to hold inquiry into Sudan child abuse', Daily Telegraph (4 January 2007) both available at www.telegraph.co.uk. That of Sudan is obviously just a single case among dozens of similar episodes. See for instance the case of the Sri Lankan UN peacekeepers accused of sexual exploitation and abuse in Haiti in 2007. According to the UN spokeswoman Michele Montas '108 of Sri Lanka's 950 soldiers in Haiti were being sent home on disciplinary grounds over allegations of "transactional sex"', also involving underage girls (C. Parsons, 'Sri Lanka peacekeepers face jail if abuse proven', Reuters, (3 November 2007), available at http://in.reuters.com/article/topNews/idINIndia-30307420071103).

4 It seems remarkable that officially the UN itself recognises to some extent its own accountability for such disgraceful behaviours occurred during peacekeeping operations and affirms to be committed in making basic assistance available to alleged victims (see, for instance, UN General Assembly, 'A comprehensive strategy to eliminate future sexual exploitation and abuse in United Nations peacekeeping operations', Report of Prince Zeid Ra'ad Zeid al-Hussein, A/59/710 (2005), paras. 37 and 52).

risk of impunity. To date, international organisations cannot be sued before regional judicial or international supervisory bodies of human rights, while Member States can. In addition, the latter may also be summoned before their own domestic courts. For that reason, finding a circuitous way (the 'Italian job') to secure indirect accountability of international organisations by bringing Member States before courts seems the most successful short-term option, as it would practically bypass immunities and jurisdictional limits enjoyed by international institutions.

This article tries to briefly explain such a solution in light of the poor internal redress mechanisms offered by international organisations and the recent domestic and international jurisprudence on the topic. A first paragraph provides a short overview of the limited remedies available to third parties against institutions vested with international legal personality. The subsequent section focuses on the potential concurrent responsibility between Member States and international organisations for wrongful acts committed during peace operations and territorial administrations, also including a few concrete examples of human rights violations. There then follow some brief remarks on how to legally assess the mandatory nature of human rights law for international organisations, as well as a short note on the extraterritorial application of human rights conventions and treaties. The fifth paragraph attempts to 'close the circle' by illustrating a few guiding principles gathered from international and constitutional jurisprudence which may support the possibility of suing Member States before courts for acts performed *by* international organisations or by State organs acting *within* their organisational framework. An analysis (and a critique) of some recent case-law is included in the final paragraph. The conclusion stresses the positive consequences of such a pragmatic approach, bearing in mind that the latter merely represents a short-term solution which reflects the lack of clarity regarding the issue of international institutions' responsibility within the international legal system. Conversely, a successful option in the long-term could be that of either establishing real external and independent claims settlement mechanisms (which may secure access to justice for third parties – individuals and legal persons – while being also truly independent from the international organisation concerned), or putting international organisations' activity under the scrutiny of international courts/supervisory bodies of human rights.

II. A FEW REMARKS ON LEGAL PERSONALITY AND ACCOUNTABILITY OF INTERNATIONAL ORGANISATIONS

A. THE ATTRIBUTION OF LEGAL PERSONALITY TO INTERNATIONAL ORGANISATIONS AND THEIR ACCOUNTABILITY TO THIRD PARTIES

The attribution of international legal personality to international organisations represents the minimal precondition to the formal establishment of any kind of international accountability towards third parties.[5] Any further rule or obligation descending from the legal personality of an international organisation, as a consequence of the provisions included in its constituent treaty, generally only binds Member States or any other State which explicitly accepted such personality.[6] On the contrary, when an international organisation is not vested with international legal personality, the only hypothetical international liability to a third party[7] is a direct one, probably joint and several, of all the participating States.[8] International institutions vested with legal personality, as subjects of law, may in principle share any potential responsibility for wrongful acts with States.[9] However, in the case of violations involving only international organisations, limited liability is recognised in the absence of a contrary indication.[10] More

5 See on the point the *Nauru Case*, in which the International Court of Justice found that the tripartite entity in charge for the administration of the territory of Nauru was not vested with a separate international legal personality as regards the three founding countries. As a consequence, the Court decided the admissibility of the petition filed by Nauru against one of them – Australia (ICJ, *Case Concerning Certain Phosphate Lands in Nauru*, Judgment on Preliminary Objections, *ICJ Rep.* (1992) para. 47 – 48. See I. Scobbie, 'Case Concerning Certain Phosphate Lands in Nauru (Nauru v. Australia), Preliminary Objections Judgment', 42(3) *International & Comparative Law Quarterly* (1993)). On the legal personality of international organisations see gen. Y.M. Kamil, 'Création et personnalité juridique des organisations internationales', in R.J. Dupuy, ed., *Manuel sur les organisations internationales* (Dordrecht, Martinus Nijhoff Publishers 1988) p. 33.

6 UN General Assembly, 'Relations Between States and Inter – Governmental Organizations', A/CN.4/195 and Add. 1 (1967), II *Yearbook of the International Law Commission* (1967) p. 138.

7 Situations concerning international organisations' liability to third parties must be distinguished from cases involving the same organisations and their staff members. In these cases, permanent entities are often established to resolve potential disputes, as for the case of the UN Administrative Tribunals (E. Gaillard and I. Pingel – Lenuzza, 'International Organizations and Immunity from Jurisdiction: to Restrict or to Bypass', 51(1) *International & Comparative Law Quarterly* (2002) p. 11). For the purposes of this essay, where not otherwise specified, responsibility refers to third parties.

8 C.F. Amerasinghe, *Principles of the Institutional Law of International Organizations*, 2nd edn. (Cambridge, Cambridge University Press 2005) p. 412.

9 International Law Commission, *Report of the Sixty-first session (4 May to 5 June and 6 July to 7 August 2009)*, UN Doc. A/64/10, pp. 83–85 (hereafter ILC (2009).

10 C.F. Amerasinghe, 'Liability to Third Parties of Member States of International Organizations: Practice, Principle and Judicial Precedent', 85(2) *American Journal of International Law* (1991) p. 275. However, specific provisions restricting Member States liability are generally

important, the issue of legal personality implies the possibility for international organisations to be the subjects of active and passive responsibility before an international body. In fact, while, to some extent, it is possible for an international institution to be sued before a domestic court for human rights violations with or without vesting any international legal personality (even if the latter possibility is rather unlikely)[11], any decision concerning its potential liability to third parties before an international supervisory or judicial body would require its previous formal recognition by the international community as a subject of international law. However, also before domestic courts, a shared consensus on the legal personality of an international organisation is often a prerequisite for any further examination of its potential responsibility towards third parties.[12]

Therefore, when addressing the accountability of an international organisation, a court should initially verify its legal personality. This implies an analysis of: (a) the wording of constituent instruments, (*b*) the capacity to enter into agreements with other international law subjects and (*c*) the possibility to exercise independent powers, distinct from those of its Member States.[13] On the other hand, it has to be pointed out that, with some exceptions, the jurisdiction normally accorded to international supervisory or judicial bodies does not go beyond the international level and generally remains a category of public international law.[14] In addition, this jurisdiction sometimes explicitly excludes

---

contained in a minority of international organisations' constituent treaties, while the founding treaties of the most important international organisations scarcely provide for an explicit discipline of responsibility to third parties (C.F. Amerasinghe, op. cit. n. 8, at p. 276 – 277). Also the existence of 'mixed entities' seems to be recognised on an international scale. In particular, they would retain a distinct legal personality but would share secondary responsibility with Member States towards third parties (I. Cheyne, 'The International TIN Council', 38(2) *International & Comparative Law Quarterly* (1989) p. 419, quoting the opinions delivered by Nourse LJ and Ralph Gibson LJ in the *Tin Council Case*, see n. 12).

11 See gen. on the matter A. Reinisch, *International Organizations before National Courts* (Cambridge, Cambridge University Press 2000) p. 233.

12 On a national scale, domestic courts normally associate the concept of the legal personality of international organisations with the principle of limited liability for shareholders in corporate law, thus normally denying concurrent legal liability of Member States for obligations contracted or acts performed by international organisations vested with international legal personality. See on the matter Corte di Cassazione (SS.UU.), *Cristiani v. Istituto italo latino americano*, Sent. No. 5819, 79(1) *Rivista di diritto internazionale* (1986) p. 146; Swiss Federal Tribunal, *Decisions Concerning Award in Westland Helicopters Arbitration*, 28(3) *International Legal Materials* (1989) p. 691; UK Court of Appeal (Civil Division), *Maclaine Watson & Co. Ltd. v. International Tin Council (No.2)*, 3 *All England Law Reports* (1988) p. 293. See on the latter I. Cheyne, loc. cit. n. 10, at p. 418; J. Cameron, 'Case Comment: International Organisations – Legal Personality – Jurisdiction to Wind – Up', 3(3) *Journal of International Banking Law* (1988) p. 104.

13 B. N. Patel, 'The Accountability of International Organizations: A Case Study of the Organization for the Prohibition of Chemical Weapons', 13(3) *Leiden Journal of International Law* (2000) p. 578.

14 See e.g. the IACHR in the *Tablada Case*, affirming that its jurisdiction does not extend to the conduct of private actors which is not imputable to the State (IACHR, *Juan Carlos Abella v. Argentina*, Case No. 11.137, 18 November 1997, available at www.cidh.org, para. 175).

international organisations[15] and in any case, it cannot include international law subjects, as international organisations themselves, which are not party to the conventions or covenants establishing such a jurisdiction or are not in any other way subjected to it.[16] Indeed, other mechanisms are often set up by the international organisations to deal with individual complaints.

B. THE ESTABLISHMENT OF INTERNAL CLAIM SETTLEMENT MECHANISMS

The concepts of judicial liability and the right to compensation for damages caused by international organisations or their agents should be maintained distinct and considered separately.[17] In fact, though the former is almost excluded because of the immunity (*de jure* or *de facto*) from courts, the latter is often secured by the establishment of mechanisms for private claim settlement.[18] The establishment of settlement claim mechanisms is regarded as mandatory in the case that an international organisation is granted immunity from domestic courts.[19] However, these mechanisms mainly consist in mere internal administrative proceedings, whose outcome would still be a decision of the organisation concerned. Conversely, Member States should in principle ensure that the procedural standards of such proceedings are equivalent to their domestic standards.[20] These standards should

15 E.g., according to the Statute of the International Court of Justice, only States can be parties before the Court (Art. 35(1)).

16 ECommHR, *Confédération française démocratique du travail (CFDT) v. Council of the European Communities*, Application No. 8030/77, 13 *ECommHR Decisions and Reports* (1978) p. 231; HRC, *H.v.d.P. v. the Netherlands*, Communication No. 217/1986, A/42/40 Supp. No. 40 (1987) para. 3.2.

17 ICJ, *Difference relating to immunity from legal process of a special Rapporteur of the Commission on Human Rights*, Advisory opinion, *ICJ Rep.* (1999) p. 88, at para. 66.

18 E.g. the UN recognises the responsibility for damages caused by peacekeeping troops under its direct command and control (UN General Assembly, 'Report of the Secretary General: Financing of the United Nations Protection Force, the United Nations Confidence Restoration Operation in Croatia, the United Nations Preventive Deployment Force and the United Nations Peace Forces headquarters', A/51/389 (1996), para. 6 – 7, reprinted in 37 *International Legal Materials* (1998) p. 702). In addition it is provided that the UN should establish appropriate models of settlement with regard to any kind of disputes (UN General Assembly, 'Convention on the Privileges and Immunities of the United Nations', 1 *UNTS* (1946) p. 15 sec. 29).

19 See on the point ECtHR, *Waite and Kennedy v. Germany*, Application No. 26083/94, 30 *EHRR* (1999) p. 261, at para. 59; ECtHR, *Beer and Regan v. Germany*, Application No. 28934/95, 33 *EHRR* (1999) p. 3, at para. 59; ECtHR, *Fogarty v. United Kingdom*, Application No. 37112/97, 34 *EHRR* (2002) p. 12, at para. 36. The International Law Association (hereafter ILA) recommends to refer 'such claims to arbitration or establish a standing claims commission or ad hoc mixed claims commissions to deal with them' (ILA, *Accountability of International Organisations: Final Report of the Berlin Conference* (2004), 1(1) *International Organizations Law Review* (2004) p. 274).

20 B. Kingsbury, N. Krisch and R. B. Stewart, 'The Emergence of Global Administrative Law', 68(3 – 4) *Law and Contemporary Problems* (2005) p. 40. See also ECtHR, *Bellet v. France*, Application No. 23805/94, *ECHR* (1995) p. 53, at para 36: 'The degree of access afforded by the

in turn encompass the right to a fair trial and the right to an effective remedy, as affirmed in the most important international human rights instruments.[21]

Indeed, the practice of creating 'international administrative law' bodies within the administrations of international institutions so far has mainly dealt with internal dispute resolutions, rather than with complaints brought forward by third parties.[22] In addition, as for the issue of immunity, it may be noted that, while in principle this has been considered essential in order to guarantee the independence and effective functioning of international organisations, nowadays the latter would hardly be threatened by an immunity restriction or by the guarantee for third parties to submit their applications to a judicial body respectful of the rule of law standards.[23] Generally it seems that as long as international organisations possess the required financial resources to settle potential claims, responsibility is not refused, even if they prefer to negotiate settlements with other subjects of international law or through local claims

---

national legislation must also be sufficient to secure the individual's "right to a court", having regard to the principle of the rule of law in a democratic society. For the right of access to be effective, an individual must have a clear, practical opportunity to challenge an act that is an interference with his rights'.

21 See ICCPR, Art. 14; ECHR, Art. 6 and 13; ACHR, Art. 8. ECtHR, *Golder v. United Kingdom*, Application No. 4451/70, 1 *EHRR* (1979–1980) p. 535, at para. 34, 1: 'In civil matters one can scarcely conceive of the rule of law without there being a possibility of having access to the courts'; ECommHR, *Dyer v. United Kingdom*, Application No. 10475/83, 39 *DR* (1984) p. 252: 'Were Article 6(1) to be interpreted as enabling a State party to remove the jurisdiction of the courts to determine certain classes of civil claims or to confer immunities from liability on certain groups in respect of their actions, without any possibility of control by the Convention organs, there would exist no protection against the danger of arbitrary power'.

22 As for the UN, for instance, the standing claims commissions, provided in para. 51 of the UN Model SOFA, have never been established. Third party claims of private law type have been mostly settled without resort to their establishment (See A/51/389 (1996), para. 22 at 705). The procedure afforded has so far consisted in proceedings before 'local claims review board', which is basically a UN administrative body operating in the host country, reporting to the UN Secretary General (K. Schmalenbach, 'Third Party Liability of International Organization', in H. Langholtz, B. Kondoch and A. Wells, eds., 10 *International Peacekeeping: The Yearbook of International Peace Operations* (2006) p. 41). In Kosovo, both UNMIK and KFOR have created their own commissions for dealing with financial and other type of claims. 'However [...] UNMIK provides no opportunity for individuals to be heard or represented by legal counsel in their proceedings and all decisions are taken by a panel of UNMIK staff members. The only appeal possible against this internal first instance decision is the sending of a "memorandum" to the UNMIK Director of Administration. In contrast, although first instance proceedings before KFOR call for a single KFOR officer to take a decision, the appeals process incorporates many elements of proper judicial proceedings, including an opportunity for individuals to be heard or legally represented' (Ombudsperson Institution in Kosovo, 'Third Annual Report, 2002 – 2003', available at www.ombudspersonkosovo.org, pp. 4–5).

23 Gaillard and Pingel – Lenuzza, loc. cit. n. 7, at p. 15. See also Judge Loucaides' dissenting opinion in the *McElhinney* case (ECtHR, *McElhinney v. Ireland*, Application No. 31253/96, 34 *EHRR* (2002) p. 341, at para. O-III5): 'Therefore, one should be reluctant to accept restrictions on Convention rights derived from principles of international law such as those establishing immunities which are not even part of the *jus cogens* norms'.

offices, rather than dealing with applications filed before judicial bodies.[24] Nevertheless, in case an obligation to compensate arises, an international organisation may in principle decide to unilaterally limit its own financial liability to third parties[25], thus practically frustrating the principle of accountability without formally infringing it.

C. 'ACCOUNTABILITY' AND 'RESPONSIBILITY'

The concept of accountability for international organisations may be extended well beyond the principles of responsibility and liability for international wrongful acts[26], embracing the notion of general answerability in the exercise of lawful powers by any kind of authority.[27] As a consequence, third parties affected by acts undertaken by international organisations might embrace any individuals or legal persons.[28] This extended notion of accountability of international organisations is mostly agreed upon by scholars, who identify three different progressive levels. While the first only includes internal accountability, the second refers to liability for unlawful acts and the last encompasses legal responsibility for breach of international obligations.[29] The latter concept has been explored by the International Law Commission (ILC) in its Draft Articles on the Responsibility of International Organizations.[30] As for the use of the term "responsibility", it seems to be the most appropriate to better address the issue of judicial or quasi-judicial

---

24 See the praise paid by the UN Secretary General in his report on the financing of peacekeeping operations to the so called 'lump-sum' agreements, by which the organisation negotiates a settlement coming from a natural person, directly with the government acting on behalf of him/her (A/51/389 (1996), para. 34, at 707).

25 For instance, in 1998 the UN General Assembly (endorsing a proposal of the Secretary General) approved temporal and financial limitations on the liability of the organisation (UN General Assembly, 'Third – party liability: temporal and financial limitations', A/RES/52/247 (1998)).

26 According to Gerhard Hafner, 'accountability' 'is a legal expression of neither the common law nor any other legal system; it cannot be translated into several languages […]. The absence of equivalent expressions in the best proof of the absence of an established meaning of accountability as a term of law' (G. Hafner, 'Accountability of International Organizations', 97 *American Society of International Law Proceedings* (2003) p. 236.

27 M.N. Shaw, *International Law*, 5th edn. (Cambridge, Cambridge University Press 2003) p. 1204.

28 S. Burall and C. Neligan, 'The Accountability of International Organizations', Berlin, GPPi Research Paper Series No. 2, 2005 p. 7. According to the Commentary of ILC draft art. 9, '(a)n international obligation may be owed by an international organization to the international community as a whole, one or several States, whether members or non – members, another international organization or other international organizations and any other subject of international law' (ILC (2009), op. cit. n. 9, at p. 78).

29 ILA, op. cit. n. 19, at p. 226. See on the point V.P. Nanda, 'Accountability of International Organizations: Some Observations', 33(3) *Denver Journal of International Law and Policy* (2005) p. 387.

30 ILC draft art. 1 (ILC (2009), op. cit. n. 9, at p. 19). For the commentary to the article see *ibid.*, pp. 40–44.

liability of international organisations[31], above all because it directly refers to a breach of law. This expression will be mainly used in the following paragraphs.

D. THE ILC DRAFT ARTICLES

1° *International organisations as subjects bound by customary human rights law*

The ILC's work on the international responsibility of international organisations may clarify some further concepts. According to the ILC, a wrongful act, which entails international responsibility, would vaguely consist in 'a breach of an international obligation' of the international organisation concerned.[32] This norm resembles the analogous provision on State responsibility.[33] Such a violation implies the non-conformity of the act or the omission committed according to what is provided for by an obligation 'regardless of its origin and character', although such obligation must be pre-existing to the act or the omission performed.[34] The obligation in question may well include human rights. On this point, it is widely known that since international organisations are normally not parties to human rights instruments, they are not bound by human rights obligations as a matter of treaty law.[35] However, this does not prevent them from being subjected to those human rights rules which have attained the status of customary law or peremptory norms (*jus cogens*).[36] Therefore, to some extent, it may be said that an international organisation vested with international legal personality, may act in breach of customary human rights law and may be held responsible for that. In this case, any violation, if authorised by the governing bodies of such organisation, is to be considered as a clear example of excess or abuse of power.[37] Nevertheless, some scholars tend to accept that these customary

---

31 As suggested by Daniela Kroslak: 'Responsibility is linked to a set of standards – legal, moral or political – by which an agent can be judged. Moreover, if responsibility is used in this sense of accountability, then it entails the notion that some consequence could have been avoided' (D. Kroslak, 'The Responsibility of Collective External Bystanders in Cases of Genocide: The French in Rwanda', in T. Erskine, ed., *Can Institutions Have Responsibilities?: Collective Moral Agency and International Relations* (New York, Palgrave Macmillan 2003) p. 162.

32 ILC draft Articles 3 and 4 (ILC (2009), op. cit. n. 9, p. 20).

33 *Ibid.*, at pp. 52–53.

34 ILC draft Articles 9 and 10 (*Ibid.*, at pp. 22, 77 and 80).

35 A. Reinisch, 'Developing Human Rights and Humanitarian Law Accountability of the Security Council for the Imposition of Economic Sanctions', 95(4) *American Journal of International Law* (2001) p. 854.

36 ILA, op. cit. n. 19, p. 250; P. Sands and P. Klein, *Bowett's Law of International Institutions*, 5th ed., (London, Sweet & Maxwell 2001) p. 458; A. Orakhelashvili, 'The impact of peremptory norms on the interpretation and application of United Nations Security Council resolutions', 16(1) *European Journal of International Law* (2005) p. 60.

37 E. Suzuki and S. Nanwani, 'Responsibility of International Organizations: The Accountability Mechanism of Multilateral Developments Banks', 27(1) *Michigan Journal of International Law* (2005) p. 195.

human rights law norms bind international organisations insofar as they are in a position to practically comply with them.[38] The mandatory nature of human rights law for international organisations is further explored in paragraph 4.

2° *Concurrent responsibility of international organisations and Member States*

As previously mentioned, the ILC specifies that a State – organisation shared responsibility may exist within several cases, in proportion to the degree of control exercised by the organisation over the Member State concerned.[39] In this respect, one can distinguish between a concurrent or subsidiary international responsibility of Member States for acts formally carried out by an international organisation[40] and the responsibility of the same international organisation for acts performed by Member States.[41] As for the former case, some authors argue that generally such concurrent or subsidiary liability should be excluded unless otherwise provided for in the organisation's constituent instruments.[42] However, scholars and practice are divided on this point.[43] Practice shows several cases in which, despite international organisations' constituent treaties that explicitly exclude concurrent or secondary liability of Member States, such liability is regarded as potentially existing by international judicial bodies.[44]

Other ILC draft Articles further refer to the issue of concurrent responsibility. Under ILC Draft Article 6, the imputability of an international organisation for acts performed by State agents becomes possible when the latter are put at disposal of the organisations concerned.[45] While in this case the potential

---

38 A. Reinisch, 'Securing the Accountability of International Organizations', 7(2) *Global Governance* (2001) p. 135.

39 ILC (2009), op. cit. n. 9, at p. 82 ff. (commentary to Chapter IV).

40 It seems important to note how draft art. 57 of the ILC Draft Articles on State Responsibility excludes the issue of the responsibility of a State for acts of an international organisation because of the 'controversial substantive questions' raised (ILC, II(2*) Yearbook of the International Law Commission* (2001) p. 362).

41 See on the matter C.F. Amerasinghe, op. cit. n. 8, at p. 413.

42 C. Brölmann, 'A Flat Earth? International Organizations in the System of International Law', 70(3) *Nordic Journal of International Law* (2001) p. 332.

43 See on the point Lord Justice Kerr's opinion and Nourse LJ's dissenting opinion in the *Tin Council Case* (UK Court of Appeal (Civil Division) *Maclaine Watson & Co. Ltd. v. International Tin Council* (No.2), 3 *All England Law Reports* (1988) p. 257), quoted in C.F. Amerasinghe, op. cit. n. 8, at pp. 417 ff. and 433 ff. See also A.H. Hermann, 'ITC Judgment Undermines Confidence in the London Market', 3(4) *Journal of International Banking Law* (1988) p. 150. The Court was disunited on this issue: Lord Justice Kerr rejected all liability on the part of the Member States, while Lord Justice Nourse alone confirmed it.

44 See C. Brölmann, loc. cit. n. 42, at p. 333.

45 ILC draft Art. 6 (ILC (2009), op. cit. n. 9, at p. 21). See the draft article's commentary at p. 62 ff. See also the commentary to Part Two, Chapter I in ILC (2009), op. cit. n., 9 at p. 51, stressing 'the existence of cases in which an organization's international responsibility may be established for conduct of a State or of another organization'.

responsibility is clarified on the basis of the effective control exercised[46], it may be attributed to the international organisation without prejudice of a potential concurrent responsibility of Member States.[47] Yet, according to Draft Article 60, a Member State may be held internationally responsible 'if it seeks to avoid complying with one of its own international obligations by taking advantage of the fact that the organization has competence in relation to the subject matter of that obligation, thereby prompting the organization to commit an act that, if committed by the State, would have constituted a breach of the obligation.'[48] The following Draft Article 61 specifies that a subsidiary responsibility also exists when a Member State '(*a*) … has accepted responsibility for that act; or (*b*) it has led the injured party to rely on its responsibility.'[49] Under Draft Article 39, Member States are required to provide international organisations with the means for effectively fulfilling their obligations.[50] However, it seems that failure to comply with this provision does not automatically imply the responsibility of Member States.[51]

---

46 C.F. Amerasinghe, op. cit. n. 8, at p. 401.

47 ILC (2009), op. cit. n. 9, at p. 56: 'Thus, attribution of a certain conduct to an international organization does not imply that the same conduct cannot be attributed to a State, nor does vice versa attribution of conduct to a State rule out attribution of the same conduct to an international organization'. On the topic, one might consider the House of Lords' ruling in *Nissan v. Attorney General* (House of Lords 11 February 1969, 1 *All England Law Reports* (1969) p. 629), in which it the British government was held liable for the actions performed by British troops in Cyprus, even if the latter were acting under the UN control. The potential State liability was also recognised in respect of British protected persons (S.A. De Smith, 'Civis Britannicus Sum', 32(4) *Modern Law Review* (1969) p. 431).

48 Prior to the provisional adoption of draft Article 60 in 2009, draft Article 28 stated that '[a] State member of an international organisation incurs international responsibility if it circumvents one of its international obligations by providing the organisation with competence in relation to that obligation, and the organisation commits an act that, if committed by that State, would have constituted a breach of that obligation.' See ILC, *Report of the Fifty-eighth session (1 May to 9 June and 3 July to 11 August 2006)*, UN Doc. A/61/10, p. 283. Interestingly, the commentary of draft art. 28 (International responsibility in case of provision of competence to an international organisation) relied on the ECtHR *Bosphorus* and *Waite and Kennedy* judgments (ILC, op. cit. in this note, at pp. 284–285). Among scholars, d'Aspremont agrees upon the rationale of this norm (J. d'Aspremont, 'Abuse of the Legal Personality of International Organizations and the Responsibility of Member States', 4(1) *International Organizations Law Review* (2007) p. 91; J. d'Aspremont, 'The Limits to the Exclusive Responsibility of International Organizations', 1(2) *Human Rights & International Legal Discourse* (2007) p. 217).

49 See also the commentary of draft art. 61 (Responsibility of a State member of an international organization for the internationally wrongful act of that organization), ILC (2009), op. cit. n., 9 at p. 166).

50 *Ibid.*, at p. 122.

51 The commentary thereto makes clear that: 'The present article does not envisage any further instance in which States and international organizations would be held internationally responsible for the act of the organization of which they are members' (*Ibid.*, at p. 123).

III. POSSIBLE RESPONSIBILITY OF UN MEMBER STATES IN PEACE OPERATIONS

A. POSSIBLE RESPONSIBILITY OF CONTRIBUTING STATES FOR VIOLATIONS COMMITTED BY UN MILITARY FORCES

In order to address the issue of the accountability of international organisations, it seems unavoidable to analyse the position of the UN *vis-à-vis* third parties during peace operations.[52] This is primarily due to the broad activities performed by the organisation in such operations, being also involved in interim/transitional territorial administrations, as well as 'loyal' to the principle of 'integrating' human rights into the organisational framework of peace operations.[53] Although it seems that there is no evidence of a presumption of an exclusive or primary responsibility for the torts caused[54], the UN has anyway accepted responsibility for acts performed by its agents or troops during peace operations.[55] Generally, when Member States place military contingents at the disposal of an organisation, they acquire a dual legal status, being official organs of both the sending States and the international organisation concerned. Even if national troops are not formally integrated into the mission's military forces, the same double status may arise if they act as such.[56] Practice shows that the UN acknowledged responsibility for activities carried out by its forces during both the United Nations Emergency Force (UNEF) and the *Opérations des Nations Unies au Congo* (ONUC).[57] As for the mission in the Congo, following a letter received by the Belgian government, the Secretary General affirmed that compensating individuals who have suffered damages for which the UN could be considered legally liable was a 'policy' of the organisation.[58] Correctly, such liability did not include acts performed during

52 We have already examined the issue in M. Tondini, 'UN Peace Operations: The Last Frontier of the Extraterritorial Application of Human Rights', 44(1 – 2) *Revue de droit militaire et de droit de la guerre* (2005) p. 191.

53 K. Månsson, 'Integration of Human Rights in Peace Operations: Is There an Ideal Model?', 13(4) *International Peacekeeping* (2006) p. 549.

54 This is the opinion of Prof. Ian Brownlie, quoted in E. Suzuki and S. Nanwani, loc. cit. n. 37, at p. 194.

55 A/51/389 (1996), para. 6, at 702. See also M. Zwanenburg, *Accountability of Peace Support Operations* (Leiden/Boston, Martinus Nijhoff Publishers 2005) p. 86.

56 K. Schmalenbach, loc. cit. n. 22, at p. 35.

57 D. Fleck, 'International Accountability for Violations of the *Ius In Bello*: The Impact of the ICRC Study on Customary International Humanitarian Law', 11(2) *Journal of Conflict & Security Law* (2006) p. 195; R. Murphy, 'International Humanitarian Law and Peace Support Operations: Bridging the Gap', 23(1) *Journal of Conflict Studies* (2003) p. 20; C.F. Amerasinghe, op. cit. n. 8, at p. 402; E. Suzuki and S. Nanwani, loc. cit. n. 37, at p. 194.

58 L.B. Sohn, ed., *Cases on United Nations Law*, 2nd edn. (Brooklyn, New York, Foundation Press 1967) p. 53. Of approximately 1,400 claims submitted by Belgian nationals, the UN accepted

combat, if justified by military necessity[59] or otherwise by actions lawfully carried out in self-defence.[60] On the contrary, compensations for accidental killings by UN forces are reported as being accorded in the course of UNEF.[61] During UNEF II, the mission's Claims Review Board was instructed to accept the organisation's liability for acts performed by UN troops, unless the latter were acting on behalf of a national government, or the government concerned had agreed to be responsible for the damages caused.[62]

Nevertheless, it should be noted that the UN would, in theory, bear exclusive responsibility only in the case of a hierarchical subordination between the organisation and the troops concerned.[63] In military terms, it would be necessary for the UN to exercise the 'operational command and control' of forces[64], since the mere 'operational control' could still leave room for a concurrent (or even primary) responsibility for sending States. Therefore, in the case of a coalition of States acting under the UN aegis, when the contributing nations maintain the full command of their forces, the military contingents deployed do not assume the status of a subsidiary organ of the organisation[65], which instead is granted

responsibility in 581 cases. Following consultations with the Government of Belgium, a final lump – sum payment of $ 1.5 million was agreed (A/51/389 (1996), at 712).

59 It seems interesting to note how in Kosovo, according to section 7 of UNMIK Regulation 2000/47, only third party claims which do not arise from 'operational necessity' can be filed against both UNMIK and KFOR to the Claims Commission. Similarly, under art. 41 AP I and art. 3 Hague Conv. (IV), states are held potentially liable to pay compensation only in case of IHL violations (see on the matter E. Schwager, 'The Right to Compensation for Victims of an Armed Conflict', 4(2) *Chinese Journal of International Law* (2005) p. 422). Given several examples taken from the past peacekeeping operations, the 'operational necessity' rule is considered by the UN as being enshrined in customary law (K. Schmalenbach, loc. cit. n. 22, at p. 44).

60 A/51/389 (1996), para. 13, at 703; C.F. Amerasinghe, op. cit. n. 8, at p. 402.

61 C.F. Amerasinghe, op. cit. n. 8, at p. 403.

62 K. Schmalenbach, loc. cit. n. 22, at p. 37.

63 See the response submitted by Mexico to the ILC with regard to the attribution of the conduct of a UN peacekeeping force to the Organization: UN General Assembly, 'Responsibility of International Organizations: Comments and Observations Received from Governments', A/CN.4/547 (2004) p. 9.

64 K. Schmalenbach, loc. cit. n. 22, at p. 36. On the semantic difference between *command* and (operational) *control* see US PDD 25 (3 May 1994), quoted in 'United States: Administration Policy on Reforming Multilateral Peace Operations', 33(3) *International Legal Materials* (1994) p. 808. 'Command' is defined as 'the authority to issue orders covering every aspect of military operations and administration', while the 'operational control' results in 'the authority to assign tasks to (national) forces, and assign tasks to (national) units led by (national) officers. […] Within the limits of operational control, a foreign UN commander cannot: change the mission or deploy (national) forces outside the area of responsibility […], separate units, divide their supplies, administer discipline, promote anyone, or change their internal organization'. The same definition is reported in the UN Civilian Police Handbook (UN/223/TH/CIPO95) (1995) p. 12.

65 J.L. Grenier, 'Extraterritorial applicability of human rights treaty obligations to United Nations – mandated forces', in A. Faite, J. and L. Grenier, eds., *Expert Meeting on Multinational*

where the UN retains both command and control.[66] In the latter situation, one might assume that any violation of international humanitarian law (IHL) or human rights law committed by UN troops in their official capacity may be attributed to the UN itself.[67] As it might be observed, the 'control' requisite remains central in determining the level of responsibility.[68] In addition, in order to address the specific responsibility for the single actions performed, one should take into account any relevant applicable agreement between the organisation, the host State and the sending State, such as a Status of Forces/Mission Agreement (SOFA/SOMA) or generally participation agreements and memoranda of understanding (MoU).[69]

However, the possibility for the UN to retain both command and control of national military forces is remote[70]: '[i]t is absolutely clear that in practice the majority of contingents reserve the right to consult their own capital, particularly in difficult operations.'[71] Generally, as was the case of the United Nations Protection Force (UNPROFOR) and the United Nations Operation in Somalia (UNOSOM) I/II, 'missions are so comparatively ephemeral that the lines of political command and control cannot be formalised and regularised before the

---

Peace Operations: Applicability of International Humanitarian Law and International Human Rights Law to UN Mandated Forces (Geneva, ICRC October 2004) p. 80.

66 A/51/389 (1996) para. 17, at 704; P. Tavernier, *Les Casques bleus* (Paris, Presses Universitaires de France 1996) p. 98; D. Shraga, 'The United Nations as an actor bound by international humanitarian law', in L. Condorelli et al., eds., *The United Nations and international humanitarian law* (Paris, Editions Pedone 1996) p. 327.

67 As it was stated by Poland before the ILC: 'the responsibility of an international organization should be restricted to cases in which peacekeeping forces act on the basis of a specific resolution of the organization, and under the command of the organization. However, the responsibility of Member States cannot be absolutely excluded if the armed forces are acting on behalf of the sending States and/or are directly controlled by officers (commanders) from the respective States' (A/CN.4/547 (2004) p. 9).

68 R. Murphy, loc. cit. n. 57, at p. 20.

69 A/51/389 (1996) para. 18, at 705. This is the position of the Democratic Republic of Congo on the issue, submitted to the ILC in 2005 (UN General Assembly, 'Responsibility of International Organizations: Comments and Observations Received from Governments and International Organizations', A/CN.4/556 (2005) p. 29). See also 'UN Model Status – of the Force Agreement for Peacekeeping Operations', A/45/594 (1990) para. 6; 'Report of the Secretary General on the Model Agreement between the United Nations and Member States Contributing Personnel and Equipment to United Nations Peace – Keeping Operations', A/46/185 (1991), Annex para. 28; UN General Assembly, 'Model Memorandum of Understanding Between the United Nations and [Participating State] Contributing Resources to [the United Nations Peacekeeping Operation]', A/51/967 (1997), Annex.

70 R. Murphy, loc. cit. n. 57, at p. 41.

71 Commission on Human Rights, *Working paper on the accountability of international personnel taking part in peace support operations submitted by Françoise Hampson* (E/CN.4/Sub.2/2005/42) (2005) p. 7. Prof. Hampson submitted her first working paper to the Commission on 13 August 2001 (E/CN.4/Sub.2/2001/WP.1).

mission's ending.'[72] This provides little clarity as to the role of the UN in truly directing the conduct of operations, thus creating possible conflicting divisions of responsibility between the UN and Member States.[73] The attribution of conduct is not established a priori, but depends on the specific circumstances of the case.[74] Hence, the possibility of a direct responsibility of national countries for any kind of violations is therefore higher, including, if applicable, breaches of human rights law. Indeed, to some extent the UN itself has also acknowledged the existence of a concurrent responsibility for Member States contributing personnel in peacekeeping operations[75] and even the possibility of seeking a recovery from them in case of wrongful acts performed by their personnel.[76] Hence, it appears difficult to understand how one could deny the possibility for third parties to claim potential breaches of human rights by directly suing the Member States concerned. Recently, the possibility of bringing civil claims against sending States before their own domestic courts has been also highlighted before the UN Commission on Human Rights.[77]

A number of additional examples, also concerning the North Atlantic Treaty Organization (NATO), confirm this scenario. In Bosnia and Kosovo, human rights violations allegedly committed by IFOR/SFOR and Kosovo Force (KFOR) troops have been investigated by the respective sending countries.[78] If the latter claim to retain the jurisdiction over cases of human rights violations, *a fortiori* they admit a possible liability.[79] Effective control was also the rationale of the allegations moved by Serbia and Montenegro against several NATO countries in the case concerning the *Legality of Use of Force*.[80] The Balkan State argued that

---

72 S. Gordon, 'Icarus Rising and Falling: The Evolution of UN Command and Control Structures', in D.S. Gordon and F.H. Toase, eds., *Aspects of Peacekeeping* (London/Portland, Frank Cass 2001) p. 21.

73 B.D. Tittemore, 'Belligerents in Blue Helmets: Applying International Humanitarian Law to United Nations Peace Operations', 33(1) *Stanford Journal of International Law* (1997) p. 85.

74 M. Zwanenburg, op. cit. n. 55, at p. 129.

75 See UN Model MoU, op. cit. n. 69, art. 9. It provides that if the cause of liability is due to 'gross negligence or wilful misconduct of the personnel provided by the government', the government is to be held liable.

76 A/51/389 (1996) para. 42, at 709.

77 E/CN.4/Sub.2/2005/42 (2005) p. 13.

78 Amnesty International, *The Apparent Lack of Accountability of International Peace - Keeping Forces in Kosovo and Bosnia - Herzegovina* (EUR 05/002/2004) (2004), p. 3; K. Schmalenbach, loc. cit. n. 22, at p. 42.

79 J. Cerone, 'Minding the Gap: Outlining KFOR Accountability in Post - Conflict Kosovo', 12(3) *European Journal of International Law* (2001) p. 486: 'The national governments of the contingents ultimately retain significant control over their soldiers, bolstering a finding of individual State accountability for the acts of the troops each State has contributed'.

80 ICJ, *Case Concerning the Legality of the Use of Force (Serbia and Montenegro v. Portugal, United Kingdom, Netherlands, Italy, Germany, Canada, France, Belgium)*, Preliminary Objections, 44(2) *International Legal Materials* (2005) p. 299. See also the commentary to the case by C. Gray in 54(3) *International & Comparative Law Quarterly* (2005) p. 787.

the whole process of targeting as well as the choice over the targets to be hit by NATO air strikes were previously and individually agreed upon among the countries whose forces participated in the actions: as a consequence it was concluded that the legal personality of NATO was limited, leaving open the possibility to hold individual States responsible.[81] As a defence, the respondent States attempted to invoke the eventual responsibility of NATO for any wrongdoing. Such arguments were so shaky[82] that their responsibility would have probably been confirmed, had the Court pronounced on the merits. On the other hand, it seems noteworthy that, given the impossibility for international organisations (like NATO) to be parties to a case before the ICJ[83], Serbia had no option other than suing Member States individually before the Court.[84] On the contrary, regarding the military operations undertaken by UN troops in Somalia, both the Human Rights Committee (HRC) and the Committee against Torture avoided considering a potential UN co-responsibility in the allegations moved to national contingents[85], though probably only for the sensitivity of the issue. However, it might be noted that, for the same human rights violations, the domestic courts of participating countries supported the rationale of State individual responsibility as demonstrated by a number of different trials.[86]

The same consequences arise when a UN military contingent, formally under the UN command and control, continues to observe orders issued directly from its government, which, therefore, might be called to respond to any violations taking place, including human rights violations.[87] As for the fall of Srebrenica, for instance, according to a report commissioned by the Dutch government, notwithstanding the formal UN control of troops, both the Netherlands (sending

---

81 ICJ, Statement by Mr. Vladimir Djerić on behalf of Serbia and Montenegro, Verbatim record, 23 April 2004, available at www.icj-cij.org/docket/files/111/4373.pdf, pp. 31 – 32.

82 ICJ, *Yugoslavia v. Canada*, CR 99/27, Request for the indication of provisional measures, Verbatim record, 12 May 1999, available at www.icj-cij.org/docket/files/106/4625.pdf, p. 10: 'Joint and several liability for acts of an international organization, or for the acts of other States acting within such an organization, cannot be established unless the relevant treaty provides for such liability'.

83 It is also well known that the ICJ merely retains the power to issue advisory opinions dealing with the rights and obligations of international organisations and only at the request of the same organisations concerned. See the Statute of the International Court of Justice, art. 34, 68, 59.

84 K. Wellens, 'Fragmentation of International Law and Establishing an Accountability Regime for International Organizations: The Role of the Judiciary in Closing The Gap', 25(4) *Michigan Journal of International Law* (2004) p. 1166.

85 F. Hoffmann and F. Mégret, 'Fostering Human Rights Accountability: An Ombudsperson for the United Nations?', 11(1) *Global Governance* (2005) p. 53.

86 For a brief list of cases see M. Tondini, loc. cit. n. 52, at p. 203.

87 D. Sarooshi, *Some Preliminary Remarks on the Conferral by States of Powers on International Organizations* (New York, Jean Monnet Working Paper No. 4/03, New York University School of Law, 2003) p. 59. Human rights violations by CIVPOL officers are reported to have taken place in Cambodia, Salvador, Haiti, Bosnia and Kosovo. Some cases of misbehaviour are reported in UN General Assembly, 'Investigation into Sexual Exploitation of Refugees by Aid Workers in West Africa', A/57/465 (2002) Annex.

State) and the UN shared the responsibility for having left the city undefended.[88] With regard to the same tragic events, it is remarkable that the Netherlands had previously claimed for a limited territorial applicability of the International Covenant on Civil and Political Rights (ICCPR) in order to avoid any liability before the Human Rights Committee.[89] A similar rationale was at the basis of a case involving the British contingent of NATO. In a judgment before the High Court of Justice, the United Kingdom admitted vicarious liability for any wrongs committed by its troops in Kosovo, the Crown retaining command of the British forces notwithstanding that they were acting under the KFOR mandate.[90] In sum, as a general rule, the level of accountability of sending States should be tied to their concrete fields of operation and to the effective level of control exercised.[91]

B. POSSIBLE RESPONSIBILITY OF MEMBER STATES FOR VIOLATIONS COMMITTED BY UN POLICE FORCES AND CIVILIAN OFFICERS

1° UN police personnel

A more complex situation to be analysed concerns the status of UN civilian or military police personnel.[92] While every situation constitutes a specific case to be separately analysed from one another, generally, civilian (including police) staff

---

88 Netherlands Institute for War Documentation, *Srebrenica, A 'Safe Area': Reconstruction Background, Consequences and Analyses of the Fall of a Safe Area*, available http://srebrenica.brightside.nl/srebrenica. See A.F. Lang, 'The United Nations and the Fall of Srebrenica: Meaningful Responsibility and International Society', in T. Erskine, ed., *Can Institutions Have Responsibilities?: Collective Moral Agency and International Relations* (New York, Palgrave Macmillan 2003), at p. 184. The thesis concerning the concurrent responsibility of both the UN and the Netherlands was rebutted in September 2008 by The Hague District Court in the *Mustafic* and *Nuhanovic* cases (see The Hague District Court 10 September 2008 *Mustafic v. the Netherlands*, Case No. 265618, http://zoeken.rechtspraak.nl/resultpage.aspx?snelzoeken=true&searchtype=ljn&ljn=BF0182&u_ljn=BF0182, para. 4.17; and *Nuhanovic v. the Netherlands*, Case No. 265615, http://zoeken.rechtspraak.nl/resultpage.aspx?snelzoeken=true&searchtype=ljn&ljn=BF0181&u_ljn=BF0181, para. 4.15.

89 M.J. Dennis, 'Application of Human Rights Treaties Extraterritorially in Times of Armed Conflict and Military Occupation', 99(1) *American Journal of International Law* (2005) p. 125.

90 High Court of Justice, 7 April 2004, *Mohamet Bici and Skender Bici v. Ministry of Defence*, EWHC 786(QB) (2004), available at www.hmcourts-service.gov.uk/judgmentsfiles/j2458/bici-v-mod.htm, para. 2.

91 J. Cerone, loc. cit. n. 79, at p. 480. *Mutatis mutandis*, this is the position held by the applicants in the Bankovic case (reported below), regarding a 'gradual approach' to the notion of jurisdiction, i.e. proportionate to the extension of the control exercised (R. Lawson, 'Life after Bankovic: On the Extraterritorial Application of the European Convention on Human Rights', in F. Coomans and M.T. Kamminga, eds., *Extraterritorial Application of Human Rights Treaties* (Antwerp, Intersentia 2004) p. 120).

92 This is the case of Multinational Specialised Units (MSU), made up of police personnel vested with military status, such as the Italian *Carabinieri*.

recruited by the organisation act in the capacity as UN agents.[93] As a consequence, they potentially entail the sole responsibility of the UN for any actions carried out while on duty.[94] In reality, as for the UN police personnel, the situation on field looks different. For instance, let us consider the condition of the International Police Units deployed until 2002 under the aegis of the UN Mission in Bosnia and Herzegovina (UNMIBH). Despite the fact that they were officially granted the status of a UN body[95], a more in depth analysis reveals that national police contingents participating in the mission often maintained strong regulating links with the respective sending States.[96] These circumstances could easily imply the responsibility of single contributing countries.[97] Generally, it may be said that once the chain of command ceases to be fully independent[98] and allows for

---

93 L. Cameron, *Accountability of International Organisations Engaged in the Administration of Territory* (Geneva, University Centre for International Humanitarian Law, 13 February 2006, available at www.adh-geneva.ch/teaching/pdf/henry-dunant/2006/Lindsey_Cameron.pdf) p. 74. See also E/CN.4/Sub.2/2005/42 (2005) p. 8.

94 The status of CIVPOL staff members is acknowledged as being that of experts on mission according to art. IV Convention on the Privileges and Immunities of the United Nations (See UN General Assembly, 'Model Status – of – Forces Agreement for Peacekeeping Operations', A/45/594 (1990) para. 26) and, according to art. 1(a)(ii) of the 1994 Convention on the Safety of United Nations and Associated Personnel, they should be considered as being totally included among the UN personnel.

95 The 'International Police Task Force' (IPTF) was established by the UN Security Council Resolution No. 1035 (1995), following the *Dayton Agreement* (General Framework Agreement for Peace in Bosnia and Herzegovina, (S/1995/999) (1995), Annex). According to Annex 11 of the Agreement, IPTF seems to have been granted the status of a UN body. See also O. Simic, 'Accountability of UN civilian police involved in Trafficking of Women in Bosnia and Herzegovina', *Peace & Conflict Monitor Special Report* (16 November 2004), available at www.monitor.upeace.org/pdf/bosnia.pdf, p. 4.

96 E.g. the *Carabinieri* contingent operating within the IPTF (UNMIBH – CC – ITALCON) hierarchically depended on the Italian defence operational command (*COI Difesa*), while the effective employment planning was decided by the Office for Planning and Military Police of the 2nd Department of the *Carabinieri* General Command. The *Carabinieri* tactical commander was also tasked to gather and share intelligence information with the G2 cell of the SFOR MSU Command in Sarajevo (G. Moscati, 'La missione ONU – IPTF in Bosnia ed Erzegovina', 50(4) *Rassegna dell'Arma dei Carabinieri* (2002) p. 27).

97 As for the uncertainty with regard to the accountability of police forces in BiH, see C. Cordone, 'Police Reform and Human Rights Investigations: The Experience of the UN Mission in Bosnia and Herzegovina', in T.T. Holm and E.B. Eide, eds., *Peacebuilding and Police Reform* (London, Frank Cass 2000) p. 207.

98 The 'CIVPOL Concept' formally includes as a basic common characteristic of its mission an independent chain of command, reporting only to the Head of Mission (H. Hartz, 'CIVPOL: The UN Instrument for Police Reform', in T.T. Holm and E.B. Eide, op. cit. n. 97, at p. 30). Sometimes, as in Mozambique, such a chain of command is separate and autonomous from the civilian pillar and the police commander reports directly to the chief of the UN mission (M. Malan, 'Peacebuilding in Southern Africa: Police Reform in Mozambique and South Africa', in T.T. Holm and E.B. Eide, op. cit. n. 97, p. 175). The CIVPOL Commissioner (the head of the police force) in UNTAES (UN Transitional Administration in East Slavonia) was himself responsible for the managerial and operational control of the international police force (T.T. Holm, 'CIVPOL Operations in Eastern Slavonia, 1992–1998', in T.T. Holm and E.B. Eide, op. cit. n. 97, p. 145).

national control (even in minor part) over the deployed police contingent[99], a potential concurrent responsibility of sending States cannot be excluded.

2° *UN civilian staff*

As previously mentioned, the actions of civil servants working in an international institution potentially entail the international responsibility of the whole organisation.[100] However, what happens if the personnel is 'associated'[101] or simply 'seconded'[102] to the organisation by a national administration? In this case, according to ILC Draft Article 6, the issue of effective responsibility is decided on the basis of the substantial control exercised. Hence, even a mere *de facto* control, carried out by the sending country, could find the case for a concurrent responsibility of both State and organisation. Some international organisations, like the Organization for Security and Co-operation in Europe (OSCE), normally hire personnel by 'secondment', which means engaging national civil servants temporarily detached from their regular posts for an assignment within the organisation. Indeed, the same OSCE has admitted that under this system '(t)he Organization has little control over who is recruited [...] and the quality of control is less effective than for contracted personnel.' Secondment is reported as 'a factor that contributes to diminished effectiveness and credibility of the Organization.'[103] On this sole legal basis, a concurrent responsibility for the respective sending States seems more than likely, notwithstanding the usual tripartite agreement between the organisation, the Member State and the staff member concerned, which should entirely regulate the issue of potential responsibilities among the players involved in international missions.[104] It may be noted that the OSCE international legal personality is still in the making. However, the same rationale may be extended to any other international organisation which employs personnel seconded from national agencies.

---

99 With regard to this, the UN seems not to have the legal authority to take punitive measures against CIVPOL monitors and any potential disciplinary proceedings for their misconduct remains in the responsibility of the contributing countries. However, the UN authorities may resort to the administrative action of repatriation; followed by a recommendation to the national authorities to take the appropriate action against the subject concerned (O. Simic, loc. cit. n. 95, at p. 19).

100 L. Cameron, op. cit. n. 93, at p. 77.

101 According to the 1994 Convention on the Safety of United Nations and Associated Personnel (art. 1(b)(i)), '"associated personnel" means: persons assigned by a Government or an intergovernmental organization with the agreement of the competent organ of the United Nations'.

102 G. Hafner, loc. cit. n. 26, at p. 239.

103 OSCE Parliamentary Assembly and Swiss Institute for World Affairs, Colloquium on "The Future of the OSCE", Washington (5 – 6 June 2005), available at www.osce.org/documents/pa/2005/06/15378_en.pdf, p. 11.

104 As for the UN see UN General Assembly, 'Personnel questions', A/RES/47/226 (1993).

C. POSSIBLE HUMAN VIOLATIONS COMMITTED BY UN TERRITORIAL ADMINISTRATIONS: THE UNMIK CASE

It is self-evident that the responsibility of international organisations cannot entirely rely on the traditional principle of territorial sovereignty. However, there are situations in which an international institution, mostly the UN, acts as an administering authority over a territory and its population (e.g. the UN Administrations in Timor Leste or Kosovo)[105], or when the same institution retains the territorial jurisdiction over its headquarters and their premises.[106] As for the first case, the concept of accountability of UN interim/transitional administrations is naturally broader than the mere legal responsibility. Acting as a quasi-state entity would in principle imply both the responsibility for any wrongs caused and the accountability for the results accomplished[107], especially when the State apparatus has collapsed and the UN acts as a *de facto* government.[108] In addition, there are situations when international organisations operate within the boundaries of a State. In this case, since such organisations would probably be immune from domestic courts, the host State should afford effective remedies for the individuals within its jurisdiction, if affected by actions carried out by the organisations concerned.[109] However, despite these assumptions, the lack of accountability for violations of human rights during UN territorial administrations is widely reported, together with the poor level of remedies adopted.[110]

105 *Ex plurimis*, R. Wilde, 'From Danzig to East Timor and Beyond: The Role of International Territorial Administration', 95(3) *American Journal of International Law* (2001) p. 583; C. Stahn, 'International Territorial Administration in the former Yugoslavia: Origins, Development, and Challenges Ahead', 61(1) *Zeitschrift für Ausländisches öffentliches Recht und Völkerrecht* (2001) p. 137. Among recent contributions see L. Cameron, 'Human Rights of International Civil Administrations to the People Subject to Administration', 1(2) *Human Rights & International Legal Discourse* (2007) p. 267; C. Stahn, *The Law and Practice of International Territorial Administration: Versailles to Iraq and Beyond* (New York, Cambridge University Press 2008) p. 598.

106 E. Suzuki and S. Nanwani, loc. cit. n. 37, at p. 193; P. C. Szasz, 'The United Nations Legislates to Limit Its Liability', 81(3) *American Journal of International Law* (1987) p. 740.

107 C. Stahn, op. cit. n. 105, at pp. 114, 137.

108 Report of the Commission of Inquiry Established Pursuant to Security Council Resolution 885 (1993) to Investigate Armed Attacks on UNOSOM II Personnel Which Led to Casualties Among Them (S/1994/653) (1994), paras. 251 – 253.

109 M. Singer, 'Jurisdictional Immunity of International Organizations: Human Rights and Functional Necessity Concerns,' 36(1) *Virginia Journal of International Law* (1995) p. 90; L. Cameron, op. cit. n. 93, at p. 85.

110 A. Abraham, 'The Sins of the Savior: Holding the United Nations Accountable to International Human Rights Standards for Executive Order Detentions in its Mission in Kosovo', 52(5) *American University Law Review* (2003) p. 1291; R. Caplan, *International Governance of War – Torn Territories* (New York, Oxford University Press 2005) p. 195. We have already tackled the subject in M. Tondini, loc. cit. n. 52, at p. 203.

As for the UN's duty to respect human rights law provisions during administrations of territories, some scholars argue that '(t)he UN's role in the creation of human rights law, the recognition of these obligations as forming international standards, and the regular application of these standards provide strong support for the use of international human rights standards as the basis for UN obligations in interim administrations.'[111] Following this rationale, the Council of Europe (CoE) Commissioner of Human Rights confirmed that the legal and political responsibility for abidance by human rights standards in the course of UN territorial administrations lies with the Special representative of the Secretary General (SRSG), being the chief of the administration.[112] While this reasoning may in principle be correct, international authorities have always refused to be bound by human rights law conventions while performing their duty.[113] Moreover, such rejection couples with the lack of external *fora* to challenge and repeal the Administrator's decisions, also ascertaining potential responsibilities.[114] The need for such a 'constitutional court' was underlined in 2004 by the CoE – *Venice Commission*[115] in respect of the UN administration in Kosovo. Following the comments raised by the Commission, mechanisms to partially hold UNMIK responsible in terms of human rights law while discharging its administrative duties (thus trying to set up an elastic and indirect form of accountability) were provided through agreements concluded between UNMIK and CoE. In August 2004 an agreement was reached between the European Committee for the Prevention of Torture and Inhuman or Degrading Treatment or Punishment (CPT) and UNMIK, providing the Committee's access to all UNMIK detention facilities.[116] Initially the agreement with UNMIK was

---

111 A. Abraham, loc. cit. n. 110, at p. 1321.

112 CoE, 'Kosovo: The Human Rights Situation and the Fate of Persons Displaced From Their Homes', 16 October 2002, *CommDH* (2002) 11, available at www.reliefweb.int/library/documents/2002/coe-kos-16oct.pdf, sec. V 1(2).

113 See in the end, the position of UNMIK on the topic, stressed in a report submitted for the first time to the Human Rights Committee in March 2006 (Human Rights Committee, 'Report Submitted by the United Nations Interim Administration Mission in Kosovo to the Human Rights Committee on the Human Rights Situation in Kosovo Since June 1999' (CCPR/C/UNK/1) (2006) p. 28, para. 123 – 124): 'These (human rights) treaties and conventions are in any way binding on UNMIK. It must be remembered throughout that the situation of Kosovo under interim administration by UNMIK is *sui generis*. Accordingly, it has been the consistent position of UNMIK that treaties and agreements, to which the State Union of Serbia and Montenegro is a party, are not automatically binding on UNMIK'.

114 On the matter UNMIK has been extremely clear in refusing the creation of such a jurisdiction, to avoid compromising the privileges and immunities accorded to the mission and to its personnel, as well as the discretion of the UN institutions to interpret the mandate conferred by the Security Council (CCPR/C/UNK/1 para. 132, pp. 29 – 30).

115 European Commission for Democracy Through Law (*Venice Commission*) 11 October 2004, 'Opinion on Human Rights in Kosovo: Possible Establishment of Review Mechanisms', CDL AD (2004)033, available at www.venice.coe.int/docs/2004/CDL-AD(2004)033-e.asp#_Toc85341413, para. 104.

116 CoE, 'Agreement between the United Nations Interim Administration Mission in Kosovo and the Council of Europe on technical arrangements related to the European Convention for the

not implemented pending the outcome of similar negotiations with NATO concerning KFOR detention facilities. The final deal with NATO took almost two years to be agreed upon. Finally, on 19 July 2006, an agreement was concluded through an exchange of letters between NATO and CoE, defining the modalities of inspections.[117] Another agreement related to the Framework Convention for the Protection of National Minorities (FCNM) was earlier signed between UNMIK and CoE in June 2004.[118]

However, it may be noted that both agreements are extremely clear in specifying that UNMIK is not a party to the human rights conventions in question. In addition, these agreements also have different 'legal weight'. While the CPT – UNMIK deal has the aim to 'promote technical cooperation'[119], the FCNM imposes a real (soft law) obligation of compliance, by means of reports to be submitted to the Committee of Ministers of CoE on a periodical basis.[120] The path towards such a limited and 'pre-packed' form of accountability found its culminating point in the adoption of UNMIK Regulations 2006/06 and 2006/12[121], the latter establishing a Human Rights Advisory Panel. The Panel encompassed a limited jurisdiction[122] as well as provided for limited remedies in respect of human rights violations.[123] Basically, the establishment of the Panel merely represented the final outcome of a political compromise between UNMIK and CoE, trying to avert possible judicial interferences by the Strasbourg court over cases which occurred in Kosovo.[124] The Panel was in fact the only quasi-judicial body available

Prevention of Torture and Inhuman or Degrading Treatment or Punishment', 23 August 2004 (hereafter CPT – UNMIK Agreement).

117 CoE, 'Council of Europe Anti – Torture Committee gains access to NATO run detention facilities in Kosovo', 19 July 2006, available at www.cpt.coe.int/documents/srp/2006-07-19-eng.htm.

118 CoE, 'Agreement between the United Nations Interim Administration Mission in Kosovo and the Council of Europe on Technical Arrangements Related to the Framework Convention for the Protection of National Minorities', 30 June 2004 (hereafter FCNM – UNMIK Agreement). Both the CPT/FCNM – UNMIK agreements are included on the CD – ROM attached to the H. Langholtz, B. Kondoch and A. Wells, eds., 10 *International Peacekeeping: The Yearbook of International Peace Operations* (2006).

119 CPT – UNMIK Agreement, Preamble.

120 FCNM – UNMIK Agreement, Art. 2.3.

121 Respectively, UNMIK, 'Regulation No. 2006/06 on the Ombudsperson Institution in Kosovo', 16 February 2006; UNMIK, 'Regulation No. 2006/12 on the Establishment of the Human Rights Advisory Panel', 23 March 2006, available at www.unmikonline.org.

122 UNMIK Reg. 2006/12, sec. 2: 'The Advisory Panel shall have jurisdiction over [...] complaints relating to alleged violations of human rights that had occurred not earlier than 23 April 2005 or arising from facts which occurred prior to this date where these facts give rise to a continuing violation of human rights'.

123 UNMIK Reg. 2006/12, sec. 17. While in fact the findings or the recommendations of the Advisory Panel are of an advisory nature, the SRSG retains the exclusive authority and discretion to decide whether to act on them.

124 The compromise seems evident: on the one hand, members of the Advisory Panel are appointed upon the proposal of the President of the ECtHR (*ibid*, sec. 5.1); on the other,

to third parties, since, following the adoption of UNMIK Regulation 2006/06, the UN Administration had been excluded from the jurisdiction of the Ombudsperson Institution, which could at best enter into a bilateral agreement with the SRSG in case of proceedings involving UNMIK.[125] The Ombudsperson was also required to enter into further agreements with KFOR and UNMIK in order to access their detention facilities.[126] Eventually, Kosovo's recent self-proclaimed independence has progressively led to the sunset of the legal and institutional system in place during the 'UN era'. So far, this has entailed the *de facto* replacement of the current UN Administration with a EU-led civilian mission (European Union Rule of Law Mission in Kosovo – EULEX) in charge of assisting Kosovo authorities, judicial authorities and law enforcement agencies.[127]

IV. SOME BRIEF REMARKS ON INTERNATIONAL ORGANISATIONS AS SUBJECTS BOUND TO HUMAN RIGHTS LAW AND EXTRATERRITORIAL APPLICATION OF HUMAN RIGHTS TREATIES

A. THE MANDATORY NATURE OF HUMAN RIGHTS LAW FOR INTERNATIONAL ORGANISATIONS

In addition to the above-mentioned customary law rules, international organisations might be considered bound by human rights law by virtue of the provisions included in their constituent instruments or further adopted documents.[128] In the light of this theory, we assume that the founding treaty serves

the creation of the Panel itself is reported to 'address the effective lack of jurisdiction of the European Court of Human Rights over Kosovo' (UNMIK, 'Press Release of 5 April 2006', UNMIK/PR/1525, available at www.unmikonline.org). Laconic are the comments raised by the Ombudsperson Institution on the establishment of the Panel: '[H]aving a Human Rights Advisory Panel to examine complaints against UNMIK is better than nothing' (Ombudsperson Institution in Kosovo, *Sixth Annual Report, 2005 – 2006*, www.ombudspersonkosovo.org, p. 26).

125 UNMIK Reg. 2006/06, sec. 3.4.

126 UNMIK Reg. 2006/06, sec. 4.9.

127 The EU Mission has become fully operational on 6 April 2009. EULEX is regarded as a technical mission which should mentor, monitor and advise whilst retaining a number of limited executive powers (see the EULEX official website at www.eulex-kosovo.eu/?id=1).

128 With regard to the UN, see UN Charter, preamble, Art. 1(3), 55(c). For the OSCE, see e.g. Helsinki Final Act, 1 August 1975, para. VII; Charter of Paris for a New Europe, 19–21 November 1990, p. 3; Lisbon Osce Summit Declaration, 12 March 1996, para. 4 and 9. For the NATO see e.g. Founding Act on Mutual Relations, Cooperation and Security between NATO and the Russian Federation, Paris, 27 May 1997, para. I, Washington Declaration, 23 April 1999, para. 1, 3 and 7; Partnership Action Plan against Terrorism, Prague, 22 November 2002, para. 4. For the ILO see e.g. the Declaration concerning the aims and purposes of the International Labour Organization, Philadelphia, 10 May 1944, art. II and the

as a constitutional framework for the organisation concerned.[129] Therefore, human rights treaties and conventions approved under the auspices of such organisation, or anyway subsequently accessed, would apply to the organisation itself[130], while the same organisation could not disrespect or derogate from these instruments unless its statute would allow such derogation.[131] The obligations arising from constituent instruments would then represent international obligations which would bind on and constraint the decision-making power of international organisations.[132] Such limits may well include human rights obligations, which will be thus mandatory for the organisation itself. On the contrary, the fact that a binding act is adopted according to the organisation's statute does not exclude possible human rights violations. In fact, even if an act undertaken by an international organisation is retained as being lawful within the international organisation's internal legal order, it does not affect a potential characterisation of the same act as being internationally wrongful under other norms.[133]

In addition, one could consider that an international organisation is a derivative subject of international law and it does not retain any original power or sovereign authority, but only the powers and authority conferred on it by Member States[134], even though the relationship established between the organisation and Member States does not simply lead to an agency rapport.[135] If the conferred powers are compelled *ab origine* in their exercise by the limits

Tripartite Declaration of Principles Concerning Multinational Enterprises and Social Policy, Geneva, November 1977 (as amended in November 2000), para. 8.

129 As for the UN, see the ICTY judgment in the *Tadić Case* (ICTY, *Prosecutor v. Tadić*, Case No. IT – 94 – 1 – AR72, 2 October 1995, Decision on the defence motion for interlocutory appeal on jurisdiction, available at www.un.org/icty/tadic/appeal/decision-e/51002.htm, para. 28). On the topic see also *ex plurimis* B. Fassbender, 'The United Nations Charter As Constitution of The International Community', 36(3) *Columbia Journal of Transnational Law* (1998) p. 529; M. J. Herdegen, 'The "Constitutionalization" of the UN Security System', 27(1) *Vanderbilt Journal of International Law* (1994) p. 150.

130 See ICJ, *Interpretation of the Agreement of 25 March 1991 between the WHO and Egypt*, Advisory Opinion, *ICJ Rep.* (1980) pp. 89 – 90: 'International organizations are subjects of international law and, as such, are bound by any obligations incumbent upon them under general rules of international law, under their constitutions or under international agreements to which they are parties'. As for the UN case, see D. Akande, 'The International Court of Justice and the Security Council: Is There Room for Judicial Control of Decisions of the Political Organs of the United Nations?', 46(2) *International & Comparative Law Quarterly* (1997) p. 324.

131 D. Akande, loc. cit. n. 130, at p. 317; M.F. Perez Solla, *The Notion of International Responsibility: A 'Classic' in Times of Change?*, paper presented at the founding conference of the European Society of International Law, Florence (15 May 2004), available at www.esil-sedi.eu/english/pdf/PerezSolla.PDF, p. 3.

132 See the Commentary to the ILC draft Art. 9, in ILC (2009), op. cit. n. 9, at p. 77; A. Reinisch, loc. cit. n. 38, at p. 136.

133 ILA, op. cit. n. 19, at p. 256.

134 ICJ, *Reparation for Injuries Suffered in the Service of the United Nations*, Advisory Opinion, *ICJ Rep.* (1949) p. 182.

135 D. Sarooshi, op. cit. n. 87, at p. 52.

imposed by human rights conventions which the founding members are themselves bound to, the organisation concerned should be considered bound by the same constraints. Lastly, it is indeed logically sound (and scholars generally agree on the point) that an international organisation should be held accountable in respect of the violations of the human rights standards it promotes and universalises.[136] As a result, any human rights violation would infringe the promotion of those same rights and thus the organisation would be acting in breach of its statute.[137] However, this theory hardly explains the concrete level of protection to be granted and does not eventually solve *the problem*, i.e. the exercise of accountability, not simply the mere confirmation of its existence.

B. THE EXTRATERRITORIAL APPLICATION OF HUMAN RIGHTS CONVENTIONS

A further issue concerns the extraterritorial application of human rights treaties.[138] Despite apprehensions and oppositions made by a few States[139],

---

136 A. Abraham, loc. cit. n. 110, at p. 1313; C. Stahn, op. cit. n. 105, at p. 150; D. Akande, loc. cit. n. 130, at p. 317, quoting Judge Bedjaoui's opinion on the issue (M. Bedjaoui, *The New World Order and the Security Council: Testing the Legality of its Acts* (Basingstoke/New York, St. Martin's Press 1994) p. 7: 'It appears less acceptable than ever that sovereign States should have created an international organization equipped with broad powers of control and sanction vìs – a – vìs themselves but *itself* exempted from the duty to respect both the Charter which gave birth to it and international law'.

137 A. Reinisch, loc. cit. n. 35, at p. 857. See also the ICJ advisory opinion in the *Effects of Awards of Compensation Case*, where the Court noted that the promotion of freedom and justice by the UN could hardly be consistent with the impossibility for its own personnel to suit the organisation before a judicial or arbitrary body in respect of any disputes arisen in the course of duty (ICJ, *Effects of Awards of Compensation Made by the United Nations Administrative Tribunal*, Advisory Opinion, *ICJ Rep.* (1954) p. 57).

138 See generally on the matter F. Coomans and M. T. Kamminga, F. Coomans and M.T. Kamminga, eds., *Extraterritorial Application of Human Rights Treaties* (Antwerp, Intersentia 2004); T. Meron, 'Extraterritoriality of Human Rights Treaties', 89(1) *American Journal of International Law* (1995) p. 78; R. Wilde, 'Opinion: The "legal space" or "espace juridique" of the European Convention on Human Rights: Is it relevant to extraterritorial State action?', 10(2) *European Human Rights Law Review* (2005) p. 115; S. Borrelli, 'Casting light on the legal black hole: International law and detentions abroad in the "war on terror"', 87(857) *International Review of the Red Cross* (2005) p. 56; M. Gondek, 'Extraterritorial Application of The European Convention on Human Rights: Territorial Focus in the Age of Globalization?', 52(3) *Netherlands International Law Review* (2005) p. 349; L. Loucaides, 'Determining the Extra Territorial Effect of the European Convention: Facts, Jurisprudence and the Bankovic Case', 11(4) *European Human Rights Law Review* (2006) p. 391. T. Schilling, 'Is the United States bound by the ICCPR in relation to occupied territories?', Emile Noel Fellows Forum (Fall 2004), available at www.jeanmonnetprogram.org/fellowsforum/Schilling%20Forum%20Paper%20100504.pdf; M.J. Dennis, loc. cit. n. 89, at p. 119.

139 This is the case e.g. of the US. In a declaration accompanying the ratification of the ICCPR, the United States affirmed that the substantive articles of the Covenant were not self executing, thereby both impeding direct effects under domestic law and preventing it from

nowadays such application (and thus the jurisdiction of the main international judicial/supervisory bodies over Member States abroad) is well established with certain requisites, i.e. the 'effective control' by States parties to such conventions over individuals or areas.[140] Such a principle also applies to peace operations.[141] In sum, if human rights treaties and provisions cease to be

being the basis for lawsuits in municipal courts. At international level, the US also contested the HRC's authority to review the legality of the reservations made by the States parties, providing in the meantime for 'few references to the implementation of the Covenant's rights' in the reports submitted to the HRC under Art. 40 ICCPR. The HRC also declared 'incompatible with the object and the scope of the Covenant' the US reservations to artt. 6(5) and 7 of the ICCPR (both of which related to the death penalty). Those reservations included statements recognizing the US Constitution as the only font of legal constraints for the US themselves (J.F. Murphy, *The United States and the Rule of Law in International Affairs* (Cambridge, Cambridge University Press 2004) p. 330).

140 ICJ, *Legal Consequences of the Construction of a Wall in the Occupied Palestinian Territory*, Advisory Opinion, *ICJ Rep.* (2004) p. 136, at para. 108; ICJ, *Democratic Republic of the Congo v. Uganda*, Judgment, *ICJ Rep.* (2005) p. 168, para. 220; House of Lords, *R. (on the application of Al-Skeini) v. Secretary of State for Defence*, (2007) *UKHL* 26, paras. 54, 88, 96, [2007] *Human Rights Law Reports*, pp. 964, 972, 975; House of Lords, *R. (On the Application of Al-Jedda) v. Secretary of State for Defence* [2007] *UKHL* 58, para. 27, [2008] *Human Rights Law Reports*, pp. 389; IACHR, *Alejandre et al. v. Cuba*, Case No. 11.589, Report No. 86/99, 29 September 1999, at para. 23; IACHR, *Coard et al. v. United States*, Case No. 10.951, Report No. 109/99, 29 September 1999, para. 37; ECommHR, *Cyprus v. Turkey*, Decision on Admissibility, 4 *European Human Rights Reports* (1982) p. 586; ECtHR, *Loizidou v. Turkey*, Application No. 15318/89, Preliminary Objections, 20 *EHRR* (1995) p. 129, at paras. 56 and 62; ECtHR, *Cyprus v. Turkey*, Application No. 25781/94, 35 *EHRR* (2002) p. 736, at para. H17; ECtHR, *Bankovic et al. v. Belgium et al.*, Application No. 52207/99, 11 *Butterworths Human Rights Cases* (2001) p. 451, at para. 71; ECtHR, *Djavit An v. Turkey*, Application No. 0652/92, 40 *EHRR* (2005) p. 1008, para. 23; ECtHR, *Ilascu v. Moldova and Russia*, Application No. 8787/99, 40 *EHRR* (2005) p. 1033, at para. 331; ECtHR, *Xenides - Arestis v. Turkey*, Application No. 46347/99, available at www.echr.coe.int, para. 27; ECtHR, *Öcalan v. Turkey*, Application No. 46221/99, 41 *EHRR* (2005) p. 1018, at para. 91; ECtHR, *Issa v. Turkey*, Application No. 31821/96, 41 *EHRR* (2005) p. 588, at para. 71; ECtHR, *Treska v. Albania and Italy*, Application No. 26937/04, Decision on Admissibility, available at www.echr.coe.int; ECtHR (GC), *Behrami & Behrami v. France*, Application No. 71412/01, and *Saramati v. France, Germany and Norway*, Application No. 78166/01, 45 *EHRR* (SE10) (2007) p. 104, at para. 71; ECtHR, *Al-Saadoon and Mufdhi v. United Kingdom*, Application No. 61498/08, Decision on Admissibility, available at www.echr.coe.int, para. 88; HRC, *López Burgos v. Uruguay*, Communication No. 52/1979 (A/36/40 Supp. No. 40) (1981), para. 12.1; HRC, *Lilian Celiberti de Casariego v. Uruguay*, Communication No. 56/1979 (A/36/40 Supp. No. 40) (1981), para. 10.3.

141 HRC, *The Nature of the General Legal Obligation Imposed on States Parties to the Covenant*, General Comment No. 31 (CCPR/C/21/Rev.1/Add.13) (2004), para. 10. Most recently, see also the HRC Concluding Observations with regard to the Report submitted by the UK, which were released on 21 July 2008 (HRC, *Consideration of Reports Submitted by States Parties under Article 40 of the Covenant, Concluding Observations of the Human Rights Committee – United Kingdom of Great Britain and Northern Ireland* (CCPR/C/GBR/CO/6) (2008), para. 14): 'The Committee is disturbed about the State party's statement that its obligations under the Covenant can only apply to persons who are taken into custody by the armed forces and held in British-run military detention facilities outside the United Kingdom *in exceptional circumstances* [...] The State party should state clearly that the Covenant applies to all individuals who are subject to its jurisdiction or control'.

localised agreements and if their binding nature extends beyond the national borders of Member States, they will naturally compel State organs operating abroad. This would take place whenever an international organisation's organ/agent accomplishes an 'effective control' on individuals or areas during peace support operations, territorial administrations or in running refugee camps.[142]

V. THE "JOB": BRINGING STATES TO COURTS

A. FINDING THE RIGHT FORUM

So far, we have established the extent to which a potential concurrent responsibility of Member States for international organisations' activities may exist. In addition, we have briefly illustrated the circumstances that justify the extraterritorial application of the main substantive rules of human rights law to their conduct. The following step would consist in finding a supervisory[143] or judicial body whose jurisdiction might encompass Member States.[144] The main rationale for this indirect approach is that although such bodies seem to be unable to directly oblige international organisations to establish external accountability mechanisms for human rights violations, they may indirectly achieve a similar goal 'by holding their Member States responsible for transferring powers to international organizations without securing effective means of redress against the exercise of such transferred powers.'[145] According to the ILA, this transfer of power cannot remove acts of the organisations from the ambit of control mechanisms established by human rights treaties nor can it

---

142 R. Wilde, '*Quis Custodiet Ipsos Custodes?*: Why and How UNHCR Governance of "Development" Refugee Camps Should be Subject to International Human Rights Law', 1 *Yale Human Rights & Development Law Journal* (1998) p. 116. See gen. G. Verdirame and B. Harrell-Bond, *Rights in Exile: Janus – Faced Humanitarianism* (New York, Berghahn Books 2005).

143 According to Prof. Reinisch, the publication of 'general comments' by supervisory bodies like the UN ECOSOC specialised committees would represent a sort of 'incidental' form of jurisdiction over international organisations (A. Reinisch, loc. cit. n. 35, at p. 868). See on the matter Committee on Economic, Social and Cultural Rights, *Implementation of the International Covenant on Economic, Social and Cultural Rights*, General Comment No. 8 (E/C.12/1997/8) (1997).

144 See ECtHR, *Klass and others v. Germany*, Application No. 5029/71, 2 *EHRR* (1979 – 1980) p. 235, at para. 55: 'The rule of law implies, inter alia, that an interference by the executive authorities with an individual's rights should be subject to an effective control which should normally be assured by the judiciary, at least in the last resort, judicial control offering the best guarantees of independence, impartiality and a proper procedure'.

145 A. Reinisch, 'Exploring the Evolution of Purposes, Methods and Legitimacy: Accountability of Intergovernmental Organizations', 94 *American Society of International Law Proceedings* (2000) p. 206.

exclude the responsibility of single Member States. Indeed, Member States themselves would retain the responsibility for filling this potential jurisdictional gap concerning the control over the exercise of the powers transmitted.[146]

Theoretically, both the domestic courts of Member States[147] and the international human rights judicial/supervisory bodies would represent suitable *fora* before which disputes regarding the accountability of single Member States may be adjudicated. In practice, several and specific encumbrances often impede the full enjoyment of the right of access to courts. As regards national courts, the most common obstacle is represented by a restrictive domestic legislation on compensation for violations committed during specific periods, together with the absence of a proper rule of law and thus the strong likelihood that the case would not receive a fair hearing.[148] On the contrary, where independence of the judiciary from the executive is firmly granted, domestic courts might represent the most suitable option to affirm State responsibility. As for the Srebrenica massacre, for instance, about 6000 victims and surviving family members recently sued both the Netherlands and the United Nations in a civil procedure before the district

146 ILA, op. cit. n. 19, p. 244. This was also the rationale of the ECJ Advocate General, Poiares Maduro, in the *Kadi* case. The latter concerned the lack of judicial oversight over UN Sanctions Committee decisions on blacklisting. According to the Advocate General: 'Had there been a genuine and effective mechanism of judicial control by an independent tribunal at the level of the United Nations, then this might have released the Community from the obligation to provide for judicial control of implementing measures that apply within the Community legal order. However, no such mechanism currently exists. [...] As a consequence, the Community institutions cannot dispense with proper judicial review proceedings when implementing the Security Council resolutions in question within the Community legal order'. (ECJ, *Kadi v. Council of the European Union and Commission of the European Communities*, Case C-402/05 P, Opinion of Advocate General Poiares Maduro, available at http://curia.europa.eu, para. 54).

147 Italian Court of Cassation (SS. UU.), *Ferrini v. Federal Republic of Germany*, No. 5044/04, para. 7.1, 87(2) *Rivista di diritto internazionale* (2004) p. 539: 'È agevole però osservare, da un lato, che l'insindacabilità delle modalità di svolgimento delle attività di suprema direzione della cosa pubblica non è di ostacolo all'accertamento degli eventuali reati commessi nel corso del loro esercizio e delle conseguenti responsabilità, sia sul piano penale che su quello civile'.

148 For instance, in several cases concerning compensation for crimes committed by Nazi troops during the World War II, at first the claimants had attempted to adjudicate their disputes in Germany but were refused access to the courts because they did not fall within the precise terms of domestic legislation on compensation for violations committed during the war (e.g. *Ferrini v. Federal Republic of Germany*, subsequently ruled in Italy; *Prefecture of Voiotia v. Federal Republic of Germany*, adjudicated in Greece; *Princz v. Federal Republic of Germany*, decided in the US). In another case (*Al-Adsani v. United Kingdom*), regarding a civil proceedings against Kuwait in English courts, the claimant argued that bringing a claim before the courts of Kuwait could not have constituted an effective remedy, due to the absence of an effective rule of law in the country (L. McGregor et al., *Considering the Relationship between State Immunity and Accountability for Torture and other Serious International Crimes* (London, The Redress Trust, December 2005) p. 19).

court of The Hague. On 10 July 2008, at the end of a preliminary hearing, the court declared that it has no jurisdiction to consider the action against the UN, being immune from domestic courts.[149] On the contrary, it allowed the civil case against the Dutch State to proceed.[150] Other two individual lawsuits – once again, against the Dutch State and the UN –were brought before the same court in 2005. In September 2008, however, The Hague District Court dismissed both the claims declaring that the actions performed by *Dutchbat* should be attributed exclusively to the United Nations.[151] Nonetheless, the court's ruling appeared as being visibly influenced by the sensitivity of the issue (i.e. the threat of millionaire compensations to thousands of victims). Indeed, according to the court, the only way to ascertain the Dutch responsibility was to prove that the *Dutchbat* either: a) 'was instructed by national authorities to ignore UN orders or to go against them', acting accordingly; or b) 'backed out of the structure of UN command, with the agreement of' Dutch authorities, considering themselves and looking as being exclusively under national command. Incredibly, the court declared that the existence of a concurrent responsibility of the Dutch government should be excluded in the case the *Dutchbat* had received 'parallel instructions' from both national and UN authorities.[152]

Ultimately, a potential British responsibility for human rights violations allegedly committed by the UK against its own servicemen abroad was recognised in May 2009 by the England and Wales Court of Appeal. The court found that State obligations under the ECHR in some cases extends beyond territorial jurisdiction, including service performed abroad by British military personnel.[153]

---

149 The Hague District Court, *The Association of Citizens 'Mothers of Srebrenica' et al. v. The State of The Netherlands*, Case No. 295247, 10 June 2008, available at www.vandiepen.com/upload/file/srebrenica/Judgement.pdf. It should be noted that the UN responded to the class action lawsuit insisting it was immune under Art. 2(2) of the 1946 Convention on the Privileges and Immunities of the United Nations (See the declarations made by Marie Okabe, Deputy Spokesperson for the Secretary-General, on 8 June 2008: Office of the Spokesperson for the Secretary-General, *Daily press briefing of 8 June 2008*, available at www.un.org/News/briefings/docs//2007/db070608.doc.htm). See on the case O. Spijkers, 'The Immunity of the United Nations in Relation to the Genocide in Srebrenica in the Eyes of a Dutch District Court', 13(1–2) *Journal of International Peacekeeping* (2009) p. 197. The Hague District Court's decision was appealed in April 2009 (see the statement of appeal at www.vandiepen.com/upload/file/srebrenica/Statement_of_Appeal_7_april_2009_Van_Diepen_Van_der_Kroef.pdf).

150 A. Hudson, 'Dutch court rejects bid to sue UN over Srebrenica', Reuters (10 July 2008), available at http://uk.reuters.com/article/latestCrisis/idUKL1043914120080710; BBC News, *Srebrenica victims cannot sue UN* (10 July 2008), available at http://news.bbc.co.uk/1/hi/world/europe/7500456.stm.

151 See *Mustafic* and *Nuhanovic*, op. cit. n. 88, at paras. 4.17 and 4.15 respectively.

152 *Ibid.*, at paras. 4.16.1 and 4.14.1, respectively.

153 England and Wales Court of Appeal (Civil Division), *Secretary of State for Defence v. Smith*, [2009] EWCA Civ 441, available at www.bailii.org/ew/cases/EWCA/Civ/2009/441.html, at para. 35.

B. INTERNATIONAL COURTS

At the international level, human rights supervisory and judicial bodies seem often reluctant to interfere with the activity of international organisations, even in cases concerning acts of Member States carried out according to the binding decisions of international organisations.[154] For many years, this irresolute approach has represented the position assumed in similar cases by the European Court of Justice in reviewing the conformity of EC acts with human rights, aiming at defending the autonomy of the *espace juridique européen* from potential interferences of constitutional and Strasbourg courts.[155] In reality, the tension generated by possible concurrent jurisdictions of national constitutional courts and international judicial bodies may play a vital role in 'closing the accountability gap.'[156] The result of such a 'judicial dialogue' might in fact form 'a useful pattern of according effective legal protection to individuals against acts of international organizations.'[157]

Among international courts, a possible 'indirect' jurisdiction over cases involving human rights violations might be that of international criminal tribunals. The jurisprudence of the International Criminal Tribunal for the Former Yugoslavia (ICTY) offers some remarkable examples in this respect, due to the special relationship established in the past with the NATO force in Bosnia (IFOR/SFOR) by the Tribunal, the former being a sort of 'enforcement agency' in investigating and executing arrest warrants issued by ICTY. More specifically, the Tribunal confirmed its authority 'to require an international organisation or its competent organ such as SFOR to cooperate with it.'[158] As a consequence, the Tribunal also

---

154 A. Reinisch, loc. cit. n. 38, at p. 141; A. Reinisch, loc. cit. n. 35, at p. 868. The author reports the ECommHR decisions in *Melchers & Co. v. Federal Republic of Germany* (9 February 1990) and *Heinz v. Contracting Parties Who Are also Parties to the European Patent Convention* (10 January 1994).

155 The *Kadi* case seems to highlight a potential change of approach by the Luxembourg Court. While in fact in the decision of first instance the CFI had ruled against the possibility for EC organs to pronounce on Security Council's decisions, even when the latter could possibly violate human rights (but not *jus cogens* norms, see CFI, Case T-315/01, *Yassin Abdullah Kadi v. Council of the European Union and Commission of the European Communities*, 21 September 2005, available at http://curia.europa.eu, at paras. 218, 221 and 226), in the following judgment of appeal, handed down by the ECJ, the court affirmed that the same decisions must be implemented within the EU territory according to community and human rights law (see ECJ (Grand Chamber), *Kadi et al. v. Council of the European Union*, Cases No. C-402/05 P and C-415/05 P, 3 September 2008, para. 326, available at http://curia.europa.eu). Eventually, this rationale has been now adopted by the CFI as well (CFI, T-318/01, *Othman v. Council and Commission*, 11 June 2009, available at http://curia.europa.eu). On the *Kadi* appellate judgment see *ex plurimis* P.J. Cardwell, D. French and N. White, 'Case Comment: Kadi v Council of the European Union (C-402/05 P)', 58(1) *International and Comparative Law Quarterly* (2009) p. 229.

156 K. Wellens, loc. cit. n. 84, at p. 1179.

157 A. Reinisch, loc. cit. n. 145, at p. 206.

158 ICTY, *Prosecutor v. Blagoje Simic, Milan Simic, Miroslav Tadic, Stevan Todorovic, Simo Zaric*, Case IT – 95 – 9, Decision on Motion for Judicial Assistance, 18 October 2000, available at www.un.org/icty, para. 48.

admitted its cognisance of potential human rights violations perpetrated by SFOR troops in undertaking the mandate received as part of the jurisdiction exercised over the case.[159] However, the Tribunal did not refer explicitly to the individual responsibility of SFOR contributing States.

Until recently, a more effective jurisdiction over human rights violations, directly involving Member States' responsibility, has been granted by the European Court of Human Rights. In fact, notwithstanding the previous calls for a progressive harmonisation of the ECHR provisions within the comprehensive international legal system (thus including an interpretation of the Convention in line with customary and treaty rules relating to State immunity)[160], currently the Court seems inclined to reaffirm its primacy in defending the full application of the Convention, being the main human rights 'constitutional instrument of European public order.'[161] Indeed, according to the jurisprudence of the Court, the transfer of powers to an international organisation is not incompatible with the ECHR as long as the organisation concerned secures a level of human rights protection (as regards both the substantive guarantees offered and the mechanisms controlling their observance) 'equivalent', i.e. 'comparable' to that granted by the Convention.[162] Hence, provided that a comparable level of human rights protection is ensured by the same organisation, a rebuttable presumption of compliance with human rights is deemed to exist. 'However any such presumption might be rebutted if, in the circumstances of a particular case, it is considered that the protection of Convention rights was manifestly deficient.'[163] In addition, Member States are held responsible for all acts and omissions of their organs regardless of whether the act or omission in question was a consequence of domestic/international law/obligations. Neither may any part of a Contracting Party's jurisdiction be excluded from the scrutiny of the Court.[164] Therefore, all

---

159 ICTY, *Prosecutor v. Dragan Nikolic*, Case IT-94-2-AR73, Decision on Interlocutory Appeal Concerning Legality of Arrest, 5 June 2003, available at www.un.org/icty, paras. 32–33: '32. In the circumstances, the evidence does not satisfy the Appeals Chamber that the rights of the accused were egregiously violated in the process of his arrest. Therefore, the procedure adopted for his arrest did not disable the Trial Chamber from exercising its jurisdiction. 33. Thus, even assuming that the conduct of Accused's captors should have been attributed to SFOR and that the latter was as a result responsible for a breach of the rights of the Accused, the Appeals Chamber finds no basis upon which jurisdiction should not be exercised'.

160 ECtHR, *Al-Adsani v. United Kingdom*, Application No. 35763/97, 34 *EHRR* (2002) p. 11, at para. 55; *Bankovic*, op. cit. n. 140, at para. 57.

161 *Loizidou*, op. cit. n. 140, at para. 75.

162 ECommHR, *Melchers & Co. v. Federal Republic of Germany*, Application No. 13258/77, 9 February 1990, 33 *Yearbook of the European Convention on Human Rights* (1990) p. 52, at para. 145; ECtHR, *Matthews v. the United Kingdom*, Application No. 24833/94, 28 *EHRR* (1999) p. 390; ECtHR, *Bosphorus Hava Yolları Turizm ve Ticaret Anonim Şirketi v. Ireland*, Application No. 45036/98, 42 *EHRR* (2006) pp. 44–45, at paras. 152 and 155.

163 *Bosphorus*, op. cit. n. 162, p. 45, at para. 156.

164 *Bosphorus*, op. cit. n. 162, p. 44, at para. 153; ECtHR, *United Communist Party of Turkey and Others v. Turkey*, Application No. 19392/92, 26 *EHRR* (1998) p. 144, at para. 29; ECtHR,

States parties to the ECHR/members of international organisations will be responsible *ratione materiae* (thus not only *ratione loci* or *personae*) for the wrongful consequences of the organisation's decisions, if they have not ensured that the rights recognised in the Convention are effectively secured in the decision-making and implementation process.[165] On the whole, Member States will be deemed responsible either for (*a*) transferring powers to international organisations without exercising the due control over their acts/decisions or for (*b*) any wrongful act and omission committed by their organs operating within the organisations concerned. Obviously, this leads to the possibility of exercising a "case by case" review in order to ascertain the alleged violation.[166]

The Strasbourg court took an approach that is similar and consistent to the one adopted by the German Federal Constitutional Court (*Bundesverfassungsgericht* - BverfG) in the *Solange II* and *Banana Market* decisions, where the BverfG held that EC law is not mainly controlled by the constitutional courts of Member States until the level of protection of fundamental rights falls below the level expected by the Constitution.[167] Similarly, at least until the Treaty of Lisbon[168] was adopted in December 2007, the EC had always averted any potential ECtHR 'interference' by affirming its commitment to secure a level of human rights protection equivalent or comparable to the one granted by the ECHR[169],

Capital Bank AD v. Bulgaria, Application No. 49429/1999, 24 November 2005, available at www.echr.coe.int, at para. 111.

165 *Matthews*, op. cit. n. 162, p. 362, at paras. 33 – 34. See also the *Senator Lines* case, in which 15 European Member States have been sued before the European Court of Human Rights by a private company, claiming they were individually and collectively responsible for the acts of the EC institutions. Although the Court failed to judge on the merits, several authoritative legal organisations admitted as third parties in the proceedings urged the Court to accept 'the possibility of Member States' responsibility for the conduct of organs of international organisations of which they are members'. ECtHR, *Senator Lines GmbH v. 15 EC Member States*, Application No. 56672/00, Decision on the Admissibility, 39 *EHRR* (SE3) (2004) p. 15, at pp. 19–20. Among the intervening organisations there were: the Council of the Bars and Law Societies of the European Union (CCBE), the European Company Lawyers Association (ECLA), the Féderation Internationale des Ligues des Droits de l'Homme (FIDH) and the International Commission of Jurists (ICJ).

166 See Judge Ress' concurring opinion in *Bosphorus*: 'The concept of a presumption of Convention compliance should not be interpreted as excluding a case by case review by this Court of whether there was really a breach of the Convention'. (*Bosphorus*, op. cit. n. 162, p. 52, para. O – II2).

167 F. Schorkopf, 'The European Court of Human Rights' Judgment in the Case of Bosphorus Hava Yollari Turizm v. Ireland', 6(9) *German Law Journal* (2005) p. 1264.

168 Treaty of Lisbon amending the Treaty on European Union and the Treaty establishing the European Community, Lisbon, 13 December 2007, *O.J. C* 306 (17 December 2007); consolidated versions of the Treaty on European Union (TEU) and the Treaty on the Functioning of the European Union (TFEU) as amended by the Lisbon Treaty are published in *O.J. C* 85 (30 March 2010). The Treaty entered into force on 1 December 2009.

169 This principle was reported, for instance, in the early version of the Charter of Fundamental Rights of the Union, which was initially included in the 'old' Treaty Establishing a Constitution for Europe (Art. II – 112(3) and II – 113, 47 C 310 *Official Journal of the European*

probably in order to harmonise the ECJ jurisprudence with that of Strasbourg, with the final aim of avoiding hazardous jurisdiction conflicts. The entry into force of the Lisbon Treaty has modified the existing legal scenario, as the Treaty provides a legal basis for the Union to accede to the ECHR.[170] This will entail subjecting the Union to the scrutiny of the Strasbourg court. In turn, the end of the EU *de facto* immunity will probably overshadow the issue of suing individually before the Court Member States implementing EU decisions (though formally this possibility will still be granted). However, much will depend on the future accession agreement between the CoE Member States and the Union itself.

VI. THE "ITALIAN JOB" IN THE MOST RECENT CASE LAW (BE ASSURED – YOUR SINS WILL FIND YOU OUT!)

Other recent national and international cases show that the possibility of suing Member States before courts/supervisory bodies, for acts performed within the operational framework of an international organisation or by the international organisation itself, is to some extent successful. Most cases concern acts concretely carried out by states' armed forces (even if operating under an external operational control). As previously noted, such acts may be easily ascribed to single participating countries. Were Member States sued for violations committed by civilian or police personnel, a more incisive result would be obtained, though the rationale would be the same. Sometimes, even though a court/supervisory body may reject the claim on its merits, the validity of this approach is confirmed. Yet, even when the individual responsibility of Member States is denied, the legal reasoning used by the court in the decision making seems so distorted that accusations of political interference cannot be avoided.

Union (16 December 2004) pp. 53–54, never entered into force). However, the same 'equivalence principle' is now embedded in the slightly modified version of the Charter, approved in December 2007 just before the adoption of the Lisbon Treaty (Charter of Fundamental Rights of the European Union, art. 52–53, 50 C 303 *Official Journal of the European Union* (14 December 2007) pp. 13–14. With the entry into force of the Lisbon Treaty, the Charter has become legally binding on the EU institutions and bodies.

170 See Art. 1(8) of the Lisbon Treaty (which amends Art. 6 of the 1992 Treaty on European Union) and the Protocol thereto (Protocol relating to Art. 6(2) of the Treaty on European Union on the Accession of the Union to the European Convention on the Protection of Human Rights and Fundamental Freedoms).

A. THE *BEHRAMI & SARAMATI* CASES

The ECtHR has lately discussed the issue of Member States' individual responsibility in the cases *Behrami & Saramati*.[171] Both cases concerned allegations of human rights violations perpetrated by NATO military personnel. The *Behrami* case dealt with the killing of a Kosovar boy and the serious wounding of his brother, due to an unexploded NATO cluster bomb submunition. The victims' relatives sued France for violation of the right to life before the Strasbourg Court since the area of the incident was within the sector of Kosovo for which a multinational brigade led by France was responsible.[172] UNMIK investigation of the case reported that the incident amounted to 'an unintentional homicide committed by imprudence.'[173] As a result, no criminal prosecution was brought on. A further petition was filed by the victims' relatives before the Kosovo Claims Office, claiming that France had not respected the de-mining provisions included in the Security Council Resolution 1244. The petition was ultimately rejected on the grounds that mine clearance had been the responsibility of the UN since 1999, while the incident occurred in 2000. In the *Saramati* case, the applicant was arrested (by a German officer) by order of the KFOR Commander (a Norwegian officer at that time, subsequently replaced by a French one) and subjected to a form of executive detention for six months without any kind of judicial oversight.[174] He was later on convicted by a Kosovar district court and transferred to a civil detention facility until his conviction was quashed by the Kosovo Supreme Court and he was eventually released from detention. Due to the nationality of KFOR commanding and arresting officers, the claimant brought a lawsuit before the Strasbourg court against France, Germany and Norway, claiming breaches of

---

171 *Behrami & Saramati*, op. cit. n. 140, at p. 85. The analysis of both cases has been already included in M. Tondini, 'Putting an End to Human Rights Violations by Proxy: Accountability of International Organisations and Member States in the Framework of Jus Post Bellum', in C. Stahn and J. Kleffner, eds., *Jus Post Bellum: Towards a Law of Transition From Conflict to Peace* (The Hague, TMC Asser Press 2008) p. 207. See also K. Mujezinović Larsen, 'Attribution of Conduct in Peace Operations: The 'Ultimate Authority and Control' Test', 19(3) *European Journal of International Law* (2008) 509; G. Verdirame, 'Breaches of the European Convention on Human Rights Resulting from the Conduct of International Organisations', 2008(2) *European Human Rights Law Review* (2008) p. 209.

172 The case was communicated to the French government on 16 September 2003 (ECtHR, Case law Information Note No. 56, September 2003). The applicants argue that the French Command failed to take any steps to remove unexploded devices which it knew were in the area in which the incident took place, in particular without informing local population of the dangers, and fence off or mark the area.

173 ECtHR, *Press Release No. 693*, 15 November 2006, available at www.coe.int.

174 During the detention, the applicant's case was transferred to the district court for trial. During each trial hearing the applicant's representatives requested his release and the trial court responded that his detention was the responsibility of KFOR. We have already examined the issue of extrajudicial detentions in Kosovo in M. Tondini, loc. cit. n. 52, at p. 204.

several ECHR provisions.[175] The application against Germany was withdrawn upon request made by the applicant in November 2006.[176] In addition to the three governments involved in the proceedings, six other European countries submitted written observations to the Court.[177] Essentially, the intervening States defended the prevalence of the obligations descending from Security Council Resolutions over other international obligations of Member States (including human rights obligations).[178] Together they also maintained the lack of jurisdiction/effective control (supposedly exercised by the UN) by the respondent States over Kosovo or otherwise in respect of the applicants.[179] In trying to influence the final verdict by recalling the harsh political consequences of an adverse decision, almost all the intervening governments also declared that exposing military operations abroad to the ECtHR scrutiny could represent a serious impediment to the organisation of future peace support operations.[180]

On 31 May 2007 the Grand Chamber rejected the admissibility of the cases against France and Norway. The final decision apparently confirms the strict *espace juridique* doctrine, which had previously emerged in the *Bankovic* case, even though initially, a first pronouncement of the Court seemed to leave the door open to a change of course.[181] The Court's decision was based on the lack of jurisdiction *ratione personae*. The Court initially noted that at the time when both events occurred, KFOR was allowed to issue detention orders, acting within the security mandate received by the Security Council. On the other hand, UNMIK was held responsible for the supervision of de-mining activities.[182] First of all, this entailed the dismissal of the application lodged by *Behrami*, the alleged human rights violations being committed by an international organisation which is not a party to the European Convention. Secondly, in order to settle the

---

175 In particular, Art. 1 ECHR (obligation to respect human rights), Art. 5 (right to liberty and security), Art. 13 (right to an effective remedy), Art. 6(1) (right to a fair trial).

176 *Behrami & Saramati*, op. cit. n. 140, at para. 64. Indeed, Saramati was not able to produce any evidence in support of the involvement of a German KFOR officer in his arrest. On the other hand, Germany declared 'that, despite detailed investigations, they had not been able to establish any involvement of a German KFOR officer in Mr Saramati's arrest'.

177 I.e. United Kingdom, Denmark, Estonia, Greece, Poland and Portugal.

178 According to Art. 25 and 103 of the UN Charter. Indeed, according to Art. 25, 'Chapter VII Resolutions' (as in the case of Kosovo) are indisputably binding on Member States. On the other hand, art. 103 is considered by authoritative scholars not just a treaty norm, but a part of *jus cogens* (see on the matter M. Tondini, loc. cit. n. 52, at pp. 196–198). This rationale has been defended by Denmark (*Behrami & Saramati*, op. cit. n. 140, at para. 97), Estonia (para. 102), Germany (para. 106) and United Kingdom (para. 113).

179 See the statements of France and Norway (op. cit. n. 171, at paras. 83 and 95), Germany (para. 107), Greece (para. 109), United Kingdom (indirectly at para. 112).

180 *Behrami & Saramati*, op. cit. n. 140, at paras. 90, 94 (France and Norway), 101 (Denmark), 108 (Germany), 111 (Poland), 115 (United Kingdom).

181 P. Leach, 'The British Military in Iraq: The Applicability of the *Espace Juridique* Doctrine Under the European Convention on Human Rights', *Public Law* (2005) p. 452.

182 *Behrami & Saramati*, op. cit. n. 140, at para. 127.

Saramati case, it became essential to address the issue of the KFOR legal status and the potential concurrent responsibility of contributing States. As for the first issue, the Court affirmed that the responsibility for any actions performed by KFOR was to be attributed directly to the UN (through the Security Council).[183] Conversely, the concurrent responsibility issue was rapidly excluded by the Court on the basis of the 'effectiveness (including the unity) of NATO's operational command… [and] control.'[184] At this point, following the rationale of *Bosphorus*, the Court should only pronounce on the existence of a possible *culpa in vigilando* for KFOR contributing States, in the event they transferred powers to NATO or the UN without exercising due control. The Court did not decide on the issue. On the contrary, it considered *Behrami & Saramati* as essentially different from *Bosphorus*.[185] The Court then restricted itself to reaffirm the prevalence of Security Council resolutions over any other treaty obligations of UN Member States.[186] This is to say that such scrutiny could not extend to "acts and omissions of Contracting Parties which are covered by UNSC Resolutions", because this would entail 'to interfere with the fulfilment of the UN's key mission in this field [and] with the effective conduct of its operations', resulting with imposing conditions on the Security Council on the implementation of its Resolutions.[187]

The Court's reasoning in the *Behrami & Saramati* cases seems illogical and bisarre. Let us consider the attribution of KFOR actions to the UN. The Resolution 1244 (1999), which mandated both KFOR and UNMIK, does not draw up any real functional or hierarchical link between the international military presence in Kosovo and the Security Council. On the contrary it merely requires KFOR to submit reports to it from time to time.[188] Moreover, since the operational command and control was in the hands of a military force mostly belonging to NATO, the attribution of the potential human rights violations solely to the UN was therefore misjudged. This would imply that the UN is, in principle, internationally liable for any KFOR action within the mandate

183 *Behrami & Saramati*, op. cit. n. 140, at paras. 133–137. According to the Court, although the Security Council retains the 'ultimate authority and control' over KFOR actions (para. 134), it has delegated the 'operational command' of forces to NATO. The latter has in turn established KFOR, also including non-Member States (para. 135). The link between KFOR and the Security Council is acknowledged in the duty for the Command of the military presence to report time by time to the Council, 'as to allow the UNSC to exercise its overall authority and control'. Yet, 'the requirement that the SG presents the KFOR report to the UNSC was an added safeguard' (para. 134).

184 *Behrami & Saramati*, op. cit. n. 140, at para. 139.

185 According to the Court, 'in the present cases, the impugned acts and omissions of KFOR and UNMIK [could not] be attributed to the respondent States', whereas in the *Bosphorus* case the alleged violations had taken place on the Irish soil and could be imputed to the Irish government (*Behrami & Saramati*, op. cit. n. 140, at para. 151).

186 *Behrami & Saramati*, op. cit. n. 140, at para. 147.

187 *Ibid.*, at para. 149.

188 S/RES/1244 (1999), para. 11.

received. However, first and foremost, this does not exclude that the responsibility for such action may also be attributable to the respondent States, nor does it address the issue of whether the applicants fell within the respondent States' jurisdiction.[189] Secondly, in referring to the mandatory nature of Security Council Resolutions, the Court did not take into account the possible application of customary human rights law and *ius cogens* provisions.[190] Thirdly, the difference between *Bosphorus* and *Saramati*, as highlighted by the Court (basically that in *Bosphorus* it was a specific Member State to carry out the alleged violations), does not affect the potential responsibility for *culpa in vigilando* of contributing States. Finally, in addressing the issue of the respondent States' potential responsibility, the Court did not consider the provisions included in ILC Draft Articles 28 and 29 (now Draft Articles 60 and 61). The decision practically results in a black cheque for any UN Member States participating in an international military operation, even if only mandated (and not directly controlled) by the Security Council.

The ECtHR decision in *Behrami & Saramati* will probably share the same fate as that in *Bankovic*. Just like the latter was practically bypassed in the following decisions of the Strasbourg Court, the most recent ECtHR case-law on the issues of jurisdiction and attribution of responsibility does not even mention the *Behrami & Saramati* cases. In *Al-Saadoon & Mufdhi*[191] the ECtHR pronounced on the admissibility of an application brought forward by two Iraqi nationals, who had been detained in a British detention facility in Iraq from 2003 to 2008 and then transferred to Iraqi authorities for prosecution. The applicants alleged that their transfer and trial (held before the Iraqi High Tribunal) were in breach

189 A. Sari, 'Jurisdiction and International Responsibility in Peace Support Operations: The Behrami and Saramati Cases', 8(1) *Human Rights Law Review* (2008) p. 159.

190 See the recent EC Court of First Instance case-law, where the Court affirmed its jurisdiction in cases concerning violations of *jus cogens* norms, occurred while implementing Security Council Resolutions (CFI, *Kadi*, op. cit. n. 155, at para. 226; CFI, Case T-306/01, *Yusuf v. Council of the European Union*, at para. 277; CFI, Case T-253/02, *Ayadi v. Council of the European Union*, at paras. 101 and 116; CFI, Case T-49/04, *Hassan v. Council of the European Union*, at para. 92. All the decisions are available at http://curia.europa.eu). See also R.S. Brown, 'Kadi v. Council of the European Union and Commission of the European Communities: Executive Power and Judicial Supervision at European Level', 4 *European Human Rights Law Review* (2006) p. 456; M. Bulterman, 'Fundamental Rights and the United Nations Financial Sanction Regime: The *Kadi* and *Yusuf* Judgments of the Court of First Instance of the European Communities', 19 *Leiden Journal of International Law* (2006) p. 753. As mentioned earlier (see n. 155), since September 2008 the *jus cogens* issue has lost much of its appeal. Currently, the Luxembourg Court itself is in fact more inclined to recognize its jurisdiction over any alleged human rights violations occurred in the implementation of Security Council Resolutions, even in the case such violations do not infringe *jus cogens* norms. This makes the ECtHR judgment in *Behrami & Saramati* even odder.

191 *Al-Saadoon and Mufdhi v. United Kingdom*, op. cit. n. 140. In this decision the *Behrami & Saramati* cases are not even quoted, apart from a short mention in a memorial submitted to the court by a third party (see at para. 82).

of a number of ECHR provisions. Not only the court confirmed its jurisdiction over the case, but it specified that 'given the total and exclusive *de facto*, and subsequently also *de jure*, control exercised by the United Kingdom authorities over the premises in question, the individuals detained there, including the applicants, were within the United Kingdom's jurisdiction' (para. 88). In other words, in *Al-Saadoon & Mufdhi* the attribution issue returns to be a pure 'matter of fact', and it is no more determined on the basis of the mere Security Council's 'overall authority and control' over the mission, as in *Behrami & Saramati*.

B. THE *AL-JEDDA* CASE

The same question examined by the ECtHR in *Behrami & Saramati* (i.e. the potential attribution of responsibility to Member States for human rights violations that may occur during peace operations mandated by the UN) was then at the centre of the House of Lords decision in the *Al-Jedda* case (12 December 2007).[192] The latter concerned the detention of an individual (Mr. *Al-Jedda*, who was also a British national) by UK forces in Iraq for security reasons, after the formal end of occupation in 2004. The Court pronounced on two pivotal issues: (*a*) whether the conduct of British forces in Iraq is attributable to the UK or to the UN, and (*b*) what the final outcome of the interplay between the obligations for Member States descending from Chapter VII Resolutions (Articles 25 and 103 of the UN Charter[193]) and the duty of securing the right to liberty under the ECHR (Article 5) is. On the former issue, the majority (four to one) ruled that the responsibility for any British forces' wrongful act in Iraq was to be attributed to the UK.[194] According to the Court, 'it cannot realistically be said that US and UK forces were under the effective command and control of the UN.'[195] It is noteworthy that the most serious obstacle for the Court to reach this

192 House of Lords, *R. (On the Application of Al-Jedda) v. Secretary of State for Defence* [2007] UKHL 58, [2008] *Human Rights Law Reports* p. 374.

193 See *supra* n. 178.

194 *R. (On the Application of Al-Jedda) v. Secretary of State for Defence*, op. cit. n. 192, at paras. 25 (Lord Bingham), 124 (Baroness Hale), 131 (Lord Carswell), 149 (Lord Brown). In the opinion of Lord Bingham (agreed by the other majority judges, with the exception of Lord Brown), the settlement of the case requires the Court to answer a number of questions: 'Were UK forces placed at the disposal of the UN? Did the UN exercise effective control over the conduct of UK forces? Is the specific conduct of the UK forces in detaining the appellant to be attributed to the UN rather than the United Kingdom? Did the UN have effective command and control over the conduct of UK forces when they detained the appellant? Were the UK forces part of a UN peacekeeping force in Iraq?' (para. 22). Indeed, Lord Bingham's answer to all these questions was in the negative.

195 *R. (On the Application of Al-Jedda) v. Secretary of State for Defence*, op. cit. n. 192, at para. 23. Lord Bingham further added 'It has not, to my knowledge, been suggested that the treatment of detainees at Abu Ghraib was attributable to the UN rather than the United States'.

apparently easy conclusion was exactly *Behrami & Saramati*.[196] Basically, the Lords tried to find a circuitous way to sidestep the Grand Chamber's decision by refusing the analogy of the situation in Iraq with that of Kosovo. Nevertheless, this revealed itself to be quite difficult, as demonstrated by the uncertainty on the issue expressed by Lord Brown in his 'postscript' to the decision. He argued that the only possible difference between Iraq and Kosovo was the absence of 'ultimate authority and control' over forces by the UN in Iraq: an expression that, as he underlined, is 'somewhat elusive.'[197] Another vague opinion was that of Lord Bingham's:

> 'The analogy with the situation in Kosovo breaks down … at almost every point. The international security and civil presences in Kosovo were established at the express behest of the UN and operated under its auspices, with UNMIK a subsidiary organ of the UN. The multinational force in Iraq was not established at the behest of the UN, was not mandated to operate under UN auspices and was not a subsidiary organ of the UN. There was no delegation of UN power in Iraq.'[198]

However, in *Behrami & Saramati* the ECtHR did not consider KFOR as being a UN subsidiary organ. So, why is this issue deemed decisive by the House of Lords?[199] In truth, at the time the alleged violations occurred, both the MNF in Iraq and the KFOR in Kosovo could be retained as being UN mandated forces, so that they should in theory be subjected to the same rules on the attribution of responsibility. Therefore following the rationale of *Behrami & Saramati*, in principle the UK should have enjoyed the same *de facto* immunity of France and Norway.[200]

The second issue examined by the Court was the legality of the appellant's detention. This entailed addressing the issue of the existing legal regime in Iraq resulting from the concurrent application of the Security Council Resolution 1546 (which imposed obligations upon Member States by virtue of Articles 25 and 103 of the UN Charter) and Article 5(1) of the ECHR. On the point, the Law Lords observed that the human rights provided in the European Convention may be modified or qualified to the extent necessary to comply with the obligations imposed by Security Council resolutions.[201] In particular, the MNF was authorised by the Security Council to 'take all necessary measures to

196 Indeed, it was just following the release of the ECtHR decision, that the British government raised the issue of the attribution of responsibility in the *Al-Jedda* case. Such an issue had never been submitted before in the previous stages of the proceedings.

197 *R. (On the Application of Al-Jedda) v. Secretary of State for Defence*, op. cit. n. 192, at para. 148.

198 *Ibid.*, para. 24.

199 K. Mujezinović Larsen, loc. cit. n. 171, at p. 526.

200 This is also the minority opinion of Lord Rodger (*R. (On the Application of Al-Jedda) v. Secretary of State for Defence*, op. cit. n. 192, at para. 91).

201 *Ibid.*, at paras. 34 (Lord Bingham), 118 (Lord Rodger), 125 (Baroness Hale), 136 (Lord Carswell), 152 (Lord Brown).

contribute to the maintenance of security and stability in Iraq'[202], including 'internment where this is necessary for imperative reasons of security.'[203] Hence, the House of Lords dismissed the appeal against the detention affirming that the deprivation of liberty suffered by the appellant was justified by 'imperative reasons of security' and this fell within the mandate received under Security Council Resolution 1546 (2004).[204]

Again, the Court's reasoning in this instance is not very convincing. In fact, Article 103 only refers to the primacy of Member States' *obligations* under the UN Charter, while the detention (as a measure required to maintain stability) was simply *authorised* by the Council. Furthermore, the British authorities failed to demonstrate the necessity of Mr. *Al-Jedda*'s internment.[205] In practice, the Court accepted the view that 'Art. 103 can act as a trump card, albeit with some qualifications.'[206]

C. OTHER RELEVANT CASES

In addition to the cases quoted hitherto, there are a number of relevant applications which have been rejected and not heard by the competent international court/supervisory body.

1° The Mehmeti case

In the *Mehmeti* case (*Mehmeti et al. v. UNMIK*), a group of Kosovar Roma residents summoned the UN Administration in Kosovo due to the diseases suffered as a consequence of the establishment of their IDP (Internally Displaced Persons) camp in a well known contaminated area near Mitrovica (*Trepca* mining complex area).[207] Since UNMIK or the UN are not parties to the ECHR, the case evidently fell outside the Court's jurisdiction, notwithstanding the

202 S/RES/1546 (2004), para. 10.

203 Letter of the US Secretary of State annexed to the Resolution 1546 (2004).

204 *R. (On the Application of Al-Jedda) v. Secretary of State for Defence*, op. cit. n. 192, at para 34.

205 See the remarks by Baroness Hale at *Ibid.*, para. 128.

206 G. Verdirame, loc. cit. n. 171, at p. 213.

207 The case, unreported, was brought before the Court on 20 February 2006 and immediately rejected. All the information mentioned in the article has been obtained from the contents of the application filed with the ECtHR by the European Roma Rights Centre (ERRC) on behalf of the applicants and obtained on file from the Centre itself (hereafter *Mehmeti* Application). The alleged violations regarded the right to life (Art. 2), prohibition of torture and inhuman or degrading treatment (Art. 3), right to a fair hearing (Art. 6), right to respect for private and family life (Art. 8), right to an effective remedy (Art. 13) and the prohibition of discriminations (Art. 14).

arguments submitted by the claimants.[208] Nevertheless, *Mehmeti* might be considered rather significant as it reveals the scarce alternative remedies available for the Kosovar population against the human rights violations purportedly committed by the UN. Indeed, in the petition filed before the Court, the applicants lamented that the harm posed by the *Trepca* complex was reported as being well known to the SRSG[209] (also because of *in loco* World Health Organization (WHO) environmental analysis[210]). The applicants also showed evidence of several appeals and inspections concerning the case made by the Ombudsperson[211], highlighting the lack of reply to most communications forwarded to UNMIK and the UN itself.[212] It is remarkable that other petitions concerning the same case brought before both the UNMIK and UN claim settlement organs have proven unfruitful.[213]

2° *Cases occurring within Haiti*

Recently, the Inter-American Commission on Human Rights (IACHR) has been invested with a case regarding the attribution of responsibility to a Member State for human rights violations allegedly committed by UN militaries. The *Jimmy Charles* case[214] concerned the illegal arrest and the murder of an employee of the Haitian telephone company. On 5 January 2005, Mr. Charles was arrested without a specific charge by Brazilian soldiers of the UN Stabilisation Mission in Haiti (MINUSTAH), who turned him over to the Haitian National Police. At

208 *Mehmeti* Application, op. cit. n. 207, at paras. 380–381: 'The applicants submit that when Serbia and Montenegro ratified the Convention, its protections automatically extended to Kosovo. Kosovo, subject to a decision on its final status, remains part of Serbia and Montenegro. Therefore, at least from that date, but for the administration of Kosovo by UNMIK, the applicants would have been covered under the Convention. Thus, unless UNMIK is held to the standards they agreed to i.e. the ECHR, the Applicants have lost their human rights which is an unacceptable result. Where UNMIK is in control, as they are in Kosovo, they are responsible. [...] Therefore, just because the government has changed to UNMIK does not change that international commitment'. The argument made by the claimants seems similar to the one reported in J. Cerone, loc. cit. n. 79, at p. 474. In another paragraph, UNMIK is described as a *de facto* sovereign State (para. 373) and the ECHR application to its soil is explained according the 'living instrument' theory, highlighted in the *Matthews* case (para. 404).

209 *Mehmeti* Application, op. cit. n. 207, at paras. 198 and 223.

210 *Ibid.*, at para. 194.

211 *Ibid.*, at para. 213.

212 *Ibid.*, at para. 417.

213 UNMIK rejected the claim concerning the case and refused to institute a specific claims commission as provided under UNMIK Regulation 2000/47. As a consequence, the representatives of the Roma people filed two additional petitions: one to the UN Office of Legal Advisor in New York (according to the Convention on Privileges and Immunities of the UN); another to the Geneva based – Office of Internal Oversight Services (OIOS) (information reported in a e-mail by ERRC on 24 October 2006).

214 IACHR, *Jimmy Charles*, Petition No. 81–06, Report No. 65/06, 20 July 2006, available at www.cidh.org/annualrep/2006eng/HAITI.81.06eng.htm.

first, Mr. Charles was brought before a judge who dismissed the case for lack of jurisdiction. Two days later, before being taken to a second court, he was found dead in the morgue of the State University Hospital by his relatives. The police authorities declared that Mr. Charles was killed during a clash between the police and 'bandits' shortly after having been released from prison. This version was lately agreed upon by the UN police authorities.

On 18 January 2006, the Institute for Justice and Democracy in Haiti and the *Bureau des Avocats Internationaux* filed a petition[215] against both Haiti and Brazil for violation of several human rights law provisions.[216] The petitioners justified the responsibility of Brazil by arguing that:

> 'In the absence of a functioning, independent human rights oversight mechanism [...] to hold the United Nations accountable for human rights violations by peace-keeping troops and other UN personal and to provide just redress and compensation to the victims, the only remaining avenue for victims to enforce compliance with human rights standards in peacekeeping missions is to invoke the responsibility of the contributing States.'[217]

In addition, since the UN SOFA in Haiti provided that contributing States retain the exclusive jurisdiction over their nationals with respect to acts performed while acting as UN officers, the petitioners maintained that such States are themselves responsible for monitoring and enforcing compliance of their troops with international human rights.[218] In the end, while the petition against Haiti was declared admissible by the IACHR, the one against Brazil was dismissed by the Commission's Secretariat for lack of previous exhaustion of domestic remedies (Article 46(1)(a) of the ACHR).[219] The Commission therefore did not question the possible attribution of responsibility to Brazil.

---

215 On file with the Institute for Justice and Democracy in Haiti (e-mail received on 5 August 2008).

216 Haiti: alleged violation of ACHR Art. 4 (right to life), Art. 5 (right to humane treatment), Art. 7 (right to personal liberty), Art. 8 (right to a fair trial), and Art. 25(1) (right to judicial protection); Brazil: alleged violation of ACHR Art. 4, 5, 7(1–2, 5) (Freedom from arbitrary arrest/detention and right to trial within reasonable time).

217 *Jimmi Charles* petition, op. cit. n. 214, at para. 56.

218 *Jimmi Charles* petition, op. cit. n. 214, at para. 57. In the further paragraph (No. 58) the petitioners recalled a statement by the HRC, in which the Committee urged ICCPR Member States to implement the Covenant during peace operations abroad (HRC, Concluding Observations (CCPR/CO/81/BEL) (2004), para. 6). As previously reported (*supra* n. 141), a similar statement is also included in the HRC General Comment No. 31.

219 Letter by the IACHR to the Institute for Justice and Democracy in Haiti, with regard to Petition No. 82–06 against Brazil, 4 August 2006 (on file with the Institute for Justice and Democracy in Haiti; e-mail received on 1 August 2008).

Jimmy Charles was not the only case on the matter to be brought to the attention of the IACHR in 2006. On 3 March 2006, *Zanmi Lasante*, a Haitian human rights organisation focusing on the right to health, with the support of two US human rights foundations requested an advisory opinion from the Commission regarding the human rights obligations of the Organization of American States (OAS) Member States participating in the UN Mission in Haiti. During the hearing, the Commission was also requested to send an onsite visit to Haiti and to appoint a special rapporteur on economic and social rights to monitor whether measurable progress in human rights protection is being made in the Caribbean State.[220]

VII. CONCLUDING REMARKS

Relying on Member States' accountability, when addressing the issue of human rights violations committed by international organisations (the 'Italian job') may be regarded as a short-term solution which reflects the lack of clarity concerning the issue of the responsibility of international institutions within the international legal order. However, to some extent it might constitute an effective means to successfully overcome the legal paradox under which States create international legal persons not bound by the same international obligations they are mandated to respect. Indeed, once judicial liability for human rights violation is established and Member States are charged accordingly, two options thus occur: either to decrease the network links between employed, seconded, assigned or other personnel that operate within an international organisation, thereby both strengthening the organisation's control over them as well as enabling it to further deny any kind of accountability; or, on the contrary, to consolidate these links and sacrifice the organisation's operational control over its personnel, in order to exercise a stricter oversight. In the (quite unlikely) first case, the organisation concerned would probably be put under more pressure by the same Member States, scared of its rising power and autonomy.[221] They would then struggle within the same organisation's internal bodies with the aim of increasing their influence in the decision-making process. Such a competition among Member States would probably lead to a reinforcement of internal and even external accountability and supervisory mechanisms (thus generating new and concurrent legal regimes). The dread of rendering international organisations too independent of Member States could also lead the latter to finally set up external and autonomous settlement claim bodies that may secure access to

220 T. Howland, 'Peacekeeping and Conformity with Human Rights Law: How MINUSTAH Falls Short in Haiti', 13(4) *International Peacekeeping* (2006) p. 472.

221 In fact some scholars consider the problem of international organizations' accountability as 'partly inspired by (States') fears of all – too – powerful organizations' (N. Blokker, 'Exploring the Evolution of Purposes, Methods and Legitimacy: Accountability of Intergovernmental Organizations', 94 *American Society of International Law Proceedings* (2000) p. 205).

justice for third parties (individuals and legal persons) while being truly independent of the international organisations concerned. Indeed, as an option, Member States could press on international organisations to accede to human rights conventions (whenever possible), as in the case of the EU under the Lisbon Treaty. This would put the international organisations under the scrutiny of the related international courts/supervisory bodies. On the other hand, strengthening State control over international organisations would result in reinforcing judicial liability of Member States, thus indirectly increasing the accountability of international institutions to third parties. For the latter, this would probably be more advantageous for several reasons, such as the extended financial liability of Member States, the possibility of bringing cases before either domestic or international courts and the existence of a well grounded case-law.

However, acknowledging judicial liability of Member States would *directly* strengthen international organisations' compliance with human rights law, bringing to light potential dilemmas occurring in the course of peace operations, e.g. as the asserted dichotomy between security and human rights.[222] At the end of the day, in a short-term perspective, for any individual subjected to the authority of an international organisation, more than the latter's eventual political accountability or judicial liability (perhaps to be established before a court located thousand of miles away from the applicant's place), an immediate fair treatment in line with human rights law is what really matters. And for such a resolution, Niccolò Machiavelli – the Italian 'Prince' of modern political thought – would probably say that '*il fine giustifica i mezzi*.'[223]

222 D. Marshall and S. Inglis, 'The Disempowerment of Human Rights – Based Justice in the United Nations Mission in Kosovo', 16 *Harvard Human Rights Journal* (2003) p. 106: 'Just before the March 2001 SG's report, an internal UNMIK document from the (Principal Deputy) SRSG's office argued that the mission was confronted with a choice between ensuring human rights and establishing security. In essence, the document asserted that human rights protection was the primary obstacle to security. This document was prepared to justify the use of the SRSG's executive power in violation of human rights principles. The fact that such a position was held by those at the highest levels of UNMIK reflected a fundamental lack of understanding of the reasoning behind the principles of human rights law'. A previous document issued by the SRSG on 12 January 2000, entitled 'Security and the Rule of Law in Kosovo', reported the need for 'flexibility' in addressing the problem of reconciling human rights protection with the promotion of public peace and order (quoted in C. Stahn, 'The United Nations Transitional Administrations in Kosovo and East Timor: A First Analysis', in J.A. Frowein and R. Wolfrum, eds., 5 *Max Planck Yearbook of United Nations Law* (2001) p. 163).

223 'The end justifies the means'. Such a sentence is erroneously attributed to Niccolò Machiavelli in 'The Prince' (XVIII Chapter).

PART II.

PEACE AND HUMANITARIAN OPERATIONS

HUMAN RIGHTS ACCOUNTABILITY OF INTERNATIONAL ORGANISATIONS IN THE LEAD OF INTERNATIONAL PEACE MISSIONS

Ulf Häußler*

I. PRELIMINARY REMARKS AND INTRODUCTION

Today's peace missions differ considerably from classical Blue Helmet peacekeeping. The task-sheet of peacekeeping operations has grown, and peace-building has emerged as a new type of operation. With or without the consent of receiving states' governments or power-brokers, the international community has frequently entrusted peacekeeping and peace-building operations with considerable transitional authority. Being deployed for extended periods of time, many of these peace missions have become increasingly embedded in receiving states' power balances, and some are expected to remain in such a position for significant periods.

The institutionalising of this transitional authority is but one factor why the human rights accountability of peace missions attracts increasing interest. Links between peace missions and counter-terrorism operations as well as cases of abuse (including sexual exploitation) of civilian individuals have highlighted the need for proper human rights protection of those affected by the actions of peace missions and the conduct of their personnel. Yet the legal framework for ensuring human rights accountability is still unsettled, and this is so for a variety of reasons. Peace missions have been launched within a variety of contexts: the UN framework; on behalf of the United Nations; or pursuant to agreements with

* At the time of writing, the author was the Legal Advisor, Joint Command Special Operations (Germany). The views expressed herein are my own; they do not necessarily correspond with the official position of Germany's Federal Government, the Federal Ministry of Defence, or the German Armed Forces. The typescript of this contribution was originally completed by the end of March 2007; it was updated, focusing for this purpose on the judgments in Behrami & Saramati (European Court of Human Rights), and Al Skeini (UK House of Lords) and relevant developments, in August 2008.

receiving states. Some are led by regional organisations (like UN peacekeeping operations, hereinafter referred to as 'international peacekeeping operations'), others by specific states within a coalition (hereinafter referred to as 'multinational peacekeeping operations'). Frequently, peacekeeping (or post-occupation stabilisation) and peace-building missions in the same receiving state are either under different lead[1] or different peace missions operate within the same receiving state.[2] No two international mandates are alike, and policies of participating regional organisations and contributing states further add to this diversity. The policy concept of human security, fundamental to all peace missions and important for the future interpretation and application of Chapter VII of the UN Charter, continues to await discussion in the UN General Assembly following up the '2005 World Summit Outcome'.

The co-ordinates of the human rights framework governing peace missions can nevertheless be identified. Analysis will have to focus on relevant standards and enforcement mechanisms. International peace missions are led by, as well as integrated within the command and control framework of international organisations. These organisations are not parties to any of the relevant law-making treaties; customary international law derived from such treaties is likewise addressed primarily at states. Accordingly, general principles of international law and of the internal law of these organisations will be the core sources of human rights and – concerning peacekeeping in particular – humanitarian law standards for reviewing action attributable to lead organisations.[3] Likewise, human rights courts and treaty bodies will only be able to review conduct attributable to lead organisations on the basis of specific agreements to that extent. Lead organisations are, however, obligated to establish appropriate internal oversight mechanisms. Moreover, they have developed professional co-operation with the International Committee of the Red Cross

---

1 The most important current and recent examples are:
- Afghanistan (NATO: ISAF; United Nations: UNAMA);
- Bosnia and Herzegovina (European Union: EUFOR ALTHEA; United Nations: High Representative and his apparatus);
- Kosovo (NATO: KFOR; United Nations: UNMIK); and
- Iraq (U.S./UK-led coalition forces; United Nations: UNAMI).

2 The most important current and recent examples are:
- East Timor (United Nations: UNAMET/UNTAET; Australian-led coalition: INTERFET);
- Democratic Republic of the Congo (United Nations: MONUC; European Union: ARTEMIS and, later, Eufor R.D. Congo);
- Sudan (African Union: AMIS – later replaced by the United Nations – African Union Mission in Darfur – UNAMID – in accordance with UNSC Resolution 1769 (2007); United Nations: UNMIS); and
- Georgia (next to UNOMIG, there is a Russian-led CIS peacekeeping force whose tasks may, as indicated by recent events, have involved a non-peacekeeping hidden agenda).

3 See U. Häußler, 'General Principles of International Humanitarian and Human Rights Law: A Tool to Overcome the War-and-Peace Divide in International Law', in C.M. Bailliet, ed., *Security: A Multidisciplinary Normative Approach* (2009), pp. 49 *et seq.*

(ICRC) in all matters equivalent to its role as a Protecting Power in the framework of armed conflict.

Human rights accountability of contributing states complements that of lead organisations. As indicated by relevant jurisprudence, conduct representing exercise of their jurisdiction at field level and participation in decision-making processes in international organisations are fully reviewable by international human rights courts and treaty bodies. The substantive provisions of relevant instruments apply directly to the exercise of authority attributable to contributing states. By contrast, limitations of substantive rights are not limited to those envisaged by the limitations clauses contained in those law-making treaties; they can also derive from UN Security Council Resolutions adopted under Chapter VII of the UN Charter. Arguably, the resulting relationship between domestic human rights and international humanitarian law is similar to that between international human rights law and international humanitarian law as defined by the International Court of Justice, viz. a relationship between a *lex generalis* and a *lex specialis*. The following analysis will focus on the accountability of international organisations. Accountability of contributing states and accountability issues pertaining to multinational peacekeeping are beyond its scope.

This contribution will discuss the legal framework of accountability of international organisations for the conduct of peace missions they have established from a practical perspective.[4] It will start with a brief typology of peace missions so as to identify certain characteristics of peacekeeping operations. An overview of the repertoire of actions of peacekeeping operations and their effects on human rights will be addressed next. Then follows the question of why, and to what extent, these actions can – and must – be attributed to the international organisation in the lead of a peacekeeping operation. After that, this contribution will identify the sources of both the authority exercised by peacekeeping forces and the limits placed thereupon. Finally, it will analyse how, on such basis, public and private interests affected by the actions of a peacekeeping operation may be balanced.

---

4 The term 'conduct' is the expression of choice used by the International Law Commission to tackle behaviour that may lead to responsibility of international organisation. As far as relevant for the present purposes, draft Article 4 of the articles on responsibility of international organizations reads as follows: 'Article 4 – Elements of an internationally wrongful act of an international organization – There is an internationally wrongful act of an international organization when conduct consisting of an action or omission: (a) Is attributable to the international organization under international law; and (b) Constitutes a breach of an international obligation of that international organization.' See International Law Commission, *Report of the Sixty-first session (4 May to 5 June and 6 July to 7 August 2009)*, UN Doc. A/64/10, at para. 51 (hereafter referred to as ILC, *Report 2009*). The ILC has particularly emphasised that '[t]he term "conduct" is intended to cover both acts and omissions on the part of the international organization […]'. See ILC, *Report 2009*, op. cit. in the same note, commentary (1) on draft Article 4, at p. 54.

II. THE INSTITUTIONALISATION OF TRANSITIONAL AUTHORITY – A BRIEF TYPOLOGY OF PEACE MISSIONS

During the Cold War, with the exception of ONUC in the early 1960s, international peace missions used to have rather limited mandates (such as to assist in the implementation of a cease-fire agreement; to observe, or monitor the activities of the armed forces of potential adversaries) – which implied smaller operations, composed mainly of military personnel and with little substantial authority. The demise of the Cold War brought with it a wind of change. Once the confrontation between the Eastern and Western blocs had ceased, the United Nations Transition Assistance Group[5] was the precedent-setting example of a new approach towards United Nations peacekeeping. The mandates adopted by the UN Security Council became increasingly ambitious, a development involving an increase in size and diversity of personnel, and of the authority entrusted in the missions in question. Although officially still referred to as 'peacekeeping operations', many contemporary peace missions established by the United Nations perform both (military) peacekeeping and (civilian) peace-building tasks[6], and consist of one or more separate components in charge thereof. Besides establishing peace missions, the United Nations has also authorised peacekeeping operations on its behalf.[7] While NATO and the European Union have long been the only international organisations in the lead of peacekeeping operations on the basis of (*inter alia*) a United Nations mandate[8,9]; various international

5 The United Nations Transition Assistance Group (UNTAG) was established by UNSC Resolution 435 (1978) for the task of supervising and controlling free elections in Namibia. Its mandate became operative upon Namibia's eventual independence from South Africa on 1 April 1989 according to UNSC Resolutions 629 and 632 (1989). On the composition and responsibilities of UNTAG see also UN Doc. S/20412 (23 January 1989).

6 See C. Gray, *International Law and the Use of Force*, 3rd edn. (Oxford, Oxford University Press 2008) at pp. 264 *et seq.* for a comprehensive overview of the United Nations peace missions combining peacekeeping and peace-building at the end of the Cold War and immediately thereafter.

7 For the need to differentiate between UN peacekeeping and peacekeeping on behalf of the United Nations, see also M. Bothe and T. Dörschel, 'The UN Peacekeeping Experiencee, in D. Fleck, ed., *The Handbook of the Law of Visiting Forces* (Oxford, Oxford University Press 2001), pp. 487–490.

8 NATO has established the original peacekeeping operation in Bosnia (IFOR/SFOR/NHQ Sarajevo), and Kosovo (KFOR); it has assumed command of peacekeeping in Afghanistan (ISAF). The European Union has established peacekeeping operations with different responsibilities in the Congo for limited periods (EUFOR ARTEMIS, 2003, and EUFOR R.D. Congo, 2006), and assumed command of peacekeeping in Bosnia and Herzegovina (when SFOR was transformed into EUFOR ALTHEA in December 2004).

9 On 6 March 2007, the African Union has launched a UN-mandated peacekeeping operation – AMISOM – in Somalia. See UNSC Resolution 1744 (2007), the Communiqué of the African Union's Peace and Security Council dated 19 January 2007 – AU document PSC/PR/

organisations[10] have launched peace missions with the consent of the government of the states receiving such missions, both with[11] and without[12] transitional authority.

Considering the diversity of their mandates it seems most persuasive to develop the typology of contemporary peace missions on the basis of their responsibilities. Military peacekeeping responsibilities comprise, but are not limited to, monitoring compliance with the terms and conditions of a peace settlement or cease-fire agreement; suppression of renewed hostilities; observing and inspecting the armed forces of potential adversaries or ex-belligerents; fulfilment of certain tasks related to disarmament, demilitarisation and reintegration; military aspects of security sector reform; and such support of civilian agencies as envisaged by the mandate or requested by the agencies in question. If no civilian agencies – in particular law enforcement agencies – exist, military peacekeepers may also be temporarily in charge of some of their responsibilities.[13] On a separate note, support to the prosecution of genocide, crimes against humanity, and war crimes can also be a part of peacekeeping realities.[14] Peace-building operations may have responsibilities up to and including all branches of government except for the defence sector and defence related aspects of the security sector. If juridical functions are exercised by internationally recruited personnel, the independence of international judges from interference by the peace-building operation is guaranteed (as evidenced e.g. by the practice of UNMIK and UNTAET). Peace-building operations are not necessarily the only

---

Comm(LXIX), and the AU Press Release concerning the Signing of the Status of Mission Agreement (SOMA) dated 6 March 2007 (on file with the author).

10 See U. Häußler, *Ensuring and Enforcing Human Security. The Practice of International Peace Missions* (Nijmegen, Wolf Legal Publishers 2007) pp. 15 *et seq.* and pp. 62 *et seq.* for further actors involved in international peacekeeping.

11 Both the NATO peacekeeping operation in Macedonia (ESSENTIAL HARVEST/ AMBER FOX/FOX/ ALLIED HARMONY) and its European Union successor (EUFOR CONCORDIA) had transitional authority to prevent hostilities between the ethnic Albanian minority and the majority population in their receiving State in accordance with the relevant requests made by the then Macedonian President Trajkovski. On the initial request see the Statement by the North Atlantic Council dated 20 June 2001 as per NATO, Press Release (2001) 093, available at www.nato.int/docu/pr/2001/p01–093e.htm).

12 For instance, AMIS Darfur does not possess the authority to enforce the peace settlement for the province. Relevant decisions of the Peace and Security Council of the African Union can be retrieved at www.africa-union.org.

13 The most prominent example, KFOR law and order mission is rooted in para 9(d) of UNSC Resolution 1244 (1999). Note the different terminology used in this paragraph ('ensuring public safety and order') and in para 11(i) concerning UNMIK's complementing responsibilities ('maintaining civil law and order'). KFOR's law and order mission is discussed in some detail in Center for Law and Military Operations, *Law and Military Operations in Kosovo* (2001), pp. 102 *et seq.*

14 See U. Häußler, 'Witness Protection by Peace Missions', in R. Arnold, ed., *Law Enforcement within the Framework of Peace Support Operations* (Leiden, Martinus Nijhoff Publishers 2008) pp. 257–307.

civilian international community actors in states receiving peace missions. Some Specialised Agencies of the United Nations prefer to establish their own presence in states receiving a United Nations peace-building operation (or might even maintain an established presence throughout the armed conflict and beyond); relevant peace-building mandates are then usually limited accordingly. From a policy perspective, however, this practice has been considered questionable.[15]

The precise range of peacekeeping and peace-building responsibilities is defined by the relevant international mandates.[16] International mandates also identify the desired end-state of a peace mission, that is, what it shall ultimately achieve by the exercise of its transitional authority. Generally speaking, such mandates aim to (re-)introduce stable constitutional democracy characterised by good governance based on human rights as well as the rule of law in the receiving state, viz. a state of affairs vital in maintaining or restoring, as the case may be, international peace and security.

The international community has entrusted particularly broad transitional authority in peacekeepers and peace-builders in the Balkans, East Timor, and Afghanistan. The relevant mandates aim(ed) at restoring peace and stability as well as supporting the growth of independent, stable, and democratic statehood, respectively. The peace process launched in Bosnia and Herzegovina after the failure of UNPROFOR – for which the fall of Srebrenica will forever be the paradigm – was supported by the North Atlantic Treaty Organization (NATO), the United Nations (including several of its Specialised Agencies), and – under

---

15 In particular, the United Nations High Commissioner for Refugees (UNHCR) and the United Nations Development Programme (UNDP) prefer to operate on their own. The High Level Panel convened by the United Nations Secretary-General has stressed, in its *Report on United Nations Peace Operations* submitted on 17 August 2000 (also known as the *Brahimi Report*), that: 'it is critical that field representatives of United Nations agencies, funds and programmes facilitate the work of an SRSG or RSG in his or her role as the coordinator of all United Nations activities in the country concerned. On a number of occasions, attempts to perform this role have been hampered by overly bureaucratic resistance to coordination. Such tendencies do not do justice to the concept of the United Nations family that the Secretary-General has tried hard to encourage.' See para. 100 of UN Doc. A/55/305 – S/2000/809.

16 International mandates are embodied in related arrangements with the receiving State or those exercising power attributable to it, and/or the relevant UNSCRs (in particular in the case of peace missions launched without any such consent, or to a failed state). If international organisations other than the United Nations participate in a UN peace mission or launch a peace mission on the UN's behalf or with the consent of the receiving state, the policy level decisions concerning their participation contribute to the international mandate, as well. Note that unless expressly required by relevant arrangements with the government and/or power brokers of the receiving state fundamental to a particular peace mission, the legality of its actions is not conditional on endorsement of its authority by the UN Security Council. UNSCRs do, however, add legitimacy to such arrangements because they ensure, by virtue of their binding force (Articles 25 and 103 of the UN Charter), universal recognition of the peace mission and its authority. Moreover, UNSCRs have the character of internal UN law and have related effects with respect to UN peace missions.

the umbrella of the latter – the Organization for Security and Co-operation in Europe (OSCE) and the European Union. It had been resting on two pillars from the beginning. The 'NATO (now also EU) pillar' consists of the military peace mission whose broad mandate covers the military aspects of the peace settlement and equally broad authority to compel[17] all military and paramilitary actors[18] within Bosnia and Herzegovina to comply with its terms. The 'UN pillar' centers around the peace-building component headed by the High Representative of the United Nations Secretary-General whose mandate and authority cover all civilian aspects of the peace settlement. In particular, decisions made by both the Force Commander and the High Representative in their respective areas of authority to implement the peace settlement have binding force on local actors.[19] This binding force is the key characteristic of transitional authority since it limits the sovereignty of the State receiving a peace mission for as long as the mandate is in force as well as it enables the peace mission to exercise its authority with direct or indirect effects on the general public in receiving states.

The 1999 settlements for Kosovo and East Timor (Timor-Leste) have entrusted transitional authority of a similar nature in the peace missions launched (KFOR and UNMIK in Kosovo, UNTAET in East Timor). As these missions started operating in situations characterised by the collapse of all previously existing government institutions which, moreover, had lost all legitimacy anyway, the exercise of their transitional authority had even more impact on the populations of Kosovo and Timor-Leste, respectively, since it initially covered the entirety of government functions.[20] All but surprisingly UNMIK and UNTAET were the

---

17 In accordance with Article VI(5) the peacekeeping Force Commander may do all he 'judges necessary and proper, including the use of military force, to protect the [peacekeeping force] and to carry out the responsibilities listed above …'. The UN Security Council has recognised this authority (see para. 5 of UNSC Resolution 1031 (1995), para. 8 of UNSC Resolution 1088 (1996), and para. 7 of UNSC Resolution 1575 (2004)) and endorsed the authorisation to use 'all necessary measures' for that purpose. See paras. 15/16/17 of UNSC Resolution 1031 (1995) – IFOR, paras. 19/20/21 of UNSC Resolution 1088 (1996) – SFOR, paras. 14/15/16 of UNSC Resolution 1575 (2004) – NHQ Sarajevo/EUFOR ALTHEA. (The SFOR and NHQ Sarajevo/EUFOR ALTHEA mandates have been renewed subsequently.).

18 The variety of military and paramilitary actors is demonstrated by Article II(1) of Annex 1A to the Dayton Agreement which defines the generic term 'Forces' as follows: 'Each Party shall ensure that all personnel and organizations with military capability under its control or within territory under its control, including armed civilian groups, national guards, army reserves, military police, and the Ministry of Internal Affairs Special Police (MUP) (hereinafter 'Forces') comply with this Annex.'

19 Technically, such decisions have the character of interpretations of the peace settlement. The Force Commander and the High Representative have final authority in theatre to interpret those aspects of the peace settlement for which they are responsible (Article XII of Annex 1A to the Dayton Agreement and Article V of Annex 10 to the Dayton Agreement, respectively). See U. Häußler, op. cit. n. 10, at p. 90 for an assessment of the nature of this authority and further references concerning the usage of this terminology.

20 This is particularly obvious from the UNMIK mandate (see para. 11 of UNSC Resolution 1244 (1999)). The United Nations Secretary-General has interpreted UNSC Resolution

first UN peace missions to determine that their actions shall comply with 'internationally recognized standards of human rights'.[21] In a similar manner, relevant NATO Operation Plans (OPLANs), Directives, and Standing Operating Procedures (SOPs)[22] for the peacekeeping forces in the Balkans (as well as Afghanistan) require compliance (either expressly or implicitly) with the spirit of international humanitarian law and respect for human rights in the course of the operations they govern.

III. THE EFFECTS OF ACTIONS OF PEACEKEEPING OPERATIONS ON HUMAN RIGHTS

The transitional authority entrusted in military peace missions has a limited material scope. Its focus rests on the military aspects of the respective peace settlement; it may also cover support of peace-building efforts and civilian actors. The act from which a peace mission derives its transitional authority limits the receiving state's sovereignty; it also places a significant degree of limitation upon the human rights of those affected by the exercise of such authority. The latter limitation is usually embodied in the authorisation of a peace mission to use all necessary means and/or measures to fulfil its responsibilities, and to protect its personnel and assets.[23] To mention the most severe effect on human rights only, peacekeepers may, in accordance with this authorisation, use force up to and including deadly force. To discuss in detail the range of action of military peace missions[24] would exceed the scope of this contribution. However, the following key examples shall suffice to demonstrate the differing practical dimensions of the exercise of transitional authority by peacekeeping operations. These examples will address the exercise of transitional authority vis-à-vis ex- and would-be-belligerents; governance institutions in receiving states; and the exercise of transitional authority directly affecting the general public. Examples pertaining to all mentioned categories represent the means and measures which peace

---

1244 (1999) so that the UN Security Council, by virtue of this resolution, 'has vested in the interim civil administration authority over the territory and people of Kosovo. All legislative and executive powers, including administration of the judiciary, will, therefore, be vested in UNMIK'. See UN Secretary-General, 'Report on the United Nations Interim Administration Mission in Kosovo', UN Doc. S/1999/779, para. 35.

21 See UN Secretary-General, op. cit. n. 20, at para. 69 and Article 1 of UNMIK Regulation 1999/24 concerning United Nations peace-building in Kosovo, and Article 2 of UNTAET Regulation 1999/1 (UN Doc. S/2000/53/Add.1) concerning United Nations peacekeeping and peace-building in East Timor.

22 See U. Häußler, op. cit. n. 10, at Chapter 6 (introducing remarks) for the role which OPLANs and SOPs play in and the framework of accountability of peacekeeping operations.

23 Depending on the policy underlying the settlement, different language, conferring less authority, may be used.

24 For a comprehensive overview and analysis, focusing on the Balkans practice, see U. Häußler, op. cit. n. 10, at Chapters 7–9.

missions have at times regarded as necessary in order to meet their responsibilities as defined in international mandates. They further illustrate the differentiation concerning the target audiences of the exercise of transitional authority and, briefly, its relationship to different threat assessments.

A. EXERCISE OF TRANSITIONAL AUTHORITY *VIS-À-VIS* EX- AND WOULD-BE-BELLIGERENTS OR GOVERNANCE INSTITUTIONS IN RECEIVING STATES

The core responsibility of both military and civilian peace missions is to prevent resumption of hostilities or return to armed conflict, as the case may be. To this end, they must ensure compliance with the terms and conditions of the peace settlement or cease-fire agreement. Usually, these instruments establish detailed obligations on the part of ex- and would-be-belligerents, and governance institutions in receiving states. *Prima facie*, these obligations require them to show certain behaviour as well as to cease certain activities (and refrain therefrom forthwith). Ultimately, however, these obligations compel such ex- and would-be-belligerents to change their attitudes towards conflict resolution. If necessary, peace missions may use means and take measures whose effects and side effects (collateral effects) on the sovereign rights of receiving states and the subjective rights of the individuals concerned might be quite intense.

1° Ex- and Would-Be-Belligerents

The category referred to as ex- and would-be-belligerents comprises all kinds of groups of individuals, regardless their formal status or informal existence, which possess the capability to pose a military or paramilitary threat to international peace and security in a peace mission's theatre of operations, including to the accomplishment, by a peace mission, of its mission. Also to this category belong all individuals showing belligerent behaviour or a belligerent attitude. As a result, the category at issue covers all kinds of armed groups addressed in GC III, and GPs I & II, as well as all individuals possessing the capability to take a direct part in hostilities. This includes non-governmental armed groups composed of civilians who have organised themselves with a view to taking a direct part in hostilities.

Peacekeepers may take action against the existence of paramilitary or military capability[25] if it is incongruent with the peace settlement, and against the use of lawfully existing military capabilities for purposes not endorsed by it. Under a

[25] For the military capability test see U. Häußler, op. cit. n. 10, at pp. 91 *et seq.*

robust mandate (Chapter VII of the UN Charter or equivalent[26]), peacekeeping operations have authority to use force against ex- and would-be-belligerents in order to compel them to act in compliance with their obligations stemming from the instrument governing the peace process. If need be – as currently throughout Afghanistan – they may engage such groups with paramilitary or military capability as attempt to escalate a still-looming conflict and return to open warfare. Obviously, any such use of force can involve adverse effects on various human rights of those affected in such cases.[27]

2° Governance Institutions

Governance institutions in receiving states (including officials holding positions therein) conducting themselves in a manner failing to comply with the requirements of the peace process can become further targets of measures taken by peace missions. In particular, the personal accountability of civilian heads and/or commanding officers of ex-belligerents and post-conflict armed forces of states receiving a peace mission is key to compliance with the obligations stemming from the legal instrument governing the peace process. Peace missions entrusted with transitional authority may withhold, or remove, from office – temporarily or irreversibly – any individual posing a threat to (in particular) the safe and secure environment, the democratic transformation of the security sector institution in question, or fulfilment of the peace mission's responsibilities in respect of the desired end-state defined by the peace settlement. In Bosnia and Herzegovina, the High Representative's 'Bonn Powers'[28] have enabled him to

26 Arguably, the extended mandate of UNIFIL is robust because UNIFIL has the authority 'to take all necessary action in areas of deployment of its forces and as it deems within its capabilities' for a number of specified purposes. This authority is not, however, based on Chapter VII of the UN Charter but on 'a request from the Government of Lebanon' rather. See para. 11 of UNSC Resolution 1701 (2006). – The consent of the receiving state's government legitimises robustness of a mandate in just the same way as a Chapter VII resolution yet it does not generate the same effects as such resolutions do in accordance with Articles 25 and 103 of the UN Charter.

27 Individual field level operations may affect not only the rights to life, physical integrity, or property but, depending on their purpose and method of execution, many more human rights. Cf. C.M. Bailliet, '"War in the Home": An Exposition of Protection Issues Pertaining to the Use of House Raids in Counterinsurgency Operations', 6 *Journal of Military Ethics* (2007) pp. 173–197.

28 The Bonn Powers are based on the High Representative's final authority in theatre to interpret Annex X to the Dayton Agreement. The international community has endorsed this mode of applying of Article V of Annex X at the Peace Implementation Council (PIC) held at Bonn in December 1997. See, most recently, para. 4 of Resolution 1639 (2005) according to which the UN Security Council *inter alia*: '*reaffirms* that under Annex 10 of the Peace Agreement the High Representative is the final authority in theatre regarding the interpretation of civilian implementation of the Peace Agreement and that in case of dispute he may give his interpretation and make recommendations, and make binding decisions as he judges necessary on issues as elaborated by the Peace Implementation Council in Bonn on 9 and 10 December 1997.' For a critical assessment see A. Schwarz and J. Zeh, 'Autorität durch

dismiss government officials (including police officers[29]) or political leaders from their posts in cases where they have acted in a manner detrimental to peace and reconciliation. In a similar manner, SFOR has vetted military officers and suspended implicated officers of Entity Armed Forces.[30] Likewise, following the independence of Kosovo, KFOR has assumed the task of vetting leadership personnel of the Kosovo Security Force established in accordance with Article 126 of the Constitution of the Republic of Kosovo.[31]

Vetting has adverse effects on the freedom to chose one's profession (or more generally termed economic freedoms) and might, considering the need to collect and evaluate relevant information, also affect privacy rights such as the protection of personal data. Moreover, since vetting decisions are based upon the final authority to interpret relevant aspects of the legal instrument governing the peace process, they are not subject to appeal in a court of law of the state receiving the peace mission. For that reason, both the procedure of their adoption and their implementation are capable of denying the individual in question the right of access to court: unless the lead organisation of the peace mission establishes a mechanism for judicial review on its own.[32]

3° Persons Indicted For War Crimes (PIFWCs)

Finally, peace missions may also take action against PIFWCs and their support networks in close co-operation with relevant criminal institutions.[33] As peacekeepers – depending on their international mandate and relevant arrangements agreed upon between the peace mission (viz. its lead organisation) and the court or tribunal concerned – may have the authority to detain PIFWCs,

Auslegung: zur Rechtsgrundlage der Macht des Hohen Repräsentanten in Bosnien-Herzegowina', in A. Schwarz and J. Zeh, *Recht und Politik: Vierteljahreshefte für Rechts- und Verwaltungspolitik* (2004), pp. 225–227 who assert that the UN Security Council's endorsement of the PIC Conclusion did not have the quality of an international mandate.

29 For an assessment, see Opinion No. 326/2004 of the Venice Commission of the Council of Europe on a possible solution to the issue decertification of police officers in Bosnia and Herzegovina, document CDL-AD(2005)024.

30 See the transcript of the International Community Press Conference of 30 May 2002, available at www.nato.int/sfor/trans/2002/t020530a.htm (last visited on 20 January 2005), detailing that COMSFOR, after analysing documents and equipment linked to non-compliant action, suspended a VRS general 'until such time as the investigation is over'.

31 An English translation of the Constitution of the Republic of Kosovo is available for download at www.kushtetutakosoves.info/repository/docs/Constitution.of.the.Republic.of.Kosovo.pdf (last visited on 14 August 2008).

32 Note that the Council of Europe's Venice Commission has accepted the lawfulness of the vetting of police officers by the International Police Task Force in Bosnia and Herzegovina. See Opinion No. 326/2004 op. cit. n. 29, at para. 39.

33 These are the International Criminal Tribunals for the Former Yugoslavia (ICTY) and Rwanda (ICTR), the Special Court for Sierra Leone (SC-SL), and the International Criminal Court (ICC).

their supporters, and suspects in a variety of cases, PIFWC operations will have adverse effects on liberty of person and, if detentions are enforced, they may, also be capable of affecting e.g. the rights to life, physical integrity, or property. Moreover, the execution of PIFWC operations may have collateral effects on subjective rights of individuals present of the scene of such operations.[34]

B. EXERCISE OF TRANSITIONAL AUTHORITY DIRECTLY AFFECTING THE GENERAL PUBLIC

Armed conflict inevitably changes the societies it affects. It compels societies as a whole and the individuals forming them to change their priorities. Frequently, the individuals affected by armed conflict will try to escape from the exercise of authority by those who will almost certainly abuse it for their own purposes. Moreover, the end of hostilities does not enable the majority of them to instantaneously return to "normal" life and its priorities. It is likely that the struggle for survival will persist, even though it might gradually be adjusted to changing realities. Mentalities, moreover, will outlive even formal peace for significant periods of time. With this in mind, reports that 'there were not any significant incidents within the area of operations' of a peace mission must not be so misconstrued as to imply that a substantial peace is within sight or has already been achieved. Rather, the existence of latent dangers is typical to post-conflict situations during extended periods; moreover, it can be camouflaged by such formulae. The latent dangers referred to specifically involve the possibility that belligerent attitudes may resurface. Even prima facie civilian threats to security might unveil their true, that is, (para-) military nature in an instant. Measures directly affecting the general public in the receiving states tackle such low- or medium-level threats as are inherent in the makeup of conflict-ridden societies. Many of these measures have a good deal in common with internal security management yet respond to the (para-) military subtext of the threats in question on the basis of a genuinely military approach.

1° Maintaining a Safe and Secure Environment (Framework Operations)

To maintain a safe and secure environment[35], the infantry units of peacekeeping forces usually conduct such operations as patrols and vehicle checkpoints. These operations involve stopping individuals in order to establish their identity, and to search items in their possession (including their clothes and means of

34 U. Häußler, loc. cit. n. 3.

35 The terminology is not fully settled in this respect. While, for instance, the mandate for IFOR/SFOR/EUFOR ALTHEA uses the phrase 'safe and secure', the KFOR mandate speaks of 'secure' only.

transport). If necessary, items capable of endangering the mission's personnel or assets, or mission accomplishment will be seized and destroyed.

The human rights potentially affected by these actions comprise freedom of movement, privacy, and property. If enforcement action is taken, adverse effects on the rights to life, physical integrity, and property might also occur. Hypothetically, individual measures taken at a checkpoint or during a patrol might also be capable of causing physical indignity or involving torturous, inhuman or degrading treatment.

2° Protecting Designated Persons and Property – Crowd and Riot Control (CRC)

Crowd and riot control operations aim to suppress outbreaks of violence, in particular ethnically and religiously motivated violence, and ultimately to prevent upheavals from crossing the threshold of non-international armed conflict. Usually, specifically trained units are charged with CRC. Crowd and riot control operations play a particular important role for the protection and defence of Property with Designated Special Status (PRDSS). KFOR used to rely on a concept of blue and red boxes[36] that addressed both the military or paramilitary nature of the threat ultimately represented by inter-ethnic violence, and the fact that usually many of those acting violently do not resort to combatant style violence. The concept of blue and red boxes aimed to enhance the protection of any key site designated as PRDSS[37] by establishing a cordon of increasingly impermeable zones around it. Unless activated, the boxes were dormant. Red boxes comprise the objects designated for protection and their immediate surroundings; in case of activation they would have been defended against entry of unauthorised individuals. Blue boxes comprise a designated area around each red box. Activation of red boxes includes activation of blue boxes which would thereupon have been protected against unauthorised entry. The notion of protecting, as opposed to defending, implies a lower level of countermeasures in case of attempted or actual intrusions. Usually, crowd and riot control measures involving the use of riot control agents and non-lethal weapons would have been taken in order to protect blue boxes. By way of contrast, defending red boxes could have involved the use of deadly force had such force been considered necessary and commensurate with the threat it responds to.

---

36 For further details see U. Häußler, 'KFOR: Current Legal Issues', *Journal of International Law of Peace and Armed Conflict* (2007) pp. 24–32.

37 The concept of blue and red boxes is not limited to cultural heritage and religious locations. In accordance with KFOR's responsibility to protect the international civil presence (para. 9(e) of UNSC Resolution 1244 (1999)) UNMIK sites may also be designated as PRDSS if so requested by the SRSG.

CRC operations, in particular those aiming to protect designated property (and, if inhabited, the individuals therein), are capable of affecting freedom of movement (by denial of access to certain areas), freedom of assembly and of speech (if demonstrations are dissolved), and, should enforcement action be considered necessary, also liberty of person and privacy (if individuals are stopped and detained) or the rights to life and physical integrity (if force is used).

3° *Support of Law Enforcement*

As indicated, peacekeeping forces may support or conduct law enforcement (if so tasked by their mandate, pending successful institution building in the receiving states). Also, local law enforcement agencies might request support once they have established initial operating capability. Such new agencies may even continue to request for support upon reaching full operational capability in order to benefit from a peacekeeping force's reputation. Actions taken by peacekeepers in support of law enforcement may affect the same human rights as does policing in a stable constitutional democracy.

4° *Operational Detention*

Much attention has recently been drawn to the legality and legitimacy of operational detention.[38] Aside from exceptional[39] cases – 'law and order missions' – peacekeeping forces detain individuals if doing so is necessary to fulfil their military responsibilities and/or tasks in accordance with the mandate, or to protect their personnel and assets. The specific 'operational' nature is rooted in the link between a detention and the defined responsibilities and tasks of peace missions.[40] As a means of peacekeeping, operational detentions are mainly conducted in the course of operations against ex- and would-be-belligerents, and during framework operations. Peace-builders, in turn, resort to operational detention when charged with policing tasks – in particular if no functioning domestic law enforcement agencies exist in the receiving state. Operational detentions reflect particularly well what it means to entrust peace missions with transitional authority.

---

38 Operational detention and related questions of judicial review are discussed in detail in Chapters 9 and 10 of U. Häußler, op. cit. n. 10.

39 To date, the KFOR law and order mission was the only one of its kind.

40 Sometimes, operational detentions are referred to as 'administrative detentions'. See, for instance, J. Pejic, 'Procedural principles and safeguards for internment/*administrative detention* in armed conflict and other situations of violence', 87 *International Review of the Red Cross* (2005) pp. 375–391 (emphasis supplied). In my view, this term is misleading; if conducted by military peacekeepers to address a threat rooted in (para-) military capabilities, detention operations have no 'administrative' characteristics at all.

Detention operations as well as other framework operations may also affect such human rights as the freedom of movement. In particular, certain measures taken from the moment of stopping and apprehension up to the point at which a decision concerning the detention or relinquishment of an individual is made, will, as a rule, affect freedom of movement rather than liberty of person. In turn, liberty of person and the right to bring *habeas corpus* proceedings in a court of law may be affected by operational detention proper. The right to judicial review may likewise be affected in the case of vetting decisions (e.g. under the Bonn Powers held by the High Representative in Bosnia and Herzegovina) involving the exercise of authority without judicial review.

C. CONCLUSION

The examples discussed show that the measures taken by peace missions in accordance with their international mandates are capable of having adverse effects on nearly all human rights guaranteed in contemporary international law. They also show that most of these measures are responses to threats to the safe and secure environment in the receiving state – they tackle military or paramilitary capability or the latent dangers inherent in a post-conflict society that has not (yet) overcome the legacy of armed conflict.

IV. ATTRIBUTION OF CONDUCT OF PEACEKEEPING OPERATIONS TO INTERNATIONAL ORGANISATIONS

Peace missions must rely on states for their funding, personnel and assets. States contribute military contingents to international peacekeeping operations as well as civilian police (CIVPOL) contingents and/or individual personnel to peace-building operations.[41] They also provide the financial resources available to international organisations. Does that practice preclude attributing the conduct of a peacekeeping operation specifically to an international organisation – typically its lead organisation? While the practice of international organisations indicates, as a matter of principle, the opposite, many details are still unclear, and the judgment in Behrami & Saramati[42] has added confusion rather than clarity to the matter.

41 Recall that many members of the personnel of peace-building operations are recruited by the respective lead organisation – in particular the United Nations and, where involved, its Specialised Agencies – on the basis of short-term contracts.

42 ECtHR, *Behrami & Behrami v. France*, Application No. 71412/01, and *Saramati v. France, Germany and Norway*, Application No. 78166/01, 45 *EHRR* (SE10) (2007) p. 85 (hereinafter referred to as '*Behrami & Saramati*').

The most prominent analysis of attribution of conduct to international organisations, including that of peacekeeping operations, was recently undertaken by the International Law Commission (ILC). In its work concerning draft articles on responsibility of international organizations, the ILC has adopted a body of provisions dedicated to this issue. As a subsidiary organ of the United Nations, the ILC has focused on UN practice for its analysis concerning attribution criteria. This section will also consider such NATO practice as is publicly accessible. It will discuss the relationship between peacekeeping operations and their lead organisations, the relationship between contributing states and lead organisations concerning peacekeeping operations, and the criteria for attribution of actions of peacekeepers to these organisations.

A. TO WHOM TO ATTRIBUTE I: PEACE MISSIONS OR LEAD ORGANISATIONS?

Attribution of conduct presupposes that the entity to whom such conduct shall be attributed is a legal person.[43] While the legal personality of international organisations should no longer be a matter of debate in contemporary international law, the proper status of peace missions might still be considered obscure depending on the analyst's perspective. For instance, the ILC has contemplated the assumption 'that the Kosovo Force [KFOR] is an international organization'. At the same time, it has also discussed the influence of the United Nations and NATO, respectively, on KFOR. The ILC has discussed whether possible KFOR misconduct might provide 'an example of two international organizations allegedly exercising direction and control in the commission of a wrongful act'; it considered that '[a] joint exercise of direction and control was probably envisaged'.[44] To add one more example, the European Court of Human Rights has held that the actions taken by KFOR be attributable to the United

---

43 The capacity of international organisations to incur responsibility is contingent on their legal personality in international law. According to the ILC Special Rapporteur on responsibility of international organizations: 'For an organization to be held as potentially responsible it should not only have legal personality and thus some obligations of its own under international law. What is required is also that in the exercise of the relevant functions the organization may be considered as a separate entity from its members and that thus the exercise of these functions may be attributed to the organization itself.' Special Rapporteur Mr. Giorgio Gaja, 'First report on responsibility of international organizations', UN Doc. A/CN.4/532, at para. 27.

44 See ILC, *Report 2009*, op. cit. n. 4, commentary (2) on draft Article 14 on responsibility of international organizations, p. 85. The passages quoted here deal with the French Government's submissions concerning the command relationships between the United Nations and NATO, respectively, and KFOR, in the ICJ case Legality of Use of Force (Yugoslavia v. France): 'NATO is responsible for the "direction" of KFOR and the United Nations for "control" of it.' See para. 45 of the French Government's Preliminary Objections quoted *ibid.* by the ILC.

Nations in its judgment in Behrami & Saramati.[45] This indicates that, as far as international peacekeeping on behalf of the United Nations is concerned, there also is a need to identify what organisation is the lead organisation for the purposes of attribution.

It is submitted that international peace missions are not subjects of international law of their own right; rather they form part of the organisational framework of their lead organisations. According to consolidated United Nations practice, UN peacekeeping operations are subsidiary organs of the world organisation.[46] This position is shared and supported by scholarly analysis.[47] Although NATO has not made an express statement of a similar nature[48], it has de facto integrated respective force headquarters into its headquarters structure; it is therefore essentially correct that NATO peacekeeping operations have been considered subsidiary organs of NATO.[49] On that basis, it is the lead organisations rather than peace mission as such to whom the conduct of the latter must be attributed.[50] The United Nations has indeed accepted international responsibility for its peacekeeping operations. The then UN Secretary-General Kofi Annan has defined 'The principle of liability' as follows: 'The international responsibility of the United Nations for the activities of United Nations forces is an attribute of its

---

45 ECtHR, *Behrami & Saramati*, op. cit. n. 42, at para. 141.

46 The references in the passages of ILC Reports to the United Nations General Assembly dealing with responsibility of international organisations contain abundant references where the character of UN peacekeeping operations as subsidiary organs of the organisation is so dealt with as if it were unquestionable and self-evident.

47 See G. Jaenicke, 'Article 7, in B. Simma, ed., *Charter of the United Nations*, 2 edn. (Oxford, Oxford University Press 2002), at paras. 17–18.

48 Note that the NATO Handbook 2006 makes no mention of the command and control relationship between NATO's permanent headquarters and NATO's field headquarters, regardless of whether headquarters of peacekeeping operations or residual headquarters like NHQs Tirana, Skopje and Sarajevo.

49 The Council of Europe's Venice Commission considers KFOR to be an organ of NATO. European Commission for Democracy through Law (Venice Commission), *Opinion on Human Rights in Kosovo: Possible Establishment of Review Mechanisms*, CDL-AD(2004)33(11 October 2004) (hereafter Venice Commission Opinion), available at www.venice.coe.int/docs/2004/CDL-AD(2004)033-e.pdf at para. 63. – Note that from a terminological perspective it might be closer to the language used in the North Atlantic Treaty to consider deployed headquarters of NATO and/or NATO-led operations, as well as forces placed under their authority by a Transfer of Authority message ('TOA Message'), to be 'subsidiary bodies' of the North Atlantic Council in the sense given to this phrase by Article 9 of the North Atlantic Treaty.

50 Note that many NATO Member States have accepted, as a matter of principle, that NATO can incur responsibility under international law. Concerning Operation Allied Force, a couple of them argued in the International Court of Justice and the European Court of Human Rights that Allied Force and individual operations in its framework were attributable to NATO. See Special Rapporteur Mr. Giorgio Gaja, 'Second report on responsibility of international organizations', UN Doc. A/CN. 4/541, at para. 7 and footnote 9 for references.

international legal personality and its capacity to bear international rights and obligations.'[51]

International Jurisprudence seems to support this position.[52] It follows from the foregoing that international peace missions must be regarded as subsidiary organs, or equivalent, of their lead organisations, and that these organisations are capable of incurring international responsibility for their conduct.

B. TO WHOM TO ATTRIBUTE II: LEAD ORGANISATIONS OR CONTRIBUTING STATES?

Referring to Article 2(1)(i) of the 1986 Vienna Convention on the Law of Treaties between States and International Organizations or between International Organizations which defines that '"international organization" means an intergovernmental organization', the ILC assumes … 'that international law endows these international organizations with legal personality because otherwise their conduct would be attributed to their members and no question of an organization's responsibility under international law would arise.'[53]

It goes without saying that this statement does not imply that peacekeeping operations can be launched in the framework of international organisations for the purpose of (inter alia) precluding international responsibility of the contributing states: if only because, as the ILC has aptly observed, there can be 'responsibility into which States may incur for activities of the organization of which they are members'.[54] The ILC, moreover, sympathetically refers to a submission made by the United Nations Legal Counsel as to the international

---

51 See UN Secretary-General Report, 'Administrative and budgetary aspects of the financing of the United Nations peacekeeping operations: financing of the United Nations peacekeeping operations', UN Doc. A/51/389, at para. 6. The quote continues: 'It is also a reflection of the principle of State responsibility – widely accepted to be applicable to international organizations – that damage caused in breach of an international obligation and which is attributable to the State (or to the Organization) entails the international responsibility of the State (or of the Organization) and its liability in compensation.'

52 The International Court of Justice has, in an *obiter dictum* in its Advisory Opinion on the Difference Relating to Immunity from Legal Process of a Special Rapporteur of the Commission on Human Rights, observed that it 'wishes to point out that the question of immunity from legal process is distinct from the issue of compensation for any damages incurred as a result of acts performed by the United Nations or by its agents acting in their official capacity. The United Nations may be required to bear responsibility for the damage arising from such acts.' ICJ, *Difference Relating to Immunity from Legal Process of a Special Rapporteur of the Commission on Human Rights* (Cumaraswamy Case), Advisory Opinion, *ICJ Rep.* (1999) p. 88, at para. 66.

53 See ILC, *Report of the Fifty-fourth session (29 April – 7 June and 22 July – 16 August 2002)*, UN Doc. A/57/10, at para. 469.

54 *Ibid.*, at para. 470.

responsibility of the world organisation: 'As a subsidiary organ of the United Nations, an act of a peacekeeping force is, in principle, imputable to the Organization, and if committed in violation of an international obligation entails the international responsibility of the Organization and its liability in compensation. The fact that any such act may have been performed by members of a national military contingent forming part of the peacekeeping operation does not affect the international responsibility of the United Nations vis-à-vis third States or individuals.'[55]

The ILC was not the only body to consider international organisations internationally responsible for the conduct of peace missions. For instance, the NATO peace missions in Kosovo and Afghanistan attracted related analysis and were dealt with in relevant international arrangements. The Council of Europe's Venice Commission, focusing on KFOR, dealt with the question how NATO's and its member states' related spheres of responsibility can be delineated.[56] Amnesty International recommended different kinds of action to NATO and ISAF troop contributing states, respectively, in its report entitled 'Afghanistan – Detainees transferred to torture: ISAF complicity?' released on 13 November 2007.[57] The Council of Europe negotiated with NATO concerning access of its Committee for the Prevention of Torture to KFOR detention facilities in Kosovo, issue on which agreement was eventually reached in 2006.[58]

Both practice and corresponding analysis demonstrate that international organisations may be internationally responsible for the conduct of international peace missions under their lead, with human rights accountability being a significant aspect of such international responsibility. The following sections of this contribution will analyse attribution criteria, the contentious issue of attribution to the United Nations in cases of delegation of Chapter VII authority, and the delineation of responsibility between the lead organisation and troop contributing states, focusing on operational control, national caveats and nationally retained powers.

1° Attribution Criteria

The International Law Commission has interpreted the quoted statement made by the United Nations Legal Counsel to the extent that '[t]he United Nations

55 See United Nations Legal Counsel's unpublished letter of 3 February 2004 to the Director of the Codification Division as quoted in Special Rapporteur Mr. Giorgio Gaja, op. cit. n. 50, at para. 36.

56 See Venice Commission Opinion, op. cit. n. 49, at para. 79, footnote 26.

57 See Amnesty International, *Afghanistan – Detainees transferred to torture: ISAF complicity*, document ASA 11/011/2007, at pp. 36 *et seq.*

58 For details see U. Häußler, loc. cit. n. 36, at pp. 26 *et seq.*

assumes that in principle it has exclusive control of the deployment of national contingents in a peacekeeping force'.[59] Translated into an attribution criterion, this observation means that the United Nations will incur responsibility for such activities of a peacekeeping force as within its 'exclusive control'. The attribute attached to the notion of control indicates that there can be different degrees of control, and that such degree of control may have an impact on attribution. In particular, where control is not exclusive, conduct, or aspects thereof, are attributable to both the lead organisation and troop contributing states. According to the Council of Europe's Venice Commission, the degree of influence over individual aspects of such conduct is the criterion for delineation of spheres of responsibility.[60] Similar considerations, although not expressly relied upon, seem to have guided Amnesty International when it devised recommendations to NATO and ISAF troop contributing states, respectively, which reflected an assessment concerning attribution of conduct on the basis of influence thereover.[61]

The examples discussed supra demonstrate that international responsibility, resulting from attribution of conduct as it does, is contingent on the degree of control of the conduct in question. They also indicate that the models of responsibility known from e.g. tort law can be adapted to the framework of international responsibility. Accordingly, as reflected in an observation made by the International Law Commission[62], conduct may be attributable to troop contributing states or international organisations alternatively, or both troop contributing states and international organisations jointly and severally. On that

---

59 See ILC, *Report 2009*, op. cit. n. 4, commentary (5) on draft Article 6 on responsibility of international organizations, at pp. 64 *et seq.* For the quotation see *supra* text accompanying footnote 55.

60 In its Opinion on Human Rights in Kosovo the Venice Commission established by the Council of Europe observed that 'acts by troops in the context of a NATO-led operation cannot simply all be attributed either to NATO or to the individual troop-contributing states'. To substantiate its point the Venice Commission discussed the example of a KFOR roadblock. In the Commission's view, 'if the KFOR Commander orders different national contingents to establish a certain number of roadblocks at certain locations this measure, in itself, must be attributed to NATO.' In the absence of a 'valid reason' for ordering the roadblocks NATO would be accountable for 'foreseeable damage' caused by the roadblock. In contrast, nations would be accountable if 'a person who happens to be searched at one of the roadblocks is mistreated by one [of] the soldiers'. The Venice Commission considered that states were not in a position to substantially influence the COMKFOR order and hence confined to opting out whereas they could influence the conduct of soldiers at the roadblocks through on-scene commanders of their own nationality. See Venice Commission Opinion, op. cit. n. 49, at para. 79, footnote 26.

61 See Amnesty International, op. cit. n. 57, at pp. 36 *et seq.*

62 As observed by the ILC: 'One of the questions which have been mostly considered in practice with regard to the responsibility of international organizations concerns the attribution of wrongful conduct either to an organization or to its member States or to some of them; in certain cases attribution could conceivably be made both to an organization and to its member States.' See ILC Report 2002, op. cit. n. 53, at para. 476.

basis, analysis of the conditions in which conduct of peace missions occurs must focus on the degree of control exercised by the states and international organisations involved; in doing so, it must extrapolate all relevant factors indicating control and examine whether control is actually associated with them in practice.

For the purposes of this analysis, the existence of a specific hierarchical structure facilitating the exercise of control is arguably the most important factor within military environments (including those of international peacekeeping operations); this factor shall hence be addressed in greater depth. As a rule, the (military) command and control framework of international peacekeeping operations comprises international headquarters[63] at the political and military strategic levels as well as the operational level.[64] Most international peacekeeping operations have international headquarters at a tactical theatre level, some of them also at a lower tactical level.[65] By contrast, units are usually mono-national but may occasionally also may be bi/multinational.[66] Command and control frameworks are established by the lead organisation; troops contributed[67] to the operation are integrated by virtue of Transfer of Authority Messages ('TOA Messages')[68] which may also reflect participating or contributing state agreements should such agreements have been concluded. As indicated by their name, TOA Messages transfer authority over the troops covered by the message

---

63 Headquarters are 'international' for the purposes of this presentation if they are organs of the international organisation. The fact that their composition is frequently referred to as 'multinational' reflects the fact that the number of states that contribute personnel to international headquarters is limited. With that in mind, the label 'multinational' does not affect the international nature of the headquarters in question.

64 Military strategic level headquarters comprise, for instance, NATO's Allied Commands Transformation (ACT) and Operations (ACO – also known as SHAPE). The European Union utilises Operation Headquarters (OHQ) established by a framework nation at operational level; these OHQ may be capable of performing military strategic functions, as well. Depending on the overall command and control structure of a mission, Joint Force Commands (JFC) and Force Headquarters (FHQ) represent the operational level. FHQ might, however, also perform tactical level tasks.

65 Some FHQs are tactical theater headquarters; Component Commands (CC) usually belong to this category, as well. Lower tactical level headquarters comprise Division (DIV) and Brigade (BDE) Headquarters. For instance, IFOR and SFOR had Multinational Divisions for significant periods of time which were first converted into Multinational Brigades and later into Multinational Task Forces.

66 Units comprise e.g. Battalions (BN) and Companies (COY).

67 Unless troop contributing states limit their contribution to specialist and headquarters personnel, they form national contingents – usually composed of units and specialist and headquarters personnel – which are then contributed to the international peacekeeping operation as a whole.

68 NATO defines transfer of authority to mean 'Within NATO, an action by which a member nation or NATO Command gives operational command or control of designated forces to a NATO Command'. *NATO Glossary of Terms and Definitions* (NATO document AAP-6(2010) – online at www.nato.int/docu/stanag/aap006/aap-6-2010.pdf) at 2-T-8 (definition adopted 9 January 1996).

to the international organisation in the lead of the peacekeeping operation. Usually, the degree of authority transferred is operational control (OPCON). From a legal perspective, transfer of authority, viz. the act of contributing military contingents to an international peacekeeping operation, is tantamount to placing organs or agents at the disposal of an international organisation. The International Law Commission's relevant analysis indicates that cases can be distinguished where the lead organisation can exclusively determine the conduct of the contingents contributed[69] and cases where the contributing states retain a certain degree of authority over their contingents.[70] This ILC analysis focuses on control of conduct of operations; as will be demonstrated shortly, the exercise of retained administrative authority, including disciplinary powers and criminal jurisdiction[71] by troop contributing states is a different matter.

Apart from TOA Messages, such factors as the command and control framework and agreed command and control doctrine of the lead organisations are key to the delineation of spheres of control of forces, attribution to lead organisations and contributing states, and associated international responsibility.

---

69 ILC, *Report of the Fifty-third session (23 April – 1 June and 2 July – 10 August 2001)*, UN Doc. A/56/10, commentary (3) on Article 57 of the articles on State responsibility, at p. 361, contains the observation that: 'if a State seconds officials to an international organization so that they act as organs or officials of the organization, their conduct will be attributed to the organization, not the sending State, and will fall outside the scope of the articles.' Moreover, the ILC has considered from a similar perspective: 'the cases in which the conduct of a State organ is mandated by an international organization or takes place in an area that falls within an organization's exclusive competence.' See ILC, *Report 2002*, op. cit. n. 53, at para. 477. Note that the ILC discussed an example derived from the United Nations Convention on the Law of the Sea to support this point.

70 With relevant practice in mind, the ILC has suggested a provision that is supposed to deal 'with the … situation in which the lent organ or agent still acts to a certain extent as organ of the lending State or as organ or agent of the lending organization'. According to the ILC: 'This occurs for instance in the case of military contingents that a State places at the disposal of the United Nations for a peacekeeping operation, since the State retains disciplinary powers and criminal jurisdiction over the members of the national contingent.' For both quotes see ILC, *Report 2009*, op. cit. n. 4, commentary (1) on draft Article 6 on responsibility of international organizations, at p. 62. – Note that, as a matter of principle, the command and control framework of all peacekeeping operations is similar, no matter whether under OPCON of the United Nations, NATO, the European Union, etc; accordingly, equivalent legal considerations apply. The draft provision reads as follows: '*Article 6 – Conduct of organs or agents placed at the disposal of an international organization by a State or another international organization.* The conduct of an organ of a State or an organ or agent of an international organization that is placed at the disposal of another international organization shall be considered under international law an act of the latter organization if the organization exercises effective control over that conduct.'

71 The *NATO Glossary of Terms and Definitions*, op. cit. n. 68, defines the notion of administrative control at 2-A-3 (definition adopted 01 April 1971) as follows: 'Direction or exercise of authority over subordinate or other organizations in respect to administrative matters such as personnel management, supply, services, and other matters not included in the operational missions of the subordinate or other organizations'. Disciplinary powers and criminal jurisdiction form part of personnel management, broadly understood.

2° *Attribution to the United Nations in Cases of Delegation of Chapter VII Authority*

The preceding considerations were based on the premise that the lead organisation to whom conduct of a peace mission is attributable is the international organisation in whose command and control framework the mission in question is integrated. This is not self-evident since e.g. in cases of international peacekeeping multiple international organisations can be involved: the United Nations by way of its Security Council adopting a resolution embodying and/or endorsing the international mandate as well as another international organisation in whose command and control structure the peacekeeping operation established in accordance with the mandate is integrated. It is obvious that questions of attribution may arise in such cases which most frequently occur as cases of exercise of delegated Chapter VII authority. Although the UN Security Council has never decided to 'delegate' Chapter VII authority in express language, doing so is part of its consolidated practice and accepted as such.[72] Accordingly, analysis of the effects of delegating Chapter VII authority on attribution requires that the notion thereof first be defined. For this purpose, the pertinent provisions of the UN Charter will be briefly analysed in the light of relevant practice.

It is obvious that the UN Security Council lacks the capability itself to implement the measures it is empowered to decide upon in accordance with Articles 39–42 and Article 51 of the UN Charter. Originally, the UN Charter envisaged two different approaches towards implementation. Although it never did in practice, the UN Security Council could have assumed command and control of forces 'placed at its disposal'[73] in accordance with Article 43 of the UN Charter.[74] In practice, however, 'the whole development of peace-keeping operations involving

---

72 Danesh Sarooshi has analysed the issue of delegation of Chapter VII powers to *inter alia* international organizations. D. Sarooshi, *The United Nations and the Development of Collective Security – The Delegation by the UN Security Council of its Chapter VII Powers* (Oxford, Oxford University Press 1999). Sarooshi has assessed the delegation of authority to NATO concerning its efforts to bring peace back to the former Yugoslavia (at pp. 253–281) as follows (at pp. 281 *et seq.*): 'The delegation of Chapter VII powers to regional arrangements is a desirable process since, as shown above, it can lead to military enforcement action being taken on behalf of the Council to achieve the Council's stated objectives.'

73 The quotation is a courtesy of Article 47(1) of the UN Charter which adequately summarises the substantive content of Article 43 of the UN Charter. – Notwithstanding the limited significance of Article 47 of the UN Charter, the International Law Commission uses its terminology in the draft articles on state responsibility and the responsibility of international organizations.

74 In my view, Article 47 of the UN Charter delineates the responsibilities of the UN Security Council and the Military Staff Committee in a similar manner as does the North Atlantic Treaty between the North Atlantic Council and the Military Committee, viz. in the UN framework the Security Council is envisaged to be de decision-maker and the Military Staff Committee an advisory body. For a similar view concerning the role of the Military

armed UN troops has bypassed the Committee'[75], resulting in the emergence of a genuine and distinct UN implementation mechanism. In using this mechanism, the UN Security Council authorises Chapter VII action, meaning that it confers the authority to perform functions which itself is incapable of performing to the appropriate subsidiary organ or the United Nations, viz. a UN peacekeeping operation. The alternative option is implementation by the UN Member States including by international organisations they may have established. As illustrated by Article 48 of the UN Charter, implementation is a matter to be taken care of – 'by all ... or by some of them', and 'directly and through their action in the appropriate international agencies of which they are members'. As Article 48 of the UN Charter aims at flexibility in the execution of enforcement measures[76], it provides sufficient cover for the delegation of Chapter VII authority to international organisations – even outside the United Nations Family – both through the UN Member States and directly.

The UN Security Council 'delegates' Chapter VII authority by way of conferring, on one or more states, or an international organisation, the right to exercise some or all of its own Chapter VII powers. In doing so, the UN Security Council has frequently limited the delegation of Chapter VII authority by virtue of determining the purposes for which conferred Chapter VII powers may be used.[77] Accordingly, the UN Security Council's approach towards delegation adapts its original authorisation technique to the peculiarities of the exercise of Chapter VII powers by a non-UN actor[78] (without, however, giving blanket authority to use force[79]). It follows that the act conferring such powers is legally

Staff Committee see B.-O. Bryde and A. Reinisch, 'Article 47', in B. Simma, op. cit. n. 47, at para 17.

75 B.-O. Bryde and A. Reinisch, loc. cit. n. 74, at para. 18.

76 B.-O. Bryde and A. Reinisch, 'Article 48', in B. Simma, op. cit. n. 47, at para. 8.

77 To give but one example, the UN Security Council has limited the delegation of Chapter VII authority concerning the military aspects of the Kosovo settlement by way of rendering the authorisation 'to establish the international security presence in Kosovo' subject to the qualification that KFOR may be established 'to fulfil its responsibilities under paragraph 9 below', that is, not for any other purposes. See para. 7 of UNSC Resolution 1244 (1999).

78 In that sense, it is correct to assert that: 'the term "authorisation" can be regarded as synonymous with the delegation of powers, at least as far as it concerns the act of conferring part or all of the UN Security Council's military power to member states or regional organizations.' See E. de Wet, *The Chapter VII Powers of the United Nations Security Council* (Oxford, Hart Publishing 2004) at pp. 259 *et seq.* where she also discusses the difference between the delegation of powers by the UN Security Council and the authorisation to perform functions which the UN Security Council itself may not perform.

79 By way of contrast, the UN Security Council usually does not limit the degree of force available when authorising international organisations (and/or states) to establish an international (or multinational) peacekeeping operation in support of a peace settlement. Rather, it authorises the use of 'all necessary means' or 'all necessary measures' to fulfil the mandate, viz. no specific limits (apart from proportionality) govern the use of means and

distinct from their actual exercise. Attribution of the exercise of Chapter VII powers by a non-UN actor must hence reflect this distinction.

The ILC has discussed attribution of the exercise of delegated authority with respect to multinational peacekeeping; in this respect, it sympathises with the view that the United Nations does not incur responsibility under international law for the conduct of peacekeeping forces whose operations it has authorised but does neither direct nor control.[80, 81] It follows that the ILC supports the principle that an entity which exercises authority delegated by the UN Security Council is internationally responsible for its actions in the course thereof.[82] Jurisprudence concerning multinational peacekeeping confirms this view. The

measures of coercion. See *infra sub specie* 'Military Necessity and Operational Necessity' for further details.

80 According to the ILC it 'appears accurate' that: '[...] insofar as "Opération Turquoise" is concerned, although that operation was "authorized" by the UN Security Council, the operation itself was under national command and control and was not a United Nations operation. The United Nations is, therefore, not internationally responsible for acts and omissions that might be attributable to "Opération Turquoise".' Unpublished letter of the United Nations Secretary-General to the Prime Minister of Rwanda, dated 11 November 1996; quoted in ILC, *Report 2009*, op. cit. n. 4, commentary (12) on draft Article 16 on responsibility of international organizations, at p. 91.

81 The ILC's Special Rapporteur on responsibility of international organizations has also discussed attribution with respect to sanctions implemented by UN Member States. Sanctions regimes and multinational peacekeeping share the absence of United Nations direction and control; the implied analogy regarding attribution does hence represent a viable approach. The Special Rapporteur has indicated that he shares the view that: 'The responsibility for carrying out embargoes imposed by the UN Security Council rests with Member States, which are accordingly responsible for meeting the costs of any particular action they deem necessary for ensuring compliance with the embargo.' See the memorandum dated 21 April 1995, submitted by the Office of Legal Affairs of the United Nations concerning a claim for reimbursement of cargo handling expenses incurred by a company during the fruitless inspection of a ship in Djibouti in the course of enforcing a weapons embargo – *United Nations Juridical Yearbook* (1995), pp. 464–465. The Assistant Secretary-General for Legal Affairs, Mr. Ralph Zacklin, reiterated in a letter of 4 May 1998 relating to the same case: 'The responsibility for implementing and enforcing mandatory sanctions imposed by the UN Security Council of the United Nations rests with States.' Both quotes are from Special Rapporteur Mr. Giorgio Gaja, op. cit. n. 50, at para. 13 and footnote 19.

82 Note, however, that the ILC has cautiously stated that: 'For instance, the articles do not say, but only imply, that conduct of military forces of States or international organizations is not attributable to the United Nations when the UN Security Council authorizes States or international organizations to take necessary measures outside a chain of command linking those forces to the United Nations. This point, which is hardly controversial, was recently expressed by the Director of the Field Administration and Logistics Division of the Department of Peacekeeping Operations of the United Nations in a letter to the Permanent Representative of Belgium to the United Nations, concerning a claim resulting from a car accident in Somalia, in the following terms: "UNITAF troops were not under the command of the United Nations and the Organization has constantly declined liability for any claims made in respect of incidents involving those troops."' See ILC, *Report 2009*, op. cit. n. 4, commentary (5) on the preliminary remarks concerning attribution of conduct to an international organization, at p. 57, quoting an unpublished letter dated 25 June 1998.

House of Lords has attributed the conduct of MNF-I to the relevant troop contributing state, relying on such conduct as orders given and actual execution of assigned tasks.[83] Both giving orders and executing certain tasks represent effective control of the conduct in question.

From such perspective, it is surprising that the ILC – concerning international peacekeeping in the case of KFOR – also voiced the consideration that '[a] joint exercise of direction and control [of KFOR by the UN and NATO] was probably envisaged'.[84] Nothing in UNSCR 1244 (1999) indicates that either NATO, once it had established KFOR as a peacekeeping operation within its command and control framework, or the states involved in establishing KFOR (who happened to be members of both NATO and the United Nations), would have to share 'direction and control', or effective control, of KFOR with the United Nations.

The opposite view, although supported by the European Court of Human Rights in Behrami & Saramati, is not convincing. According to the Strasbourg Court: 'delegation must be sufficiently limited so as to remain compatible with the degree of centralisation of UNSC collective security constitutionally necessary under the Charter and, more specifically, for the acts of the delegate entity to be attributable to the UN.'[85]

This dictum tackles two separate concerns, viz. 'centralisation of UNSC collective security' and attribution of 'the acts of the delegate entity' to the United Nations. This position, particularly in its capacity as a premise for the subsequent reasoning of the European Court of Human Rights, is rather questionable. First, it is within the UN Security Council's remit to decide how it wants international peace and security to be maintained or restored. Collective Security within the framework of the UN Charter requires decisions to be made by the UN Security Council; it does not require such decisions to be carried out in any particular manner as long as their implementation fits the aforementioned co-ordinates defined by Article 48 of the UN Charter and/or reflected in consolidated UN Security Council practice under the UN Charter. Second, the Strasbourg Court asserts rather than explains why 'delegation must be sufficiently limited ... for the acts of the delegate entity to be attributable to the UN'. This part of the

83 See the judgment of the House of Lords, *R (on the application of Al-Jedda) (FC) v Secretary of State for Defence*, [2007] *UKHL* 58, at paras. 22–25. The House of Lords has stressed that the UK government's assertion that an analogy can be drawn between KFOR and UNMIK on the one hand, and MNF-I on the other hand, 'breaks down on almost every point'. In particular, MNF-I 'was not established at the behest of the UN, was not mandated to operate under UN auspices and was not a subsidiary organ of the UN. There was no delegation of UN power in Iraq.' *Ibid.*, at para. 24 (per Lord Bingham of Cornhill). This assessment contains a proper summary of the key differences between international and multinational peacekeeping.

84 See *supra* text accompanying footnote 44.

85 ECtHR, *Behrami & Saramati*, op. cit. n. 42, at para. 132.

quoted dictum indicates that, in the court's view, that 'the acts of the delegate entity' ought to 'be attributable to the UN' in order to maintain the 'collective' nature of security whereas only 'the multilateral and complex nature of such security missions renders necessary some delegation of command'.[86] Implied in this passage is the assumption that 'some delegation of command' is the exception rather than the rule[87] and that attribution of the exercise of delegated authority to the United Nations must hence be ensured. This position lacks the necessary support from the ordinary meaning to be given to the terms of the UN Charter in their context and in the light of the UN Charter's object and purpose. As discussed, the UN Charter has established the options for implementation of Chapter VII UNSCRs as matters of equal choice, not as rule and exception. Moreover, its consolidated interpretation and application by the UN Security Council – to which States have not objected and which hence represents subsequent practice in the application of the UN Charter which establishes the agreement of the parties regarding its interpretation – demonstrates that the act conferring powers (i.e. delegating authority) is legally distinct from their (the authority's) actual exercise. The European Court of Human rights fails to recognise this distinction; it is on this basis that it proposes that 'the acts of the delegate entity' (the acts of exercise of delegated authority) ought to 'be attributable to the UN' where this requirements only covers the act of delegation.[88]

In the light of the foregoing, it is of limited surprise that the Strasbourg Court needed to resort to an unusual degree of innovationism in its reasoning. The range of surprising innovations is broad. The Court has, e.g., in invented the notion of 'ultimate authority and control'[89] where no such command relationship exists in either military doctrine or practice.[90] It has also read much into the fact that the UN Security Council had resolved to remain 'actively seized of the matter' in para. 21 of UNSCR 1244 (1999)[91] although this passage merely means that the matter shall remain on its agenda rather than be struck off it. Moreover, the Strasbourg Court has also attached a substantial meaning to a usual formality, viz. the reporting requirement under para. 20 of UNSCR 1244 (1999), requirement that limits the UN's role to receiving and evaluating the reports

86 *Ibid.*

87 This understanding of the court is supported by its pointing at 'the absence of Article 43 agreements' (*ibid.*) which the court apparently considers the rule.

88 Arguably, the Strasbourg court's position is even based on a *petitio principii* because it argues in favour of a requirement that the attributability of the acts of exercise of delegated authority to the United Nations must be maintained, and later holds that these acts are indeed so attributable.

89 ECtHR, *Behrami & Saramati*, op. cit. n. 42, at para. 133.

90 See U. Häußler, 'Regional Human rights vs. International Peace missions: Lessons learned from Kosovo', *Journal of International Law of Peace and Armed Conflict* (2007) p. 238, at p. 240.

91 ECtHR, *Behrami & Saramati*, op. cit. n. 42, at para. 134.

from the leadership of the international security presence (through its lead organisation's chain of command[92]) rather than retaining effective UN control.

The reporting requirement demonstrates the limited role retained by the United Nations with respect to the exercise of transitional authority by KFOR particularly well. It is true that a peacekeeping force's report enables its recipient to assess its authors' compliance with the relevant mandate. However, unlike suggested by some authors, receiving reports does not obligate the recipient to take action[93]; even the question of whether the UN Security Council wants to conclude that a peacekeeping operation has exceeded its mandate remains at its discretion.[94] As a result, receiving reports must not be misunderstood as indicative of the exercise of effective control, the UN Security Council's power to cancel a delegation of Chapter VII authority as well as to seize effective control *ex nunc* notwithstanding. Unless, however, the UN Security Council so re-establishes effective United Nations control it must be deemed to have accepted that the exercise of any delegated authority will be reviewed by the lead organisation through which UN member states have chosen to act (Article 48(2) of the UN Charter). NATO practice in relation to KFOR confirms this legal assessment; it demonstrates that the North Atlantic Council, after in effect establishing KFOR as a subsidiary body in the sense of Article 9 of the North Atlantic Treaty (or equivalent) by virtue of its relevant decisions taken in accordance with the North Atlantic Treaty as well as para. 7 of UNSCR 1244 (1999)[95], has exercised political direction and control of KFOR by virtue of e.g. approving the strategic Operation Plans for the NATO Balkans operations.[96]

---

92 The UN Secretary-General receives the KFOR reports concerning the situation in Kosovo from the NATO Secretary-General; it can be assumed that this involves approval both through the military chain of command (JFC Naples, SHAPE) and, at the political level, by the North Atlantic Council.

93 This is, however, the quintessence of Danesh Sarooshi's analysis (op. cit. n. 72). See also the position of E. de Wet, op. cit. n. 78, at pp. 320 *et seq.*

94 This follows *a contrario* from the fact, highlighted by the discussions concerning the responsibility to protect, that the UN Security Council is not even considered legally obligated to take determined action to repress genocide, crimes against humanity, or war crimes. The continued reluctance of certain permanent members of the UN Security Council to approve a Chapter VII UNSC Resolution authorising a peace mission with such mandate and capabilities as necessary for this purpose and also to enforce existing and future indictments issued by the International Criminal Court in relation to the situation in the Sudanese province of Darfur, demonstrates that, regrettable as it may be, the broad discretion enjoyed by the UN Security Council is still supported by practice, and must hence still be considered good law.

95 See U. Häußler, op. cit. n. 10, at pp. 48 *et seq.*

96 See U. Häußler, loc. cit. n. 90, at p. 241.

By way of conclusion, comprehensive delegation of authority – as usually is the case of both international and multinational peace missions – does not relieve the United Nations of all responsibility under international law. However, the world organisation is, as a rule, only accountable for the act of delegation. Arguably, it would also incur international responsibility in the event of total inaction on the part of the UN Security Council despite having received compelling evidence that an organisation entrusted with delegated Chapter VII authority deliberately exercises such authority in an illegal manner.

3° *Operational Control, National Caveats, and Nationally Retained Powers*

Whatever measure of control international organisations may have of peacekeeping forces, none of them has ever enjoyed exclusive control of each and every action forming part of the conduct of peacekeeping forces in practice. In particular, troop contributing states have always retained certain powers – in particular administrative authority, including disciplinary powers and criminal jurisdiction – over their contingents; some conduct might hence be attributable to these states.[97] As far as disciplinary powers and criminal jurisdiction are concerned, attribution is most often rooted in the failure to act where action is otherwise deemed obligatory – in particular, where international law imposes 'prevent and punish' obligations on states, or requires them to investigate alleged violations of human rights.[98] Apart from that, deficient pre-deployment training and/or provision of insufficient equipment to fulfil the mandate may also incur international responsibility on the part of troop contributing states, including human rights accountability where protection of human rights is an obligation under the mandate.

Besides retaining administrative authority, including disciplinary powers and criminal jurisdiction, troop contributing states sometimes notify national

97 Discussing 'the control that the contributing State retains over disciplinary matters and criminal affairs', the ILC has observed that: 'Attribution of conduct to the contributing State is clearly linked with the retention of some powers by that State over its national contingent and thus on the control that the State possesses in the relevant respect.' See ILC, *Report 2009*, op. cit. n. 4, commentary (6) on draft Article 6 on responsibility of international organizations, at pp. 65 *et seq.*, referring to relevant Contributing State Agreements and an opinion of the United Nations Office of Legal Affairs concerning troop contributing states' obligation to ensure compliance with obligations under the 1973 Convention on International Trade in Endangered Species of Wild Fauna and Flora (quoted from *United Nations Juridical Yearbook* (1994) at p. 450)

98 For a recent example of deployed forces' failure to report alleged human rights violations through the national chain (in addition to reports appropriately made through the operational chain) as well as that failure's attribution to a troop contributing state see the UN Committee Against Torture's Concluding Observations concerning Sweden (UN Doc. CAT/SWE/CO/5, at para. 19.

caveats[99] or, as shown by various examples, even retain powers over national contingents contributed to international peacekeeping forces in clear contradiction to relevant contributing state agreements.[100] In these cases, the exercise of the lead organisation's command and control as well as the exercise of retained authority by the troop contributing states may be hard to distinguish when assessing the exercise of transitional authority by the international peacekeeping force – if only because of they are too closely interwoven. The classified nature of many relevant documents may add to this challenge; in some cases it might even preclude that an assessable distinction can established.

It is in these cases where, as the ILC has accurately identified, the need to 'inquire whether there is a joint or a joint and several responsibility or whether the member States' responsibility is only subsidiary'[101] is most pressing – yet where such an inquiry is also prone to fail. A possible remedy could be to rely, for the purpose of attribution, upon such rebuttable presumptions as can be derived from the definition of the relevant command and control relationship in the lead organisation's military doctrine.

As indicated earlier, states usually contribute their contingents to a peacekeeping force on the basis of a transfer of operational control. Transfer of OPCON preserves troop contributing states' ability to exercise administrative authority, including disciplinary powers and criminal jurisdiction. Given the absence of such powers and jurisdiction on the part of lead organisations, the requirements

99 The *NATO Glossary of Terms and Definitions* (op. cit. n. 68) contains a recently agreed definition of 'caveat' at 2-C-2 (adopted 20 June 2006)): 'In NATO operations, any limitation, restriction or constraint by a nation on its military forces or civilian elements under NATO command and control or otherwise available to NATO, that does not permit NATO commanders to deploy and employ these assets fully in line with the approved operation plan. – Note: A caveat may apply inter alia to freedom of movement within the joint operations area and/or to compliance with the approved rules of engagement.'

100 See the examples discussed in the ILC, *Report 2009*, op. cit. n. 4, commentary (7) on draft Article 6 on responsibility of international organizations, at pp. 65 *et seq*. and U. Häußler, 'Command Responsibility in Combined Environments', 44 *The Military Law and the Law of War Review* (2005) pp. 143–167.

101 See ILC Report 2002, op. cit. n. 53, at para. 479. See also *ibid*., para. 482: 'Should one consider that the conduct of an organ of a State is attributed to the same State even when conduct is mandated by an international organization, the issue whether the organization is responsible in this case would have to be considered together with the instances of aid or assistance, direction and control, or coercion of a State by an organization over the commission of an internationally wrongful act.' Moreover, compare commentary (6) on draft Article 3 on responsibility of international organizations: 'The fact that an international organization is responsible for an internationally wrongful act does not exclude the existence of parallel responsibility of other subjects of international law in the same set of circumstances. For instance, an international organization may have cooperated with a State in the breach of an obligation imposed on both.' ILC, *Report 2009*, op. cit. n. 4), at p. 53.

of the doctrine of command responsibility[102] compel them to do so. Apart from that, as demonstrated by relevant definitions in military doctrine[103], troop contributing states' authority over their forces is fairly limited after transfer of authority. In particular, operational planning and decision-making is internationalised as a result of the transfer of OPCON. Accordingly, the phrase contained in the NATO definition that commanders exercising OPCON 'may accomplish specific missions or tasks which are usually limited by function, time, or location; to deploy units concerned, and to retain or assign tactical control of those units' sounds more limiting than it actually is. Considering that OPCON is exercised in accordance with an OPLAN agreed upon at international level (i.e. approved by the North Atlantic Council in the case of NATO), all 'specific missions or tasks' are predetermined by this OPLAN. As a result, the internationally agreed OPLAN and the transfer of OPCON taken together as a whole afford significant authority to commanders of international peacekeeping forces. As a result, the exercise of such transitional authority as has been entrusted in the peacekeeping force should hence be presumed attributable to the lead organisation.

The presumption thus established is rebuttable, in which event attribution may shift away from the lead organisation. In such cases, international legal responsibility rests with either the lead organisation and the troop contributing state jointly and severally, or with the troop contributing state alone. For rebuttal, it must be established that the lead organisation has not controlled exclusively the conduct of operations whose attribution is at issue. The object of exclusive control in this context is post-TOA in-theatre conduct; troop contributing states' decisions concerning pre-deployment training, force composition, and provision

102 On the importance of the doctrine of command responsibility in this respect see U. Häußler, op. cit. n. 10, at pp. 51 *et seq.* and pp. 79 *et seq.*

103 The *NATO Glossary of Terms and Definitions*, op. cit. n. 68, defines OPCON at 2-O-3 (definition adopted 01 October 2001) as follows: 'The authority delegated to a commander to direct forces assigned so that the commander may accomplish specific missions or tasks which are usually limited by function, time, or location; to deploy units concerned, and to retain or assign tactical control of those units. It does not include authority to assign separate employment of components of the units concerned. Neither does it, of itself, include administrative or logistic control.' The definition of OPCON in the *Department of Defense Dictionary of Military and Associated Terms* is as follows (Joint Publication 1–02 as amended through April 2010 – online at www.dtic.mil/doctrine/new_pubs/jp1_02.pdf – at p. 343): '[...] Operational control is the authority to perform those functions of command over subordinate forces involving organizing and employing commands and forces, assigning tasks, designating objectives, and giving authoritative direction necessary to accomplish the mission. Operational control includes authoritative direction over all aspects of military operations and joint training necessary to accomplish missions assigned to the command. [...] Operational control normally provides full authority to organize commands and forces and to employ those forces as the commander in operational control considers necessary to accomplish assigned missions; it does not, in and of itself, include authoritative direction for logistics or matters of administration, discipline, internal organization, or unit training. Also called OPCON.'

of equipment cannot affect the effectiveness of the lead organisation's measure of control – although e.g. tactics, techniques and procedures not properly trained are likely to be deficiently implemented, and under-staffed and/or under-equipped forces may fail to accomplish their mission.

As indicated, troop contributing states may be able to influence the conduct of operations by way of exercising of retained administrative authority, including disciplinary powers and criminal jurisdiction. To begin with retained administrative authority, its exercise covers e.g. provision of supply and services, personnel management (of which decisions concerning repatriation may bear particular importance), medical support, base management and in some cases walking-out policies. As a rule, exercise of this kind of authority exerts no more than fairly indirect influence on the conduct of operations. In a similar manner, the exercise of disciplinary powers and criminal jurisdiction cannot either exert direct influence on the conduct of operations in light of its retrospective nature. The fact that peacekeepers may be likely to yield to the threat that misconduct will have adverse consequences for them is not so measurable as to permit assessing its influence as direct. As a result, the inherent limits of OPCON associated with retained administrative authority, including disciplinary powers and criminal jurisdiction, should not be overestimated. In this respect, the ILC Special Rapporteur has aptly observed that … '[i]t would be going too far to consider that the existence of disciplinary power and criminal jurisdiction on the part of the contributing State totally excludes forces being considered to be placed at the disposal of the United Nations'.[104] As a result, disciplinary powers and criminal jurisdiction enable contributing states to maintain conditions conducive to abidance by the orders given at higher levels of command within the scope of conferred OPCON, and to react to misconduct of individual peacekeepers. They do not, however, empower *de jure* or enable *de facto* contributing states (including national contingent commanders acting in that capacity) to influence the content of the orders received from superior international headquarters.

To conclude, as it is for the international chain of command to tailor troops to tasks, taking into account the factors at issue, the exercise of retained administrative authority is not per se capable to rebut the presumption that conduct of operations is attributable to the lead organisation. (This assessment is without prejudice to attribution, and associated human rights accountability, of conduct occurring on base or during walk-out, which will, as a rule, be attributable to troop contributing states.)

---

104 Special Rapporteur Mr. Giorgio Gaja, op. cit. n. 50, at para. 40.

By way of contrast, field level commanders have direct influence on the conduct of operations through operational and tactical planning – both at the core of OPCON – and supervising and/or directing the execution of such Concepts of Operations (CONOPS) as they may approve. Operational and tactical planning enable the responsible commander to take precautions aiming at preventing such misconduct as would incur responsibility on the part of the lead organisation; such precautions may include the adoption of Standing Operating Procedures, Tactical Directives, and individual orders concerning inter alia appropriate in-theatre training and rehearsals of the tactics, techniques and procedures specified therein. Relevant general principles of international humanitarian law require precisely that – as demonstrated by e.g. the written rules concerning the avoidance, or minimisation, of incidental loss of civilian life, injury to civilians, damage to civilian objects, or a combination thereof. It follows that in most cases the only option left to troop contributing states to influence individual field level operations is to pull their forces out of them. It is worthwhile recalling in this respect that policy debates concerning e.g. German caveats limiting the use of force[105] and deployment to ISAF operations in southern Afghanistan[106] indicate what political price states might have to pay if their decisions create the impression, rightly or wrongly, that they do not want to participate fully in the mission they have decided to contribute troops to.

The foregoing indicates that, while conduct of peacekeeping operations cannot usually be fully attributed to either the lead organisation or one or more troop contributing states, most of it is attributable to lead organisations. By way of contrast, joint and several attribution is the exception rather than the rule in operational matters.

---

105 The German weekly 'Der Spiegel' has reported in an article entitled 'Not Licensed to Kill – German Special Forces in Afghanistan Let Taliban Commander Escape' (19 May 2008) that Germany has notified – '"clarification notes" to NATO with far-ranging instructions for their soldiers which expressly contradict the usual procedures: "The use of lethal force is prohibited unless an attack is taking place or is imminent." Sources in NATO circles regard the confidential document as a "national exception," a caveat which places restrictions on operational capability' and that '[t]he German government considers its allies' approach as "not being in conformity with international law."' The weekly believes that the quoted passages stem from the 'secret document' containing the German caveat. See www.spiegel.de/international/world/0,1518,druck-554033,00.html (last visited on 11 August 2008). Whether or not the report is in fact true and the quotations are correct is beyond the scope of this contribution.

106 The German National ISAF Mandate limits deployment outside Regional Commands Capital and North to cases of limited measures in support of operations for limited periods: provided that such support is indispensable to fulfill ISAF's overall mission, being, however, without prejudice to German participation in ISAF command and control. See e.g. Bundestagsdrucksachen 15/5996, 16/2573, 16/4298, and 16/6460.

The suggested rebuttable presumption notwithstanding, it seems imperative to attribute individual conduct of peacekeepers on the basis of assessments of each given case separately, taking the complexity of command and control relationships duly into account. In this context, attribution to either the lead organisation or the respective contributing state is only possible 'insofar as it is possible to distinguish ... areas of effective control respectively pertaining to the United Nations [i.e. lead organization] and the contributing State'.[107] In other cases, as will be demonstrated in the following paragraphs, attribution to the lead organisation is presumed.

In accordance with the position voiced by the International Law Commission, attribution is contingent on whether the relevant contributing state or the lead organisation has effective control of actions taken in the course of an individual field level operation.[108] In particular, the existence and degree of control of individual conduct must be established. For that purpose, both a formal and a factual test can be applied. The formal test for attribution of the conduct of peace missions is the command relationship between the lead organisation and forces on the ground. This criterion is addressed in a statement of the International Law Commission where the ILC expressly refers to cases 'when the Security Council authorizes States or international organizations to take necessary measures outside a chain of command linking those forces to the United Nations'.[109] The ILC's reference reflects, moreover, consolidated practice of international peacekeeping.[110] Lead organisations (including the United Nations) always

107 See ILC, *Report 2009*, op. cit. n. 4, commentary (8) on draft Article 6 on responsibility of international organizations, at p. 66. – Note that the ILC seems to agree with the United Nations Secretary-General's view (expressed in respect of UNOSOM II) that: 'In joint operations, international responsibility for the conduct of the troops lies where operational command and control is vested according to the arrangements establishing the modalities of cooperation between the State or States providing the troops and the United Nations. In the absence of formal arrangements between the United Nations and the State or States providing troops, responsibility would be determined in each and every case according to the degree of effective control exercised by either party in the conduct of the operation.' *Ibid.*, quoting UN Doc. A/51/389 at paras. 17–18.

108 Note, however, that the ILC's considerations might create the impression of a *petitio principii*: 'The criterion for attribution of conduct either to the contributing State or organization or to the receiving organization is based [...] on the factual control that is exercised over the specific conduct taken by the organ or agent placed at the receiving organization's disposal. [...] In the context of the placement of an organ or agent at the disposal of an international organization, control [...] concern[s] the issue [...] to which entity – the contributing State or organization or the receiving organization – conduct is attributable.' See ILC, *Report 2009*, op. cit. n. 4, commentaries (3) and (4) on draft Article 6 on responsibility of international organizations, at p. 63.

109 See ILC, *Report 2009*, op. cit. n. 4, commentary (5) on draft Article 6 on responsibility of international organizations, at p. 64.

110 The KFOR mandate is a typical example for the authorisation of action outside a chain of command linking the operation directly to the United Nations. The UN Security Council has authorised 'Member States and relevant international organisations to establish the

establish a chain of command between their supreme headquarters and the peacekeeping forces on the ground. To assess attributable actions, the military strategic (and operational, as the case may be) level decisions that bind upon field level commanders must be assessed in connection with the doctrinal definition of the existing command and control relationship to establish what degree of control a commander at a given level may exercise.

In the light of the limited influence troop contributing states retain once they have transferred OPCON, it seems appropriate to assert that there exists a rebuttable presumption that a lead organisation exercising OPCON is fully responsible for the effects of actions taken and omissions occurring in the course of an operation. The United Nations has accepted this in principle with respect to private law claims.[111] The ILC Special Rapporteur suggests that, regardless of this background of the responsibility for damage caused in the course of an operation, 'it is implied that the same principle concerning attribution of conduct would apply in relation to responsibility under international law'.[112] Considering the fact that certain private law claims are rooted in human rights[113] this position is convincing since they are, by virtue of these roots, closely linked to relevant general principles of international humanitarian and human rights law.[114]

international security presence in Kosovo ... with all necessary means to fulfil its responsibilities under paragraph 9 below' (see para. 7 of UNSC Resolution 1244 (1999)). Note that the authorisation to establish KFOR with all necessary means implies necessarily that KFOR may also use the means at its disposal (unless otherwise directed).

111 See the memorandum of the Office of Legal Affairs concerning an accident that occurred to a British helicopter which had been put in Cyprus at the disposal of the United Nations Peacekeeping Force in Cyprus (UNFICYP) – *United Nations Juridical Yearbook* (1980) pp. 184 *et seq.*: 'The crew members of the helicopters are members of the British contingent of UNFICYP and the helicopter flights take place in the context of the operations of UNFICYP. Through the chain of command, the operations in which the helicopters are involved take place under the ultimate authority of the UNFICYP Force Commander and are the responsibility of the United Nations. The circumstances under which the British-owned helicopters are put at the disposal of UNFICYP thus lead to the conclusion that these helicopters should be considered as United Nations aircraft. As the carrier, it is the United Nations that could and normally would be held liable by third parties in case of accidents involving UNFICYP helicopters and causing damages or injuries to these parties; therefore third-party claims should normally be expected to be addressed to the United Nations.'

112 Special Rapporteur Mr. Giorgio Gaja, op. cit. n. 50, para. 36.

113 From the perspective of human rights doctrine, the protection of such private interests as in particular life, liberty, and property must be effectuated by way of appropriate legislation given the lack of direct horizontal applicability of human rights in relationships between non-governmental entities (unless provided otherwise in the relevant human rights instrument).

114 Note that Contributing State Agreements do not usually deal with international responsibility vis-à-vis individuals for damage caused during an operation. The ILC has drawn attention to the relevant framework of UN peacekeeping: 'For example, according to the model contribution agreement relating to military contingents placed at the disposal of the United Nations by one of its Member States, the United Nations is regarded as liable towards third parties, but has a right of recovery from the contributing State under circumstances such as "loss, damage, death or injury [arising] from gross negligence or wilful misconduct of the

The factual test for attribution of conduct of peacekeeping operations relies on the information necessary to determine whether the presumption that such conduct is attributable to the lead organisation is rebutted. For the purposes of this test, it does not suffice to establish that individual peacekeepers, units or headquarters dominated by a particular troop contributing nation have deviated from the superior – international – commander's intent. Related information must also support, with sufficient evidential value, the assumption that the deviation in question is rooted in national policy. The presumption in favour of attribution of peacekeeping conduct to the lead organisation would only be rebutted if national caveats that prevent the full implementation of the respective commander's course of action have not been integrated in the decision-making process within the lead organisation.[115] As a matter of principle, it seems inappropriate to differentiate between caveats that preclude certain conduct for policy reasons and the reluctance to contribute certain capabilities with similar effect.[116] While it is true that troop contributing states frequently use some legal reasoning in support of caveats they might notify, they do not usually rely on legal obligations proper but on such interpretations of relevant legal instruments as developed for domestic policy reasons.

The aforementioned presumption does not cover cases where the lead organisation expressly requires subordinate command levels to make decisions in accordance with national policy. In this respect, based on KFOR practice, the

personnel provided by the Government". The agreement appears to deal only with distribution of responsibility and not with attribution of conduct. At any event, this type of agreement is not conclusive because it governs only the relations between the contributing State or organization and the receiving organization and could thus not have the effect of depriving a third party of any right that that party may have towards the State or organization which is responsible under the general rules.' See ILC, *Report 2009*, op. cit. n. 4, commentary (2) on draft Article 6 on responsibility of international organizations, at p. 62, quoting Article 9 of the model contribution agreement (A/50/995, annex; A/51/967, annex).

115 If compared with similar policy patterns in the framework of the law of treaties, the character of national caveats oscillates between invocations of internal law for the failure to perform treaty obligations and reservations. Arguably, as long as national caveats are not integrated in the decision-making process of the lead organisation, they have much in common with invocations of internal law; conduct based on them would then be attributable to the state in question. (It is submitted that Article 27 of the Vienna Convention on the Law of Treaties, according to which '[a] party may not invoke the provisions of its internal law as justification for its failure to perform a treaty', contains an implicit rule of attribution in the term 'failure'.) If, by way of contrast, national caveats are integrated in the decision-making process of the lead organisation, the conduct reflecting them is attributable to the lead organisation because the acceptance of the caveat modifies the rights and obligations both of the lead organisation and the contributing state as regards the use of the troops contributed.

116 The practical effect is similar regardless of whether a troop contributing state notifies a caveat according to which the troops it contributes may not perform e.g. certain reconnaissance tasks or whether it contributes troops without the training and/or equipment necessary to perform them. In either case the responsible commander cannot use the troops in question to perform the reconnaissance tasks at issue.

decision-making process concerning operational detention provides a good example. Decisions concerning operational detention taken by organs of the lead organisation[117] or commanders holding a position within its command and control framework[118] are attributable to the organisation in question. As far as decisions made at lower levels of command are concerned, attribution depends on actual control. Such decisions do not affect attribution to the lead organisation if they merely implement superior directives or procedures at a lower level of command or apply them to an individual case. By way of contrast, should a directive or procedure delegate discretionary authority to subordinate commanders, attribution then depends on whom it defines as the repository of such discretion.[119] Force Commanders may also delegate detaining authority, even – unlike in the context of KFOR – accepting that it be exercised in accordance with national policy, yet retain the authority to release detainees. Similarly, while basic principles and rules concerning the treatment of detainees are usually defined in directives or procedures issued by the Force Commander, it is frequently a matter of contributing state policy – triggered, for example, by a delegation of relevant authority to national contingent commanders – to determine the particulars of treatment and, more specifically, the establishment and operation of holding facilities.[120]

C. FURTHER ATTRIBUTION CRITERIA

As indicated, the main attribution criterion derives from a proper analysis of command and control structures of a peace mission.[121] This is congruent with the draft articles on responsibility of international organisations. According to

117 In particular, strategic OPLANs of NATO peacekeeping operations including the Rules of Engagement are approved by the North Atlantic Council. The relevant procedure is defined in the NATO Use of Force Concept. Although this concept is perceived as a policy document, its practical effects are so as if it were a procedural enactment if only because deviation from the procedure specified would require a unanimous decision.

118 In particular, directives and procedures implement the ROE, introduce additional constraints, or amplify them to the extent necessary.

119 If the exercise of discretion is exclusively governed by concerns defined by lead organisation policy, detention decisions will be attributed to the lead organisation alone. If it is governed by concerns defined by contributing state policy, a decision will be attributed to the state in question. If both lead organisation and contributing state concerns impact a decision it will be attributable to both the organisation and the state. Technically, it will make a difference whether the extent that respective policies have indeed governed a decision can be established. If not so, the decision can be attributed to the organisation and the state jointly; each of them can then be held fully accountable for the decision and they must then determine how they share responsibility.

120 This practice reflects the basic attribution principle concerning treatment of prisoners of war specified in Article 12 of GC I and *inter alia* civilian internees (as a subcategory of protected persons) specified in Article 29 of GC IV.

121 See also U. Häußler, op. cit. n. 10, at pp. 52 *et seq.*

the ILC, conduct is attributed to an international organisation if it is performed by an organ of a State or an organ or agent of another international organisation placed at the disposal of the organisation in question – viz., for the present purposes, the lead organisation of a peacekeeping operation – even if such conduct happens to be *ultra vires*, provided that the organisation in question exercises effective control over it.[122]

Attribution of conduct to an international organisation is also contingent on its occurrence in the performance of functions, as defined by rules of the organisation, by an organ or agent[123] of the organisation in question.[124] Conversely, *ultra vires* conduct not linked to the lead organisation by effective control will be attributed to the state (or organisation) whose organ or agent has exceeded their authority, or has contravened instructions[125], i.e. conduct beyond the scope of the organ's or agent's official functions.[126] As regards peacekeeping, according to the ILC: 'While the "off-duty" conduct of a member of a national contingent would not be attributed to the organisation, the "on-duty" conduct may be so attributed. One would then have to examine in the case of *ultra vires* conduct if it related to the functions entrusted to the person concerned.'[127]

Apart from such a scenario, it is without legitimate doubt that conduct deemed non-attributable to the lead organisation under scrutiny – and within the criteria

---

122 See ILC, *Report 2009*, op. cit. n. 4, draft Articles 6 and 7 on responsibility of international organizations, p. 62 *et seq.*

123 The notion of 'agent' covers any person through which an international organisation acts. The ILC has relied on the International court of Justice's Advisory Opinion of 11 April 1949 in ICJ, *Reparation for Injuries Suffered in the Service of the United Nations, ICJ Rep.* (1949) pp. 174–177 in this respect. See ILC, *Report 2009*, op. cit. n. 4, commentaries (2) and (5) of draft Article 5 on responsibility of international organizations, at pp. 58 and 60. – As a result, it is linked to the mission rather than to formal status. See ILC, *Report 2009*, op. cit. n. 4, commentary (2) of draft Article 5 on responsibility of international organizations, at p. 59, relying on the ICJ's Advisory Opinion on 14 June 1989 in ICJ, *Applicability of article VI, section 22, of the Convention on the privileges and immunity of the United Nations, ICJ Rep.* (1989) p. 177, paras. 48 and 47, respectively. It follows that any person 'acting for the United Nations on the basis of functions conferred by an organ of the organization' is considered an agent. See ILC, *Report 2009*, op. cit. n. 4, commentary (3) of draft Article 5 on responsibility of international organizations, at p. 59.

124 See ILC, *Report 2009*, op. cit. n. 4, draft Article 5 on responsibility of international organizations, at p. 58.

125 *Ibid.*, draft Article 7 on responsibility of international organizations, at p. 70, and commentary (6) on draft Article 7 (*ibid.* at pp. 72 *et seq.*), quoting the International Court of Justice's Advisory Opinion of 20 July 1962 in ICJ, *Certain Expenses of the United Nations, ICJ Rep.* (1962) at p. 168.

126 ILC, *Report 2009*, op. cit. n. 4, commentary (9) on draft Article 7 on responsibility of international organizations, at p. 73.

127 *Ibid.*, commentary (9) on draft Article 7 on responsibility of international organizations, at p. 74.

previously discussed – is attributable to that organisation to the extent that it organisation acknowledges and adopts the conduct in question as its own.[128]

Finally, it should be stressed that attribution to NATO of responsibility for the use of means and measures of coercion by peacekeeping operations led by it is not contingent on whether the UN Security Council expressly mentions NATO in the mandate or subsequent resolutions. Considering their legally inextricable connection, decisions of the North Atlantic Council launching a peacekeeping operation and decisions of the Member States to transfer authority (OPCON) over peacekeeping forces to NATO, considered as a whole, imply NATO accountability by necessity. It is noteworthy in this context that NATO Member States can only be held accountable for their policy decision to transfer such authority if they fail to create proper NATO mechanisms to deal with this accountability; in accordance with relevant human rights jurisprudence, they must ensure that NATO adheres to standards of protection substantially equivalent to those binding upon them.

D. CONCLUSION

Policy level, military strategic level, operational level, and field level decisions as well as field level actions of international peace missions are all capable of affecting a variety of human rights. Decisions at all levels will most likely affect human rights by way of actualising existing limitations; policy decisions taken under Chapter VII authority may, as will be demonstrated shortly, add further limitations of human rights for the purposes of achieving the desired end-state of the peace mission. Field level action will usually affect the human rights of those individuals exposed to them directly or indirectly.

V. DEFINING THE LIMITS OF TRANSITIONAL AUTHORITY OF PEACEKEEPING OPERATIONS

When is an action taken by a peacekeeping force in breach of the human rights of an individual in the receiving state it affects? Even under Chapter VII of the UN Charter, the transitional authority of international peace missions is not unlimited. In general terms, the International Court of Justice has identified the sources of obligations of international organisations as follows: 'International

---

128 *Ibid.*, draft Article 8 on responsibility of international organizations, at p. 74. The ILC has discussed this issue with respect to the ICTY Trial Chamber II's decision of 9 October 2002 on the defence motion challenging the exercise of jurisdiction in *Prosecutor v. Dragan Nikolic* – Case No. IT-94–2-PT (concerning *ultra vires* conduct during an SFOR detention).

organizations are subjects of international law and, as such, are bound by any obligations incumbent upon them under general rules of international law, under their constitutions or under international agreements to which they are parties.'[129]

International organisations are governed by the principle of conferred powers; apart from implied powers, they have only such powers as conferred on them by their constituent treaty.[130] As a result, the UN Security Council's powers under Chapter VII of the UN Charter demarcate the outer limit of possible peacekeeping authority under a UN mandate.[131] Apart from that, receiving states can confer additional powers on a peace mission by virtue of consent; the exercise of such powers has, however, no *erga omnes* effects under the Chapter VII mandate. Likewise, the consent of the state receiving a peace mission of specific actions taken by it precludes (though only) that such actions violate the sovereignty of the state in question.[132]

Further limits of the authority of peace missions are inherent in their mandates; in particular, they derive from the definition of the substantial scope of the responsibilities. In addition, the emerging customary international law of peace missions and relevant general principles of international humanitarian and human rights law[133] generate rules which also bind upon lead organisations and accordingly limit the transitional authority of peace missions.

---

129 ICJ, *Interpretation of the Agreement of 25 March 1951 Between the WHO and Egypt*, Advisory Opinion, *ICJ Rep.* (1980) p. 73, at para. 37.

130 The International Court of Justice has summarised this principle as follows: '[I]nternational organizations [...] do not, unlike States, possess a general competence. International organizations are governed by the 'principle of speciality', that is to say, they are invested by the States which create them with powers, the limits of which are a function of the common interests whose promotion those States entrust to them.' See the ICJ's Advisory Opinion of 8 July 1996 in ICJ, *Legality of the Use by a State of Nuclear Weapons in Armed Conflict, ICJ Rep.* (1996) p. 226, at para 25.

131 Cf. the characterisation of delegation of authority as 'the transferral of the Security Council's military power to member states or regional organizations' by E. de Wet, op. cit. n. 78, at pp. 259 *et seq.*

132 See ILC, *Report 2009*, commentary (3) on draft Article 19 on responsibility of international organizations, at p. 94: 'As an example of consent that renders a specific conduct on the part of an international organization lawful, one could give that of a State allowing an investigation to be carried out on its territory by a commission of inquiry set up by the United Nations Security Council.' The ILC has referred, concerning the requirement of consent, to para 6 of the Declaration annexed to General Assembly resolution 46/59 of 9 December 1991. The ILC has also drawn attention to the consent to the deployment of the Aceh Monitoring Mission in Indonesia, following an invitation addressed in July 2005 by the Government of Indonesia to the European Union and seven contributing States. See *ibid.*, noting that a reference to the invitation by the Government of Indonesia may be found in the preambular paragraph of the European Union Council Joint Action 2005/643/CFSP (9 September 2005) *OJ L* 234/13.

133 The ILC has addressed customary international law and general principles of international law implicitly, observing that an international [...] 'obligation may result either from a treaty

A. THE EMERGING CUSTOMARY INTERNATIONAL LAW OF PEACE MISSIONS

The ILC has observed, in discussing the notion of rules of an international organisation[134], that the following categories must be considered: 'in particular: the constituent instruments; decisions, resolutions and other acts taken by the organization in accordance with those instruments; and established practice of the organization.'[135]

Practice, one of the two constituent elements of customary international law[136], is particularly important in respect of international peace missions. To date, there exist no codifications of international law which specifically deal with peace missions. Existing jurisprudence deals with the conduct of states during armed conflict rather than the conduct of international organisations in peace missions.[137] Moreover, practice is continually developing because of the variety of conflict and post-conflict scenarios and the differing policy concepts applied to resolve them. International organisations involved in international peace missions try to tailor mandates and the policy guidance for their implementation as closely to the practical realities at field level as possible in the prevailing political and operational environment. A thorough analysis of the practice of international peace missions is particularly important where international organisations label their decisions as expressions of policy[138] rather than acts adopted in accordance with their constituent treaties, and where they establish

binding the international organization or from any other source of international law applicable to the organization.' See ILC, *Report 2009*, op. cit. n. 4, commentaries (1 and 2) on draft Article 4, at p. 54.

134 The 'rules' of an international organisation create obligations on its part under international law. See ILC, *Report 2009*, op. cit. n. 4, commentary (4) on draft Article 9 on responsibility of international organizations, at p. 78.

135 The ILC has relied on Art. 2(1)(j) of the Vienna Convention on the Law of Treaties between States and International Organizations and between International Organizations which states that: '"rules of the organization" means, in particular, the constituent instruments, decisions and resolutions adopted in accordance with them, and established practice of the organization.' See ILC, *Report 2009*, op. cit. n. 4, commentary (15) on draft Article 2 on responsibility of international organizations, at pp. 49 *et seq.*

136 The ILC has justified the relevance of practice (as opposed to the 'rules enshrined in the constituent instruments and formally accepted by members of the organization') with a view to 'the need for the organization to develop as an institution'. See ILC, *Report 2009*, op. cit. n. 4, commentary (16) on draft Article 2 on responsibility of international organizations, at p. 50. It is submitted that this observation focuses on the internal law of international organisations rather than addressing their conduct with effects on states and other international organisations.

137 U. Häußler, op. cit. n. 10, at pp. 71 *et seq.*

138 Note that there used to be a tendency to deny that certain organisations have obligations under international law at all: cf. the observations concerning NATO made by M. Zwanenburg, *Accountability of Peace Support Operations* (Leiden, Martinus Nijhoff Publishers 2005) pp. 179 *et seq.* This point of view is surprising in light of NATO's legal personality, on which see *ibid.* at 64–68.

subsidiary organs (or equivalent) whose conduct follows certain rules that are not generically regarded as part of the internal law of the organisation in question. Considering that no international organisation operates in a legal vacuum, the validity of such claims is rather doubtful if the organisation in question implements, in its decisions, general principles of international humanitarian and human rights law and such implementation amounts to consolidated practice; such practice may then indicate that *opinio juris* exists even if policy statements to the opposite extent are made. By contrast, decisions are usually matters of policy where an international organisation imposes standards exceeding those contained in general principles of international humanitarian and human rights law for a specific theatre of operations.

Since the end of the Cold War, certain basic co-ordinates of a prospective international law of peace missions have emerged. At policy level, the practice of the UN Security Council, the North Atlantic Council, and increasingly the Peace and Security Council of the African Union, have particular importance. The UN Security Council has repeatedly authorised the use of all necessary means or all necessary measures by peacekeeping forces with full knowledge of field level practice under this authorisation. It follows that the UN Security Council has endorsed the operational patterns identifiable in relevant field level practice and that these patterns represent subsequent consolidated practice in the application of international mandates whose value is equivalent to agreement of the parties regarding interpretation of related resolutions of the UN Security Council and, ultimately, Chapter VII of the UN Charter (cf. Article 31(3)(b) of the Vienna Convention on the Law of Treaties). In particular, the practice concerning operational detention has such character.[139]

Relevant practice of the North Atlantic Council is embodied in the consent to OPLANs of NATO peacekeeping operations which include the Rules of Engagement (ROE) for these operations. An OPLAN contains the strategic commander's direction and guidance; it defines the peacekeeping force's centre of gravity. ROE, usually contained in a distinct annex to the OPLAN, are defined as '[d]irectives issued by competent military authority which specify the circumstances and limitations under which forces will initiate and/or continue combat engagement with other forces encountered'.[140] ROE are influenced by a variety of factors, among which international law is the most prominent.[141] The North Atlantic Council has repeatedly required NATO peacekeepers under its

139 See U. Häußler, op. cit. n. 10, at pp. 137–145 for a detailed analysis of relevant practice and the conclusion summarised here.

140 See the *NATO Glossary of Terms and Definitions*, op. cit. n. 68, at 2-R-8.

141 The Introduction of the NATO Use of Force Concept mentions international law as the first influencing factor and observes that the North Atlantic Council provides political direction of the use of force through ROE '[w]ithin this legal framework'.

political direction and control to comply with the spirit of relevant international humanitarian law.[142] As a result, it is consistent practice of both the UN Security Council and the North Atlantic Council to integrate relevant general principles of international humanitarian law in the legal framework of peacekeeping operations in particular. Mainly at theatre level, both NATO and the United Nations have also translated relevant principles into such rules binding upon peacekeeping forces as define their authority and its limits.

B. GENERAL PRINCIPLES OF INTERNATIONAL HUMANITARIAN AND HUMAN RIGHTS LAW

Practice reinforces the relevance of general principles of international humanitarian and human rights law as sources of rules demarcating or limiting the authority of peace missions. Although prima facie separate subject-matters of international law, international humanitarian and human rights law cannot be thought apart as far as international peace missions are concerned. The international community decides whether it launches peace missions regardless of the character of the situation in the receiving state under international law.[143] This practice reflects the fact that Article 39 of the UN Charter has established a test for coercive action which bridges the traditional doctrinal gap between the states of war and peace. For that reason, Chapter VII mandates adopted by the UN Security Council frequently create the legal framework for a peace mission by way of merging (at least implicitly) relevant aspects of the law of armed conflict – also known as international humanitarian law (LOAC/IHL) and the law of peace. In particular, UN Security Council mandates authorising the use of 'all necessary means' or 'all necessary measures' empower peace missions to make use of their full repertoire of armed force and do hence imply that their actions be governed by LOAC/IHL. On that basis, unless expressly laid down in policy decisions that express the *opinio juris* of the lead organisation, the limits of the authority entrusted in international peace missions derive from relevant general principles

---

142 In a recent Standardization Agreement (STANAG) NATO has expressed the view that the law of armed conflict, as it is referred to, does not apply 'as a matter of law' to peacekeeping operations. At the same time, the STANAG reaffirms that it is NATO policy that peacekeepers will comply with the spirit and principles of the law of armed conflict. STANAG No. 2449 'Training in the Law of Armed Conflict' (29 March 2004) NATO/PfP Unclassified. The approach combining inapplicability of international humanitarian law 'as a matter of law' with the (allegedly politically) binding effect of its 'spirit and principles' correctly reflects the fact that NATO is not party to relevant treaty law; however, it fails to honour the legally binding force of general principles of (*inter alia*) international humanitarian law on NATO in their capacity as general principles of international law and, as I would submit, general principles of NATO's internal law as well.

143 For instance, international peace missions were deployed to Bosnia and Herzegovina prior to and after the conclusion of the General Framework Agreement for Peace (also known as the Dayton Agreement), viz. both during open armed conflict and after restoration of formal peace.

of international humanitarian and human rights law. Apart from such abstract principles as proportionality, general principles expressed in certain provisions that protect private interests (human rights) or public interests (e.g. protection of the natural environment) must be duly considered during the planning processes and implemented in the conduct of international peace missions.

The practice of lead organisations (both at policy and field levels) and relevant jurisprudence of international courts indicate that international humanitarian and human rights law can jointly contribute to the legal framework of peace missions. As regards human rights law, particular consideration should be given to the fact that decision-making in the field of contemporary peace missions involving the exercise of transitional authority is in many respects similar to supranational decision-making. In the light of these similarities it can hardly be doubted that the general principles of human rights law derived from the lead organisation's Member States' common ground in matters of human rights[144] will apply.[145] Note that both NATO and the United Nations have adopted various binding human rights related policies, including policy documents aiming to prevent or suppress sexual abuse.[146] Concerning LOAC/IHL, the United Nations – similar to NATO practice already discussed – requires peacekeepers' compliance with the spirit of international humanitarian law.[147] Note that recently the UN Security Council has expressly 'call[ed] upon all parties [operating in Afghanistan] to uphold international humanitarian and human rights law and to ensure the protection of civilian life' in the course of 'address[ing] the threat to the security and stability of Afghanistan posed by the Taliban, Al-Qaida, other extremist groups and criminal activities'.[148] This demand might indicate an increasing awareness of the need that inter alia international peacekeeping operations should honour express commitments to adherence to general principles of international humanitarian and human rights law.

---

144 Cf. Article 6(2) of the Treaty on European Union (24 December 2002) *O.J. C* 325. For a detailed assessment see U. Häußler, op. cit. n. 10, at pp. 64 *et seq.* and pp. 71 *et seq.* This provision has been recently modified by the Treaty of Lisbon, which entered into force on 1 December 2009 (Treaty of Lisbon amending the Treaty on European Union and the Treaty establishing the European Community, Lisbon, 13 December 2007, *O.J. C* 306 (17 December 2007); consolidated versions of the Treaty on European Union (TEU) and the Treaty on the Functioning of the European Union (TFEU) as they are amended by the Lisbon Treaty are published in O.J. C 85 (30 March 2010)).

145 This does not, however, preclude that transitional authority entrusted by a Chapter VII mandate adopted by the UN Security Council comprises mission specific powers of limiting such general principles of international human rights law as apply to the conduct of the mission.

146 U. Häußler, op. cit. n. 10, at pp. 81 *et seq.*; R. Arnold, 'The NATO Policy on Human Trafficking: Obligation to Prevent, Obligation to Repress', in R. Arnold, ed., *Law Enforcement within the Framework of Peace Support Operations* (Leiden, Martinus Nijhoff Publishers 2008) pp. 351–379.

147 This is evidenced by the Secretary-General's Bulletin on Observance by United Nations forces of international humanitarian law – UN Doc. ST/SGB/1999/13, 6 August 1999.

148 See e.g. UNSC Resolution 1746 (2007) para. 25.

C. CONCLUSION

In the light of the absence of specific law-making treaties, the legal framework of international peace missions is based on customary international law and general principles of international law. The practice of lead organisations of peace missions indicates that international humanitarian and human rights law are duly considered – although this assessment does not immunise the decisions taken against criticism. The legal sources governing the operations of international peace missions are not different from those generally relevant in international law and defined in Article 38(1) of the ICJ Statute.

VI. BALANCING PUBLIC AND PRIVATE INTERESTS IN THE FRAMEWORK OF INTERNATIONAL PEACEKEEPING

The merger of international humanitarian and human rights law for the purposes of international peace missions can be visualised best in the context of balancing public and private interests. Balancing consists of three elements. It requires identification of the public interest that shall be achieved by an intended action, and of the private interest affected by the action in question. Then, the respective weight of these interests must be assessed: in an abstract manner if policy or leadership decisions are taken, and with a view to the on-scene situation if field level actions are at issue. Finally, should the public interest prevail, it must be determined how the core of the specific human right affected may be protected – as a matter of principle, unless dictated by the behaviour of the individual concerned, no one may be completely deprived of their human rights. The following examples indicate how an equitable balance between public and private interests can be achieved at different levels.

A. SELF-DEFENCE

Rules of Engagement are without prejudice to the right of individual and extended self-defence; they may only limit extended self-defence but must not deprive any peacekeeper of their right to individual self-defence.

The ILC has discussed self-defence in a manner identifying the conceptual challenges linked to this right. As regards practice, the ILC has observed that: 'In the practice relating to United Nations forces, the term "self-defence" has often been used in a wider sense, with regard to situations other than those contemplated in Article 51 of the United Nations Charter. References to "self-defence" have been made also in relation to the "defence of the mission".'[149]

The ILC has stressed that in this context, the notion of self-defence 'is given a meaning that encompasses cases which go well beyond those in which a State or an international organization responds to an armed attack by a State'. It has, at the same time, upheld the differentiation between self-defence against an armed attack (as addressed by Article 51 of the UN Charter) and self-defence of a peace mission in accordance with its mandate: 'At any event, the question of the extent to which United Nations forces are entitled to resort to force depends on the primary rules concerning the scope of the mission ...'[150]

Arguably, the International Law Commission should have differentiated more clearly between the different repositories of the right to self-defence. Self-defence of a peace mission is not a matter of Article 51 of the UN Charter. From the perspective of international law, it seems unlikely that either the lead organisation or the troop contributing states of a peacekeeping operation are quintessentially taken to war in case of an armed attack inflicted by ex- or would-be belligerents in the given theatre of operations on 'their' peacekeepers. In a peacekeeping context, self-defence – both individual and extended – against such acts is a response to an imminent threat to life and limb of individuals, or to items in the property of individuals, troop contributing states, or the lead organisation. The right of self-defence in this sense is protected by a general principle of international law since, notwithstanding the differences concerning practical details, all known legal orders permit self-defence. For the individual peacekeeper, the exercise of the right to self-defence is governed by their home state's criminal law. In light of this understanding, there is no such justification for the use of force as 'defence of the mission'. This phrase represents an innovative (yet ultimately futile) attempt to enable UN peacekeeping operations whose mandate did not contain enforcement authority based on Chapter VII of the UN Charter to empower themselves and seize de facto authority with similar effects. By way of contrast, in robust ROE like those usually authorised by the North Atlantic Council, the use of force in situations not triggering self-defence[151] is covered by specific rules that permit a specified degree of force to prevent all or designated kinds of interference with peacekeepers during the conduct of their mission. To conclude, while individual self-defence of peacekeepers is subject to the balancing requirements of the criminal law of the

149 See ILC, *Report 2009*, op. cit. n. 4, commentary (3) on draft Article 20 on responsibility of international organizations, at p. 96.

150 *Ibid.*, p. 97.

151 Note that gaps between different concepts of self-defence can be closed by way of authorising the ROE permitting a response to hostile acts and demonstrations of hostile intent. Cf. U. Häußler, op. cit. n. 10, at pp. 94 *et seq.*

relevant contributing state, extended self-defence is generally a matter of ROE decision-making. Those responsible must consider whether certain means or measures might be excessive and should hence be prohibited by virtue of pertinent ROE or implementing direction and guidance. As a result, individual peacekeepers must not only abide by relevant (domestic) criminal law but also by relevant ROE – either in their capacity as, or as implemented by, superior orders.

B. MILITARY NECESSITY AND OPERATIONAL NECESSITY

From an abstract perspective, all known proportionality tests comprise, among others, the criterion of necessity. In the present context, the notion of necessity must be rendered more precisely such as to refer to military necessity, or, as the case may be, operational necessity. The ILC Special Rapporteur's analysis of the criterion 'necessity' (draft Article 24 on responsibility of international organisations[152]) has drawn attention to this specification. Unlike the ILC in its related commentaries, the Special Rapporteur has discussed the concepts of 'operational necessity' and 'military necessity' in the context of draft Article 24. The Special Rapporteur noted that '[a] more significant element of practice is given by statements that assert that United Nations forces may invoke "operational necessity" or "military necessity"'.[153]

152 Draft Article 24 on responsibility of international organizations deals with 'necessity' as a ground for precluding the wrongfulness of an act not in conformity with an international obligation by way of specifying situations in which necessity may not be invoked as a ground for precluding the wrongfulness of an act performed.

153 See the Special Rapporteur Mr. Giorgio Gaja, 'Fourth report on responsibility of international organizations', UN Doc. A/CN.4/564, at para. 37. The Special Rapporteur quoted a Report submitted by the United Nations Secretary-General and memorandum prepared by the United Nations Office of Legal Affairs. The Secretary-General's report indicates that he regards operational necessity as an exception from (civil) liability for property loss and damage caused by peacekeeping forces in the course of action taken in accordance with their mandates: 'The liability of the Organization for property loss and damage caused by United Nations forces in the ordinary operation of the force is subject to the exception of 'operational necessity', that is, where damage results from necessary actions taken by a peacekeeping force in the course of carrying out its operations in pursuance of its mandates.' See para 13 of the *report on financing several UN peacekeeping operations in the former Yugoslavia*, UN Doc. A/51/389. – The memorandum referred to deals with a different situation, namely the legality of the occupation of a compound by UNOSOM II for reasons of force protection: 'If it is established [...] that occupation of the compound by hostile factions would have exposed UNOSOM II to serious threat so that effective protection to "the personnel, installations and equipments of United Nations and its agencies, ICRC as well as NGOs" [...] could not have been assured without UNOSOM II taking physical possession of the compound, the occupation thereof may be considered as an act of military necessity to ensure the achievement of the objectives laid down in Security Council resolution 814 (1993). From this perspective, the occupation of the compound may be considered legal.' See *United Nations Juridical Yearbook* (1994) at pp. 403–405.

The concepts of 'operational necessity' and 'military necessity' are derived from international humanitarian law; the language of Chapter VII mandates indicates that the UN Security Council frequently has this specific category of necessity in mind when it authorises the use of all necessary means or the taking of all necessary measures.[154] It is submitted that, unlike implied in the Special Rapporteur's opinion, the concepts at issue do not serve to justify internationally wrongful acts. The concepts of 'military necessity' and 'operational necessity' address the specific public interests which govern military operations, i.e. interests which are lawful and legitimate in an armed conflict or during a peacekeeping operation entrusted with transitional authority.[155] They do so in such a manner as to enable military commanders to balance these public interests with the private interests of civilian individuals who might be directly or indirectly affected by the operations they command and control. From a human rights perspective, these concepts have a nature equivalent to a general limitations clause. This quasi-limitations clause is actualised for the purposes of peacekeeping operations by the authorisation of all necessary means or measures in the international mandate.

The military/operational necessity limitations clause deserves further analysis concerning its proper source in international humanitarian law. For the purposes of this contribution, analysis will focus on GP I. Translated into human rights terminology, GP I reflects the premise that 'military necessity' limits, as a matter of principle, all human rights affected by military action. GP I introduces, however, certain limits of this limitations clause: it determines that certain military actions with direct or indirect adverse effects on the sustenance of the civilian population may only be performed 'where required by'[156], or 'in case of[157] imperative military necessity'. The qualification 'imperative' embodies the limit of the quasi-limitations clause in the relevant provisions of GP I.

[154] U. Häußler, op. cit. n. 10, at pp. 71 *et seq.* (the concluding remarks in particular).

[155] From the perspective of legal method the concepts of 'military necessity' and 'operational necessity' do not have the character of an exception to a rule, i.e. need not be construed narrowly in accordance with the *singularia non sunt extendenda* principle. As a matter of principle, it is legitimate and legal in the context of both an armed conflict or a robust peacekeeping operation to cause such damage and harm as is necessary to accomplish the mission. International humanitarian law is not only without prejudice to this premise, it is actually based upon it.

[156] Article 55(5) of GP I: taking out objects indispensable to the survival of the civilian population on a Party's national territory under its own control in the defence against invasion.

[157] Article 62(1) of GP I: denying civilian civil defence organizations the right to perform their civil defence tasks; Article 67(5) of GP I: diverting material and buildings of military units permanently assigned to civil defence organizations and exclusively devoted to the performance of civil defence tasks who have fallen into the hands of an adverse Party; Article 71(3) of GP I: limiting the activities or restricting the movement of relieve personnel by a Party in receipt of relief consignments.

The construction of the phrase 'military necessity' suggested here for the purpose of international peace missions derives further support from provisions of GP I that contain guidance for the process of balancing competing public and private interests in operational planning. It may, for instance, be militarily necessary to lead an 'attack'[158] in such a manner that civilian casualties and/or collateral damage cannot be precluded. GP I requires military commanders and their operational planners to take precautions to prevent such effects from being 'excessive in relation to the concrete and direct military advantage anticipated'.[159] The criterion 'excessive' belongs to the specific proportionality test utilised in military operational planning. It affords increased weight to the public interest to achieve operational success, namely a 'concrete and direct military advantage'. Increased weight means that military commanders and their operational planners may even launch an 'attack' if its effects are disproportionate to the military advantage anticipated: provided that they are not so extremely disproportionate as having to be considered excessive.

As a result, within the scope of the authorisation to use all necessary means, ROE decision-makers, operational planners, and peacekeepers on-scene may attach, as a matter of principle, additional weight to the exigencies of the mission defined by the international mandate, and assume that the relevant public interest prevails over competing private interests protected by human rights. They must, however, respect the prohibition of taking action with adverse effects on the sustenance of the civilian population embodied in GP I – it is submitted that there can hardly be 'imperative military necessity' justifying such effects in a peace mission, and that such effects would run counter to the mission's desired end-state and hence lack all legitimacy anyway.

Moreover, even if militarily/operationally necessary, adverse effects on private interests protected by human rights must not be excessive – regardless of whether civilian injuries or casualties or collateral damage to civilian property – in

---

158 Article 49(1) of GP I defines that '"Attacks" means acts of violence against the adversary, whether in offence or in defence.'

159 Article 51(5)(b) of GP I specifies that 'an attack which may be expected to cause incidental loss of civilian life, injury to civilians, damage to civilian objects, or a combination thereof, which would be excessive in relation to the concrete and direct military advantage anticipated' is considered as indiscriminate and hence prohibited in accordance with Article 51(4) of GP I. Article 57(2)(a)(iii) of GP I requires, as a precautionary measure, 'those who plan or decide upon an attack' to 'refrain from deciding to launch any attack which may be expected to cause incidental loss of civilian life, injury to civilians, damage to civilian objects, or a combination thereof, which would be excessive in relation to the concrete and direct military advantage anticipated'. In addition, Article 57(2)(b) of GP I requires military commanders to cancel or suspend an attack if it has such undesired effects. Moreover, if such effects are launched in the knowledge that it will have the effects referred to is a grave breach of international humanitarian law (Article 57(3)(b) of GP I) and an international crime in accordance with Article 8(2)(b)(iv) of the ICC Statute.

accordance with relevant general principles of international humanitarian law codified in GP I. In consequence, high intensity operations will only be an option of choice for a peacekeeping operation in response to activities of such groups with paramilitary or military capability as attempt to escalate a still-looming conflict and return to hostilities.

C. CLAIMS

As indicated in the previous section, militarily/operationally necessary actions taken by peace missions on the basis of a robust mandate are not illegal but represent legitimate and lawful limitations of applicable human rights. Notwithstanding this legal qualification the use of force may nevertheless cause damage to civilian property or the physical integrity or life of civilian individuals. In light of the fact that peace missions intend to restore peace and stability such adverse effects are capable of having a negative impact on mission accomplishment: from the perspective of those suffering loss, it does not make a real difference whether such loss was caused in a lawful manner or is the effect of an illegal action. Like visiting forces[160], many peacekeeping forces have addressed this dilemma by introducing claims policies under which they make ex gratia payments in lieu of damages: they award an equitable payment on the basis of an assessment of the damage caused without even starting to think whether such damage was caused lawfully or illegally.[161] Note that this practice has certain similarities with e.g. the German approach to damage caused to individuals by lawful government action: if the damage in question falls outside the range of loss typically incurred by such actions, i.e. amounts to an inequality, it constitutes a 'Sonderopfer' and an equitable payment will be awarded regardless of the legality of the causative action.

Practice differs concerning the mechanism of processing claims related payments. Preferably, decisions concerning claims should be made on the basis of a uniform claims policy adopted by the Force Commander. Oftentimes, a specific claims office is established, or a claims officer contributed to the Legal Office of the peacekeeping operation, for that purpose. Practice with respect to implementation of claims decisions, however, varies. Some payments are made by the peacekeeping operation or its lead organisation, others are made by the

---

160 See, for instance, Article VIII of the *Agreement Between the Parties to the North Atlantic Treaty Regarding the Status of Their Forces* (19 June 1951), available at www.nato.int/docu/basictxt/b510619a.htm.

161 See also para. 51 of the *UN Model Status of Forces Agreement* which deals with the standing claims commission to be established by a UN peacekeeping operation and to be composed of members appointed by the United Nations Secretary-General, the government of the receiving state, and both actors jointly (UN Doc. A/45/594).

contributing state whose personnel has actually caused the damage in question. In some cases, troop contributing states even treat claims as part of their administrative control.

From the perspective of the lead organisation, a positive claims decision made by its in-theatre Headquarters always involves the adoption as its own of the causal action.[162] It does not, however, imply acceptance of the action's illegality even if so alleged by the claimant. This practice, regardless of whether labelled as a matter of policy, can therefore be relied upon for the purposes of determining whether certain – intended or unintended – (side-) effects of an action taken by a peacekeeping operation are attributable to the lead organisation. It deserves particular mention in this context that the practice that payments are frequently made by troop contributing states is without prejudice to the accountability of the lead organisation.[163] This practice reflects a mechanism aimed to facilitate expeditious payment because some international organisations do not have the necessary budgetary resources to make claims related payments, if only because of the disinclination of their Member States to provide them with adequate funding.[164] Even if implementation of the claims decision is contingent on a positive decision to endorse it, to be made by the relevant troop contributing state, would attribution of the causative action to that state, assuming it was not *ultra vires* action, hardly be possible if the state in question has transferred OPCON over its contingent to the lead organisation.[165]

162 This is the essence of UN policy concerning claims for damage caused by UN peacekeeping forces as summarised by the United Nations Secretary-General as follows: 'In recognition of its international responsibility for the activities of its forces, the United Nations has, since the inception of peacekeeping operations, assumed its liability for damage caused by members of its forces in the performance of their duties. [...] The undertaking to settle disputes of a private law nature submitted against it and the practice of actual settlement of such third-party claims [...] evidence the recognition on the part of the United Nations that liability for damage caused by members of United Nations forces is attributable to the Organization.' UN Secretary-General, 'Report on financing of United Nations peacekeeping operations', UN Doc. A/51/389, paras. 7 and 8.

163 In particular, the settlement of the claim of the Government of China in relation to the bombing of China's embassy in Belgrade on 7 May 1999 through a bilateral agreement between China and the United States cannot be relied upon as a precedent for attribution of this incident to the United States.

164 Cf. relevant submissions made to the International Court of Justice in the proceedings leading to the ICJ, *Effect of Awards of Compensation Made by the United Nations Administrative Tribunal*, Advisory Opinion, *ICJ Rep.* (1954) p. 47 and ICJ, *Certain Expenses of the United Nations*, op. cit. n. 125, at p. 151.

165 It is submitted that as long as payments are made in accordance with the Force Commander's claims policy the technical question of what entity makes such payments cannot be qualified as indicating that the conduct that gave rise to the claim is attributable to the state which had contributed the troops who performed it.

As a result, claims policies adopted by international peace missions can be characterised as a proper mechanism to compensate individual loss in cases where the human rights to life, physical integrity, and property are adversely affected, though need not necessarily violated, by actions taken by mission personnel in performance of their functions.

D. JUDICIAL REVIEW OF OPERATIONAL DETENTION?

As previously discussed, operational detention usually involves that detainees are placed in a holding facility without access to judicial oversight. The legitimacy of this practice has attracted criticism after the U.S. detention practices at Guantánamo Bay in the course of the 'Global War on Terror' became public, and allegations were made that individuals detained by NATO peacekeeping operations had been handed over to the U.S. and brought there. Although these allegations have not been confirmed, the NGO and press efforts associated with them have prompted lead organisations to refine their detention policies such as to balance more properly the human rights of liberty of person and access to court with the public interest that justifies operational detention.[166] The review mechanisms created by peacekeeping operations are modelled on the limitations of the human rights referred to as contained in international humanitarian law. By tailoring these review mechanisms to the particular factual framework of peacekeeping operations the lead organisations have both (implicitly) accepted the applicability of the human rights at issue (though adapted to the specific legal framework governing international peace missions) and utilised the authority to use all necessary means – i.e. to take action, if militarily necessary, in accordance with general principles of international humanitarian law.

As indicated, the review mechanisms reflect the doctrine of command responsibility to the extent that Force Commanders usually retain final decision-making authority. For their decisions, commanding officers at all levels concerned rely extensively on legal advice. While advisory bodies are, as a general rule, composed of the representatives of multiple staff sections – usually the Chiefs of Military Police and Security and the Legal Advisor – the legal assessment contributed by the latter is the core factor in decision-making. Thus, military lawyers have, as a matter of practice, not only been members of the teams of staff officers charged with establishing any relevant facts but have also made the final recommendation which forms the basis of the commander's decision on whether an individual should be ordered detained or relinquished, or whether certain treatment should be continued or changed. It is, moreover, consistent practice that military lawyers do not receive orders from their

166 On the importance of NGO and press control see U. Häußler, op. cit. n. 10, at pp. 148 *et seq.*

commanders concerning the assessment of pertinent legal principles and rules.[167] Oftentimes, moreover, internal appeals mechanisms have been included in relevant detention directives or procedures. Appeals are usually reviewed at a higher level of command. Reporting requirements up to the military strategic or policy levels may also be in place. Furthermore, external oversight by the International Committee of the Red Cross helps ensuring that detaining authority is not abused in individual cases.[168] As far as it is possible to establish, files of detention decisions and detention review are made available to ICRC delegates upon request.

As a result, detention oversight in peace missions seems capable of striking a fair balance between the requirements of force protection and accomplishment of the mission on the one hand, and, on the other hand, liberty of person and the right of access to court of individuals ordered detained. It is also transparent within the chain of command and vis-à-vis the International Committee of the Red Cross. The fact that transparency vis-à-vis NGOs or the general public is limited is clearly justifiable by operation security concerns – in particular, certain information which might support a detention order is usually classified. As long as latent dangers to the peace process prevail, such security concerns should not be taken lightly. Considering the crucial role of military lawyers, detention oversight mechanisms that possess the characteristics specified above should, consequently, be regarded as sufficient to comply with the essence of relevant access to court requirements in human rights law on account of their quasi-judicial[169] nature: provided they meet the requirements associated with the notion of 'tribunal' in relevant LOAC/IHL. – In addition to the external oversight by the International Committee of the Red Cross, international human rights treaty bodies might also get such access in accordance with arrangements concluded with a peace mission's lead organisation.[170]

---

167 I have never experienced or heard of situations where a Commander wanted to substitute his assessment of the law for my own or the one of the colleagues I spoke with. Doing so would be contrary to the professional ethics of a commanding officer, and accepting orders concerning interpretation and application of the law to individual cases from a commander would be contrary to the professional ethics of a military lawyer. The concern expressed by the Venice Commission that it is not institutionally ensured that Commanders receive independent legal advice (Venice Commission Opinion, op. cit. n. 49, at para. 129) is, accordingly, not supported by practical realities.

168 On the role of the ICRC see U. Häußler, op. cit. n. 10, at p. 136.

169 The core difference between a court of law and the boards of staff officers preparing decision briefs in matters of operational detention lies in the fact that commanding officers retain final decision-making authority in accordance with the doctrine of command responsibility. By way of contrast, the involvement of the Chiefs of Military Police and Security is equivalent to the position of lay judges in an ordinary court of law.

170 On international oversight of field level practice see U. Häußler, op. cit. n. 10, at p. 9.4 and the analysis of the arrangement between NATO and the Council of Europe concerning visits of the Council of Europe Committee for the Prevention of Torture to KFOR detention facilities in U. Häußler, loc. cit. n. 36, at pp. 26 *et seq.*

Operational detention will always be a significant command responsibility challenge with major legal ramifications. For anyone accustomed to the environment of a stable constitutional democracy, it sounds quite challenging that detentions should be possible without a judicial review of each individual case. Too many cases are known where individuals simply disappear and never return. None of these cases, however, involves actions taken by a peace mission. In light of the external oversight – which also covers internal review and appeals decisions – effective independent oversight of action attributable to international organisations is ensured. However, it is beyond doubt that lead organisations could establish enhanced internal appeals mechanisms which would also add legitimacy to long-term operational detentions.

VII. CONCLUSION

As illustrated, international peace missions do not operate in a legal vacuum. Their lead organisations have demonstrated that they are prepared to assume responsibility for (most of) the actions taken by the deployed personnel under their command and control. Decisions made at all relevant levels – political strategic, and military strategic, operational, and tactical – illustrate that lead organisations try to establish an equitable balance between the public interests supported by the peace mission and the human rights affected by the exercise of the mission's transitional authority. It is beyond doubt that the answer to the question of whether or not lead organisations meet this challenge – both at policy level and at the differing levels of military command – is also a matter of perspective. Only the exposure to a post-conflict area brings the latent dangers that prevail in such areas for extended periods to full awareness. My own practical experience is that once one is so aware, one's assessment of the differing weights of competing private and public interests will no longer be the same. Perhaps it is a paradox: peace missions must limit human rights more intensely than what is regarded as usual 'at home' in a stable constitutional democracy, but they must do so lest stable constitutional democracy will never even have a chance to grow out of the devastation, physical as well as in people's minds, left behind by armed conflict. As long as peace missions keep in mind that they neither operate in a legal vacuum nor may extend the unprotected situation of the inhabitants of the receiving state, they will be able to accomplish their mission, that is, help the receiving state to reach the desired end-state defined by the peace settlement they support.

ACCOUNTABILITY OF THE UNITED NATIONS: THE CASE OF SREBRENICA

Peter R. Baehr*

> 'Through error, misjudgement and an inability to recognize the scope of the evil confronting us, we failed to do our part to help save the people of Srebrenica from the Serb campaign of mass murder [...]. The tragedy of Srebrenica will haunt our history for ever.'[1]

I. INTRODUCTION

In June 1995, some 7600 male Muslim civilian inhabitants of the enclave of Srebrenica in Bosnia were brutally murdered by Bosnian Serb forces under the command of General Ratko Mladić. This happened almost under the very eyes of a small Dutch peacekeeping force that was part of the United Nations Protection Force (UNPROFOR) that had been deployed there to guard the enclave as a 'safe area'. These events led to extensive and recurrent debates in Dutch society and parliament on the question of who was responsible and whether the dismal result could have been prevented. In April 2002, the Netherlands Institute for War Documentation (NIOD) published a study that had been commissioned by the Dutch government.[2] This publication led to the

* Peter R. Baehr (political science) professor of international relations at the University of Amsterdam, executive secretary (later member) of the Scientific Council for Government Policy (WRR), The Hague, professor of human rights, Universities of Leiden and Utrecht, director of the Netherlands Institute of Human Rights (SIM), Utrecht. Books. *Human Rights. Universality in Practice; Human Rights in the Foreign Policy of the Netherlands* (with Monique Castermans-Holleman and Fred Grünfeld); *The Role of Human Rights in Foreign Policy* (with Monique Castermans-Holleman); *The United Nations: Ideal and Reality* (with Leon Gordenker); *Non-Governmental Human Rights Organizations in International Relations*. The author thanks Philip Everts, Otto Spijkers, Fred van Staden en Leon Gordenker for their comments on an earlier version of this contribution.

1 UN Secretary-General, 'Report of the Secretary-General Pursuant to General Assembly Resolution 53/35', A/54/549 (hereafter cited as UNSG Report), at para. 503.

2 NIOD, *Srebrenica: Een "Veilig" Gebied: Reconstructie, Achtergronden, Gevolgen en Analyses van de Val van een Safe Area* (Amsterdam, Nederlands Instituut voor Oorlogsdocumentatie 2002) (hereafter cited as NIOD Report; an English version of the report is accessible on the internet: www.niod.nl: J.C.H. Blom and P. Romijn, *Srebrenica, a Safe Area: Reconstruction, Background, Consequences and Analyses of the Fall of a Safe Area*, (Amsterdam 2002)).

resignation of the cabinet of Prime Minister Wim Kok, shortly before the parliamentary elections, in April 2002.

A major issue in the discussions involved the question of and the degree to which the United Nations (UN) had failed to carry out it tasks, among other ways by letting the Dutch send a small, lightly armed military contingent to the area and by refusing to allow air strikes to be made against the attacking Bosnian Serb forces.

This contribution deals with the question of to what extent the UN was – directly or indirectly – accountable for the massacre. On this issue Secretary-General Kofi Annan has already given his view of the situation in an extensive report.[3] This will be compared to the findings in the NIOD report, the report by the French National Assembly[4], the inquiry by the Dutch parliament[5] and the secondary literature on the subject. The aim of this contribution is manifestly *not* to describe once again all that happened at Srebrenica in 1995. Rather, its focus is on the issue of accountability. However, to thoroughly pursue this subject, it will first be necessary to summarise briefly the events for which accountability is sought.

II. WHAT HAPPENED AT SREBRENICA

To determine the accountability of the UN, it is, first of all, important to establish who represents or acts on behalf of the UN. Formally, that would be its highest executive officer, the Secretary-General. However, UNPROFOR commander, the French General Philippe Morillon, stated at a public gathering in Srebrenica in front of television cameras on 13 March 1993, that the people of Srebrenica were henceforth under UN protection and 'that he would not abandon them.'[6] He was at that moment clearly speaking on behalf of the organisation he served, the UN. As his words were later neither withdrawn, nor

3 UNSG Report, op. cit. n. 1.

4 French National Assembly, *Rapport d'Information*, No. 3413 (22 November 2001) [hereafter cited as Report French National Assembly].

5 Dutch Parliament, *Enquête Srebrenica*, Tweede Kamer, vergaderjaar 2002–2003, 28506, No. 2–3 (hereafter cited as Dutch Parliamentary Inquiry).

6 UNSG Report, op. cit. n. 1, at para. 38 and Report French National Assembly, op. cit. n. 4, at p. 18. His visit to Srebrenica was termed a 'political error' in the Report French National Assembly, p. 17: 'to the extent that the general would find himself compelled to enter, on behalf of the international community, into an engagement he would not be able to fulfil, thus deceiving the civilian populations and perhaps leading to increase the catastrophe of 1995.' [translated from the original French]. See also NIOD Report, op. cit. note 2, p. 3133 and E. Rijsdijk, 'Srebrenica, Genocide en de Reterritorialisering van Internationale Verantwoordelijkheid' ['Srebrenica, Genocide and the Reterritorialisation of International Accountability'], 32(3) *Vrede en Veiligheid* (2003) p. 307.

objected to by higher placed UN officials, the inhabitants of Srebrenica could in good faith expect to be henceforth protected from their enemies by the UN.[7] Their expectation seemed to be confirmed when the UN Security Council adopted on 16 April of that year resolution 819, declaring the city of Srebrenica a 'safe area'. The people of Srebrenica were in due time dismally disappointed in their expectations.

Although the Security Council confirmed the allocation of Srebrenica as a 'safe area' in subsequent resolutions 824 and 836, the latter resolution in the words of the UN Secretary- General, explicitly eschewed the use of the words 'protect' or 'defend' and asked UNPROFOR only 'to occupy some key points on the ground' and linked the use of force to the phrase "acting in self-defence"'.[8]

Two days later, a token force of approximately 170 Canadian UNPROFOR soldiers was deployed in the Srebrenica area.[9] The Canadian troops remained in Srebrenica until elements of a battalion of the Netherlands armed forces ('Dutchbat') were deployed there in January 1994.[10] Since these troops can be seen as the local representatives of the UN, it is useful to have a brief look at the reaction of the Dutch UNPROFOR troops at the time of the fall of Srebrenica.

The Dutch force that was sent to Srebrenica was small and lightly armed. The NIOD report discusses at length the reasons for selecting a small calibre machine gun for the 49 armoured infantry vehicles rather than the more customary 25 mm guns.[11] One of the arguments used by the government was that the weaponry had to be light when operating in a UN context; another that the Serbs should not be provoked, as it had to be clear to them that the weaponry was merely intended for self-protection, not for the military defence of the enclave. The main argument seems to have been that the airmobile battalion must not be allowed to resemble an armoured infantry battalion.[12]

The Secretary-General's report offers four reasons why no close combat air strikes were ordered against the advancing Bosnian Serb forces: (1) the UN would be perceived as having entered a war against them, which was not authorised by the Security Council; (2) the risk of losing control over the process would imply

7 The Secretary-General's report confirms this expectation: 'The fall of Srebrenica is also shocking because the enclave's inhabitants believed that the authority of the United Nations Security Council, the presence of UNPROFOR peacekeepers and the might of NATO air power, would ensure their safety.' (UNSG Report, op. cit. n. 1, at para. 468).

8 UNSG Report, op. cit. n. 1, at para. 79.

9 *Ibid.*, at para. 61.

10 *Ibid.*, at para. 104.

11 NIOD Report, op. cit. n. 2, at pp. 1122–1129.

12 *Ibid.*, at p. 1127. See also Dutch Parliamentary Inquiry, op. cit. n. 5, at pp. 71–74.

possible grave consequences for the UN troops; (3) the use of air power might endanger the humanitarian mission of UNPROFOR and (4) the fear of Serb reprisals against UN troops.[13]

The role that the Dutch battalion was to fulfil was obscure from the beginning as the concept of 'safe areas' remained unclear.[14] In the NIOD Report that notion is compared to the earlier one of 'safe havens':

> 'The concept of 'Safe Areas' had already been raised in connection with the conflicts in the former Yugoslavia, but it was a new and as yet undefined notion. The UN had a 'safe haven' concept, but this would have required a greater number of troops than were actually available. In searching for ways forward despite the limited resources (based on the belief that 'something had to be done'[15]), the term 'Safe Area' was coined. This remained a vague notion since it was a term *sui generis* which, even when adopted in the resolutions of the Security Council, remained applicable only to Bosnia.'[16]

The idea was manifestly *not* to defend the enclave militarily, since the Dutch forces were clearly too weak for that purpose. It was more 'to deter by presence' a possible attack. Its presence should be seen as a kind of tripwire against potential invaders, which if transgressed should alarm the world in general and the UN in particular.[17] 'The peacekeeping force did not command the means to enforce

---

13 UNSG Report, op. cit. n. 1, at para. 482.

14 *Ibid.*, at para. 51: 'The force commander of UNPROFOR was concerned that the nature of the safe area mandate which was being proposed would be inherently incompatible with peacekeeping. [...] [O]ne cannot make war and peace at the same time.' Also UNSG Report para. 150 referring to a report by the Secretary General of 9 May 1994: 'The Secretary-General then noted 'the failure of the parties to understand or fully respect the safe-area concept' and that ÚNPROFOR found itself in a situation where many safe areas were not safe.' See also Dutch Parliamentary Inquiry, op. cit. n. 5, at p. 423.

15 This was also a major reason for the Dutch decision to send troops to Srebrenica; see: Dutch Parliamentary Inquiry, op. cit. n. 5, at p. 416.

16 NIOD Report, op. cit n. 2, at p. 3133. According to the Report of the French National Assembly it was originally a French concept: 'It translated the will of our diplomacy to have a preponderant role in dealing with the conflict without having the means to put its initiatives at work.' (Report French National Assembly, op. cit. n. 4, at p.122; translated from the original French.). In David Rohde's words it was a 'vaguely worded measure' of which 'no one was quite sure what it meant.' D. Rohde, *A Safe Area: Srebrenica: Europe's Worst Massacre Since the Second World War* (London etc., Pocket Books 1997) p. 48. The co-chairman of the International Conference on the Former Yugoslavia, British Lord David Owen, called the safe areas 'flawed in concept' (UNSG Report, op. cit. n. 1, at para. 48).

17 NIOD Report, op. cit. n. 2, at 3133. The Dutch parliamentary inquiry was rather critical on this point: 'It must be acknowledged that the contents of the concept of "deterrence by presence" was unclear. This lack of clarity leads to differences of interpretation by various involved persons with regard to the precise meaning of the protection of the population by Dutchbat.' (Dutch Parliamentary Inquiry, op. cit. n. 5, at p. 422; translated from the original Dutch).

demilitarisation, whereas the idea that UNPROFOR by its very presence could deter military aggression against a safe area turned out to be a misconception.'[18] In the words of the NIOD Report: 'Altogether the proclamation of the territory as a *Safe Area* was thus on the one hand a signal for potential attackers, but it created on the other hand a feeling of security for the population that was illusory in fact.'[19]

What happened at Srebrenica in the beginning of July 1995 is by now well-documented. In the early morning of 6 July, the Bosnian Serbs began their attack on the town, which they easily captured on 11 July. The Dutch UNPROFOR troops, having eagerly – but in vain – waited for NATO air strikes against the attackers, were not in a position nor even tried to defend the town.[20] One Dutch soldier, retreating in an armed vehicle from an observation post that he had manned, was killed. The Dutch military officers negotiated with the Bosnian Serbs, headed by General Ratko Mladić for the evacuation of the 25000 Muslim refugees. Over the objections of the Dutch peacekeepers, the Muslim men were separated from the women and children. Some 7600 of them were taken away in buses by the Bosnian Serbs and summarily executed. They had first allegedly been screened for having committed war crimes, but these interrogations were not really meant to distinguish the guilty from the innocent; everyone was slated for execution. There is no doubt that these killings constituted a major crime against humanity.

What had happened was described succinctly and very clearly in the indictment of the Yugoslavia Tribunal against Radovan Karadžić and Ratko Mladić:

> 'After Srebrenica fell to besieging Serbian forces in July 1995, a truly terrible massacre of the Muslim population appears to have taken place. The evidence tendered by the prosecutor describes scenes of unimaginable savagery: thousands of men executed and buried in mass graves, hundreds of men buried alive, men and women mutilated and slaughtered, children killed before their mothers' eyes, a grandfather forced to eat the liver of his own grandson. These are truly scenes from hell, written on the darkest pages of human history.'[21]

---

18 F. Baudet, 'Srebrenica, een "Veilig Gebied": Het Laatste Woord over de Val van een *Safe Area?*' ['Srebrenica a Safe Area: The Final Word about the Fall of a Safe Area?'] in F. Ankersmit et al., eds., 'Het Drama Srebrenica: Geschied-theoretische Beschouwingen over het NIOD Rapport', 116(2) *Tijdschrift voor Geschiedenis* (2003) p. 197.

19 NIOD Report, op. cit. n. 2, at p. 3133.

20 See J.W. Honig and N. Both, *Srebrenica: Record of a War Crime* (London, Penguin Books 1996) pp. 3–27.

21 Judge Riad of ICTY on 16 November 1995 as cited by the UNSG Report, op. cit. n. 1, at para. 2.

III. THE ROLE OF DUTCHBAT

Should the Dutch peacekeepers in any way be held accountable for what had happened? The Secretary-General's report was relatively mild about the role of the Dutch: 'Ultimately, it is not possible to say with any certainty that stronger actions by the Dutch would have saved lives, and it is even possible that such efforts could have done more harm than good.'[22]

The Secretary-General found it 'harder to explain', however, why the Dutch battalion did not report more fully the scenes that had unfolded following the fall of Srebrenica. Although they did not witness directly the mass killings, they were aware of 'some sinister indications'. The Secretary-General did not rule out the possibility that, if the Dutch had reported more fully and in detail about these 'sinister indications', the UN might have 'responded more robustly and more quickly' and that lives might have been saved.[23]

In the epilogue to the NIOD report the question is raised whether the Dutch peacekeepers could not have done more to avoid what happened. The answer given is that, without outside help, the Dutch would have stood little chance against the Bosnian Serb forces and that moreover, its UN mandate was meant to deter by its presence rather than by the actual use of arms: 'The rules did not explicitly exclude an armed response, but required that this should be a last resort and only in self-defence.'[24] The NIOD Report argues that, militarily speaking, any Dutch action would have been 'doomed to failure'.

However, on a political and psychological level, 'it might not have been unthinkable' that General Mladić would have shied away from a conflict in which UNPROFOR casualties would have fallen.[25] Moreover, one may also consider that perceived military inferiority need not always lead to inaction. For

---

22 UNSG Report, op. cit. n. 1, at p. 109.

23 *Ibid.*, at p. 109. See also Dutch Parliamentary Inquiry, op. cit. n. 5, at p. 443.

24 NIOD Report, op. cit. n. 2, at p. 3142. However, Faber considers this a 'typically Dutch position', which he compares unfavourably with the British who fought at Gorazde as well as the French who protected the area around Sarajevo. See M.J. Faber, *Srebrenica: De Genocide die Niet Werd Voorkomen* ['Srebrenica: the Genocide that Was Not Prevented'] (The Hague, Interkerkelijk Vredesberaad 2002) p. 109. French officers, who testified before the French National Assembly, asserted that they would have fought: 'If one receives an order to bar one direction, one fights, that is one's mission. We would have fought and everything would have changed.' (Report French National Assembly, op. cit. n. 4, at p. 97; translated from the original French). The commander of Dutch, lieutenant-colonel Karremans, testified before the Dutch parliamentary inquiry as follows: 'The culture of the Dutch military in general is different from that of the British and the French. (...) The French have had a number of killed in action. That I have always greatly questioned, but I think it has to do with culture, with the French way of operating.' (Dutch Parliamentary Inquiry, op. cit. n. 5, at p. 185; translated from the original Dutch).

25 NIOD Report, op. cit. n. 2, at p. 3143.

instance, in May 1940, the Dutch forces defending the Netherlands against the invasion of the country were clearly, by military terms, no match for the attacking German forces. Some 2,300 Dutch soldiers lost their lives in May 1940 in what can be seen as from the beginning having been a hopeless battle. In the eyes of those responsible, the difference with Srebrenica appears to have been that, whereas soldiers' lives may be risked in the defence of their own country, that risk was not acceptable in the defence of the citizens of another country. Moreover, in 1940 the Dutch hoped that, if they resisted the German onslaught, British and French forces might come to their assistance.

Much has been made of the fact that the massacres took place under the very eyes of the Dutch peacekeepers, which did not report thereafter on what they had observed. The American human rights organization Human Rights Watch described a (destroyed) video tape as 'showing Bosnian Serb soldiers engaged in extrajudicial executions as Dutch U.N. troops looked on'.[26] This accusation is, however, strongly rejected by the NIOD Report: 'The march and the ensuing mass executions were events outside the battalion's field of vision. The conclusion that Muslims had been killed 'under the very eyes of Dutchbat' is therefore inaccurate'.[27] Perhaps indeed not *literally* under their eyes, but it was certainly very close by and, as the Secretary-General has said, there were at least those 'sinister indications' which the Dutch could have reported on, but chose not to do. In the words of a Dutch military officer: 'We accepted that the men faced an uncertain fate and that they might indeed come to suffer the most appalling conditions'.[28] Although the NIOD Report says that the overall impression created by Dutchbat 'was not particularly favourable', it nevertheless comes to the somewhat surprising conclusion 'that most tasks were nevertheless carried out competently'.[29]

Both the Secretary-General's report and the NIOD Report present roughly the following assessment of the Dutch performance: they *could* not defend their exposed position, therefore they *should* not have done so. The then director of the Netherlands Institute of International Relations, 'Clingendael', Alfred van Staden, shared that opinion: 'Some critics have afterwards put demands to the "Dutchbatters" that in fact amounted to a far going measure of self sacrifice, even

---

26 Human Rights Watch, *Bosnia-Herzegovina: The Fall of Srebrenica and the Failure of U.N. Peacekeeping* (2 October 1995).

27 NIOD Report, op. cit. n. 2, at p. 3153.

28 *Ibid.*, at pp. 3157–3158.

29 *Ibid.*, at p. 3162. The original Dutch text says 'min of meer naar behoren', of which the literal translation is 'more or less as it should be'. However, '[o]ne has some difficulty in understanding what led Mrs. Albright to salute the courage and the efficacy of the Dutch contingent in the Security Council, on 12 July 1995.' (Report French National Assembly, op. cite n. 4, at p. 43; translated from the original French).

to martyrdom. Others consider the absence of a heroic defence by the Dutch in the light of its probable pointlessness. And thus the debate continues.'[30]

Nevertheless, the inaction on the part of the Dutch could be described as surprising, as earlier, in May 1995, the Dutch government had strongly rejected an idea of General Bernard Janvier, in which he was supported by Secretary-General Boutros-Ghali, to give up the UN presence in the enclaves altogether, in view of their indefensibility.[31] This idea was, however, rejected by the members of the Security Council. At the time, the Netherlands government also rejected this view:

> 'When it appeared that Boutros-Ghali wanted to withdraw UNPROFOR from the eastern enclaves,[32] the Dutch government openly distantiated [sic!] themselves. The ministers Voorhoeve [defence] and Van Mierlo [foreign affairs] gave notice of objection to the statements by the UN Secretary-General. They opposed reduction of UNPROFOR and the possible withdrawal from the eastern *Safe Areas*, because that would endanger the safety of the population. The Dutch commitment was that 'of course' the population in the enclaves deserved special attention, according to Voorhoeve. UN observers in the eastern enclaves as Boutros-Ghali wanted, could offer the population insufficient safety, Voorhoeve thought. If the UN moved out, the Bosnian Serbs could take the enclave without hardly any resistance, which would cause an exodus of Displaced Persons.'[33]

In view of these (in my view correct) positions, one might conclude that the Dutch military might at least have made an effort to defend the people that had come under their protection. The more so, as the prior position of the Netherlands government was that, if the UN troops left the enclaves, they would have to take along the local population.[34] Apparently, the Dutch were at first not aware of what had happened 'under their very eyes'. Otherwise, it cannot be explained why they celebrated their safe withdrawal to Zagreb. They were given a heroes' welcome in

30 A. van Staden, *De Fuik van Srebrenica: Een Bijdrage aan Nadere Oordeelsvorming* ['The Fyke of Srebrenica: A Contribution to Forming a Closer Judgment'] (The Hague, Instituut Clingendael 1997) p. 27; translated from the original Dutch.

31 NIOD Report, op. cit. n. 2, at pp. 1752–1757. 'All the military that were consulted supported the thesis of the indefensibility of the enclaves in the absence of adequate means.' (Report French National Assembly, op. cit. n. 4, at p. 80; translated from the original French. See also NIOD Report, op. cit. n 2, at pp. 88 and 188).

32 'UN Secretary-General Boutros-Ghali himself also made an effort to find ways to prevent muddling through. In the Security Council he and General Janvier defended the plan to withdraw UNPROFOR from the eastern enclaves to reduce the vulnerability of UNPROFOR. That would make more 'forceful' action against the Bosnian Serbs possible. However, this plan was rejected in the Security Council because it was not in line with the positions of the countries concerned, and also because it meant loss of face for the UN Security Council if the eastern enclaves were abandoned.' (NIOD Report, op. cit. n. 2, at p. 1839).

33 NIOD Report, op. cit. n. 2, at p. 1759, citing *de Volkskrant* (Amsterdam) (18 May 1995).

34 NIOD Report, op. cit. n. 2, at p. 1775.

the presence of Crown Prince Willem Alexander, Prime Minister Wim Kok and Minister of Defence Joris Voorhoeve: 'A party, complete with a forty-two-piece brass band playing Glen Miller songs, cases of beer and drunken Dutch soldiers dancing in a chorus line, was thrown that afternoon.'[35] The NIOD report's account of that party, published almost seven years after the event, is more sober, stressing its private nature and the fact that the participating soldiers were not aware of what had happened:

> 'Before long the images made it unto Dutch television as well. They prompted widespread disgust, even more so in the light of the information about the scale of the Srebrenica tragedy that had been emerging in the months since the fall. That was accompanied by a growing tendency towards anachronism in the media's approach to the subject, giving rise to the suggestion that the troops in the party were fully aware of the mass murders that had taken place. This was just as fallacious as the incorrect assumption that the party had taken place before the eyes of the assembled media.'[36]

For the Dutch, the events in Srebrenica turned out to be a national experience of traumatic proportions.[37] Since the Second World War, the Netherlands had always prided itself on its commitment to the UN and the protection and promotion of human rights in the world at large. The Netherlands Constitution even charges the government to contribute to the promotion of an international legal order.[38] By participating in UNPROFOR the Netherlands had tried to do both: helping the UN to promote and protect human rights in the 'safe area' of Srebrenica. The failure of that operation was widely seen in the Netherlands as a failure to accomplish two basic tenets of its foreign policy. It destroyed the Dutch self-image of being 'a force for the good'. These were some of the reasons why the Netherlands government commissioned the study by NIOD in 1996. That assignment was at the time seen by many observers (including this author) as a method to avoid, or at least postpone for the time being, a full-scale political debate.

35 D. Rohde, op. cit. note 16, p. 325.

36 NIOD Report, op. cit. n. 2, at p. 2932.

37 Eleven years later, a government proposal to decorate the members of Dutchbat still caused controversy in the Netherlands. See S. Leydesdorff, 'Dutchbatter Past Geen Lintje' ['Dutchbatter Does Not Deserve A Decoration'], *de Volkskrant* (Amsterdam) (13 November 2006); P. Ego, 'Onderscheiding is Wel Terecht' ['Decoration Is Correct Indeed'], *de Volkskrant* (Amsterdam) (18 November 2006). The decorations – or rather 'badges' as they were officially called – were handed out by the minister of Defence on 4 December 2006. Relatives of the victims protested against the event and it was also criticised by the government of Bosnia Herzegovina. See *NRC Handelsblad* (Rotterdam) (4 December 2006) and *De Volkskrant* (Amsterdam) (5 December 2006).

38 The Netherlands Constitution, art. 90.

Although the NIOD Report stressed that it was a 'factual, historical account which does not attempt to arrive at political conclusions or to pass judgment'[39], its publication led directly to the resignation of the entire Dutch cabinet.[40] Prime Minister Wim Kok, in his abdication speech to parliament, emphasised that the responsibility for the massacre lay with the Bosnian Serbs, and General Mladić more in particular. However:

> '[T]he international community failed to offer sufficient protection to the people in the so-called safe area. Therewith, also the Netherlands Government, as a member of that international community has failed (...) The Netherlands explicitly does not take the blame for the horrible murder of thousands of Bosnian Muslims in 1995. It does show the political co-responsibility of the Netherlands for the situation in which this could happen. The international community is anonymous and cannot take upon itself the responsibility, responsibility vis-à-vis the victims and their next of kin of Srebrenica. I can do that and will do so.'[41]

With the benefit of hindsight it remains somewhat surprising that *all* members of the cabinet resigned, including those who had nothing to do with the events in Srebrenica. It would have been more understandable if, next to the prime minister, only the ministers of defence and of foreign affairs had resigned. However, by their collective resignation, the members of the cabinet clearly wanted to express their solidarity with the prime minister. It was a dramatic gesture, unique in Dutch constitutional history.

IV. THE ROLE OF THE 'INTERNATIONAL COMMUNITY'

Should the 'international community' be held accountable for the massacre in Srebrenica?

Manifold are the references in the Secretary-General's report and in other sources to the 'international community' on whose behalf UNPROFOR was supposed to act or failed to act. Yet, it is never made entirely clear what this 'international community' precisely entails. Is there such a thing? In his book *Power Politics*, first published in 1941, George Schwarzenberger, basing himself on the writings of the German sociologist Ferdinand Tönnies, introduced the distinction between 'international society' that did and the 'international community' that, he argued, did not exist. In his words:

---

39 NIOD Report, op. cit. n. 2, at p. 3125.

40 This fact becomes somewhat less impressive if one realises that it happened some six weeks before the national elections, which would have led to the resignation of the cabinet anyway.

41 Speech by Prime Minister Kok in Parliament, 16 April 2002; translated from the original Dutch.

> 'The criterion by which a society can be distinguished from a community may be formulated in a variety of ways. While a society is the means to an end, a community is an end in itself. Whereas a society is based on interest and fear, a community requires self-sacrifice and love. In the words of Toennies, the members of a society remain isolated in spite of their association, and those of a community are united in spite of their separate existence.'[42]

Clearly, since then, i.e. in 1995 (or today for that matter) the world has not yet made much progress. It has not reached the community stage, but is still, as in 1941, at the society stage. Nevertheless, politicians, diplomats and journalists alike are keen to suggest otherwise and to employ the term 'international community'. The Secretary-General's report contains many references to this alleged international community, without ever defining the term more concretely.[43] At one point the report even refers to the debate within the international community *and* within the UN[44], implying that the international community is something different from or beyond the UN.

Non-governmental organisations such as Human Rights Watch and Amnesty International too refer, in their reports about the conflict in the former Yugoslavia on many occasions to the activities or lack of activities of the 'international community'. Thus, for instance, Human Rights Watch, in its report on Srebrenica stated that 'the international community has failed to fulfil its moral and legal duty to prevent genocide and to insist that those commit acts of genocide (…) be brought to justice'.[45] Amnesty International devoted even an entire report to 'The International Community's Responsibility to Ensure Human Rights'.[46] On 18 October 1995, it presented a 10-point program for the international community to implement human rights in Bosnia and Herzegovina, which included: the international community should provide adequate, secure long term funding for human rights implementation and the international community must resolve cases of 'disappeared' and 'missing' persons as a matter of urgency to bring those responsible to justice and determine the fate of those persons.

42 G. Schwarzenberger, *Power Politics: A Study of World Society*, 3rd ed., (London, Stevens & Sons Ltd. 1964) p. 12.

43 UNSG Report, op. cit. n. 1, at paras. 6, 45, 49, 71, 127, 129, 130, 195, 321, 371, 372, 408, 415, 446, 452, 465, 474, 487, 497, 501, 502, 503, and 504. See also Report French National Assembly, op. cit. n. 4, at pp. 13, 20, 41 and 83; and Dutch Parliamentary Inquiry, *passim*.

44 UNSG Report, op. cit. n. 1, at para. 132; italics supplied.

45 Human Rights Watch, op. cit. n. 26, at p. 2 See also: Human Rights Watch, *World Report 2001 Bosnia and Herzegovina*, p.1: 'The international community's close involvement continued to be necessary to move the peace process along […] However, many in the international community were losing patience with the slow progress in Bosnia, and international attention was shifting to other areas.'

46 Amnesty International, *The International Community's Responsibility to Ensure Human Rights*, http://web.amnesty.org/library/print/ENGEUR63014196. Internet page last visited on 1 September 2006.

However, neither Human Rights Watch nor Amnesty International made clear to whom exactly they were addressing their recommendations.

The NIOD Report also refers in a number of places to the 'international community'.[47] However, in its epilogue the authors of the Report show their awareness of the difficulties in using the term:

> 'The decision-making processes within what we sometimes rather presumptuously refer to as 'the international community' are, almost by definition, slow and faltering. The governments and international organisations concerned have a marked tendency to "wait and see", postponing any actual decision as they carefully weigh up their own interests and determine their own positions. Intervention is therefore almost always reactive rather than proactive. Preventive action taken before major disruptions occur is largely unheard of.'[48]

The term 'international community', if not properly defined, is a vague concept that is used for all kinds of objectives. For instance, the international community was supposed to defeat finally and decisively the Taliban in Afghanistan. In 1999, it was the international community on whose behalf the Americans and British (as well as the Dutch), acting within the framework of the NATO alliance, intervened in Kosovo in order to defeat the oppressive regime of Slobodan Milosević, without authorisation by the UN Security Council. It is never made clear what the term precisely means and should therefore be banned from academic discourse.[49] It cannot be held accountable for the massacre in Srebrenica.

V. ACCOUNTABILITY

The academic literature on the subject can be criticised for other reasons as well. Erna Rijsdijk questions the fact that the use of violence before the fall of Srebrenica was described as a 'humanitarian disaster' rather than as a 'humanitarian crime' or 'genocide':

> 'By not describing the previous acts of violence in terms of universal crimes could and can the question not be raised which are or ought to be the matching international

47 NIOD Report, op. cit. n. 2, at pp. 1727, 1753, and 1778,.

48 NIOD Report, op. cit. n. 2, at p. 3130. See also: D. Rieff, *A Bed for the Night: Humanitarianism in Crisis*, (London, Vintage 2002) p. 8: '[...][W]hat thinking person can take seriously the idea that there is such a thing as the international community?.'

49 See also: D. Hellema, 'De Internationale Gemeenschap Bestaat Niet' ['The International Community Does Not Exist'], *NRC Handelsblad* (Rotterdam) (9 April 2004); P. Baehr, 'De Internationale Gemeenschap Bestaat Niet – De VN Wel' ['The International Community Does Not Exist – the UN Does'], 27(5) *Idee* (October 2006) pp. 54–57.

obligations. Therefrom [sic] we can conclude that academic analyses, consciously or not, can play an important role in hiding international accountability with regard to violence in Bosnia in general and in Srebrenica in particular.'[50]

The UN Secretary-General did admit in his report, however, that the UN at least shared in the responsibility for the massacre: 'There is an issue of responsibility and we in the United Nations share in that responsibility, as the assessment at the end of this report records.'[51] While the principal responsibility for the failure to act lies, as Van Staden has stressed, with the member-states[52], but he also argues that the UN bureaucracy showed itself unable to lead a complex and relatively large-scale peacekeeping operation in which enforcement actions might have been applied.[53]

When discussing responsibility and accountability, one should not forget that the first and foremost responsibility lies with the perpetrators, the Bosnian Serbs and the Serbian political leadership:

> 'As for final culpability, this must rest squarely on the shoulders of the most senior Serbian politicians and officers. They authorised and organized the crime. Their responsibility is clearly shown by a careful analysis of the crime [...]. The crime's systematic nature, the indications of extensive planning and carefully followed procedures, all point to the direct responsibility of the Bosnian-Serb leadership and the collusion, at the very least, of the Serbian leadership in Belgrade.'[54]

Doubtlessly the Bosnian Serbs under the leadership of General Mladić were first and foremost directly accountable for what happened in Srebrenica. He remains the person who was mainly responsible and who should face trial before the Yugoslavia Tribunal.

---

50 E. Rijsdijk, loc. cit. n. 6, at pp. 316–317; translated from the original Dutch. See also D. A. Leurdijk, *The United Nations and NATO in Former Yugoslavia, 1991–1996* (The Hague, Netherlands Atlantic Commission/Netherlands Institute of International Relations "Clingendael" 1996), p. 75, note 101: 'To the surprise of many, the fall of Srebrenica never led to an extensive debate in the Security Council on the events preceding and following the fall of Srebrenica.'

51 UNSG Report, op. cit. n. 1, at para. 5.

52 The then UN High Commissioner for Refugees, Sadako Ogata, was also very clear on this point: 'The secretary-general requested additional troops to be deployed to the safe areas, but there was no response. By taking a stand without substantive backup, the council revealed its limit in both strength and authority.' (B. Urquhart, 'Humanitarianism is Not Enough', 52(9) *The New York Review of Books*, (26 May 2005). Urquhart adds by way of comment: 'The members of the Security Council, and especially the permanent members, sometimes lack the sense of urgent international responsibility that, in situations when action is desperately needed could, at least for a short time, override their disagreements or intransigent national policies.'

53 A. Van Staden, op. cit. n. 30, at p. 29.

54 J.W. Honig and N. Both, op. cit. n. 20. See also Report French National Assembly, op. cit. n. 4, at p. 185.

An international community does not exist. Thus no international community can be held accountable for what happened in Srebrenica.

The Netherlands was at least indirectly involved through the presence of 'Dutchbat'. The least the Dutch military should have done is to report more extensively about what happened under (or at least very close to) their very eyes. Thus the Netherlands shares at least some of the responsibility for what happened.[55]

What about the UN?

The Secretary-General's report was remarkably candid about the failures of his organisation to protect the civilian population of Srebrenica. It was, 'with hindsight' wrong to declare repeatedly in public that it was not going to use airpower against the Serbian attackers, 'except as a last resort'.[56] The deployment of a peacekeeping force was not a coherent response to the problem: 'Lightly armed, highly visible in their white vehicles, scattered across country in numerous indefensible observation posts, they were able to confirm the obvious: there was no peace to keep.'[57]

The UN Secretariat was clearly not prepared to oppose a policy of 'ethnic cleansing': 'The civilian inhabitants of the enclaves were not the incidental victims of the attackers; their death or removal was the very purpose of the attacks upon them.'[58]

However, in the view of the Secretary-General, the main culprits were neither the Dutch peacekeepers nor the UN hierarchy that gave them their orders, but the Security Council that made 'fundamental mistakes': 'The safe areas were established by the Security Council without the consent of the parties and without providing any credible military deterrent.'[59] This led to the 'cardinal lesson of Srebrenica' that a deliberate and systematic attempt to terrorise, expel or murder an entire people must be met decisively with all necessary means, and with the political will to carry this policy through to its logical conclusion.[60]

---

55 Former Minister of Defence Joris Voorhoeve later reached the conclusion that he should have resigned at the time, see R. van den Boogaard, 'Tien Jaar na de Val van Srebrenica: Schuld of Boete', ['Ten Years after the Fall of Srebrenica: Culpability or Atonement'], *NRC Handelsblad Monthly M* (Rotterdam) (4 June 2005).

56 UNSG Report, op. cit. n. 1, at para. 483.

57 *Ibid.*, at para. 492.

58 *Ibid.*, at para. 495.

59 *Ibid.*, at para. 499.

60 *Ibid.*, at para. 502.

Ten years after the event, the Secretary-General insisted, 'we cannot evade our own share of responsibility'. Referring to his 1999 Report, he repeated that the UN 'made serious errors of judgement', rooted in a philosophy of impartiality and non-violence, which was 'unsuited to the conflict in Bosnia'.[61] His conclusions were in fact also highly critical of the actions of the highest civilian representative, Yasushi Akashi, and the military commander, Lieutenant-General Janvier. This tallied with the analysis by outside observer David Rohde, who wrote:

> 'Whether Janvier was cynical or misguided, he is more responsible than any other individual for the fall of Srebrenica. The restrictions on the use of airpower that he actively endorsed and his decision not to approve Close Air Support on Monday, July 10, had disastrous results.'[62]

The report of the French National Assembly stresses the wish on the part of the UN hierarchy in Zagreb to protect the French UNPROFOR soldiers that had been taken hostage by the Bosnian Serb forces: '[T]he responsible French military were obsessed by the protection of their men, which is quite normal, at the expense of that of the civilian populations, which poses the problem.'[63]

The Secretary-General admitted the UN's share of responsibility to what he clearly termed 'mistakes', when faced with a determined attacker. The Security Council itself never went so far. It neither discussed the Secretary-General's Report, nor admitted its own share of responsibility. The main culprits, General Ratko Mladić and his political superior Radovan Karadzić, though both indicted by the Yugoslavia Tribunal, were never arrested by the NATO military who regularly encountered them.[64] In other words: while the UN bureaucracy, represented by the Secretary-General did account for its mistakes, the members of the UN, who were in fact his superiors, never did so.

In view of this failure of the Security Council to admit its responsibility, the conclusion by David Rieff, laying all the blame on the shoulders of the organisation, i.e. the UN Secretariat, would not seem to be justified: 'Bosnia was

---

61 Message of the Secretary-General to the ceremony marking the 10th anniversary of the Srebrenica massacre, 11 July 2005. The Report of the French National Assembly even speaks of an 'institutional culture' of the UN to stay neutral, which prevented it from acting (Report French National Assembly, op. cit. n. 4, at p. 187).

62 D. Rohde, op. cit. note 16, p. 368.

63 Report French National Assembly, op. cit. n. 4, at p. 191; translated from the original French.

64 The Report of the French National Assembly ends with an urgent call on the French, British and Americans to devote all necessary means 'to capture these criminals against humanity' (Report French National Assembly, op. cit. n. 4, at p. 192; translated from the original French). For a similar call see Dutch Parliamentary Inquiry, op. cit. n. 5, at p. 452.However, as is well-known, on 21 July 2008, Karadzić was arrested by Serbian forces and transferred the following week to The Hague to be tried by the International Criminal Tribunal for the Former Yugoslavia.

the place where the world organization definitely lost its moral compass. For to have behaved as the U.N. did in Bosnia [...] is a disgrace from which the U.N. may not recover, or deserve to recover.'[65]

Rieff wrote these words three years before the Secretary-General's report was published. He was plainly wrong to conclude 'that the United Nations is quite simply the only body devised by human beings in the history of the world that can never be held accountable for its actions.'[66]

In 2007, a group, called the 'Mothers of Srebrenica' asked a Dutch court to indict the UN for its failure to prevent the slaughter and asked for financial compensation. In July 2008, the court ruled that it had no jurisdiction as the UN had full immunity from actions by national courts.[67] The 'Mothers of Srebrenica' appealed the decision, but on 30 March 2010, the Court of Appeal of The Hague upheld the 2008 ruling of the District Court. It considered that it did not have jurisdiction to hear the case because of the immunity from prosecution of the UN.[68] The lawyers of the group declared that they may bring the case to the Dutch Supreme Court or to the European Court of Justice.[69]

Srebrenica survivors and victims' families also filed a claim for compensation against the Dutch government arguing that the Dutch troops failed to take effective action to prevent the massacre. On 10 September 2008, the Hague District Court rejected the claim for compensation and ruled that the Dutch government could not be held responsible for this since the Dutch battalion was under UN command.[70] Consequently, the Dutch state had transferred its security and freedom competences to the UN and could not be liable for any violation committed during UN operations.

This case was the first attempt to hold a state participating in a peacekeeping force responsible for failing to protect the civilians.

---

65 D. Rieff, 'The Institution that Saw No Evil', *The New Republic* (12 February 1996) p. 19. See also F. Ajami, 'The Mark of Bosnia: Boutros-Ghali's Reign of Indifference', 75(3) *Foreign Affairs* (1996) p. 164: 'The moral indifference and callousness of the secretary-general was contagious [...]. But in Bosnia this secretary-general forfeited the organization's principal asset, its moral standing to speak out on the great issues of the day.'

66 D. Rieff, op. cit. n. 48, p. 20.

67 District Court in The Hague, 295247/HA ZA 07-2973 (10 July 2008).

68 Court of Appeal in The Hague, The Netherlands, *The Association of Citizens Mothers of Srebrenica v. The Netherlands and the UN (Appeal)*, 200.022.151/01, 30 March 2010.

69 The Hague Justice Portal, 'Mothers of Srebrenica cannot sue UN for compensatory damages', 30 March 2010, available at www.haguejusticeportal.net/smartsite.html?id=11576.

70 District Court in The Hague, 265618 / HA ZA 06-1672 (10 September 2008); District Court in The Hague, 265615 / HA ZA 06-1671 (10 September 2008).

VI. CONCLUSION

At Srebrenica, the UN personnel themselves were not involved in any acts amounting to human rights violations. What it was responsible for, were more actions of omission rather than of commission. The Dutch soldiers may be blamed for looking away, preferring not to see what they should have seen and reported on. It would seem fair, as has been suggested, that they should at least have insisted on an escort for the Muslim prisoners by the International Red Cross. The 'tripwire concept' clearly did not work.

Should 'Dutchbat' – outmanned and outgunned as it was – have put up more than a token resistance? That is hard to say even with the benefit of hindsight of more than eleven years. It would be far too facile to reach the judgment that men and women in a very difficult position should have acted as heroes (or even martyrs, as Van Staden has suggested), the more so as they had never been instructed to do so. What can be said – and what is hardly a new insight – is that both the UN and the Dutch government should have been much clearer in their instructions.

The UN Security Council established a 'safe area', without ever making clear what that concept meant, suggesting at least to the local population that they would be protected from their enemies. When the attack took place, no air support was provided which could have helped the Dutch and which might have been effective in repulsing the Bosnian Serbs. The Dutch, for their part, would have avoided much trouble if they had never gone to Srebrenica in the first place, but that would certainly not have helped the local population. Moreover, there was a widespread feeling in the Netherlands in those years that 'something should be done'. That this something ended in dismal failure could hardly have been foreseen at the time.

Secretary-General Kofi Annan has, through his report, squarely shouldered the blame on behalf of the organisation. It remains to be seen, however, whether the lessons learnt will be put into practice, should another 'Srebrenica' occur. Recent developments in West Darfur in Sudan would seem to provide little reason for optimism in this respect.

ON THE SOCIAL LIFE OF INTERNATIONAL ORGANISATIONS: FRAMING ACCOUNTABILITY IN REFUGEE RESETTLEMENT

Kristin Bergtora Sandvik*

I. INTRODUCTION

The legal and social status of international organisations is increasingly subjected to academic scrutiny. Largely ignored until recently, particular focus is now directed at international organisations as human rights *violators*. As evident from this edited volume, this critical interest spawns scholarship on international law and political science as well as a range of social science disciplines. Taking an empirical approach to the study of international organisations, this contribution explores the everyday life of humanitarian international organisations through a sociolegal lens. The contribution represents an attempt to think about the role of international organisations from a slightly different perspective than a strictly normative. Rather, the linkages that I identify do not explicitly register as transgressions of international law, they nonetheless inform us about something of the complex forms of dominance embedded in the contemporary practice of international organisations.

The starting point for the inquiry is the crisis of confidence that hit international humanitarianism beginning from the mid 1990s onwards. What is today known as 'New humanitarianism' came about as an antidote to this crisis: to establish renewed legitimacy, humanitarianism went through a transformation that

* I became interested in the social life of international organisations while working as a resettlement intern for UNHCR BO Kampala in 2004. This contribution draws on fieldwork in Kampala in 2005, where I was affiliated with the Refugee Law Project, and archival research at the Oxford Refugees Studies Centre, where I was a visiting researcher in 2006. My research was made possible by research grants from Harvard Law School, the University of Oslo and the Norwegian Research Council. I am grateful to the conference organisers for inviting me. As of May 2009, I am working as senior researcher with the Security Program at The International Peace Research Institute, Oslo (PRIO) and my e-mail is bergtora@prio.no.

included legalisation of procedures and the emergence of an institutional rapprochement between human rights and humanitarianism. Central to both of these efforts is the emphasis on administrative accountability. Through an examination of how the legal protection officers of the United Nations High Commissioner for Refugees (UNHCR) and urban refugees in Kampala, Uganda, negotiate access to third-country resettlement, the contribution explores certain facets of the new 'bureaucracies of virtue'[1] engendered by this rapprochement. By investigating how soft law rules and soft governance standards 'create' victims of torture and violence in refugee resettlement, the contribution questions the role of procedural accountability in the organisation of humanitarian projects. I describe how the content of the accountability-mechanisms at work in UNHCR's resettlement-operations inadvertently shifts towards processes for determining applicant credibility. I ask whether such conceptual instability may adversely result in the displacement of responsibility and the entrenchment of extra-democratic relationships.

The contribution proceeds in six parts. Section II develops the problem further. Section III frames legal humanitarianism, while section IV lays out the tenants of accountability in humanitarianism. Section V continues with a mapping of resettlement as humanitarian practice. In section VI, I describe the category 'survivor of torture and violence'. Section VII interrogates the social life of accountability in humanitarianism. Finally, in Section VIII, I offer a set of concluding observations.

II. THE PROBLEM

The impetus for the reform that spurred the rapprochement between humanitarianism and the human rights regime was initially motivated by the global public's growing unease regarding the legitimacy of an expansionist international humanitarian bureaucracy. Today, this enterprise is a reform project infused with pragmatism. Additionally, in the contemporary political climate, a human rights profile has become an essential communicative resource for international organisations.[2] There is a rhetorical demand for *engagement* in particular ethical conversations, creating an expectation that international players such as UNHCR coach their staff-client relationships in human rights

---

1 M. Jacob & A. Riles, 'The New Bureaucracies of Virtue: Introduction', 30 *Political and Legal Anthropology Review* (2007) pp. 181–191.

2 K. Kenny, 'When Needs are Rights: an Overview of UN Efforts to Integrate Human Rights in Humanitarian Action', Providence, The Thomas J. Watson Jr. Institute for International Studies, Occasional Paper Nr. 38, 2000, p. 4; D. Rieff, *A Bed for The Night, Humanitarianism in Crisis* (New York, Simon & Schuster 2003); M. Duffield, *Global Governance and the New Wars: The Merging of Development and Security*, (London, Zed Books 2001).

language as opposed to a philanthropic vocabulary or realist power-talk. In these conversations, a plethora of discourses about the content of the core human rights 'values' shape the expectations and demands of the participants. The international human rights regime has created a demand for *institutionalised* responses that conform to human rights 'standards', and which incorporates an appetite for dynamic inclusion of marginalised identities and groups. The *accountability* of decision makers – such as that of UNHCR's legal protection officers – is central to this framework and has consequently emerged as a prominent topic in drafting and programming humanitarian policy. In this contribution I explore the deployment of accountability to allay political and popular concerns about interventionist humanitarianism.

The literature on public accountability explains the disagreements and confusion surrounding the concept of 'accountability' by pointing to conceptual misunderstandings. The actors have diverging, though implicit forms of accountability in mind. Thus, initiatives to improve humanitarian governance are frequently stranded upon misconstrued standards to be implemented, or questions over 'how' to evaluate ongoing or completed projects.[3] My argument is that a framing of the discussion about the meaning of accountability as a contest between *competing* models offers an incomplete view. Rather, I suggest that we need to direct attention at the fit between the versions of accountability formally at work and the changing internal constellation of the background rules. Accountability measures are governance tools with complex effects. Devised as *means* to achieve greater legitimacy for bureaucratic interventions – by way of installing institutional cultures of human rights and administrative justice – these measures may themselves be transformed into instrumental ends through everyday practice. Using the refugee resettlement procedure as example, I will try to show how this reconfiguration may play out.

I propose that in the case of refugee resettlement, the content of accountability standards undergoes periodic shifts. This opens the possibility for the gradual displacement of the original normative intentions underlying the humanitarian renewal project. Democratic legitimacy for international organisations increasingly hinges on designing appropriate accountability structures and integrating these into programming. Yet, in the case of UNHCR, the current global climate of fear and xenophobia[4] has allowed for a bureaucratic transference

3 M.W. Dowdle, 'Introduction: on the crisis in public accountability', in M.W. Dowdle, ed., *Public Accountability, Designs, Dilemmas and Experiences* (Cambridge, Cambridge Studies in Law and Society 2006).

4 UN General Assembly, First Committee 11th Meeting (AM), 'New Security Paradigm Needed Following 11 September Terrorist Attack, First Committee Told, as General Debate concludes', available at www.un.org/News/Press/docs/2001/gadis3206.doc.htm, last visited on 4 February 2009.

of the rationale for accountability mechanisms onto a set of law-like requirements for determining the credibility of the refugees` narrative of suffering. The impetus to realise accountability through accuracy assessments has developed into a key interpretive principle in resettlement proceedings, which anchors accountability in the emphasis put on the *trustworthiness* of the applicant, and the *veracity* of his or her narrative.

III. FRAMING LEGAL HUMANITARIANISM

This contribution is not concerned with spectacular infringements on integrity or the slow path to obliteration through structural violence, though these are certainly possible and plausible perspectives on the nature of humanitarian governance. Rather, it is about the predicament of humanitarian presence. Judith Butler recently observed that 'petty bureaucrats are the new sovereigns'[5] and nowhere do such comments resonate more than in the administrative structures of international humanitarian organisations. I am interested in how the ambiguity of these structures functions as a source of informal power which simultaneously escapes and twists the logic of New humanitarianism.

The primary subject of responsibility under international law remains the nation-state, but over the past two decades humanitarianism has undergone an explosive normative and institutional expansion, as well as an intensive legalisation of routines and technical operations.[6] A parallel international governance structure has appeared which at once *cooperates* and *competes* with domestic government ministries and civil society organisations in the Global South.[7] Today, UNHCR holds many administrative, judicial, or quasi-judicial powers over refugee populations.[8] As an international organisation, UNHCR is not a *de jure* sovereign authority with territorial jurisdiction.[9] Yet, in practice UNHCR is widely

5 J. Butler at the Society for Anthropology of Religion, American Ethnological Society Invited Session: *Theologies of the Political: Thinking Across Practices of Governance*. American Anthropological Association, annual meeting November 2006, San Jose, California.

6 J. Goldstein, M. Kahler, R. O. Keohane, and A. Slaughter, 'Introduction: Legalization and World Politics' 54(3) *International Organization* (2000) pp. 385–399; L. Minear, *The Humanitarian Enterprise, Discoveries and Dilemmas*, (Bloomfield, CT Kumarian Press 2002).

7 D. Kennedy, 'Challenging Expert Rule: The Politics of Global Governance', 27(1) *Sidney Law Review* (2005).

8 For example, as pointed out by R. Wilde, '*Camps* are invariably located in states, but camp management and many other activities of core importance for the welfare of hundreds of thousands of people take place according to UNHCR guidelines, and do not engage with municipal law.' R. Wilde, 'Quis Custodiet Ipsos Custodes?: Why and How UNHCR Governance of "Development" Refugee Camps Should be Subject to International Human Rights Law', 1(5) *Yale Human Rights and Development Law Journal* (1998) pp. 110–111.

9 A. Betts, 'International Cooperation Between North and South to Enhance Refugee Protection in Regions of Origin', 25 *Oxford, RSC Working Paper* (2005) p. 2.

understood to operate with a 'sovereign face', managing the lives of millions.[10] As of 2005, UNHCR operated in 116 countries, and managed a budget of Annual Programme Budget of $1,145.3 million. It had 6,540 employees, and is responsible for a refugee population of 19.2 million.[11]

Aptly conceptualised by Kingsbury *et al* as a 'global administrative space'[12], this kind of social field is marked by unresolved legal disputes over the sovereignty and immunity of international organisations.[13] Continuous negotiations over the allocation of resources, personal relationships and discursive meanings characterise the relationship between humanitarian staff and their clients. Despite the interpersonal quality of these exchanges and the enormity of what is at stake for the refugee clients, this relationship is located *outside* the jurisdictional reach of domestically formulated accountability systems, and is only subjected to non-binding international frameworks.[14] Hence, to manage and secure legitimacy for this evolving transnational structure, the international community promotes the idea of administrative accountability for material and procedural operations.

Critical reflections on humanitarian governance tend to make grand claims about global governance[15], to leap into abstractions[16] or to rely upon a set of well-worn examples from the academic cottage industry dealing with Rwanda, Bosnia and Kosovo. Aiming for a more grounded understanding, this contribution uses aspects of the everyday interactions between UNHCR and sections of the urban refugee community in Kampala as an empirical lens. Dominating this interaction is the pursuit of refugee resettlement to a Western country. Having become an institutionalised practice, with an ever-expanding number of countries partaking in the resettlement program, resettlement is a particularly illustrative example of the growing regulatory power of international 'soft governance' regimes. At face

---

10 M. Barnett, 'Humanitarianism with a sovereign face: UNHCR in the global undertow', 35(1) *The International Migration Review* (2001) pp. 244–76; B.S. Chimni, 'From Resettlement to Involuntary Repatriation-Towards a Critical History of Durable Solutions', 23(3) *Refugee Survey Quarterly* (2004) pp. 55–73.

11 UNHCR, Annual Programme Budget (2006) A/AC.96/1011, 30 August 2005, available at www.acnur.org/biblioteca/pdf/3699.pdf#search=%22UNHCR%20annual%20budget%202006%22, last visited on 4 February 2009.

12 B. Kingsbury, N. Krisch and R.B. Stewart, 'The Emergence of Global Administrative Law', 68 *Law and Contemporary Problems* (2005) pp. 15–62.

13 The nuts and bolts of these disputes are subjected to extensive doctrinal discussions in international law journals and will not be reiterated here.

14 M. Pallis 'The Operation of UNHCR's Accountability Mechanisms', 37 *New York University Journal of International Law and Politics* (2005) pp. 869–918.

15 Typically, M. Hardt and A. Negri, *Empire* (Cambridge, Mass. Harvard University Press 2000).

16 D. Kennedy, *The Dark Sides of Virtue, Reassessing International Humanitarianism*, (Princeton University Press 2004).

value, resettlement represents a field of *shared* interests between UNHCR and refugees: according to NGOS, resettlement quotas remain unfilled, year after year, to the detriment of both parties.[17] However, the selection process remains traversed by competing visions of fairness. Given the difficult socioeconomic situation and increasingly bleak political prospects in Uganda, urban refugees conceive the move to a third country as one of few possible means of obtaining freedom and security. From the humanitarian perspective, fairness springs from the legal ordering of resettlement. Humanitarians have become managers of memberships to the protected communities of Western nation states. The general availability of this type of membership hinges on the perceived diligence of the institutional actors involved.[18]

Whereas UNHCR defines and communicates the standards of protection as universal across geographical boundaries, the organisation has in practice come to inhabit a dual role as advocate in the North and adjudicator in the South. In locations such as Uganda the predicament of power is acutely present for UNHCR legal protection officers. Unwilling and unable to embrace power openly, they frame the encounter with refugees as a regulated bureaucratic process. In response to criticism arising from past instances of mismanagement and corruption, enhanced internal monitoring systems have been developed, and the merits of material resettlement decisions are reviewed in regional hubs.[19] Nevertheless, administrative practices remain largely outside organisational oversight, and country operations largely lack effective channels for hearing and addressing the grievances of client groups.[20]

IV. CONTEXTUALISING ACCOUNTABILITY

Formulating a working concept of accountability, and of its deficits, remains a challenge. The concept of accountability is generally based on the idea that actors have obligations to act in ways that are consistent with accepted standards of behaviour and that other actors will sanction them for failures to do so. *Legal accountability* refers to the requirement that agents abide by formal rules and are prepared to justify their actions in those terms, in courts or quasi-judicial arenas. Public officials, like anyone else, can be 'held accountable' for their actions both

---

17 Part 8: The NGO Perspective Global Consultations on International Protection Third Track, Theme 3: 'The Search for Protection-Based Solutions: NGO Statement on Resettlement (22–24 May 2002)', 22(2–3) *Refugee Survey Quarterly* (2003) pp. 432–441.

18 Following the scandal surrounding the migration practices of the British home office in April 2006, public confidence plummeted. *See* H. Mulholland, 'Reid promises 'fundamental reform' of Home Office', *Guardian Unlimited,* 19 July 2006.

19 P. Browne, *The Longest Journey, Resettling Refugees From Africa,* (UNSW Press 2006).

20 M. Pallis, loc. cit. n. 14.

through administrative and criminal law.[21] Michael Dowdle suggests that international regimes operate with an idea of accountability inherited from Anglo-American ideas of public accountability. According to Dowdle, this idea is not so much the product of extrapolation from core conceptual principles as an accretional *layering* of responses to the periodic crisis of legitimacy experienced by Anglo-American societies. He argues that from a participant's perspective, there are critical aspects of bureaucratic accountability that are likely to escape detection by design-based perspectives. Such aspects are present in the irreducible complexities of social interaction. Accountability means different things to different actors. For example, Dowdle suggests to us, human rights activists see accountability principally in terms of popular participation in and supervision of political decision-making. In the developing world, members of civil-society protest against public actors who hinder the implementation of emerging public international norms, and against transnational regulatory actors seen to illegitimately interfere in domestic political matters. Yet another perspective is offered by human rights international organisations, whose staff generally includes a high number of persons with legal training, and thus tend to prefer juridical modes of public accountability.[22]

Traditionally, international organisations have been viewed as both progressive and powerless. Their mere presence in sub-Saharan countries was seen as an assurance of at least some stability and development. Under international law, international organisations were agents of the state, not actors in their own right. As an international organisation, UNHCR enjoys immunity under the 1946 UN Privileges and Immunities act.[23] Under the standard agreements between the host country and UNHCR, the government agrees to grant to UNHCR and its personnel such additional privileges and immunities as may be necessary for the effective exercise of the international protection and humanitarian assistance functions of UNHCR.[24] Ongoing debates in international law discuss whether a move from absolute to functional/proportionate immunity for international organisations would be desirable. The International Law Commission has pointed out that there is a widely perceived need to improve methods for settling

21 R.W. Grant and R.O. Keohane, 'Accountability and Abuses of Power in World Politics', 99(1) *American Political Science Review* (2005); E. Rubin, 'The myth of non-bureaucratic accountability and the anti-administrative impulse' in M.W. Dowdle, ed., *Public Accountability, Designs, Dilemmas and Experiences*, (Cambridge, Cambridge Studies in Law and Society 2006) p. 52.

22 M.W. Dowdle, loc. cit. n. 3, at p. 6, n. 6.

23 See the Convention on the Privileges and Immunities of the United Nations, 1946. Section 2 provides that the UN "shall enjoy immunity from every form of legal process" unless it waives its immunity.

24 UNHCR's standard host country agreement. Articles X (1)(b); VII (2), available at www.unhcr.md/article/host.htm, last visited on 4 February 2009.

disputes about the responsibility of international organisations.[25] Because of the essential features of the judicial function, the remedial potential of judicial remedies is crucial for the entire accountability regime.[26]

Despite a constrained mandate, UNHCR has been able to operate with considerable flexibility and obtain legitimacy for a host of engagements. As noted by James Hathaway, '[I]n practice, and despite the externally imposed limits on its authority, there is no doubt that UNHCR plays an absolutely vital role in promoting respect for refugee rights around the world'.[27] Article 35 of the 1951-refugee convention endows UNHCR with a capacity to supervise 'the applications of the provisions of this Convention.' According to the preamble of the 1951 Convention relating to the Status of Refugees, contracting parties are under the obligation to cooperate with UNHCR, by 'recognizing that the effective co-ordination of measures taken to deal with this problem will depend upon the co-operation of States with the High Commissioner.'[28] The international refugee law regime is under severe pressure, and the contents of the refugee definition and of the durable solutions have shifted substantially over the past decade, mostly independent of UNHCR's advice.[29] Particular groups have gained expanded legal recognition both in international refugee law and in national immigration legislations. Nevertheless, the general trend is that administrative courts, appeal courts and constitutional reviews in the West are increasingly constrained by restrictive immigration policies. In this harsh political climate, UNHCR often operates as a dynamic advocate for the plight of refugees.[30] A very different set of concerns applies to UNHCR's activities in the developing world.

---

25 International Law Commission, Working Group on Responsibility of International Organizations, General Assembly A/CN.4/L.622 (1995) at p. 9. As matters stand at present, see International Law Commission, *Report of the Sixty-first session (4 May to 5 June and 6 July to 7 August 2009)*, UN Doc. A/64/10, chapter IV, paras. 31–51.

26 A. Reinisch, *International Organizations Before National Courts*, (Cambridge, Cambridge University Press 2000) p. 313.

27 J.C. Hathaway, *The Rights of refugees Under International Law* (Cambridge, Cambridge University Press 2005) p. 993.

28 W. Kählin, 'Supervising the 1951 Convention Relating to the Status of Refugees: Article 3 and beyond', in E. Feller et al., eds., *Refugee Protection in International law: UNHCR's Global Consultations on International Protection* (Cambridge, Cambridge University Press 2003).

29 J.C. Hathaway & R.A. Neve, 'Making International Refugee Law Relevant Again: A Proposal for Collectivized and Solution-Oriented Protection', 10 *Harvard Human Rights Journal* (1997) p. 115.

30 See for example UNHCR's amicus brief submitted before the United Kingdom's House of Lords in the *Islam* and *Shah* cases, providing relevant guidance with respect to domestic violence as a ground for asylum. House of Lords, *Islam (A.P.) v. Secretary of State for the Home Department* and *Regina v. Immigration Appeal Tribunal and Another Ex Parte Shah (A.P.)*, Conjoined Appeals available at www.publications.parliament.uk/pa/ld199899/ldjudgmt/jd990325/islam01.htm.

With the past decades of institutional expansion, the distributive consequences of the encounters between humanitarian staff and marginalised groups in the Global South have greatly reinforced the need to address questions of accountability and democratic participation.[31] The power struggles humanitarian organisations engage in are often of local nature, while the everyday behaviour of humanitarian officials is coupled with transnational immunity. Scholarship has criticised the growing dominance of the 'humanitarian international',[32] the upshot of which is the gradual disempowerment of national authorities.[33] Different from other UN organisations, UNHCR has no budgetary funding from the general assembly, and relies upon Western countries for continuous economic support. While mandated to 'protect refugees', UNHCR finds itself in cyclical financial difficulties and continuously under strong pressure from its Western donors. Consequently, since the early 1990s, the organisation has gradually moved away from the protection mandate, in favour of a 'lead agency' approach geared towards direct service provision on the ground.[34] Critics acknowledge that international organisations such as UNHCR face extensive organisational challenges, with employment policies and human resource management prohibiting the development of reform.[35] However, they emphasise that a consequence of this is the sidelining of the national governments in favour of ultimately unaccountable international charity. For example, studies have shown that the risk of procedural failure during the refugee status determination

---

31 A. Reinisch, 'Securing the Accountability of International Organization', 7 *Global Governance* (2001) p. 131.

32 A.D. Waal, *Famine crimes, Politics & The Disaster Relief Industry in Africa* (Indiana, Indiana University Press 1997). B. Harrell-Bond, *Imposing Aid* (Oxford, Oxford University Press 1984); M. Barnett and M. Finnemore, *Rules for the World: International Organisations in Global Politics* (Ithaca, Cornell University Press 2004); F. Terry, *Condemned to Repeat? The Paradox of Humanitarian Action,* (Ithaca and London, Cornell University Press 2002).

33 Liisa Malkki's informants in the Mishamo camp in Tanzania gave a favourable assessment of UNHCR, while they deplored the 'malign' Tanzanian camp administration. In her account of the handover of Kyriandongo Refugee Settlement from UNHCR to the Ugandan government, Kaiser describes how 'the prospects of being left in the hands of the local government left the refugees with fear and trepidation.' Reflecting over UNHCR's position in Kenya, the Refugee Consortium of Kenya suggests that UNHCR has in effect assumed the role of a government ministry. In so doing, the organisation has seriously compromised its autonomy and its effectiveness in providing refugee protection. L. Malkki, *Purity in Exile, Violence, Memory, and National Cosmology among Hutu Refugees in Tanzania* (Chicago, The University of Chicago Press 1995); T. Kaiser, 'The handover of Kyriandongo; The Anatomy of a Takeover', 21(1–2) *Refugee Survey Quarterly* (2003); The Refugee Consortium of Kenya, 'Refugee management in Kenya', 16 *FMR* (2003) p. 17.

34 G. Loescher, *The UNHCR and World Politics- A Perilous Path* (Oxford, Oxford University Press 2001); M. Barutciski, 'A Critical View of UNHCR's Mandate Dilemmas' 14(2/3) *Journal of Refugee Law* (2002) p. 365.

35 M. Walkup, 'Policy dysfunction in humanitarian organizations: the role of coping strategies, institutions, and organizational culture', 10(1) *Journal of Refugee Studies* (1997); G. Verdirame & B. Harrell-Bond, *Rights in Exile, Janus-Faced Humanitarianism* (New York, Oxford, Berghahn Books 2005); B. Harrell-Bond, 'Can Humanitarian Work with Refugees be Humane?' 24(1) *Human Rights Quarterly* (2002) pp. 51–85.

procedure is not merely a theoretical possibility.[36] Criticism also continues to be levied against UNHCR to make the organisation accept legal representation in *refugee status determination hearings.*[37]

V. RESETTLEMENT AS HUMANITARIAN PRACTICE

The international refugee law regime under the auspices of UNHCR foresees three, non-hierarchical durable solutions for refugees, leading to a satisfactory situation which enables the refugee to integrate into *a* society. Refugees may integrate locally, on a voluntary basis or because of cessation of their refugee status. The second solution is voluntary return to the country of origin. The third solution, for refugees who have special needs which cannot be met adequately in the country of refuge, is resettlement. Every year, UNHCR resettles thousands of refugees from war-torn poverty-stricken countries in the global south, to wealthy countries in the North. The UNHCR resettlement program is based on the voluntary participation of states. In 2005, 30,500 refugees were resettled with UNHCR's assistance (80,800 in total), and sixteen countries participated in UNHCR's resettlement program. The largest resettlement countries by far are the United States, Australia and Canada, followed by the Scandinavian countries, The Netherlands and New Zealand. Still, this number accounted for less than 0.5% off the total refugee population of almost nine million.[38]

According to the definition used by UNHCR, resettlement involves the selection and transfer of refugees from a state in which they have initially sought protection to a third state that has agreed to admit them with permanent residence status.[39] Resettlement is primarily a solution for those refugees with 'legal and physical protection needs', whose fundamental human rights are at risk in the country of refugee. However, over the past decade, seven other categories have also come into use. Eligible for resettlement are also survivors of torture and violence, medical needs, women-at-risk, family reunification,

---

36 M. Kagan, 'Is Truth in the Eye of the Beholder? Objective Credibility Assessment in Refugee Status Determination', 17(3) *Georgetown Immigration Law Journal* (2003).

37 In a paper based on evidence gathered from UNHCR's refugee status determination activities in Egypt and Jordan, Michael Kagan set out a number of grave procedural failings. Specific reasons for rejection are not provided to asylum seekers; evidence considered in cases is withheld from applicants concerned; critical parts of standard operating procedures are withheld from the public; most appeals are rejected without an in-person re-hearing and appeals are not considered by a fully independent unit. M. Kagan, 'Frontier Justice: Legal Aid and UNHCR Refugee Status Determination in Egypt', 19 *Journal of Refugee Studies* (2006) p. 45.

38 UNHCR, 'Refugees by Numbers' (2006 edition), available at www.unhcr.org.

39 J. Van Selm, 'The Strategic Use of Resettlement: Changing the Face of Protection'. The Strategic Use of Resettlement: A Discussion Paper Prepared by the Working Group on Resettlement WGR/03/04.Rev3 (2003).

children and adolescents, elderly refugees and refugees without local integration prospects. As previously indicated, this contribution centres on the bureaucratic constitution of survivors of torture and violence.

The international refugee regime frames the hierarchical relationships between humanitarians and their clients in two modes: through quantitative techniques such as statistical methods and 'headcounts',[40] and by way of a broader arsenal of qualitative approaches, with legal measures as one such component. Based on the 1951 Convention, regional instruments and soft law documents, displaced people are distributed into categories such as 'asylum seekers', 'irregular movers', 'bona fide refugees' and 'internally displaced people'. These groups are then allocated to various 'solutions'. Foregrounding the legal and bureaucratic structure creates an idea of fair and ordered access and distribution.

Resettlement is not a recognised legal procedure under international law, but in line with the general legalisation of the activities of international organisations, resettlement has been redesigned from a tool for transferring large populations, to a process governed by juridical ideas. The standards of procedure are set out in a regularly updated *Resettlement Handbook*, which was first introduced in 1997. In the 2004 handbook, UNHCR states that '[a] rational and transparent approach will, furthermore, strengthen the credibility of UNHCR in general and widen the confidence of refugees, resettlement countries and other partners, which in turn should help to ensure that resettlement can be done efficiently and effectively.'[41] For UNHCR, a well-managed resettlement program is essential to maintain the appearance of efficiency and integrity traditionally associated with the organisation; playing up the image of a carefully determined *legal* credibility as the benchmark for the selection process becomes a visible manifestation of the fulfilment of a humanitarian mandate.

According to a modest estimate, Uganda is home to some 250,000 refugees, produced by the many conflicts of geopolitical character that has plagued this part of Africa. While the vast majority comes from Sudan, thousands of refugees from Burundi, DR Congo, Eritrea, Ethiopia, Rwanda and Somalia have also sought protection in the country.[42] A significant percentage of the displaced populations have been victim of or witness to war crimes and other human rights

40 Jeff Crisp argues that prior to the 1990s, UNHCR's capacity and commitment in the area of refugee statistics was by any standard weak. Since 1994, UNHCR has published an annual statistical overview of 'refugees and others of concern to UNHCR'. In 1994, the review consisted of 32 pages and included 15 tables. By 1998, the publication had grown to 104 pages and included 32 tables, and is widely distributed within and outside the organisation in a number of formats. J. Crisp, 'Who has counted The Refugees? UNHCR and the politics of numbers', *New Issues in Refugee Research, Working Paper No. 12* (Geneva, UNHCR, 1999) at pp. 18–20.

41 UNHCR, Resettlement Handbook and Country Essays (2004) at p. 34.

42 UNHCR, Global Appeal (2006).

violations. Most refugees in Uganda are in a 'protracted' situation, meaning that they have lived in exile for more than five years, and that they still have no immediate prospect of finding a *durable solution* to their plight.[43] Attempting to overcome their dire situations and thwart the bleak prospects of continued exile, or return, many refugees, particularly those residing in and around the capital Kampala, still pursue any prospect of 'getting out', of leaving, of going somewhere else, by whatever means available. 'Somewhere else' is ideally the West, where social goods like security, health care, education, housing and work are perceived to be readily available, and where ones children, if not oneself, can embark on an life of 'human flourishing', exerting themselves to the fullest of their capabilities.[44] During the time of fieldwork, the number of individuals resettled from Uganda was surging. For 2006, the numbers were projected at 2500, up from 1500 the year before and 35 in 1997.[45]

Asylum seekers are entitled to have their refugee claims determined through an administrative or legal process. However, while durable solutions are designated to provide formal solutions to the refugee problem, no solid connection is made between the right to status determination, and need for an accepted refugee to find a long-term solution. Unlike the refugee status determination procedure, whose bureaucratic structure rests upon treaty obligation, resettlement is a *contract* based on a principle of burden-sharing. The legal basis for resettlement is the tripartite agreements between host states, receiving countries and UNHCR. The amalgam of humanitarian principles and human rights norms has served as a convincing frame for the argument that transnational relocation is an effective means of diminishing human tragedy. Importantly, this strategy simultaneously responds to a host of other policy objectives. The rhetoric of 'protection', prominent as a strategic tool, takes on a fluid shape in everyday life. The limited resettlement quota, the inadequate bureaucratic capacity, the complex structures of access, the material requirements and the significance of submission under priority-category all contribute to give meaning to the idea of 'protection' harboured by refugees.

VI. SURVIVING TORTURE CREDIBLY

Refugees who are 'survivors of torture and violence' are eligible for resettlement, yet some of the features of torture as a practice of violence make the requisite storytelling difficult. This section explores how bureaucratic recognition becomes

---

43 J. Crisp, 'No Solution in Sight: The Problem of Protracted Refugee Situations in Africa', *New Issues in Refugee Research, Working Paper No. 75* (Geneva, UNHCR, 2003).

44 A. Sen, *Development as Freedom* (New York, Random House 1999).

45 UNHCR, Global appeal (2006).

a Weberian iron cage of rationally demarcated suffering. The refugee must convince UNHCR staff that she or he is a survivor of torture and violence, yet the act of listening itself becomes problematised within the specific criteria and expectations of UNHCR staff as well as the troubling thematics that torture stories often produce. The experience of suffering and its long-term traumatic effects significantly affects the ability to communicate ones story. In her classic work, *The Body in Pain: The Making and Unmaking of the world*, Elaine Scarry proposed that: 'pain destroys language and dissolves the world of the victims. Pain and suffering create conditions of radical epistemological doubt, which may not be possible to articulate by the sufferer, or knowable by the "other".'[46] Yet, the existence of this condition of apathy is also circulated knowledge, and impacts how UNHCR's protection officers gauge the comportment of their clients.

The resettlement handbook bases its conception of torture on the definition promulgated in the *1984 Convention against Torture and Other Cruel Inhuman or Degrading Treatment or Punishment* (CAT).[47] Priority is given to refugees with medical problems directly related to persecution and flight, for example, psychological trauma, torture, war-inflicted disabilities, and rape.[48] The handbook explains that '[i]n cases of refugees who sustained torture but do not show obvious consequences of it, one should always consider the risk of latent effects.'[49] It is not clear how many of the refugee population in Uganda have suffered torture in their country of origin, but observers believe that the number is high. According to REDRESS, 'torture is a systemic problem in Uganda, as an instrument of political repression, as a tool used in law-enforcement, and as one of the methods employed in the conduct of war'.[50]

In theory, a donor-funded replica of the whole gamut of the western therapeutic cycle caters to victims of human rights violations with psychosocial problems.

---

46 As cited by Richard Ashby Wilson on Humanitarian Responses to Narratives of Inflicted Suffering, available at www.humanrights.uconn.edu/conf_2006.htm, last visited on 4 April 2007.

47 According to CAT Article 1, Torture means 'any act by which severe pain or suffering, whether physical or mental, is intentionally inflicted on a person for such purposes as obtaining from him or a third person information or a confession, punishing him for an act he or a third persons has committed or is suspected of having committed, or intimidating or coercing him or a third person, or for any reason based on discrimination of any kind, when such pain or suffering is inflicted by or at the instigation of or with the consent or acquiescence of a public official or other person acting in an official capacity. It does not include pain or suffering arising only from, inherent in or incidental to lawful sanctions.'

48 UNHCR, Resettlement Section, 'Opinion Resettlement: An Instrument of Protection and a Durable Solution', 9(4) *International Journal of Refugee Law* (1997).

49 UNHCR, Resettlement Handbook 2004(8).

50 There are several reports of Congolese detainees who have been tortured while in detention in Uganda. Human Rights Watch, 'State of Pain: Torture in Uganda' (2004); REDRESS, 'Torture in Uganda, A Baseline Study on the Situation of Torture Survivors in Uganda' (2007).

Refugee informants gave extensive accounts of routine shuttling between governmental and voluntary institutions to obtain medical care and documentation of torture. At the centre of these efforts is the ACTV (the Africa Centre for Treatment of Torture Victims), which is a professional centre for the rehabilitation of victims of torture and violence, which moulds its work on CAT.[51] According to ACTV, out of its 752 clients in 2005, 52 came from DRC, mainly from Eastern DRC, 18 from Rwanda, 9 were Burundians 9 Sudanese, 4 Ethiopian, 2 Tanzanian and 1 from Somalia.[52] Urban refugees who are torture survivors are particularly vulnerable due to their uncertain legal status and the dire socioeconomic situation they often have to cope with. A 1999 study revealed that most of these torture survivors developed various psychological disorders including chronic (and complex) posttraumatic stress disorder (75.4%), depression (28%), anxiety disorders (17%), somatoform disorders (32%) and chronic pain disorders/syndromes 82%. A number of patients also had physical signs of torture including fractures (43.5%) hernias (7.7%) and sexually transmitted diseases (60%) contracted through rape.[53]

As mentioned in the beginning of this section, effective storytelling does not happen by way of silence or accounts of aimless night-time roaming through the slums of Kampala. The international protection framework envisions a certain type of survivor, of which is required a particular legal performance. I will just briefly outline the main points here: this performance should trigger specific cultural sensibilities. The right narrative brings out empathy, trepidation and hope in equal measures: exaggeration and internal imbalance should be avoided. As Thomas Spijkerboer pertinently points out in his description of testimonies by female refugees: '[a]n applicant who does not show any emotion when speaking of sexual violence is deemed incredible; a restrained display of emotions is deemed eminently credible; and showing an excess of emotions is seen as play acting.'[54]

Thus, neither conspicuously moving testimonies, nor passivity will work towards a successful resettlement candidacy. If we suppose that credibility is intrinsically connected to a particular mode of mediating knowledge, it becomes possible for

---

51 The ACTV was formed in Kampala in 1993 by a Ugandan medical doctor, himself a torture survivor, under the guidance of the Danish-based International Rehabilitation Centre for Torture Victims (IRCT). Today those who come to ACTV are 'ordinary' people tortured by the army, police and prison service, political victims engaged in opposition to the current Government, and refugees tortured in Uganda's neighbouring countries (REDRESS, op. cit. n. 50).

52 REDRESS, op. cit. n. 50, at p. 19–20.

53 S. Musisi, E. Kinyanda, R. Mayengo-Kiziri and H. Liebling, *Post-Traumatic Torture Disorders in Uganda: A 3-Year Retrospective Study of Patient Records at a Specialised Torture Treatment Centre in Kampala, Uganda, 1999.*

54 T. Spijkerboer, 'Stereotyping and Acceleration' in G. Noll, ed., *Proof, Evidentiary Assessment and Credibility in Asylum Procedures* (Leiden, Martinus Nijhoff Publishers 2005).

a credibility assessment to contribute to the fulfilment of the demands for accountable global governance, and to make the humanitarian a deeply unjust ruler in the local context. Paradoxically, the initiative required to succeed inevitably engenders a moral switch: efforts to induce credibility are perceived to be antithetical to the image of sincerity and trustworthiness, which overlaps so much of the legal conceptualisation of credibility. Commentators occasionally point out that the 'marginality' set forth in the resettlement handbook has become a market opportunity for refugees, and UNHCR frets about the danger of creating 'pull factors'. However, the marginality imagined in the resettlement handbook embeds itself in social life in intricate ways: crafty impostors sometimes cunningly play with these legal constructs. However, more often than not, human vulnerability is twisted and turned.

In its *Note on Burden and Standard of Proof in Refugee Claims*, UNHCR states that 'Credibility is established where the applicant has presented a claim which is coherent and plausible, not contradicting generally known facts, and therefore is, on balance, capable of being believed.'[55] Western legal culture considers spontaneity and immediacy in the communication of suffering as indications of genuineness.[56] In the encounter between humanitarian and refugees, this translates into a demand for authenticity. Nevertheless, such performances are rarely unplanned events. ACTV spends considerable resources on documenting torture of refugees by way of medical reports or photographic evidence, and this evidence is actively used by refugees during resettlement interviews. On the other hand, through ACTVs initial screening process, many refugees discover that the physical and sexual violence they are victims of falls *outside* the torture definition. To be a credible torture victim means the ability to produce both the appropriate injury, and to establish causality between the action, the agent/institution and oneself. The competent management of speech and technology, and the generation of artefacts, figure prominently in the tactics refugees use to obtain legal assistance, or to gain access to administrative legal processes such as resettlement. These are also crucial in establishing a level of credibility *during* resettlement interviews.

According to procedural standards, once the refugee status is determined, the next step is the search for durable solutions. The individual UNHCR Legal protection officer makes the determination of whether resettlement is the appropriate solution during a face-to-face encounter, or through a facilitator. Successfully making ones plight and persona known to any possible facilitator

55 M. Kagan, loc. cit. n. 36, at p. 381.

56 See Juliet Cohen for an analysis of the complexities involved in credibility-determinations. J. Cohen, 'Questions of credibility: omissions, discrepancies and the errors of recall in the testimony of asylum-seekers', 3(3) *International Journal of Refugee Law* (2001) pp. 293–309.

will result in a letter, phone call or informal/formal conversation with UNHCR staff about a potential resettlement claim. With luck and skill, this transmission of information will result in a 'note for the file', which recommends that a resettlement-case should be opened. Subsequently, a screening interview is scheduled. The responsible officer makes the decision about whether to proceed. Depending on the outcome on the case assessment and verification, the refugee will then start the procedure, which may take anywhere from weeks to years.[57]

UNHCR employs a number of different staff positions to run its program smoothly. The focus is on professional expertise as a guarantee for credibility; while actually intrinsic to the selection process, the bureaucrats construe client expertise in *opposition* to the marginal position appropriate resettlement candidates are expected to occupy. For refugees, the absence of a right to access *any* form of permanent solution is a core concern. The lack of a predictable avenue of access to resettlement means that significance of agency is even stronger. Where access is qualified upon identification of need by UNHCR, through sub-contracted entities (implementing partners) or recommendation of influential/legitimate local actors (government, other international staff, missionaries etc), *two* versions of the deserving client have to be performed. The refugee client must first let him or herself passively get selected for screening. He or she must then promptly discard this passive attitude, in order to push pro-actively for his or her candidature, and by compellingly navigating the material criteria.

VII. DOING AND LIVING ACCOUNTABILITY STANDARDS

An empirical interrogation of UNHCR's performance suggests that humanitarians and client groups offer radically divergent accounts of the social nature of resettlement. The tension between UNHCR's managerial mode and its humanitarian ideals are reflected in the shift away from administrative accountability *towards* the credibility of the client group. This quest for legitimacy mediates between local and transnational entities. Both refugees and humanitarians struggle to meet the external benchmarks for legitimacy imposed through the human rights framework, and are hard at work constructing 'credible'

[57] Following the interview, the resettlement officers compile the resettlement registration form and review the quality of the submission. Subsequently, they identify the category of submission as 'normal', 'urgent' or 'emergency'. If accepted by the regional hub, in the present case UNHCR BO Nairobi, the resettlement dispatch is submitted to a possible resettlement country. States may accept or reject cases referred by UNHCR, and can also decide to admit refugees under other resettlement programs. UNHCR handles the departure in cooperation with IOM, which facilitates travel and arranges for medical screenings. Once a refugee arrives in a resettlement country, the domestic social system assumes responsibility.

resettlement identities. While refugees have to display a sufficient level of credibility in their interaction with UNHCR staff, this staff has to perform a balance act to satisfy the demands for a credible and accountable operation posed by their superiors in Geneva, and the donor community/international humanitarian community at large.

According to the argument outlined above, accountability is *performed* when humanitarian organisations are seen to engage in careful legal analysis. General principles of international law, as well as the legal instruments specific to UNHCR, most crucially the resettlement handbook, demarcate and organise the resettlement-process. A form of market accountability infuses legal humanitarianism, where 'reputation, transparency and efficiency impact the resource-inflow'.[58] When suffering is mediated by humanitarian organisations, personalised images of pain and distress are intrinsic to its effectiveness as a mode of communication. Carefully calculating the response of their audience, UN agencies and NGOs spend considerable resources framing their message in a suitable manner. Peter Redfield describes the strategic mobilisation of suffering as highly scripted and mediated representations. He observes that his research subject, *Medicine Sans Frontiers* 'prize immediacy of contact and direct quotations seeking to maintain some semblance of specificity of voice amid a wash of routinized images'.[59] Redfield's observations resonate also with the activities of UNHCR.

A complex set of background rules determines the legal organisation of migration flows, of which only elements surface as official motivation.[60] By channelling both domestic demands for orderly admission and charitable interventionism into a quasi-legal selection procedure, Western governments are able to combine and re-label policy objectives as human rights projects. For UNHCR, financial insecurity and the drive towards bureaucratic expansion create an interest in sustaining labour intensive protection procedures, but in order for the organisation to be legitimate, their arrangements must be seen as transparent and accountable. The emphasis on human rights functions instrumentally towards shoring up legitimacy, by offering an ethical, procedural and substantive framework for legal interpretation. Credibility-assessments are demarcated as the dual qualifying element for legal protection *and* a proxy for accountability. Resettlement constitutes an important symbolic component within the

58 For a disaggregation of the complex forms of global accountability in the absence of global democracy, R.W. Grant and R.O. Keohane, loc. cit. n. 21, at p. 18.

59 P. Redfield, 'A Less Modest Witness Collective advocacy and motivated truth in a medical humanitarian movement', 33(1) *American Ethnologist* (2006) pp. 3–26.

60 G. Troeller, 'UNHCR Resettlement: Evolution and Future Direction', 14 IJRL (2002) pp. 85–89.

humanitarian toolkit and is framed as a strategic and resource-intensive effort by the international community to offer human rights protection.

The notion of a *conflation of interest* between resettlement-countries, humanitarians and refugees, functions as a charter-myth in resettlement. An idealised perception of practice informs the official promotion of humanitarian ideology *and* structures rationalisation-processes among humanitarians in a way that largely eliminates theoretical disturbances and which transforms normative tension into technical discrepancies.[61] The frustration and anger expressed towards humanitarians must be understood in the context of the unstable bureaucratic culture of the government and UNHCR.[62] A closer examination of these complaints help us appreciate better how perceptions about accountability are squared with the credibility demanded *from* refugees, to form a more comprehensive picture of how refugees construe humanitarianism. As ideals, human rights concepts have penetrated social discourse to a considerable degree. Refugees frequently understand UNHCR's staffs attempt to highlight institutional limitations as 'delaying tactics' which prevent refugees from obtaining their 'human rights'. Refugees conceive of their relationship with UNHCR as structured along the lines of extreme imbalance, partly upheld by the humanitarian insistence on rhetorical equality and legal formalism.

Much of the mistrust between refugee organisations and humanitarians is based on misunderstandings, lack of manpower as well as real and perceived arrogance on the part of humanitarians. Listening to such stories predictably yields a *long* list of grievances about UNHCR and its shortcomings: refugees routinely accuse humanitarians of evasion, intrusion or tokenism. A Congolese refugee organisation gave this laconic assessment:

> 'Make the refugees believe that you are putting a lot of effort into working for them and they should really be appreciative. It is particularly rewarding when they thank you. Tell them that you have a number of cases you are working on, running up and down; your time is so limited... Promise them but don't achieve. Use only demagogy in conversation with refugees. This strategy can create hope in them because they are hopeless in advance.'[63]

---

61 In his analysis of the rules of exchange and distribution of power in the partnership between UNHCR and NGOs in northern Uganda, Mommers describes how UNHCR staff portrays UNHCR and NGOs being equal partners, and how their overall perceptions in terms of equality in decision-making and power closely resembled the official discourse on partnership. Mommers suggest that the power of UNHCR over NGOs has become such an enduring, if implicit, part of the relationship, that it mostly works unnoticed. C. Mommers, 'Partnership from Rhetoric to reality, field level partnerships between NGOs and UNHCR in northern Uganda', Ph.D. Thesis at the Vrije Universiteit Amsterdam, *unpublished* (2005).

62 REDRESS notes that the refugees interviewed were wary of UNHCR staff, who are not seen as very helpful (REDRESS, op. cit. n. 50, at pp. 19–20).

63 PPDR 20 Points, on file with author.

The participation of international organisations and their staff, in local power struggles, further divorces the operation of resettlement from any legal/administrative form. One of the most important communal lines of narrative in the urban refugee community, concerns the conduct and attitude of the individuals employed in the various organisations at any given time. Colourful narratives lend an almost mythical character to some particularly unpopular officers. The facelessness (and unaccountability) caused by frequent turnover of staff, compounds the difference in power. Together, these experiences exacerbate the acutely felt sense of rightlessness and exclusion.

I would argue that neither humanitarians nor refugees perceive legal procedure as the only, or even predominant *normative* framework within which negotiations over narrative and credibility are taking place. According to Michael Herzfeld, bureaucracy is a phenomenon only noticed when it appears to violate its own alleged ideals. He argues that where the state is supposed to be a respecter of persons, *rejecting* the hateful formalism of bureaucracy is itself a conventional, formal act, and identifies areas of tension between official norms and more localised social values. In postcolonial settings, the problem is rather a *lack* of formalism.[64] This observation offers insights into UNHCR's practice as well. One of the greatest sources of frustration in the relationship between the UNHCR and the refugee community is the lack of procedural transparency. Generally, unsuccessful resettlement applicants receive a standardised letter of rejection, which make it impossible to determine the reason for rejection more precisely.[65] This leaves the individual in question and his or her surrounding community as bewildered about the particular rejection as about the nature of resettlement as a bureaucratic process more generally.

Furthermore, the opportunity for private and professional gain for humanitarians is obvious to all involved. Thus, refugees understand the principle of illegality to form an intrinsic part of how international law operates. Numerous rumours about fraudulent activities have created an understanding that 'international law' is a matter of negotiation and possibly commercial transaction. While investing substantial effort in managing resettlement-identities, refugees also criticise UNHCR for buying into these tactics, and not being legalistic in their approach: 'Dans les camps, ces officiers commencent à accorder la réinstallation aux réfugiés qui ne remplissent même pas de critère et qui ne sont donc pas éligibles. Ils le font seulement de manière sentimentale et subjective pour juste attirer

64 M. Herzfeld, *The Social Production of Indifference, Exploring the Symbolic Roots of Western Bureaucracy* (New York, St. Martins press 1992).

65 Human Rights Watch, 'Hidden in Plain View: Refugees Living Without Protection in Nairobi and Kampala' (2002), available at www.hrw.org/reports/2002/kenyugan/, last visited on 28 August 2008.

l'attention des réfugiés urbains vers les camps.'[66] As a general consequence, misinformation and lack of a clear procedure hampers the bureaucratic process and creates a situation where numerous refugees who do not have credible claims for resettlement submit applications, resulting in a massive backlog of cases that UNHCR officials must examine.[67]

VIII. CONCLUDING OBSERVATIONS

In this contribution, I have put forward the idea that a dislocation between the objective to secure legitimacy and the deployment of accountability structures happens simultaneously at two levels. The political rationale of humanitarian organisations is constituted according to a matrix of converging and diverging institutional and individual interests. As noted by Dorothea Hilhorst, while organisational interests may very well coincide with humanitarian principles, such as the desire to appear professional, they can also be at variance.[68] My claim has been that the protestations of humanitarianism to have embraced ideals of human rights, the rule of law and the ethics of good governance sit somewhat uneasily with the continued predominance of an emergency ethos, and needs further scrutiny. Furthermore, as the empirical example has illustrated, I think there are multiple ways of interpreting how accountability measures actually work in practice. The shaping of behaviour through legal mechanisms enables the characterisation of social conflicts or disagreements as lacks/wants, gaps, violations or problems of implementation. Underlying rationales are removed from scrutiny. Because of the unexamined tensions embedded in legal humanitarianism, protection-mechanisms in international law function ambiguously on the ground, paving way for the entrenchment of new power relationships through old colonial-like formats. A human rights approach to humanitarianism produces several protected categories, and demands that the implementation of these follow particular procedures. My claim is that when accountability becomes an end in itself, it allows for a *reconstitution* of protected categories.

I have suggested that the primary interpretive consideration, which drives the resettlement-process, is the appropriation of humanitarian ethos to pursue *other* organisational interests. The account of evolving refugee protection takes the shape of a historical progress narrative, with each new development carefully

66 CAR (Pseudonym for Congolese refugee association), 'Rêve ou réalité: mise en lumière des difficultés socio-économiques et sécuritaires vécues par les réfugiés francophones en Ouganda.' [sic] (On file with the author, Personal Communication, 20 September 2005).

67 G. Verdirame & B. Harrell-Bond, op. cit. n. 35.

68 D. Hilhorst, 'Dead letter or living document? Ten years of the Code of Conduct for disaster relief' 29(4) *Disasters* (2005) pp. 351 and following at p. 355.

formatted as the unfolding of a wider scheme of justice. In this larger frame, the expansion of the resettlement-scheme is an expression of bureaucratic efficiency and state-commitment to ideals of compassion and solidarity. By drawing on a particular stratification between humanitarians and marginalised groups and individuals, this contribution has explored 'accountability' as a fundamentally unstable concept. When applicants invent and perform extensive renditions of substantive categories, the process gains legitimacy through the procedural structure. The agency needed to participate in the resettlement process is fundamentally at odds with the performance of victimicy required by humanitarian discourse. I have argued that this steady transference of the moral burden towards applicants represents a form of subjection, which comes into view more clearly set against the backdrop of past, colonial interactions. This stratification may also be read as a dominant institutional expression of postcolonial relationships, where imperial salvation has become the main *modus operandi*. This form of human rights-based humanitarianism represents both a place of fantasy and operates according to the principles of interpellation: for humanitarians, the humanitarian imperative, coupled with the inspirational impulses of human rights discourse constitute an ideological renewal. For refugees, it works as an occasional grammar of hope. Together, these perspectives force the question of how we can think about the existence of contrasting perceptions of social contracts embedded in resettlement. This contribution has suggested that real accountability is contingent upon both the awareness of, and openness towards such types of friction in the practice of international organisations.

PART III.

INTERNATIONAL CIVIL ADMINISTRATION

UNDERSTANDING THE INTERNATIONAL TERRITORIAL ADMINISTRATION ACCOUNTABILITY DEFICIT: TRUSTEESHIP AND THE LEGITIMACY OF INTERNATIONAL ORGANISATIONS

Ralph Wilde*

I. INTRODUCTION

When the UN took on the role of territorial administrator in Kosovo and East Timor in 1999, attention was initially focused mostly on the formidable practical challenges raised by these missions.[1] Over time, and particularly in relation to the activities of the United Nations Interim Administration Mission in Kosovo (UNMIK), commentary shifted into the normative terrain of accountability. Often, concerns were raised about the lack of national or international review mechanisms and/or the bars to the exercise of jurisdiction by such mechanisms created by immunity law, and substantive complaints were made about particular practices conducted, notably the use of security detentions in Kosovo.[2]

Such criticism came from both academics and expert bodies such as the office of the independent Ombudsperson in Kosovo and the Venice Commission of the Council of Europe. Invariably, wry remarks were made about the irony of the United Nations seeking to promote democracy, human rights and the rule of law

* UCL Faculty of Laws, www.ucl.ac.uk/laws/wilde. Internet pages last visited on February 2010. Thanks to Dr Silvia Borelli for research assistance. This research was supported by the UK Arts and Humanities Research Council. This piece is a reproduction of a contribution published in 12 *International Peacekeeping: The Yearbook of International Peace Operations* (2008) p. 93. Some of the ideas herein are also discussed in Wilde, below n. 1, chap. 8 and 9.

1 On these missions and the commentary on them, see R. Wilde, *International Territorial Administration: How Trusteeship and the Civilizing Mission Never Went Away* (Oxford, Oxford University Press 2008), Chapter 1 and the academic commentary listed in sections 5.1 and 5.2 of the List of Sources.

2 See the sources cited *ibid.*, List of Sources, section 5.2.7.

while acting in a manner that is undemocratic, violative of human rights, and above the law.[3]

The office of the Independent Ombudsperson in Kosovo, for example, stated in its second annual report in 2002 that,

> 'UNMIK is not structured according to democratic principles, does not function in accordance with the rule of law, and does not respect important international human rights norms. The people of Kosovo are therefore deprived of protection of their basic rights and freedoms three years after the end of the conflict by the very entity set up to guarantee them.
> [...]
> It is ironic that the United Nations, the self-proclaimed champion of human rights in the world, has by its own actions placed the people of Kosovo under UN control, thereby removing them from the protection of the international human rights regime that formed the justification for UN engagement in Kosovo in the first place.'[4]

Underlying such commentary is the widely-held assumption that International Territorial Administration (ITA) should be made fully accountable, particularly through domestic institutions.[5] If the UN is acting as the government, then it should be subject to the same checks and balances as any other government.

Should, then, ITA be made accountable and, if so, why have the accountability mechanisms operating in relation to it been so inadequate? In this piece I will suggest that to answer these questions, it is necessary to place the projects in a broader historical context. In particular, it is important to consider the extent to which they are similar or different from analogous activities conducted by states operating on the basis of 'trusteeship.' The concept of trusteeship, and the relative distinctions made in normative understandings of states, on the one hand, and international organisations, on the other hand, as trustees, are central in explaining both how ITA should be rendered accountable and, conversely, why this has not happened properly.[6]

---

3 See *ibid.*, Chapter 1, n. 26 and sources cited therein.

4 Ombudsperson Institution in Kosovo, *Second Annual Report 2001-2002*, 10 July 2002, obtainable from www.ombudspersonkosovo.org, pp. 3 and 7 respectively.

5 On International Territorial Administration, see generally R. Wilde 'From Danzig to East Timor and Beyond: the Role of International Territorial Administration', 95 *American Journal of International Law* (2001) p. 583; R. Wilde, op. cit. n. 1 and sources cited therein. For a list of academic commentary covering issues of accountability, often including calls for greater accountability, see *ibid.*, List of Sources, section 5.2.7.

6 The following analysis is drawn from the ideas set out in more detail *ibid.*, Chapter 8.

II. TRUSTEESHIP

A. COLONIAL TRUSTEESHIP

At its core, trusteeship denotes a relationship of care whereby a trustee or guardian exercises control over a beneficiary or ward, acting on behalf of the latter entity, not in its own interest.[7]

On the international level, the concept of trust became associated with certain forms of colonialism, as illustrated in Edmund Burke's influential recitation of the concept in relation to British rule in India in 1783, formulated in the gendered language of his day as follows:

> 'all political power which is set over men […] being wholly artificial, and for so much a derogation from the natural equality of mankind at large, ought to be some way or

---

7 For commentary on the concept of international trusteeship conducted by individual states, mostly concerned with either or both of colonialism and the Mandates and Trusteeship systems, see, e.g., P.H. Kerr, 'Political Relations between Advanced and Backward Peoples', in A.J. Grant, A. Greenwood, J.D.I. Hughes, P.H. Kerr and F.F. Urquhart, eds., *An Introduction to the Study of International Relations* (London, Macmillan 1916) p. 141; C.G. Fenwick, *Wardship in International Law* (Washington, US Government Printing Office 1919); A.H. Snow, *The Question of Aborigines in the Law and Practice of Nations* (Washington, US Government Printing Office 1919); M.F. Lindley, *The Acquisition and Government of Backward Territory in International Law: Being a Treatise on the Law and Practice Relating to Colonial Expansion* (Longmans, Green & Co. 1926); F.D. Lugard, *The Dual Mandate in British Tropical Africa*, 3rd edn., (London, Blackwood 1926); Q. Wright, *Mandates Under the League of Nations* (Chicago, University of Chicago Press 1930), Chapter 1; K.E. Robinson, *The Dilemmas of Trusteeship: Aspects of British Colonial Policy Between the Wars* (London, Oxford University Press 1965); R.N. Chowdhuri, *International Mandates and Trusteeship Systems: A Comparative Study* (The Hague, M. Nijhoff Pub. 1955) pp. 13–6, 20–4, 35–6; R.H. Jackson, *Quasi-States: Sovereignty, International Relations and the Third World* (Cambridge, Cambridge University Press 1990), pp. 71–4; B. Ashcroft, G. Griffiths and H. Tiffin, *Post-Colonial Studies: The Key Concepts* (London, Routledge 2000) p. 47; A.W.B. Simpson, *Human Rights and the End of Empire: Britain and the Genesis of the European Convention* (Oxford, Oxford University Press 2001) pp. 291–5; R.H. Jackson, *The Global Covenant: Human Conduct in a World of States* (Oxford, Oxford University Press 2000) Chapter 11; S. Schama, *A History of Britain, Volume 3: The Fate of Empire 1776 – 2000* (New York, Miramax Books 2002) pp. 269–70; W. Bain, *Between Anarchy and Society. Trusteeship and the Obligations of Power* (Oxford, Oxford University Press 2003); R.E. Gordon, 'Saving Failed States: Sometimes a Neocolonialist Notion', 12 *American University Journal of International Law & Policy* (1997) p. 903, p. 926; A. Anghie, 'Finding the Peripheries: Sovereignty and Colonialism in Nineteenth-Century International Law', 40 *Harvard International Law Journal* (1999) p. 62–5 and sources cited therein; N. Tsagourias, 'Humanism and the Mandates System: Its Modern Revival', 13 *Hague Yearbook of International Law* (2000) p. 97. See also the separate opinion of Judge Sir Arnold McNair in ICJ, *International Status of South West Africa*, Advisory Opinion, *ICJ Rep.* (1950) p. 128, and in particular 149. Trusteeship is of course related to the concept of paternalism. On the latter concept see, e.g. G. Dworkin, 'Paternalism', in R.A. Wasserstrom, ed., *Morality and the Law* (Belmont Calif., Wadsworth Publishing Company 1971) p. 107.

other exercised ultimately for their benefit. If this is true with regard to every species of political dominion [...] then such rights, or privileges, or whatever you choose to call them, are all, in the strictest sense, a *trust*.'[8]

Trusteeship was adopted in Article IV of Chapter I of the General Act of the Berlin Conference of 1884–1885, under which the colonial powers in Africa were bound to '[...] watch over the preservation of the native tribes, and to care for the improvement of the conditions of their moral and material well-being.'[9] Later, in the UN Charter of 1945, the Declaration on Non-Self-Governing Territories (i.e., colonies) stated that '[...] the interests of the inhabitants of these territories are paramount [...]' and that the colonial powers, 'accept as a sacred trust the obligation to promote to the utmost [...] the well-being of the inhabitants.'[10]

The concept was adopted as the explicit basis for the Mandate and Trusteeship systems after the two World Wars of the twentieth century, which were conceived

8 E. Burke, 'Speech on Mr Fox's East India Bill, 1 December 1783', reproduced in E. Burke, *The Speeches of the Right Honorable Edmund Burke in the House of Commons, and in Westminster-Hall*, vol. II (London, Longman & Ridgeway 1816) p. 406, at p. 411 (emphasis in original). In its 1923 parliamentary White Paper on Kenya, the British Government stated that they 'regard themselves as exercising a trust on behalf of the African population'; 'Indians in Kenya', *Parliamentary Papers* Cmd. 1922 (1923) p. 10 quoted in W. Bain, op. cit. n. 7, p. 62. On this statement see, e.g., R. Hyam, *Britain's Imperial Century, 1815 – 1914*, 3rd ed. (New York, Palgrave MacMillan 2002) p. 265 and A.W.B. Simpson, op. cit. n. 7, p. 291. So for Brian Simpson, in the case of British colonial ideology, '[...] the basic justifying conception, derived from the common law tradition, was trusteeship; colonial peoples were the beneficiaries, the colonial power the trustee.' A.W.B. Simpson, op. cit. n. 7, p. 291. The association of the concept of trust with colonial ideology was taken up by the international lawyers of the time, as reflected in the statement of Joseph Hornung in 1885 that '[w]e accept the hegemony and trusteeship of the strong but only in the interests of the weak and in view of the full future emancipation.' J. Hornung, 'Civilisés et barbares' (Part 3), 17 *Recueil de Droit International* (1985) p. 559, quoted in M. Koskenniemi, *The Gentle Civilizer of Nations* (Cambridge, Cambridge University Press 2002) p. 130. On this generally, see, e.g., the discussion in A. Anghie, *Imperialism, Sovereignty and the Making of International Law* (Cambridge, Cambridge University Press 2005) Chapter 2 and M. Koskenniemi, op. cit. n. 8, Chapter 2. Edmund Burke is popularly regarded as the original theorist of colonial trusteeship, but the concept is evident in the ideas of Francisco de Vitoria and Bartolomé de Las Casas in relation to Spanish colonialism in the 16th Century. See F. de Vitoria, 'On the American Indians' (1539), in *Vitoria - Political Writings* (A. Pagden and J. Lawrance eds. and transl., Cambridge, Cambridge University Press 1991) p. 231 and, for commentary, the discussion in R.N. Chowdhuri, op. cit. n. 7, pp. 20–4; A. Anghie, op. cit. in this note, Chapter 1; A. Anghie, 'Francisco de Vitoria and the Colonial Origins of International Law', 5 *Social & Legal Studies* (1996) p. 321; W. Bain, op. cit. n. 7, pp. 15 *et seq.*

9 General Act of the Conference respecting (1) Freedom of Trade in the Basin of the Congo; (2) the Slave Trade; (3) Neutrality of the Territories in the Basin of the Congo; (4) Navigation of the Congo; (5) Navigation of the Niger; and (6) Rules for Future Occupation on the Coast of the African Continent, signed at Berlin, 26 February 1885, 165 *CTS* 485 (hereinafter 'Berlin Conference General Act'), Chapter I, Art. VI.

10 UN Charter, Art. 73. For commentary, see, e.g., U. Fastenrath, 'Article 73', in B. Simma, ed., *The Charter of the United Nations: A Commentary*, 2nd ed., vol. 2 (Oxford, Oxford University Press 2002) p. 1089 and sources cited therein.

in relation to the detached colonies of the defeated powers.[11] According to Article 22 of the League Covenant, the people of Mandated territories were deemed 'not yet able to stand by themselves' and the administration of the Mandates was to be a 'sacred trust of civilization.' In the UN Charter, the concept of trust is reflected in the name given to the arrangements; the designation of incapacity, by contrast, was made by implication, in the provision for trusteeship itself, and the objectives for trusteeship administration such as the promotion of development.[12] So the imperial concept of colonial trusteeship was refashioned as the explicit basis for a set of modified colonial arrangements.[13]

The colonial concept of trust was often understood to have a two-part character in terms of the role of the trustee: first, to care for the ward, and second, tutelage of the ward in order that it can mature and eventually care for itself. In the context of colonialism, then, the idea of the 'civilizing mission' was to govern so as to address the perceived incapacity for self-government, or at least governance that meets the standard of civilization, and also to build up local capacities, sometimes with the aim that self-administration, meeting the standard, is eventually possible.[14]

The general contours of this two-part conception of trusteeship are evident in the earlier quotation from the General Act of the Berlin Conference, with its obligation to 'watch over' and 'care for [...] improvement'.[15] In the same way, Article 22 of the League Covenant articulates the 'sacred trust of civilization'

---

11 On the Mandates and Trusteeship systems, see the sources cited in Wilde, op. cit. n. 1, Chapter 5, n. 43 and 44 respectively.

12 On the common origins and bases for both systems, see, e.g., R.N. Chowdhuri, op. cit. n. 7, *passim* and especially pp. 8–12 and chap. III; R.Y. Jennings and A. Watts, *Oppenheim's International Law*, 9th ed., vol. 1 (London, Longman 1992) para. 89; D.J. Harris, *Cases and Materials on International Law*, 6th ed. (London, Sweet & Maxwell 2004) p. 130. On the origins of the Mandates system, see Q. Wright, op. cit. n. 7, Chapter I. On the origins of the Trusteeship system, see R.N. Chowdhuri, op. cit. n. 7, pp. 27–35. On the provisions for trusteeship and development for Trust Territories, see UN Charter, Art. 76.

13 The notion that the Mandates were a class of colonies is illustrated, for example, in the sub-title of James Hales' study of the Mandates arrangements: 'A Study in International Colonial Supervision'; see J.C. Hales, 'The Creation and Application of the Mandate System. (A Study in International Colonial Supervision)', 25 *Transactions of the Grotius Society* (1939) p. 185.

14 See generally the sources cited *supra* n. 7. For Bill Ashcroft, Gareth Griffiths and Helen Tiffin, through the civilizing mission, '[...] colonialism could be (re)presented as a virtuous and necessary civilizing task involving education and paternalistic nurture'; B. Ashcroft, G. Griffiths and H. Tiffin, op. cit. n. 7), at p. 47. Antony Anghie describes the civilizing mission as the idea of 'extending Empire for the higher purpose of educating and rescuing the barbarian'; A. Anghie, *Imperialism*, op. cit. n. 8, p. 96; see also *ibid.*, p. 96 more generally, *et seq.*; M. Koskenniemi, op. cit. n. 8, pp. 145, 147, 168.

15 Berlin Conference General Act, op. cit. n. 9, Chapter I, Art. VI. In its 1923 parliamentary White Paper on colonial rule in Kenya, the British Government stated that the 'object' of the trust exercised by the Crown in Kenya was the 'protection and advancement of the native races'; 'Indians in Kenya', op. cit. n. 8, p. 10.

forming the basis for the Mandate arrangements in terms of the 'well-being and development' of the people in Mandated territories.[16] The provisions of the UN Charter concerning Non-Self-Governing Territories and Trust Territories are similarly concerned with ideas of both care and advancement.[17]

B. INTERNATIONAL TERRITORIAL ADMINISTRATION AS A FORM OF TRUSTEESHIP

ITA similarly manifests the central elements for a trust relationship – the idea of the 'ward' placed under the care of another actor, who performs this role not for its own gain but in the ward's own interest.[18] Like colonial trusteeship, ITA is often associated with the dual objective of remedying perceived incapacities for governance – whether in relation to governance *per se*, or governance that conforms to certain policy objectives – and also transforming the situation locally so that these problems no longer exist and the local population can run their own affairs.[19]

In East Timor, for example, UN administration was introduced on the basis that, in the short term, local people were deemed incapable of self-administration, the objective being to both provide governance and build up local capacities.[20] In Bosnia and Herzegovina, the Office of the High Representative (OHR) has exercised purported powers to legislate and remove elected governmental officials in order to further a particular agenda for the economic and political system in the state.[21] So, for example, elected officials have been removed from office when they have been deemed to be acting to undermine the integrity of Bosnia and Herzegovina as single state.[22]

C. THE PROGRESSIVE INTERNATIONALISATION OF TRUSTEESHIP

This role for ITA can be seen as the ultimate internationalised manifestation of trusteeship. Initially internationalisation occurred through the articulation of ideas of trusteeship as legal obligations operating in relating to colonial rule in

16 On this, see further the dictum of the International Court of Justice in the case *International Status of South West Africa*, op. cit. n. 7, at p. 131.

17 For Non-Self-Governing Territories, see UN Charter, Art 73; for Trust Territories, see *ibid.*, Art 76.

18 See further R. Wilde, op. cit. n. 1, Chapters 1 and 2.

19 See *ibid.*, Chapter 6.

20 See *ibid.*

21 See *ibid.*

22 See *ibid.*

the Berlin Final Act. With the Mandates and Trusteeship systems, this idea was again adopted in relation to an entire class of territories, but at the commencement of their administration by the victorious states rather than, as with colonialism, after foreign administration had been introduced. Moreover, unlike with the Berlin Final Act, an overall structure was created to supervise these arrangements.[23] As far as internationalisation is concerned, then, the focus moved beyond the basis for administration to include a regime of accountability.

ITA takes things one step further by internationalising the actor involved in conducting territorial administration. However, as will be illustrated below, conversely it involves a step backwards in terms of the quality of international supervision provided. Understanding why this has happened requires further consideration of the idea of trusteeship administration and how its normative character is understood in the case of ITA.

III. ACCOUNTABILITY UNDER TRUSTEESHIP

A. HUMANISING COLONIALISM

The concept of trust was understood by its proponents as a means of placing colonial rule by European states on an ethical, humanitarian footing.[24] In some cases the need for this arose in part from concerns related to that which 'trusteeship' administration was called upon to replace: earlier forms of state colonialism and/or control by corporate entities like the trading companies understood in terms of neglect, exploitation, profit and general irresponsibility.[25]

---

23 See the discussion in Q. Wright, op. cit. n. 7, Chapters 1 and 2. In the words of William Bain, '[t]he mandates system reaffirmed the principle of trusteeship enshrined in the Berlin Act; but it went further than the arrangements of Berlin in specifying procedures of international supervision.' W. Bain, op. cit. n. 7, at p. 79. See also *ibid.*, at p. 102.

24 See, e.g., W. Bain, op. cit. n. 7, *passim*, especially 1, 53 *et seq.*, Chapter 2.

25 Indeed, in the case of British colonialism, ideas of trusteeship originated in attempts to regulate the activities of the British East India Company, the perceived failure of which lead to calls for rule by the crown and the eventual dissolution of the Company. See generally the discussion in W. Bain, op. cit. n. 7, Chapter 2; A. Anghie, *Imperialism*, op. cit. n. 8, at p. 69, and sources cited therein at n. 104; A. Anghie, 'Finding the Peripheries', loc. cit. n. 7. Antony Anghie reports that '[b]y the end of the nineteenth century [...] [the] direct involvement of European States in the whole process of governing resulted in a shift in the ideology justifying Empire from the vulgar language of profit to that of order, proper governance and humanitarianism.' *Ibid.*, at p. 37. In 1945 the international lawyer Philip Marshall Brown stated that: '[a]rbitrary rule and selfish exploitation has gradually given way to the recognition of the right of such [colonial] peoples to attain self-government and enjoy their own material resources. The present war has given a great impetus to the acceptance of the principle that colonial administration must be considered as a trusteeship in [sic] behalf of the subject peoples.' P.M. Brown, 'Editorial Comment: Imperialism', 39 *American Journal of International Law* (1945) p. 85. On the notion that trusteeship administration would replace control by

B. REQUIREMENT OF ACCOUNTABILITY

Most obviously, trusteeship requires accountability because of the imbalance in the power relationship between the trustee and the ward, and the resulting possibilities for abuse. As Michael Reisman observes in his discussion of the law applicable to trusteeship arrangements, the requirement of accountability is rooted in the fact that 'the power relationship between the parties concerned is manifestly asymmetrical'.[26] In other words, it is not enough to humanise forms of foreign domination to ensure that they operate for the benefit of the local population; there must also be mechanisms to ensure that the humanitarian standards are adhered to. So Edmund Burke regarded accountability to be 'of the very essence of every trust.'[27] Those who advocated reconceiving colonialism to operate on the basis of trust did so in part because this would provide a basis for subjecting colonial administration to third party review.[28] To whom, then, should international trusteeships be accountable?

C. ACCOUNTABILITY IN THE TRUSTEESHIP CONTEXT

Richard Caplan asks:

> 'Whose opinion should count [...]? International transitional authorities cannot function as governments answerable *primarily* to the people whose territories they administer. International trusteeships are not representative democracies [...].'[29]

Even if the international administrators have not been elected by the people they govern, does this necessarily mean that they should not be answerable to them? Simon Chesterman argues that

> '[...] final authority remains with the international presence and it is misleading to suggest otherwise. If the local population had the military and economic wherewithal to provide for their security and economic development then a transitional

---

'private companies that pursue no other objective than immediate personal enrichment'; C. Salomon, *L'Occupation des territoires sans maître* (Paris, Giard 1889) p. 186; see, e.g., the discussion in M. Koskenniemi, op. cit. n. 8, pp. 118, 144. On the general idea of the civilizing mission as a shift towards a humanitarian ethic for colonialism, see also D.K. Fieldhouse, *Colonialism 1870–1945: An Introduction* (London, Weidenfeld and Nicolson 1981), p. 173; Koskenniemi, op. cit. n. 8, pp. 151, 129–30.

26 W.M. Reisman, 'Reflections on State Responsibility for Violations of Explicit Protectorate, Mandate, and Trusteeship Obligations', 10 *Michigan Journal of International Law* (1989) p. 231, at p. 233.

27 E. Burke, loc. cit. n. 8, p. 406, at p. 411 (emphasis in original).

28 See the sources cited *supra*, n. 7.

29 R. Caplan, *International Governance of War-Torn Territories: Rule and Reconstruction* (Oxford, Oxford University Press 2005) p. 246, emphasis added, footnote omitted.

administration would not have been created. Where a transitional administration is created, its role is – or should be – precisely to undertake military, economic, and political tasks that are beyond existing capacities.'[30]

The suggestion is that direct accountability is at odds with the underlying enterprise: international organisations have taken over control of governance because of a judgment concerning the inability or unwillingness of the local population to perform this role themselves – at all, or in a manner that conforms to certain policy objectives. To render the projects directly accountable to the local population in any meaningful way – i.e., in a way that meant policies were altered to take into account the views of that population – would be to miss the point of the enterprise. In Bosnia and Herzegovina, for example, as previously discussed the High Representative sometimes removed elected officials from office, *inter alia* because the policies espoused by the officials in question, such as what was deemed to be extremist nationalism, ran counter to the political agenda OHR has for Bosnia and Herzegovina. Necessarily this goes against the popular will insofar as it was meaningfully exercised in the vote that brought the official in question to office in the first place.

Even on its own terms, however, such an argument goes only so far. It only applies to those ITA policies concerned with remedying problems associated directly with the local population. For missions concerned with, for example, enabling the transfer of the territory from one political group to another, such as UNTAES in Eastern Slavonia transferring control from local Serbs to Croatia, there is nothing contradictory with the mission's objective in making the policies it promotes during the period of administration accountable directly to the local population.[31] The fact that a mission is intended to hand the territory over to another sovereign after an interim period does not by itself necessitate, for example, an ability to make decisions about the economy of the territory during that period without having to account to the local population in doing so.

Even in ITA mandates responding to perceive problems with the way local actors carry out governance, the mandate itself should not be taken for more than it is. A mandate to foster economic development and reconstruction, for example, does not by itself presuppose that the economic model being implemented in the territory should not be determined by the local population. In East Timor, for example, development was needed because the East Timorese had been denied self-determination, not because the local population were deemed incapable of making decisions on economic matters. Part of the answer to the accountability

30 S. Chesterman, *You, the People: The United Nations, Transitional Administrations, and State-Building* (Oxford, Oxford University Press 2004) p. 143.

31 On UNTAES, see the discussion in R. Wilde, op. cit. n. 1, Chapters 2 and 6, *passim*.

issue, then, concerns the scope of the mandate and what this means in terms of decision-making.[32]

More fundamentally, however, accountability issues run much wider than the particular policies being promoted: corruption, mismanagement and human rights abuses are not part of the mandate of the projects, and to exercise scrutiny over them is not to undermine the policy objectives of the mission. Effective accountability mechanisms concerning such matters are not incompatible with the idea of ITA itself. Indeed, for those projects concerned with transforming the politics of the territory to promote the rule of law and human rights, a key component of 'tutelage' is leading by example.

A range of commentators have discussed the nature of the accountability mechanisms operating in relation to the current and recent ITA projects. Reflecting the sentiments expressed in the above quotation from the office of the Independent Ombudsperson in Kosovo, the general conclusion is that accountability mechanisms operated by third parties in relation to ITA have been inadequate.[33] In understanding why this is the case, again a focus on the trust nature of the activity under evaluation can be illuminating.

IV. REVIVING THE TRUSTEESHIP COUNCIL

A. INTERNATIONAL OVERSIGHT OF STATE-CONDUCTED TRUSTEESHIP

As mentioned earlier, the key internationalised feature of trusteeship with the Mandates and Trusteeship systems was to supplement the legalisation of trusteeship as an obligation with specific institutional mechanisms to enforce this obligation. These mechanisms were intended to provide, in the words of Article 22 of the League Covenant relating to the Mandates arrangements, 'securities for the performance of this trust'.

With the Mandates, oversight of different kinds was provided by the League of Nations Assembly, the Council, the Permanent Mandates Commission (to whom individuals in the Mandates could bring petitions), the Mandates section of the Secretariat, other League bodies and the possibility that issues relating to the Mandates could be brought before the Permanent Court of International

32 In both Kosovo and East Timor, the UN set up bodies to which certain prerogatives were devolved, but final authority on decision making always resided in the head of the UN mission. See the discussion *ibid.*, Chapter 1, notes 1 and 2.

33 See the commentary listed *ibid.*, List of Sources, section 5.2.7.

Justice.[34] Oversight was exercised in relation to Trust Territories by the UN General Assembly and the Trusteeship Council and through the possibility that issues relating to Trust Territories could be brought before the International Court of Justice.[35] Oversight was exercised in relation to Non-Self-Governing territories through the reporting obligations under Art. 73(e) of the Charter.[36]

For all the main forms of state-conducted trusteeship, then, dedicated international mechanisms of oversight operated as integral parts of the two main international organisations of the 20th Century.[37]

B. THE TRUSTEESHIP COUNCIL AND ITA

The UN Trusteeship System was mothballed with the termination of the final Trust territory, Palau, in 1994. However, under the Charter it was and continues to be open to territories, 'voluntarily placed under the system by States responsible for their administration',[38] and the administering authority can be individual states or the UN itself.[39] East Timor fitted into the category of a Trust territory: it had been detached from what was in effect a colonial power; its people enjoyed a right of self-determination; it was not under the sovereignty of any other actor but rather had distinct legal personality by virtue of the self-determination entitlement; and the East Timorese were deemed incapable of self-administration in the short term following Indonesian withdrawal.[40]

Despite this fit between East Timor and the Trusteeship model, the Trusteeship Council was not revived for the East Timor administration project. Nonetheless, commentators have proposed that the Trusteeship Council should be revived to provide oversight to ITA missions.[41] However, there seems to be a general international consensus that the Council be abolished, as proposed by Kofi Annan and endorsed by the General Assembly in 2005.[42] Attention has shifted

34 See *ibid.*, Chapter 8, n. 411 and sources cited therein.

35 See *ibid.*

36 See *ibid.*

37 Critics did, however, argue that these mechanisms had important limitations. See *ibid.*, Chapter 8, n. 412 and sources cited therein.

38 UN Charter, Art. 77.

39 UN Charter, Art. 81.

40 On the legal status of East Timor during the period of UN administration, see the discussion in R. Wilde, op. cit. n. 1, Chapter 5, section 5.7.

41 M. Ruffert, 'The Administration of Kosovo and East Timor by the International Community', 50 *International & Comparative Law Quarterly* (2001) pp. 613, 631; T. Parker, *The Ultimate Intervention: Revitalising the UN Trusteeship Council for the 21st Century* (Sandvika, Norwegian School of Management 2003) pp. 43–50.

42 See UN Secretary-General Report, 'In Larger Freedom, Towards Development, Security and Human Rights for All', UN Doc. A/59/2005, 21 March 2005, Chapter V, Section B, paras.

towards the Peacebuilding Commission as a body that might become involved in such oversight.[43]

Why was the Trusteeship Council not revived for East Timor? Why, given the existence of the Kosovo and East Timor UN projects, and the role of OHR in Bosnia and Herzegovina, did states nonetheless wish to see it abolished? Is this because of a view that the Peacebuilding Commission would necessarily provide an equivalent role?

In the case of East Timor, clearly several potentially mediating factors are in play, including the fact that East Timor had already been officially classified within the UN as a 'Non Self-Governing Territory' as a former colony.[44] However, two such factors that are generally relevant to ITA can be seen in the light of what has been previously said about the 'trusteeship' nature of the activity involved.

V. SELF-DETERMINATION AS AN EXPLANATION FOR THE LACK OF ACCOUNTABILITY

A. THE REPUDIATION OF TRUSTEESHIP

The first factor is found, paradoxically, in the self-determination entitlement which is necessarily sidelined, even if ostensibly on a temporary basis in most cases, in relation to ITA. The call for self-determination amounted to a repudiation of foreign territorial administration.[45] Administration by an outside

165–6 and section F, para. 218; UN General Assembly, '2005 World Summit Outcome', GA Res. 60/1, 16 September 2005, para. 176.

43 The creation of the Peacebuilding Commission was recommended by the General Assembly in 2005; see UN General Assembly, op. cit. n. 42, at para. 176, paras. 97–105; on the establishment of the Commission, see UN Security Council, SC Res. 1645 (2005), 20 December 2005; UN Security Council, Res. 1646 (2005), 20 December 2005; UN General Assembly, GA Res. 60/180, 30 December 2005. On the Peacebuilding Commission see, in general, www.un.org/peace/peacebuilding/.

44 See the discussion in R. Wilde, op. cit. n. 1, Chapter 5, section 5.7.

45 On self-determination, see UN Charter, Arts 1(2) and 55; International Covenant on Civil and Political Rights, 16 December 1966, 999 *UNTS* 171, Art. 1; International Covenant on Economic, Social and Cultural Rights, 16 December 1966, 993 *UNTS* 3, Art. 1; UN General Assembly, GA Res. 1514 (XV), 14 December 1960; UN General Assembly, GA Res. 1541 (XV), 15 December 1960; UN Security Council, SC Res. 183, 11 December 1963, para. 4; UN General Assembly, GA Res. 2621 (XXV), 12 October 1970; UN General Assembly, 'Declaration on Principles of International Law Concerning Friendly Relations and Cooperation among States in Accordance with the Charter of the United Nations ("Friendly Relations Declaration")', GA Res. 2625 (XXV), 24 October 1970; UN General Assembly, GA Res. 3103 (XXVIII), 30 December 1973; ICJ, *Legal Consequences for States of the Continued Presence of South Africa in Namibia (South West Africa) Notwithstanding Security Council Resolution 276 (1970)*, Advisory Opinion, *ICJ Rep.* (1971) p. 16 (hereinafter '*Namibia Advisory Opinion*'); ICJ,

actor, necessarily preventing self-administration, was considered *ipso facto* objectionable.[46]

In the particular case of foreign administration introduced on a trusteeship basis because of the perceived incapacity for self-administration, independence was no longer to be granted if and when the stage of development had reached a certain level. Rather, it was an automatic entitlement. Thus even if there was not much local capacity for governance, self-administration would take place unless the people of the territory decided otherwise.[47] Under paragraph 3 of General Assembly Resolution 1514 of 1960, '[i]nadequacy of political, economic, social or educational preparedness should never serve as a pretext for delaying independence.'[48] As Robert Jackson states, 'Independence was a matter of political choice and not empirical condition.'[49] In the words of William Bain,

> '[...] decolonization abolished the distinction upon which the idea of trusteeship depended. There were no more 'child-like' peoples that required guidance in becoming 'adult' peoples: everyone was entitled by right to the independence that came with adulthood. Thus it no longer made any sense to speak of a hierarchical world order in which a measure of development or a test of fitness determined membership in the society of states.'[50]

Western Sahara, Advisory Opinion, *ICJ Rep.* (1975) p. 12; ICJ, *East Timor (Portugal v. Australia)*, Judgment, *ICJ Rep.* (1995) p. 90; ICJ, *Legal Consequences of the Construction of a Wall in the Occupied Palestinian Territories*, Advisory Opinion, *ICJ Rep.* (2004) p. 136; Supreme Court of Canada, *Reference re Secession of Quebec*, 28 August 1998, [1998] 2 RCS 217, 37 (1998) *ILM* 1340; for academic commentary, see the sources in R. Wilde, op. cit. n. 1, List of Sources, section 5.4.

46 In the words of Robert Jackson, '[...] for several centuries prior to the middle of the twentieth century, an activist doctrine of military intervention and foreign rule was a norm that was imposed by the West on most of the world. By 1960 that old doctrine had been completely repudiated by international society. That was not because trusteeship could not produce peace, order, and good governance in some places. It was because it was generally held to be wrong for people from some countries to appoint themselves and install themselves as rulers for people in other countries ... Self-government was seen to be morally superior to foreign government, even if self-government was less effective and less civil and foreign government was more benevolent. Political *laissez-faire* was adopted as the universal norm of international society.' R.H. Jackson, *Global Covenant*, op. cit. n. 7, p. 314. In the words of William Bain, 'the idea of trusteeship [...] was relegated to the dustbin of history along with the legitimacy of empire' because of a 'normative shift whereby independence became an unqualified right and colonialism an absolute wrong'; W. Bain, op. cit. n. 7, pp. 4 and 134 respectively.

47 For Robert Jackson, decolonisation thus shifted from being 'evolutionary', i.e. depending on improvements in and capacity for self-administration, to being 'accelerated' and 'precipitous'; R.H. Jackson, *Quasi-States*, op. cit. n. 7, pp. 95–102.

48 UN General Assembly, GA Res. 1514 (XV), 14 December 1960, para. 3.

49 See R.H. Jackson, *Quasi States*, op. cit. n. 7, p. 95. Of course, which particular associations of people could claim or, put differently, which territorial units would form the basis for independence was in part a matter of the 'empirical condition'.

50 W. Bain, op. cit. n. 7, at p. 135.

Concerns by western states about 'underdevelopment' in the global south, and activities by them to try and 'improve' this situation shifted into the arena of what is now called 'aid' or 'development assistance'.[51]

B. THE LINK WITH ACCOUNTABILITY

Given this normative position, it can be speculated that, although, in fact, trusteeship continued in its fully internationalised form, this only happened in a few places; more generally there is considerable international resistance to it as a general idea, particularly amongst G77 states.[52]

To revive the Trusteeship Council or to explicitly provide for oversight of ITA by the Peacebuilding Commission would be to accept that the self-determination paradigm has somehow become qualified – that trusteeship is back as a legitimate feature of international public policy. Formalising an accountability mechanism would inevitably represent the formalising and legitimising of the trusteeship paradigm itself. If there is no general acknowledgment that trusteeship is back, then one cannot invoke this as the basis for greater accountability. The denial of accountability, then, is in this sense structurally tied to the self-determination entitlement.

VI. THE 'LEGITIMACY' OF INTERNATIONAL ORGANISATIONS AS AN EXPLANATION FOR THE LACK OF ACCOUNTABILITY

A second explanation for the inadequate nature of accountability in relation to ITA can be found in normative treatment of state-conducted trusteeship and political ideas about the legitimacy of international organisations.

---

51 For an example of commentary on this link between contemporary notions of development assistance and the activities of colonial trusteeship, see, e.g., W. Bain, op. cit. n. 7, at p. 7.

52 See further International Commission on Intervention and State Sovereignty, *The Responsibility to Protect*, December 2001, available at www.iciss.ca/pdf/Commission-Report.pdf, at p. 43, para 5.2.4; M. Ruffert, loc. cit. n. 41, p. 631; S. Chesterman, *You, the People*, op. cit. n. 30, p. 33; S. Chesterman, 'Virtual Trusteeship' in D. Malone, ed., *The UN Security Council: From the Cold War to the 21st Century* (Boulder, Lynne Rienner 2004) p. 219, at p. 222; S. Chesterman, 'Occupation as Liberation: International Humanitarian Law and Regime Change', 18(3) *Ethics & International Affairs* (2004) p. 51, at p. 58.

A. NORMATIVE IDEAS OF STATE-CONDUCTED TRUSTEESHIP

One central critique of colonialism was that the colonial states were acting in their own interest.[53] Colonialism was often associated explicitly with policies concerning the interests of the colonial state, its settlers, and corporate interests, from wealth extraction to opening markets and protecting traders.[54] This was critiqued as a perversion of the concept of trust, contradicting the idea that the trustee is supposed to be acting selflessly, in the interests of the beneficiary only and not also for its own sake.[55] It was argued that the humanitarian civilizing policies associated with colonialism were often invoked in bad faith. In reality, then, there was little else being done other than the promotion of the state's interests; the actuality of trusteeship was, therefore, largely a fiction.

Critiques focusing on the self-serving nature of colonialism went beyond accusations of bad faith, of course: for many, as far as its effect on the local population, colonialism was nothing short of exploitation. In the words of Kwame Nkrumah,

> '[b]eneath the 'humanitarian' and 'appeasement' shibboleths of colonial governments, a proper scrutiny leads one to discover nothing but deception, hypocrisy, oppression, and exploitation.'[56]

In many instances the people of colonial territories were treated in a discriminatory, oppressive and sometimes violently brutal manner, from structural arrangements that privileged settlers over 'natives' to specific atrocities such as the suppression of the Mau Mau rebellion in Kenya and generalised

---

53 For critiques of colonialism generally, see the discussion in R. Wilde, op. cit. n. 1, Chapter 8, section 8.5 and sources cited therein, and the sources cited in *ibid.* List of Sources, sections 5.3.1, 5.3.3 and 5.3.4. On the critique alleging self-serving motivations in particular, see, e.g., K. Nkrumah, *Towards Colonial Freedom: Africa in the Struggle Against World Imperialism* (London, Heinemann 1962) and especially pp. 1–6 and 35. Antony Anghie defines colonialism as '[t]he conquest of non-European peoples for economic and political advantage [...]'; A. Anghie, *Imperialism*, op. cit. n. 8, p. 32. For Bipan Chandra, '[...] the fundamental aspects of the colony's economy and society are determined...by the needs and interests of the metropolitan economy and its capitalist class [...] subordination of the colony's economy and society is the crucial or determining aspect [...]'. B. Chandra, *Essays on Colonialism* (Sangam Books, 1999) p. 10. For Jürgen Osterhammel, colonial territories were 'transformed according to the needs and interests of the colonial rulers'; J. Osterhammel, *Colonialism: A Theoretical Overview* (trans. S.L. Frisch) (Princeton, Markus Wiener Publishers 1997) p. 15.

54 Anthony Anghie identifies the 'central importance of colonial possessions for the economic well being of the metropolitan power'; A. Anghie, *Imperialism*, op. cit. n. 8, p. 142. Bill Ashcroft, Gareth Griffiths and Helen Tiffin report the 'perception of colonies as primarily established to provide raw materials for the burgeoning economies of the colonial powers'; B. Ashcroft, G. Griffiths and H. Tiffin, op. cit. n. 7, p. 46.

55 See, e.g., W. Bain, op. cit. n. 7, p. 130.

56 K. Nkrumah, op. cit. n. 53, xvi, cited in W. Bain, op. cit. n. 7, p. 130.

systems of oppression such as the introduction of bonded labour, or slavery, in the Belgian Congo.[57]

B. NORMATIVE IDEAS OF INTERNATIONAL ORGANISATIONS

One powerful way in which ITA is distinguished from colonialism is through a distinction in the normative character of international organisations when compared with states.

The normative character of the two is often understood by way of a sharp contradistinction operating between them.[58] In this Manichean, two-legs-bad four-legs-good vision, whereas states are considered to be potentially 'imperial,' self-interested and exploitative, international organisations are presented as selfless and humanitarian.

Such relational positioning, however simplistic, is a powerful aid in distinguishing international territorial administration from colonialism in that it enables the activity of territorial administration when conducted by international organisations to be disassociated, normatively, from the same activity when performed by states, which would always be vulnerable to suspicions of bad faith and self-serving motivations.

There are two interrelated aspects to this idea. In the first place, on a political level the reification of the 'international' in the form of international organisations permits the notion of a distinct actor, created by, but separate from, states. This enables international organisations to be presented as independent from states, as impartial manifestations of the global community.[59] Actions

---

57 On settler privileges, see, e.g., A.W.B. Simpson, op. cit. n. 7, p. 318 and A. Anghie, *Imperialism*, op. cit. n. 8, p. 176. For a discussion of the use of security detentions, restrictions on freedom of expression and collective punishments in British colonies, see A.W.B. Simpson, *ibid.*, pp. 317–21. On the Mau Mau rebellion, see, e.g., D. Anderson, *Histories of the Hanged: Britain's Dirty War in Kenya and the End of Empire* (London, Weidenfeld & Nicholson 2005); C. Elkins, *Imperial Reckoning. The Untold Story of Britain's Gulag in Kenya* (New York, Henry Holt 2005). On the Congo, see, e.g., F. Cattier, *Etude sur la situation de l'Etat indépendant du Congo*, 2nd edn., (Bruxelles, Larcier and Pedone 1906); R. Anstey, *King Leopold's Legacy: The Congo under Belgian Rule, 1908–1960* (London, Oxford University Press 1966); A. Hochschild, *King Leopold's Ghost* (New York, Houghton Mifflin 1999) see also M. Koskenniemi, op. cit. n. 8, p. 158.

58 See the discussion in R. Wilde, op. cit. n. 1, Chapter 8, text accompanying n. 501 *et seq.* and sources cited therein.

59 See S. Vohra, 'Impartiality in United Nations Peace-Keeping', 9 *Leiden Journal of International Law* (1996) p. 63; M. Von Grunigen, 'Neutrality and Peace Keeping', in A. Cassese, *United Nations Peace-Keeping: Legal Essays* (Alphen aan den Rijn, Sijthoff & Noordhoff 1978) p. 125.

conducted by such actors are 'public' in the sense that they are not conducted by an individual member of the international 'polity' (a particular state) but rather the 'polity' as a whole.

In the second place, on a normative level, states and international organisations are set up as binary opposites. Whereas states are suspected of acting for self-serving motives, international organisations are considered selfless, neither representing the interests of particular states,[60] nor pursuing any self-interested objectives other than what is for the benefit of the so-called 'international community' as a whole.[61] Equally, the suspicion of self-interest on the part of states leads to a fear that states' actions outside their territory will be exploitative of the population in those territories. International organisations, by contrast, are presented as intrinsically humanitarian and benign. ITA projects, therefore, are acts not of conquest but of charity.

This essentialised portrayal of the normative difference between international organisations and individual states, however simplistic and potentially problematic, is of significant purchase when understanding ideas of legitimacy associated with ITA, especially when a comparison is made with colonial arrangements.[62]

---

60 As for independence in terms of Member States, Article 100 of the UN Charter states that '1. In the performance of their duties the Secretary-General and the staff shall not seek or receive instructions from any government or from any other authority external to the Organization. They shall refrain from any action which might reflect on their position as international officials responsible only to the Organization. 2. Each Member of the United Nations undertakes to respect the exclusively international character of the responsibilities of the Secretary-General and the staff and not to seek to influence them in the discharge of their responsibilities.' The UN Staff Regulations state that the responsibilities of UN staff 'are not national but exclusively international,' and must declare that they will regulate their conduct 'with the interests of the United Nations only in view'; UN Secretary-General Bulletin, 'Staff Regulations of the United Nations', ST/SGB/2000/7, 23 February 2000, Regulation 1.1. See also *ibid.*, Regulation 1.2. For commentary, see, e.g., C. Schreuer and C. Ebner, 'Article 100', in B. Simma, ed., *The Charter of the United Nations: A Commentary*, 2nd edn., vol. 2 (Oxford, Oxford University Press 2002) p. 1230, at pp. 1232–51 and sources cited therein. On the 'impartiality' of UN peace operations, see, e.g., S. Vohra, loc. cit. n. 59 and sources cited therein.

61 See, for example, the award of the Nobel peace prize to the UN and its Secretary-General in 2001, 'for their work for a better organized and more peaceful world'; see Norwegian Nobel Committee, Press Release, 'The Nobel Peace Prize 2001', 12 October 2001, obtainable from www.nobel.se/peace/laureates/2001/press.html.

62 Steven Ratner finds that the 'tar of colonialism is not sticking' to ITA and speculates that one possible reason for this is the 'the absence of an exploitative economic motive'; S.R. Ratner, 'Foreign Occupation and International Territorial Administration: The Challenges of Convergence', 16 *European Journal of International Law* (2005) p. 695, at p. 696. Considering ideas of impartiality associated with the United Nations and their significance for the use of the 'occupation' label in relation to ITA projects, he states that '[…] from this perspective, state occupiers, even so-called 'coalitions of the willing,' lack the broad multinationality of the UN; they are in a confrontational relationship with the population, self-interested, and in

Just as territorial administration by foreign states was presented as essentially unjust in the era of decolonisation, so this activity performed by international organisations is sometimes considered essentially legitimate because it is conducted by international organisations. At the very least, the presumption is reversed; what was presumed to be illegitimate is now presumed to be legitimate. Mathias Ruffert, for example, essentialises the normative tenor of 'international administration' in terms of a 'benevolent character'.[63]

For the purposes of the present enquiry on accountability, a key consequence of these ideas is the notion that the use of a humanitarian actor as the administering authority is seen by some as obviating the need for the same kinds of accountability that would be in order were states to be involved. The dominant normative portrayal of international organisations as selfless and humanitarian operates as a powerful alternative source of legitimization. Whereas colonial trusteeship was seen as requiring international oversight through the Mandates and Trusteeship systems because of concerns that, without such checks and balances, states would act in a self-interested and exploitative manner, the same concerns in the context of ITA are addressed through the choice of the administering actor, rather than the introduction of an oversight mechanism.

The disregard for the Trusteeship Council when UN administration was planned for East Timor underlines the normative distinction between states and international organisations. Now that the administering actor *is* the United Nations – the very actor that would safeguard the interests of the people through supervising the conduct of administration by individual states – the need for a supervisory mechanism is obviated. While with states, good faith and selflessness is questioned, with the United Nations it is assumed.

The start of this contribution quoted the office of the independent Kosovo Ombudsperson to the effect that it is ironic that the UN, the champion of human rights, has placed the people of Kosovo into a governmental structure that is not subject to human rights protections. Given what has been said about the normative portrayal of the UN, perhaps this is less of a surprise. The lack of accountability can be understood to be bound up in the UN's identity as the champion of human rights.

---

need of reining in. In contrast, the UN, thanks to its multinationality, can only be working for loftier goals to benefit the population: thus its operations cannot be termed occupations.' S.R. Ratner, *ibid.*, pp. 711–712. See also W.J. Durch, 'Building on Sand: UN Peacekeeping in the Western Sahara', 17 *International Security* (1993) p. 151; R. Caplan, op. cit. n. 29, pp. 4 and 34; N. Tsagourias, loc. cit. n. 7, *passim*.

63 M. Ruffert, loc. cit. n. 41, p. 629. See the discussion in A. Orford, *Reading Humanitarian Intervention: Human Rights and the Use of Force in International Law* (Cambridge, Cambridge University Press 2003), p. 142.

VII. CONCLUSION

This contribution has focused on the normative identity of the United Nations and the general denial of the legitimacy of international trusteeship as a way of understanding why the accountability structures operating in relation to ITA have been inadequate. The point of this analysis has been exclusively explanatory, however. It has not been suggested that the explanations offered necessarily legitimate the inadequacy of the accountability structures. Rather, the explanations illustrate two of the broader issues – the global self-determination entitlement and the legitimacy of international organisations – that will be implicated in attempts seeking to change the situation. Because of the significance of the second issue in particular, such attempts should form part of the broader enterprise – a key component of efforts to critically evaluate the accountability of international organisations generally – to challenge dominant understandings of the political character of such actors so as to better acknowledge their normatively complex position.

HUMAN RIGHTS ACCOUNTABILITY OF INTERNATIONAL ADMINISTRATIONS: THEORY AND PRACTICE IN EAST TIMOR

Eric De Brabandere*

I. INTRODUCTION

Following the conduct of a popular consultation, through which the East Timorese expressed their clear wish to begin a process of transition towards independence, the Security Council established the 'United Nations Transitional Authority in East Timor' (UNTAET)[1], an international operation endowed with full executive and legislative powers. UNTAET functioned as a government for almost three years, during which the international presence gradually transferred authority to the East Timorese institutions it had been asked to set up. On 20 May 2002, the new nation achieved independence, changed its name to Timor-Leste and became the 191st UN Member State on 27 September 2002. The exercise of such vast administrative powers by an international organisation in a state or territory is far from ground-breaking. The UN, as well as its predecessor the League of Nations, had previously been involved in the administration of territory. Whereas many of these former international administrations were envisaged either as a solution for territorial questions, or to facilitate transition towards independence in the decolonisation era[2], the current use of international administration needs to be seen as a method of post-conflict peace-building. Having started out as missions in which no administrative power was exercised by international organisations, UN-led operations have become involved in long-term reconstruction projects, necessitating the grant of far-reaching administrative powers to UN subsidiary organs in order to exercise the functions entrusted to it by the Security Council. This evolution in peacekeeping mandates

* Lecturer in International Law, Leiden University.

1 UN Security Council, Res. 1272, UN Doc. S/RES/1272 (1999).

2 For an overview of these historical precedents, see M. Ydit, *Internationalised Territories: from the "Free city of Cracow" to the "Free city of Berlin". A study in the Historical Development of a modern Notion in International Law and International relations (1815–1960)* (Leyden, A.W. Sijthoff 1961).

which started with the UN experience in Cambodia is explicitly aimed at creating stable and democratic societies[3], and therefore tackling the root-causes of conflicts.[4] Although the creation of UNTAET can be said to have partly its roots in the decolonisation process, it nevertheless needs to be situated within this context. The final objective of the mission in East Timor is of course independence, but UNTAET clearly had many features of post-conflict peace-building included in its mandate, going well beyond merely facilitating the state's transition towards independence.

The recent revival of such activities by international organisations has of course resulted in an expanding debate on the concept of the administration of territory by an international entity and the legal framework applicable to such intrusive operations. The combination of post-conflict peace-building and the legal rules pertaining to the exercise of administrative functions by an international organisation results in an applicable legal framework that is complex and far from self-evident. In addition, local laws and the specific situation of the state or territory under administration play a fundamental and often disregarded role. The application of human rights to international administrations is only one element of the legal framework, and thus cannot be isolated from the broader legal context.

Issues of accountability (or the lack there of) with foreign actors involved in international administrations have been frequently raised to criticise the grant of such intrusive powers to international organisations.[5] The appropriateness or suitability of requiring international actors not to violate human rights, given that they are mandated to introduce and implement human rights in the

---

3 See on the link between democratic governance and post-conflict peace-building: M. Cogen and E. De Brabandere, 'Democratic Governance and Post Conflict Reconstruction', 20 *Leiden Journal of International Law* (2007) p. 669 and J. d'Aspremont, 'Post-Conflict Administrations as Democracy-Building Instruments', 9 *Chicago Journal of International Law* (2008) p. 1. See generally E. De Brabandere, *Post-conflict Administrations in International Law. International Territorial Administration, Transitional Authority and Foreign Occupation in Theory and Practice* (Boston/Leiden, Martinus Nijhoff Publishers 2009).

4 UN Secretary-General Report, 'The rule of law and transitional justice in conflict and post-conflict societies', UN Doc S/2004/616, 23 August 2004, at para. 4.

5 See for example F. Mégret and F. Hoffmann, 'The UN as a Human Rights Violator? Some Reflections on the United Nations Changing Human Rights Responsibilities', 25 *Human Rights Quarterly* (2003) p. 330; F. Rawski, 'To Waive or Not to Waive: Immunity and Accountability in U.N. Peacekeeping Operations', 18 *Connecticut Journal of International Law* (2002–2003) p. 103; E. Abraham, 'The Sins of Saviour: Holding the United Nations Accountable to International Human Rights Standards for Executive Order Detentions in its Mission in Kosovo', 52 *American University Law Review* (2003) p. 1291; C. Bongiorno, 'A culture of impunity: applying international human rights law to the United Nations in East Timor', 33 *Columbia Human Rights Law Review* (2001–2002) p. 643; M. Tondini, 'Putting and end to human rights violations by proxy: Accountability of International Organizations and Member States in the Framework of a Just Post Bellum', in C. Stahn and J. Kleffner, eds., *Just Post Bellum* (The Hague, T.M.C. Asser Press 2008).

territories under administration, is not the equivalent of a clear legal foundation. It is therefore imperative to start with the question whether and on what ground human rights are, as a matter of law rather than policy, applicable to international organisations when exercising administrative functions. The question of how to establish or enhance the accountability of these actors for alleged violations of human rights obligations can only be addressed in line with the conclusion of the first question. We will thus start with an analysis of the legal framework applicable to international administrations, with a focus on the human rights obligations of the UN presence in East Timor. In the next part, we will examine how UNTAET dealt with human rights issues in practice by reviewing mechanisms made available to the East Timorese in order to examine alleged human rights violations by the UN-led administration.

II. HUMAN RIGHTS OBLIGATIONS OF INTERNATIONAL ORGANISATIONS

While it might seem appropriate to require international actors to not violate human rights, since they are mandated to implement human rights in the territories under administration, the legal foundation for this assertion is not self-evident. At present, no international organisation is a party to an international human rights treaty, as human rights instruments are in general open only to States. The International Covenant on Civil and Political Rights[6], for example, provides that the Convention is open for signature by any UN Member State or member of any of its specialised agencies, by any State Party to the Statute of the International Court of Justice and by any other State which has been invited by the General Assembly of the United Nations to become a Party to the Covenant.[7] A similar limitation is contained in the European Convention for the Protection of Human Rights and Fundamental Freedoms[8], which is open for signature only by states members of the Council of Europe.[9]

None of the resolutions establishing international administrations explicitly confirm the application of internationally recognised human rights standards to the administering authority. Several approaches have thus been explored in an attempt to validate the theory that human rights apply to international

[6] International Covenant on Civil and Political Rights (19 December 1966), 999 *UNTS* (1966) p. 171 (hereafter ICCPR).

[7] See article 48, para. 1, ICCPR.

[8] European Convention for the Protection of Human Rights and Fundamental Freedoms and its protocols, (4 November 1950) 213 *UNTS* (1950) p. 222, hereafter ECHR.

[9] See article 59, ECHR.

organisations.[10] The first approach we will focus on consists of an examination of the UN's constitutional treaty, to see whether such an obligation to respect human rights can flow from the UN's own obligations under the UN Charter. The second theory hinges on the binding character of customary human rights norms. We will later turn to the question of the application of human rights to military components, which to a certain extent differs from the civilian components, and questions relating to the attribution of conduct.

A. THE UN CHARTER

Although certain 'programmatic' provisions contained in the UN Charter can certainly create an obligation to respect human rights *as a matter of policy*, it is far from clear that the Charter contains any *legal* obligation in this respect.[11] The preamble to the UN Charter emphasises the determination of the United Nations 'to reaffirm faith in fundamental human rights.' Article 1 further declares one of the purposes of the United Nations to be 'achieve international co-operation in solving international problems of an economic, social, cultural, or humanitarian character, and in promoting and encouraging respect for human rights and for fundamental freedoms for all without distinction as to race, sex, language, or religion.' This commitment is reaffirmed again in Article 55: '[...] the United Nations shall promote [...] universal respect for, and observance of, human rights and fundamental freedoms for all without distinction as to race, sex, language, or religion.' These explicit commitments by the UN have directed several scholars to conclude that the organisation has an obligation to respect human rights law.[12] However, the provision contained in Article 1 seems to be at most a non-compulsory commitment of the UN to establish international consciousness of basic human rights standards. The same objection can be made for the provision contained in Article 55, which merely includes an obligation for the UN to *promote* respect for human rights standards. Consequently, a textual interpretation of this provision would underpin the non-compulsory character of such obligations. From a strictly legal point of view, the UN Charter cannot function as a legal basis for the application of human rights standards to the

10 For an overview of other additional approaches than those discussed in this contribution, trough member state's treaty obligations for instance, see L. Cameron, 'Human Rights Accountability of International Civil Administrations to the People Subject to Administration', 1 *Human Rights & International Legal Discourse* (2007) p. 267.

11 R. Kolb, G. Porretto and S. Vité, *L'application du droit international humanitaire et des droits de l'homme aux organisations internationales: Forces de paix et administrations civiles transitoires* (Bruxelles, Bruylant 2005) p. 259.

12 See for instance, J. Cerone, 'Minding the gap: outlining KFOR accountability in post-conflict Kosovo', 12 *European Journal of International Law* (2001) p. 469, at p. 473. See also Z. Stavrinides, 'Human Rights Obligations under the United Nations Charter', 3 *International Journal of Human Rights* (1999) p. 38.

UN.[13] On the other hand, one must be sensitive to the argument that it is hardly imaginable that the UN, while having the responsibility to promote and encourage respect for human rights, would consider itself not to be bound by these standards when it comes down to its own activities.[14]

Nevertheless, such a consideration will not be very helpful to understand the human rights obligations of an international administration that operates in a post-conflict environment. Equally, such a policy argument ignores the legal rules applicable under international administration, which cannot be limited to human rights obligations. The respective obligations of international administrations are more complex than would seem at first hand and are not limited to the international organisation's constitutional obligations.[15] Questions of international legal personality and the legal character of human rights obligations need to be carefully examined.

B. HUMAN RIGHTS AS CUSTOMARY INTERNATIONAL LAW

While it can be no longer doubted that at least certain human rights have achieved customary status in international law, the application of these customary rules to international organisations proves to be more challenging. As stated by the International Court of Justice in the *Reparation for Injuries* case, 'the Organization is an international person. That is not the same thing as saying that it is a State, which it certainly is not, or that its legal personality and rights and duties are the same as those of a State. (…) What it does mean is that it is a subject of international law and capable of possessing international rights and duties.'[16] The UN thus has international legal personality distinct from that of its Member States. The international personality of an organisation is in addition not identical to the legal personality of a State, but it is limited by the organisation's competences.[17] The distinct legal personality of an international organisation, originally developed by the Court for the UN, is a general principle of international law, and applies to other international organisations which are

13 See for an extensive discussion R. Kolb, G. Porretto and S. Vité, op. cit. n. 11, at pp. 259 *et s.*

14 Cf. T.H. Irmscher, 'The Legal Framework for the Activities of the United Nations Interim Administration Mission in Kosovo. The Charter, Human Rights, and the Law of Occupation', 44 *German Yearbook of International Law* (2001) p. 353, at p. 369 and R. Kolb, G. Porretto and S. Vité, op. cit. n. 11, at p. 259.

15 In that regard, we should emphasise that the enumerated provision of the UN Charter are generally not considered to contain a legal obligation on the Member States to observe international human rights. Cf. M.N. Shaw, *International Law* (Cambridge, Cambridge University Press 2003) p. 258.

16 ICJ, *Reparation for Injuries Suffered in the Service of the United Nations*, Advisory Opinion, *ICJ Rep.* (1949) p. 174.

17 *Ibid.*

presumed to possess international legal personality.[18] International legal personality confers not only rights, but also, as a counterpart, the duty to respect international law.[19] This principle has equally been confirmed by the International Court of Justice: 'International Organizations are subjects of international law and, as such, are bound by any obligations incumbent upon them under general rules of international law, under their constitution or under agreements to which they are parties.'[20] An analysis of the fairly theoretical question of whether the capacity to possess rights and duties is a consequence of the international legal personality, or conversely, it flows from the organisation's status as a subject of international law as opined by the ICJ, is beyond the scope of this contribution. Whatever the case may be, international organisations can be considered bound by customary international law or general international law.

At this stage, several internationally recognised human rights standards, such as the prohibition of prolonged arbitrary detention, the prohibition of retroactive penal laws and the core due process guarantees, have without doubt attained customary status in international law.[21] Regarding the Universal Declaration of Human Rights (UDHR)[22], which is formally not a legally binding instrument, several authors have even claimed that the overwhelming majority of states who voted in favour of it and the continuous affirmation over the years transformed it – or at least part of it – into customary international law.[23] In addition, several 'hardcore' provisions of human rights law, among which are the prohibition of torture and inhumane or degrading treatment, the prohibition of racial discrimination and the prohibition of slavery, are generally considered norms of

---

18 M. Bettati, 'Création et personnalité juridique des organisations internationales', in R.-J. Dupuy, ed., *Manuel sur les organisations internationales – A Handbook on International Organizations* (Dordrecht/Boston/London, Martinus Nijhoff Publishers 1998) pp. 51–52.

19 P.-M. Dupuy, *Droit international Public* (Paris, Dalloz 2000) p. 175.

20 ICJ, *Reparation for Injuries Suffered in the Service of the United Nations*, op. cit. n. 16, at para. 90.

21 Cf. T. Meron, *Human Rights and Humanitarian Norms as Customary Law* (Oxford, Clarendon Press 1989) pp. 94–96; J. Cerone, 'Reasonable Measures in Unreasonable Circumstances: a Legal Responsibility Framework for Human Rights Violations in Post-conflict Territories under UN Administration', in N.M. Blokker and H.G. Schermers, eds., *Proliferation of International Organizations – Legal Issues* (The Hague/London/Boston, Kluwer Law International 2001); The American Law Institute, *Restatement of the Law, Third, Foreign Relations Law of the United States* (St. Paul, American Law Institute Publishers 1987) para. 702 and, for a commentary on the Restatement, L. Henkin, 'Restatement of the Foreign Relations Law of the United States (Revised): Tentative Draft No. 3', 76(3) *American Journal of International Law* (1982) p. 653.

22 UN General Assembly, Resolution A/217 (III), *Universal Declaration of Human Rights*, UN Doc. A/RES/3/217 A, 10 December 1948.

23 See in particular H. Hannum, 'The Status of the Universal Declaration of Human Rights in National and International law', 25 *Georgia Journal of International & Comparative Law* (1995–1996) p. 287, at p. 322 and C. Tomuschat, *Human Rights: Between Idealism and Realism Actors* (Oxford, Oxford University Press 2003) p. 4.

jus cogens.[24] As far as these peremptory norms of international law are concerned, it is generally admitted that they bind international organisations[25], insofar as the rule can be applied to the organisation.

However, the defined customary rules of international human rights law are without doubt principally addressed to States, and have therefore become customary law because of *State* practice and corresponding *opinio juris.* The question thus remains whether an international organisation can be bound by customary norms, which have become binding because of *State* practice. One approach to the issue is to consider the customary norms of human rights as customary law of the international organisation itself, and more specifically, the UN. This is difficult to ascertain, however, especially with regard to UN-led international administrations, as the recent relevant practice is limited to the latest cases of Kosovo and East Timor. Previous experience in the administration of territory[26] is insufficient to establish a customary legal obligation relative to the application of human rights to transitional administrations.[27] These recent cases could perhaps be considered relevant practice for an *emerging* customary obligation, although a detailed analysis of the practice of international administrations shows that they are reluctant to accept explicitly that human rights are binding upon them. The following approach seems more convincing. Several scholars have argued that once a norm has become customary international law it applies to all subjects of international law, irrespective of their nature.[28] The rights and obligations of international organisations would

24 See B. Kondoch, 'Human Rights Law and UN Peace Operations in Post-Conflict Situations', in N.D. White and D. Klaasen, eds., *The UN, Human Rights and Post-Conflict Situations*, (Manchester, Manchester University Press 2005) p. 36 and P.-M. Dupuy, op. cit. n. 19, at p. 175. See also ICJ, *Certain Expenses of the United Nations (Article 17, paragraph 2, of the Charter)*, Advisory Opinion, *ICJ Rep.* (1962) p. 151.

25 H.G. Schermers, 'The Legal Bases of International Organization Action', in R.-J. Dupuy, ed., *Manuel sur les organisations internationales – A Handbook on International Organizations* (Dordrecht/Boston/London, Martinus Nijhoff Publishers 1998) p. 402; H.G. Schermers and N.M. Blokker, *International Institutional Law* (Boston/Leiden, Martinus Nijhoff Publishers 2003); P.-M. Dupuy, op. cit. n. 19, at p. 175. See also ICJ, *Certain Expenses of the United Nations (Article 17, paragraph 2, of the Charter)*, op. cit. n. 24, at p. 151.

26 Previous practice can be found with regard to the proposed administrations of Trieste and Jerusalem, although these cases were never implemented. With regard to West Irian, human rights observance was mainly limited to the respect by the United Nations Temporary Executive Authority (UNTEA) of the rights the citizens enjoyed before the take-over of the administration. UNTEA was however also requested to ensure *inter alia* the rights to freedom of expression and association. The UN administration in West Irian lasted only eight months.

27 See also R. Kolb, G. Porretto and S. Vité, op. cit. n. 11, at p. 264.

28 H.G. Schermers, loc. cit. n. 25, at p. 402, para. 2. See also C. Tomuschat, 'International Law: Ensuring the Survival of Mankind on the Eve of a New Century: General Course on Public International Law', 281 *Recueil des Cours de l'Académie de Droit International* (2001) pp. 134-135. See also G. Buzzini, on the formation of what the author calls 'droit objectif', which the author considers to be applicable '*(...) à tous les sujets d'un ordre juridique, indépendamment de leur assentiment individuel à être soumis à ces règles*", (G. Buzzini, 'La théorie des sources

thus be the consequence of the organisation's 'subjectivity' or 'legal personality'. Hence, international organisations, while not directly participating in the formation of custom, could be considered bound by customary law, including human rights law, even though they have not participated in the creation of it. However, customary rules can obviously only bind an international organisation to the extent that these rules can be applied to the organisation. In order to establish the exact contents of the international organisation's obligation, one has to go back to the specific international legal personality of international organisations, drawn from the aforementioned *Reparations* case.

While an international organisation's rights under international law need to be interpreted in function of its competences, the same is true with regard to its duties or obligations under international law. The possession of international legal personality does not imply that the organisation enjoys the same rights and duties as a State. In our view, and in the same line as the international organisation's general obligation to respect international law, an international organisation's human rights obligations need to be examined in function of the performed activity. Human rights are mainly intended to regulate the exercise of public authority, and are therefore primarily intended to regulate State conduct. In the case of international administrations, an international organisation assumes direct responsibility for the administration of a territory, thus replacing the government of a State or territory in the exercise of public authority. When international administrations are entrusted with legislative and executive powers, they exercise competences that are usually a State's exclusive prerogative. The same can be said when international organisations perform more limited administrative functions. Considering the nature of the performed activity, it can therefore be concluded that, taking into account the competences exercised by the international organisation, an international organisation is bound by *customary* human rights standards as it performs administrative functions in place of a State.[29] The exercise of state function thus encompasses an obligation to respect human rights in the same way as the national administration and government's obligations. Such an approach has the advantage of being 'universal', in the sense that this obligation does not flow from an international organisation's constitutional treaty.

In practice, the international administration in East Timor has adopted several regulations stating that human rights laws apply throughout the territory. The first regulation adopted by the Special Representative of the Secretary-General set out the framework for UNTAET's authority and powers. It provided that in

face au droit international général', 106 *Revue Générale de Droit International Public* (2002) p. 582).

29 See also T.H. Irmscher, loc. cit. n. 14, at p. 370 and C. Bongiorno, loc. cit. n. 5, at pp. 643–644.

exercising their functions, all those undertaking public duties or holding public office in East Timor shall observe internationally recognised human rights standards reflected, *inter alia,* in the UDHR and the ICCPR.[30] It is interesting to note that in its 2006 report submitted to the Human Rights Committee on the Human Rights in Kosovo, the international administration in Kosovo explained that, while international human rights treaties were a part of the applicable law, 'this does not imply that these treaties and conventions are in any way binding on UNMIK. It must be remembered throughout that the situation of Kosovo under interim administration by UNMIK is *sui generis.* Accordingly, it has been the consistent position of UNMIK that treaties and agreements, to which the State Union of Serbia and Montenegro is a party, are not automatically binding on UNMIK. In each case, a specific determination as to the applicability of the principles and provisions must be made.'[31] While it is not clear on what basis this assertion was made, it nevertheless seems obvious that reliance on the *sui generis* character of the mission is certainly insufficient. Nevertheless, the statement does not seem to exclude any application of human rights to the administration as a matter of customary law, as it only relates to international *treaty* law.

C. HUMAN RIGHTS AND MILITARY CONTINGENTS

The status of foreign military contingents participating in international operations is different from that of civil presence in terms of an applicable legal framework. The same reasoning we held in respect of the civil components of international administration can of course be applied to military forces if they can be regarded as UN subsidiary organs, and if they exercise functions to which human rights can be applied. This would for instance be the case if military personnel would run detention facilities or exercise policing activity. Contrary to the UNMIK in Kosovo, established a few months before UNTAET, the military component in the East Timor mission was part of the UN administration and therefore under the direct authority of the Special Representative. In that case, the military component is formally a UN subsidiary organ. However, an often-overlooked issue is the possible concomitant application of the laws of armed conflict in certain cases, namely when there is an armed conflict or a situation of occupation. In that case, the legal framework applicable in armed conflict or under occupation needs to be regarded as a *lex specialis.* A detailed analysis of this issue would be beyond the scope of this contribution, but we can briefly mention the growing

---

30 UNTAET, Regulation No. 1999/1 on the Authority of the Transitional Administration in East Timor, UN Doc. UNTAET/REG/1999/1, 27 November 1999.

31 Human Rights Committee, 'Report Submitted by the United Nations Interim Administration Mission in Kosovo to the Human Rights Committee on the Human Rights Situation in Kosovo since June 1999', UN Doc. CCPR/C/UNK//1, 13 March 2006, paras. 123–124.

consensus in favour of the applying human rights law to situations of occupation.[32] This was confirmed by the International Court of Justice in its advisory opinions in the 'Legality of the Threat or Use of Nuclear Weapons' case[33] and in the case concerning the 'Legal Consequences of the Construction of a Wall in the occupied Palestinian Territory'.[34] The Human Rights Committee similarly confirmed the complementary character of both legal frameworks.[35]

The human rights obligations of such military contingents can also be tackled from the perspective of obligations of the individual states to observe human rights law.[36] Military contingents are indeed composed of national forces which have international obligations, including respect for the laws of armed conflict.[37] In principle however, the scope of application of the main human rights instruments is limited to persons who are subject to the jurisdiction of a State party to these instruments, but the extraterritorial application of human rights treaties has recently been reaffirmed. Several decisions or recommendations have extended the application of human rights to the agents of a State, party to one of these human rights treaties, for acts committed on the territory of another State. With regard to the ICCPR, the Human Rights Committee has repeatedly argued that the state jurisdiction can be extended beyond the territorial boundaries of the State party to the ICCPR. In 'Delia Salidas Lopez v. Uruguay', where a Uruguayan national living in Argentina was captured and tortured, the Committee held that the violation by Uruguay of certain rights enshrined in the Covenant could not be waived by reason of the fact that the violations were committed outside its territory.[38] Although this case concerned the violation of rights of a state's *own* citizens residing on foreign territory, the principle posed by the Committee is considered broad enough to include all violations of the ICCPR on foreign territory by a State party.[39]

---

32 S.R. Ratner, 'Foreign Occupation and International Territorial Administration: The Challenges of Convergence', 16 *European Journal of International Law* (2005) p. 697; R. Wilde, 'The Applicability of International Human Rights Law to the Coalition Provisional Authority (CPA) and Foreign Military Presence in Iraq', 11 ILSA *Journal of International and Comparative Law* (2005) pp. 489–490.

33 ICJ, *Legality of the Threat or Use of Nuclear Weapons*, Advisory Opinion, *ICJ Rep.* (1996) p. 226.

34 ICJ, *Legal Consequences of the Construction of a Wall in the occupied Palestinian Territory*, Advisory Opinion, *ICJ Rep.* (2004) p. 136.

35 Human Rights Committee, 'General Comment 31: Nature of the General Legal Obligation on States Parties to the Covenant', UN Doc. CCPR/C/21/Rev.1/Add. 13 (2004), para. 11.

36 See J. Cerone, loc. cit. n. 12, at p. 475.

37 M. Sassoli, 'Droit international pénal et droit pénal interne: le cas des territoires se trouvant sous administration internationale', in M. Henzelin and R. Roth, eds., *Le droit pénal à l'épreuve de l'internationalisation* (Paris/Brussels/Geneva, LGDJ/Bruylant/Georg 2002) p. 143.

38 Human Rights Committee, *Delia Salidas de Lopez v. Uruguay*, Communication No. 52/1979, UN Doc. CCPR/C/OP/1, 29 July 1981, para.12.3.

39 J. Cerone, loc. cit. n. 12, at p. 476.

As far as the ECHR is concerned, the European Court of Human Rights extensively examined the extraterritorial application of the convention in the landmark case of 'Loizidou v. Turkey'.[40] The case concerned alleged violations of the ECHR, such as unlawful detention and denial of access to property, by the Turkish presence in Northern Cyprus. Turkey invoked declarations it had made restricting the application of the Convention to acts or omissions of public authorities in Turkey performed within the boundaries of the national territory of the Republic of Turkey. The Court explicitly linked the obligation to ensure the application of the ECHR to the 'effective control' over the territory.[41] The developed 'effective control' criterion was confirmed by the same Court in the 'Bankovic' case.[42] The Court subsequently examined whether the applicants were capable of coming within the jurisdiction of the respondent State, and concluded that the victims of the bombing of the RTS in the Federal Republic of Yugoslavia by NATO Air Forces were not within the jurisdiction of a Contracting State.[43]

A similar approach was followed by the Inter-American Commission of Human Rights in 'Coard et al. v. the United States'. The Commission held that 'each American State is obliged to uphold the protected rights of any person subject to its jurisdiction. (…) (This) may, under given circumstances, refer to conduct with extraterritorial locus where the person concerned is present in the territory of one state, but subjected to the control of another state – usually through the acts of the latter's agent abroad.'[44] The threshold applied by the Inter-American Commission is lower than that by the European Human Rights Court, as it requires effective control over an individual, irrespective of his nationality or geographical location.[45] The International Court of Justice equally confirmed the extraterritorial application of human rights standards in its 2004 Advisory Opinion on the *Legal Consequences of the Construction of a Wall in the occupied Palestinian Territory*. The International Court contended that the ICCPR, the ICESCR and the Convention on the Rights of the Child applied to Israel's conduct in the occupied Palestinian Territory.[46] With respect to the ICESCR, however, the Court asserted that, while it does not contain a provision on its

---

40 ECtHR, *Loizidou v. Turkey*, Application No. 15318/89, Preliminary Objections, para. 56 and 62, 20 *EHRR*(1995) p. 129.

41 *Ibid.*, para. 62.

42 ECtHR, *Bankovic et al. v. Belgium et al.*, Application No. 52207/99, para. 71, 11 *Butterworths Human Rights Cases* (2001) para. 61.

43 *Ibid.*, paras. 74–75.

44 IACHR, *Coard et al. v. the United States*, Case 10.951, Report No. 109/99, 29 September 1999.

45 Cf. J. Cerone, 'The Application of Regional Human Rights Law Beyond Regional Frontiers: The Inter-American Commission on Human Rights and US Activities in Iraq', *American Society of International Law Insights* (2005), available at www.asil.org/insights/2005/10/insights051025.html.

46 ICJ, *Legal Consequences of the Construction of a Wall in the occupied Palestinian Territory*, op. cit. n. 34, para. 111.

scope of application and although the rights guaranteed therein are essentially territorial, "it is not to be excluded that it applies both to territories over which a State party has sovereignty and to those over which that State exercises territorial jurisdiction."[47] Interestingly, the Court linked the application of the ICESCR to the exercise of *territorial* jurisdiction, and thus not *individual* jurisdiction.

The abovementioned principles, applied to recent cases in which a military component was concomitantly established, would have encompassed an obligation for the military components to observe the human rights contained in the instruments discussed, on the condition that the sending States were bound by them.[48] Although the application of the 'effective control' test might not have resulted in an overall obligation for all contingents to ensure respect for human rights law, the jurisdiction of military forces over individuals, and especially detainees in the emergency phases, was unquestionable.[49] However, the diversity of the military contingents often leads to difficult application of these instruments. In East Timor for example, not all troop contributing States had signed or ratified the ICCPR.[50] The application of *customary* human rights to military components however remains incontestable.

D. OBSERVATIONS ON THE ATTRIBUTION OF CONDUCT

The attribution of conduct is a separate and more difficult question which is often mistaken with the human rights obligations of international actors. In the case of a subsidiary organ of the UN, the conduct of that organ is without doubt attributable to the UN. This principle is incorporated in the draft articles with regard to the responsibility of international organisations which are currently being developed by the International Law Commission (ILC). Although these draft articles cannot be considered as representing a codification of customary international law, there does not seem to be an obstacle in accepting a *mutatis mutandis* application of the relevant rules of attribution of conduct in case of state responsibility. According to Draft Article 5, '(t)he conduct of an organ or agent of an international organization in the performance of functions of that

47 *Ibid.*, para. 112.

48 For a similar conclusion, with regard to KFOR in Kosovo, see J. Cerone, loc. cit. n. 12, at pp. 479–480.

49 See for overview of the issue of detainees: M.J. Kelly, 'INTERFET Detainee Management Unit in East Timor', *Paper presented at the Swiss Seminar on the Law of Armed Conflict, Chavannes-de-Bogis*, (27 October 2000), available at www.jsmp.minihub.org.

50 In East Timor, for example, the States, which contributed to the military component, were Australia, Bangladesh, Bolivia, Brazil, Chile, Denmark, Egypt, Fiji, Ireland, Japan, Jordan, Kenya, Malaysia, Nepal, New Zealand, Norway, Pakistan, Philippines, Portugal, Republic of Korea, Russian Federation, Singapore, Slovakia, Sweden, Thailand, Turkey, the United Kingdom, the United States and Uruguay.

organ or agent shall be considered as an act of that organization under international law whatever position the organ or agent holds in respect of the organization.'[51] According to the ILC draft articles, the UN can in addition be held responsible for the *ultra vires* conduct of one of its agents or organs when acting in its official capacity.[52] On the other hand, 'off-duty' conduct of UN staff cannot entail the responsibility of the UN.[53]

Regarding military contingents placed at the disposal of the UN, the model contribution agreement relating to military contingents provides that the UN is liable to third parties. This is, however, more a question of attribution of responsibility than attribution of conduct, and has legal effects only between the parties to the agreement.[54] If the conduct of military contingents is attributable to the sending State, then the responsibility of that state can be engaged, although the UN will in that case bare the ultimate responsibility *vis-à-vis* third states. According to the Draft Article 6, the criterion to see whether the conduct of organs or agents of a State placed at the disposal of an international organisation is attributable to that organisation, is the exercise of 'effective control'.[55]The 'effective control' criterion should be analysed in the light of the factual circumstances. If the UN is considered to be in effective control of the military operation, then the conduct of that military component is directly attributable to the UN. This seems to have been the approach followed by the European Court of Human Rights in the 'Behrami and Saramati' case.[56] The first case concerned the death of a Kosovar citizen by reason of the presence of an unexploded cluster bomb unit and the inadequate demining of the territory by both UNMIK and KFOR. The second case related to the alleged unlawful arrest of a citizen by the UNMIK Police following an order issued by the KFOR Commander. In both cases, the applicants submitted that the actions involved the responsibility of the sending states. The Court found that the responsibility for demining fell solely into the hands of UNMIK, while detention fell within KFOR's mandate. The Court concluded that both UNMIK and KFOR action were in principle attributable to the UN. UNMIK was rightly considered a subsidiary organ of the UN. Although one can criticise the factual appraisal by the Court of the entity having 'effective control' in the case of the military contingents, KFOR's actions were equally considered by the Court to be attributable to the UN because KFOR

51 ILC, *Report of the Sixty-first session (4 May to 5 June and 6 July to 7 August 2009)*, UN Doc. A/64/10, p. 21 (hereafter ILC, *Report 2009*).

52 Draft article 7, *ibid.*, p. 21. See also ICJ, *Difference relating to immunity form Legal Process of a Special Rapporteur of the Commission on Human Rights*, Advisory opinion, *ICJ Rep.* (1999), para. 66.

53 ILC, *Report 2009*, p. 73.

54 *Ibid.*

55 *Ibid.*, p. 61.

56 ECtHR, *Behrami & Behrami v. France*, Application No. 71412/01, and *Saramati v. France, Germany and Norway*, Application No. 78166/01, 45 *EHRR* (SE10) (2007) p. 85.

exercised lawfully delegated Chapter VII powers of the Security Council, which held ultimate control over the operation.[57] While the Court's underlying legal reasoning in respect of the attribution of conduction might indeed seem feeble, the Court equally indicated that relevant Security Council Resolutions are the primary source for analysing the human rights obligations of the international administration. The Court opined that the European Convention cannot 'impos[e] conditions on the implementation of a UNSC Resolution which were not provided for in the text of the Resolution itself.'[58]

The question remains how the organisation should deal with alleged breaches of human rights obligations of its subsidiary organs in practice. The immunity system will often bar individuals from directly addressing claims to national judicial bodies. Often alternative mechanisms need to be put in place concomitantly to address alleged human rights violations. The possibility of creating such mechanisms in post-conflict societies, however, is not an easy task.

III. IMMUNITY AND ACCOUNTABILITY MECHANISMS IN EAST TIMOR

According to Security Council Resolution 1272, UNTAET was 'endowed with overall responsibility for the administration of East Timor and will be empowered to exercise all legislative and executive authority, including the administration of justice'.[59] UNTAET's responsibility for the administration of East Timor during its transition to independence encompassed an all-inclusive mandate in order to provide security and maintain law and order, to establish an effective administration, to assist in the development of civil and social services, to ensure the co-ordination and delivery of humanitarian assistance, rehabilitation and development assistance, and to support capacity-building for self-government.[60] More specifically in respect of human rights, Security Council Resolution 1272 asked UNTAET to develop an independent East Timorese human rights institution.[61] As already briefly noted, the Security Council failed to specify the administration's obligations regarding human rights law.

57 *Ibid.*, para. 140.
58 *Ibid.*
59 UN Security Council, Resolution 1272, op. cit. n. 1, para. 1.
60 *Ibid.*, para. 2.
61 *Ibid.*, para. 8.

A. UNTAET'S HUMAN RIGHTS OBLIGATIONS

The first regulation adopted by the Special Representative of the Secretary-General, Regulation 1999/1, set out the framework for UNTAET's authority and powers. It affirmed, on the one hand, that all legislative and executive authority was vested in UNTAET, and on the other hand, that in exercising their functions, all those undertaking public duties, or holding public office in East Timor had to observe internationally recognised human rights standards reflected, *inter alia* in the UDHR and the ICCPR.[62] Regulation 1999/1 equally contains an explicit reference to the prohibition of discrimination.[63] One can thus conclude from the above that the international administration was bound by human rights, either from an international legal point of view, as a UN subsidiary organ, but also from the perspective of the administrator's first regulation.

However, in practice the applicable law in territories under UN administration must be taken in to account when considering the available review mechanisms. One of the recurrent problems in international administrations is the definition of the applicable legal framework. Apart from defining the human rights obligations of the official institutions, the first UNTAET regulation also adopted the principle that the whole body of Indonesian law would apply in East Timor, provided that it did not conflict with the enumerated internationally recognised human rights standards.[64] On that basis, several Indonesian laws were immediately repealed as they manifestly conflicted with these human rights standards.[65] The task of identifying those provisions of the applicable Indonesian law that violated human rights standards was obviously difficult, if not almost impossible, as there were no functioning judicial system, let alone experienced lawyers upon which to rely. This complication lead UNTAET to focus on adopting new legislation compliant with international human rights standards, instead of trying to review the whole Indonesian legal system in function of international human rights standards.[66]

However, although UNTAET sought to adopt regulations consistent with international human rights standards, violations of human rights can never be ruled out. The question really is which review mechanisms were available to

---

62 UNTAET, Regulation 1999/1 on the Authority of the Transitional Administration in East Timor, UNTAET/REG/1999/1, 27 November 1999, Section 1.

63 *Ibid.*, Section 2.

64 UNTAET, Regulation 1999/1 on the Authority of the Transitional Administration in East Timor, UNTAET/REG/1999/1, 27 November 1999, Section 3.

65 *Ibid.*, Section 3.2.

66 See J. Morrow and R. White, 'The United Nations in Transitional East Timor: International Standards and the Reality of Governance', 22 *Australian Yearbook of International Law* (2002) p. 1, at pp. 9 *et s.*

alleged violations of human rights by the international presence. In addition to the institution of the Ombudsperson, a certain role can be played by national courts and tribunals in the judicial review of official acts issued by the administration. However, before turning to these mechanisms, we will start with an overview of the immunities system that applies both to international staff and to international organisations, and thus bars a direct access to judicial mechanism by individuals.

B. IMMUNITY OF INTERNATIONAL ACTORS

Unlike UNMIK, the UNTAET Special Representative, Sergio Viera de Mello, did not issue a specific regulation to confirm UNTAET's jurisdictional immunity. The UN and its international staff are nevertheless generally considered to have immunity. This draws from the UN Charter itself, which explicitly stipulates that 'the Organization shall enjoy in the territory of each of its Members such privileges and immunities as are necessary for the fulfilment of its purposes. [...] [O]fficials of the Organization shall similarly enjoy such privileges and immunities as are necessary for the independent exercise of their functions in connexion with the Organization.'[67] In addition, the Convention on Privileges and Immunities of the United Nations[68] provides for a complete immunities system, including provisions with respect to immunity for 'UN officials' and functional immunity for 'experts on mission' for the UN.[69] In both cases, the Secretary-General has the power to waive their immunity.[70] In general, claims against the organisation cannot be brought before national courts.[71] It should be immediately emphasised that immunity is distinct from the question of compensation by the UN in case of harm caused by the act in question, which should be considered according to the relevant rules of attribution discussed above.

Certain participants in peacekeeping forces, such as military observers, and civilian police officers can be considered experts on mission, falling under Section 22 of the UN Convention.[72] The immunities system therefore applies to all UN staff provided that the individual is not acting *ultra vires*, that is, not outside the scope of his or her mandate. The 'Model status of forces agreement

67 Art. 105 UN Charter.

68 Convention on the Privileges and Immunities of the United Nations (13 February 1946), 1 *UNTS* 15.

69 *Ibid.*, Articles V and VI.

70 *Ibid.*

71 This has expressly been confirmed by the ICJ: 'any such claims against the United Nations shall not be dealt with by national courts (...)'. ICJ, *Difference Relating to Immunity from Legal Process of a Special Rapporteur of the Commission on Human Rights*, Advisory Opinion, *ICJ Rep.* (1999) p. 66.

72 H.G. Schermers and N.M. Blokker, op. cit. n. 25, p. 255.

for peace-keeping operations' provides that, in the case of a criminal offence, the host country can exercise jurisdiction after a waiver of immunity.[73] However, the formal application of the UN Convention on Privileges and Immunities is not always self-evident. In the case of East Timor, the convention did not formally apply in the territory. Indonesia had ratified the convention, but the state's title over the territory was extremely dubious, and only recognised by Australia. Military members of national contingents do not in principle fall under the UN Convention, although in practice the distinction between 'experts on mission' and members of national contingents is not always easy to make.[74] As members of a military contingent are concerned, the model agreement provides for an exclusive jurisdiction of the troop-contributing country.[75]

Privileges and immunities are often also negotiated and incorporated into a Status of Forces Agreement or a Status of Mission Agreement, with the UN or with individual troop contributing states. Prior to the establishment of UNTAET, Australia had, for example, signed a Status of Forces Agreement with Indonesia to regulate the deployment of Australian troops for the INTERFET mission, which provided several privileges and immunities for the military and civilian staff, including those provided for by the UN Convention.[76] The problem however, was again the contested Indonesian title over East Timor. The New Zealand forces were obviously not bound by the Status of Forces Agreement concluded between Australia and Indonesia. However, New Zealand did not sign an agreement with Indonesia. Instead, the official New Zealand position was that the New Zealand Defence Forces were immune from local jurisdiction as a matter of customary international law.[77] In addition, it seems that, upon deployment of the international presence, no Status of Forces or Status of Mission Agreement concerning the status of UNTAET was signed. Obviously, such an agreement could not have been signed between the UN and Indonesia, since UN organs had repeatedly challenged Indonesian title over East Timor. The official position of the UNTAET Principal Legal Advisor, as reported by Rawski, was that that the Convention on the Privileges and Immunities of the UN applied

---

73 See Article 47, Model status of forces agreement for peace-keeping operations, UN Doc. A/45/594, 9 October 1990.

74 See for and overview and examples: A.J. Miller, 'United Nations Experts on Mission and their Privileges and Immunities', 4 *International Organizations Law Review* (2007) pp. 30–32.

75 See Article 48, Model status of forces agreement for peace-keeping operations, UN Doc. A/45/594, 9 October 1990. For an example of case in which the sending State exercised jurisdiction for a criminal offences, see e.g. CBC News, 'US Soldier Gets Life for Kosovo Rape and Murder' (1 August 2000), available at www.cbc.ca.

76 See for an overview: M.J. Kelly, T.L.J. Mccormack, P. Muggleton and B.M. Oswald, 'Legal aspects of Australia's involvement in the international force for East Timor', 841 *International review of the Red Cross* (2001) p. 101.

77 *Ibid.* See also P.-M. Dupuy, op. cit. n. 19, at p. 188 and with regard to UNTAET, see C. Bongiorno, loc. cit. n. 5, at p. 661.

fully to UN staff.[78] As the Convention could in our view not apply as a matter of treaty law, UNTAET immunity could only be based on customary law.

The problem often raised is whether the immunities system is appropriate when the UN is performing administrative functions in a state or a territory. Immunity is often waived in case of (serious) criminal offences.[79] In the case of a traffic accident involving an UNTAET staff member resulting in the death of an East Timorese citizen, the Special Representative insisted that the Secretary-General waive the staff member's immunity.[80] In several other cases, immunity has also been waived or declared inapplicable.[81] In addition, from a legal point of view, immunity is not applicable for acts committed by experts on mission outside the performance of their mission.[82] Under UNTAET, for instance, in a case of rape involving a Jordanian CIVPOL officer, the individual's immunity was declared inapplicable, as the alleged act was considered to have been committed outside official functions.[83] In other cases of criminal offences, immunity can be waived by the Secretary-General.

Apart from the waiver or inapplicability of immunities, one should remember that immunities in fact serve a purpose. The main rationale behind the immunities system is to protect international staff from taunting claims by the host State and to guarantee the independence of the UN and its agents.[84] The independence of a UN mission as an institution and its international staff is crucial and, indeed needs to be preserved. The European Court of Human Rights, in *Waite and Kennedy v. Germany*[85], pointed out that 'the attribution of privileges and immunities to international organisations is an essential means of ensuring the proper functioning of such organizations free from unilateral interference by individual governments. [...] [T]he rule of immunity from jurisdiction, [...], has a legitimate objective.'[86] The question, according to the

---

78 F. Rawski, loc. cit. n. 5, at p. 118.

79 *Ibid.*

80 UNTAET, Daily Press Briefing, 'SRSG Briefs National Council', 13 December 2000, available at www. un.org/peace/etimor/DB/Db131200.htm. See also J. Morrow and R. White, loc. cit. n. 66, at p. 24 and F. Rawski, loc. cit. n. 5, at p. 120.

81 J. Morrow and R. White, loc. cit. n. 66.

82 Section 22, b), Convention on the Privileges and Immunities of the United Nations (13 February 1946), 1 *UNTS* 15.

83 ECOSOC, Commission on Human Rights, 'Administration of Justice, Rule of Law and Democracy, Working paper on the accountability of international personnel taking part in peace support operations submitted', UN Doc. E/CN.4/Sub.2/2005/42, 7 July 2005, para.31. See also F. Rawski, loc. cit. n. 5, at p. 120.

84 The International Court of Justice confirmed this in its *Reparation for injuries* advisory opinion: ICJ, *Reparation for Injuries Suffered in the Service of the United Nations*, op. cit. n. 16, at p. 183.

85 ECtHR, *Waite and Kennedy v. Germany*, Application No. 26083/94, *ECHR* (1999-I) p. 13.

86 *Ibid.*, para. 63.

European Court of Human Rights, is whether reasonable alternative means are available effectively to protect the individual's human rights.[87] Although this jurisprudence relates to the European Convention on Human Rights, and therefore has a limited scope of application, in our view the Court's findings could be applied to international administrations. The problem is thus not the immunities system itself, but the availability of alternative means and mechanisms to protect human rights under international territorial administration. Such an alternative mechanism is even more necessary when the international administration as such is suspected to have violated certain human rights, as in that case, the immunity of the organisation will bar any proceedings against the UN or its subsidiary body.

C. ALTERNATIVE ACCOUNTABILITY MECHANISMS

A recently re-emerged method of enabling individuals to bring claims against UN staff or the organisation itself is the institution of the 'ombudsperson'. An ombudsperson's office was established in Kosovo to investigate complaints concerning human rights violations and actions constituting an abuse of authority by UNMIK or any other official institution.[88] Although cooperation with UNMIK has apparently not always been successful, the UNMIK Ombudsperson was generally seen as an effective mechanism to address human rights violations in general.[89] However, when the Ombudsperson institution was remodelled in 2006, its jurisdiction in respect to UNMIK action was brought to an end[90] and replaced by a 'Human Rights Advisory Panel'. UNTAET created a comparable ombudsperson, which became operational only 17 months after the arrival of the administration.[91] The UNTAET Ombudsperson's official mandate, however, was not founded on an UNTAET Regulation. Its functioning, effectiveness and achievements are difficult to assess. However, from the UNTAET Daily Briefings it can be deduced that complaints against UNTAET, the Transitional Administration, the Cabinet, and agencies, programmes and institutions which collaborate with the Government could be accepted by the Ombudsperson, but the number of claims submitted prove that the local population was not fully aware of the

87 *Ibid.*, para. 68.

88 UNMIK, Regulation No. 2000/38 on the establishment of the Ombudsperson Institution in Kosovo, UN Doc UNMIK/REG/2000/38, 30 June 2000.

89 See for example Ombudsperson Institution in Kosovo, *Fourth Annual Report* (2003–2004) addressed to the Acting Special Representative of the Secretary General of the United Nations, p. 23, available at www.ombudspersonkosovo.org.

90 UNMIK, Regulation No. 2006/6 on the Ombudsperson Institution in Kosovo, UN Doc. UNMIK/REG/2006/6, 16 February 2006.

91 Cf. UNTAET, Daily Briefing, 'Twenty Cases Examined by Ombudsperson', 1 June 2001, available at www.un.org/peace/etimor/DB/Db010601.htm.

mechanism.[92] The Ombudsperson in East Timor was generally described as ineffective, and it is clear that he did not have the same effect as in Kosovo.[93]

An effective Ombudsperson can play an important role in upholding human rights during international territorial administration. The creation of such an ombudsperson at the level of the UN, solely responsible for considering alleged human rights violations by UN staff in transitional administrations, can be a possible alternative if a national ombudsperson proves to be ineffective.[94] Nevertheless, this kind of 'universal' institution at the UN level also comprises certain difficulties, as the threshold will be even higher than at the national level. Equally, ombudspersons are generally nationals of the territory concerned or of neighbouring states and are familiar with local custom, speak the language of the territory and are, as local actors, independent *vis-à-vis* the international administration and the international organisation in charge of administering the territory.

Another possible method of ensuring accountability for human rights violations can be judicial review of official acts issued by the administration before national courts and tribunals. The exercise of public authority by an international organisation and the acts issued by these international administrations are characterised by what can be called 'functional duality'.[95] On the one hand, an international administration is a subsidiary organ of an international organisation and, on the other hand, it functions as the government of a territorial entity. The acts of the international administration are thus both international acts of the international organisations and internal acts of the state or territory. As such, functional duality is not an innovative concept where the administration of territory is concerned. Virally, discussing the administration of Germany after the Second World War, noted that 'en réalité, les autorités alliées de contrôle en Allemagne possèdent une double nature : ce sont des autorités territoriales (...) et ce sont des autorités nationales. Suivant le titre auquel elles agissent, elles sont autorités nationales ou étrangères, soit à l'égard du droit allemand, soit à l'égard du droit interne des Etats alliés.'[96]

Although viewed from a national perspective, as the Allies were not at that time an international organisation with a distinct legal personality, the author already

92 *Ibid.*

93 S. Chesterman, *You The People – The United Nations, Transitional Administration, and State-Building*, (Oxford, Oxford University Press 2004) p. 150.

94 See for example F. Mégret and F. Hoffmann, loc. cit. n. 5.

95 See on the concept of 'functional duality' in post-conflict situations, the contributions by R. Wilde and G. Verdirame in N.D. White and D. Klaasen, eds., *The UN, Human Rights and Post-Conflict Situations*, (Manchester, Manchester University Press 2005).

96 M. Virally, *L'administration internationale de l'Allemagne du 8 mai 1945 au 24 avril 1947* (Paris, Pedone 1948) para. 46.

stressed the fact that decisions taken by the international administration needed to be seen as part of the German legal system.[97] The same principle of 'functional duality' can be applied in relation to acts issued under international administrations. The regulations which UNTAET adopted, for example, are international acts of a subsidiary organ of an international legal person, yet the act in question produces effects in the territory in question, thus forming an integral part of the East Timorese legal system. These acts conserve their validity even after the resumption of governmental functions by the territorial entity itself. The theory of the 'functional duality' of international administrations and the acts issued by them has been developed and applied by the Constitutional Court of Bosnia and Herzegovina with regard to the review by the Court of the Law on State Border Service enacted by the High Representative of the International Community.[98] The Court observed:

> 'Such a situation amounts to a sort of functional duality: an authority of one legal system intervenes in another legal system, thus making its functions dual. [...] [T]he High Representative [...] has been vested with special powers by the international community and his mandate is of an international character. In the present case, the High Representative – whose powers under Annex 10 to the General Framework Agreement, the relevant resolutions of the Security Council and the Bonn Declaration as well as his exercise of those powers are not subject to review by the Constitutional Court – intervened in the legal order of Bosnia and Herzegovina substituting himself for the national authorities. In this respect, he therefore acted as an authority of Bosnia and Herzegovina and the law which he enacted is in the nature of a national law and must be regarded as a law of Bosnia and Herzegovina.'[99]

This kind of competence presupposes, on the one hand, the existence of a functioning judicial system and, on the other, a court or tribunal having the competence to review the international administration's acts. Often the first condition cannot be met, as the judicial system is usually collapsed or non-existent at the establishment of the majority of the peace-building missions. The difficulty of the exercise can be further illustrated by two cases dealing with by Timorese courts under UNTAET's mandate. In both cases, the court apparently lacked the necessary competence to review the legislation. In addition, the two cases both clearly include misinterpretations of existing legislation. Moreover, the Special Representative's immunity was disregarded in one of the cases, as a claim had been brought against him personally for issuing an executive order. Even so, both cases indicate that judicial review of official acts could be an interesting alternative to provide an effective remedy

97 *Ibid.*

98 Constitutional Court of Bosnia and Herzegovina, Decision U9/00, 3 November 2000, available at www.ustavnisud.ba/eng/odluke/.

99 *Ibid.*, para. 5.

for alleged violations of human rights standards, provided that the necessary conditions are met.

The *Victor Alves* case[100] concerned the application of UNTAET Regulation 2000/14[101] adopted by the Special Representative to clarify and adjust the basic judicial system as laid out in Regulation 2000/11.[102] In addition to clarifying the role and powers of the investigating judges and the procedure relating to pre-trial detention, the regulation extended the detention time-limits. Furthermore, the Regulation was adopted with immediate effect the day before the Dili District Court was to hear the case of a former FALINTIL member, Victor Alves, whose detention had exceeded the limits set by the Indonesian Code of Criminal Procedure, which was applicable in accordance with Regulation 1999/1. The Judge refused to apply the newly passed Regulation 2000/14, as he found that the extension of the detention limits was both a violation of fundamental human rights and an impermissible interference by the executive power in order to influence the case. The Judge therefore found that Victor Alves had been unlawfully detained. Clearly, this case highlights the difficulty of judicial review of regulations adopted by international administrations. A clear separation of powers would have prevented such a decision in which a judge simply refused to apply the law. Moreover, it seems that the judgment comprised various misinterpretations of the applicable legal instruments.[103] The case does indicate the need to have an official institution to evaluate conformity with international human rights standards of the legislation adopted by international administrations.

In another case, a Japanese national, Takeshi Kashiwagi, had made a claim against the Special Representative of the Secretary-General, the Minister of Justice of East Timor, the Prosecutor General and a judge, based on alleged unlawful detention.[104] Kashiwagi, a freelance journalist, had been arrested

---

100 For a comprehensive overview and report of this unpublished case see S. Linton, 'Rising From The Ashes: The Creation of a Viable Criminal Justice System In East Timor', 25 *Melbourne University Law Review* (2001) p. 140.

101 UNTAET, Regulation No. 2000/14 Amending Regulation No. 2000/11, UN Doc. UNTAET/REG/2000/14, 10 May 2000.

102 UNTAET, Regulation No. 2000/11 on the organization of courts in East Timor, UN Doc. UNTAET/REG/2000/11, 6 March 2000.

103 See S. Linton, loc. cit. n. 100, at pp. 140–143.

104 For an extensive overview and discussion of the case, see Amnesty International, *East Timor, Justice past, present and future*, Report Nr. ASA 57/001/2001, 27 July 2001; Article 19, 'Freedom of Expression and the Media in Timor Leste', December 2005, available at www.article19.org; C. Bongiorno, loc. cit. n. 5, at pp. 666 *et s.*; S. Linton, loc. cit. n. 100, at pp. 140–143; M.A. Fairlie, 'Affirming Brahimi: East Timor makes the Case for a Model Criminal Code', 18 *American University International Law Review* (2003) p. 1059, at pp. 1087 *et s.*; D. Zaum, *The Sovereignty Paradox: The Norms and Politics of International Statebuilding* (Oxford, Oxford University Press 2007) p. 201.

following allegations of defamation and making threats to the life of the president, which was a criminal offence under the applicable Indonesian Criminal Code. The Special Representative intervened by issuing an executive order decriminalising defamation, upon which Kashiwagi was released. Kashiwagi nevertheless decided to take his case to the Dili District Court, alleging a violation of the relevant provisions of the Indonesian Criminal Code, which admits criminal defamation cases only after a *complaint* by the victim. The Dili District Court, by applying similar reasoning to that in the previous case, concluded that the executive order was illegal as is sought to override an UNTAET Regulation and therefore constituted an impermissible interference by the judiciary. The Court equally found that the procedure contained in the Indonesian Criminal Code had not been followed correctly, and therefore found all defendants liable for following incorrect procedures. Surprisingly, the Special Representative of the Secretary-General was equally found *personally* liable for issuing an executive order which conflicted with the Indonesian Criminal Code. The Court failed to recognise that the transitional administrator had diplomatic immunity and, ironically, condemned the transitional administrator for violating Kashiwagi's human rights, even though the executive order issued by the transitional administrator was aimed at protecting these same rights. The case was appealed, and the Court of Appeal overturned the lower court's decision by stating that such a case should have been brought against the UN instead of against individuals. Kashiwagi's compensation claim was dismissed, although he was finally awarded compensation outside the court process.[105]

These two cases demonstrate the complexity of reviewing official acts by nascent judicial systems which are characterised by a lack of trained and qualified judicial personnel. The functional duality theory applied by the Supreme Court of Bosnia and Herzegovina can be effective in assuring the compatibility of regulations with international human rights standards. However, once more, the situation 'on the ground' does not always allow for this kind of review. Under the thorny circumstances in which these operations need to manoeuvre, a local court can often not be utilised to guarantee the implementation of human rights. However, in some cases, a certain review mechanism was set up within the international presence. For example, under at least two UNTAET Regulations, persons were authorised to apply in writing to the Deputy Transitional Administration for a review of decisions taken by an UNTAET subsidiary unit.[106] The Deputy Transitional Administration is neither neutral nor a judicial

105 ECOSOC, Commission on Human Rights, 'Administration of Justice, Rule of Law and Democracy, Working paper on the accountability of international personnel taking part in peace support operations submitted', E/CN.4/Sub.2/2005/42, 7 July 2005, at para. 50.

106 UNTAET, Regulation No. 2000/17 on the prohibition of logging operations and the export of wood from East Timor, UN Doc. UNTAET/REG/2000/17, 8 June 2000, Section 6.1. and

institution. In many cases, one would thus need to rely on more effective means of ensuring an official and impartial review mechanism.

IV. CONCLUSION

The accountability of international organisations raises many questions in relation to effective implementation of possible responsibility of international actors engaged in the administration of foreign territory. In our view, the immunities system as such is not threatening and does provide certain guarantees with regard to the independence of UN personnel in the exercise of their function. Equally, we pointed out that in cases of reported serious criminal offences, immunity has been waived, or has been declared inapplicable because the conduct was considered to have taken place 'off-duty'.

Nevertheless a real concern relates to the question of compatibility of certain official acts with internationally recognised human rights standards. This is particularly imperative with regard to detention as the right to challenge one's detention before a Court can be considered as a general principle of international law. When analysing the review mechanisms that have been put in place, we can only find that they have been insufficient, as witnessed by the reported cases. The Ombudsperson institution in East Timor was not able to provide adequate review. Furthermore, the discussed cases prove that judicial review of official acts is not always feasible, and the two mentioned examples illustrate the difficulty of this exercise when a clear legal framework is lacking. On the other had, effective mechanisms should indeed be introduced to examine alleged human rights violations by international administrations, and to ensure compliance of official acts with international human rights standards. Obviously, the fact that the UN has only been recently involved in post-conflict administration has contributed to the unavailability of adequate mechanisms. At the same time, important lessons can be learned from these cases, and the experiences in Kosovo and East Timor might lead more efficient mechanisms in future operations.

UNTAET, Regulation No. 200/19 on protected places, UN Doc. UNTAET/REG/2000/19, 30 June2000, Section 8.4.

SHOULD THE UNITED NATIONS CREATE AN INDEPENDENT HUMAN RIGHTS BODY IN A TRANSITIONAL ADMINISTRATION?

The Case of the United Nations Interim Administration Mission in Kosovo (UNMIK)

Remzije ISTREFI*

I. INTRODUCTION

Lately the role of international organisations on the international scene has increased to such an extent that, due to their functional authority, they have even been referred to as occupiers of a territory.[1] As such, international organisations very often are in a position – through their actions and omissions – to affect individuals' human rights, especially, in the territories that they administer. Until recently, few thought of an international organisation as a human rights violator.[2] However, the United Nations Interim Administration Mission in Kosovo (UNMIK) is one of the examples where the United Nations (UN) as an

---

* Professor at the Department of Political Science, University of Prishtina. This contribution was written while accomplishing the Fulbright Fellowship at the Human Rights Centre of the Duke University, Durham, N.C., U.S.A. The extended version of the idea for creation of an independent human rights body in Kosovo was introduced in R. Istrefi, 'Human Rights Accountability Regime of the UNMIK; A proposal for Establishing non legal Alternative Remedy', *Policy Development*, pp. 263–287.
All opinions and errors in this contribution are mine and do not represent the views of the institution to which I am currently affiliated. All internet pages were last visited in March 2010.

1 S.R. Ratner, 'Foreign Occupation and International Territorial Administration: The challenge of Convergence', 16 *European Journal of International Law* (2005), p. 695, the term 'occupation' is used to describe functional control of a territory.

2 See F. Mégret and F. Hoffmann, 'The UN as a Human Rights Violator? Some Reflections on the United Nations Changing Human Rights Responsibilities', 25 *Human Rights Quarterly* (2003) p. 334.

international organisation, exercised direct administration of a territory and where violations of individuals' rights occurred due to its institutional and operational activity.[3] This recent situation where the UN plays a governmental role capable of violating human rights has raised much interest and criticism among different international bodies and legal scholars. UNMIK has been criticised for not being able to deal properly with the violations that have occurred[4] because it does not have the proper human rights accountability mechanisms. At the same time, this unregulated situation poses many legal questions, among which the most challenging is how to create the most adequate human rights mechanism based on the specific situation in Kosovo.[5]

On 17 February 2008 Kosovo's parliament in an extraordinary session formally approved its declaration of independence and officially declared Kosovo's independence from Serbia.[6] With the declaration of independence[7] a new political reality in the territory of the Republic of Kosovo was created;[8] however,

---

3 In Kosovo, reports also alleged human rights violations committed by UN authorised security forces known as Kosovo Forces (KFOR) operating under the North Atlantic Treaty Organisation (NATO).

4 Council of Europe, Parliamentary Assembly, Committee on Legal Affairs and Human Rights, 'Protection of human rights in Kosovo', Doc. 10393, 6 January 2005; Amnesty International, Federal Republic of Yugoslavia, 'Kosovo, Setting the Standard? UNMIK and KFOR's Response to the Violence in Mitrovica', AI Index EUR 70/13/00, March 2000; Ombudsperson Institution in Kosovo, 'Special Report No. 1 on the Compatibility with Recognized International Standards of UNMIK Regulation No. 2000/47 on the Status, Privileges and Immunities of KFOR and UNMIK and their Personnel in Kosovo (18 August 2000) and on the Implementation of the Above Regulation', 26 April 2001, available at www.ombudspersonkosovo.org/repository/docs/E4010426a.pdf.; Ombudsperson Institution in Kosovo, 'Special Report No. 4, Certain Aspects of UNMIK Regulation No. 2001/18 on the Establishment of a Detention Review Commission for Extra-Judicial Detentions Based on Executive Orders', 12 September 2001, available at www.ombudspersonkosovo.org/repository/docs/E4010912a.pdf.

5 This question is of great importance to the Kosovar population and it does not in any case diminish its importance for all other similar UN missions. See European Commission for Democracy through Law (Venice Commission), *Opinion on Human Rights in Kosovo: Possible Establishment of Review Mechanisms,* CDL-AD (2004) 33 (11 October 2004) (hereafter Venice Commission Opinion), available at www.venice.coe.int/docs/2004/CDL-AD(2004)033-e.pdf.

6 See Kosovo Declaration of Independence (17 February 2008), available at www.assembly-kosova.org/?krye=news&newsid=1653&lang=en. This was the second declaration of independence by Kosovo Institutions, the first having been proclaimed on 7 September 1990. See B. Reka, *UNMIK as an International Governance in Post-War Kosova: NATO's Intervention, UN Administration and Kosovar Aspirat*ions (Skopje, Logos A 2003), pp. 31–69.

7 By 12 July 2010, the Republic of Kosovo had been recognised by 69 states of which 21 are European Union Member States. For a list of recognitions see: www.kosovothanksyou.com/.

8 UN Secretary-General Ban Ki-moon stated that 'given the new reality in Kosovo, UNMIK can no longer efficiently carry out its tasks as a transitory administration.' In his report on Kosovo, the Secretary-General said that 'Pristina's declaration of independence disabled UNMIK and that the mission has been "fundamentally challenged, owing to actions taken by the authorities in Pristina and the Kosovar Serbs"'. The UN Secretary-General has instructed his special representative in Kosovo, Lamberto Zannier, to initiate UNMIK's reconfiguration so the mission can adapt to the new situation on the ground. With this reconfiguration, UNMIK

the issue of the lack of accountability for the alleged human rights violations by UNMIK remains.

The territory of Kosovo was governed by UNMIK under Security Council (SC) Resolution 1244.[9] The mission was established within the UN framework for peacekeeping operations[10] to administer Kosovo until the final status was determined.[11] The main responsibilities of the interim administration enumerated in section 11 of the resolution provided for extensive powers in all fields: governing, establishing civil administration, reconstruction and maintenance of public utilities, establishing economic growth, establishing a judicial system and the rule of law, and also, in conjunction with the international security forces known as the Kosovo Force (KFOR), establishing peace and security, and respect for human rights.

Despite the unquestioned benefits of UNMIK efforts in creating a stable, functioning and viable society in Kosovo, UNMIK's governmental authorities have been subject to criticism.[12] Concretely, UNMIK was criticised with regard to the process of applying the concept of democracy and respect for human

is stripped of most of the administrative competences, but will allow a limited political role and political mentoring. In April 2007, UN special envoy Martti Ahtisaari recommended and proposed internationally supervised independence for Kosovo. The Comprehensive Proposal For the Kosovo Status Settlement (2 February 2007), the Ahtisaari plan, which was supported by the United States and most of the Member States of the European Union, but opposed by Serbia and Russia, provides for the authorised transfer of rule of law responsibilities from UNMIK to a new European Union Mission (EULEX) in the territory of the Republic of Kosovo, a plan which has started to take place. See UNMIK Online News Coverage, available at www.unmikonline.org/news.htm#1707. Also, South East European Times, 'UN secretary-general says UNMIK unable to carry out tasks efficiently', available at www.setimes.com/cocoon/setimes/xhtml/en_GB/features/setimes/newsbriefs/2008/07/18/nb-01.

9 UN Security Council, Res. 1244, UN SCOR, UN Doc. S/Res/1244 (1999).

10 UN Charter, Chapter VII.

11 UNMIK, Regulation No. 1999/1 on the Authority of the Interim Administration in Kosovo, 25 July 1999. Since 1999, UNMIK has performed basic civilian administrative functions, has organised and overseen the development of the provisional institutions for democratic self-government, elections have been held, it has established a police force, was involved in drafting the Constitutional Framework with which it has transferred certain powers to Provisional Institutions for Self Government (PISG), it has organised the return of refugees and it has assisted the PISG in the process of status negotiations.

12 M.J. Matheson, 'United Nations Governance of Post Conflict Societies', 95 *American Journal of International Law* (2001) p. 76; R. Wolfrum, 'International Administration in Post -Conflict Situations by the UN and Other International Actors', 9 *Max Planck Yearbook of United Nations Law* (2005) p. 649; S. Chesterman, *You the People: The United Nations, Transitional Administration and State Building* (Oxford, Oxford Univ. Press 2004); E. Abraham, 'The sins of the Saviours: Holding the United Nations Accountable to International Human Rights Standards for Executive Orders Detention in its Mission in Kosovo', 52 *American University Law Review* (2003), p.1291; R. Everly, 'Reviewing Governmental Acts of the United Nations in Kosovo', 8 *German Law Journal* No. 1, 1 January 2007, available at www.germanlawjournal.com/article.php?id=794; F. Mégret and F. Hoffman, loc. cit. n. 2, pp. 314–342.

rights. The entire legislative, administrative and executive power rested with the Special Representative of the Secretary-General (SRSG), who headed UNMIK. UNMIK, as an authority, issued binding decisions for the inhabitants of Kosovo and it claimed that human rights enshrined in international human rights law were applicable in Kosovo.[13] Very often UNMIK has been accused of violating those same rights it was charged to foster and uphold.

With the promulgation of the Constitutional Framework for Provisional Institutions of Self-Government in 2001 (Constitutional Framework), UNMIK has transferred certain powers to the newly created Provisional Institutions for Self Government (PISG).[14] Still, UNMIK and the SRSG had expressly reserved their authority through Chapters 8 and 12 of the Constitutional Framework under which the SRSG and UNMIK had the authority to override every decision of the Kosovar elected institutions.[15] UNMIK for almost a decade continued to exercise its governmental role in the territory of Kosovo under the so-called 'reserved powers' and still continues to be unaccountable for its acts. This unregulated situation caused considerable confusion among the inhabitants of Kosovo and it has raised an equal degree of criticism among various international bodies and the legal community. The Opinion expressed by the Venice Commission of the Council of Europe[16] for the establishment of human rights review mechanisms had raised significant hopes for the Kosovar community, but at the same time the issuance of UNMIK Reg. 2006/12,[17] on the establishment of the Human Rights Advisory Panel (Advisory Panel) was greeted with considerable scepticism. According to this new regulation any person that claims that his/her fundamental rights have been violated by UNMIK is able to complain, after exhausting domestic remedies, to this Advisory Panel, which will express an opinion as to whether or not UNMIK has committed a human rights breach. Although this opinion will not be legally binding, it will be made public in all three languages and, if there was a violation, will put pressure on UNMIK to redress the situation.

---

13 UNMIK, Regulation No. 1999/24 on the Applicable Law in Kosovo, 12 December 1999. The applicable human rights standards include: The Universal Declaration of Human Rights; The European Convention for the Protection of Human Rights and Fundamental Freedoms; The International Covenant on Civil and Political Rights; The International Covenant on Economic, Social and Cultural Rights; The Convention on the Elimination of All Forms of Racial Discrimination; The Convention on the Elimination of All Forms of Discrimination Against Women; The Convention Against Torture and Other Cruel, Inhuman or Degrading Treatment or Punishment; The Convention on the Rights of the Child; the regulations adopted by UNMIK are available at www.unmikonline.org/.

14 UNMIK, Regulation No. 2001/9 on the Constitutional Framework for Provisional Self Government in Kosovo, 15 May 2001.

15 UNMIK Regulation No. 2001/9, op. cit. n. 14, Chapters 8 and 12.

16 Venice Commission Opinion, op. cit. n. 5.

17 UNMIK, Regulation No. 2006/12 on the Establishment of the Human Rights Advisory Panel in Kosovo, 23 Mar. 2006.

UNMIK Reg. 2006/12 provides that the Advisory Panel only has competence to examine complaints about actions/omissions of UNMIK dating from 23 April 2005. To some extent this takes over the authority to review complaints that used to belong to the Ombudsperson Institution,[18] since the Ombudsperson Institution is based on the Assembly Law and it no longer has the competence to examine complaints against UNMIK.[19] Two years after the promulgation of UNMIK Reg. 2006/12, the Advisory Panel became functional and has received cases.[20] However, the Human Rights Advisory Panel as the only human rights mechanism in existence that deals specifically with human rights violations allegedly committed by or attributable to a United Nations field mission set the date of 31 March 2010 as the last date for receiving complaints.

Therefore, this contribution argues that it is highly desirable that UNMIK establish human rights mechanisms to address UNMIK's human rights accountability for all alleged violations that occurred while present in Kosovo; is the Advisory Panel an adequate mechanism to deal with alleged human rights violations in Kosovo? Should UNMIK consider the creation of another model for a human rights mechanism based while present in Kosovo, and what kind of human rights mechanism would be 'ideal' for Kosovo? These are issues that this contribution will focus on.

II. UNMIK'S MANDATE AS A CAUSE OF HUMAN RIGHTS VIOLATIONS

UNMIK's mandate with all its powers and responsibilities constitutes a unique example of an international administration.[21] From a legal and political point of view very often UNMIK's mandate is compared to the equivalent of the powers of a true state.[22] UNMIK's mandate falls in the category of administrative missions that is characterised by a 'temporary but complete take-over of

---

18 UNMIK, Regulation No. 2000/38 on the Establishment of the Ombudsperson in Kosovo, 30 June 2000.

19 UNMIK, Regulation No. 2006/6 on the Ombudsperson in Kosovo, 16 February 2006.

20 For the work and other information on the Human Rights Advisory Panel, read its website, www.unmikonline.org/human_rights/about.htm. The issue of functionality of the Human Rights Advisory panel is very controversial. Very few people in Kosovo are aware that the Advisory Panel is functional, including those who continuously research the issue.

21 UN Secretary-General, 'Report on the United Nations Interim Mission in Kosovo', S/1999/779, 12 July 1999, available at www.un.org/Docs/sc/reports/1999/s1999779.htm.

22 Ombudsperson Institution in Kosovo, *Special Report No. 1*, op. cit. n. 4, refers to UNMIK as a surrogate state. Also A.M. Novicki, 'The Presentation before the Reporting Group for Democratic Stability of Council of Ministers of Council of Europe' according to the Albanian version, published in *Koha Ditore* (27 June 2002), p. 10 quoted in B. Reka, op. cit. n. 6. See J. Nilsson, 'UNMIK and the Ombudsperson Institution in Kosovo: Human Rights Protection in a UN "surrogate State"', 22(3) *Netherlands Quarterly of Human Rights* (2004) pp. 389–411.

governmental functions by the organization guaranteeing a normal functioning of the state until national reconstruction has advanced to a point where democratically elected institutions may resume their functions'.[23] In terms of its mandate UNMIK is the most complex and extensive mission to date.[24] It differs considerably from previous UN missions in several respects: UNMIK was responsible for the entire rebuilding of a legal, yet ambiguously defined province on the territory of the former Federal Republic of Yugoslavia; UNMIK included the involvement of international organisations other than the UN, each working within its specialised field;[25] and UNMIK had the broad powers and responsibilities that were vested in the SRSG.

UNMIK Resolution 1244 has granted all legislative and executive powers in the SRSG that headed the interim civil administration, including the administration of the judiciary.[26] In essence, UNMIK exercised *de facto* governmental functions in the territory of Kosovo and, as such, was in the position to violate international human rights standards. Many examples support this assertion: UNMIK police have been accused of brutality and the use of excessive force and in particular, during the March Riots[27] were also accused of violating individuals' property rights;[28] UNMIK has been accused of violating detainees' rights under the

---

23 C. Stahn, 'International Territorial Administration in the former Yugoslavia: Origins, Developments and Challenges ahead', 61 *Zeitschrift für ausländisches öffentliches Recht und Völkerrecht* (2001) p. 108, p. 129 (footnote omitted).

24 Other operations with similar authorities include United Nations Transitional Administration for Eastern Slavonia, Baranja and Western Sirmium (UNTAES) that took place in Eastern Slavonia from 1996 to 1998 and United Nations Administration in East Timor (UNAET) that took place from 1999–2002. Still, UN Security Council Resolution 1244 differs from the previous and subsequent Security Council Resolutions that provide for International Territorial Administrations. See for example, Resolution 1727 on the establishment of the UNTAET. Also the UNTAES was given significant powers: even though the transitional administrator alone had executive powers his powers had to be devolved to Croatia in a two-phase exit strategy – first the civil administration functions and second executive functions. See also the High Representative in Bosnia and Herzegovina that represented the ultimate authority in relation to local government bodies, mostly on issues concerning implementation of the Dayton Agreement, though the scope of such powers is much narrower than UNMIK's. See in general the OHR Office of the High Representative website, available at www.ohr.int/ohr-info/gen-info.

25 UN Secretary-General, 'Report on the United Nations Interim Mission in Kosovo', op. cit. n. 21. The Report's Introduction and Overall Structure of the Mission provides that the structure consists of four pillars: Police and Justice UN (Pillar I); the UN Interim Administration, which heads the civil administration (Pillar II); the OSCE, responsible for institution building, democratisation and human rights (Pillar III); and the European Union (EU) that heads the economic reconstruction (Pillar IV). The four pillars cooperated through the Executive Committee, appointed by the SRSG, which brings together on a daily basis the SRSG, his Principal Deputy and the four Deputy Special Representatives representing the four pillars of UNMIK.

26 UN Security Council, Res. No. 1244, op. cit. n. 9, at para. 35.

27 Amnesty International, op. cit. n. 4.

28 US Department of State, Country Reports 2000, *Yugoslavia 2001*.

executive order detention;[29] and most notably, UNMIK was accused of violating the right to have an effective remedy.[30] Even though Resolution 1244 does provide that human rights protection and promotion is one of its main responsibilities, UNMIK has not established any judicial mechanisms for enforcing human rights against the acts of its personnel or the personnel of the NATO led security presence KFOR. With the establishment of the Ombudsperson Institution in Kosovo the powers and responsibilities of UNMIK were limited; however, the Ombudsperson did not have the power to compel the SRSG to follow its recommendations. Also, Resolution 1244 provides that the international presence will respect and promote human rights.[31] While UNMIK's mandate was to rebuild an entire public administration in Kosovo, it is questionable whether the fulfilment of such a mandate must tolerate violations of individuals' human rights.

III. THE APPLICABLE LAW IN KOSOVO AND UNMIK ACCOUNTABILITY

International human rights standards that are supposed to regulate the conduct of public authorities in relation to the citizens – at least on paper – are directly applicable in Kosovo's legal system based on the wording of UNMIK Regulation 2000/59.[32] Section 1 of this regulation states that all persons undertaking public duties or holding public office in Kosovo in exercising their functions shall observe internationally recognised human rights standards. The same section makes it clear that, among others, those human rights standards contained in the European Convention on Human Rights (ECHR) and the International Covenant on Civil and Political Rights (ICCPR) must apply. Also, UNMIK

---

29 OSCE Mission in Kosovo, Department of Human Rights and Rule of Law, *Kosovo, Review of the Judicial System* (October 2001), available at www.osce.org/documents/mik/2001/11/966_en.pdf; Ombudsperson Institution in Kosovo, *First Annual Report* (2000–2001), available at www.ombudspersonkosovo.org/repository/docs/E6010718a.pdf.

30 See in general the Ombudsperson Reports; R. Murphy, *UN Peacekeeping in Lebanon, Somalia and Kosovo*, (Cambridge, Cambridge University Press 2007) p. 281. See also: ICRC, *Expert Meeting on Multinational Peace Operations, Applicability of International Humanitarian Law and International Human Rights Law to UN Mandated Forces* (Geneva 11–12 December 2003), available at www.icrc.org/Web/Eng/siteeng0.nsf/htmlall/p0912/$File/ICRC_002_0912.PDF!Open.

31 In his report, the Secretary-General to the Security Council states that: '[I]n assuming its responsibilities, UNMIK will be guided by internationally recognized standards of human rights as the basis for the exercise of its authority in Kosovo.' UN Secretary General, 'Report on the United Nations Interim Mission in Kosovo', op. cit. n. 21.

32 UNMIK, Regulation No. 2000/59 amending UNMIK Regulation No. 1999/24 of 12 December 1999 on the Applicable Law in Kosovo, 27 October 2000.

Regulation 2000/47[33] in its section 3(5) obliges UNMIK personnel to respect the laws of Kosovo and to refrain from any action incompatible with that law. The applicability of international human rights standards in Kosovo is confirmed further in the Constitutional Framework.[34] The effectiveness of the existence of these standards is diminished due to the non-existence of proper mechanisms for rendering UNMIK accountable when accused of being a violator of these standards. Even though in Kosovo a judicial system has been established, it can not hear cases against UNMIK because of the broad immunity granted to the SRSG and to UNMIK's assets and personnel as a whole.[35]

IV. UNMIK ACCOUNTABILITY AT THE DOMESTIC LEVEL

A. JUDICIAL REVIEW

Under the UNMIK administration, there was no constitutional court in Kosovo nor any equivalent body in the legal system that could test the legality of any legislative or executive act of UNMIK.[36] The Special Chamber for Constitutional matters provided for by the Constitutional Framework in Chapter 9.4.11 is a body that could possibly have competence to determine the legality of the SRSG's decisions for detentions under executive orders or any other decision in question, but it was not established while under UNMIK administration. The Supreme Court of Kosovo established that according to the Constitutional Framework, it has the authority to preside only over inter-institutional disputes concerning the Constitutional Framework and it does not have authority over decisions or actions of UNMIK or KFOR.

33 UNMIK, Regulation No. 2000/47 on the Status, Privileges and Immunities of KFOR and UNMIK and Their Personnel in Kosovo, 18 August 2000.

34 Constitutional Framework in Chapter 3 provides that the following international human rights documents are aplicable in Kosovo: a) The Universal Declaration on Human Rights; (b) The European Convention for the Protection of Human Rights and Fundamental Freedoms and its Protocols; (c) The International Covenant on Civil and Political Rights and the Protocols thereto; (d) The Convention on the Elimination of All Forms of Racial Discrimination; (e) The Convention on the Elimination of All Forms of Discrimination Against Women; (f) The Convention on the Rights of the Child; (g) The European Charter for Regional or Minority Languages; and (h) The Council.

35 Ombudsperson Institution in Kosovo, *Special Report No. 1*, op. cit. n. 4.

36 The new Constitution of the Republic of Kosovo promulgated on 15 June 2008 provides for the creation of the Constitutional Court of the Republic of Kosovo. The Constitutional Court of the Republic of Kosovo was established and became functional as of 1 September 2009.

B. OMBUDSPERSON INSTITUTION IN KOSOVO

Initially the Ombudsperson Institution in Kosovo (OIK)[37] was established in June 2000.[38] The Ombudsperson was competent to 'receive and investigate complaints against any person or entity in Kosovo concerning human rights violations and actions constituting an abuse of authority by the interim civil administration or any emerging central and local institution'.[39] Although the UN accepted that the complaints against UNMIK officials can be received, KFOR was left outside the scrutiny of the Ombudsperson. The Ombudsperson, as the only non-judicial institution where Kosovar people could make a complaint against UNMIK, could 'receive complaints, monitor, investigate, offer good offices, take preventive steps, and make recommendations and advice on matters'.[40] The Ombudsperson's highest sanction was to draw the SRSG's attention to the matter and to make public statements about it.[41] Since its establishment, the Ombudsperson has received many applications where it has taken a very critical position towards UNMIK, while it has also criticised the content of several UNMIK regulations for the lack of compliance with international human rights standards.[42] The Ombudsperson issues annual reports and also has issued special reports on specific issues for the SRSG's attention.[43] It can also issue *ex officio* investigations and interim measures. In the majority of cases raised by the Ombudsperson the respondent parties did not respond at all.[44] While the Ombudsperson reported that 'recently, the cooperation with UNMIK as a respondent party has improved',[45] UNMIK on 16 February 2006 promulgated new Regulation 2006/6[46] on the establishment of the Ombudsperson Institution in Kosovo. With this regulation, the Ombudsperson became a solely Kosovar institution with a local Kosovar

37 Until December 2005, Mr. Marek Antoni Nowicki served as international Ombudsperson. Mr. Novicki was appointed as Ombudsperson in Kosovo on 11 July 2000 by the SRSG Mr. Bernhard Kouchner, upon the recommendation of the Chairman in Office of the OSCE. The process of recruitment of the new local Ombudsperson is still going on. Since January 2006 Mr. Hilmi Jashari, a deputy Ombudsperson, is acting Ombudsperson.

38 UNMIK, Regulation No. 2000/38, op. cit. n. 18. The Ombudsperson's general mandate is to protect and promote human rights and fundamental freedoms as provided in international standards especially in the ECHR and its Protocols and the ICCPR.

39 *Ibid.*, section 3.1.

40 *Ibid.*, section 4.1.

41 *Ibid.*, section 4.11.

42 In particular, the Ombudsperson has strongly criticised the SRSG issuance of executive orders and on the compatibility with recognised international standards of UNMIK Regulation No.2000/47 on the Status, Privileges and Immunities of KFOR and UNMIK and their personnel in Kosovo.

43 *Ibid.*

44 Interview with the acting Ombudsperson, Mr. Hilmi Jashari, 12 November 2007.

45 Ombudsperson Institution in Kosovo, *Fifth Annual Report* (2004–2005) addressed to the Special Representative of the Secretary-General of the United Nations, 11 July 2005, at p. 24.

46 UNMIK, Regulation No. 2006/6, op. cit. n. 19.

Ombudsperson. Most importantly, with this regulation UNMIK has excluded itself from the Ombudsperson's jurisdiction. This regulation provides under section 3 (3.4) that '[t]he Ombudsperson may enter into a bilateral agreement with the SRSG on procedures for dealing with cases involving UNMIK'.[47] From the previous experience of the Ombudsperson where the respondent party was UNMIK it is hardly to be considered that UNMIK will show goodwill by engaging itself in any agreement with the Ombudsperson Institution, in which it will subject itself to the jurisdiction of the Ombudsperson Institution as a local Kosovar institution. Strangely enough, in a letter addressed to Human Rights Watch on 9 November 2007,[48] the SRSG confirmed that the Ombudsperson Institution in Kosovo still had jurisdiction over the applications against UNMIK and that this jurisdiction would continue until the new Ombudsperson is appointed.[49] In the same letter SRSG assures Human Rights Watch that the 'office of the SRSG shall meet requests from Ombudsperson in a timely manner'. However, the reality is that since the promulgation of UNMIK Reg. 2006/6 on 'Kosovarisation' of the Ombudsperson Institution there has been no response to any of the letters that the Acting Ombudsperson has addressed to UNMIK concerning human rights violations by UNMIK.[50] Although the Ombudsperson has a very important role in human rights protection and promotion it cannot become an effective remedy as provided in international human rights standards.

V. UNMIK'S ACCOUNTABILITY AT THE INTERNATIONAL LEVEL

For the time being, there is no international judicial mechanism that can hear complaints concerning alleged breaches of international human standards by UNMIK.[51] Even though there were attempts by Kosovars to bring applications against UNMIK before the European Court of Human Rights in Strasbourg,

---

47 UNMIK, Regulation No. 2006/6, op. cit. n. 19, section 3.3.4.

48 Letter addressed to Mr. Benjamin Ward, Associate Director, Europe and Central Asia, Division, Human Rights Watch, by SRSG Joachim Rucker on file with author.

49 *Ibid.* On 4 June 2009, the Assembly of Kosovo elected Mr. Sami Kurteshi as the first local Ombudsperson in Kosovo for a mandate of five years.

50 Interview with the acting Ombudsperson, Mr. Hilmi Jashari, 12 November 2007. See also generally: Republic of Kosovo Ombudsperson, Eighth Annual Report 2007–2008 addressed to the assembly of Kosovo 21 July 2008 available at www.ombudspersonkosovo.org/repository/docs/EIGHT%20ANNUAL%20REPORT%202007-2008.doc#_Toc204321601.

51 H.H. Perritt, 'Providing Judicial Review for Decisions by Political Trustees', 15 *Duke Journal of Comparative and International Law* (2004) at p. 32. The UN Inspector General apparently has authority to revive the conduct of UN established bodies including political trustees like UNMIK, but the limited role of this office could not be extended. See generally Inspector General Act 1978, *Public Law* No 95–452 11,92 Stat. 1101(1978).

they were rejected due to the lack of jurisdiction over UNMIK.[52] The only international organ that is in a position to deal with the accountability of UNMIK is the UN Security Council to which the SRSG is responsible.

Also, at present, the provisions of the Statute of the International Court of Justice (ICJ) do not provide for the possibility to raise an application against the UN or UNMIK for violations of international human rights standards. However, it has been argued that the ICJ provisions create the possibility for the UN itself to ask for a non-binding advisory opinion that would relate to a case regarding the UN's own activities.[53] At this stage, in order to be able to raise an individual complaint application to any of the existing international mechanisms, their Statutes need to be amended with provisions that allow for this. Currently only the internal UNMIK claims office is mandated to settle certain third-party claims for property loss or damage that arise from or may be directly attributed to UNMIK or its personnel.[54]

The interesting development in relation to the international human rights mechanisms is that UNMIK has signed two agreements with the Council of Europe regarding oversight of UNMIK by international human rights monitoring bodies, that of the Framework Convention on the Protection of National Minorities and that of the Convention against Torture and Other Cruel and Inhuman and Degrading Treatment.[55] In the case of the Framework Convention on the Protection of National Minorities, the UNMIK/PISG authorities have submitted the required compliance report, but with regard to monitoring by the European Committee for the Prevention of Torture under the Torture Convention there have been problems in its application.[56] In addition, the UN Human Rights Committee of the ICCPR and monitoring committee of the ICESCR have requested UNMIK to report on the human rights situation in Kosovo. Both reports have been submitted and have been commented on by the mentioned bodies.[57]

52 ECtHR (GC) 31 May 2007 *Behrami & Behrami v. France*, Application No. 71412/01, and *Saramati v. France, Germany and Norway*, Application No. 78166/01, 45 *EHRR* (SE10) (2007) p. 85. Also the European Court in Strasbourg rejected the application made from the European Centre for Roma Rights against UNMIK due to the lack of jurisdiction. LAJM, Daily Kosovar newspaper, 27 February 2006, at p. 1.

53 R. Wilde, Accountability and International Actors in Bosnia and Herzegovina, Kosovo and East Timor, 7 *ILSA Journal of International and Comparative Law* (2001) p. 455.

54 Ombudsperson Institution in Kosovo, *Fourth Annual Report* (2003–2004) addressed to the Acting Special Representative of the Secretary-General of the United Nations, at p 16.

55 Ombudsman Institution in Kosovo, *Fifth Annual Report* (2004–2005), op. cit. n. 45, at p. 27.

56 *Ibid.*

57 Human Rights Committee, Concluding Observations, CCPR/C/UNK/CO/1, 14 August 2006.

A. IS THE ADVISORY PANEL AN ADEQUATE MECHANISM TO DEAL WITH ALLEGED HUMAN RIGHTS VIOLATIONS IN KOSOVO?

The inadequate legal situation in UN administered Kosovo concerning human rights has raised significant interest among different international bodies and the legal community in exploring possible alternative solutions.[58] The possibility of extending the jurisdiction of the European Court of Human Rights to UNMIK and KFOR was mentioned[59]; also the creation of a Court in parallel to the system of the European Convention for Human Rights was discussed; and, as it was found more appropriate, the setting up of an advisory panel as a provisional short-term solution. The Venice Commission Opinion[60] for the establishment of possible human rights mechanisms was welcomed by the Kosovar community, but the issuance of the UNMIK Reg. 2006/12 on the establishment of the Advisory Panel raised many criticisms.[61] UNMIK Reg. 2006/12 provides for the creation of an institution of an unusual nature and shape. Perhaps this was the most suitable proposal that the UN could offer considering the then current political and legal environment in UNMIK administered Kosovo. UNMIK Reg. 2006/12 provides that the Advisory Panel will be an institution of an advisory nature and shall have competence over the whole territory of Kosovo but with a time restriction over the period when the violation occurred.[62] It will examine complaints from 'any person or group of individuals' after 'available avenues for review have been pursued'.[63] The Advisory Panel will be composed of three international jurist members, one of which shall be a woman.[64] The three members will be appointed by SRSG upon the proposal of the President of the European Court of Human Rights for a two-year term with the possibility of renewal for another two-year term.[65] Even though UNMIK Reg. 2006/12

58 See Council of Europe Parliamentary Assembly, Resolution 1417, 25 January 2005, at para. 4; Council of Europe Parliamentary Assembly, Recommendation 1691, 25 January 2005, at para. 2. Interestingly, the Parliamentary Assembly at the same time recommended UNMIK and KFOR to co-operate with the Council on a study of a possible *interim* extension of the jurisdiction of the ECtHR to all inhabitants of Kosovo.

59 Council of Europe Parliamentary Assembly, Resolution 1417, op. cit. n. 58, at para. 5 (as regards reforming/establishing the advisory board of KFOR), see para. 6; Council of Europe Parliamentary Assembly, Recommendation 1691, op. cit. n. 58, p. 25, at para. 2; Report of the Legal Affairs and Human Rights Committee, Doc. 10393, 6 January 2005, at paras. 39–47 (as regards KFOR, see paras. 19–22).

60 Venice Commission Opinion, op. cit. n. 5.

61 UNMIK, Regulation No. 2006/12 on the Establishment of the Human Rights Advisory Panel was promulgated on 23 March 2006, almost two years after the Opinion of the Venice Commission. UNMIK, Regulation No. 2006/12, op. cit. n. 17.

62 Chapter 1 at section 2 provides that the Advisory Panel only has competence to examine complaints about actions/omissions of UNMIK dating from 23 April 2005.

63 In light of this provision there are in fact no available effective remedies for breaches of human rights standards committed by UNMIK.

64 Chapter 2 of UNMIK Reg. No. 2006/12, op. cit. n. 17, at section 4 (4.1), (42).

65 *Ibid.*, section 5 at 5.1, 5.2.

provides that the advisory panel shall have its seat in Prishtina,[66] it is not clear whether the three panel members will be in Prishtina and work on a daily basis or only come to Kosovo from time to time to reach decisions on cases prepared for them by a permanent Secretariat.[67] This raises the following practical question: 'Does the UN have a budget for this?'[68] The Advisory Panel will issue findings and recommendations of whether there has been a human rights violation and these will be submitted to the SRSG. Even with the creation of this institution the question of the existence and availability of effective remedies for Kosovars remains to be answered. This question is particularly relevant after the SRSG's intervention in the work of the Advisory Panel in the most outspoken cases raised by Kosovars against UNMIK, as the case of Mon Balaj (deceased), Arben Xheladini (deceased), Zenel Zeneli and Mustaf Nerjovaj against UNMIK[69], involving serious injuries inflicted by UNMIK police on 10 February 2007. In this case the SRSG intervened by issuing an 'administrative direction' for cancellation of the public hearing that was scheduled on 4 June 2009.[70] The 'administrative direction' was never enacted publicly but the Advisory Panel has decided to permanently cancel any further public or private hearing of the case on 12 May 2009.[71] This SRSG's undertaking demonstrates again that the right to an effective remedy for Kosovars against UNMIK is infringed.

B. CREATION OF A HUMAN RIGHTS PROTECTION MECHANISM: A *SUI GENERIS* BODY FOR KOSOVO

The creation of any judicial or quasi-judicial mechanism as a human rights mechanism in Kosovo is not an ordinary undertaking.[72] Being aware of the extraordinary nature of UNMIK and the absence of a 'normal' relationship between governmental decisions and courts as with an ordinary government, it remains only to synthesise a possible human rights mechanism. The UN is known for its efforts to create international and national human rights bodies and commissions. One would expect that the UN SC would itself initiate the creation of a human rights mechanism to deal with UNMIK accountability while

---

66 *Ibid.*, section 4 at 4 1

67 *Ibid.*, section 9.

68 *Ibid.*, section 8.

69 *Balaj and others v. UNMIK* (complaint no.04/07), available at www.unmikonline.org/human_rights/documents/PR/pr-hrap190309-eng.pdf.

70 Press Conference, 4 June 2009, at the Grand Hotel in Prishtina on the cancellation of the Human Rights Advisory Panel's public hearing in the case of the deaths and serious injuries inflicted by UNMIK police on 10th February 2007.

71 *Ibid.*, Document containing press conference comments prepared by Paul Troop, Jude Bounting, Tooks Chambers London (in file with the author).

72 See in general R. Istrefi, 'Human Rights Accountability Regime of the UNMIK; A proposal for Establishing non legal Alternative Remedy', *Policy Development*, pp. 263–287.

present in Kosovo through the issuance of a general resolution whereby it gives the power to the human rights mechanism to adjudicate cases of alleged violations of human rights by the UNMIK administration.[73] The question of the existence of political will of Member States in order to undertake efforts to create a less formal, *ad hoc,* specialised human rights commission for Kosovo (hereinafter the UN Commission for Kosovo) is something that would need to be answered. It is not the aim of this contribution to provide a doctrinal solution for UN accountability. Creation of the UN Commission for Kosovo is a proposal presented as a practical option for correcting alleged human rights violations by UNMIK.

The creation of a UN Commission for Kosovo should be requested by the SRSG and UNMIK's Human Rights Oversight Committee,[74] and/or by the Ombudsperson Institution. Also the courts and civil society should actively participate in this process. The request for the creation of a UN Commission for Kosovo could be contained in the SRSG's regular report to the SC and should be supported by shadow reports from civil society and the Ombudsperson. It is for the UN SC and UN Member States to make a decision on the establishment of such a body. The UN Commission for Kosovo needs to be a mechanism of a hybrid nature that would combine elements of an Ombudsman Institution and an UNMIK claims office in order to be able to investigate alleged violations, make determinations of a violation of human rights and also to award compensation for the damage that has occurred, as appropriate decisions taking into consideration the nature of human rights obligations. The threshold for interventions of the UN Commission for Kosovo must have a narrow and clear *focus operandi* that will allow the Commission to deal only with such complaints against UNMIK that have resulted from the exercise of its functional mandate while discharging public authorities and not against any UNMIK individual or a Member State of the UN. The UN and UNMIK should support the creation of the UN Commission for Kosovo – mainly for the benefit of Kosovo individuals

73 The Security Council has the power to establish judicial bodies; it has created the International Criminal Tribunal for the Former Yugoslavia (ICTY). See ICTY, *Prosecutor v. Dusko Tadic*, Decision on the Defence Motion on Jurisdiction, IT-94-1, 10 August 1995, at paras. 20–40 (reviewing the legitimacy of the SC decision creating it) available at www.un.org/icty/tadic/trialc2/decision-e/100895.htm; also, for the role of the United Nations in promoting the National Human Rights Institutions read more at S. Cardenas, 'Global Norms: The United Nations and National Human Rights Institutions', paper presented at the Academic Council of the United Nations System/American Society of International Law Workshop, University of Warwick, summer 2000.

74 This body was set up in June 2002 and is composed of the Principal Deputy of the SRSG, the heads of the four Pillars, the Legal Advisor, the Director of UNMIK Public Affairs, the Director for UNMIK Office for Returns and Communities, the Head of Office of the UN High Commissioner on Human Rights, the Chief of UNMIK Office of Gender Affairs, the Deputy Commander of KFOR (observer) and the Department of Human Rights and Rule of Law of OSCE.

– because their position is not very favourable knowing the existence of the inherent imbalance of powers between them as individuals and UNMIK as an International Mission. Therefore the UN and UNMIK should provide a mechanism that is 'favourable' to Kosovo citizens in order to meet the parameters of an adequate alternative mechanism. The principle of effectiveness as a remedy should be the fundamental base of this particular mechanism in relation to the current state of human rights in Kosovo given that the major procedural obstacles mentioned above are still existent.

C. THE AUTHORITY FOR ESTABLISHING THE UN COMMISSION FOR KOSOVO

The UN Commission for Kosovo could derive its formal authority from the UN Charter (Art. 55 and 56), UN Resolution 1244 and all UN human rights treaties, as well as of the ECHR, which are included in the applicable law in Kosovo. The Commission should have a legislative basis within the domestic legal order of Kosovo as an UNMIK regulation. The authority to conduct investigations should derive from its statutory standing as independent body. It can initiate inquiries at the request of the Ombudsperson Institution or based on individual petitions. The Commission must be enabled to invite or summon witnesses and interrogate them, while it can also ask for access to documents relevant to the case.

D. THE MANDATE AND STRUCTURE OF THE UN COMMISSION FOR KOSOVO

The mandate of the UN Commission for Kosovo would be designed based on the role and the mandate of UNMIK. Therefore, this body should review only the actions and omissions of UNMIK that have resulted in human rights violations and that fall within UNMIK's authority. The human rights Commission for Kosovo should be an independent institution operating on a temporary mandate but with a retroactive effect. In its constituent instrument it should be provided that the functions of the UN Commission for Kosovo will be concluded when UNMIK's mandate ends. In this case it will be difficult and perhaps irrelevant to classify the UN Commission for Kosovo as either an international or a local mechanism because it will need to have elements of both. The UN Commission for Kosovo should be sited in Kosovo, with international and local experts who will apply national and international law.[75]

[75] Because of their respective expertise in international/local law and experience in other international and/or national human rights bodies as well as to fulfil the criterion of impartiality.

E. COMPOSITION OF THE UN COMMISSION FOR KOSOVO

The UN Commission for Kosovo should be composed of international and local commissioners (multiethnic composition) recognised as well-known human rights and judicial experts. The process for hiring the commissioners should be advertised and it should be transparent. Screening and selection of the commissioners should be made by another body[76] but approved by the UN Secretary-General. The UN Commission for Kosovo should comprise fourteen commissioners, seven of them to be international and seven local experts (multiethnic and gender-balanced composition).[77] The UN Commission for Kosovo should operate in two chambers, one (small) chamber consisting of three commissioners and a (big) chamber of seven commissioners. The law to be applied by the UN Commission for Kosovo should be the applicable law in Kosovo as promulgated by UNMIK, which contains all international standards. The applications can be submitted by individuals and the Ombudsperson Institution. The decisions of the body should be both declaratory and obligatory on the existence of a human rights violation and also provide for compensation. An order by this body for the repeal or alteration of measures taken by UNMIK to implement an institutional act that has been declared in violation of human rights would constitute an example of a legal *restitutio in integrum*. The reparation of damages caused by that same act or decision of UNMIK would be material *reistitutio in integrum*. The UN Commission for Kosovo should hear also the applications against KFOR, if a possible agreement with the Member States of NATO is agreed for respecting the applicable law in Kosovo. In general the aim of this body is to provide for the possibility for Kosovar inhabitants to have a mechanism which would provide for an acceptable outcome through a procedure initiated by the injured party. The UN SC needs to take up the role of the decision enforcement mechanism for the UN Commission for Kosovo in order to ensure the full functioning of this body.

F. PROCEDURAL RULES OF THE UN COMMISSION FOR KOSOVO

The constitutive document of the UN Commission for Kosovo should provide for the creation of its own work and procedural rules that would provide an opportunity for individuals to be heard or represented by a legal representative. This body should be led by the principle of determining whether a particular act

[76] The Venice Commission in its Opinion for establishing human rights bodies for Kosovo for example proposes that the selection of the judges for the Kosovo Human Rights Chamber is made by the Council of Ministers of the Council of Europe.

[77] This composition and structure will enable the commission to function full time and on a regular daily basis.

can be classified as a human rights violation attributed to the UNMIK authorities. This would have a psychological effect because it frequently happens that individuals are satisfied that their cases are heard. The body should have a two-level approach. The first one should analyse any alleged violation of fundamental rights through interviews and independent investigation and decide on whether it constitutes a violation or not, and the second level is the undertaking of a remedial action of a positive, corrective and compensatory nature.[78]

The UN Commission for Kosovo should be supported by an administrative office that would be mandated to administer its own budget and other administrative requirements. The UN SC should allocate a solid budget to UNMIK to establish a fund that will allow for the payment of the compensation awards but under independent control. Also an appeal mechanism should be put in place – perhaps the Secretary-General himself can have a role in this instance. A very relevant feature of this body should be the transparency of its work; as to the number of claims that are always received and pending, considering that the extent of this transparency will not harm the processes.

G. JURISDICTION OF THE UN COMMISSION FOR KOSOVO

The UN Commission for Kosovo should have jurisdiction over concrete human rights violations that have occurred since UNMIK started its administration in Kosovo, including procedural irregularities and decisional irrationalities in relation to human rights. It should address all internationally recognised human rights norms except for property rights, since this issue needs to be regulated further given the specific circumstances of this right in Kosovo. It is to be expected that this Commission would be dealing more with civil and political rights but also the possibility for dealing with economic, social and cultural rights should be available in those cases over which UNMIK has authority. The UN Commission for Kosovo will not consider applications that pertain to political, military and security matters. Also the Commission will not be entitled to review UNMIK statements with no legal effect, UNMIK decisions that do not affect the legal interests of individuals such as statements or unexecuted intentions of UNMIK. The principle of exhaustion of remedies in this case is irrelevant, since there is no effective remedy available in Kosovo to deal with human rights cases attributed to UNMIK. The UN Commission for Kosovo should have a regulative impact because its key function in the protection and promotion of the human rights norms will be designed based on the specific

78 With this structure there is going to be a split between admissibility of a complaint and a determination of a complaint with award of compensation.

nature of UNMIK and UNMIK's obligation to exercise its authorities in conformity with international human rights and rules.

H. UNMIK'S ACCOUNTABILITY IN FRONT OF THE UN COMMISSION FOR KOSOVO

The most important role of the UN Commission for Kosovo has to be the independent assessment of UNMIK's compliance with human rights norms that are provided for in the applicable law in Kosovo. This includes holding UNMIK accountable for the violations attributed to UNMIK since it entered Kosovo. This entails accepting and investigating complaints of human rights abuses. In the course of investigating complaints the Commission can gather information from the parties concerned and check documents, examine witnesses, and can issue binding decisions. The UN Commission for Kosovo should regularly and publicly report about their work and findings. The UN Commission for Kosovo should be guided by the objective of international human rights law the objective of which is not to punish the violator but to provide reparation for the damages resulting from the acts of the responsible authorities[79] as well as to encourage changes in legislation, policies and actions to ensure that similar violations do not occur in future.

VI. CONCLUSION

The creation of a review mechanism that will handle the alleged human rights violations attributed to UNMIK is neither an easy nor an ordinary undertaking. In order to justify its intervention in Kosovo and to endorse the respect for human rights in Kosovo, the international community, in particular the UN, should show the political will and develop a strategy for the creation of such a mechanism. The creation of such a mechanism will strengthen Kosovars' trust in the existence of the rule of law and respect for human rights principles embodied in the UN Charter and other UN human rights documents. In addition, the proposed model of the UN Commission for Kosovo can serve as a model for the creation of future mechanisms in places where the UN exercises authority through its missions.

[79] IACtHR, *Velasquez -Rodriguez case*, 28 *ILM* (1989) p. 291, at para. 134.

THE OMBUDSPERSON INSTITUTION *VS* THE UNITED NATIONS MISSION IN KOSOVO (UNMIK)

Gjylbehare Bella MURATI*

I. INTRODUCTION

The Ombudsperson Institution (hereinafter 'the OIK') is the only mechanism offering human rights protection to individuals in Kosovo. It provides protection to all those who consider themselves to be victims of violations of human rights or abuses of authority by public institutions. Courts, which in 'ordinary' circumstances are considered to be the best protectors of human rights, proved to be incapable of performing this duty[1] and no other non-judicial institutions have been developed yet. Such reluctance should be seen as a consequence of the system which never sufficiently relied on accepted principles of international human rights law, and has continuously suffered from corruption, a dysfunctional administration of justice and a lack of transparency. However, while rule of law was given a priority by UNMIK, the international administration in postwar Kosovo, those whose responsibility it was to enforce such principles lacked a meaningful and coherent legal framework of how to perform their respective duties.

The objective of this contribution is to analyse the role played by the OIK as a non-judicial mechanism with regard to the human rights violations committed by UNMIK administration. This analysis will be based upon a discussion of the nature of the violations and their legal implications.

* Ph.D. candidate at the University of Ghent, Belgium. She held the position of the Senior Investigating Lawyer with the Ombudsperson Institution in Kosovo from April 2003 until February 2009. The opinions expressed in this contribution are solely those of the author and do not necessarily represent the views of the Ombudsperson's Institution.

1 It has been argued that Judges cannot be considered to be automatically responsible for implementing and protecting human rights but, however, they are required to ensure that their approach to interpretation and to the implementation of human rights is compatible with provisions of national and international law.

For the purpose of this contribution three issues of human rights violations have been chosen which I consider have cast a dark shadow over the functioning of the UN administration in Kosovo. The three issues are the protection of residential property, the right to liberty and security of person, and the right to freedom of expression, which has drawn the special attention of the OIK.

The contribution is based upon the analyses conducted by the OIK, which are available to the public.[2]

Yet prior to this analysis, background information on both the international community's engagement and the mandate of the OIK will first be given.

II. THE UNITED NATIONS MISSION IN KOSOVO

A. THE LEGAL FRAMEWORK GOVERNING UNMIK

The role of the United Nations Interim Administration Mission in Kosovo (UNMIK) has been subject to a wide discussion since its establishment. Given a role of a surrogate state empowered to exercise all legislative and executive authority and to take responsibility for the administration of justice[3], UNMIK has brought to the surface new sets of issues in international law that occupy an important place in international discourse.

Established on 10 June 1999, under the UN Charter and pursuant to Security Council Resolution 1244, it was empowered to temporarily exercise complete sovereignty over the territory of Kosovo. Until 2005, its structure comprised four pillars, each assigned to different tasks[4]: Pillar I was in charge of Police and Justice and Pillar II of Civil Administration, both under the direct leadership of the Special Representative of the UN Secretary-General (SRSG), who represents the United Nations in Kosovo; Pillar III was responsible for Democratisation and

2 Information taken from the OIK website, www.ombudspersonkosovo.org.

3 See UNMIK, Regulation No. 1999/1 on the authority of the Interim Administration in Kosovo, 25 July 1999, at para. 1.1: 'All legislative and executive authority with respect to Kosovo is vested in UNMIK and is exercised by the Special Representative of the Secretary – General'. All UNMIK Regulations can be found at www.unmikonline.org.

4 The major tasks of UNMIK included: 'Performing basic civilian administrative functions where and as long as required; Organising and overseeing the development of provisional institutions for democratic and autonomous self-government pending a political settlement, including the holding of elections; Transferring, as these institutions are established, its administrative responsibilities while overseeing and supporting the consolidation of Kosovo provisional institutions and other peace-building activities; Supporting the reconstruction of key infrastructure and other economic reconstruction; Maintaining civil law order, including establishing local police forces and meanwhile through the deployment of international police personnel to serve in Kosovo; Protecting and promoting human rights.'

Institution Building and led by the Organization for Security and Co-operation in Europe (OSCE); Pillar IV, led by the European Union (EU), was in charge of Reconstruction and Economic Development.[5] Following the ongoing transfer of powers into local hands, currently UNMIK's structure comprises the Democratisation and Institution Building Pillar led by the OSCE.

Soon after the proclamation of independence[6] UNMIK was expected to fully cede power to the EU, but legal grounds for a structured transition have been lacking. The lack of unanimity within the United Nations Security Council to endorse the new resolution which would establish the legal grounds for deploying a new EU mission in Kosovo has brought new sets of problems to the functioning of the newly created state. However, until a temporary solution is found, the UN Secretary General has made a decision on the basis of UN Security Resolution 1244 to reconfigure the United Nations presence in Kosovo and as such enable the deployment of a new EU mission.

In light of the above, the EU's Rule of Law mission (EULEX) in Kosovo has been deployed. It formally operates under the authority of the reconfigured UNMIK[7] and at the same time retains a neutral stance towards Kosovo

---

5 Pursuant to UNMIK Regulation 2001/9 on the Constitutional Framework for Provisional Self-Government in Kosovo, 15 May 2001, a number of competencies were transferred to local government institutions. In particular, most of the competencies under Pillar II have been or are in the process of being transferred to local structures. However, some major responsibilities remain in the hands of the SRSG. Those 'reserved powers and responsibilities' include: 'Exercising powers and responsibilities of an international nature in the legal field; Exercising authority over law enforcement institutions and the correctional service; Concluding agreements with states and international organisations in all matters within the scope of UNSCR 1244 (1999); and External relations, including with states and international organisations, as may be necessary for the implementation of [the SRSG's] mandate.' Hence, the responsibilities and powers held and exercised by Pillar I are among those remaining in the hands of UNMIK until the final status of Kosovo is determined.

6 In 2005, the UN Secretary General appointed the former Finish President, Mr. Marti Ahtisaari as Special Envoy for the Kosovo status process which is to determine the future political status of the UN administered territory. On 15 March 2006, Mr. Ahtisaari announced the settlement proposal which involved the internationally supervised independence of the country. Almost a year later on 17 February 2007, the Kosovo Parliament declared independence. The proposed settlement places Kosovo under the EU supervision comprising an International Civilian mission (ICO) responsible for implementing the above mentioned plan and EULEX, the law and order mission responsible for administering and developing the rule of law in the country.

7 The very process of reconfiguration of UNMIK lacks transparency and clarity. On 18 August 2008, an agreement was signed between UNMIK and EULEX on the transfer of certain parts of UN mission property to EULEX. It relates to the transfer or sale of certain assets, vehicles and facilities which were used by UNMIK. Due to the lack of transparency, the public still lacks clarity about the content of this very agreement. For the majority of people it has been understood as a document which stipulates the details of the reconfiguration process, however, it has been stressed by the UNMIK spokesperson that this is a pure technical agreement and that the signing of the Memorandum of Understanding between UNMIK and EULEX on the transfer of competences is a separate issue and it has still not been scheduled.

status.[8] As a consequence, UN Security Council Resolution 1244, which has created UNMIK, is still in force and it remains to be seen what tools will be used to enforce the resolution's legal requirements. The new EU mission is widely rejected by the Serb minority which suddenly shows willingness to accept UNMIK's authority and there is a probability that the future role of UNMIK will be more concentrated on the Serbian enclaves and as such it might retain a certain level of responsibility in the future.

B. THE LEGAL IMPLICATIONS ARISING FROM UN SC RESOLUTION 1244

UN SC Resolution 1244 ensures the sovereignty and territorial integrity of the Federal Republic of Yugoslavia (FRY) and regards Kosovo as still being part of the FRY.[9] At the same time, its provisions clearly show that FRY[10] cannot be held accountable for violations committed on the territory of Kosovo as it no longer exercises jurisdiction over this territory within the meaning of Article 1 of the European Convention on Human Rights (ECHR).[11]

The Resolution, which was strictly designed for the UN mission in Kosovo, empowered UNMIK to exercise public authority over the mandated territory; intervene in its politics, economy and legislation; as well as represent the territory outside its boundaries. By becoming a state actor, UNMIK was empowered to enact laws, conduct judicial and law enforcement reforms, support civil society and establish transitional justice mechanisms aiming to create a democratic system and strengthen the rule of law.

It was entitled to enter into international treaties without being a state and as such be bound by the rules arising from a particular treaty. In this context, UNMIK was engaged in performing both state functions attributed to the State and on the other side fulfil obligations borne by the international organisation in relation to the implementation of human rights treaties.[12]

8 UNMIK has also taken a neutral position regarding Kosovo's unilaterally declared independence.

9 See introductory part of Security Council Resolution 1244 UN, SCOR, UN Doc. S/Res/1244 (1999).

10 On 27 April 1992, under a new constitution, Serbia and Montenegro established the Federal Republic of Yugoslavia (FRY). On 4 February 2003, the FRY ceased to exist and was succeeded by a new state called simply Serbia and Montenegro. After the proclamation of independence of Montenegro, on 21 May 2006, Serbia was obliged to officially proclaim its independence on 5 June 2006, as the successor state to the State Union of Serbia and Montenegro. However, Serbia was assumed to be the legal successor of the dissolved/divorced state.

11 Article 1 of the ECHR stipulates that '[t]he High Contracting party shall secure everyone within their jurisdiction the rights and freedoms defined in Section I of this Convention'.

12 See R. Wilde, 'International territorial administration and human rights', in N.D. White and D. Klaasen, eds., *The UN, Human Rights and Post-conflict Situations* (Manchester, Manchester University Press 2005) p. 15.

These United Nations-made state actors are not bound by the same human rights standards designed for States, although they have acknowledged and have been very vocal about the relevance of these standards.[13] As a consequence, no supervisory body was established to supervise their acts with regards to its compatibility with human rights standards.[14]

Consequently, Kosovan citizens lack and will continue to lack an effective mechanism enabling individuals to initiate proceedings against the international authorities who have violated their rights in order to obtain just compensation. Although the Constitutional Framework[15] provided for the establishment of a Special Chamber whose task would be to determine the compatibility of adopted laws with the Constitutional Framework, it did not authorise this body to review cases involving alleged human rights violations.

As already mentioned, the new EU mission in Kosovo, envisaged to take over UNMIK's mandate over the territory will, like UNMIK, operate on the basis of Resolution 1244, the resolution which recognises Serbia's territorial integrity and sovereignty over Kosovo. It remains to be seen how it will exercise its mandate.

C. THE UNITED NATIONS DOMESTIC LAWMAKING

The applicable law in Kosovo consists of laws issued in the form of UNMIK Regulations[16], laws passed by the provisional Assembly of Kosovo and promulgated by UNMIK and of certain non-discriminatory provisions taken from those Yugoslav laws that are not in contradiction with accepted international human rights standards.[17]

---

13 See UNMIK, Regulation No. 2000/59 amending UNMIK Regulation 1999/24 on the law applicable in Kosovo, 27 October 2000; all persons, undertaking public duties or holding public office in Kosovo shall observe internationally recognised human rights standards as reflected in: the Universal Declaration on Human Rights, the International Covenant on Civil and Political Rights, the European Convention on Human Rights, the International Covenant on Economic, Social and Cultural Rights, the Convention on Elimination of All Forms of Racial Discrimination, the Convention on Elimination of All Forms of Discrimination against Women, the Convention against Torture and Other Cruel and Inhumane or Degrading Treatment or Punishment and the International Convention on the Right of the Child.

14 It is common knowledge that the SRSG often interfered in the course of justice as well as in the procedure of passing of laws, adopted by the Assembly, which he considers to be in contradiction with Security Council Resolution 1244 or the Constitutional Framework. Corrections and amendments of those laws are often conducted without further consultations with the Assembly.

15 The Framework Convention is not in force any longer as it was replaced by the State Constitution which came into effect on 15 June 2008.

16 The UNMIK Regulations will continue to form part of the applicable law.

17 The laws enacted prior to the NATO strike (23 March 1999) remained in force insofar as they did not conflict with international human rights standards.

Since 1999, Kosovo has been undergoing a rapid process of legislative and institutional reform. The legislative reforms within the areas of competence reserved for UNMIK were drafted directly by UNMIK and issued as UNMIK regulations. Until recently, laws relating to issues within the PISG's areas of responsibility were passed by the Assembly of Kosovo, and then forwarded to the SRSG for review and formal promulgation as UNMIK regulations.

Laws passed by the Kosovo Assembly were initiated by the Assembly itself or by the responsible PISG ministry. Generally, the processes by which laws were promulgated were too long and complicated. The first draft laws were mainly prepared by the legal department of the relevant ministry and then further submitted to the Office of the Prime Minister, which established a working group to review the law. The working group included a UNMIK legal adviser, and representatives from NGOs, municipalities and experts. Some, though not all, proposed legislation preferred by the working group to public debate and civil society input. The final stage required all legislation to be reviewed for compliance with the Constitutional Framework and international human rights instruments before it was finalised.[18]

However, due to the unclear roles and responsibilities of the PISG and UNMIK, as well as the relationship between them (or for other reasons), the legislation has nonetheless in numerous cases contained serious gaps, overlaps, inconsistencies or even internal incompatibilities.

The limited involvement of civil society in the process of legislative and policy development has contributed to a lack of awareness and knowledge about the existing legislation among the general population.

All this has led to a situation with serious gaps in the development of subsidiary legislation. Only in a very few cases has the passing of laws in the Kosovo Assembly been followed by limited efforts to develop further binding instruments to ensure full and consistent implementation of the law.

D. UNMIK AND ITS ROLE IN THE JUDICIARY

Besides exercising legislative and executive authority, the UN Security Council empowered UNMIK with the responsibility for the administration of justice.[19]

---

18 Administrative Instruction on Procedures for Drafting and Submitting Draft Laws to the Government and Assembly (Draft), January 2004.

19 See UNMIK, Regulation No. 1999/1, op. cit. n. 3, at para. 1.1: 'all legislative and executive authority with respect to Kosovo is vested in UNMIK and is exercised by the Special Representative of the Secretary-General'.

UNMIK thus had an enormous task, which *inter alia* involved the re-creation of the judiciary. From the outset, UNMIK has focused on improving the effectiveness of the judiciary by establishing a legal framework, re-activating the judicial staff and establishing a police force. The reform in question is still being conducted with the active participation of regional organisations, non-governmental organisations and the legal technical assistance of the international community, involving reforms of substantive and procedural laws, as well as education and training of judges and public prosecutors in order to reform the court administration in general.[20]

In general terms, an independent judiciary is commonly viewed as the strongest guarantee to upholding the rule of law and the protection of human rights.[21]

The major problem with UNMIK's judiciary in Kosovo was the ignorance of the principle of the separation of powers, a fundamental principle designed for the functioning of a political system of a modern democracy. It is known that the principle of the separation of powers is the best guarantee to prevent judges from acting as an extension of the legislative or executive branches.

UNMIK, on the contrary, did not recognise the division of powers; all three powers were concentrated in a single authority, the SRSG. This has discouraged the entire society since it undermined the independence of the judiciary.

The methods of selection and appointment of judges may in some circumstances endanger the principle of separation of powers and consequently the independence of the judiciary; therefore security of tenure proved to be a necessary element to secure the independence and impartiality of judges.[22] In the previous system of the Federal Republic of Yugoslavia, judges were appointed for a life-term by a parliamentary panel based on a list drawn up by the Ministry of Justice. One of the main criteria for their nomination was loyalty to the government. Judges were politically influenced and under constant pressure.[23]

20 The Organization for Security and Co-operation in Europe (OSCE) is directly involved in helping to re-establish the judicial system in Kosovo. For more details about OSCE activities in Kosovo see the OSCE website: www.osce.org/kosovo/mandate.

21 See D.C. Prefontaine, Q.C. and J. Lee, 'The Rule of Law and the Independence of the Judiciary', Paper prepared for the World Conference on the Universal Declaration on Human Rights, Montreal (7–9 December 1998), available at www.icclr.law.ubc.ca/Publications/Reports/RuleofLaw.pdf.

22 Office for Democracy and Governance, Bureau for Democracy, Conflict, and Humanitarian Assistance, U.S Agency for International Development, *The Guidance for Promoting Judicial Independence and Impartiality*, Washington, DC 20523–3100, Revised Edition, January 2002, p. 13.

23 Mr. Nike Lumezi, an attorney at law with diverse legal experience in former Yugoslavia (former Deputy Ombudsperson in Kosovo, former President of the Supreme Court, former Head of the Legislation Secretariat) says: 'Interference was always present during politically motivated trials. During such trials, a judge was not only obliged to follow the law (which was

Because of the lack of separation of powers in that system, there was little need for judges to be independent; loyalty to the government was valued far higher than independence or competence.[24]

However, during UNMIK's mandate, the procedure for the appointment of local judges was conducted by the Kosovo Judicial and Prosecutorial Council (hereinafter KJPC), an advisory body with no real power established pursuant to Regulation 2001/8 (6 April 2001)[25] which advised and made recommendations to the SRSG concerning the appointment of professional judges, lay judges and prosecutors.[26] Until recently the SRSG was the body which would make a final selection from a list of candidates proposed by the KJPC and endorsed by the Assembly, with a reserved right to remove local judges and prosecutors without any prior consultation with the KJPC.[27]

The period for which judges are appointed was a matter of concern since the beginning of UNMIK's mission. Initially, local judges were appointed for six-month terms but later it was changed and their terms were set to last until the end of the UN mission.[28] International judges[29] were appointed through a UN procedure in New York and were subject to six months' renewable terms of office.[30] The appointment procedure lacked clarity as it was totally invisible to the outside world.[31] Moreover, there were no clear criteria on which to base their appointment. UNMIK Regulation 2000/06 on the Appointment and Removal

very tough on offences affecting the values of the communist system) but to defend the communist ideology as well.' The interview with Mr. Lumezi was conducted on 26 October 2004 in Prishtina. All interviews were conducted for the purpose of writing a conference paper (The Independence of Judiciary and its Role in the Protection of Human Rights under UN Administration, using the case of Kosovo) organised by the European Society of International Law, 13–15 May 2004, Florence.

24 On 28 May 1998, the Yugoslav Minister of Justice, Mr. Dragoljub Jankovic, in a speech during a nomination ceremony, addressed the newly appointed judges by saying: 'Your duty is not only to protect the constitutionality and legislation of this country, but also to love this country, therefore do not forget your roots...We will be fighting terrorism' Ljudska prava u Jugoslaviji 1998, Pravo Praksa i Pravna Svest u Saveznoj Republici Jugoslaviji i Medjunarodni Standardi Ljudskih Prava, pg.214, Beogradski Centar za Ljudska Prava, Beograd (1999) p. 215.

25 Judicial Councils are mechanisms for selecting judges and prosecutors that can be found in many European countries. For more details see *supra* n. 22, at p. 14.

26 Since the independence of the country the SRSG is no longer involved in the process of appointing judges and prosecutors.

27 See D. Marchal and S. Inglis, 'The Disempowerment of Human Rights-Based Justice in the United Nations Mission in Kosovo', 16 *Harvard Human Rights Journal* (2003) p. 121.

28 It remains to be seen what will be the length of the judges' and prosecutors' appointments after the departure of UNMIK.

29 A considerable number of UN judges and prosecutors in Kosovo have been replaced by EU judges and prosecutors.

30 See the OSCE Mission in Kosovo, Department of Human Rights and Rule of Law, *Review of the Criminal Justice System* (September 2001- February 2002) p. 32, available at www.osce.org/documents/mik/2002/04/965_en.pdf.

31 See D. Marchal and S. Inglis, loc. cit. n. 27, at p. 124.

from Office of International Judges and Prosecutors failed to include general provisions as to qualifications for judicial appointment of the international judges and prosecutors.[32]

The lack of security of tenure made both international and, until recently, local judges automatically vulnerable to the influence of those who may have affected their employment prospects.[33] Furthermore, the failure to establish a legal mechanism to address the complaints involving international judges has raised serious concerns with regard to the transparency of the system as a whole.[34]

Even after ten years in power, UNMIK has still not managed to establish full control over the judicial system in Kosovo. Two parallel judicial systems emerged which continue to claim absolute and exclusive jurisdiction over the territory. A number of previous formal municipal courts in Kosovo are still working under the auspices of the Serbian authorities, applying Serbian laws and are located in the northern part of Mitrovica town, Leposavic and Zubin Potok, where the Serbian minority population lives. At the same time, there is a parallel structure of district courts acting in Serbia proper, so-called courts in exile. Nowadays they mainly deal with property issues. However, until 2003, they also exercised jurisdiction over criminal and minor offences, which in some cases caused the overlap of jurisdictions and led to double jeopardy.[35]

Neither UNMIK nor PISG authorities have yet made a decision with regard to the legal validity of decisions issued by parallel courts, especially between 1999 and 2002, when they were most active.[36]

---

32 Amended by UNMIK Regulation 2000/34 of 15 February 2000 and UNMIK Regulation 2001/2 of 12 January 2001; the issue of appointment of international judges has been widely criticised by the Ombudsperson Institution in Kosovo; see OIK 5th and 6th Annual Report, available at www. ombuspersonkosovo.org.

33 Security of tenure involves a long-term appointment; it guarantees that a judge can be removed from his/her position only for good cause, such as the breach of ethical rules. For more details see *supra* note 17, p. 19.

34 During the interview with Mr. Thomas Monaghan the issue of the disciplinary mechanism by which the complaints can be brought against international judges was raised. No concrete answer was provided. The interview with Mr. Monaghan was conducted on 28 October 2004.

35 Following an order issued in 2003 by KFOR authorities, the parallel courts inside Kosovo stopped handling criminal cases. Nevertheless, the courts in exile operating within Serbia proper had continued to deal with criminal cases, in particular those involving war crimes and inter-ethnic crimes, asserting jurisdiction over the accused individuals against whom had been issued indictments. As soon as they were found in Serbia, they were arrested and subjected to trial. Several Kosovan politicians who used to serve as members of the Kosovo Liberation Army have been indicted by the Serbian authorities, among them previous and current Prime Ministers. Moreover, there have been some trials which have been held *in absentia*. For additional information, see E. Baylis, 'Parallel Courts in Post Conflict Kosovo', 32 *Yale Journal of International Law* 1 (2007) pp. 1 and following.

36 See the OSCE Mission in Kosovo, Department of Human Rights and Rule of Law, *Parallel Structures in Kosovo* (October 2003), p. 26, available at www.osce.org/documents/mik/2003/10/698_en.pdf.

It is becoming increasingly clear that the future challenges will not be easier than the previous ones. Currently Kosovo's biggest challenge will be the establishment of a new EU mission, originally envisaged to take over UNMIK's mandate in 2008, but now in a more unclear position.

In the framework of this new EU mission, the judicial system will continue to be supported by a new contingent of international judges and prosecutors. Initially, over 40 judges and roughly 18 prosecutors have been deployed all over Kosovo, and more are expected to be deployed in the near future.[37] They will be subordinated to the President of the Assembly of EULEX judges and the Chief of the EULEX prosecutors acting under the Head of the Justice Component.[38] The EULEX judges will have jurisdiction and competence over any case investigated or prosecuted by the Special Prosecution Office of the Republic of Kosovo (SPRK). The President of the Assembly of the EULEX judges holds the competence to assign a EULEX judge to any stage of the criminal proceedings investigated or prosecuted by the SPRK, as well as to decide that an EULEX judge should not be assigned to a certain stage of the criminal proceedings. Though the aim is full integration into the Kosovo judicial system, they will be acting under totally separate authority, the Head of the Justice Component.

It remains to be seen whether the EULEX judges and prosecutors are going to be subjected to quality control, and if so, what will be the legal regulatory mechanism to address complaints in cases alleging misconduct of judges.

Overall, it is important that the new EU mission takes into account all the shortcomings and gaps made by UNMIK and tries to build an accountable and transparent mission.

III. THE OMBUDSPERSON INSTITUTION

The OIK was established by UNMIK Regulation 2000/38 on 30 June 2000, 'for the purpose of enhancing the protection of human rights in Kosovo'.[39] The role of the Institution was confirmed by the Constitutional Framework for Kosovo, which gave this institution an important position in the new postwar legal order.[40]

37 Interview with Mr. Bernard Rabatel, Justice Expert, EULEX Mission in Kosovo (July 2008).

38 See Law on Jurisdiction, Selection and Case Allocation of the EULEX Judges and Prosecutors in Kosovo No.D-.019-2008, (15 June 2008); see also Law on the Prosecution Office of the Republic of Kosovo, No. DL-018-2008, (15 June 2008).

39 UNMIK, Regulation No. 2000/38 on the Establishment of the Ombudsperson Institution in Kosovo, 30 June 2000.

40 The institution was led for five years by the International Ombudsperson, the Polish Human Rights Lawyer, Marek Antoni Nowicki.

As an independent entity, the OIK has the mandate to engage in human rights and rule of law issues in relation to both international administration[41] and emerging local institutions.

The jurisdiction of the OIK covers issues concerning human rights violations and actions constituting abuse of authority. The main reference instruments are the European Convention on Human Rights and its Protocols and the International Covenant on Civil and Political Rights. While the OIK does not have the power to issue binding decisions, its findings are addressed in the form of special reports which cover general situations and individual case reports, based on an individual complaint or ex-officio.

The OIK is considered to be the most effective mechanism for the protection of human rights in Kosovo today. It is directly involved in monitoring, protecting, investigating and reporting human rights violations by public institutions. After the promulgation of the new UNMIK Regulation 2006/6[42] the mandate of the Institution became constricted and, as it stands, no longer endows the automatic right to review and redress acts of omissions/decisions constituting an abuse of authority or a violation of human rights by UNMIK. Although the OIK refrains from commenting upon draft laws, when it comes to already promulgated laws it has proved to be very vocal. It always limits itself to comments addressing compliance with the adopted regulations of international standards.

The independence of the OIK is ensured by Section 2 of Regulation 2000/38 which provides, that '[t]he OIK shall act independently. No person or entity may interfere with his her functions' and it has been confirmed by Regulation 2006/06 section 2.1 using similar wording.

The new Regulation 2006/6 which excludes UNMIK from the OIK jurisdiction has weakened the institution in the eyes of the citizens who vested their hopes in this institution for seeking justice for the acts committed by UNMIK officials.[43]

Instead, it foresees a possibility of concluding bilateral agreements between the OIK and UNMIK authorities, which turns OIK into a contracting party whose main business is 'human rights protection in an administered territory'.[44]

41 Under the old Regulation 2000/38 the OIK had the mandate to investigate complaints against administrative bodies (UNMIK).

42 UNMIK, Regulation No. 2006/6 on the Ombudsperson Institution in Kosovo, 16 February 2006.

43 See Ombudsperson Institution in Kosovo, *Fifth Annual Report* (2004 – 2005) addressed to the Special Representative of the Secretary General of the United Nations, 11 July 2005.

44 The Regulation has been subject to a criticism by the Acting Ombudsperson, who immediately after being informed of the promulgation of this Regulation sent a letter to the SRSG in which he expressed his concerns/comments about the decision to narrow the mandate of the

The OIK is awkwardly squeezed between its narrow mandate and the wide expectations coming from the victims of violations, since no other effective alternative remedy has been established yet. Faced with such a legal cocktail together with the lack of accountability of the actors involved, it continues to struggle to build paths promoting and protecting human rights in Kosovo.[45]

A. PROTECTING RESIDENTIAL PROPERTY (HOUSING AND PROPERTY DIRECTORATE AND HOUSING AND PROPERTY CLAIMS COMMISSION)

The following section discusses the OIK's procedure concerning property restitution and its legal implications. It aims at providing an overview of the property claims processing before an ad hoc administrative and quasi-judicial body.

Among other consequences of the 1998–1999 Kosovo war and the following period, the issues surrounding housing and property rights[46] have been a matter of particular concern for UNMIK from the very beginning and have been given an important place on its agenda.

Thousands of houses were destroyed during the war and many of them usurped.[47]

Institution; 'we consider it problematic that the OIK no longer has automatic jurisdiction over UNMIK bodies, given that there are still a considerable number of areas that remain under reserved powers, in particular matters pertaining to the protection of minority communities. One specific example of this would be Northern Mitrovica, where the PISG do not operate and concerns would need to be brought directly to the attention of UNMIK,' said the Acting Ombudsperson. A letter was sent on 22 February 2006 and is available at the OIK website www.ombudspersonkosovo.org.

45 It was not clear for a long time whether the Acting Ombudsperson who was appointed by the SRSG can exercise his oversight functions over UNMIK following the long transition period from internationally to locally appointed Ombudsperson. After one year, on 9 November 2007, finally it was clarified that the Acting Ombudsperson will continue to exercise his functions and responsibilities over UNMIK upon the appointment of a new Ombudsperson.

46 In the former Yugoslavia, two types of property were recognised: socially and privately owned.

47 Regarding residential property usurpation it is necessary to stress that in some cases usurpation resulted from the need for shelter as many houses had been burnt during a war. In some other cases, usurpation of property was done based on the claim that the alleged property was taken unlawfully from the Albanians during the Milosevic regime and as such he/she is entitled to have it back. In other cases, another motive was invoked (revenge, greediness). In the Northern part of Mitrovica, the usurpation came as a result of revenge and to some extent as a need for shelter since many Serbs after the war had to move to this part of Kosovo leaving behind their residential property.

Such a situation required an urgent response and a solution was found in the establishing of administrative mechanisms, the Housing and Property Directorate (hereinafter HPD)[48], entitled to receive and process property claims, and the independent quasi-judicial body, the Housing and Property Claims Commission (hereinafter HPCC), to adjudicate such claims.[49]

The creation of these mechanisms resulted in the removal of jurisdiction from the courts for the cases which concerned the residential property rights on the territory of Kosovo, categorised in three groups: Category A) encompasses claims by individuals who lost their property as a result of discriminatory laws after 1989; Category B) claims by individuals who entered into unofficial transactions for the sale of their property; Category C) claims brought by internally displaced persons and refugees who lost possession of their property.

The procedure before the HPD involved several stages, claim registration, notification, verification, rejection, mediation and the referral of cases to the Commission.

Prior to submission of the claim, a claimant was required to give an interview before a clerk/officer, and then fill in a form and submit the necessary documents. Soon after, the claimant, respondent and the person who had legal interest in the dispute were notified about the process. The respondent was also required to submit a claim in reply to the claimant within the time limit provided for by the Regulation.[50] After a thorough verification of the submitted documents, it considered the possibility of initiating mediation.[51] However, when a case was not settled by mediation[52], the claim was submitted to the legal officer for review, who after thorough examination of the file wrote a referral report. The referral report contained the basic findings, conclusion and recommendations and once finalised, was subjected for an additional review to the case manager. After the examination by the case manager, the referral report was forwarded to the Register Adjudication for the final review who had to assess if everything had been done in accordance with the existing rules, and if so, the case was submitted to the Commission.[53] The claims were submitted electronically to the international members of the Commission as the Commissioners were expected to do preparatory and supplementary work at their home base, for most of the

48 Mechanisms established by UNMIK, Regulation 1999/23 on the establishment of the Housing and Property Directorate and the Housing and Property Claims Commission, 15 November 1999.

49 Pursuant to UNMIK Regulation No. 2006/10, the Housing and Property Directorate has been replaced by the Kosovo Property Agency which assumed its responsibility on 4 March 2006.

50 UNMIK Regulation 2000/60, Section 8.9.

51 Section 10.

52 There is no information available regarding the practice of mediation.

53 UNMIK Regulation 2000/60, Section 7.8.

time. Basically, the Commission relied on the submissions received from the HPD.

The proceedings before the Commission were carried out based on the written submissions. In this context, parties could not argue before the Commission, since oral hearings were excluded. In certain cases, the Commission would delegate certain claims to the Register Adjudication who submitted a claim to the local Commissioner for review, and in case of any comments it was sent to the full panel. It is necessary to stress that the Commission had developed cover decisions for claims involving similar legal issues. This was used for a so-called 'mass claims' approach, which involved the collection of several cases which share similar facts and subsequently making of a decision.[54]

Yet, in some cases, it could refer specific separate parts of claims to local courts or administrative bodies and also issue provisional measures of protection.[55] The final decisions issued by the HPCC were binding and enforceable, and were not subject to judicial or administrative review.[56]

The enforcement of the decisions was conducted through the execution of evictions pursuant to an eviction order issued by the Directorate. The execution was assigned to the Enforcement Unit according to the HPD standard operational procedures.[57]

The right to property[58] is often considered a highly complex and controversial right whose parameters have been very difficult to establish.[59] It includes a wide range of economic interests including movable and immovable property, tangible or intangible interest[60] and as such requires a proper degree of protection.

In the Kosovo context, interpretation of property laws is especially complicated because it lacks an adequate legal framework and property rights are governed

---

54 See A.R. Smitt, 'Housing and property Restitution and IDP return in Kosovo', 44(3) *International migration* (2006) p. 68.

55 Section 1.2 UNMIK Regulation 1999/23.

56 Section 2.7 UNMIK Regulation 1999/23.

57 Information regarding proceedings before the HPD/HPCC are taken from B. Vagle and F. de Medina-Rosales, *An evaluation of the Housing s and Property Directorate in Kosovo*, NORDEM Report 12, (2006), pp. 26 and 52.

58 Article 1 of Protocol 1 offers a broad definition of property: '[e]very natural or legal person is entitled to the peaceful enjoyment of his possessions. No one shall be deprived of his possessions except in the public interest and subject to the conditions provided for by law and by the general principles of international law'.

59 T.R.G. van Banning, *The Human Right to Property* (Antwerpen, Intersentia 2002) p. 79.

60 M. Carss-Frisk, 'A guide to the Implementation of article 1 of Protocol 1 to the European Convention of Human Rights', 4 *Human Rights Handbook* (2001) p. 12.

by several bodies of laws.[61] These include pre-1989 Yugoslav law, laws issued between 1989 and 1999 to the extent that they do not enter into conflict with the accepted standards of the international human rights law, UNMIK regulations and laws passed by the new Kosovo Assembly.[62]

In addition, two laws have been entirely repealed, as they proved to be discriminatory. "The following laws, which do not comply with the standards referred to in section 2 of UNMIK Regulation No. 1999/1, are repealed in Kosovo: The Law on Changes and Supplements on the Limitation of Real Estate Transactions (Official Gazette of Republic of Serbia, 22/91 of 18 April 1991); The Law on the Conditions, Ways and Procedures of Granting Farming Land to Citizens Who Wish to Work and Live in the Territory of the Autonomous Province of Kosovo and Metohija (Official Gazette of Republic of Serbia, 43/91 of 20 July 1991) [...]."[63]

Nevertheless, the failure to issue clear guidance on the way to identify which laws or parts of laws are inconsistent with internationally recognised standards, has led to a problematic and nurtured confusion. The claims within the 'Category A' defined as 'claims by individuals whose ownership, possession or occupancy rights to residential real property have been revoked on the basis of legislation which is discriminatory in its application or intent'[64], have proved to be the most complicated ones. Indeed, it was difficult to assess claims where complainants alleged to have been deprived of their property in a discriminatory manner because of the complexity arising from the subtle actions of the discriminatory regime.[65]

---

61 The legal framework governing the property rights in Kosovo consists of the following laws: a) Law on Basic Property Relations (Official Gazette of SFRY No.6/80), b) Law on Transfer of Real Property (Official Gazette of SAP Kosovo No.45/81 and 28/88), c) Law on Expropriation (Official Gazette of SAP Kosovo No. 37/71), Law on Construction of Annexes to Buildings and Conversion of Common Premises into Apartments) Official Gazette of SAP Kosovo No 14/88), Law on Construction of Facilities for Investment-Commercial Purposes (Official Gazette of SAP Kosovo No 5/86), Law on Co-Ownership of an Apartment (Official Gazette SAP Kosovo No 43/80 and 22/87), Law on Expropriation, (Official Gazette SAP Kosovo No.21/78 and 46 /86), Law on Forests (Official Gazette SAP Kosovo No 46/86 and 10/87), Law on Housing Relations (Official Gazette SAP Kosovo No 11/83, 29/86 and 42/86), Law on Land for Construction (Official Gazette SAP Kosovo No 14/80 and 42/86), Law on Registration of Real Properties in Social Ownership (Official Gazette SAP Kosovo No 37/71), Law on Transfer of Real Property (Official Gazette SAP Kosovo No 45/81, 29/86 and 28/88), UNMIK Regulation 2006/10, and UNMIK Regulation 2006/50.

62 See UNMIK Regulation 1999/01.

63 See UNMIK Regulation 1999/10.

64 Article 1.2, UNMIK Regulation 2000/60

65 See OIK Report, Osman Kozmaqi, Avni Kumnova, Fatmir Dragaj, Hamdi Zenelaj and Asim Rragoni against the HPD. See also OIK Report, Hatixhe Rexhaj Avdyli against the HPD, available at www.ombudspersonkosovo.org.

It should be stressed that both HPD and HPCC were composed of a mixture of international and local staff members. Since international members came from different countries, they often faced difficulties in identifying legal gaps in an 'improvised law', particularly regarding discriminatory provisions that posed serious obstacles to the rule of law.[66] Moreover, local members who only experienced the old communist regime were totally unfamiliar with international human rights law.[67]

Although it was expected to follow procedural rules akin to the court and uphold the principles of fair trial, the procedure before the HPCC was purely administrative and lacked transparency. While the initial phase before the HPD was foreseen to be of an administrative nature, the proceedings and adjudication of the claims before the HPCC required a court-like approach.

The manner in which these proceedings were handled clearly shows that the HPCC failed to uphold basic principles of a fair trial.

Such situations have created significant problems for both claimants and respondents. Many of them have approached the Ombudsperson Institution to seek redress. Most of the complaints brought before the Institution involved the length of the proceedings, the delays in the delivering of decisions made by the HPPC, the non-enforcement of the final decisions and discrimination. In the view of the Ombudsperson, the delays caused during the deliberation made the entire process ineffective.[68]

The roughness of this process became even more evident when it came to its execution.[69] The decisions were executed with delays because the HPD/HPCC lacked funds to employ eviction officers entitled to execute the eviction.[70] It frequently happened that illegal occupants of apartments/houses that were once

66 See D. Marchal and S. Inglis, loc. cit. n. 27, at pp. 97. Authors mainly refer to the international judges who are acting pursuant to UNMIK Regulation No. 2000/64; however the same should apply to the HPD and HPCC panel.

67 Kosovo did not have an Anti –Discrimination Law until 2005 and as such society including the judiciary was not familiar with issues involving discrimination. Consequently, this also influenced the work of the HPD and HPCC. The lack of human rights knowledge and the complexity of the existing law might have led to the difficulties and eventual errors in determination of presumption of the discrimination during the claim proceedings.

68 Ombudsperson Institution in Kosovo, *Fourth Annual Report* (2003–2004) addressed to the Acting Special Representative of the Secretary General of the United Nations, p. 23, available at www.ombudspersonkosovo.org.

69 Most of the complaints involved the length of the proceedings and the issues related to discrimination. See reports, *N. Korca against HPD* issued on 24 September 2004; *Ismet Ukqa and others against HPD*, issued on 12 November 2004; *Jusuf Gashi and others against HPD*, issued on 16 November 2004.

70 L. Carlowitz, 'Settling Property Issues in Complex Peace Operations: The CRPC in Bosnia and Herzegovina and the HPD/CC in Kosovo', 17 *Leiden Journal of International Law* (2004) p. 612.

evicted, later came back to threaten the rightful owners, or in the worst cases to burn or destroy the apartments or houses.[71] Moreover, in many cases, the eviction was delayed for security reasons.

Such ineffectiveness could be blamed on the failure of UNMIK Regulation 2000/60 on Residential Property Claims and the Rules of Procedure and Evidence of the HPD and HPCC to provide that the execution of HPD decisions would be 'thwarted in such a tenuous and lawless manner'.[72]

According to the OIK the inability to efficiently respond to the claims of the rightful owners to repossess their property jeopardises the effectiveness of the entire mechanism.[73]

Bearing in mind that the United Nations Administration had experienced similar problems in Bosnia with the Commission for Real Property Claims (CRPC), the question of the appropriateness of continuing with the same procedure in Kosovo arises.

It is argued that the mass claims mechanisms are an exception to the domestic courts for the benefit of justice in exceptional situations;[74] however, the Kosovo experience proves that this might not be an appropriate option.[75]

In the view of the legal experts, these bodies cannot ensure the sustainability of the decisions and secure the best long-term results, since there is a risk that a series of property determinations carried by the Commission will be later overturned by the future legal regime of Kosovo.[76]

Another issue raised by the OIK involving property rights was the promulgation of Regulation 2001/17 (Regulation 2001/17 on the registration of contracts for the sale of real property in specific Geographical Areas of Kosovo).[77]

---

71 Ombudsperson Institution in Kosovo, *Fourth Annual Report* (2003–2004), op. cit. n. 68, p. 23.

72 *Ibid.*

73 *Ibid.*

74 J.M. Arraiza and M. Moratti, 'Getting the Property Question Right: Legal Policy Dilemmas in Post-Conflict Property Restitution in Kosovo (1999–2009)', 21 *International Journal of Refugee Law* 3 (2009) at p 449.

75 B. Vagle and F. de Medina-Rosales, *An evaluation of the Housing and Property Directorate in Kosovo*, Nordem Report 12 (2006), pp. 10–11.

76 *Ibid.*, pp. 11–12.

77 The content of the above-mentioned regulation has been widely criticised by the Ombudsperson Institution. For a detailed analysis see Ombudsperson Institution in Kosovo, *Special Report No. 5 on Certain Aspects of UNMIK Regulation No. 2001/17 on the Registration of Contracts for the Sale of Real Property in Specific Geographical Areas of Kosovo (22 August 2001)*, 29 October 2001, available at www.ombudspersonkosovo.org/repository/docs/E4011029a.pdf.

During the period between 1999 and 2001 the number of sales of real properties owned by Serbs/Montenegrins has increased. Since many of them fled to Serbia and Montenegro they were trying to sell their property and start a new life there.

Such a rapid sale of property soon had become a matter of concern for the international community as it posed an obstacle to their aim of establishing a multicultural society in Kosovo. In order to prevent the Serbian/Montenegrin minority from leaving Kosovo territory UNMIK promulgated the above Regulation, which forbids the sale of property in areas inhabited by the Serbian/Montenegrins community. From a human rights perspective the regulation proved to be incompatible with the recognised human rights standards especially those enshrined in the European Convention on Human Rights. It directly violates the individual's right to a peaceful enjoyment of possession[78], the right to respect for private and family life and home[79], the right to choose one's place of residence[80], the prohibition against discrimination[81] and the prohibition against imposing restrictions on rights for a purpose other than those prescribed.[82]

An overall impression in terms of resolving property issues in postwar Kosovo proved to have not been effective and efficient enough. Although the whole matter has required urgent action, it showed that urgency in resolving a situation should not validate the shortening of legal paths as it might negatively affect standards of fairness.

B. PROTECTING THE RIGHT TO LIBERTY AND SECURITY OF PERSON

The following section aims at providing an overview on the SRSG's interference in the course of justice through examples of executive orders which directly affected individuals' right to liberty and security.

Protection of the liberty and security of person occupies an important place in human rights law. The European Court in its case law has stressed on several occasions that the fundamental importance of Article 5 of the ECHR is 'securing the rights of individuals in a democracy to be free from arbitrary detention at the hands of the authorities'.[83]

78 The right is guaranteed by Article 1 of the Additional Protocol to the Convention.
79 The right is guaranteed by Article 8 of the Convention.
80 The right is guaranteed by Article 2 of Protocol No. 4 of the Convention.
81 The right is guaranteed by Article 14 of the Convention.
82 The right is guaranteed by Article 18 of the Convention.
83 ECtHR, *Akdeniz and others v. Turkey*, Application No. 23954/94, *ECHR* (2001) p. 353.

The European Convention establishes clear grounds under which detention is permissible with a very narrow margin of appreciation for States. In this regard, to be lawful any and all detentions must fall within a scope of at least one of the 15 purposes listed in paragraph 1 of Article 5 and may only be justified if based on clearly established legal grounds of domestic law.

Bearing in mind the importance of the rights enshrined in this article, the Ombudsperson has strongly opposed the practice of detaining criminal suspects under Executive Orders issued by the SRSG.[84] Although now abandoned as a practice, executive orders have left a deep mark in the judicial system of Kosovo.

Several individuals against whom international prosecutors and judges found insufficient evidence to support their detention have been detained for many months solely on the strength of such orders.

The case of Afrim Zeqiri[85] is the best example for elaborating the executive orders practice.[86] On 29 May 2000, Afrim Zeqir had voluntarily reported to the police after being informed that an arrest order had been issued against him for being suspected of committing a murder. After being questioned by the UNMIK police he was arrested and sent to the detention centre in Bondsteel.[87] He was suspected of murdering three Serbs and attempted murder of two others in the village Cernica. From 29 May until 25 July he was held in detention, which was based on judicial orders. The investigating judge decided to suspend the case and terminate detention as it was found that there were no grounds for proceeding with the prosecution.[88]

Nevertheless, such a decision was not acceptable to the SRSG office, so the following day on 26 July, SRSG issued an Executive Order, ordering the continuation of the detention for 30 days[89], pursuant to UNMIK Regulation 1999/26.[90] On 18 August a second Executive Order was issued asking for another 30 days of detention.

84 See Ombudsperson Institution in Kosovo, *Special Report No. 3 on the Conformity of Deprivations of Liberty under 'Executive Orders' with Recognised International Standards* (29 June 2001), available at www.ombudspersonkosovo.org/repository/docs/E4010629a.pdf.

85 See UNMIK, Press release PR/394, 18 October 2000.

86 See Ombudsperson Institution in Kosovo, *Report on Afrim Zeqir against UNMIK*, 30 May 2003.

87 Bondsteel belongs to the American KFOR and is situated in the area of Ferizaj/Urosevac.

88 See Ombudsperson Institution in Kosovo, *Report on Afrim Zeqir against UNMIK*, op. cit. n. 86, at paras. 20–21.

89 Executive order was issued by SRSG, Mr. Bernard Kouchner.

90 See UNMIK, Regulation No. 1999/26 on the Extension of Periods of Pre-Trial Detention, 22 December 1999.

On the request of an international investigating prosecutor the international judge issued a decision permitting extension of detention without specifying the exact detention period or providing any information about available legal remedies to challenge the detention time.[91] Another series of Executive Orders were issued (13 January 2001 and 20 February 2001) and the reason for doing so was 'the threat that the accused poses to public order and safety'.[92]

After a series of Executive Orders and judicial decisions had been exhausted, Afrim Zeqiri was finally released on 11 February 2002 because of a lack of evidence against him.

In the OIK's report issued for the purpose of the above-mentioned case, it was made clear that 'the practice of keeping a person in detention because of a lack of clear rules governing the detainee's situation, whereby a person may be deprived of his liberty for an unlimited period without *judicial* authorisation, is incompatible with the principles of legal certainty and the protection from arbitrariness, which are common threads throughout the Convention and the rule of law.'[93]

However, the case of Afrim Zeqiri was not the only one where persons were detained based on Executive Orders. Almost the same procedure was applied in the case of Çelë Gashi, Avdyl Behluli and Jusuf Veliu, which involved the bombing of the ***Nis Express bus***[94] where around ten people were killed and a large number of others injured. The above-mentioned individuals were suspected to be involved in this incident. Three of them have been detained without clarification of the legal basis for the detentions and have remained in custody based on successive Executive Orders. In all three cases, the OIK found that their deprivation of liberty was not in conformity with Article 5 paras. 1, 3 and 4 of the Convention.[95]

As a result of being exposed to widespread criticism the SRSG ultimately issued a regulation establishing an international commission for review of extra-judicial detentions, including those which were subject to OIK's investigation.[96]

---

91 See Ombudsperson Institution in Kosovo, *Report on Afrim Zeqir against UNMIK*, op. cit. n. 86, at paras. 26–27.

92 *Ibid.*, at paras. 43–46.

93 *Ibid.*

94 On 16 February 2001, a bus driving from Gracanica to Niš was attacked with bombs near Podujeva and as a consequence ten persons were killed and several heavily injured.

95 See Ombudsperson Institution in Kosovo, *Report on Cele Gashi, Avdyl Behluli and Jusuf Veliu*, 12 September 2001.

96 See UNMIK, Regulation No. 2001/18 on the Establishment of a Detention Review Commission for Extra-Judicial Detentions based on Executive Orders, 25 August 2001.

Nevertheless, in the view of the OIK, the establishment and nature of this commission still failed to meet the relevant international human rights standards.[97] The situation lacked legal clarity, sufficient independence and a necessary guarantee that procedures would be conducted in an impartial manner.[98]

C. PROTECTING FREEDOM OF EXPRESSION

This section deals with the practice of restricting the right to freedom of expression in Kosovo and with the legal implications arising from this practice.

The expressing of free opinions, participating in public debates and maintaining conflicting opinions are fundamental elements of a democratic state. Such elements derive from the principles that govern the protection of human rights which form the basic foundation for the functioning of democracy.

For this very reason international human rights law calls upon states to undertake all measures necessary and ensure proper protection of the rights enshrined in international human rights law on behalf of its citizens. Among these, the right to freedom of expression is given the highest degree of protection.[99] Taken together with other supporting rights such as freedom of thought, freedom of association and the right to vote, it recognises the ability for both individuals and democratic society in general to form and express opinions, even when they prove to be controversial.[100]

To this extent, Article 10 of the European Convention on Human Rights covers a broad range of utterances/speeches. Political expression, which includes expression concerning the public interest, criticism of the government, and

---

97 See Ombudsperson Institution in Kosovo, *Special Report No. 4 on Certain Aspects of UNMIK Regulation No. 2001/18 on the Establishment of a Detention Review Commission for Extra-judicial Detentions Based on Executive Orders (25 August 2001)*, 12 September 2001, available at www.ombudspersonkosovo.org/repository/docs/E4010912a.pdf.

98 The Detention Review Commission was only used in one case. It convened on 20 September 2001 to determine whether the detention of three suspects in connection with the Niš bus bombing was justified. Following the review of available information, the panel determined that the detention of three suspects based on executive order was justified. It stated that there were 'reasonable grounds to suspect that each of the detained persons has committed a criminal act and that circumstances exist which suggest the strong possibility of flight'. No appeal was allowed against this decision

99 Universal Declaration of Human Rights (Article 19), International Covenant on Civil and Political Rights (Article 19), European Convention for the Protection of Human Rights and Fundamental Freedoms (Article 10).

100 N. Jayawickrama, *The Judicial Application of Human Rights Law* (Cambridge, Cambridge University Press 2002) p. 666.

criticism of politicians and public figures are the most protected forms of freedom of speech.[101]

The standard test of the justification or lawfulness of any interference with the right to respect for freedom of expression requires that a) any restriction must be clearly prescribed by law, b) the restriction must be justified by one of the legitimate aims recognised under the European Convention, and c) the restriction must be shown to be "necessary in a democratic society".[102]

The right to freedom of expression was widely violated during the period of the Milosevic regime. Together with other human rights it was conveyed as a Western product aiming to poison the socialist order and the principle of 'brotherhood and unity' on which the socialist order was established. By its mandate of exercising the role of a surrogate state, UNMIK is seen by the majority in Kosovo as a possibility to enhance individual liberty, democratic participation and social diversity.

In 2005, a group of young protesters from the VETEVENDOSJE movement[103] started to protest all over Kosovo in opposition to the decision of the international community to enter into negotiations with Serbia regarding Kosovo's future status. In this regard they organised peaceful protests the purposes of which were manifested in the slogans, '*Jo negociata – Vetëvendosje*' ('*No negotiations – Self Determination*') sprayed on the walls of public and private buildings.[104] From the start of their activities, activists of the movement have been subjected to ill-treatment and unwarranted arrests. The Ombudsperson Institution has from the outset expressed its concern and on several occasions requested the responsible authorities to refrain from such actions and undertake all possible measures to conduct investigations for alleged ill-treatment.[105] The OIK's investigation merely focused on examining whether measures taken by local police officers and UNMIK Police amount to an interference with the activists'

---

101 ECtHR, *Vgt Verein gegen Tierfabriken v. Switzerland,* Judgment of 28 June 2001. See also ECtHR, *Özgür Gündem v. Turkey,* Judgment of 16 March 2000. At para. 60 of this judgment, the Court states that '[t]he authorities of a democratic State must tolerate criticism, even if it may be regarded as provocative or insulting'.

102 ECtHR, *The Sunday Times v. United Kingdom,* Judgment of 27 April 1979, 2 *EHRR* (1979–1980) p. 245; ECtHR, *Handyside v. United Kingdom,* Judgment of 7 December 1976, 1 *EHRR* (1979–1980) p. 737.

103 The VETEVENDOSJE movement strongly opposed the negotiations as a form of resolving Kosovo status. They call on the international community to immediately recognise Kosovo's right to self-determination. More details about this movement can be found on the following website: www.levizjavetevendosje.org.

104 The slogans on the private buildings were written with the consent of the owners. Interview with Mr. Glauk Konjufca, member of the VETEVENDOSJE movement, November 2005.

105 See the letter that the ombudsperson sent to SRSG Mr. Soren Jessen Peterssen, 25 October 2005, available at www.ombudspersonkosovo.org.

right to freedom of expression under Article 10 of the European Convention on Human Rights.

In this regard it was found that in several places, the protesters were ill-treated and more than 100 of them arrested or alternatively received fines amounting to 150 euros.[106]

Legal grounds for police intervention and courts' deliberation have been found in the provisions of the Law on Public Peace and Order[107], which is known to the public to have always been in contradiction with international human rights standards as it directly violates the right to freedom of expression and the right to assembly.

In his letter to the SRSG, the Ombudsperson said:

> 'I believe that we all agree that the freedom of expression constitutes an essential foundation of each democratic society and is one of the basic conditions for its progress and for each individual's right to exercise the freedom of expression. Any interference with this right must pursue a legitimate aim and must be proportionate to this aim, due regard being given to the importance of freedom of expression.
>
> While I do agree that public authorities enjoy a certain margin of appreciation in assessing whether and to what extent to interfere with the exercise of the right to freedom of expression, I would like also to remind you that this margin of appreciation is very limited when talking about the freedom of political speech.
>
> In a democratic system, every person's right to express his/her political opinion, in particular regarding matters of common public interest, falls under the special protection of the freedom of speech guaranteed by Article 10 of the ECHR.'[108]

The aim was to make it clear to the authority that the writing of slogans on walls is a form by which activists have chosen to express their political opinion while taking part in the current public debate, and that such form lies solidly within the limits accepted in a democratic society. According to the OIK 'there is no difference whether it is expressed in the form chosen by the activists or in interviews with political leaders or during round table discussions' so the aim of the activity was to convey their opinion which is of an expressive content. Surprisingly, neither law enforcement agencies nor courts have so far considered the possibility of writing slogans on public buildings as amounting to an offence that constitutes damage to property.[109]

---

106 *Ibid.*

107 The law is very old; it was enacted in 1981 and contains provisions which are not consistent with international human rights law.

108 See the letter that the ombudsperson sent to SRSG Mr. Soren Jessen Peterssen, op. cit. n. 105.

109 *Ibid.*

Based on the inquiries conducted for this contribution the UNMIK Police Commissioner has shown a willingness to initiate investigations into this matter, but so far no concrete steps have been taken.[110]

Despite the intervention and recommendations issued by the OIK[111] in which he strongly requested that the SRSG intervene in this matter and take all necessary measures to stop further interference with the protestors' right to freedom of expression and any similar cases in the future which involve freedom of expression, unfortunately no positive steps have been taken and, as a consequence of such reluctance, the situation has worsened, as will be shown.

On 10 February 2007, a new demonstration was organised by the same movement, the main goal of which was to express resistance towards the proposal of the UN Special Envoy Mr. Martti Ahtisaari concerning the future status of Kosovo. As a result of excessive force used by both international and local police to disperse the group, two people were killed, 87 injured and several of them arrested including the leader of the movement.[112] The police intervention was widely criticised both inside and outside Kosovo and all parties pushed for an independent and impartial investigation to be carried out pursuant to the UN Principles on the Effective Prevention and Investigation of Extra-legal Arbitrary and Summary Executions.[113]

The OIK had urged the relevant authorities to establish an independent commission and ensure an independent and transparent investigation into this matter.[114] However, despite OIK's call as well as other entities – both national and international – to establish an independent commission to investigate the above-mentioned event, such a commission was never established. Instead, the investigations were carried out by an international prosecutor and later on by the Police Inspectorate of Kosovo (PIK).[115] Although investigations have been completed, no one has yet been brought to justice.[116]

---

110 Interview with Mr. Avni Hasani, the OIK lawyer (January 2007).

111 The case has been brought to the attention of the Public Prosecutor by the OIK asking him to initiate proceedings against police officers involved in ill-treatment. Interview with Mr. Avni Hasani, the OIK lawyer, January 2007, op. cit. n. 110.

112 Information taken from Daily Newspaper, *Gazeta Express* available at www.gazetaexpress.org.

113 Statement issued by Amnesty International, 15 February 2007.

114 Letter sent by the Acting Ombudsperson to the SRSG, dated 13 February 2007.

115 In this *Special Report 008/2007* (paras. 90, 91, 92) the OIK stated: 'the preliminary investigations initiated by PIK were conducted by police organ and thus can not be held to be completely independent'. It further notes: 'At the same time, the investigations conducted by an international prosecutor also cannot be deemed to be completely independent since international prosecutors and judges are appointed by the SRSG, who is also the final supervisor of the UNMIK Police and KPS'.

116 On 17 April 2007, the Special Prosecutor Robert Dean submitted his interim report to SRSG regarding the death and injuries of protestors during the 10 February 2007 protests. In his

In October 2006, parents of the victims submitted a complaint before the Human Rights Advisory Panel[117], which is still under examination pending a final decision.

IV. CONCLUSION

Having been continually exposed to a wide range of atrocities, not the least during Milosevic's brutal rule over Kosovo, many Albanians regarded the international community's instalment in Kosovo in 1999 as a salvation of the Albanian nation. The population perceives both UNMIK actors and KFOR forces as liberators, who not only brought peace and security but also democracy and human rights. For this reason, the Albanian community has never felt comfortable with reporting violations committed by their 'saviours', thinking that such actions may signal ingratitude, irritate the 'saviours', compel them to leave, and as such cause the widely feared return of the Belgrade regime.[118] Crucially, the population in Kosovo believes that human rights require obedience and somehow need to be deserved. This false thinking comes from a lack of awareness of the functioning of the human rights system.

OIK has promoted human rights in Kosovo but is nonetheless not an effective remedy for human rights violations. Regardless of the legal, financial and cultural settings in which OIK works and regardless of the current state of democratisation in today's Kosovo, OIK has been persistent in seeking ways to defend Kosovans' rights against unfair acts of both the UNMIK administration and local actors.

---

report Prosecutor Dean concluded that the Romanian gunners attached to the Romanian Police Unit (FPU) are responsible for the death of two and two seriously wounded persons. Nevertheless, despite his findings no criminal charges have been brought against the responsible persons. The only person who was brought to justice is the VETEVENDOSJE leader, Mr. Albin Kurti whose trial has been suspended due to collective refusal of Kosovan lawyers to act as Mr. Kurti's defence lawyer which came in support of Mr. Kurti's call issued upon his arrest, asking all Kosovan lawyers not to accept the court assignment in his case as he does not want to actively cooperate with the UNMIK's court. Mr. Kurti's trial has been perceived by the majority in Kosovo as politically motivated.

117 A Human Rights Advisory Panel was established in 2006 pursuant to UNMIK Regulation 2006/12 for the purpose of providing an effective means of redress for an alleged violation of human rights attributable to UNMIK. Established by UNMIK regulation and run by members appointed by SRSG and whose procedure will be subject to amendment by UNMIK, there is little hope that it can function independently. For more information see Human Rights Watch, *Report Better Late than Never*, June 2007.

118 Furthermore, the involvement of the international community in determining the future status of the territory has deepened a fear in society.

Being the only non-judicial mechanism for promoting human rights in Kosovo, the institution has been trying to enhance its sphere of activity from that of the transitional watchdog guarding against human rights abuses. It has been supervising with utmost care the activities of the UNMIK administration by trying to prevent them from violating the law. Although not having the authority to correct UNMIK official abuses, it at least raises it voice whenever it comes across a violation.

During the tenure of the International Ombudsperson, the institution was highly critical of UNMIK, and has contributed enormously towards a better understanding of UNMIK's mandate. Through its critical viewpoints, it tried to raise awareness among the population of ongoing violations and progressively stood to defend the rights of the victims.

The OIK was among the first to point to the negative effects of the immunity of international institutions upon the people of Kosovo. Through its commitment it is trying to make people understand that UNMIK cannot be perceived as an Almighty Authority but instead is called upon to promote and protect their rights.

It remains crucial that the new Ombudsperson continues to follow the paths built by the International Ombudsperson, is able to preserve its independence and act in an impartial manner, both for the sake of the citizens of Kosovo and the public respect for the local and international authorities administering it.[119]

---

119 The Institution was run by the Acting Ombudsperson since the departure of the International Ombudsperson in July 2005. In April 2009, after four failed attempts, the Kosovo Assembly finally appointed Mr. Sami Kurteshi as Ombudsperson.

PART IV.
ECONOMIC GOVERNANCE

ACCOUNTABILITY OF INTERNATIONAL ORGANISATIONS: AN ANALYSIS OF THE WORLD BANK'S INSPECTION PANEL

Rekha OLESCHAK-PILLAI*

> 'Large parts of the public no longer believe that their interests are represented in institutions such as the [...] World Bank [...] or that the institutions are adequately accountable for what they do.'[1]

Calls for accountability of international organisations are increasingly found in international legal and political discourse.[2] This contribution looks at one aspect of these calls for accountability, i.e. accountability of international organisations for human rights violations in development projects. Specifically, it seeks to examine to what extent the World Bank's Inspection Panel[3] constitutes an accountability mechanism under international law. The contention is that although the Inspection Panel is an innovative model of accountability in international law, it does not always have positive impacts on outcomes in bank-financed projects. This argument is supported by examining the role, reports and outcomes of four cases investigated by the Inspection Panel relating to India.

The first part of the contribution looks at the concept of accountability in international law and provides a short overview of various accountability mechanisms available. The second part of the contribution examines the World Bank[4] as an international organisation and its involvement in human rights

---

* Senior Research Fellow, Institute of Federalism, Fribourg, Switzerland. A first version of this contribution was presented at the International Conference on Accountability for Human Rights Violations by International Organisations, Brussels March 2007. The author extends heartfelt gratitude to Prof. Dr. Anne van Aaken and participants at the Conference for comments and questions. Internet pages last visited in August 2009.

1 UNDP, *Human Development Report* (New York, Oxford University Press 2002) p. 112.

2 See ILA, Committee on the Accountability of International Organisations, *Third Report* (2002); K. Wellens, *Remedies Against International Organisations* (Cambridge, Cambridge University Press 2002).

3 Hereafter referred to as the Inspection Panel or the Panel.

4 The World Bank group consists of five Organisations, the International Bank for Reconstruction and Development (IBRD) and the International Development Association (IDA); the International Finance Corporation (IFC); the Multilateral Investment Guarantee Agency (MIGA); and the International Centre for Settlement of Investment Disputes (ICSID).

abuses. The third part introduces the Inspection Panel, its functioning, limitations and how it is perceived in international legal discourse. This section will also examine the Operational Standards of the World Bank, which form the normative basis of the Inspection Panel's work. The fourth part examines each of these previous investigations in the light of specific case-studies and attempts to find the common thread running through all the cases. The final section extracts the outcomes in the cases examined in order shed light on these unique, yet similar effects.

I. ACCOUNTABILITY IN INTERNATIONAL LAW

In international legal discourse the term 'accountability'[5] has been applied to: individuals[6], States[7], non-governmental organisations[8], multinational corporations[9], peace support operations[10] as well as international organisations.[11] However, the concept itself is not a well-developed one in international law. To a minimal degree, accountability may be referred to as 'the various norms, practices, and institutions whose purpose is to hold public officials (and other bodies) responsible for their actions and for the outcomes of those actions.'[12] According

Since the Inspection Panel's mandate is limited to the activities of the International Development Association (IDA) and International Bank for Reconstruction and Development (IBRD), the term World Bank in this contribution refers to either IDA or IBRD or both. See *infra* n. 32 and related text.

5 See generally D. Held and M. Koenig-Archibugi, *Global Governance and Public Accountability* (Malden, Blackwell Publishing 2005).

6 See S. Ratner and J. Abrams, *Accountability for Human Rights Atrocities in International Law: Beyond the Nuremberg Legacy*, 2nd ed. (Oxford, Oxford University Press 2001).

7 See Statement by the American Civil Liberties Union to the 87th Session of the Human Rights Committee regarding the US Government Compliance with the International Covenant on Civil and Political Rights, available at www.aclu.org/files/images/asset_upload_file321_26097.pdf.

8 See S. Charnovitz, *Accountability of Nongovernmental Organizations (NGOs) in Global Governance*, (GWU Law School Public Law Research Paper No. 145), April 2005, available at http://papers.ssrn.com/sol3/papers.cfm?abstract_id=716381.

9 See O. de Schütter, 'The Accountability Of Multinationals For Human Rights Violations In European Law', in P. Alston, ed., *Non-State Actors and Human Rights* (Oxford, Oxford University Press 2005); D. Weissbrodt and M. Kruger, 'Human Rights Responsibilities of Businesses as Non-State Actors', in P. Alston, ed., *Non-State Actors and Human Rights* (Oxford, Oxford University Press 2005).

10 See M. C. Zwanenburg, *Accountability of Peace Support Operations* (Leiden, Martinus Nijhoff Publishers 2005); L. Cameron, *Accountability of International Organisations Engaged in the Administration of Territory* (Geneva, University Centre for International Humanitarian Law), 13 February 2006, available at www.ucihl.org/teaching/Henry_Duannt_2006b_LCameron.pdf.

11 See K. Wellens, op. cit. n. 2; A. Clapham, *Human Rights Obligations of Non-State Actors* (Oxford, Oxford University Press 2006).

12 A. Schedler, 'Conceptualizing Accountability', in A. Schedler, L. Diamond and M.F. Plattner, eds., *The Self-Restraining State: Power and Accountability in the New Democracies* (Boulder, CO, Lynne Rienner 1999) p. 14.

to the International Law Association, '[p]ower entails accountability; that is the duty to account for its exercise'.[13] Thus, the notion of accountability relates to a broader concept than the concept of 'responsibility'[14] or of 'liability'[15] under international law.

There are various accountability mechanisms in the international arena. Those relating to accountability of individuals include the International Criminal Court[16], the International Criminal Tribunal for Former Yugoslavia[17] and the International Criminal Tribunal for Rwanda.[18] Responsibilities of states *vis-à-vis* individuals are dealt with by regional human rights bodies[19] and international human rights bodies.[20]

Accountability mechanisms of international organisations *vis-à-vis* non-state actors are a new development. These are the accountability mechanisms at multilateral development banks, of which the World Bank's Inspection Panel is one example. This type of accountability has been termed 'judicial-style accountability'.[21] Such mechanisms function in a judicial style, in that they can be approached by interested actors; a petition is submitted by which an investigation may be conducted. However, the Inspection Panel is not a judicial organ and its independence is not absolute as it requires permission from the Board to conduct an investigation. Furthermore, its findings are not binding on the Bank and it does not have follow-up or monitoring powers.

13 ILA, *Third Report*, op. cit. n. 2, at p. 2.

14 For example the concept of state responsibility under international law refers to responsibility of states for breach of an international obligation. There are clearly defined parameters for violations or breaches and remedies. See International Law Commission, *Draft Articles on State Responsibility*, Official Records of the General Assembly, Fifty-sixth Session, Supplement No. 10, A/56/10, 2001, available at www.un.org/documents/ga/docs/56/a5610.pdf.

15 Liability under international law is usually applied in international environmental law. See ILC's Draft principles on the allocation of loss in the case of transboundary harm arising out of hazardous activities, with commentaries (2006), available at http://untreaty.un.org/ilc/texts/instruments/english/draft%20articles/9_10_2006.pdf.

16 Set up under the Rome Statute of the International Criminal Court, A/CONF.183/9.

17 Set up under the Statute of the International Criminal Tribunal for the Former Yugoslavia.

18 Set up under the Statute of the International Criminal Tribunal for Rwanda.

19 The European Court of Human Rights, the Inter-American Court of Human Rights, the African Commission and recently established African Court on Human Rights.

20 The Human Rights Committee which monitors the implementation of the International Covenant on Civil and Political Rights, the Committee Against Torture (Convention on the Prevention of Torture); the Committee on the Elimination of Racial Discrimination (Convention on the Elimination of All Forms of Racial Discrimination); Committee on the Elimination of Discrimination against Women (Convention on the Elimination of all Forms of Discrimination Against Women); Committee on the Rights of the Child (Convention on the Rights of the Child); Committee on Migrant Workers (International Convention on the Protection of the Rights of All Migrant Workers and their Families).

21 See UNDP, *Human Development Report*, op. cit. n. 1, at p. 116.

A. ACCOUNTABILITY OF INTERNATIONAL ORGANISATIONS

The necessity for accountability of international organisations initially came about due to the increasing proliferation of international organisations and their involvement in a large number of areas and activities, which subsequently increased the likelihood of international organisations being involved in human rights violations. This development, coupled with the near-total immunity afforded to them started being questioned by international civil society.[22] As the ILA's Committee on the Accountability of International Organisations opined: '[t]here is no reason at all, as a matter of principle, why [international Organisations] could or should not be held accountable for disadvantages and repercussions resulting from their acts or omissions and normally based upon the authority and power granted to them.'[23]

As international organisations hold international personality, it necessarily follows that they too have international obligations. This was stated by the International Court of Justice in its advisory opinion in the *Reparations case*[24], and reiterated in its *Advisory Opinion in the WHO and Egypt* case[25], where it held that: 'International Organizations are subjects of international law and, as such, are bound by any obligations incumbent upon them under general rules of international law, under their constitutions or under international agreements to which they are parties.'

Whereas the law relating to State responsibility is relatively well-developed[26], the law relating to the responsibility of international organisations[27] is less developed and the concept of "accountability" of international organisations even less so.[28] The International Law Commission has adopted the topic of responsibility of

22 See K. Wellens, 'Fragmentation Of International Law And Establishing An Accountability Regime For International Organizations: The Role Of The Judiciary In Closing The Gap', 25 *Michigan Journal of International Law* (2004) pp. 1159–1182.

23 ILA, Committee on the Accountability of International Organisations, *First Report* (1998) p. 14.

24 ICJ, *Reparation for Injuries Suffered in the Service of the United Nations*, Advisory Opinion, *ICJ Rep.* (1949) p. 173.

25 ICJ, *Interpretation of the Agreement of 25 March 1951 Between the WHO and Egypt*, Advisory Opinion, *ICJ Rep.* (1980), pp. 89–90.

26 See ILC, *Articles on Responsibility of States for Internationally Wrongful Acts*, available at http://untreaty.un.org/ilc/texts/instruments/english/draft%20articles/9_6_2001.pdf.

27 The International Law Commission is working on the topic of responsibility of international Organizations. As matters stand at present, see International Law Commission, *Report of the Sixty-first session (4 May to 5 June and 6 July to 7 August 2009)*, UN Doc. A/64/10, chapter IV, paras. 31–51.

28 See ILA, *First Report*, op. cit. n. 23 and ILA, *Third Report*, op. cit. n. 2; K. Wellens, 'The Primary Model Rules of Accountability of International Organisations: the Principles and Rules Governing the Conduct or the Yardsticks for Their Accountability', in N. Blokker and

international organisations in its programme of work and the International Law Association has recently published its report on the accountability of international organizations.[29] These developments demonstrate a weakening of the argument that international organisations need to have absolute immunity to carry out their functions and a shift in the notion that the concept of 'power entails responsibility' is inapplicable to international organisations.

As the concept of accountability is broader than that of 'responsibility'[30] under international law, this distinction can problematise putting into operation such a concept. Thus, it is useful to take the approach adopted by Barberis in operationalising accountability. He asks five questions to make the concept workable, namely:

- Who is accountable;
- For what;
- To whom;
- Through what mechanisms; and
- With what kind of accountability outcomes[31]

This contribution will use this framework to find out whether the World Bank's Inspection Panel constitutes an effective accountability mechanism.

Before embarking on this task it would be pertinent to note the limitations of the contribution: it looks only at a few cases and does not provide a comprehensive study of all the cases which have been investigated by the Inspection Panel. This is not an empirical study, but illustrates the limitations of the Panel through specific case-studies. Further, the activities of the International Finance Corporation and Multilateral Investment Guarantee Agency or the International Centre for the Settlement of Investment Disputes are not under consideration in this contribution. This is due to the fact that the Inspection Panel's work itself is limited to activities arising out of IDA and IBRD operations.[32]

H.G. Schermers, eds., *Proliferation of International Organizations* (The Hague-London-Boston, Kluwer Law International 2001) p. 434.

29 The ILA report is very broad-based and uses a framework which unfortunately is quite difficult to use and operationalise.

30 See *supra* n. 14; see also ILC, *Report of the Fifty-fifth session*, UN Doc. A/58/10 (2003) and ILC, *Report of the Fifty-eighth session*, UN Doc. A/61/10) (2006).

31 P. Barberis, 'The New Public Management and a New Accountability', 76 *Administration* (1998) pp. 451–470, at p. 466.

32 World Bank, Resolutions Nos. IBRD 93–10 and IDA 93–6 of September 1993 establishing the Inspection Panel are only applicable to the IDA and IBRD. Hereafter referred to as the "Resolution".

Returning again to Barberis' framework to the World Bank, one can answer the above questions as follows:

B. WHO IS ACCOUNTABLE?

The World Bank, namely the IDA and IBRD[33] should be held accountable. Although the Bank consists of five difference institutions, the IDA and IBRD are involved in project lending which directly affects people.[34]

C. FOR WHAT?

The Bank should be held accountable for violations of human rights under the International Bill of Rights.[35] In addition to the principle of non-intervention as enshrined in Article 2(4) of the UN Charter[36], the World Bank relies on its Articles of Agreement[37] to assert its independence of human rights considerations defined as 'political considerations'[38] and its reliance only on economic rationale in its activities. As many authors have opined, this contention does not hold much water.[39] In spite of statements by the Bank concerning human rights[40], it has consistently maintained the position that, as non-members to the 1966 human rights covenants and other human rights treaties, it is not bound by these

33 For the reason mentioned above.

34 The IFC also is involved in such lending, but since it has its own compliance mechanism, the Ombudsman, it is not taken into consideration in this contribution.

35 The International Bill of Rights: The Universal Declaration of Human Rights; the International Covenant on Civil and Political Rights; the International Covenant on Economic Social and Cultural Rights and the First Optional Protocol to the ICCPR.

36 Article 2(4) of the Charter states: 'All Members shall refrain in their international relations from the threat or use of force against the territorial integrity or political independence of any state, or in any other manner inconsistent with the Purposes of the United Nations.'

37 Section 10 of the Articles of Agreement of the IBRD states 'The Bank and its officers shall not interfere in the political affairs of any member; nor shall they be influenced in their decisions by the political character of the member or members concerned. Only economic considerations shall be relevant to their decisions, and these considerations shall be weighed impartially in order to achieve the purposes stated in Article I.' Similarly, Section 6 of the Articles of Agreement of the IDA prohibits the Bank from engaging in any political activity.

38 See I.F.I. Shihata, 'Democracy and Development', 46 *International and Comparative Law Quarterly* (1997) pp. 635–643.

39 See S.I. Skogly, 'Structural Adjustment and Development: Human Rights – An Agenda for Change', 15(4) *Human Rights Quarterly* (1993) pp. 751–778; S.I. Skogly, *The Human Rights Obligations of the World Bank and the International Monetary Fund* (London, Cavendish 2001); A. Clapham, op. cit. n. 11; D. Clark, 'The World Bank and Human Rights: The Need for Greater Accountability', 15 *Harvard Human Rights Law Journal* (2002) p. 205.

40 World Bank, *Development and Human Rights: the Role of the World Bank* (Washington DC 1998).

instruments.[41] However, a change in this attitude within the Bank regarding its role in upholding human rights is becoming visible.[42] For example, with regard to the Chad-Cameroon pipeline, the Management acknowledged that the Bank was 'concerned by human rights in Chad as elsewhere', even though 'its mandate [did] not extend to political human rights.'[43] Further, even the Inspection Panel found the need to speak of the general human rights situation in the country.[44]

However, if one were to take a very narrow position (without getting into the debate of whether the Bank is bound by human rights obligations[45] or not) and only demand compliance with the Bank's internal policies, then the Bank is to be held accountable for non-compliance with Bank policies.

D. TO WHOM?

To answer the question to whom the Bank should be accountable, one needs to take into consideration the main actors involved. They are:

- donor countries,
- borrowing countries,
- people affected by Bank projects.

As an international organisation, the World Bank is accountable to its Member States.[46] Member States can influence policies and decisions of the World Bank.[47]

---

41 See I.F.I. Shihata, 'The World Bank and Human Rights', 17 *Denver Journal of International Law and Policy* (1989) p. 40; R. Kneller, 'Human rights, Politics, and the Multilateral Development Bank', 6 *Yale Studies in World Public Order* (1980) p. 361.

42 In his note 'The Legal Aspects of the World Bank's Work on Human Rights', Roberto Dañino, Former Senior Vice President and General Counsel, The World Bank (2003–2006) takes the position that 'human rights are at the very core of the World Bank's mandate'. R. Dañino, *The Legal Aspects of the World Bank's Work on Human Rights* (2006), available at www.devoutreach.com/oct06/SpecialReport/tabid/1518/Default.aspx.

43 World Bank Inspection Panel, Investigation Report, Cameroon: Petroleum Development and Pipeline Project (Loan No. 7020-CM) and Petroleum Environment Capacity Enhancement (CAPECE) Project (Credit No. 3372-CM) (May 2003) p. 74.

44 World Bank Inspection Panel, Investigation Report op. cit. n. 43, at p. 76.

45 See A. Reinisch, 'Securing the Accountability of International Organizations', 7 *Global Governance* (2001) p. 131; P. Armstrong, 'Human rights and Multilateral Development Banks: Governance Concerns in Decision Making', 88 *American Society of International Law Proceedings* (1994) p. 271; D.D. Bradlow, 'The World Bank, the IMF and Human Rights', 6 *Transnational Law and Contemporary Problems* (1996) p. 47; S. Schlemmer-Schulte, 'The World Bank and Human Rights', 4 *Austrian review of International and European Law* (1999) p. 230; S.I. Skogly, op. cit. n. 39.

46 The IBRD has 188 member countries while the IDA has 166 member countries.

47 The voting power at the Bank is skewed in favour of seven countries, the US; Japan, France, UK; Saudi Arabia, Germany and the Russian Federation which account for 46% of the voting power.

Another constituency involved is the borrowing countries. These are usually bound by the international agreements with the Bank. By virtue of being a specialised agency of the UN and of its Articles of Agreement[48], the Bank enjoys immunity from challenges by its Member States. Therefore, as it is impossible (even in theory) to challenge the Bank, there have been no incidents where these states have challenged the Bank in any domestic or international fora. No legal challenges are possible against officials of the Bank, except in cases where the Bank waives its immunity.[49] The final group of actors is people affected by projects of the Bank. Any accountability towards people affected negatively by decisions and projects of the World Bank was not even contemplated till the 1990s. However, increasing pressure and various scandals did open up the Bank to external scrutiny and the setting up of the Inspection Panel was one step in giving third parties access to demand accountability.

E. BY WHAT MECHANISMS?

Since this contribution only deals with one constituency – the people affected by Bank project – only the operations of the Inspection Panel shall be examined.

F. WITH WHAT OUTCOMES?

Outcomes of a normal judicial procedure would be the redress of grievances as well as adequate reparation. However, it is this final stage which in my opinion is the main shortcoming of the Inspection Panel. Thus, to showcase the limitations of the Inspection Panel, four reports of the Panel shall be examined.

II. WORLD BANK AND HUMAN RIGHTS VIOLATIONS

The World Bank's involvement in financing infrastructure projects puts it at the forefront of human rights violations in development projects.[50] The Sardar

---

48 Article VII of IBRD; Article VIII of IDA.

49 Article VIII, section 8 of the IDA; Article VII, section 8 of the IBRD.

50 For accounts of various projects involving the Bank and human rights violations see B. Rich, *Mortgaging The Earth: The World Bank, Environmental Impoverishment, And The Crisis Of Development* (Boston, Beacon Press 1994); D. Djiraibe, K. Horta and S. Nguiffo, 'Access to Justice from Local Village to Global Boardroom: An Experience in International Accountability The World Bank Inspection Panel and the Chad-Cameroon Oil and Pipeline Project' (2004), available at www.edf.org/documents/4065_AccessToJustice.pdf; K. Horta, 'Rhetoric and Reality: Human Rights and the World Bank', 15 *Harvard Human Rights Journal* (2002) p. 227; G. Brodnig, *The World Bank and Human Rights: Mission Impossible?* (Carr

Sarovar Dam Project in India[51], the Polonoroeste Project in Brazil[52], the Chixoy Dam[53] in Guatemala are few examples of projects where the World Bank was involved, of which carried with it massive human rights violations. It is not contended that the Bank as such is engaged in human rights violations. However, by financing projects in which the host state is involved in routine human rights violations – for example, India's record of forced evictions is very high and its record of resettlement of displaced populations is pathetically low – the Bank exposes itself to being complicit in these human rights violations. Further, it is submitted that even if the Bank cannot act as a police force and force host states to comply with certain minimum standards of treatment – either by not condemning these violations or by overlooking such violations during the implementation of its projects – the Bank thus accrues secondary responsibility for its host state's activities.

III. INSPECTION PANEL

The World Bank Inspection Panel[54] was established by the board of the World Bank in 1993[55] after facing harsh criticism over the Sardar Sarovar Dam[56] project in India and initiatives for reforms and greater accountability within the World Bank.[57] The Inspection Panel's formal mandate is to make specific

Center for Human Rights Policy Working Paper T-01-05) available at www.ksg.harvard.edu/cchrp/Web%20Working%20Papers/BrodnigHR&WorldBank.pdf.

51 For different problems relating to the Sardar Sarovar Project see W. Fischer, *Toward Sustainable Development? Struggling Over India's Narmada River* (New York, M.E. Sharpe 1995) and for the Bank's role and involvement see B. Morse and T. Berger, *Sardar Sarovar: Report of the Independent Review.* (Ottawa, Resources Futures International 1992).

52 B. Rich, op. cit. n. 50, at pp. 26–28.

53 See C. Chen, 'The Chixoy Dam Case: Submission to the World Commission on Dams' (1999), available at www.dams.org/kbase/submissions/showsub.php?rec=soc073; see also Petition submitted to the Inter-American Commission on Human Rights by the Centre on Housing Rights and Evictions (COHRE) on behalf of the Survivors of the Río Negro community and similarly situated communities in Guatemala (Petitioners) online at www.cohre.org/store/attachments/G4b-Chixoy_Petition.pdf.

54 For more information see, www.worldbank.org/inspectionpanel.

55 Resolution of the Executive Directors establishing the Inspection Panel for the International Bank for Reconstruction and Development (IBRD) (No. 93-10) and the International Development Association (IDA) (No. IDA 93-6), Docs. Sec M93-988 (IBRD) and Sec M93-313 (IDA) of 22 September 1993, available at www.worldbank.org. For a detailed account of the setting up of the Panel, see A. Umana, *The World Bank Inspection Panel: The First Four Years (1994–1998)* (Washington D.C.,The World Bank 1998); K. Treakle, *Accountability at the World Bank, What does it Take? Lessons from the Yacyreta Hydroelectric Project Argentina/Paraguay* (Washington D.C., Bank Information Center 1998) and D. Clark & D. Hunter, *The World Bank Inspection Panel: Amplifying Citizen Voices for Sustainable Development* (Washington D.C., Center for International Environmental Law 1998).

56 See I.F.I. Shihata, loc. cit. n. 38, at pp.635–643 and references therein.

57 The Wapenhans Report, authored by a Bank vice-president Willi Wapenhans, criticised the Bank's pervasive 'culture of approval', in which the incentive structure encouraged staff to

recommendations to the Bank's board arising from complaints by people claiming to suffer of materially adverse effects from the failure by the Bank to follow its operational policies and procedures with respect to the design, appraisal, or implementation of a project. The panel comprises of three members nominated by the President. The basic operating procedure of the Panel is guided by Bank Resolution 93–10 and the Inspection Panel Operating Procedures.[58]

There are several ways of bringing a claim to the Inspection Panel. An 'affected party', namely two project-affected persons, may bring a claim to the Inspection panel alleging violation of the Bank's internal policies in a bank-funded project on its own behalf.[59] Or a local representative, for example an NGO may bring a claim on behalf of project-affected people.[60] In exceptional circumstances, an international NGO may bring a claim, given that a local representative is unable to do so and with proof of authorisation.[61] A claim may also be brought by an Executive Director who may, 'in special cases of serious alleged violations of such policies and procedures',[62] request the Inspection Panel for an investigation. To be eligible for investigation, a request must fulfil certain criteria[63]:

1. they are two or more people with common interests or concerns living in a country or an area affected by a Bank-financed project;
2. the Bank has violated its policies and procedures, and they have or are likely to suffer material adverse effects as a result of those policy violations;
3. they have attempted to raise their concerns with Bank Management and are not satisfied with the response;

move large amounts of money quickly without adequate attention to the social and environmental implications of projects. See D. Clark, *Citizens Guide To The World bank Inspection Panel*, 2nd ed., (Washington D.C., Center for International Environmental Law 1999); See also J. Fox and L. David Brown, eds., *The Struggle for Accountability: The World Bank, NGOs and Grassroots Movements* (Cambridge, MIT Press 1998); I.F.I. Shihata, 'The World Bank Inspection Panel: Its Historic, Legal and Operational Aspects', in G. Alfredsson and R. Ring, eds., *The Inspection Panel of the World Bank: A Different Complaints Procedure* (The Hague-London-Boston, Martinus Nijhoff Publishers 2001) pp. 7–46.

58 Resolution of the Executive Directors establishing the Inspection Panel, op. cit. n. 55.

59 Section II A. (4) of the Resolution.

60 Such claims will be admitted only with proper authorisation.

61 This is extremely restricted as the Board must approve of the non-local or international representative (Section VI, 39 of the Resolution). This provision is probably intended to ensure that international NGOs (mostly Northern ones) do not take up claims on behalf of project-affected people. This factor could be one which extremely restricts the number of petitions being filed. One example of where a northern NGO was allowed to bring a request was in the China Western Poverty Reduction Project. In this case, the claim was filed by a US-based NGO acting on behalf of affected people in Tibet and the names were kept confidential because of fear of reprisals.

62 Section II A. (d) of the Resolution.

63 Section I.1 and 2 of the Resolution.

4. and the project is under consideration or has been approved by the Bank, and the loan has not yet been substantially disbursed.[64]

The Inspection Panel makes a preliminary assessment of the complaint and also takes into account the management's responses to the complaint.[65] The Panel can then recommend to the executive board that it conducts a full investigation. It is within the board's powers to launch full investigations and to make final decisions based on the findings of the panel and the managements' recommendations. Although the Panel has been created as an independent body, its powers are quite restricted. For example, it can only undertake site visits with prior consent of the host country.[66] In the 1999 Clarification of the Board's Second Review of the Inspection Panel, the Board found it necessary to mention that '[t]he Panel's methods of investigation should not create the impression that it is investigating the borrower's performance.' This statement reflects the dilemma faced by the Panel. A strict separation of analysis of the Bank's performance (whether by acts or omissions) without looking at the performance of the Borrower is a difficult if not impossible task.

A. PERCEPTIONS IN INTERNATIONAL LEGAL DISCOURSE

The Inspection Panel has received much attention in international legal discourse.[67] Benedict Kingsbury's illuminating article perceives the Inspection Panel as 'an innovative means of introducing a degree of independent scrutiny and public accountability for compliance by an international agency with its own

---

64 For example, the Sardar Sarovar Dam Project would not be eligible for consideration by the World Bank because the funding has stopped, even though compliance with the resettlement policies is non-existent.

65 The Management is required to respond to the Panel's request for information regarding a request for inspection. It needs to provide evidence that:
   i. it has complied with the relevant Bank operational policies and procedures; or that
   ii. there are serious failures attributable exclusively to its own actions or omissions in complying, but that it intends to comply with the relevant policies and procedures; or that
   iii. the serious failures that may exist are exclusively attributable to the borrower or to other factors external to the Bank; or that
   iv. the serious failures that may exist are attributable both to the Bank's non-compliance with the relevant operational policies and procedures and to the borrower or other external factors. Section 3 of 1999 Clarification of the Board's Second Review.

66 Those borrowers who certainly do not want an investigation of the reality on ground would not grant permission for the Panel members to visit the affected people.

67 D. Hunter and L. Udall, *The World Bank's Inspection Panel: Will it Increase Accountability?*, available at www.ciel.org/Publications/issue1.html; D.D. Bradlow, 'International Organizations and Private Complaints: The Case of the World Bank Inspection Panel', 34 *Virginia Journal of International Law* (1994) p. 553.

policies.'[68] The Panel is innovative due to the fact that it allows direct claims from affected people and is the first international organisation to do so.[69] It has been said to have 'fundamentally altered the relationship between international organizations on the one hand and private individuals and groups on the other.'[70] Other scholars, notably those associated with the World Bank have been consistent in pointing out that the Inspection Panel does not represent 'a legal remedy mechanism through which positions described in the Bank's policies or rights [...] could be enforced against the Bank.'[71] On the contrary, they argue that it does provide a mechanism for increased scrutiny of bank activities and its operations.[72]

Other multilateral organisations involved in development work adopt and emulate World Bank practices. Various multilateral development banks have followed the example of the World Bank and created similar accountability mechanisms.[73] International civil society seems to be sceptical about the Inspection Panel and its effectiveness.[74] The fact that 58 requests for inspection have been filed shows that affected people are using the mechanism.[75] However, the question is – how effective is this mechanism?

68 B. Kingsbury, 'Operational Policies of International Institutions as Part of the Law-Making Process: The World Bank and Indigenous Peoples', in G.S. Goodwin-Gill and S. Talmon, eds., *The Reality of International Law: Essays in Honour of Ian Brownlie* (Oxford, Clarendon Press 1999) pp. 323–342.

69 See also L. Boisson de Chazournes, 'Compliance with International Standards: The Contribution of the World Bank's Inspection Panel', in G. Alfredsson and R. Ring, eds., *The Inspection Panel of the World Bank: A Different Complaints Procedure* (The Hague-London-Boston, Martinus Nijhoff Publishers 2001) pp. 67–86.

70 E. Suzuki and S. Nanwani, 'Responsibility Of International Organizations: The Accountability Mechanisms Of Multilateral Development Banks', 27 *Michigan Journal of International Law* (2005), p. 177, at p. 188.

71 S. Schlemmer-Schulte, 'The World Bank Inspection Panel: A Record Of The First International Accountability Mechanism and Its Role for Human Rights', *Human Rights Brief* 6 No. 2 (1998), available at www.wcl.american.edu.

72 See I.F.I. Shihata, 'Human Rights, Development, and International Financial Institutions', in I.F.I. Shihata, *The World Bank in a Changing World: Selected Essays and Lectures,* Volume II (The Hague, Martinus Nijhoff Publishers, 1995).

73 Asian Development Bank; Inter-American Development Bank, the African Development Bank, European Bank for Reconstruction and Development.

74 J. Fox and L. D. Brown, op. cit. n. 57.

75 Of course given the extend to which the IDA and IBRD are involved in project financing, this is probably not a great number. But as the UNDP has noted, 'not everyone is in a equal position to use the procedures-not just in lodging formal complaints but also in ensuring that the threat of such actions makes officials mindful of their powers and their Organizations' rules'. UNDP, *Human Development Report*, op. cit. n. 1, at p. 117; See also J. Fox, 'The World Bank Inspection Panel: Lessons from the First Five Years', 6 *Global Governance* (2000) p. 279, at p. 300 for difficulties related to actual use of the Panel as an accountability mechanism.

B. OPERATIONAL STANDARDS AND POLICIES

The Inspection Panel's mandate is limited to examining whether operational policies and procedures of the World Bank have been complied with.[76] These policies and procedures that are based upon different subject matters nonetheless apply to all projects funded by the World Bank.[77] These operational policies reflect a growing need for the inclusion of social and environmental criteria into decision-making which was earlier restricted to only technical details. Earlier, environmental and social impact assessments were rarely carried out and did not play a major role in decision making of whether or not to fund the project. However, the Bank faced criticisms, which rested mainly on the areas of destruction of the environment and of development-induced displacement. It was accused of 'bankrolling disasters.'[78] Stark criticisms regarding socially and environmentally destructive projects, from project-affected peoples, NGOs and even donor countries, forced the World Bank to adopt in the 1980s a series of standards which were aimed at remedying some of the issues raised by the critics.[79] There are at present 10 safeguard policies[80], namely: environmental assessment[81]; natural habitat[82]; forests[83]; pest management[84]; physical cultural

76 Inspection Panel's Operating Procedure, Article I (1) states that the request should concern 'an actual or threatened material adverse effect on the affected party's rights or interests arises directly out of an action or omission of the Bank to follow its own operational policies and procedures during the design, appraisal and/or implementation of a Bank-financed project'.

77 The policies and procedures consist of several groupings, named, operational policies, bank procedures, good practices, operational directives, and operational memoranda. This classification is very important due to the fact that some are binding and others are not. The Inspection Panel only takes into account the binding policies and procedures.

78 J. Fox and D. Brown, op. cit. n. 57, Introduction at p. 1; See also B. Rich, 'The Multilateral Development Banks, Environmental Policy and the United States', 12 *Ecology Law Quarterly* (1985); S. Schwartzmann, *Bankrolling Disasters: International Development Banks and the Global Environment* (San Francisco, Sierra Club Books 1986).

79 There are ten so-called safeguard policies aimed at preventing and mitigating undue harm to people and environment in the development process. These policies are online at http://go.worldbank.org/WTA1ODE7T0.

80 See the website of the World Bank, and more precisely at http://web.worldbank.org/WBSITE/EXTERNAL/PROJECTS/EXTPOLICIES/EXTSAFEPOL/0,,menuPK:584441~pagePK:64168427 piPK:64168435~theSitePK:584435,00.html

81 Operational Policy (OP)/Bank Procedure (BP) 4.01: Environmental Assessment.

82 Operational Policy 4.04: Natural Habitats.

83 Operational Policy/Bank Procedure 4.36 Forests; to be read in conjunction with OB/BP 4.04 Natural Habitats.

84 Operational Policy 4.09: Pest Management.

resources[85]; involuntary resettlement[86]; indigenous peoples[87]; safety of dams[88]; international waterways[89] and disputed areas.[90]

These safeguard policies are very important as they provide concrete points to raise when seeking to prove the harmful effects of Bank financed projects. However, as mentioned earlier[91], not all of the operational policies are binding on Bank staff and only these binding policies and standards are applied by the Inspection Panel.[92]

From an international law perspective, one could term these policies as those dealing with the obligation to protect the environment[93] and other natural habitats. They deal with the protection of cultural resources[94], with the right to an adequate standard of living and livelihood[95], as dealing with the rights of indigenous peoples[96] and so on. However, the terminology used by the Bank expressly disregards the usage of the term 'rights'. Thus when a person is forcibly evicted from her home, it is not a violation of the *right* to housing, but rather a technical step in the process of involuntary resettlement. Especially in cases of displacement, the term 'involuntary resettlement' assumes that forced evictions always result in resettlement.

However, does it really make a substantial difference whether or not the language used mentions 'a right to something'?[97] Would the situation be at all different if one were to use a rights-based language in its operational policies? In my opinion, 'yes', a right necessarily entails a corresponding duty[98], for when a right is violated one is entitled to an effective remedy. This is, however, not the situation with the Bank's policies. The violation (or non-compliance) with the Bank's

---

85 OP/BP 4.11 on Physical Cultural Resources.

86 Operational Policy 4.12: Involuntary Resettlement.

87 OP/BP 4.10, Indigenous Peoples; OP/BP 4.10 replaced the OD 4.20 Indigenous Peoples from 1991 and is applicable to all projects starting after 01 July 2005.

88 Operational Policy (OP) 4.37: Safety on Dams.

89 Operational Policy (OP)/Bank Procedure (BP) 7.50: Projects on International Waterways.

90 Operational Policy (OP)/Bank Procedure (BP) 7.60: Projects in Disputed Areas.

91 *Supra* n. 77.

92 The Operational Policies and Bank Procedures are binding on Bank staff, while the Good Practices are not.

93 The OP on Environmental Assessment mentions specifically that the Bank shall not fund any projects in contravention of international environmental agreement.

94 The OP on Cultural Property makes explicit reference to obligations under the 1972 Convention Concerning the Protection of World Cultural and Natural Heritage.

95 The OP on Involuntary Resettlement relates to the rights under the International Covenant on Civil on Political Rights and the Covenant on Economic Social and Cultural Rights.

96 ILO Indigenous and Tribal Peoples Convention, 1989 (No. 169) and ILO Convention 107.

97 Thanks to Prof. Koen de Feyter for this question.

98 Or according to H. Shue, three duties see *infra*.

policy enables affected people to approach the Inspection Panel. It does not go further in terms of remedies.

As Henry Shue opines: 'simply to provide something is not the same as to provide it as a right. To provide something as a right means to provide social guarantees against its enjoyment against standard threats, and these guarantees must include arrangements for the effective performance of three types of correlative duties.'[99]

These duties are the:

1. duties to avoid depriving
2. duties to protect from deprivation
3. duties to aid the deprived.[100]

To provide something which one is not entitled to through a right, means that it may be taken away without any claim on the part of the deprived.[101] If a rights-language were to be used by the Bank, it would entitle rights-holders to effectively challenge any and all subsequent violations thereof.

IV. INVESTIGATIONS BY THE INSPECTION PANEL

As of August 2009, the Panel has received 58 requests for inspection. Of these, the Panel has investigated around 24. A total of seven requests have been filed from India.[102] This contribution examines four of these cases from India i.e. NTPC Power Generation Project (1997), Ecodevelopment Project (1998), Coal India Project (2001), and the Mumbai Urban Transport Project (2004).

The purpose behind examining these cases is to find out how effective the Inspection Panel's work is when a powerful borrower country is involved.[103] India, as a rising economic power is engaged in rapid infrastructure development. These development projects carry with it also quite a few negative effects on both people and the environment. One of the main effects on people is displacement.

---

99 H. Shue, *Basic Rights: Subsistence, Affluence and US Foreign Policy* (Princeton, Princeton University Press 1980) p. 76.

100 *Ibid.*, at p. 52.

101 S.I. Skogly, loc. cit. n. 39, at p. 769.

102 These are Uttaranchal Decentralised Watershed Development Project (2007); Mumbai Urban Transport Project (I and II) (2004); Coal Sector Environmental and Social Mitigation Project and Coal Sector Rehabilitation Project (2001); NTPC Power Generation Project (not registered) (2000); Ecodevelopment Project 1998; NTPC Power Generation Project (1997).

103 For a discussion of borrower country's powers, see J. Fox, loc. cit. n. 75.

Increasing population pressures as well as the necessity of land for rapid economic development has led to the situation where a very high number of people are being displaced. India has the largest number of development projects in the world and, quite possibly, the largest number of development-induced displaced persons in the world as well.[104] During the last 50 years, an estimated 25 million have been displaced by development projects,[105] of which less than 25% have been resettled.[106] Use of force to quell protests and suppress dissent is almost routine in these situations. The latest displacement-inducing projects relate to Special Economic Zones (SEZs) and industrial development. There have been several reports of displaced people protesting against displacement and excessive use of police forces to quell these protests.[107] Although India has a vibrant judiciary, displaced persons have little recourse to challenge their displacement.[108] Given the fact that India's record with resettlement is quite bad and the Bank is aware of this situation, it is surprising that time and again it is ready to accept promises of comprehensive resettlement policy with little implementation on the ground. Therefore, this contribution seeks to find out whether the Inspection Panel contributes to any improvement of the situation.

A. INDIA ECODEVELOPMENT PROJECT (1998)

The India Ecodevelopment Project was funded by the World Bank and the Global Environment Facility. The beneficiaries of the project were to 'globally important

---

104 W. Courtland Robinson, 'Risks and Rights: The Causes, Consequences, and Challenges of Development-Induced Displacement', available at www.brook.edu/fp/projects/idp/articles/didreport.pdf.

105 L.K. Mahapatra, 'Testing the Risks and Reconstruction Model on India's Resettlement Experiences', in M. Cernea, ed., *The Economics of Involuntary Resettlement: Questions and Challenges* (Washington D.C., World Bank 1999) as cited in W. Courtland Robinson, loc. cit. n. 104.

106 See World Commission on Dams, *Dams and Development: A New Framework for Decision-Making* (2000) p. 108.

107 Amnesty International, *India: Deaths in West Bengal due to police firing during protests against new industrial project*, ASA 20/008/2007 (Public) News Service No: 050, 15 March 2007; Amnesty International, *India: Deaths in West Bengal during protest against new industrial project*, ASA 20/004/2007 (Public)News Service No: 006, 11 January 2007; Amnesty International, *India: Kalinga Nagar police firing one year on – Orissa must ensure speedy justice for adivasi victims and address their concerns over displacement*, ASA 20/001/2007 (Public) News Service No: 001, 2 January 2007; Amnesty International, *India: Concerns over harassment and continued detention of protestors against Dadri displacement in Uttar Pradesh*, ASA 20/029/2006 (Public) News Service No: 268, 17 October 2006. All these reports are available on the Amnesty International Website, www.amnesty.org.

108 This is due to the fact that most land acquisition laws are placed under Schedule IX of the Constitution, which exempts these from judicial review. Where petitioners have challenged displacement on the basis of violation of their fundamental rights, the judiciary has not been very receptive to their cause. See Supreme Court of India 18 October 2000 *Narmada Bachao Andolan v. Union of India and Others*, Writ Petition (C) No. 319 (1994).

protected area ecosystems' and 'people in and around these areas.'[109] In India, as in many other countries with indigenous populations dependent on the forests for their lives and livelihood, clashes between environmental protection agencies and indigenous peoples[110] are common. India's biodiversity protection legislation affords little space for forest-dependent indigenous peoples.[111] In 2006, a law recognising the traditional rights of forest-dwellers has been enacted, yet it is too early to make any statements on its implementation or effectiveness.[112] The Ecodevelopment Project, however, was according to the World Bank not only beneficial to the environment but also to human beings: '[t]he project's human beneficiaries, tribal peoples, and forest fringe villagers, belong to the poorest sections of society. About 39 percent of the beneficiaries are tribal. Tribal development concerns are integrated under the rubric of social impact, participation and equity, rather than as a subsidiary tribal development plan or component. The project also incorporates specific measures to safeguard the interests of the landless and women.'[113]

In 1998, the Nagarahole Budakattu Janara Hakkusthapana Samithy (NBJHS) filed a request for Inspection to the World Bank's Inspection Panel. The petition alleged that the World Bank had violated its own policies on Indigenous Peoples and Involuntary Resettlement. It also alleged violation of a number of human rights norms, including the UN Declaration on Forced Evictions to which India is a signatory as well as violations of several provisions of the ILO Convention 107, including respect for customary land ownership, protection of indigenous property rights etc. It also alleged that Indian constitutional law protections have been violated.

However, as the Inspection Panel's terms of reference are limited and because its mandate does not include investigating any human rights violations under international law, the Inspection was limited to whether or not World Bank

---

109 World Bank, *India Ecodevelopment Project*, Project Document (1996); The project was to be implemented through (i) a process of village level planning (microplanning) 1 through which individual families and groups can express their needs and get financial support for improved stoves, fodder planting, weaving, tailoring, mushroom cultivation, electric fences, training as nature guides, developing tourist accommodation etc.; and, (ii) a Protected Area Management planning process through which local people can increase their involvement in overall park planning and management and resolve conflicts. See World Bank, *India Ecodevelopment Project*, Management Response (1997), p. 2, para.5.

110 The Government of India uses the word Tribals to denote the indigenous populations. They are also termed as 'Adivasi' (which means 'first peoples') in local parlance and by the people themselves. For a legal analysis see B. Kingsbury, 'Indigenous People' in International Law: A Constructivist Approach to the Asian Controversy', 92(3) *American Journal of International Law* (1998).

111 Under the provisions of the Wildlife Protection Act (1972), no human habitation is allowed within a national park.

112 The Scheduled Tribes (Recognition of Forest Rights) Act (2006).

113 President's Memorandum (MOP) 6.

Directives have been violated. The Requesters alleged the violation of the two World Bank Directives

a. The World Bank Operational Directive 4.20 on Indigenous Peoples[114]
b. The World Bank Operational Directive 4.30 on Involuntary resettlement[115]

The Inspection Panel in its preliminary investigation found that the World Bank OD 4.20 on Indigenous Peoples had been violated.[116] It stated that the IDA's broad objective towards indigenous people is '[...] to ensure that the development process fosters full respect for their dignity, human rights, and cultural uniqueness' and that '[...] the objective at the centre of this directive is to ensure that indigenous peoples *do not suffer adverse effects during the development process*[117], particularly from Bank-financed projects, and that they receive culturally compatible social and economic benefits.'

Inter alia the Panel found[118] that Management, in spite of having been aware of the paucity of information and research at the appraisal stage, allowed the debate about the potential conflict between the two main thrusts of the project to be conducted on the basis of predetermined views and unsubstantiated claims. For example, the Panel found that the widespread view shared by the Forest Department of Karnataka was that the tribal population living inside the park constitutes the main source of biodiversity degradation in the protected area. However, when the Panel requested studies which had analysed the impact of the tribal population on the ecology of the region, it was informed that none had been undertaken. Further, the Panel was told that the tribals within the park have no cattle and no grazing rights. Yet, the larger populations living in peripheral communities graze thousands of heads of cattle in the park and this was agreed upon by all to be a major threat. Again no studies had been conducted on the comparative impacts of the tribal and peripheral communities. It further found that the 'identification of local preferences through direct consultation' was not carried out and neither were the GEF guidelines on local 'participation' followed. By doing this the Panel found that the IDA denied 'the adivasi peoples of the park any significant input on the basic assumptions and concepts underlying the indicative plan, including the traditional rights of the adivasi to use the resources of the park, the nature of future microplanning processes, and their role in the future management of the park.'[119]

---

114 OD 4.20 has been replaced by Operational Policy 4.20 in 2005.
115 OD 4.30 has been replaced by Operational Policy 4.12.
116 World Bank Inspection Panel, *Report and Recommendation on Request for Inspection, India Ecodevelopment Project Rajiv Ghandi (Nagarahole) National Park (Eligibility Report).*
117 Emphasis added.
118 These observations can be found in the Inspection Panel's Investigation Report, op. cit. n. 116.
119 *Ibid.*, para. 78.

The Bank Management admitted that no separate Indigenous Peoples Development Plan was prepared during the appraisal stage, as required by OD 4.30. The Panel noted: 'if an Indigenous People's Development Plan had been prepared, it would have further exposed the tension between biodiversity protection objectives and the condition and aspirations of the indigenous people at Rajiv Gandhi National Park. It would have enabled significant input on the basic assumptions and concepts underlying the Ecodevelopment Project. And it may well have exposed the weakness of some of the premises under which the Project was conceived, at least for this particular park.'[120]

One of the fundamental premises underlying the Project was that the population residents in the park, including all the Adivasi, have a choice whether to stay or to leave. They can choose to stay in their communities within the park, or they can choose to voluntarily resettle in communities adjacent to, though outside the park. Moreover, the Project was based on the further premise that these two options are true options.[121] However, the Panel found that this did not accurately reflect the reality on the ground for several reasons, namely: the Wildlife Protection Act[122]; preference not to relocate; lack of usufruct and property rights; difference in expectations of the Bank Management and of local implementation authorities, namely State forest departments. The Panel found that 'certain key premises underlying the design phase of the Project at the Nagarhole site are flawed, as a result of which there is a significant potential for serious harm'.

The Panel recommended that the Executive Directors authorise an investigation into this case. However, according to a press release of the Bank, 'the Board decided, and the Panel agreed, that no investigation was necessary at this time.'[123] The implementation of the project does not seem to have changed because of the intervention of the Inspection Panel.[124] There have been reports of violence and intimidation of the tribal population and filing of false criminal cases against them.[125] The Bank's website does not provide any follow up on the case.[126]

---

120 *Ibid.*, para. 79.

121 *Ibid.*, para. 31 and Management Response to Inspection Panel (5 May 1998), para. 20.

122 *Supra* n. 111.

123 Emphasis supplied. World Bank Inspection Panel, Press Release announces results of review of India Ecodevelopment Project (22 December 1998).

124 Forest Peoples Programme, *Indigenous and tribal communities, biodiversity conservation and the Global Environment Facility in India* (2005) online at www.forestpeoples.org/documents/ifi_igo/gef/gef_ecodev_india_may05_eng.pdf and see also S. Mathews, 'Imperial Imperatives and the Global Financing of Protected Areas Ecodevelopment and the Resistance of Adivasis of Nagarhole National Park, India', (1) *Law, Social Justice & Global Development Journal (LGD)* (2005), available at www.go.warwick.ac.uk/elj/lgd/2005_1/mathews.

125 Forest Peoples Programme, op. cit. n. 124.

126 Although the Bank has expanded its Information Disclosure Policy considerably, some documents are still not freely accessible.

B. NTPC PROJECT (1997)

The NTPC Thermal Power Generation Project[127] was a $400-million World Bank loan given to the National Thermal Power Corporation to expand Rihand Vindhyachal coal-fired thermal power plant. The project also comprised *inter alia* of the implementation of an environmental action plan (EAP) which was to provide assistance for strengthening of NTPC environmental and resettlement and rehabilitation (R&R) management. The main problems connected with the project were environmental degradation and the forced eviction of people, resulting from the acquisition of land to construct new ash dykes. The region of Singrauli has six thermal power stations, nine open cast coal mines, an aluminium extraction project, a pesticide manufacturing industry, several explosive factories, three cement manufacturing units, hundreds of stone crushing units besides the Rihand and Obra dams.[128] When the request for Inspection was filed by people living in the Singrauli region, the Inspection Panel asked the Management for a response. Not being satisfied with the same, the Panel recommended an investigation into the shortcomings of the project. The Board only allowed the Panel to do a desk-study (which meant that the Panel was not allowed to witness and record first hand the situation on the ground). In spite of this, the Panel submitted its Report criticising severely the non-compliance with Bank policies.

According to the request submitted on behalf of the affected people,[129] forced eviction of people was taking place without adequate alternative housing and livelihood opportunities.[130] The complaint alleged that protestors were beaten up

---

127 The objectives of the project were i.) help improve commercial discipline in the power system through the implementation of new commercial and investment policies; ii) help NTPC meet its targets for capacity additions through increased mobilisation of resources from internal resources, domestic and foreign capital markets as well as from the private sector though joint venture operations; iii) upgrade environmental performance of NTPC power stations and makes its new power stations environmentally more sustainable; and iv) strengthen environmental management and resettlement and rehabilitation management capability."

128 World Bank Inspection Panel, *Request for Inspection, NTPC Power Generation Project Cr. 3632*, available at http://siteresources.worldbank.org/EXTINSPECTIONPANEL/Resources/NTPCRequestforInspection.pdf.

129 See Centre for International Environmental Law, *Villagers Challenge World Bank Role in Thermal Power Projects in Singrauli, India*, (28 April 1997), available at www.ciel.org/Publications/sing1.html.

130 The requesters alleged violations of the World Bank policies on:
- Economic evaluation of investment operations (OD10.04)
- Environmental Assessment (OD 4.01)
- Involuntary Resettlement (OD 4.30)
- Indigenous Peoples (OD 4.20)
- Bank Project Supervision (OD 13.05).

and false cases were filed against them.[131] Human Rights Watch[132] has reported that arbitrary detentions, degrading treatment in custody, and indiscriminate use of force was used against protestors in the Singrauli region.

The Panel found serious violations of policies and procedures on participation and consultation of affected peoples as required by ODs 4.01 and 4.30. In respect of the policy on Involuntary Resettlement, the Panel found that it is '*prima-facie* evident that many of the involuntary actual or potential displacees affected by this project have or are likely to have suffered as a result of an alleged failure by the Bank to comply with OD4.30.'[133] It also found that violation of policies and procedures could be attributed to 'pressure from Senior Regional Management to accelerate the process of loan approval.'[134]

The Panel did not address the allegation of violation of the policy on Indigenous Peoples as it accepted the management's statement that no indigenous people were affected. As was the case in the Ecodevelopment Project,[135] the Panel's somewhat naïve acceptance of management's statement backed by the Borrower's responses makes the investigation less trustworthy than it otherwise should have been.

Regarding the environmental issues, the Panel found that the Bank did not consider all possible or feasible alternate technologies. The Panel agreed that the creation of ash dykes can create health hazards to the population because of emissions of hazardous substances. However, it could not estimate whether the risks are high or damage has taken place because of the inexistence of a health database. Instead of asking the Bank to ask the borrower to create such a database or to monitor the conditions on the ground, the Report simply lets the issue drop on the basis of the inexistence of a health database.[136]

The Panel's Report in the NTPC mentions that 'India's democratic system with its respected independent judiciary allows PAPs to question their R&R treatment'. This statement gives the impression that there are local remedies available. However, what is not evident is the fact that although project-affected persons

131 See CIEL, op. cit. n. 129.

132 See Human Rights Watch, *Letter to President Wolfensohn*, available at www.hrw.org/press98/aprl/memorandum.htm; See also Human Rights Watch, *World Bank Should Monitor Abuses In India*, available at http://hrw.org/english/docs/1998/04/21/india1083.htm.

133 World Bank Inspection Panel, *Report on Investigation, India: NTPC Power Generation Project (Loan 3632-IN)* (22 December 1997) (hereafter Report Singrauli), p. 34, at para. 81.

134 Report Singrauli, op. cit. n. 133, p. 8, at para. 16.

135 The Management stated that there were no issues of resettlement involved since there was not going to be any involuntary relocation.

136 The Panel has the power to hire external consultants under the Resolution. Therefore it is somewhat surprising that no such assistance was availed of.

(PAPs) can question the treatment meted out to them, they cannot question the land acquisition itself.[137] The National Human Rights Commission (NHRC) has also seized on this matter, but did not find merits in the case. According to Human Rights Watch, the NHRC's investigation did not include any interviews with the affected people. Similarly, the affected people have the right to approach the Panel and ask for compliance with Bank policies, however, they do not have the opportunity to actually challenge the project or funding provided. The existence of several projects in the same area with different agencies resulted also in disparate conditions of resettlement. The resettlement package offered by the World Bank had certain elements which other resettlement packages did not have, thus creating the situation where people could be considered 'lucky' to lose their homes because of a Bank funded project and not one funded by the Government of India.

The outcome of the Inspection Panel's Report in this case was that an Independent Monitoring Panel (IMP) consisting of eminent citizens was set up. The IMP found the rehabilitation package to be inadequate and implementation of the rehabilitation policy to be inadequate.[138] However, it is not clear whether the Monitoring Panel's findings resulted in any improvement of the situation. As in the Ecodevelopment Project area, threats of intimidation and violence were reported.[139]

C. COAL INDIA PROJECT (2001)

This Request for Inspection was filed by the Chotanagpur Adivasi Sewa Samiti (CASS) and local NGO on behalf of the residents of the Parej East Coal Mining Project Area.[140] The Parej East Mine is an opencast coalfield which is operated by Central Coalfields Limited. There were a total of 818 PAPs to be resettled, of whom 418 were entitled to rehabilitation.[141] The Requesters stated that the

137 All state and national level land acquisition laws are placed under Schedule IX of the Constitution which effectively removes any judicial intervention.

138 Center for International Environmental Law, *Singrauli and Yacyreta Update: Action Needed Now*, 13 May 1998, available at www.ciel.org/Ifi/pryacsin.html.

139 See Center for International Environmental Law, *Statement of Madhu Kohli World Bank Executive Board of Directors*, 3 February 1998, available at www.ciel.org/Ifi/madhu.html.

140 For an analysis of this Investigation by the Panel, see X. Dias, 'World Bank in Jharkhand: Accountability Mechanisms and Indigenous Peoples', 1(1) *Law, Environment and Development Journal* (2005), available at at www.lead-journal.org/content/05071.pdf, p. 05071.

141 The credit of 63 million USD was to finance the Coal Sector Environmental and Social Mitigation Project (CSESMP). Another IBRD credit of 530 million and an IDA credit of 2 million USD was granted to India to help finance the Coal Sector Rehabilitation Project. The objective of this program was to assist CIL in making coal production more environmentally and socially sustainable through technical assistance to enhance the company's capacity to deal with environmental and social issues. That meant that CIL would be assisted in the

objectives of the CSESMP for them would mean that 'the quality of their lives would improve and that they would share in the benefits of the mining project, that their displacement and relocation would be undertaken as a development programme, that their former living standards, income earning capacity and production levels would be restored if not improved.' However, the result was that the project had failed and that the guarantees given 'were used as levers to win consent to give their land and livelihood for the CSRP Project'[142] The request alleged violation of a number of policies, including Environmental Assessment[143], Indigenous Peoples[144], Involuntary Resettlement[145], Disclosure of Operational Information[146], Management of Cultural Property[147] and Project Supervision.[148]

The Panel found that the Resettlement Action Plan for the Parej East mines did not reflect the reality on the ground and therefore was in violation of the OD on Involuntary Resettlement. Further, it found that Project Affected Persons were not being adequately compensated for the loss of their land and that the only option for redress was to approach the Tribunal constituted under the Coal Bearing Areas Act.[149] This is a lengthy judicial process which also costs money and not all PAPs are in a situation to approach this Tribunal. The Panel criticised the Bank in its handing out monetary compensation. In the words of the Panel '[...] it is difficult, if not impossible to reconcile the Bank's aim of development with a one-time cash grant for acquisition of home and land. Presenting an oustee, whose previous source of survival included a small patch of land, with a check maybe a legal way of getting them to move on, but it should not be confused with development.'[150] The Panel also found violated the requirement that people holding customary rights over land should be compensated before relocation. It further found non-compliance with policy requirements relating to access to forest produce, which has a very important role in subsistence-economies. Lastly, it found inadequate attention paid to income restoration and that this has subsequently caused harm to the project-affected people.

implementation of the Environmental Action Plans (EAP); Rehabilitation Action Plan (RAP) and Indigenous Peoples Development Plans (IPDP).

142 Request for Inspection, Coal India Project, p.1.

143 OD 4.01.

144 OD 4.20.

145 OD 4.30.

146 BP 17.50.

147 OPN 11.03.

148 OD 13.05.

149 Coal Bearing Areas (Acquisition and Development) Act, 1957.

150 World Bank Inspection Panel, *Coal Sector Environmental and Social Mitigation Project (Credit No. 2862-IN)*, Investigation report, para. 20.

The Management Response to the Inspection Panel's report[151] stated that of the 52% of project-affected families to be displaced have shifted. Of these only 27% have relocated to the resettlement sites. While 69% have opted to receive cash compensation and relocate to a site of their own choosing.[152] This development was seen as 'provid[ing] some grounds for optimism that the resettlement process will encounter less resistance in future.'[153] The Management acknowledged that the situation had not improved regarding the social and environmental issues, but that they decided against suspending the loan as it would have adversely affected the mitigation efforts. To prevent this '[...] Management decided to continue to actively work with Coal India Limited (CIL) to help develop practical solutions to improve environmental and social mitigation at the mine and corporate level, and to achieve compliance with Bank policies.'[154] 'It would have been worse without us', as justification has been used by the Bank time and again in order to avoid the use of sanctions, i.e. loan suspension. The Panel recommended the setting up of an Independent Monitoring Panel to monitor the situation. However, this was not accepted by the Government of India.[155]

The Board decided that the project would be supervised 'as long as necessary to ensure that the outstanding issues relating to resettlement and environment are substantially resolved in order to appropriately safeguard the interests of the project-affected people'.[156] Its Board also came to the conclusion that 90% of the project affected persons had improved or been restored to their previous income levels.[157] However, NGOs challenge the claim of the Bank on numbers regarding improvements in economic situation.[158] According to the FIAN[159], CIL is not implementing the agreed standards and that the Bank does not take any decisive action to remedy the suffering of the displaced.[160] In 2005, an update on the

151 World Bank Inspection Panel, *Coal Sector Environmental and Social Mitigation Project (Credit No. 2862-IN) Coal Sector Rehabilitation Project (Loan No. 4226-IN)*, Management Response to the Inspection Panel, 19 July 2001.

152 *Ibid.*, at p. 9.

153 *Ibid.*, at p. 9.

154 *Ibid.*, at p.13.

155 According to the Government of India, the 'circumstance on ground do not warrant the constitution o f an independent monitoring panel and that regular Bank supervision missions may suffice to provide the necessary monitoring.' See World Bank Inspection Panel, *India: Coal Sector Environmental and Social Mitigation Project*, Management Report on Status of Outstanding Issues following the Inspection Panel Investigation Report and Management's Response, 5 April 2005.

156 World Bank, News Release, *World Bank Board Discusses Coal Project Findings* (25 July 2003).

157 *Ibid.*

158 Bretton Woods Project, *Coal India: Rehabilitation claims linger on unaddressed*, available at www.brettonwoodsproject.org/art.shtml?x=84224.

159 Food First Information and Action Network.

160 FIAN, *Globalising Economic and Social Human Rights by Strengthening Extraterritorial State Obligations*, available at www.eed.de/fix/files/doc/eed_fian_bfdw_case_studies_human_rights_05_eng.pdf.

monitoring of the social and environmental issues[161] identified four main challenges that affected the Bank's efforts to resolve the issues, one of which was 'speculative expectations of some of the key stakeholders regarding the benefits that would accrue to them due to the Bank's continued involvement.'[162] It is interesting that the Bank identifies this as a challenge when the Bank itself refused to suspend the loan on the ground that the Bank's disengagement would make the situation worse. The Bank also found that 'misinformation campaign in the village regarding the Panel's findings and the scope of the Bank's continued involvement' was a challenge.

Overall, it can be concluded that although the Investigation provided some impetus for monitoring and supervision, civil-society actors seem unconvinced of the results presented by the Bank. According to one activist, the impact of the Report on the Inspection Panel on the Bank has been fruitless.[163]

D. MUMBAI URBAN TRANSPORT PROJECT (2004)

This investigation by the Inspection Panel was carried out on the basis of several separate requests for inspection filed by local residents, NGOs and shop owners associations regarding the Mumbai Urban Transport Project which was partly financed by the IBRD.[164] The Project consisted of three main components, the Rail Transport, Road Transport and Resettlement and Rehabilitation. The Project was expected to involve displacement of around 77,000 people, which categorised the project as Category A according to the OD on Environmental Assessment.

The requesters claimed that the displacement due to the project would hurt their livelihoods and that the Bank had not complied with various policies including those of involuntary resettlement and environmental assessment. This case is quite different from the others previously examined in that the people who were being displaced did not belong to the poorest segments of the society. Many were middle income shopkeepers. This was, however, not the position taken by the Bank at the beginning. The project appraisal document stated that '[m]ost of the affected persons are slum dwellers and squatters living in poor and unhealthy housing conditions and lack basic amenities. As a result of project intervention,

161 World Bank Inspection Panel, op. cit. n. 155.

162 *Ibid.*

163 Xavier Dias states that in October 2004, a World Bank representative visited Pindra (a resettlement colony) and later the CASS offices, where she indicated a zero when asked about the Inspection Panel's report. See X. Dias, loc. cit. n. 140, at p. 78.

164 The objective of the Project is 'to facilitate urban economic growth and improve quality of life by fostering the development of an efficient and sustainable urban transport system including effective institutions to meet the needs of the users in the Mumbai Metropolitan Region (MMR).'

the affected persons are expected to receive higher standards of alternative houses with improved basic amenities.' It further stated that '[l]oss of income and livelihood opportunities is not a major issue in this project since the affected persons will be relocated within a close proximity of the existing locations, thus enabling them to retain the site related opportunities. All those loosing[sic] petty shops and business units will be offered alternative shops to enable them to re-establish their shops.'

Examining the request for Inspection, the Panel expressed its concern that the 'lack of sufficient analysis and consideration of the many risks of resettlement may be at the root of many problems facing the people affected by the Project'. It criticised the use of local NGOs to carry out surveys and assessments, which transferred the huge responsibility of implementation from the state government to NGOs with insufficient institutional capacity and knowledge to deal with the problems. There were discrepancies in the appraisal of number of people to be displaced. The Panel also found a lack of consultation with shopkeepers as well as other project-affected people. The project had as part of its set up a grievance redress mechanism. The Panel found that it 'lacks clear responsibilities, procedures and rules and has not been independent'.[165] As a result of the Panel's findings, in March 2006, the Bank temporarily suspended the disbursement of the loan citing outstanding concerns regarding equitable treatment of people.[166] This development was greeted by a local official as a 'blessing in disguise'.[167] However three months later, the Bank decided to lift the suspension.[168]

The Management submitted its First Progress Report to the Board of Executive Directors on 1 March 2007.[169] Management reported that progress had been made in resolving several issues but also acknowledged that progress had been 'slower than anticipated' in several areas and that some challenges remained. Following this Report, the Inspection Panel issued a Progress Report on 5 June 2007 in which it noted the considerable efforts of the Bank Management.

---

165 World Bank Inspection Panel, *India: Mumbai Urban Transport Project*, Investigation Report (2005), p. 104, para. 416.

166 World Bank, News Release, *World Bank Suspends Support to Major Indian Urban Transport Initiative*, No. 2006/293/SAR, 2 March 2006.

167 According to a news report Metropolitan, Commissioner T. Chandrasekhar called the decision a blessing in disguise and said the authority will look to Japanese banks for funds for the Metro rail project. 'The World Bank has a lot of harsh, impractical conditions," he said. "They want us to use global laws for local conditions', available at www.dnaindia.com/report.asp?NewsID=1015967.

168 See World Bank, Press Release, *World Bank lifts suspension*, 30 June 2006, No. 2006/519/SAR.

169 World Bank Inspection Panel, *India: Mumbai Urban Transport Project (Loan No.4665-IN; Credit No. 3662-IN)*; follow up to the Meeting of the Executive Directors of the World Bank (28 March 2006) on the Inspection Panel Investigation Report No. 34725 and Management Report and Recommendation; Progress Report on Implementation of the Action Plan, dated 1 March 2007.

However, some problems still had to be resolved notably the resettlement of shopkeepers, the appointment of a post-resettlement agency, improvement of the database, etc. Concerning the redress mechanism, the project affected people repeatedly complained about a high number of pending grievances, about the slow process of complaints and about the fact that the verification process of grievances was carried out by the same NGOs, who they claimed had done the incorrect surveys which caused the grievances.[170]

On 13 November 2007, the Management submitted a Second Report on the implementation of the Action Plan. It reported further progress made in the implementation of the Action Plan, notably that the Mumbai Metropolitan Region Development Authority had made noteworthy progress in reaching mutually acceptable and compliant solutions with the shopkeepers.[171] A Third Progress Report has been submitted on 13 March 2009, which stated that '[m]ost of the activities proposed in the Action Plan have either been completed or substantially completed. However several resettlement challenges remain that are linked to the resolution of cases involving court litigation and relocation of community structures. Bank Management will report in a year's time on progress made in implementation of the Action Plan. If Management determines that satisfactory closure has been reached regarding the shopkeepers and long-term sustainability of post-resettlement activities, the next progress report would be the last.'[172]

On 29 May 2009, the Inspection Panel received a new Request for Inspection related to this project. The Requesters announced their wish to see their particular problem resolved in negotiation with the Mumbai Metropolitan Region Development Authority with possible assistance of the World Bank. The Panel noted that 'the chances of an expedient resolution of the case brought forward by the Requesters appear promising.'[173]

170 World Bank Inspection Panel, *Progress Report India: Mumbai Urban Transport Project (IBRD Loan No. 4665-IN, IDA Credit No. 3662-IN)*, available at http://siteresources.worldbank.org/EXTINSPECTIONPANEL/Resources/FINALMUTP-panelreport-june5.pdf.

171 World Bank Inspection Panel, *India: Mumbai Urban Transport Project (Loan No.4665-IN; Credit No. 3662-IN)*; follow up to the Meeting of the Executive Directors of the World Bank (28 March 2006) on the Inspection Panel Investigation Report No. 34725 and Management Report and Recommendation, Progress Report on Implementation of the Action Plan, dated 13 November 2007.

172 World Bank Inspection Panel, *India: Mumbai Urban Transport Project (Loan No.4665-IN; Credit No. 3662-IN)*; follow up to the Meeting of the Executive Directors of the World Bank (28 March 2006) on the Inspection Panel Investigation Report No. 34725 and Management Report and Recommendation; Third Progress Report on Implementation of the Action Plan, dated 13 March 2009.

173 World Bank Inspection Panel, Re: Request for Inspection, *INDIA – Mumbai Urban Transport Project (Loan No. 4665-IN; Credit No. 3662-IN)*, Notice of Registration, available at http://siteresources.worldbank.org/EXTINSPECTIONPANEL/Resources/MUMBAI_Final_NOR.pdf.

V. OUTCOMES AND CONCLUDING REMARKS

The red thread running through all these decisions is that issues of displacement and environmental degradation feature routinely in bank-financed projects. However, the issues are treated in an ad-hoc manner and without real consideration of whether the borrower has the capacity and/or the will to implement the policies. Different implementing authorities at the domestic level seem to take the same position as regards implementation of agreed policies and packages. On a procedural issue, consultation with affected people is lacking. Although the Panel's Reports points out time and again that there should be meaningful consultation, it is rarely seen in practice.

The Bank pays little attention or deliberately ignores issues of domestic law and their incompatibility with its own Operational Standards. For example in the Coal India Project, the Coal Bearing Areas Act, precludes the possibility of providing long-term leases to project affected and this is part of the agreed resettlement package.[174] In the Ecodevelopment Project, clashes with Indian laws relating to biodiversity conservation and Bank policies were inevitable. And while, the Inspection Panel's Reports point this out, changes are not possible.

Furthermore, recommendations from the Panel are not always accepted by the Board. In cases like the Mumbai Urban Transport Project where the Bank temporarily suspended the loan on account of the Panel's Report seem to be an exception, which of course is not really an exception. The Bank lifted the suspension after three months, which seems to be a pretty short period of time to evaluate all the issues and be convinced of progress. Thus, the borrowing country remains unaccountable and devoid of sanctions for non-implementation. It can be seen that although the Bank's experience with resettlement issues in India is poor, the Bank will not antagonise India, one of its largest borrowers.[175]

Non-implementation of any policy of the Bank does not hold any real sanction, either for the borrower or for the Bank. Consequently, the reports of the Inspection Panel are in some senses creating a source of legitimacy for the operations of the Bank, in that they make pretence of dealing with the issues. In reality however, implementation remains poor. The Inspection Panel's credibility is at stake mainly because of the Board's refusal to change positions.

---

174 However, the Bank itself admits that although amendments to the law have been proposed it is unclear whether these amendments will pass, and in what timeframe. See World Bank Inspection Panel, op. cit. n. 155.

175 In the fiscal year 2006, new lending by the Bank to India amounted to USD 2.131 billion. Information from World Bank website. available at http://web.worldbank.org/WBSITE/EXTERNAL/COUNTRIES/SOUTHASIAEXT/0,,contentMDK:20889253~pagePK:146736~piPK:146830~theSitePK:223547,00.html.

In a paper reviewing the first five years of the Inspection Panel, J. Fox comments that 'transnational civil society pressure led some nation-states to create the panel, but other nation-states and Bank management have managed to prevent it from having significant impact most of the time.' This situation does not seem to have changed much in recent years. As has been observed from the cases, the Panel's findings have had equivocal outcomes.

The World Bank needs to wake up to the fact that merely the existence of the Inspection Panel does not alone create accountability. It also needs to show that the policies reflect international minimum standards and those are actually implemented. As Handl states: 'While each [Multilateral Development Bank's] MDB's inspection procedure will ostensibly focus on whether the existing operational policies and procedures have been followed with regard to bank-financed projects, at the end of the day, it will call attention also to the very existence of international obligations incumbent upon the MDB concerned and to the degree to which these obligations are reflected in the institution's by-laws and policies in the first place.'[176]

As a few years ago, the creation of a mechanism like the Inspection Panel was largely unthinkable, similarly it will not be unthinkable for us in the coming years to regard the Inspection Panel with the ability to actually enforce its findings.

176 G. Handl, 'The Legal Mandate of Multilateral Development Banks as Agents for Change toward Sustainable Development', 92 *American Journal of International Law* (1998) p. 642.

THE ACCOUNTABILITY OF THE INTERNATIONAL MONETARY FUND FOR HUMAN RIGHTS VIOLATIONS

Pierre SCHMITT*

The International Monetary Fund (IMF or the Fund) is an international organisation which has notably been established 'to promote international monetary cooperation through a permanent institution, which provides the machinery for consultation and collaboration on international monetary problems.'[1] Human rights are not mentioned in its Articles of Agreement, which has lead G.B. Taplin, formerly Assistant Director at the IMF's Geneva office, to state before the United Nations (UN) Sub-commission for the Promotion and Protection of Human Rights that the Fund, in a strict sense, does not have a mandate to promote human rights. It is not bound by the various human rights declarations and conventions.[2] As a consequence, the idea of accountability of the IMF for human rights violations may sound far-fetched.

Nevertheless, the separation between the IMF's activities and human rights is not tight and the practice reveals cases in which the IMF was confronted with the question whether it should take into account human rights factors in its decisions. A recent example is provided by Sri Lanka's request in early 2009 to the IMF for a US$ 1.9 billion emergency support loan to cover the costs of immediate government functions and to pay for post-conflict resettlement. The Sri Lankan government searched for funds to reconstruct the Northern Province

* Research Fellow, Leuven Centre for Global Governance Studies and Institute for International Law, University of Leuven (K.U.Leuven). The author thanks Dominic Coppens, Kathleen Gutman and Nicolas Hachez for their helpful comments on a preliminary draft. Internet pages have been last visited on 30 March 2010.

1 Article I, Section 1 of the Articles of Agreement of the International Monetary Fund, 27 December 1945, 60 Stat. 1401, 2 *UNTS* 39 (as amended in 1969, 1978, 1992 and 2009).

2 G.B. Taplin, 'Speaking Points: Globalization and its Impacts on the Full Enjoyment of Human Rights', Speech to Sub-Commission on the Promotion and Protection of Human Rights, 8 August 2001, available at www.unhchr.ch/huricane/huricane.nsf/view01/7A33AABB095C51F3C1256AA300282C86; See also G. Capdevila, 'IMF Not Taking into Account Human Rights Issues', 13 August 2001, available at www.globalpolicy.org/component/content/article/209/42944.html.

and to bring a sustainable solution to the conflict. The struggle between government forces and the separatist Liberation Tigers of Tamil Eelam (LTTE) had caused many civilian casualties and internally displaced persons; the humanitarian situation in northern Vanni was disastrous. UN High Commissioner on Human Rights N. Pillay declared that 'certain actions being undertaken by the Sri Lankan military and by the LTTE may constitute violations of international human rights and humanitarian law. We need to know more about what is going on, but we know enough to be sure that the situation is absolutely desperate.'[3] On 23 March 2009, Human Rights Watch wrote a letter to the IMF to express its concern that this loan 'will not achieve its intended objectives unless the Sri Lankan government takes serious steps to safeguard the rights of internally displaced persons and ensure an effective humanitarian response to the immediate conflict and post-conflict situations.'[4] On 27 July 2009, the IMF approved a 20-month Stand-By-Agreement for Sri Lanka in the amount of approximately US$ 2.6 billion to support the economic reform program.[5] Managing Director Dominique Strauss-Kahn wrote to Human Rights Watch on 5 November 2009 to explain that

> '[t]he Sri Lankan economy is facing a serious crisis and regardless of one's opinion of the human rights situation in that country, the collapse of the economy cannot be considered a reasonable outcome. [...] The aim of our support, therefore, is to provide the resources necessary to prevent a full-blown economic crisis, contribute to reconstruction efforts, and sustain social spending aimed at protecting the poor. In addition, this program also provides the necessary framework without which international donors would be unable to provide assistance in the areas of infrastructure, roads, hospitals, and schools.'[6]

It is not the subject of this analysis to discuss the conflict in Sri Lanka, but this case illustrates the need to clarify the relationship between the IMF and human rights in order to assess the Fund's accountability for human rights violations. In this example, Human Rights Watch considers that the IMF should take human rights in consideration in its decisions. This raises several questions, namely whether the IMF itself is bound by any human rights obligations, whether the

---

3 N. Pillay, 'Serious violations of international law committed in Sri Lanka conflict: Pillay', 13 March 2009, available at www.unmultimedia.org/radio/english/detail/71133.html.

4 Human Rights Watch, 'Letter to the International Monetary Fund (IMF) on Sri Lanka's Emergency Support Loan Request', 23 March 2009, available at www.hrw.org/en/news/2009/03/23/letter-international-monetary-fund-imf-sri-lankas-emergency-support-loan-request.

5 IMF, 'IMF to Lend $2.6 Billion to Sri Lanka', 29 July 2009, available at www.imf.org/external/pubs/ft/survey/so/2009/car072809a.htm.

6 IMF, 'Letter from IMF Managing Director to Human Rights Watch', 5 November 2009, available at www.imf.org/external/np/vc/2009/110509.htm.

IMF has the mandate to lawfully deal with human rights factors and whether it is obliged to promote human rights through its operations.

The first part of this contribution examines whether the IMF is bound by any human rights obligations. The IMF is not party to any human rights agreements. Yet, three separate arguments have been advanced to sustain that the IMF has to respect some human rights obligations in its operations.[7]

The second part assesses the content of these obligations and their significance. As will be seen, it has been argued that the IMF has an obligation to respect human rights, but not to protect or to promote human rights, since such obligations would exceed its legal mandate.[8] However, this issue remains much debated and deserves examination in the light of recent developments in this area. I will analyse this issue from three angles, namely the mandate of the IMF (section A), its practice (section B) and the recent evolution of both the mandate and the practice of the IMF (section C).

The third part presents the available accountability mechanisms and the proposals made to improve the system. Since the accountability mechanisms for human rights violations may not be entirely dissociated from a broader study of accountability of the IMF for any types of violations, this part will also address features of the general accountability system of the IMF. In the first section (A), I will explore the existing accountability system and assess why it is probably the weakest aspect of IMF governance. In the second section (B), I examine the internal mechanism adopted by the IMF to improve its accountability, namely the Independent Evaluation Office (IEO), which has issued interesting recommendations to improve the accountability of the IMF (subsection 1). Some scholars have criticised internal accountability mechanisms because of the decision-making process within the IMF. I assess these views in relation to the recent developments in this area (subsection 2). Finally, proposals to create external accountability mechanisms will be examined in the third section (C). These proposals include the establishment of an external complaint mechanism, namely an ombudsman or an inspection panel (subsection 1), the creation of a working group within the UN Commission on Human Rights (subsection 2) and the accountability of individual Member States (subsection 3).

7 S.I. Skogly, 'The Human Rights Obligations of the World Bank and the IMF', in W. van Genugten, P. Hunt and S. Mathews, eds., *World Bank, IMF and Human Rights* (Nijmegen, Wolf Legal Publishers 2003) pp. 46–50.

8 S.I. Skogly, *The human rights obligations of the World Bank and the International Monetary Fund* (London, Cavendish 2001) p. 193.

I. THE SOURCES OF THE INTERNATIONAL HUMAN RIGHTS OBLIGATIONS OF THE IMF

Prior to addressing the question whether the IMF may be held accountable for human rights violations, one has to analyse whether the IMF is bound by international human rights law. The IMF has traditionally denied applicability of international human rights law to its operations, since its Articles of Agreement do not contain any human rights references. Moreover, the IMF, as an international organisation, is not a party to international human rights conventions and hence seems not to be bound by these conventions.

Yet, three separate arguments could be advanced that the IMF has to respect some human rights obligations in its operations.[9]

First, such an obligation could derive from the international legal personality that the IMF seems to have.[10] If international legal personality was not specifically conferred upon the IMF under its Articles of Agreement, there is no doubt that the IMF possesses this separate personality from its Member States. The resolution of this question is a matter of construction. The IMF is an international organisation established by treaty conferring powers, functions and a capacity to create international rights and obligations.[11] Moreover the extensive immunities and privileges foreseen in its Articles of Agreement are a sign of the IMF's international legal personality. All these factors indicate international legal personality separate from its members.[12]

As a consequence, the Fund has to fulfil its mandate within the framework of international law and notably to respect general rules of international law.[13] These include international human rights which are part of customary

---

9 S.I. Skogly, 'The Human Rights Obligations of the World Bank and the IMF', in W. van Genugten, P. Hunt and S. Mathews, eds., *World Bank, IMF and Human Rights* (Nijmegen, Wolf Legal Publishers 2003) pp. 46–50.

10 A. Broches, *Selected Essays: World Bank, ICSID and Other Subjects of Public and Private International Law* (Dordrecht, Martinus Nijhoff Publishers 1995) p. 22; J. De Gregorio, B. Eichengreen, T. Ito and C. Wyplosz, *An independent and accountable IMF* (Geneva reports on the World economy, Oxford, Information Press 1999).

11 This presupposes international legal personality. See ICJ, *Reparation for Injuries Suffered in the Service of the United Nations*, Advisory Opinion, *ICJ Rep.* (1949) p. 174.

12 S.I. Skogly, op. cit. n. 8, at pp. 63–71; M. Darrow, *Between Light and Shadow: the World Bank, the International Monetary Fund and International Human rights Law* (Oxford, Hart Publishing 2003) p. 126; M. Darrow, 'Human rights Accountability of the World Bank and the IMF: Possibilities and Limits of Legal Analysis', *Social Legal Studies* (2003) p. 133; B. Ghazi, *The IMF, the World Bank Group and the Question of Human rights* (Ardsley, Transnational 2005) pp. 102–106.

13 ICJ, *Interpretation of the Agreement of 25 March 1991 between the WHO and Egypt*, Advisory Opinion, *ICJ Rep.* (1980) p. 73.

international law. Therefore, one has to examine whether international human rights may be considered as such international custom. The Universal Declaration of Human Rights (UDHR) lists fundamental human rights to be universally accepted. 'The Universal Declaration and the International Covenants represent minimal standards of conduct of all people and all nations. Intergovernmental organisations are inter-state institutions and they too are bound by the generally accepted standards of the world community.'[14] Though it is only a declaration, most authors agree that substantial parts of the UDHR constitute customary rules[15] or general principles of international law.[16] However, the IMF has continually denied to be bound by the rights contained in the International Covenant on Civil and Political Rights (ICCPR) and the International Covenant on Economic, Social and Cultural Rights (ICESCR). Former IMF General Counsel F. Gianviti argued that the ICESCR is a treaty among States without any status under international general law.[17] This reasoning is mainly based on obiter dicta in the judgment of the International Court of Justice in the *Barcelona Traction* case.[18] In this judgment, the Court drew a distinction between obligations owed by States to the community as a whole – *erga omnes* – and obligations owed by one State to another. The Court established a list of examples of general obligations owed to the international community. However, this list was not a closed one.[19] Moreover, one should remember that the above mentioned judgment dates from 1970, and one may question whether it is still relevant nowadays. As noted by H. Hannum, certain economic, social and cultural rights in the Declaration 'enjoy sufficiently widespread support as to be at least potential candidates for rights recognized under customary international law [...].'[20] Furthermore, the IMF General Counsel did not rule out the possibility that the IMF may take into account 'the relationship between its activities and the achievement of social rights contained in the covenant.'

---

14 M. Cogen, 'Human rights, prohibition of political activities and the lending policies of Worldbank and International Monetary Fund', in S.R. Chowdhury, E. Denters and P.J.I.M. de Waart, eds., *The Right to Development in International Law* (Dordrecht, Kluwer/Martinus Nijhoff Publishers 1988) p. 387.

15 M. Darrow and L. Arbour, 'The pillar of glass: human rights in the development operations of the United Nations', 103 *AMJIL* (2009) p. 470; A. Clapham, *Human Rights Obligations of Non-State Actors* (Oxford, Oxford University Press, 2006) p. 144.

16 B. Simma and P. Alston, 'The Sources of Human Rights Law: Custom, Jus Cogens and General Principles', 12 *Australian Yearbook of International Law* (1988–1989) p. 82.

17 F. Gianviti, 'Economic, Social and Cultural Rights and the International Monetary Fund, Submission by IMF General Counsel to the UN Committee on Economic, Social and Cultural Rights, 7 May 2001, available at www.imf.org/external/np/leg/sem/2002/cdmfl/eng/gianv3.pdf.

18 ICJ, *Barcelona Traction, Light and Power Company, Limited*, Judgment, *ICJ Rep.* (1970) p. 3.

19 A. Clapham, op. cit. n. 15, at p. 147.

20 H. Hannum, 'The Status of the Universal Declaration of Human Rights in National and International Law', 25 *Georgia Journal of International and Comparative Law* (1995–1996) p. 349.

Second, the IMF is a specialised agency, having entered into a relationship agreement with the UN in accordance with the UN Charter Articles 57 and 63.[21] This is a second path linking the IMF to human rights standards, since it implies that the IMF is to act in accordance with the UN Charter.[22] For P. Alston, 'the IMF is a United Nations body and must therefore be bound by the principles stated in the UN Charter. Among these principles and purposes of the organisation is the promotion of respect for human rights. It is not therefore a political objective, but a legally mandated one.'[23] Former IMF General Counsel Gianviti rejected this argument since the IMF is not exactly a UN body but an intergovernmental agency. Besides, he argued that the Fund's agreement with the UN mentions in its Article 1(2) that 'by reason of the nature of its international responsibilities and the terms of its Articles of Agreement, the Fund is, and is required to function as, an independent international organisation.'[24] Nevertheless, the IMF remains a specialised agency of the UN, and it seems hardly conceivable that an organisation created by the UN may undertake activities undermining one of the most important missions of the UN, namely the protection of human rights.[25]

The third argument is based on the IMF's composition of Member States having international human rights obligations. According to Article 103 of the UN Charter, '[i]n the event of a conflict between the obligations of the Members of the United Nations under the present Charter and their obligations under any other international agreement, their obligations under the present Charter shall prevail.'[26] When representatives of Member States determine the policies of the IMF, they are bound by the States' international obligations, including those arising from international human rights law. Some authors have considered that in concluding agreements with the members, the IMF shall respect the

21 Agreement between the United Nations and the International Monetary Fund, 15 November 1947, available at www.imf.org/external/pubs/ft/sd/index.asp?decision=DN19.

22 United Nations Economic and Social Council, Commission on Human Rights, Report of the Secretary-General, *Question of the Realization in All Countries of the Economic, Social and Cultural Rights Contained in the Universal Declaration on Human Rights and in the International Covenant on Economic, Social and Cultural Rights, and Study of Special Problems Which the Developing Countries Face in Their Efforts to Achieve These Human Rights: Ways and Means to Carry out a Political Dialogue Between Creditor and Debtor Countries in the United Nations System, Based on the Principle of Shared Responsibility*, UN Doc. E/Cn.4/1996/22 (1996) at para. 50.

23 P. Alston, 'Symposium: 1986 World Food Day and Law Conference: "The Legal Faces of the Hunger Problem: IX Immediate Constraints on Achieving the Right to Food: the International Monetary Fund and the Right to Food"', 30 *Howard Law Journal* (1987) pp. 473–479.

24 F. Gianviti, loc. cit. n. 17.

25 R. Abouharb and D. Cingranelli, 'IMF programs and human rights, 1981–2003', 4(1) *Review of International Organizations* (2009) p. 69.

26 United Nations Charter, 26 June 1945, 59 Stat. 1031, T.S. 993.

obligations of the members according to Article 103 of the UN Charter, which include giving priority to the respect for human rights.[27]

A group of experts met in October 2001 and April 2002 at Tilburg University in the Netherlands to study the relations between international financing institutions and human rights. They particularly discussed the possible redress of adverse human rights implications of the activities of the financial institutions and summarised their conclusions in 'the Tilburg Guiding Principles on World Bank, IMF and human rights'. In accordance with these guiding principles,

> 'the responsibility for implementing human rights is universal and concerns all – state and non-state – actors whose activities may affect people's lives. The primary responsibilities and obligations in the field of domestic human rights enjoyment, however, remain with the state: states cannot "delegate" human rights obligations to, for instance, international institutions and free themselves from these obligations. As international legal persons, the World Bank and the IMF have international legal obligations to take full responsibility for human rights respect in situations where the institutions' own projects, policies or programs negatively impact or undermine the enjoyment of human rights.'[28]

There seems to be an emerging consensus among scholars that the IMF is under some obligation to abide by fundamental principles of human rights[29] and that human rights are part of a larger framework of international law in which all legal actors operate.[30]

Despite this obligation, the IMF continues to operate with little regard for human rights concerns. This may be partly explained by the fact that the IMF is more concerned with implementing macroeconomic policies for short periods of time, which seems to have 'sheltered the IMF from a direct linkage to human rights violations for longer than the World Bank or regional development banks.'[31]

---

27 S.I. Skogly, loc. cit. n. 7, at pp. 48–50.

28 W. van Genugten, P. Hunt and S. Mathews, eds., *World Bank, IMF and Human Rights* (Nijmegen, Wolf Legal Publishers 2003) p. 248.

29 A. Clapham, op. cit. n. 15, at p. 144

30 S.I. Skogly, op. cit. n. 8, at pp. 56–71.

31 C. Ochoa, 'Advancing the language of human rights in a global economic order: an analysis of a discourse', 23 *Boston College Third World Law Journal* (2003) pp. 57–114.

II. THE SIGNIFICANCE OF THE HUMAN RIGHTS OBLIGATIONS OF THE IMF

In the previous part, I concluded that the IMF is under some obligation to abide by fundamental principles of human rights. Yet, the concrete significance of this obligation remains to be examined in order to define its scope.

In her book entitled *The human rights obligations of the World Bank and the International Monetary Fund*, Sigrun I. Skogly[32] followed the theory of obligations developed by Asbjørn Eide[33], who identified three levels of obligations: an obligation to respect, an obligation to protect and an obligation to fulfil. The first requires the obligation holder to guarantee that the human rights situation is not deteriorating and to observe human rights. The second obliges its holder to ensure that third parties do not violate human rights, while the third requires positive actions ensuring the improvement of human rights. Sigrun I. Skogly argued that the IMF has an obligation to respect human rights, but not to protect or to fulfil human rights, since such obligations would exceed its legal obligations. As stated by the author, 'to argue that respecting human rights has become part of international customary law, or general rules of international law, seems plausible and reasonable.'[34] However, arguments have been raised in recent years towards progressive inclusion of human rights considerations within IMF policies, particularly in the light of studies on the interplay between IMF programs and human rights.[35] In this part, I examine the scope of the IMF's human rights obligations from three angles, namely the mandate of the IMF, its practice, and the evolution of both mandate and practice in order to identify the content of the human rights obligations of the IMF.

A. THE MANDATE OF THE IMF

Article I of the Articles of Agreement of the IMF states:

'The purposes of the International Monetary Fund are:

i) To promote international monetary cooperation through a permanent institution which provides the machinery for consultation and collaboration on international monetary problems.

---

32 S.I. Skogly, op. cit. n. 8.

33 A. Eide, 'Realisation of social and economic rights and the minimum threshold approach', 10(1–2) *Human Rights Law Journal* (1989) p. 37.

34 S.I. Skogly, op. cit. n. 8, at p. 151.

35 See notably R. Abouharb and D. Cingranelli, *Human Rights and Structural Adjustment* (Cambridge, Cambridge University Press 2008) p. 4; S.I. Skogly, 'Structural Adjustment and Development: Human Rights – An Agenda for Change', 15(4) *Human Rights Quarterly* (1993) p. 754.

ii) To facilitate the expansion and balanced growth of international trade, and to contribute thereby to the promotion and maintenance of high levels of employment and real income and to the development of the productive resources of all members as primary objectives of economic policy.
iii) To promote exchange stability, to maintain orderly exchange arrangements among members, and to avoid competitive exchange depreciation.
iv) To assist in the establishment of a multilateral system of payments in respect of current transactions between members and in the elimination of foreign exchange restrictions which hamper the growth of world trade.
v) To give confidence to members by making the general resources of the Fund temporarily available to them under adequate safeguards, thus providing them with opportunity to correct maladjustments in their balance of payments without resorting to measures destructive of national or international prosperity.
vi) In accordance with the above, to shorten the duration and lessen the degree of disequilibrium in the international balances of payments of members.

The Fund shall be guided in all its policies and decisions by the purposes set forth in this Article.'

The pursuit of human rights is not mentioned in the Articles of Agreement of the IMF. These require the Fund to 'respect the political and social policies' of its Member States.[36] This has been interpreted as precluding the IMF from applying any political criteria including those relevant to civil and political rights to any lending or surveillance decisions.[37] For the World Bank, Article IV, Section 10 of the IBRD Articles and its IDA equivalent state that 'the Bank and its officers shall

---

36 Article IV, Section 3 of the Articles of Agreement of the International Monetary Fund states: 'Surveillance over exchange arrangements, (a) The Fund shall oversee the international monetary system in order to ensure its effective operation, and shall oversee the compliance of each member with its obligations under Section 1 of this Article. (b) In order to fulfil its functions under (a) above, the Fund shall exercise firm surveillance over the exchange rate policies of members, and shall adopt specific principles for the guidance of all members with respect to those policies. Each member shall provide the Fund with the information necessary fur such surveillance, and, when requested by the Fund, shall consult with it on the member's exchange rate policies. The principles adopted by the Fund shall be consistent with cooperative arrangements by which members maintain the value of their currencies in relation to the value of the currency or currencies of other members, as well as with other exchange arrangements of a member's choice consistent with the purposes of the Fund and Section 1 of this Article. These principles shall respect the domestic social and political policies of members, and in applying these principles the Fund shall pay due regard to the circumstances of members.' Articles of Agreement of the International Monetary Fund, 27 December 1945, 60 Stat. 1401, 2 *UNTS* 39 (as amended in 1969, 1978, 1992 and 2009).

37 M. Allen, 'The International Monetary Fund and the Promotion of Human rights', Presentation for Wilton Park Conference on 'Human rights and Global Economic Governance', 16–19 October 2000, available at www.hcci.gouv.fr/travail/actes_seminaires/upload/mallen.pdf.

not interfere in the political affairs of any member; nor shall they be influenced in their decisions by the political character of the member or members concerned. Only economic considerations shall be weighed impartially in order to achieve the purposes stated in Article I.'[38] Nevertheless, as noted by A. Clapham, '[t]he political affairs prohibition cannot be read as excluding concern that governments comply with their international human rights obligations. And, in any event, the prohibition on interference in the political affairs of a state cannot be read to mean that the Bank and IMF have no human rights obligations of their own.'[39]

As previously mentioned, former Assistant Director at the IMF's Geneva office G.B. Taplin considered that the IMF does not have a mandate to promote human rights. They are not mentioned in its Articles of Agreement and human rights issues were not raised in the process of amending these Articles on several occasions. Furthermore, the autonomy of the IMF with regard to the UN was established in their agreement of 1947.[40]

B. THE PRACTICE OF THE IMF

Though he rejected the idea that the IMF has a mandate to promote human rights, G.B. Taplin added that

> 'this is all too narrow – the question might be, what is the Fund effectively doing to promote human rights? And I would confidently claim that the Fund is indeed promoting human rights through a variety of channels. The emphasis by the Fund on poverty reduction, higher spending on education and health, the preparation of PRSPs [i.e. Poverty Reduction Strategy Papers] in a broad participatory process with active involvement of civil society, the enhancement of governance through all possible channels (improvements in information availability to facilitate accountability and dialogue, the strengthening of the rule of law, the promotion of transparency in government policies), and the push for a reduced role of the state in economic activity are all critical areas for the empowerment of the civil society and preconditions for the attainment of human rights in their broad sense.'[41]

---

38 Article IV, Section 10 of the Articles of Agreement of the International Bank for Reconstruction and Development (IBRD). Articles of Agreement of the IBRD, 27 December 1945, 60 Stat. 1440, Articles of Agreement of the IBRD, 27 December 1945, 60 Stat. 1440, TIAS No. 1502, 2 *UNTS* 134 (as amended in 1965 and 1989). On the relationship between human rights and the World Bank, see D. Kinley, 'Human rights and the World Bank: Practice, Politics and Law', in A. Palacio, C. Sage and M. Woolcock, eds., *The World Bank Legal Review: Law, Equity and Development* (The Hague, Martinus Nijhoff Publishers 2006) pp. 353–383; G.A. Sarfaty, 'Why culture matters in international institutions: the marginality of human rights at the World Bank', 103 *American Journal of International Law* (2009) pp. 647–683.

39 A. Clapham, op. cit. n. 15, at p. 144.

40 G.B. Taplin, loc. cit. n. 2.

41 *Ibid.*

In practice, one notices that the IMF has increased the issues it takes into consideration in its consultations and operations[42], as for instance in its financing negotiations with borrowing members, such as via the mandatory PRSP framework. When seriously indebted countries apply for debt relief from the international financial institutions or for concessional lending facilities, they have to prepare a PRSP.[43] This document is issued by the relevant country and developed through a participatory process with, among others, the civil society, whereby the country summarises its national strategy on how it will tackle poverty. The country has to present its PRSP for approval both to the IMF and to the World Bank. The international financial institutions will decide on the basis of an assessment called the 'Joint Staff Assessment'. Guidelines have been adopted for this assessment, but do not contain any references to human rights obligations.[44] There is consequently no obligation to take into account the human rights obligations of the borrower.[45] Nevertheless, the borrower may voluntarily include human rights considerations in its PRSP. For instance, the Islamic Republic of Afghanistan issued an interim PRSP in June 2006 based on three independent pillars of activity among which one pillar concerned governance, rule of law and human rights.[46] In May 2000, a PRSP of Burkina Faso placed a high priority on human rights in its development and structural adjustment efforts.[47] F. Cheru, the independent expert of the UN Commission on Human rights, considers that too much emphasis is given to macroeconomic considerations and heavily indebted poor countries may feel that increasing human rights obligations in their PRSP is not particularly helpful in convincing the international financial institutions to provide debt relief.[48] Therefore, the UN High Commission on Human Rights issued a report providing guidelines for the

---

42 D.D. Bradlow and C. Grossman, 'Limited Mandates and Intertwined Problems: A New Challenge for the World Bank and the IMF', 17 *Human rights Quarterly* (1995) p. 432; J. Gold, 'The rule of law in the International Monetary Fund', 32 *International Monetary Fund Pamphlet Series* (1980) pp. 59–60.

43 IMF, 'World Bank and IMF Endorse Country-Owned Poverty Reduction Strategies', Press release n° 99/65, 22 December 1999, available at www.imf.org/external/np/sec/pr/1999/PR9965.HTM.

44 Annex 2 to IMF/IDA, Poverty reduction strategy papers. Progress in implementation, Washington: IMF/IDA, 2001, pp. 22–27.

45 K. de Feyter, 'Self-regulation', in W. van Genugten, P. Hunt and S. Mathews, eds., *World Bank, IMF and Human Rights* (Nijmegen, Wolf Legal Publishers 2003) p. 92.

46 IMF, 'Country Report n°06/194', 2006, available at www.imf.org/external/pubs/ft/scr/2006/cr06194.pdf.

47 S. Pereira Leite, 'Human Rights and the IMF', *38 Finance & Development* 4, 2001, WL 19654133.

48 The Highly Indebted Poor Countries (HIPC) Initiative: a human rights assessment of the Poverty Reduction Strategy Papers (PRSP), Report submitted by Mr. Fantu Cheru, independent expert on the effects of structural adjustment policies and foreign debt on the full enjoyment of all human rights, particularly economic, social and cultural rights, UN Commission on Human rights, 2001, available at www2.ohchr.org/english/issues/development/debt/annual.htm.

implementation of a human-rights based approach to PRSPs. 'The draft guidelines are intended to assist countries, international agencies and development practitioners to translate human rights norms, standards and principles into pro-poor policies and strategies.'[49]

Furthermore, the IMF itself has increasingly integrated political considerations in its negotiations, particularly on good governance and transparency. The Executive Board of the IMF adopted in 1997 a guidance note on the role of the IMF in governance issues, which considered as legitimate 'for management to seek information about the political situation in member countries as an essential element in judging the prospects for policy implementation.'[50] Thus, poor governance may be addressed by the IMF if it has a significant impact on the macroeconomic situation, as for instance in its relationship with the government of Angola. At the end of the 1990s, the country had a considerable amount of debt and the IMF was crucially important for the government. The Fund conditioned its cooperation to improved transparency. Consequently, the relations between the Angolan government and the IMF have been very tense, alternating from periods during which the government was sincerely negotiating a reform program to periods where the government decided to withdraw these reforms. As noted by Human Rights Watch, it seems clear that the IMF has been one of the most consistent and forceful proponents for government transparency in Angola.[51]

Yet, increased conditionality has raised some criticisms. Joseph Stiglitz notably considers that this conditionality is generally a failure as a policy tool because the IMF considers a liberalised financial system as an end in itself.[52] He notably reproaches the IMF for not sufficiently taking into consideration the concrete situation of developing countries in order to search for appropriate and tailor-made economic policies rather than abstract policies which may be harmful in early stages of economic development.[53]

---

49 UN High Commission for Human Rights, 'Draft Guidelines: A Human Rights Approach to Poverty Reduction Strategies', available at www.unhchr.ch/pdf/povertyfinal.pdf.

50 IMF, 'The Role of the IMF in Governance Issues: Guidance Note' (Approved by the IMF Executive Board on 25 July 1997), available at www.imf.org/external/pubs/ft/exrp/govern/govindex.htm.

51 Human Rights Watch, 'Some Transparency. No Accountability. The Use of Oil Revenue in Angola and Its Impact on Human rights', 12 January 2004, available at www.hrw.org/en/reports/2004/01/12/some-transparency-no-accountability-0.

52 J. Stiglitz, *Globalization and its Discontents* (New York, Norton 2002) p. 31.

53 D. Gualerzi, 'Stiglitz on Globalization and Development with an Eye to Keynes', 17(2) *Review of Political Economy* (2005) pp. 317–329.

C. EVOLUTION OF THE MANDATE AND THE PRACTICE OF THE IMF

As noted by former IMF General Counsel Gianviti, though the purpose of the IMF has not changed, both its practice and mandate have evolved to meet the needs of its members.[54] The Fund 'has slowly mutated from a monetary organisation into a macro-economically oriented development financing institution.'[55] Though the IMF is continuously denying the role of development institution[56], Article I of its Articles of Agreement notably indicates that the purposes of the IMF are 'to facilitate the expansion and balanced growth of international trade, and to contribute thereby to the promotion and maintenance of high levels of employment and real income and to the development of the productive resources of all members as primary objectives of economic policy.'[57]

This evolution of the IMF mandate has been accompanied by an increasing awareness of the importance of human rights and their relevance to help the IMF achieve its goals. The Committee on Economic, Social and Cultural Rights has stated that 'the realms of trade, finance and investment are in no way exempt from human rights obligations and principles, and that the international organisations with specific responsibilities in these areas should play a positive and constructive role in relation to human rights.'[58] This view seems to be shared by former World Bank General Counsel R. Dañino who acknowledged that '[a]s the concept of development evolved, human rights and international human rights law have become increasingly relevant to helping the Bank achieve its mission and fulfil its purposes' and that 'it is now evident that human rights are an intrinsic part of the Bank's mission.'[59]

---

54 F. Gianviti, loc. cit. n. 17.

55 D.D. Bradlow, 'The Governance of the IMF: The Need for Comprehensive Reform', September 2006, available at www.g24.org/brad0906.pdf, pp. 1–2.

56 IMF, 'What is the IMF?', 30 September 2006, available at www.imf.org/external/pubs/ft/exrp/what.htm.

57 Article I of the Articles of Agreement of the International Monetary Fund, 27 December 1945, 60 Stat. 1401, 2 *UNTS* 39 (as amended in 1969, 1978, 1992 and 2009). See also J.M. Boughton and D. Lombardi eds., *Finance, Development and the IMF* (Oxford, Oxford University Press 2009).

58 Sub-Commission resolution 1998/12, United Nations, Economic and Social Council, Sub-Commission on Prevention of Discrimination and Protection of Minorities, *Human rights as the primary objective of trade, investment and financial policy*, UN Doc. E/CN.4/Sub.2/Res/1998/12, 20 August 1998.

59 R. Dañino, 'Legal Opinion on Human Rights and the Work of the World Bank by the Senior Vice President and General Counsel', 27 January 2006, available at www.ifiwatchnet.org/sites/ifiwatchnet.org/files/DaninoLegalOpinion0106.pdf. He added, that '[w]here violations or non-fulfillment of obligations are at issue, and where these have an economic impact, the Bank should take these into consideration. Furthermore, if a human rights violation leads to a breach of international obligations relevant to the Bank, such as those created under binding decisions of the UN Security Council, the Bank should also take those violations into account.'

At the IMF, former General Counsel Gianviti indicated that human rights policies of may be relevant in some cases.

> 'Another basis for Fund involvement is its assessment, as a condition for its assistance, that the member's program is viable and likely to be implemented. This means that, if a program is so strict that it is likely to generate strong popular opposition, it may not be implemented, and the Fund should not support it. It also means that, if egregious or systematic violations of human rights lead foreign governments or creditors to suspend their financial assistance or other forms of external financing, the program may not be implemented, and the Fund should not support it. Clearly this does not establish a direct link with the objectives of the Covenant [on Economic, Social and Cultural Rights]. However, to the extent that major violations of economic and social human rights trigger civil unrest or a lack of foreign financing, there would be at least an indirect link. Whether or not a program may create such problems is a matter of judgment for the Managing Director when transmitting the member's request to the Executive Board and for the Executive Board when deciding on the request.'[60]

Moreover, the interdependency of economic development and human rights has been noted by numerous authors, considering on one hand that 'economic development is a means to promote human rights.'[61] As stated in the Human Development Report 2000, 'a decent standard of living, adequate nutrition, health care, education and decent work and protection against calamities are not just development goals – they are also human rights.'[62] On the other hand, research has shown that respect for human rights facilitates economic development.[63] Development is not only measured in economic terms[64] and is to be understood as 'a comprehensive economic, social, cultural and political process, which aims at the constant improvement of the well-being of the entire population and of all individuals.'[65] As a consequence, increasing the protection of human rights serves to promote economic growth. M. Robinson, former UN High Commissioner for Human Rights, declared that while eradicating poverty

60 F. Gianviti, loc. cit. n. 17, at para. 51.

61 P. Alston and M. Robinson eds., *Human rights and Development. Towards Mutual Reinforcement* (Oxford, Oxford University Press 2005); S.I. Skogly, loc. cit. n. 35, at p. 754.

62 UNDP, Human Development Report, *Human Rights and Development*, 2000 p. 8.

63 D. Kaufmann, 'Human rights and governance: The empirical challenge', in P. Alston and M. Robinson, eds., *Human rights and Development. Towards Mutual Reinforcement* (Oxford, Oxford University Press 2005) pp. 352–402; A. Sen, *Development as freedom* (New York, Knopf 1999).

64 S.I. Skogly, loc. cit. n. 35, at p. 754.

65 *Declaration on the Right of Development*, adopted by General Assembly Resolution 41/128 of 4 December 1986.

must be our first goal in this new millennium, poverty cannot be eradicated without the realisation of human rights.[66]

Rodwan Abouharb and David Cingranelli conducted a study on the impact of structural adjustment programmes on human rights in 131 developing countries between 1981 and 2003. This study showed that on average structural adjustments had led to less respect for economic and social rights, and worker rights. 'Compliance with structural adjustment conditions causes governments to lessen respect for the economic and social rights of their citizens, including the rights to decent jobs, education, health care and housing.'[67] They concluded that 'equitable economic development efforts would be more efficient and many of the negative impacts of World Bank and IMF loans and grants would be mitigated or eliminated if the IFIs pursued a human-rights based strategy of development assistance.'[68]

Among scholars, many arguments have been raised towards the progressive inclusion of human rights considerations within IMF policies. It has been suggested that such policies should take into account their impact on human development objectives, including human rights. Some authors have encouraged the development of operational policies to ensure that the projects and programs are both in conformity with their human rights obligations and 'do not undermine the ability of other subjects of international law to act in conformity with their own legal obligations.'[69] International financial institutions should have with respect to human rights generally a 'duty of vigilance' to ensure that actions do not have negative effects on the human rights situation in its borrowing members.[70] Others go further and consider that the IFIs substantial influence in borrowing countries make it becoming 'increasingly untenable that the IFIs should function without human rights responsibilities within their spheres of influence, and without accountability for the impact of their economic decisions on the exercise of human rights.'[71]

66 UN High Commission for Human Rights, 'Draft Guidelines: A Human Rights Approach to Poverty Reduction Strategies', available at www.unhchr.ch/pdf/povertyfinal.pdf.

67 R. Abouharb and D. Cingranelli, op. cit. n. 35, at pp. 4–5.

68 *Ibid.*, p. 13.

69 D.D. Bradlow, 'The World Bank, the IMF, and human rights', 6 *Transnational Law & Contemporary Problems* (1996) pp. 48–89; A. McBeth, 'Breaching the Vacuum: A Consideration of the Role of International Human rights Law in the Operations of the International Financial Institutions', *International Journal of Human rights* (2006) pp. 385–404

70 P. Klein, 'La responsabilité des organisations financières internationales et les droits de la personne', *Revue Belge de Droit International* (1999) p. 97.

71 M.E. Salomon, 'International Economic Governance and Human rights Accountability', in M.E. Salomon, A. Tostensen and W. Vandenhole, eds., *Casting the Net Wider: Human rights, Development and New Duty-Bearers* (Antwerp, Intersentia 2007) p. 27.

These arguments seem to plead for an integration of human rights within IMF policies. However, from a strict legal point of view, this theory is difficult to reconcile with the IMF's constitutional mandate. What is the exact scope of the IMF's obligation towards human rights? The view expressed by M. Dañino in relation to the World Bank is revealing since, though he recognises the importance of human rights as an intrinsic part of the Bank's mission, he considers that the role of the Bank (and by analogy, the Fund) 'is not that of an enforcer of human rights obligations.' Indeed, enforcement 'is primarily the responsibility of member countries and of other, non-financial entities, such as the United Nations treaty monitoring bodies and regional human rights organizations.'[72] In 2001, the IMF still considered that it did not have to take into consideration human rights in its activities, given that 'it has no general mandate to ensure that its members abide by their international obligations', including human rights obligations.[73] S. Peereira Leite, Assistant Director at the IMF Office in Europe declared that 'while human rights advocates should be given every opportunity to participate in the PRSP consultations, they should not expect the IMF to impose human rights conditions on its assistance to member countries. The IMF does not have the expertise required to make judgments in this area.'[74]

Almost ten years after this statement, the question arises whether the IMF would still have the same perception of its relations with human rights nowadays.

One may be tempted to advocate a more active participation of the IMF in the promotion of human rights in following a human rights-based development strategy. As argued by R. Abouharb and D. Cingranelli, the goals of the World Bank and the IMF should be the 'equitable economic development, defined as the simultaneous achievement of economic growth and advancement in protection of economic and social rights of citizens.'[75] Following these authors, the Fund should establish a minimal level of respect for human rights as a necessary condition to enter into negotiations, analyse the human rights impact assessment of its activities and support national authorities to make progress in the protection of human rights.

Yet, in the actual situation, there is no legal argument obliging the IMF to follow these prescriptions. As a consequence, the debate remains open and mainly depends on the political will of both the authorities and the Member States of the IMF to clarify this issue.[76]

---

72 R. Dañino, loc. cit. n. 59.

73 F. Gianviti, loc. cit. n. 17, at p.28.

74 S. Pereira Leite, loc. cit. n. 47.

75 See notably R. Abouharb and D. Cingranelli, op. cit. n. 35, at p. 34.

76 Z.F. Kabasakal Arat, 'Human Rights and Structural Adjustment', 7(4) *Journal of Human Rights* (2008) pp. 397–399.

III. MECHANISMS OF ACCOUNTABILITY

A. ACCOUNTABILITY: PROBABLY THE WEAKEST ASPECT OF IMF GOVERNANCE[77]

Though the obligation to promote human rights is still debated, the obligation of the IMF to respect human rights in its activities should not be questioned anymore. The recognition of this obligation requires the establishment of mechanisms of accountability. Indeed, the effectiveness of obligations relies on an accessible, transparent and effective accountability system. The study of accountability mechanisms for human rights violations may not be entirely dissociated from a broader study of accountability mechanisms for any types of violations. This part will consequently also address features of the general accountability system of the IMF.

The IEO defines accountability in relation to the IMF as 'the ability of shareholders (and possibly other stakeholders) to hold the IMF and its decision makers to a set of standards, to judge whether they are meeting those standards, and to set rewards or sanctions accordingly. Accountability requires a set of benchmarks against which to judge performance, good reporting and monitoring mechanisms, clear lines of authority, and the capacity to sanction an agent whose performance does not meet agreed standards.'[78]

To enable the Fund to fulfil its functions, its Articles of Agreement provide for a certain degree of immunity from judicial process in connection with its activities on the territory of its Member States. Indeed, the Fund, its property, its assets and its staff enjoy immunity from any form of judicial process, unless it expressly waives such immunity.[79] Given this status of immunity from judicial process within the territory of its Member States, the accountability of the IMF may not be engaged before national courts but exclusively through other mechanisms.

The creators of the IMF have designed a system in which the IMF is accountable to its Member States through their representatives in the Board of Executive Directors and the Board of Governors. These representatives are accountable in turn to their governments and finally to their citizens through elections.

77 IMF, Independent Evaluation Office, 'Governance of the IMF – an evaluation', 2008, available at www.ieo-imf.org/eval/complete/pdf/05212008/CG_main.pdf.

78 *Ibid.*

79 Article IX, Section 3 of the Articles of Agreement of the International Monetary Fund, 27 December 1945, 60 Stat. 1401, 2 *UNTS* 39 (as amended in 1969, 1978, 1992 and 2009).

The Board of Governors is the highest decision-making body of the IMF and has responsibility for its direction and performance. It delegates most of its powers to the IMF's Executive Board, which is accountable to the Board of Governors. However, there is only one formal mechanism of accountability, namely the requirement that the Board of Executive Directors reports annually on the state of the IMF and the international financial system. This does not permit an effective assessment of the Executive Board's performance, especially since the Board of Governors meets only once a year and is not an appropriate body to challenge individual operational management decisions.

As emphasised by Daniel D. Bradlow, the Board of Executive Directors does not constitute an effective accountability channel either. Indeed, most consumer States are not directly represented within this Board and the programs developed by the Fund have become too numerous and complex to be effectively controlled by the Executive Board.[80]

If this indirect form of accountability was considered to be sufficient in the 1950s, this is not valid anymore because of the evolution of the IMF's mission and its active participation in the policy-making process within the Member States. Indeed, the shift from a monetary institution to a development financing institution has brought the IMF to develop policies which directly affect people in its Member States. Yet, there is no direct means for individuals to hold the IMF accountable.

As denounced by the IEO, 'accountability is probably the weakest aspect of IMF governance. There are no agreed standards against which to assess the actions of the IMF and no adequate mechanisms for the organisation and its governing bodies to be held accountable by the membership or by appropriate stakeholders.'[81]

With regard to its human rights obligations, the IMF has consequently enjoyed unaccountable freedom over the past 60 years.[82] As stated by Bahram Ghazi, the actual lack of any possibility of bringing a claim for a violation of human rights by the IMF constitutes a denial of justice.[83] People may only inform Governors,

80 D.D. Bradlow, 'The Changing Role of the IMF in the Governance of the Global Economy and its consequences', Workshop, *New rules for Global Finance*, 9 June 2006, available at www.new-rules.org/docs/imfreform/bradlow.pdf, pp. 29–32.

81 IMF, Independent Evaluation Office, loc. cit. n. 77.

82 C. Tan, 'Mandating Rights and Limiting Mission Creep: Holding the World Bank and International Monetary Fund Accountable for Human rights', 2(1) *Human Rights and International Legal Discourse*, 2008, p. 86.

83 B. Ghazi, op. cit. n. 12, at p. 240.

Executive Directors, IEO or parliamentarians and hope that this channel will produce effective results.[84]

Several actions have been suggested to improve the accountability of the IMF, both through internal and external accountability mechanisms.

B. INTERNAL ACCOUNTABILITY MECHANISM

The IMF has tried to avoid external accountability by developing self-regulatory mechanisms. One should mention the work of the IEO and its recommendations to improve the accountability of the IMF (Subsection 2.1). Yet, internal accountability mechanisms are exposed to severe criticisms due to the asymmetrical decision-making process of the IMF. These criticisms have to be assessed in relation to the recent developments in this area (Subsection 2.2).

1° The Independent Evaluation Office

In 2000, the IMF established an evaluation office to systematically conduct objective and independent evaluations of its activities: the IEO.[85] It regularly reviews compliance with operational policies and makes recommendations to the Executive Board for remedial action and/or revision of the operational policies.

In accordance with the IEO's terms of reference, the Director of the IEO is appointed by the Executive Directors. 'In carrying out its mandate, including the preparation of its Work Program, IEO will be free to consult with whomever and whichever groups it deems necessary, both within and outside the Fund.' The IEO will publish reports (within the constraints imposed by the need to respect the confidentiality of the information provided to the Fund by the Member States) presenting its conclusions. In conducting its work, the IEO should avoid interfering with operational activities, including programs, or attempting to micro-manage the institution.[86]

As denounced by Bahram Ghazi, '[a]ll these elements together make it hard for the IEO to work without pressure [...] Another very important criticism is the fact that it is not currently envisaged that those most directly affected by the

84 J.A. Scholte, 'Civil Society and IMF Accountability', CSGR Working Paper 244/08, May 2008, available at www2.warwick.ac.uk/fac/soc/csgr/research/workingpapers/2008/24408.pdf.

85 IMF, Independent Evaluation Office, loc. cit. n. 77.

86 IMF, Independent Evaluation Office, 'Terms of Reference for the Independent Evaluation Office of the International Monetary Fund' (Revised on 16 November 2004), available at www.ieo-imf.org/about/tor.pdf.

IMF's operations will be granted any formal right to participate in the work of the evaluation office. This creates the risk that the office will not have great credibility with outsiders, and so can be safely ignored by the IMF staff and management.'[87]

The IEO only has the competence to make recommendations, subject to the IMF's commitment to enforce them in order to have effective results. In 2008, the IEO issued a report on the governance of the IMF[88], in which it recommended *inter alia* the following reforms:

- The roles and responsibilities of the IMF's governance bodies, namely the Board and the Management must be clarified.[89] In addition to strengthening the IMF's effectiveness and facilitate accountability, this clarification also aims to minimise overlaps and address possible gaps.
- The Fund needs more systematic ministerial involvement. Currently, the International Monetary and Financial Committee (IMFC) is an advisory body which lacks a mandate for setting strategic decisions and providing high-level oversight of the IMF. The IEO therefore calls for the activation of a Council as a Ministerial Governance Body. This ultimate decision-making body should be given the explicit mandate to exercise oversight over the IMF on behalf of the Board of Governors.[90]
- 'The Board's effectiveness is hindered by excessive focus on executive, rather than supervisory, functions. The Board should reorient its activities towards a supervisory role, playing a more active part in formulating strategy, monitoring policy implementation to ensure timely corrective actions, and exercising effective oversight of Management. To this end, the Board would need to change many of its working practices, shifting away from executive, day-to-day operational activities, including through more delegation to comities and possibly to Management.'[91]
- The Management has to be made accountable for its performance within a framework establishing a process and criteria for regular assessments.[92]

These recommendations deemed to improve the IMF's accountability need to be combined with an institutional commitment on the part of managers to implement these recommendations. The Executive Board agreed in January 2007 to a more systematic approach and stronger monitoring of the implementation of Board-endorsed IEO recommendations. A first Management Implementation Plan was

87 B. Ghazi, op. cit. n. 12, at p. 237.
88 IMF, Independent Evaluation Office, loc. cit. n. 77.
89 *Ibid.*, p. 19 *et seq.*
90 *Ibid.*
91 *Ibid.*, p. 1.
92 *Ibid.*, p. 19 *et seq.*

produced by the IMF staff in response to Board-endorsed recommendations and the first Periodic Monitoring Report on the state of implementation of previous recommendations was released by the IMF staff during the financial year 2008. In its annual report of 2008, the IEO welcomed 'this new framework as an important step forward in maintaining an effective institutional accountability framework, as well as promoting a strong learning culture at the IMF.'[93]

These foregoing developments may indicate the inclination of the IMF management to take into consideration the recommendations of the IEO, which would certainly improve the accountability of the IMF. Yet, its mandate does not permit interested parties to challenge IMF programs but solely to address public concerns about accountability. Consequently, there is still a need to establish a complaint office.[94]

2° *Asymmetrical accountability*

Internal accountability mechanisms have been criticised by many scholars because of the decision-making process within the IMF. Voting power within the IMF is tied to the size of the country in the global economy, reflected in a quota for which the country has to pay subscriptions. As a consequence, decisions are mostly taken by a small group of states, namely the most industrialised countries, while the IMF's clients are mainly developing countries. R. Wade, for instance, denounced the 'asymmetrical accountability', in which a group of members – the developing countries – is governed by rules established by other members – Western NGO Watchdogs and most industrialised countries – who do not have to comply with these rules.[95]

More specifically on human rights violations, Celine Tan has stated that '[a] fundamental limitation of reliance on internal mechanisms for redressing human rights violations within the Bank and the Fund has been the asymmetrical structure of decision-making – and hence, norm creation – at the institutions, which concentrates far too much discretionary power in the hands of both the institutional bureaucracy and the political governors representing the major shareholding countries.'[96]This has given rise to instances in which financing has been used to further geo-strategic or commercial objectives of these major

93 IMF, Independent Evaluation Office, 'Annual Report', 2008, available at www.ieo-imf.org/pub/ar/pdf/2008Report.pdf.

94 W. van Genugten, 'Tilburg Guiding Principles on World Bank, IMF and Human rights', in W. van Genugten, P. Hunt and S. Mathews, eds., *World Bank, IMF and Human Rights* (Nijmegen, Wolf Legal Publishers 2003).

95 R. Wade, 'Tighter Accountability? Some Dangers', in B. Carlin and A. Wood, eds., *Accountability of the International Monetary Fund* (Ottawa, Ashgate and the International Development Research Centre 2006) pp. 108–114.

96 C. Tan, loc. cit. n. 82, at p. 92.

shareholders in infringement of fundamental norms of human rights and other principles of general international law.[97]

The IMF has acknowledged the need to reform its decision-making process. On 28 April 2008, an important quota and voice reform has been adopted by the Board of Governors of the IMF. This reform of the institution's governance structure aims to realign quota and voting shares of Member States with their relative importance in the world global economy and consequently enhance the participation of emerging market and low-income countries. The quota will be increased for 54 countries and the basic votes will be tripled for low-income countries.[98] Moreover, an additional Alternate Executive Director will be created for the two African chairs at the Board. Finally, this reform envisages realignments of quota and voting shares every five years. The reform is not yet effective since it has first to be accepted by at least three-fifths of IMF members representing 85 percent of the total voting power.[99]

Despite its presentation as a far-reaching reform enhancing legitimacy and credibility, the proposed changes have been criticised by many experts for being too modest. A major problem is the formula proposed for calculating the quota and voting shares which, taken on its own,

> 'generates changes in shares that move away from rather than toward a closer alignment of voting power with economic realities. The proposed package as a whole achieves its very modest improvements only because the formula is overridden with one-time, ad hoc adjustments that mask the unpalatable consequences of the formula and because the basic votes allocated to each member are tripled. Worse still, the new formula is not a viable basis for making future adjustments in quotas and votes that will adequately reflect changes in relative positions in the world economy.'[100]

---

97 C. Tan, loc. cit. n. 82, at p. 93 quoting for example C. Aid, *Enough is Enough: The Debt Repudiation Option* (London, Christian Aid 2007); S. George and F. Sabelli, *Faith and Credit: The World Bank's Secular Empire* (Boulder and London, Westview Press 1994); J. Hanlon, '"Illegitimate" Loans: Lenders, Not Borrowers, Are Responsible', 27 *Third World Quarterly* (2006) pp. 211–226; N. Woods, *The Globalizers: The IMF, the World Bank and their Borrowers* (Ithaca and London, Cornell University Press 2006) pp. 22–24.

98 IMF, 'Quota and Voice Publications', 13 June 2008 available at www.imf.org/external/np/fin/quotas/pubs/index.htm.

99 According to the IMF's website, as of early March 2010, 65 members representing about 70 percent of total voting power had accepted. See IMF Factsheet, 'IMF Quotas', 11 March 2010, available at www.imf.org/external/np/exr/facts/quotas.htm.

100 N. Birdsall, C. Bradford, R. C. Bryant, J. M. Griesgraber, H. Kharas, J. Linn, E. M. Truman and J. Williamson, 'Letter to the Executive Directors of the IMF and their Governments', 26 March 2008, available at www.brookings.edu/opinions/2008/~/media/Files/rc/opinions/2008/0409_imf_linn/letter_imf_quota_reform.pdf.

On 4 September 2008, D. Strauss-Kahn, Managing Director of the IMF, announced the appointment of a committee of eminent persons to assess the adequacy of the Fund's current framework for decision-making and advice on any modifications that might enable the institution to fulfil its global mandate more effectively. He added that 'the committee's perspective [...] will provide yet another important input to our reform efforts, which have benefited recently from important work by many groups and individuals, including the Fund's Independent Evaluation Office; the Fund's Executive Directors, who have formed a working group to focus on these issues; numerous academics and analysts; and civil society groups.'[101]

One may hope that these developments will lead to improvements in the accountability of the IMF. Yet, in the present state of things, these developments are not sufficient and do not elude the criticisms raised against internal accountability mechanisms. It seems consequently that the IMF should rather seek to establish external accountability mechanisms.[102] These external accountability mechanisms will be studied in the following section of this contribution.

C. EXTERNAL ACCOUNTABILITY MECHANISMS

There is a need for stronger accountability mechanisms at the IMF.[103] Actions have to be taken to correct this situation, among which the creation of an external complaints mechanism should be envisaged. An ombudsman or an inspection panel should be assigned to receive and investigate complaints brought by any person, organisation, or state, against the IMF (Subsection 3.1).

Focusing on human rights, one should mention the possible role of the UN structures to improve the IMF's accountability, as suggested by Sigrun I. Skogly. For instance, the UN Human Rights Commission could establish a working group or a sub-commission which would have to deal with complaints concerning human rights impacts of the IMF's activities (Subsection 3.2).

Furthermore, the accountability of individual Member States for actions of the IMF may be taken into consideration (Subsection 3.3). Indeed, some members of the IMF may abuse its personality and initiate or support decisions leading to human rights violations. The accountability of these Member States could be

101 IMF, Press Release 08/200, 'Managing Director Strauss-Kahn Appoints Committee on IMF Governance Reform', 4 September 2008, available at www.imf.org/external/np/sec/pr/2008/pr08200.htm.

102 By external accountability mechanisms, I refer to mechanisms through which people affected by the operations of the IMF can make it accountable.

103 IMF, Independent Evaluation Office, loc. cit. n. 77.

established on the basis of international obligations, as well as domestic ones. Moreover, some Member States have imposed national human rights obligations on the state organ directing the vote on the IMF Board.

1° *Need for an External Complaints Mechanism: inspection panel or ombudsman*

The IMF lacks a mechanism like an inspection panel or an ombudsman. An internal ombudsperson has existed since 1999 to handle employment-related problems for IMF staff[104], but there is no specific office where external stakeholders can submit allegations of harm or misconduct.

The World Bank has established an inspection panel[105] in 1993 where groups of at least two persons can file claims for actual or likely harms resulting from failure by the Bank to act in accordance with its policies and procedures. This inspection panel primarily focuses on compliance review. This panel may not be considered as a human rights accountability mechanism as such since it has no mandate to consider the Bank responsible for human rights violations. In some cases, requesters have invoked human rights at the panel, which has substantively responded to these claims. Nevertheless, the inspection panel verifies the accordance of Bank actions with its operational policies and not human rights law. 'Human rights violations are only relevant to the extent that they result in non-compliance with the operational policies.'[106]

According to Daniel D. Bradlow, '[t]he model that is most suited to the IMF's needs is an ombudsman.'[107] In addition to the function exercised by the inspection panel, namely the compliance review, the ombudsman would also be entitled to engage in solving problems of affected people and to give the IMF the possibility of learning lessons about the implications of its operations in reality. Such ombudsman should be independent of the IMF board and management. Moreover, he should be entitled to receive and investigate complaints launched by any person, organisation, or state, against the IMF. However, in this proposal, the jurisdiction of the ombudsman should be limited to cases of non-compliance with the institution's operational policies and procedures in order to avoid any

104 IMF, 'Ombudsperson's Terms of Reference', 30 June 1999, available at www.imf.org/external/hrd/ombuds.htm.

105 International Bank for Reconstruction and Development, International Development Association, Resolution No. IBRD 93-10, Resolution No. IDA 93-6, 'The World Bank Inspection Panel', available at http://siteresources.worldbank.org/EXTINSPECTIONPANEL/Resources/ResolutionMarch2005.pdf.

106 K. de Feyter, loc. cit. n. 45, pp. 79–137, especially at p. 119.

107 D.D. Bradlow, 'Operational Policies and Procedures and an Ombudsman', in B. Carin and A. Wood, eds., *Accountability of the International Monetary Fund* (Ottawa, Ashgate and the International Development Research Centre 2005) p. 105.

encroachment on the Member States' sovereignty. Since the IMF has not adopted any human rights policy, this limited jurisdiction precludes the ombudsman from constituting an effective accountability mechanism in the fields of human rights. Such mechanism should have human rights specifically mentioned in its mandate.

As to the form, both accountability mechanisms – the ombudsman and the inspection panel – have advantages and disadvantages. An ombudsman is a very flexible mechanism, which allows notably for mediation and is generally oriented towards a conflict resolution. However, it may be considered as too weak, as denounced by civil society organisations during the debates preceding the establishment of an inspection panel at the World Bank.[108] On the opposite, an inspection panel follows a clear procedural process and constitutes a stronger mechanism. Yet, it does in principle not engage in mediation nor in monitoring to ensure that victims have received redress. Neither the ombudsman – as proposed by Daniel D. Bradlow – nor the World Bank inspection panel has a power of enforcement.[109]

Ideally, an independent inspection panel should be established with a clear mandate in the area of human rights. It would provide for a strong external complaint mechanism for individual victims of human rights violations attributable to the IMF. In addition, an independent monitoring panel could be established to monitor the situation and provide victims with reparation.

The High-Level Panel on IMF Board Accountability convened by the 'New Rules for Global Finance' coalition[110] was not of one mind regarding an external complaint mechanism for the Fund. Its participants admitted that the Fund has been involved in a number of controversial programs that may have resulted in substantial complaints about its functioning. There was a consensus that given the centrality of the contemporary principles of accountability to stakeholders, the Fund should engage in an experimental approach. Therefore, the Panel recommended that

> 'as a first step, the Fund should hold public sessions, conducted by an independent body, to review some of the most important controversies in its recent history.

108 S. Park, 'Designing accountability, international economic organisations and the World Bank's Inspection Panel', 64(1) *Australian Journal of International Affairs* (2010) pp. 13–36, at p. 27.

109 In D.D. Bradlow's proposal, the ombudsman makes a report which is publicly available to the Executive Board. At the World Bank, the inspection panel issues recommendations and the Bank management has to report its plans to improve the compliance. However, none of these mechanisms may enforce its decisions

110 The 'New Rules for Global Finance' is a coalition of development, human rights, labor, environmental, and religious organizations and scholars analysing and suggesting reforms of the global financial architecture. This coalition has convened a panel of experts with diverse backgrounds to assess how the governance of the IMF could be improved and to establish recommendations to the IMF.

> Interested stakeholders should be able to participate in these public sessions. There will be public reports upon the conclusion of these sessions. The purpose of these public sessions should not only be to provide an independent report on the selected controversies, but also to give the IMF some experience in dealing with an external complaints mechanism.'[111]

2° *United Nations Human Rights Commission*

Nowadays, there is no organ within the UN where individuals can bring cases of human rights violations by the IMF. Sigrun I. Skogly proposes that the UN Commission on Human Rights should deal with the observance of the human rights obligations of the IMF (and of the World Bank). Since the IMF would probably take criticism from a high level UN group of experts seriously, 'one could establish a working group that would receive communications from individuals and organisations, point to adverse effects of the operations of the two institutions, and discuss this publicly.'[112] As pointed out by the author, it would be difficult, however, to use this model in order to obtain an individual or even group redress. Moreover, and one could fear that the demands would be excessive.

3° *Accountability of individual Member States*

In addition to the accountability of the IMF, one should examine the question whether the conduct of Member States within the IMF may be taken into consideration in the case of human rights violations attributable to the IMF. Indeed, many decisions of the IMF may be initiated or supported by some of its members, especially those who control the IMF. Member States should not be shielded from culpability in case of human rights-violating acts or omissions.

J. d'Aspremont has argued in favour of concurrent or joint responsibility of Member States having an *effective* and *overwhelming* control over the decision-making process of the organisations in cases where such acts would constitute a breach of their international obligations if they were committed by themselves and where the international personality of the organisation has been abused by these Member States.[113]

---

111 High-Level Panel on IMF Board Accountability, 'Key Findings and Recommendations', *New Rules for Global Finance*, 10 April 2007, available at www.new-rules.org/docs/imf_board_accountability.pdf.

112 S.I. Skogly, op. cit. n. 8, at pp. 186–188.

113 J. d'Aspremont, 'The Limits of Exclusive Responsibility of International Organizations', 1(2) *Human Rights and International Legal Discourse* (2007) pp. 217–229.

Such mechanism would certainly increase the oversight of the IMF's operations. It would probably be even more efficacious if national or regional mechanisms could be taken into consideration to establish improper behaviour.[114]

Some Member States of the IMF have adopted national human rights legislation imposing certain obligations on the Executive Directors representing them. For instance, the UK Human Rights Act obliges all UK government departments to pursue respect of human rights in their work. As a public authority, the Department for International Development (DFID) is bound by the Human Rights Act. It issued a Guidance Note on the Human Rights Act in 2005, which stated that if an act or a failure to act is incompatible with the European Convention on Human Rights, a 'human rights claim' can be brought against the Secretary of State.[115] As M.E. Salomon notes,

> 'executive directors acting on behalf of the UK in the Bank and Fund are bound to comply with their national and international human rights obligations in the policies they pursue that impact on the exercise of those rights in developing countries, the approval vote cast by their representative constituting a state act and thus subject to human rights law and the general law on state responsibility.'[116]

In the United States, the US Code, Chapter 7, Section 262d entitled *Human Rights and United States Assistance policies with international financial institutions* states that

> 'the United States government, in connection with its voice and vote in [...] the International Monetary Fund shall advance the cause of human rights, including by seeking to channel assistance towards countries other than those whose governments engage in – (1) a pattern of gross violations of internationally recognised human rights, such as torture or cruel, inhumane, or degrading treatment or punishment, prolonged detention without charges, or other flagrant denial to life, liberty, and the security of person; [...] The United States Executive Directors are authorized and instructed to oppose any loan, any extension of financial assistance, or any technical assistance to any country [...], unless such assistance is directed specifically to programs which serve the basic human needs of the citizens of such country.'[117]

114 C. Tan, loc. cit. n. 82, at pp. 113–114.
115 The Human Rights Act: Building a Culture of Respect for Human Rights in DFID, Guidance Note, 2005.
116 M.E. Salomon, loc. cit. n. 71 (footnotes omitted).
117 Section 701 of the International Financial Institutions Act (22 U.S.C. 262d).

Human rights groups have criticised the selective application of this provision by the United States[118], which added to the general suspicion of IMF circles towards human rights.[119]

In cases of non-compliance with national human rights legislation, victims may seek to obtain judicial review of the decisions taken by the state organ who directs the vote of the Executive Directors on the IMF Board. One could argue that the accountability of individual Member States would run counter to the legal personality of the Fund and the theory of organs. However, these theories do not imply that the state is immune from any legal responsibility for its acts when it exercises effective control over the international organisation. The European Court of Human Rights has stated that the transfer of powers of a state to an International Organisation does not necessarily preclude the human rights responsibility of the Member States with regard to the exercise of these powers.[120] Moreover, the Court decided that 'state action taken in compliance with such legal obligations is justified as long as the relevant organisation is considered to protect fundamental rights, as regards both the substantive guarantees offered and the mechanisms controlling their observance, in a manner which can be considered at least equivalent to that for which the Convention provides.'[121] Following this jurisprudence, the responsibility of Member States for acts within the IMF could be tackled if the decisions taken by the IMF do not offer protection which is 'comparable' to human rights standards by which the Member States are bound.

A similar reasoning may be found with regard to the International Covenant on Economic, Social and Cultural rights. Indeed, this treaty contains an obligation of international assistance and cooperation in Article 2(1). The Committee on Economic, Social and Cultural Rights has interpreted that provision in its concluding observations in 2000 on many industrialised countries and notably Belgium as follows:

> 'the Committee encourages the Government of Belgium, as a member of international organizations, in particular the International Monetary Fund and the World Bank, to do all it can to ensure that the policies and decisions of those organizations are in conformity with the obligations of states parties to the Covenant, in particular the obligations contained in article 2.1 concerning international assistance and cooperation.'[122]

---

118 Human Rights First, *The World Bank: Governance and Human Rights*, 2nd ed. (New York, Human Rights First 1995).

119 A. Clapham, op. cit. n. 15, at p. 141.

120 European Commission of Human Rights, *M. & Co. v. Germany*, 9 February 1990, *DR* 64, p. 138.

121 ECtHR, *Bosphorus Airways v. Ireland*, Application No. 45036/98, 30 June 2005.

122 CESCR, 'Concluding Observations: Belgium', UN Doc. E/C.12/1/Add.54, 2000, available at http://sim.law.uu.nl/SIM/CaseLaw/UNCom.nsf/804bb175b68baaf7c125667f004cb333/4013ee3b71f0d4c2c12569ce004d6ae2?OpenDocument.

IV. CONCLUSION

There is a general trend toward the recognition of the contribution of human rights to the development and poverty reduction process, which are intrinsic parts of the IMF mandate. However, the exact role of the IMF remains unclear within this evolution. Given its substantial influence on borrowing countries, one can hardly accept that the IMF does not bear any responsibility for human rights.

Despite the IMF's reluctance to consider itself bound by any human rights provisions, there is a general consensus emerging among scholars that the IMF is under some obligation to abide by fundamental principles of human rights[123] and that human rights are part of a larger framework of international law in which all legal actors operate.

In addition to this obligation to respect human rights, the obligation to promote human rights gains ground. The IMF objects that this does not feature in its Articles of Agreement and that it does not have sufficient expertise to impose human rights conditions in its decisions. Indeed, there is no binding commitment obliging the IMF to promote human rights. As a consequence, the debate remains open and mainly depends on the political will of the authorities and the Member States of the IMF to clarify this issue.

If one considers the Fund to be bound by these obligations, the question of the accountability of the Fund for human rights violations arises. Major changes in the governance of the Fund are required to reinforce its accountability and to continue its role as global financial stability promoter. The recent developments and the ongoing reform within the IMF seem to indicate an increasing awareness within the IMF of the necessity to reform its accountability system and its decision-making process.

Finally, the absence of an external accountability mechanism may be detrimental to upholding individual's human rights. An inspection panel should be established to receive and investigate complaints launched by any person against the IMF in the fields of human rights. In addition, an independent monitoring panel should ensure that victims receive redress.

123 M. Darrow, loc. cit. n. 12, at pp. 133–134.

THE WORLD TRADE ORGANIZATION: AN OBSTACLE TO ENFORCING HUMAN RIGHTS OBLIGATIONS?

Jeroen DENKERS and Nicola JÄGERS*

I. INTRODUCTION

Legal scholars increasingly claim that international organisations can be held responsible for human rights violations in their international operations. At the same time it should be acknowledged that not all international organisations have autonomous powers that, when exercised, directly violate human rights. Legally speaking, international organisations can only be held accountable if they have actual duties in international law, which they violate rather than the Member States acting collectively.[1] The relevant question in this respect is whether the organisation under scrutiny bears separate rights and duties under international law. In this context, the World Trade Organization (WTO) as an international organisation cannot be compared to other international organisations such as the World Bank or the International Monetary Fund (IMF). Whereas these organisations, independently from Member States, develop policies which can at times directly violate human rights, the WTO as an organisation does not. This stems from the fact that the WTO is not much more than a negotiating forum in which Member States negotiate on international trade rules which regulate their domestic trade policies. Thus, if the implementation of these trade policies violates human rights obligations the responsibility should be with the WTO Member States and not the organisation as such. Yet, there are autonomous activities that the organisation employs which may have implications for the protection of human rights. One of those activities

* Nicola Jägers is associate professor of international law at the Center for Transboundary Legal Development, Tilburg University, The Netherlands. Jeroen Denkers completed his PhD at Tilburg University (published as: *The World Trade Organization and Import Bans in Response to Violations of Fundamental Labour Rights* (Antwerp, Intersentia 2008). He now works for the Dutch Ministry of Justice. The opinions expressed in this contribution are the authors own and do no not represent the view of the Ministry of Justice in any way.

1 C.F. Amerasinghe, *Principles of the Institutional Law of International Organizations* (Cambridge, Cambridge University Press 1996) p. 78.

is the WTO Trade Policy Review Mechanism (TPRM). Under this system trade policies of Members are reviewed on a regular basis. This review is done by the WTO General Council that meets as the Trade Policy Review Body on the basis of a report prepared by the government of the State of which trade policy is being examined and a report prepared by economists of the WTO secretariat. The relevant question in this respect is whether the WTO secretariat should take human rights into account in their review. Currently, this is not the case. However, it is not uncommon that States actually pose questions with regard to compliance with core labour standards in the TPRM. In the review of Chinese trade policy, for instance, the European Community (EC) posed questions on supervision of labour standards and asked which initiatives China had taken to ensure respect for labour standards in Export Processing Zones (EPZs).[2] Obviously, such questions may contribute in pressuring States to comply with core labour rights. The effect of such reviews, however, should not be overestimated: first, as a best case scenario least-developed countries are reviewed every six years – though these intervals are typically longer. Second, apart from raising awareness by 'naming and shaming' there are no consequences attached to the structural denial of labour rights in the trade policy reviews. The TPRM is of a purely political nature and Members are free to ask questions on all kind of issues.

Dispute settlement is another activity – the most important one – that the WTO autonomously employs and which may have implications for the protection of human rights. Therefore, the role that the WTO dispute settlement mechanism may have in the protection of human rights will be clarified in this contribution. This will be done by using an example of a country where serious violations of fundamental workers' rights occur. This will set the stage for a broader discussion on the potential conflict between the enforcement of fundamental norms and international trade law.

II. AN EXAMPLE: BRAZIL

Although it cannot be denied that some improvement has been made in recent years, forced labour is still a serious problem in Brazil. A report by the International Labour Organization (ILO) published in 2005, estimates that at

2 Trade Policy Review Body WT/TPR/M/161/Add.2, *Minutes of Meeting Trade Policy Review of People's Republic of China* (11 September 2006) p. 87. The EC asked questions such as: 'Is China taking initiatives aimed at ensuring respect for labour standards in Export Processing Zones (EPZs)?' and 'How does China intend to ensure that employment standards covered in national employment legislation (e.g. minimum wages, working hours, health and safety at work) are respected in all companies including in those directly or indirectly engaged in international trade?'

least 25000 people in the country work under slavery-like conditions.[3] In 2008 Brazilian authorities rescued over 4500 slaves from captivity but it is estimated that between 25000 and 40000 people continue to work as bonded labourers.[4] Most workers, often entire families, are persuaded to work in rural areas and once they start working they are told that they have to pay off their debts for the transport, food and housing to the employer. Their salaries, however, rarely cover the costs that the employer charges them.[5] Such practices of debt bondage are known to occur in activities such as charcoal production.[6] The charcoal is used to produce steel in blast-furnaces mainly for export purposes. It is American and European corporations that benefit from these practices through the import of the low-priced steel for the production of cars.[7] Similar conditions exist for the Brazilian sugar industry. The people working the sugar plantations are held under slavery-like conditions. And again, it is the large multinational corporations such as Coca-cola that benefit most from the low-priced sugar.[8]

As these examples show, corporations play a pivotal role in the violation of basic labour rights. In 2005, the ILO published a report entitled 'A Global Alliance against Forced Labour' which reveals that out of the 12.3 million people that are victims of forced labour worldwide nearly 10 million people are exploited through forced labour in the private economy. The remaining 2.5 million are forced to work by the State or rebel groups.[9] This raises the question if and to what extent corporations can be held accountable for violations of basic workers' rights. Currently, there is no international mechanism to hold multinational corporations to account for human rights violations. The lack of an international enforcement mechanism must however not be mistaken for a lack of applicable norms.[10] In recent years the traditional State-centric approach to international

3 ILO Report, *A Global Alliance Against Forced Labour*, ILC, 93rd session 2005, para. 190.

4 T. Phillips, 'Brazilian taskforce frees more than 4,500 slaves after record number of raids on remote farms, *The Guardian*, Saturday 3 January 2009.

5 B. Sharma, 'Anti-Slavery International, Contemporary Forms of Slavery in Brazil' (2006), available at www.antislavery.org/english/resources/reports/download_antislavery_publications/latin_america_reports.aspx (last visited 19 August 2009).

6 International Confederation of Free Trade Unions (ICFTU), 'Internationally Recognised Core Labour Standards in Brazil', Report for the WTO General CouncilReview of the TradePolicies of Brazil, Geneva (29 November and 1 December 2004), available at www.icftu.org/www/pdf/clsbrazilenglish2004.pdf#search=%22brasil%20ilo%20forced%20labour%22 (last visited 19 August 2009).

7 NRC Handelsblad, *Marta's longen zijn kapot van as en rook*, 12 June 1996.

8 NRC Handelsblad, *Zo helpen we de arme suikerboeren niet*, 24 June 2005.

9 ILO Report, op. cit. n. 3. The report further shows that the numbers are highest in Asia with nearly 9,5 million victims almost two-thirds of which fall victim to economic exploitation by private actors. About one fifth is imposed by the State in countries such as Burma (Myanmar).

10 N.M.C.P. Jägers, *Corporate Human Rights Obligations. In Search of Accountability* (Antwerp/Oxford, Intersentia 2002); A. Clapham, *Human Rights Obligations of Non-State Actors* (Oxford, Oxford University Press 2006) pp. 195–267.

law which leaves little room for scrutiny of private actors has been breaking down. Support for direct applicability of human rights norms to non-State entities can be found in several international documents[11] and it is clear that extending human rights obligations on to corporations does not meet with conceptual obstacles.[12] Evidence of the applicability of international human rights norms to corporations is most prevalent at the domestic level especially in the United States under the Alien Tort Claims Act (ATCA).[13] Be that as it may, at the international level corporations cannot be held accountable for human rights violations.

The question is therefore posed: what measures States can take in order to control undesirable corporate behaviour. States are the bearers of human rights obligations which are seen as having a tripartite character: States are required to respect, protect and fulfil the enjoyment of human rights by persons within their jurisdiction.[14] The obligation to protect implies that States must protect persons against human rights violations committed by third parties.[15] In the example used in this contribution this implies that the government of Brazil must protect the workers against the economic exploitation by corporations. Brazil has ratified

11 Most commonly referred to is the paragraph in the preamble of the Universal Declaration of Human Rights (UDHR) which states: 'that *every individual and every organ of society*, [...] shall strive [...] to promote respect for these rights and freedoms and by progressive measures, national and international, to secure their universal and effective recognition and observance [...].' Every organ of society includes corporations.

12 The idea of 'corporate human rights obligations' challenges several traditional concepts, for one, the idea that States are the only subjects of international law. International law however already addresses corporations most notably when it comes to protecting their interests. International arbitration where corporations have legal standing such as the International Center for the Settlement of Investment Disputes (ICSID) of the World Bank is an example. Also in the realm of international human rights law corporations can be seen as participants. They can invoke human rights protection as frequently happens before the European Court of Human Rights in Strasbourg. See, *inter alia*, N.M.C.P. Jägers, op. cit. n. 10; International Council of Human Rights Policy, *Beyond Voluntarism: Human Rights and the Developing international legal obligations of companies*, (Geneva 2002); and the *UN Norms on the Responsibilities of Corporations and other Business Entities with regard to Human Rights*, UN Doc. E/CN.4/Sub.2/2003/12/Rev.2 (2003).

13 For a thorough overview see: S. Joseph, *Corporations and Transnational Human Rights Litigation*, Chapter 2, (Oxford, Hart Publishing 2004).

14 H. Shue, *Basic Rights. Subsistence, Affluence, and U.S. Foreign Policy* (Princeton, Princeton University Press 1980); A. Eide, *The Right to Food*, UN. Doc.E/CN.4/Sub.2/1987/23 (7 July 1987).

15 The importance of this State obligation to protect in the field of corporate social responsibility has been underlined by the United Nations Special Representative of the Secretary General on Human Rights and Transnational Corporations and other Business Enterprises, Professor John Ruggie. In 2008, he published the report 'Protect, Respect and Remedy: A Framework for Business and Human Rights', UN Doc. A/HRC/8/5, 7 April 2008. In this report the state duty to protect against human rights violations by or involving corporations is identified as the prime pillar in the framework for corporate accountability for human rights. The other two pillars are the corporate responsibility to respect human rights and greater access by victims to effective remedy, judicial and non-judicial.

the international documents prohibiting such practices. To name a few examples: the ICCPR, the ICESCR[16] and the ILO Convention no. 29 on Forced Labour.[17] However, States where corporations operate in violation of human rights are often unable or unwilling to take steps to ensure respect for human rights by these corporations. In this light, we will discuss the question what *other* States can do to influence the situation; more specifically we will examine the particular State response of import bans.[18] As the examples show, human rights may be violated in the production process of products that are intended to be exported. Import bans are therefore a logical reaction. More concretely, Europe or the US for instance could ban the import of low-priced steel or sugar from Brazil. The US, for example, has adopted domestic legislation that allows trade sanctions if particular workers' rights in exporting countries are denied. As a result of the US Omnibus Trade and Competitiveness Act (OTCA) of 1988 amending Section 301 of the 1974 Trade Act, the systematic denial of worker rights (the right to form trade unions and to engage in collective bargaining, the prohibition of forced labour, a minimum employment age, and the establishment of minimum working conditions and pay levels) are considered an unreasonable trade practice and countries that engage in such practices can face retaliatory measures.[19]

However, the question is whether responding to these situations by adopting import bans is in conformity with international trade law. This particular matter will be discussed in the first section. Subsequently, the article explores whether international law provides a legal basis for adopting import bans in response to violations of basic workers' rights. If that is the case then a conflict with

16 Brazil ratified both documents on 24 January 1992.

17 Ratified by Brazil on 25 April 1957.

18 States can be induced to comply with their human rights obligations by using the "stick" of trade-restrictive measures such as a total import ban discussed in this contribution or by using the 'carrot' such as granting additional tariff preferences. The latter is allowed towards developing countries under the Enabling Clause which should be seen as an exception to Article 1 of the GATT. Appellate Body Report WT/DS246/AB/R, European Communities – Conditions for the Granting of Tariff Preferences to Developing Countries, 7 April 2004, paragraph 99. See further, J.P. Denkers, *The World Trade Organization and Import Bans in Response to Violations of Fundamental Labour Rights* (Antwerp, Intersentia 2008) pp. 24–25.

19 G. Caire, 'Labour Standards and International Trade' in W. Sengenberger and D. Campbell, eds., *International Labour Standards and Economic Interdependence* (Geneva, International Institute for Labour Studies 1994) pp. 303–304; P. Alston, 'Labor Rights Provisions in U.S. Trade Law' in L.A. Compa and S.F. Diamond, eds., *Human Rights, Labor Rights, and International Trade* (Philadelphia, University of Pennsylvania Press 1996) p. 73; R.M. Gadbaw and M.T. Medwig, 'Multinational Enterprises and International Labor Standards: Which Way for Development and Jobs?' in L.A. Compa and S.F. Diamond, eds., *Human Rights, Labor Rights, and International Trade* (Philadelphia, University of Pennsylvania Press 1996) p. 151. Gadbaw and Medwig show how the OTCA provides that labour rights violations will not be seen as unreasonable if the country where the violations take place can demonstrate significant progress or if the practice is not inconsistent with the level of economic development of the country.

international trade law may arise. Lastly, in the event of a potential conflict the question of how the WTO dispute settlement mechanism should deal with it will be answered.

III. THE PERMISSIBILITY OF IMPORT BANS ON SUGAR AND STEEL FROM BRAZIL UNDER WTO LAW

In order to answer the question of whether an import ban on steel or sugar from Brazil allegedly violates WTO law, the interplay between Article I, III, and XI of the General Agreement on Tariffs and Trade (GATT) should be looked into. Non-discrimination is the most important principle underlying Articles I and III. Article XI is based on the principle of market access.

A. ARTICLE XI OF THE GATT

Article XI prohibits quantitative restrictions. Therefore any ban on a particular product such as sugar or steel from Brazil violates this provision (a ban is zero quota). Import bans, however, may be covered by Article III of the GATT, which allows non-discriminatory internal regulations, rather than by Article XI. In this sense, import bans may be reallocated from the scope of Article XI to Article III. Furthermore, such bans may violate Article I of the GATT.

B. ARTICLE I OF THE GATT

Article I of the GATT contains the Most Favoured Nation (MFN) treatment principle, which means that States cannot treat the same product from different Members or non-Members differently. The purpose of Article I of the GATT is to prohibit discrimination between similar products from different countries.[20] It applies to *de jure* as well as to *de facto* discrimination.[21] A measure that does not allow import of jeans from Member A, for instance, violates Article I of the GATT if jeans from other countries do get market access. A measure that does not explicitly distinguish between goods from different countries and thus seems origin-neutral may violate Article I if the effect of the ban is discriminatory. An import ban on blue jeans, for instance, although at first sight origin-neutral, may violate Article I if country A produces blue jeans and other countries produce

---

20 M. Matsushita, T.J. Schoenbaum and P.C. Mavroidis, *The World Trade Organization. Law, Practice and Policy*, 2nd edn. (New York, Oxford University Press 2006) p. 215.

21 Appellate Body Report WT/DS139/AB/R, *Canada – Certain Measures Affecting the Automotive Industry*, 31 May 2000, at para. 78.

black jeans. If the differently coloured jeans are seen as the same product, the effect of the measure would be *de facto* discriminatory against jeans from Member A. Moreover, it seems that in order to find a violation of Article I of the GATT it is not necessary to prove trade effects; if a measure creates more favourable competitive opportunities for producers in a foreign country, for instance, by making certification for producers from one country easier without granting the same benefit to producers from all Members, it violates Article I.[22]

For present purposes, this means an import ban against sugar or steel from Brazil violates Article I of the GATT if similar ('like') products from other countries do get market access. This raises the question of when two products are considered to be alike; can differences in the production process, such as the violation of labour rights, cause two products otherwise alike to be seen as 'unlike'? The 'likeness' test, which can be found in Articles I:1, III:2 and III:4 may differ. In WTO case law it has been recognised that the meaning of the 'like products' term depends on the product and the legal provision at issue.[23] It has no fixed meaning: 'the concept of "likeness" is a relative one that evokes the image of an accordion. The accordion of "likeness" stretches and squeezes in different places as different provisions of the *WTO Agreement* are applied. The width of the accordion in any one of those places must be determined by the particular provision in which the term "like" is encountered as well as by the context and the circumstances that prevail in any given case to which that provision may apply.'[24]

Because of limited WTO case law on the issue, most scholars refer to GATT case law to determine the meaning of 'likeness' under Article I:1.[25] It is argued that it is inescapable that if a WTO Panel would have to decide on the likeness of two products under Article I:1, it will take other factors such as consumer preferences into account in its analysis.[26] This suggests that the factors that are usually considered in the 'likeness' test of Article III:4 of the GATT may be of relevance for the 'likeness' test under Article I. Therefore, the 'likeness' test under Article

---

22 Panel Report WT/DS27/R, EC – *Regime for the Importation, Sale and Distribution of Bananas*, 22 May 1997, at para. 7.239.

23 See for instance the *Asbestos* case in which the Appellate Body held that the obligations in Articles III:2 and III:4 both apply to 'like products', but that the text of both paragraphs differ. This textual difference has considerable implications for the meaning of the term 'like products' in these provisions. Moreover, it held that an assessment of likeness has to be made on a case-by-case basis. Appellate Body Report WT/DS135/AB/R, *EC – Measures Affecting Asbestos and Asbestos Containing Products*, 12 March 2001, at paras. 94–95, p. 101.

24 Appellate Body Report WT/DS8/AB/R, WT/DS10/AB/R, WT/DS11/AB/R, *Japan – Taxes on Alcoholic Beverages*, 4 October 1996, at p. 23.

25 P. Van den Bossche, N. Schrijver and G. Faber, *Unilateral Measures Addressing Non-Trade Concerns* (The Hague, The Ministry of Foreign Affairs of the Netherlands 2007) pp. 22–23; M. Matsushita, T.J. Schoenbaum and P.C. Mavroidis, op. cit. n. 20, at pp. 209–210.

26 P. van den Bossche, N. Schrijver and G. Faber, op. cit. n. 25, at p. 23.

I:1 will be elaborated on more fully when discussing the likeness test under Article III:4 of the GATT in the following section. Yet, it should be stressed from the outset that the term may still have a different meaning under the different provisions of the GATT.

C. ARTICLE III:4 OF THE GATT

Similar to Article I:1, Article III:4 of the GATT prohibits *de jure* discrimination as well as *de facto* discrimination.[27] Thus, once goods are imported they should be treated no less favourably than similar locally produced goods.[28] Basically, its purpose is to ensure that market access commitments made by Members cannot be done away with by imposing discriminatory domestic taxes or similar measures.

A regulatory measure that explicitly discriminates between foreign and domestic goods is considered to be *de jure* discriminatory. This type of discrimination was dealt with in *US – Gasoline* because the US had set a different, potentially more burdensome standard for foreign gasoline suppliers.[29] Setting different standards for foreign products compared to domestic products is not prohibited as long as it does not modify the conditions of competition to the detriment of foreign products.[30]

A regulatory measure is *de facto* discriminatory if it seems to be origin-neutral (it does not explicitly distinguish between foreign and domestic goods) but has a disproportionate impact on foreign goods. For instance, a measure that holds that only yellow flowers may be sold and producers in the importing country, unlike those in the country it imports from, predominantly grow yellow flowers. Such a measure will be suspect of *de facto* discrimination under Article III.

At first sight it seems that any import ban enforced at the border falls within the scope of Articles I and/or XI of the GATT. However, Article III of the GATT, which prohibits discriminatory domestic regulations (taxes sub 2 and non-fiscal measures sub 4), may also be applicable if internal regulations are enforced at the border. The Interpretative Note to Article III holds that this provision applies to

---

27 On the coverage of Article I of GATT see: Appellate Body Report WT/DS139/AB/R, *Canada – Certain Measures Affecting the Automotive Industry*, 31 May 2000, para. 78.

28 The National Treatment principle can be found in Article III of the GATT, Article XVII of the GATS and Article 3 of the TRIPS.

29 WTO Appellate Body Report WT/DS2/AB/R, *United States – Standards for Reformulated and Conventional Gasoline*, 29 April 1996.

30 Appellate Body Report WT/DS161/AB/R, WT/DS169/AB/R, *Korea – Measures Affecting Imports of Fresh, Chilled and Frozen Beef*, 11 December 2000, para. 144.

such measures if the national treatment standard of Article III is met.[31] This was the case in *Argentina – Hides and Leather*, in which the Panel held that Argentinean fiscal provisions which applied to imported goods at the time of their importation were nevertheless to be considered an 'internal tax' within the meaning of Article III:2 of the GATT because a similar measure was imposed on the like domestic product.[32] Pursuant to the Interpretative Note this conclusion can also be drawn if it does not concern taxes but other internal measures. Slightly reworded, if State A prohibits the import of wine this measure can be treated as an internal regulation rather than a border measure if the sale of domestically made wine is also prohibited. If such a situation would occur, it is likely that a complainant would argue that the measure it challenges violate Article III:4 of the GATT and/or Article XI of the GATT.[33] It is then up to the Panel to examine the challenged measure under any of these two provisions.[34]

In this light, it seems that an import ban based on the way a product is produced (a process-based ban) can be treated as a domestic regulation if a similar prohibition is in force for like domestic products. For present purposes this would mean that an import ban on products made in forced labour camps could be seen as an internal regulation if the importing State does not allow its own producers to engage in such practices. In such a case, the import ban will have to be examined under Article III and is therefore only incompatible with the GATT if it does not meet the requirements of that provision. As was shown in the previous section, Article I of the GATT requires a comparison between the treatment of 'like' goods from different countries upon importation. The analysis under Article III:4 attempts to reveal a different type of discrimination: it requires a comparison between the treatment of imported and domestic 'like' products.

The question remains whether differences in production processes may cause 'unlikeness'. If this is accepted, then different treatment of the product made with the disfavoured process would be allowed. The question of whether two products are considered to be 'like' depends on a number of factors. These factors

---

31 See: Interpretative Note to Article III in Annex I to the GATT. Its function is to reallocate measures from the scope of Article XI to Article III. See also: C. M. Vázquez, 'Trade Sanctions and Human Rights – Past, Present, and Future', 6 *Journal of International Economic Law* (2003) pp. 797 and 811.

32 Panel Report WT/DS155/R, *Argentina – Measures Affecting the Export of Bovine Hides and the Import of Finished Leather*, 19 December 2000, para. 11.145.

33 This is what Canada argued in *EC – Asbestos*.

34 It should be noted that in cases where it found a violation of Article III:4 of the GATT it did not continue to examine the challenged measure under Article XI of the GATT as well. See: Panel Report WT/DS135/R, *EC – Measures Affecting Asbestos and Asbestos Containing Products* (18 September 2000), para. 8.159; Panel Report WT/DS161/R, WT/DS169/AB/R, *Korea – Measures Affecting Imports of Fresh, Chilled and Frozen Beef*, 31 July 2000, para. 639.

are usually related to detectable product characteristics. Consumer preferences, however, may also play a role in the determination of 'likeness'. On this basis it has been argued that differences in the production process which are not detectable in the product itself (such as the violation of labour rights) may cause physically similar products to be considered 'unlike' because of consumer preferences alone. In *EC – Asbestos*, consumer preferences were affected by detectable characteristic: (the toxicity) of the product. It remains unclear whether consumer preferences alone are a strong basis for considering physically similar products to be unlike. There has been a growing trend of thought which recognises that there are situations where consumer preferences alone can change the competitive relationship of two products otherwise alike.[35] For this to be the case, however, quantitative evidence should prove that a large majority of consumers are willing to pay more for products made with the favoured process. However, if this cannot be proven, then a ban against products from one country violates Article I of the GATT if physically similar products from other countries do gain market access. To illustrate, if a Member exports only carpets which are made by children then a ban against all products from this country violates Article I of the GATT when carpets that are made by machines from other countries do get in. Since the products are physically similar (in contrast to the way they are produced) they should be treated similarly.

It seems that a ban on steel or sugar from Brazil, if it is covered by Article III:4 of the GATT, violates this provision because the regulation is not origin-neutral: it is not based on an objective requirement. Thus, a ban on sugar from Brazil will also affect Brazilian producers who use the favoured production process. Domestic producers who use the same production process are allowed to sell on the importing State's market. Therefore, the measure discriminates between domestic products and foreign products.

Summarising, it seems that an import ban on sugar and steel from Brazil raised by an importing WTO Member violates the substantive obligations of the GATT. This means that such measures may be challenged before the WTO dispute settlement system.

IV. WTO DISPUTE SETTLEMENT AND HUMAN RIGHTS

The reform of the old GATT dispute settlement mechanism is commonly seen as one of the most important achievements of the Uruguay Round which led to the establishment of the WTO. This is not strange considering that a strong dispute

35 P. Van den Bossche, N. Schrijver and G. Faber, op. cit. n. 25, at p. 64.

settlement mechanism is a prerequisite for a smooth functioning of the international trade system. The new WTO dispute settlement mechanism has limited but compulsory jurisdiction. It is limited in that it has the competence to deal with claims under the WTO Agreements only.[36] More specifically, the claims over which it has jurisdiction are categorised into 'violation claims', 'non-violation claims' and 'situation claims'.[37] The first type is the most common one and flows from the alleged failure of another Member to carry out its WTO obligations. The second type rarely occurs and follows from the application of a measure by another Member which undermines market access commitments. The third type of claim is the most vague one and has, to date, never been used.

The jurisdiction of the WTO dispute settlement mechanism is compulsory or exclusive because Members are obliged to have recourse to the WTO dispute settlement process to the exclusion of other jurisdictions when they seek redress of a WTO law violation.[38] Taken together, this means that if a Member unilaterally adopts trade restrictive measures in response to human rights violations that take place in another Member's territory the latter can go to the WTO in Geneva to complain.

For instance, the question of whether the implementation of selective public procurement policies, which prohibit State agencies from contracting with corporations doing business in a country where gross human rights violations take place, violate WTO law has already been raised in the Massachusetts case. The European Union and Japan claimed that the selective public procurement policy implemented by Massachusetts was in violation of the WTO Government Procurement Agreement[39] as it imposed conditions that were not essential to fulfil the contract and were based on political instead of economic considerations.[40] The EU therefore requested consultation in the WTO.[41] The

36 Those Agreements have been enumerated in Appendix 1 to the Dispute Settlement Understanding (DSU).

37 Article XIII of the GATT.

38 Panel Report WT/DS152/R, *United States – Sections 301–310 of the Trade Act of 1974*, 22 December 1999, para. 7.43.

39 Agreement on Government Procurement, opened for signature 15 April 1994 (entered into force on 1 January 1996), 1915 UNTS 103. Public procurement is exempted from the GATT. Contrary to the GATT the Agreement on Public Procurement is a plurilateral treaty and therefore only enforceable against member States, which currently are Canada, European Communities, Hong Kong China, Iceland, Israel, Japan, Korea, Liechtenstein, Netherlands with respect to Aruba, Norway, Singapore, Switzerland, United States.

40 The EU and Japan considered this to be a violation of articles VIII (b), X and XIII of the WTO Agreement on Government Procurement. WT/DS88/1, GPA/DS2/1, *United States – Measure Affecting Government Procurement*, Request for Consultation by the European Communities, 26 June 1997.

41 WT/DS88/1, GPA/DS2/1, *United States – Measure Affecting Government Procurement*, Request for Consultation by the European Communities (26 June 1997).

Massachusetts law was also challenged in the domestic courts of the United States by the National Foreign Trade Council (NFTC), a coalition of corporations, which claimed that the Massachusetts law was unconstitutional as it infringed on the federal governments' exclusive authority to regulate foreign affairs.[42] The case went to the Supreme Court which ruled in favour of the NFTC. The EU then decided to withdraw their request for consultations and the case did not proceed any further within the WTO. As a result the WTO dispute settlement system has not yet had the opportunity to address the question whether public procurement policies that are selective in view of protecting human rights abroad are in violation of WTO law. Although there never has been a case concerning import bans taken in response to human rights violations, it is not unlikely that the WTO dispute settlement mechanism may, at some point, be confronted with a case in which an import ban in response to human rights violations is challenged. With respect to our previous examples from the Brazilian sugar and steel industries, when a ban is imposed and this measure is challenged, how should a WTO Panel or the Appellate Body deal with the case? It was argued that such a ban violates the substantive provisions of the GATT. This immediately raises the question of the possible lines of defence that the defendant may raise to justify the ban. In this context, it will be examined in the next section if and to what extent general international law allows States to impose import bans in response to human rights violations in the production process.

V. IMPORT BANS AS COUNTERMEASURE

A brief look into State practice suggests that it is not unheard of for States to adopt trade restrictions in response to a prior breach of international law.[43] The US in 1978 adopted a trade embargo which violated their GATT obligations against Uganda in response to genocide committed by the Ugandan government. Without relying on GATT exceptions the US claimed that it 'should take steps to dissociate itself from any government which engages in the international crime of genocide'.[44] In April 1982, when Argentina took control over part of the Falkland Islands, the European Community, Australia, New Zealand and Canada adopted trade sanctions, including a temporary import barrier against Argentinean products in violation of their GATT obligations. Another example is the rather unique case of Burma (Myanmar). Here, the International Labour Conference for the first time in its history *recommended* States, employers and

---

42 Supreme Court of the United States, *National Foreign Trade Council v. Baker*, 26 F. Supp. 2d 287, 291 (Mass. 1998).

43 J. Crawford, 'Third Report on State Responsibility addendum', A/CN.4/507/Add.4, 4 August 2000, p. 14. Crawford cites the Uganda Embargo Act.

44 *Ibid.* Note that in this case the US did not rely on GATT exceptions but on its obligations under general international law.

workers to 'review [...] the relations they may have with the member State concerned and take appropriate measures to ensure that the said Member cannot take advantage of such relations to perpetuate or extend the system of forced or compulsory labour referred to by the Commission of Inquiry and to contribute as far as possible to the implementation of its recommendations.'[45]

As a result of the International Labour Conference recommendation the US adopted the Burmese Freedom and Democracy Act which prohibits all imports from Burma.[46] These examples – and many more like them – seem to suggest that, in specific circumstances, importing States can and will unilaterally use import restrictions in response to prior breaches of international law (including labour rights) by the exporting State. Because of the lack of any other justification in international law, such measures will have to be seen as countermeasures if they violate international law, i.e., as lawful action because it is a response to a prior breach by the State against which the countermeasure is adopted. The adoption of countermeasures including import bans which are originally a form of self-help to induce another State to comply with its obligations has always been a popular enforcement mechanism in the international legal order. Such measures may also have other aims than inducing compliance: they can be used to induce another State to appear before an international tribunal or to make another State comply with a ruling of an international adjudicating body. Moreover, they can be used to break with a particular regime that is involved in serious human rights violations. Countermeasures taken with regard to the breach of a particular obligation (say, violation of fundamental labour rights) may be an action which violates another obligation rather than the same (e.g. lead to a violation of the GATT).

The two prerequisites for a measure to be seen as a legitimate countermeasure in international law are: (1) a prior obligation towards the State that adopts the countermeasure has been breached and (2) State action taken in response breaches an international law obligation.[47] It was demonstrated that an import ban on sugar and steel from Brazil would violate the substantive provisions of the GATT, so the second prerequisite seems to have been met. In the following section, it will be examined to what extent importing States are entitled under

45 ILC, *Resolution Concerning the Measures Recommended by the Governing Body under Article 33 of the ILO Constitution on the Subject of Myanmar*, 88th session, June 2000, para. 1(b). Also see: F. Maupain, 'Is the ILO Effective in Upholding Workers' Rights? Reflections on the Myanmar Experience', in P. Alston, ed., *Labour Rights as Human Rights* (New York, Oxford University Press 2005) pp. 85–142; A. Vandaele, *International Labour Rights and the Social Clause: Friends or Foes* (London, Cameron 2005) p. 629.

46 Burmese Freedom and Democracy Act, H.R. 2330, 2003.

47 The countermeasure must also be directed against the State that has breached this obligation. ICJ, *Gabčikovo-Nagymaros Project (Hungary v. Slovakia)*, Judgment, *ICJ Rep.* (1997) p. 7, para. 83.

general international law to react against exporting States by means of countermeasures in the form of import bans. If it can be established that importing States indeed have such a right or obligation under general international law, an inconsistency may arise between the WTO Members' obligations under WTO law and their rights or obligations under general international law.

For the sake of clarity, it should be noted at the outset that the term 'countermeasure' in legal literature is frequently equated with the term 'sanction'. As the International Law Commission (ILC) points out, the terms 'legitimate reprisal' or measures of 'self-help' are historically considered to be the more usual terminology.[48] The term 'sanction' is more appropriate when it concerns measures taken by the United Nations (UN) Security Council under Chapter VII of the UN Charter.[49]

VI. LEGAL STANDING

As the ICJ clarified in the *Gabčikovo-Nagymaros Project* case, the first prerequisite for any lawful countermeasure is the breach of a prior international obligation.[50] Thus, if a prior obligation owed to the State that takes the measure is breached, then such measures will have to be seen as countermeasures.[51] This traditional narrow approach to legal standing poses problems if one applies it to human rights law. This is the result of the particular nature of human rights obligations.

---

48 ILC, *Draft Articles on Responsibility of States for Internationally Wrongful Acts with Commentaries*, II(2) *Yearbook of the International Law Commission* (2001) p. 75.

49 *Ibid.*

50 Pauwelyn sees customary international law and general principles of law as the sources of general international law. J.H.B. Pauwelyn, *Conflict of Norms in Public International Law* (Cambridge, Cambridge University Press 2003) p. 148. The rules on countermeasures as described in the present Chapter are considered to be part of general international law because, as rules of customary international law, they bind all States. As will be argued at a later stage, the source of general international law cannot be customary international law or general principles of law only. As will be elaborated on in Chapter IV, it can no longer be denied that conventional law can contribute to the birth of a general international law norm as well. In such a case, the near universal adherence would become the pivotal requirement for a conventional rule to become part of general international law. Brownlie explains that 'treaties binding a few states are only dubbed "particular international law" as opposed to "general international law" comprising multilateral "law-making" treaties to which a majority of states are parties'. I. Brownlie, *Principles of Public International Law*, 5th edn., (Oxford, Clarendon Press 1998) p. 4.

51 Obviously, such justification may not be necessary if the measure can be justified by the GATT exception clauses. These exception clauses will be discussed in Chapter V. For now, suffice it to say that in Chapter V the question will be addressed of whether these exception clauses may justify measures that may otherwise be justified by referring to general international law. In other words, to what extent can they serve as a conflict avoidance tool?

They are considered to be owed to individuals rather than to States. Thus in case of violations it is not States but individuals who are affected in their legal positions. In 1970 the International Court of Justice (ICJ), however, in its dictum in the *Barcelona Traction* case made clear that certain obligations exist, the violation of which would affect the international community as a whole. This immediately raises question as to the legal consequences of the existence of such obligations *erga omnes*? More specifically, does it entitle States to impose an import ban on sugar and steel from Brazil? In the attempt to answer this question, the (draft) Articles on Responsibility of States for Internationally Wrongful Acts (ASR) formulated by the ILC can provide a useful framework of reference. Although these articles do not constitute a binding legal instrument as such it may be considered an influential source since they are an attempt to reflect State practice. According to these Articles States have legal standing in a limited number of situations. A State that is specially affected as a result of a collective obligation has legal standing.[52] This will only be the case if in addition to a violation of a collective obligation a bilateral obligation is breached. If Dutch workers would work in slavery-like conditions in Brazil, the Netherlands would be able to exercise its right of diplomatic protection because Brazil has breached the right of the Netherlands that its nationals are treated well within Brazilian territory.[53] In such case, the Netherlands would be allowed to resort to countermeasures to secure compliance of its right.

It is unclear, however, if States are entitled to adopt countermeasures as a reaction to a violation of an obligation *erga omnes* if such link does not exist. The ILC deliberately left this question unanswered by stipulating in its Commentary to the ASR that 'the resolution of the matter should be left to the further development of international law'.[54] The reason why the ILC was so reluctant can be explained by the high risk of abuse it may bring about.[55] Yet, the acknowledgement of such a right may be good from the perspective of law enforcement. In order to determine whether all States in contemporary international law indeed have a right to take countermeasures as a response to the violation of an obligation *erga omnes*, both Dzida and Tams have examined State practice and evidence for *opinio juris* in this area.[56] Both conclude that

52 Article 42 ASR.

53 Article 44 ASR.

54 ILC, op. cit. n. 48, p. 139.

55 C.J. Tams, *Enforcing Obligations* Erga Omnes *in International Law* (Cambridge, Cambridge University Press 2005) p. 199.

56 In order for a rule of customary international law to arise, there must be State practice guided by *opinio juris*, i.e., the belief that it is legally obligatory to act in this manner. See: ICJ, *North Sea Continental Shelf Case (Federal Republic of Germany v. Denmark; Federal Republic of Germany v. the Netherlands)*, Judgment, *ICJ Rep.* (1969) p. 3; ICJ, *Case Concerning Military and Paramilitary Activities in and against Nicaragua (Nicaragua v. USA)*, Judgment, *ICJ Rep.* (1986) para. 97.

individual States are allowed to take countermeasures (within the same limits that general international law sets out for countermeasures within a bilateral relationship) in response to systematic or large-scale, i.e., serious,[57] breaches of an obligation *erga omnes*.[58] In addition, Dzida remarks that a similar tendency can be found for 'non-serious' or 'normal' violations of an obligation *erga omnes*. In his view, a right for all States to take countermeasures in such cases is most likely to develop into international customary law in the foreseeable future.[59]

The second issue that needs to be resolved here is the question of whether the State practice referred to is guided by *opinio juris*. In order for a rule of customary international law to arise, there must be State practice guided by the belief that this practice is based on a legally binding norm.[60] For this requirement to be met, the objections of other States to situations where a State has responded by means of countermeasures are relevant.[61] In most cases, if not all, in which countermeasures were adopted in response to human rights violations, States have not protested, which can be explained by the importance of the obligations breached and the gravity of the breaches. What is more, Tams claims that the countermeasures taken in the examples he refers to are predominantly based on legal considerations: 'Western States publicly condemned previous breaches of international law – often specifically referring to, for example, the freedom of expression and association [...] or the prohibition against the use of force [...] – and claimed to act in defence of international law. While their decision to resort to countermeasures (as opposed to other forms of response) might have been influenced by political considerations, their assessment of the underlying dispute thus was legally relevant.'[62]

The foregoing suggests that countermeasures can be taken if structural violations of an obligation *erga omnes* take place in the exporting country. It cannot be denied that in the case of Myanmar, for instance, where the military regime has set up a system of forced labour, general international law allows States to react

57 Note that Article 40(2) of the Draft Articles defines a serious breach as follows: 'A breach of such an obligation is serious if it involves a gross or systematic failure by the responsible State to fulfill the obligation.'

58 C.J. Tams, op. cit. n. 55, p. 249.

59 B. Dzida, *Zum Recht der Repressalie im heutigen Völkerrecht, eine Bewertung anläßlich* der *Diskussion innerhalb* der *International Law Commission über ‚countermeasures'* im *Konventionsentwurf* zur *Staatenverantwortlichkeit* (Frankfurt am Main, Lang 1997) p. 265.

60 See Article 38 of the Statute of the ICJ; see also: *North Sea Continental Shelf Case (Federal Republic of Germany v. Denmark; Federal Republic of Germany v. the Netherlands)*, op. cit. n. 56, p. 3, para. 77; ICJ *Case Concerning Military and Paramilitary Activities in and against Nicaragua (Nicaragua v. USA)*, op. cit. n. 56, p. 14; ICJ, *Continental Shelf Case (Libya v. Malta)*, Judgment, *ICJ Rep.* (1985) p. 29.

61 M.N. Shaw, *International Law*, 5th edn. (Cambridge, Cambridge University Press 2003) p. 85.

62 C.J. Tams, op. cit. n. 55, p. 239.

by means of import bans. They are not under an obligation to act in this manner but they have the right to do so when it comes to large-scale violations of an obligation *erga omnes*. This leads to the following question in the light of the example used throughout this contribution: is the prohibition of forced labour an obligation *erga omnes*? If the answer is affirmative, it can be argued that States are allowed to adopt an import ban against sugar and steel from Brazil.

VII. DOES THE PROHIBITION OF FORCED LABOUR ENTAIL AN OBLIGATION *ERGA OMNES*?

Forced labour is defined in the Forced Labour Convention of 1930 (ILO Convention No. 29) as 'all work or service which is exacted from any person under the menace of any penalty and for which the said person has not offered himself voluntarily'. Often, forced labour is said to coincide with slavery.[63] This comparison is relevant because the prohibition of slavery has been recognised to entail an obligation *erga omnes* by the ICJ in the *Barcelona Traction* case.[64] Consequently, if forced labour is regarded as being tantamount to slavery, the peremptory character of the prohibition of forced labour can easily be proved.[65] Yet, a closer reading of, for instance, the Slavery Convention of 1926 reveals that forced labour may not be identical to slavery. Nevertheless, the 1926 Convention recognises that forced labour practices may easily become slave-like practices.[66]

Given the relevance of the issue for the determination of the *jus cogens* status of the prohibition of forced labour, in the present section, an attempt will be made to answer the question of when forced labour may change into slavery. First, the two concepts must be defined. In the League of Nations Slavery Convention of 1926, slavery was defined for the first time as 'the status or condition of a person over whom any or all of the powers attaching to the right of ownership are

63 *Ibid.*, pp. 158–160; see also N. Lassen, 'Slavery and Slavery-Like Practices: United Nations Standards and Implementation', 57 *Nordic Journal of International Law* (1988) p. 205.

64 Note that the Slavery Convention of 1926 has only been ratified by 95 States. See: www.unhchr.ch/html/menu3/b/treaty3.htm (accessed on 25 March 2008). On the emergence of the prohibition of slavery as a peremptory norm, see M. Ragazzi, *The Concept of International Obligations Erga Omnes* (Oxford, Clarendon Press 1997) pp. 105–117.

65 For present purposes, we consider the concept of *jus cogens* (or peremptory norms) and the concept of an obligation *erga omnes* as different aspects of the same rule. Whereas the *jus cogens* status refers to the non-derogability of the norm, the concept of *erga omnes* refers to legal standing when the norm has been breached. See further: J.P. Denkers, op. cit. n. 18, at pp. 91 *et seq.*

66 The Preamble of the Convention, for instance, reads 'that it is necessary to prevent forced labour from developing into conditions analogous to slavery' which suggests that forced labour and slavery do not overlap. In the same vein, according to Article 5, Contracting Parties must 'take all necessary measures to prevent compulsory or forced labour from developing into conditions analogous to slavery'.

exercised'.[67] It is assumed that the powers attaching to the right of ownership were the authority of the master over the slave in Roman law.[68] One of the important elements of the traditional concept of ownership is that the servile status is permanent, i.e., it cannot be terminated by the individual, solely by the owner. This component of ownership causes difficulties in determining whether other slavery-like practices may fit within the definition of the 1926 Convention. Technically, ownership cannot be proven when elements of free choice can be found. Therefore, the scope of the 1926 Convention was expanded in the Supplementary Convention of 1953 to include debt bondage,[69] serfdom,[70] servile forms of marriage,[71] and the exploitation of children.[72, 73] Strictly speaking, these practices as such do not seem to fall within the 1926 definition of slavery and the Supplementary Convention did not broaden this definition. Yet, it cannot be denied that, for instance, the effect of certain forms of debt bondage, although it implies elements of free choice, is hardly distinguishable from slavery.[74] The same applies to some forms of forced labour. This is the result of the fact that the pivotal elements of the two concepts are closely related; the "involuntary nature" is the most important element of forced labour,[75] whereas "ownership" is the most central element of slavery. Vandaele observes that the notion of

67 Article 1 of the Slavery, Servitude, Forced Labour and Similar Institutions and Practices Convention of 1926 (Slavery Convention of 1926), 60 *LNTS* p. 253, entered into force on 9 March 1927. This definition was not changed in the UN Supplementary Convention on the Abolition of Slavery, the Slave Trade, and Institutions and Practices Similar to Slavery, 226 *UNTS* p. 3, entered into force on 30 April 1957. See also: M. Cherif Bassiouni, 'Enslavement as an International Crime', 23 *New York University Journal of International Law and Politics* (1991), pp. 445, 455.

68 N. Lassen, loc. cit. n. 63, at p. 204.

69 According to Article 1(a) of the Supplementary Convention, this is 'the status or condition arising from a pledge by a debtor of his personal services or of those of a person under his control as security for a debt, if the value of those services as reasonably assessed is not applied towards the liquidation of the debt or the length and nature of those services are not respectively limited and defined'.

70 According to Article 1(b) of the Supplementary Convention, this is 'the condition or status of a tenant who is by law, custom or agreement bound to live and labour on land belonging to another person and to render some determinate service to such other person, whether for reward or not, and is not free to change his status'.

71 According to Article 1(c) of the Supplementary Convention, this is a practice whereby '(i) [a] woman, without the right to refuse, is promised or given in marriage on payment of a consideration in money or in kind to her parents, guardian, family or any other person or group; (ii) The husband of a woman, his family, or his clan, has the right to transfer her to another person for value received or otherwise; or (iii) A woman on the death of her husband is liable to be inherited by another person'.

72 According to Article 1(d) of the Supplementary Convention it concerns practices whereby: 'Any institution or practice whereby a child or young person under the age of 18 years, is delivered by either or both of his natural parents or by his guardian to another person, whether for reward or not, with a view to the exploitation of the child or young person or of his labour.'

73 M. Cherif Bassiouni, loc. cit. n. 67, at p. 455.

74 N. Lassen, loc. cit. n. 63, at p. 208.

75 A. Vandaele, op. cit. n. 45, at pp. 154–155.

involuntariness is considered to be broader and more flexible than the concept of ownership.[76] Nevertheless, the distinction between the notions of involuntariness and ownership, however, cannot always easily be made since ownership suggests involuntariness.

Since involuntariness may not always be so easily distinguished from ownership, our Brazilian example brings this point into greater relief. As ILO sources show, bonding workers through debts is a widespread form of forced labour in Brazil.[77] Basically, recruiters bring workers to remote areas where they have no choice but to buy essentials from their employers at high prices. Due to the fact that the workers simply do not earn enough money and the prices of these essentials are too high, they pay their employer back in labour. Employers claiming that their employees are free to leave often threaten or pressure them not to terminate the employment. Such a situation may not, technically speaking, fit within the concept of ownership because it suggests elements of free choice, but it cannot be denied that they are tantamount to slavery. Some scholars therefore claim that the inability to control the working conditions and to terminate the employment not only proves involuntariness on the part of the employee, but constitutes a form of ownership on the part of the employer.[78] Admittedly, it can be argued that some forms of forced labour, although it is not slavery in itself, can be seen as a contemporary form of slavery.[79] In this context, Vandaele claims that in order to assess whether a certain practice can be defined as slavery or forced labour, it is necessary to look at the individual situation at stake.[80] Of particular relevance here is that the ILO Commission of Inquiry that has examined the situation in Myanmar observed that 'there exists now in international law a peremptory norm prohibiting any recourse to forced labor and that the rights not to be compelled to perform forced or compulsory labor is one of the basic human rights'.[81]

76 *Ibid.*, p. 160.

77 ILO, *Brazil, Combating Forced Labour*, April 2002 – April 2007, available at: www.ilo.org/dyn/declaris/DECLARATIONWEB.PROJECTDETAILS?var_Language=EN&var ID=191. (accessed 19 August 2009).

78 M.E. Gorden, 'Haitian Forced Labor in the Dominican Republic', 15 *Comparative Labor Law Journal* (1994) p. 218.

79 N. Lassen, loc. cit. n. 63, at p. 206.

80 A. Vandaele, op. cit. n. 45, at p. 160.

81 ILO, *Forced Labour in Myanmar (Burma).* Report of the Commission of Inquiry appointed under article 26 of the Constitution of the International Labour Organization to examine the observance by Myanmar of the Forced Labour Convention, 1930 (No. 29). Geneva (2 July 1998) para. 203; see also S. Bal, 'International Free Trade Agreements and Human Rights: Reinterpreting Article XX of the GATT', 10 *Minnesota Journal of Global Trade* (2001) p. 95.

VIII. CAN GENERAL INTERNATIONAL LAW SERVE AS AN AUTONOMOUS DEFENCE IN WTO DISPUTE SETTLEMENT?

In the preceding sections, it was shown that, by approving the WTO rules, its Members seem to have 'contracted out' of (i.e., intended to modify) their sovereign right to determine what can and what cannot be imported. Making such contracts in itself would not cause any problems and is perfectly normal in the international legal order. However, just as private contracts cannot contract out of criminal law on the domestic level, so too allowing States to develop, apply and to derogate from the general rules of State responsibility by agreements among themselves also cannot be unlimited. As the Study Group of the ILC on the fragmentation of international law claims, 'the rules that derogate must have at least the same rank as those they derogate from. It is hard to see how States could, for example, derogate from those aspects of the general law on State responsibility that define the conditions of operation of "serious breaches of obligations under peremptory norms of general international law".'[82]

It has been generally accepted that States cannot 'contract out' of the system of international law,[83] the reason being that States cannot modify the *pacta sunt servanda* principle in international law.[84] It is this principle that is at the basis of the international legal order.[85] Shaw claims that 'the principle that agreements are binding (*pacta sunt servanda*) upon which all treaty law must be based cannot itself be based upon consent'.[86] Therefore, it seems impossible to modify this principle, which is claimed to be positioned at the first level within the international legal order, on the basis of consent.[87] Treaties and customs, all founded on this principle, are within the second level of the international legal order. This theoretical framework can serve to make it clear that norms at the second level cannot modify norms at the first level. For our present purposes, this would mean that WTO norms, which are at the second level, cannot contract out of norms *juris cogentis*, which are at the first level. This also raises the question of whether or not the legal consequences of a violation of such norms can be modified. The answer to this question may lie in the phrase 'conditions of

---

82 Report of the Study Group of the International Law Commission, *Fragmentation of International Law: Difficulties Arising from the Diversification and Expansion of International Law*, A/CN.4/L.682, 13 April 2006, para. 64.

83 J.H.B. Pauwelyn, op. cit. n. 50, p. 37.

84 Report of the Study Group of the International Law Commission, op. cit. n. 82, para. 176.

85 This principle is codified in Article 26 of the Vienna Convention on the Law of Treaties which reads: 'Every treaty in force is binding upon the parties to it and must be performed by them in good faith.'

86 M.N. Shaw, op. cit. n. 61, p. 10.

87 *Ibid.*, p. 49.

operation' in the above-quoted passage. What is meant by this? In a footnote to the passage, the Study Group refers to Articles 40, 41, and 48 of the ASR. Articles 40 and 41 deal with the legal consequences of a serious breach of a peremptory norm. Article 48 deals with the invocation of responsibility by States other than the injured State. This seems to suggest that the study group is of the opinion that States cannot deviate from the whole system dealing with serious violations of a peremptory norm as set out in the preceding sections. The enforcement of peremptory norms is of vital importance to the international community of States as a whole. It would be absurd if States, by unilateral action or agreement, could actually nullify the, albeit rather primitive, enforcement system of general international law. This suggests that, when it comes to a dispute, the Panels or Appellate Body will have to apply non-WTO law as an autonomous source which trumps WTO law. This raises the question of whether the WTO Panels can do that.

As seems to follow from *Mexico – Soft Drinks* that non-WTO law cannot be applied as an independent defence against a violation claim. In this case, Mexico had imposed trade-restrictive measures against the US because it claimed that the latter had not complied with its obligations under NAFTA, a regional trade agreement. Essentially, the trade restriction thus constituted a countermeasure to induce the US to comply with its NAFTA obligations. When the US brought the case before the WTO adjudicating body, Mexico claimed as a defence that its WTO obligations were not applicable in the dispute.[88] The Appellate Body, however, claimed that accepting this argument 'would entail a determination whether the United States has acted consistently or inconsistently with its NAFTA obligations. We see no basis in the DSU for Panels and the Appellate Body to adjudicate non-WTO disputes. Article 3.2 of the DSU states that the WTO dispute settlement system "serves to preserve the rights and obligations of Members under the *covered agreements*, and to clarify the existing provisions of *those agreements*". (…) Accepting Mexico's interpretation would imply that the WTO dispute settlement system could be used to determine rights and obligations outside the covered agreements.'[89]

This passage suggests that Article 3(2) DSU should be seen as a substantive jurisdictional limitation of the WTO adjudicating bodies. In this view, non-WTO law cannot be applied as an independent defence against a violation claim.[90] Accepting this view in all circumstances is troublesome for two reasons.

88 Appellate Body Report WT/DS308/AB/R, *Mexico – Tax Measures on Soft Drinks and Other Beverages*, 6 March 2006, para. 55.

89 Appellate Body Report WT/DS308/AB/R, op. cit. n. 88, at para. 56.

90 It should be noted here that Mexico also invoked Article XX(d) of the GATT. As will be discussed in the next chapter, non-WTO law can be taken into account, in the interpretation of the GATT exception clauses.

First, it would mean that any subsequent agreement between some WTO Members which allows for trade restrictions in specific circumstances cannot be applied by a WTO Panel. Evidently, from the perspective of international law-making, this view is problematic: WTO law is bilateral in nature and thus Members should be allowed to modify their international trade obligations just like in any other branch of international law. It would be absurd to accept that a dispute settlement mechanism can be set up that has no jurisdiction to apply later *inter se* modifications. Since there was no such agreement that modified WTO obligations between the US and Mexico, the decision in *Mexico – Soft Drinks* is not problematic; even if it was accepted that Article 3(2) DSU does not constitute a substantive jurisdictional limitation, the outcome of the dispute would be the same. In this specific case, a trade-restrictive countermeasure was challenged by the US. It can be argued that WTO law seems to have 'contracted out' of this type of countermeasures. Put differently, WTO Members can still impose different kinds of countermeasures such as freezing assets or denying landing rights in response to violations of bilateral non-WTO law (e.g., obligations under the NAFTA) but they cannot take measures that violate the GATT. In this respect, WTO law would thus take precedence over the general international law on countermeasures. This may be different if a (later) modification agreement does exist. In such an event, the Appellate Body would have to apply the modification agreement on the basis of any of the conflict rules of international law. If the WTO judiciary maintains, however, that they have a substantive jurisdictional limitation, then *inter se* modifications can never be applied and thus not prevail over the older WTO law. This seems to run contrary to the system of international law-making.[91]

Second, when a peremptory norm is seriously violated, States are not allowed to contract out of the legal consequences thereof. In such cases, resorting to countermeasures including import bans should remain an option. Therefore, WTO law cannot be regarded as 'contracting out' of this particular part of international law. Consequently, it seems that creating an adjudicating body with limited jurisdiction with the effect of diminishing the legal consequences of large-scale breaches of a peremptory norm is not allowed from the perspective of international law. Accordingly, Article 3(2) of the DSU, whether it should be understood as a conflict clause or a limitation of jurisdictional competence in favour of WTO law, cannot have legal force if this diminishes the legal consequences of large-scale breaches of a peremptory norm. Therefore, WTO Panels and the Appellate Body will have to directly apply the general international

---

91 It should nevertheless be stressed here that the conflict rules (which let modifications of WTO law prevail) will not have to be applied if a conflict can be avoided by means of interpretation. In such a case, WTO law will have to be interpreted harmoniously with general international law on countermeasures. See further: J. P. Denkers, op. cit. n. 18, Chapter V.

law on countermeasures as an independent defence against a violation claim in the event of conflict. Surely, applying non-WTO law as an autonomous source brings about the risk of misinterpretation of this non-WTO law. Yet, Pauwelyn is of the opinion that such a misinterpretation would be the lesser evil: the alternative would be to ignore non-WTO law altogether.[92] Furthermore, this potential evil can be reduced by appointing Appellate Body Members with knowledge of international law and by requesting expert advice in case of any ambiguity.[93] It should nevertheless be stressed that, in practice, the situation where a WTO Panel would have to decide on compliance with a norm *juris cogentis* and the legal consequences thereof on its own will rarely if ever occur. In the case of Myanmar, for instance, ILO reports may be used to determine the seriousness of the situation. Consequently, it is highly unlikely that the WTO dispute settlement mechanism will have to independently determine whether a *jus cogens* norm has been breached.

Another option would be for a Panel to decline jurisdiction because the case concerned claims under other international law rather than WTO law.[94] In *Mexico – Soft Drinks*, where Mexico had adopted countermeasures against the US because the latter had not complied with its NAFTA obligations, Mexico requested the Panel to decline jurisdiction in favour of an Arbitral Panel under the NAFTA. The Panel responded that it had no discretion to decide whether or not to exercise jurisdiction in a case before it.[95] This conclusion was upheld by the Appellate Body for this specific case, but it expressed 'no view as to whether there may be other circumstances in which legal impediments could exist that would preclude a panel from ruling on the merits of the claims that are before it'.[96] Dunoff points out that other international adjudicating bodies have increasingly disposed of contentious issues on grounds of jurisdiction.[97] There is no apparent reason why the WTO judiciary cannot employ the same strategy. If a WTO Panel does not decline jurisdiction, however, there is another option: the WTO Panels could attempt to avoid the conflict by means of interpretation. In other words, they might be able to prevent the situation from getting to the conflict stage where they would have to apply general international law (and may

92 J.H.B. Pauwelyn, 'How to Win a World Trade Organization Dispute Based on Non World Trade Organization Law?', 37 *Journal of World Trade* (2003) p. 1030.

93 *Ibid.*

94 J.H.B. Pauwelyn, 'Human Rights in WTO Dispute Settlement' in T. Cottier, J. Pauwelyn and E. Bürgi Bonanomi, eds., *Human Rights and International Trade* (Oxford, Oxford University Press 2005); J.H.B. Pauwelyn, loc. cit. n. 92.

95 Panel Report WT/DS308/R, *Mexico – Tax Measures on Soft Drinks and Other Beverages*, 7 October 2005, para. 7.1.

96 Appellate Body Report WT/DS308/AB/R, *Mexico – Tax Measures on Soft Drinks and Other Beverages*, 6 March 2006, para. 54.

97 J. L. Dunoff, 'The Death of the Trade Regime', 10 *European Journal of International Law* (1999) p. 758.

possibly also have to decide on compliance with substantive non-WTO law). In such a case, both norms continue to apply and States will not be confronted with a conflict in the applicable law. The most obvious means to do this would be to interpret Article XX of the GATT in such a manner so as to allow from import bans imposed in response to serious violations of a peremptory norm.[98]

IX. CONCLUSION

The WTO differs from many other international organisations as it does not independently from its Members develop policies that may directly violate human rights. Nevertheless, some autonomous activities of the WTO may have implications for the protection of human rights. This article's focus has been on dispute settlements, one of the WTO's most important activities. It was demonstrated that the dispute settlement body may find that import bans adopted by States aimed at influencing the human rights situation abroad are in violation of substantive international trade law, more specifically of articles I, III, and XI GATT. However, general international law does provide a basis for adopting countermeasures in response to structural violations of an obligation *erga omnes*. The prohibition of forced labour can entail such an obligation and it can therefore be argued that under general international law States are allowed to adopt an import ban on products produced in a country where the prohibition of forced labour is structurally violated. It is questionable whether the violations of the prohibition of forced labour in Brazil are of such a structural nature to entitle other States to raise import bans on Brazilian steel and sugar. If the violations do reach this level, the Dispute Settlement Body may be confronted with a conflict between general international law and international trade law. In such an event, it will have three options. First, it can decide to decline jurisdiction. Second, it must attempt to interpret WTO law in harmony with general international law. Third, if the previous option fails then general international law will have to be applied as an autonomous source that trumps WTO law. It would be incongruous when in the case of large-scale breaches of an obligation *erga omnes* the WTO Dispute Settlement Body would be able to nullify the legal consequences of such breaches. If this would be the case, the WTO indeed becomes an obstacle to enforcing human rights obligations.

---

[98] On this matter, see J. P. Denkers, op. cit. n. 18, Chapter V.

TRIPs AND HUMAN RIGHTS: ACCESS TO CHEAPER AIDS MEDICINES

Stefaan Smis, Stephen Sevidzem Kingah and Christine Janssens[1]

'Trade has the power to create opportunities and support livelihoods; and it has the power to destroy them. Production for export can generate income, employment, and the foreign exchange which poor countries need for their development. But it can also cause environmental destruction and a loss of livelihoods, or lead to unacceptable levels of exploitation. The human impact of trade depends on how goods are produced, who controls the production and marketing, how the wealth generated is distributed, and the terms upon which countries trade. The way in which the international trading system is managed has a critical bearing on all of these areas.'[2]

I. INTRODUCTION

Recent strictures have shown that international trade can have an impact on human rights in various ways. Although the majority of economists hold the view that globalisation and liberalisation of trade have had a positive effect upon human rights, some instances have shown the opposite to be the case.

The negative effects of globalisation and liberalisation of trade can be found in the relation between the Agreement on Trade-Related Aspects of Intellectual Property (TRIPs or TRIPs Agreement) and human rights, in particular, the right to health. The TRIPs Agreement, mainly negotiated in the interest of the leading pharmaceutical and technological multinationals, has had a negative influence in accessing medicines, in particular medicines related to HIV/AIDS in poorer nations. Nonetheless, Article 27 of the Universal Declaration of Human Rights (UDHR) that probably has a status of customary international law states that 'everyone has the right to the protection of the moral and material interests

1 Stefaan Smis is Professor of International Law at the Vrije Universiteit Brussels (VUB), Reader at the School of Law of the University of Westminster and Guest Lecturer at the University of Ghent. Stephen S. Kingah is Doctor in Law and researcher at the Institute for European Studies (IES) of the VUB. Christine Janssens is a PhD candidate at the Faculty of Law and Criminology of the VUB.

2 The Oxfam Poverty Report.

resulting from any scientific, literary or artistic production of which he is the author' and by this one can argue that the TRIPs Agreement should also take into account human rights. If human welfare is the main goal of the TRIPs Agreement, this is also the case with human rights: the UDHR refers in its preamble to the promotion of 'social progress and better standards of life' and to 'a common standard of achievement for all peoples and all nations'. Even though, both rights have the same interest, reality demonstrates that intellectual property rights sometimes undermine these objectives: 'while private rights may support and protect individual owners of patents and copyrights, they also occasion significant challenges to assuring that welfare gains can be meaningfully realized by the poor nations of the world.'[3]

This contribution deals with the issue of conflicting rights. In the present case, one is at the same time confronted with intellectual property rights, such as patents, as well as with access to cheaper medicines. Our approach will be to balance both rights. The right to health, however, can only be effectively protected if it is supported by mechanisms of accountability. The general idea, stated by Lloyd, is that 'all actors involved in the process of developing and implementing solutions to global challenges need to be accountable and responsive to the people and communities they affect.'[4]

The focus will be centred upon the manner in which intellectual property (IP) rules can impact health, in particular attention is placed on access to affordable health care for HIV/AIDS patients. We will present the international normative frameworks in terms of human rights that are applicable to patients (right to health) and to intellectual property holders. The contribution also considers ways of balancing both forms of rights. Moreover, potential accountability mechanisms for the World Trade Organization (WTO) will be analysed. We will then conclude by proposing an enhanced framework for the right to health.

II. THE DEVELOPMENT OF INTELLECTUAL PROPERTY PROTECTION

The election of former US President Ronald Reagan in 1980 in the US heralded a new era in terms of intellectual property protection. Reagan replaced Jimmy Carter whose presidency had upheld the respect of human rights as a hallowed

---

3 R.L. Okediji, 'Securing intellectual property objectives: new approaches to human rights considerations', in M.E. Salomon, A. Tostensen and W. Vandenhole, eds., *Casting the Net Wider: Human Rights, Development and New Duty-Bearers* (Antwerp/Oxford, Intersentia 2007) p. 226.

4 R. Lloyd, 'Promoting global accountability: the experiences of the Global Accountability Project', 14 *Global Governance* (2008) p. 274.

pursuit. The spirit of deregulation that accompanied the advent of Reagan, as well as Thatcher in the UK underscored a sense of heightened individualism in this era. Within international law governments were increasingly regarded as the problem rather than the solution to many issues. The Keynesian-Miltonian equilibrium between greater regulation and increased liberalism shifted towards the celebration of individual enterprise. The translation of this shift in reality was a re-balancing of the priorities of capitalist governments. Individuals would become much more aware of their rights in terms of their artistic or scientific output. It mattered less whether individual creativity had to be harnessed for the greater good of the community in terms of access to better health care, affordable education or better food. It is this same spirit of Reaganomics that Newt Gingrich and Dick Armey used in the 1990s to lead the Republican onslaught in Congress pushing Democrats into a minority corner. Under the Reagan presidency, US firms projected this new sense of assertive individualism onto the international scene by extending American based IP rules into the international trade agenda. The culmination of this was the codification of enforceable IP rules at the international level with the TRIPs. Although a trade agreement, TRIPs has had wide ranging impacts on social conditions and welfare broader than could have been initially imagined when the text was being negotiated in the 1980s and 1990s. The rules of the treaty increasingly impact upon the capacity of individuals and governments to ensure sustainable provision of public goods in terms of health care, education and food.

III. THE RIGHTS TO ACCESS AIDS MEDICINES, TRIPs AND PATENT RATIONALE

HIV/AIDS has been having a serious impact on human rights, especially the rights of women.[5] Advocates of better treatment for HIV/AIDS patients stoutly defend their positions because they believe that issues regarding access to affordable medicines are at the very core of what human rights are all about. Their fervent aspirations are grounded upon a vision of a world in which people are neither deprived of health care nor medication due to poverty. More often than not, the case for better and affordable access to HIV/AIDS medication is couched in terms of a dialectical friction between the vulnerable patients who live mainly in poor countries, on the one hand, and the big research-based pharmaceutical companies mainly located in rich countries, on the other. So how is the balance of interests to be crafted? In addressing this issue it is important to revisit the nature of the interests claimed by patients and patent

[5] J.M. Spectar, 'The Hydra Hath But One Head: The Socio-Cultural Dimensions of the AIDS Epidemic and Women's Right to Health', 21 *Boston College Third World Law Journal* (2001) pp. 1–34.

owners. At the very core of this debate is calibrated the importance of human rights in safeguarding the right to life on the one hand, and defending the right to intellectual property (patents) on the other. To adequately address this issue it is vital to critically examine what patent advocates tender as arguments for upholding intellectual property rights.

Firstly, research on new medicines is expensive. So, investments for further research of better medicines have to be recouped in order to fund further research. This is the crux of the argument that big research pharmaceutical companies[6] advance in order to defend their use of patent protection for medicines in general and for second line antiretroviral drugs (ARVs) in particular. Although the issue of patent protection is often presented in simple terms, it is foundational to a much wider debate on the rationale for introducing the TRIPs Agreement in the international trading system.[7] As aforementioned, developed countries in Europe, North America and South Asia (especially Japan) (where most big industries are concentrated) backed the introduction of the multilateral intellectual property protection regime. The main advocates for incorporating intellectual property in the international trading system were from industry officials. Intellectual property was already well developed in the richer countries, but the approach to the issue in developing countries was considerably less so.[8] Thus, one of the compromises that was struck within the framework of the TRIPs (in particular regarding pharmaceutical patent

6 There are basically two main kinds of pharmaceutical companies. First, research based pharmaceutical companies are those that invest stupendous sums of money in order to develop new medicines. Examples of such companies include Pfizer (USA), Abbott (USA), Merck (USA), GSK (UK), Novartis (Switzerland), AstraZeneca (UK), Boehringer Ingelheim (Germany), Hoffman La Roche (France-Switzerland), Sanofi Synthelabo (France). Second, the generic based companies are those that do not invest heavily on innovative research on new drugs as do the research based companies. Rather they often come into the market to mass produce the drugs of the research-based companies once the term of the patent expires for any given drug. Good examples of generic based pharmaceutical companies are Ranbaxy and Dr Reddy's (India) as well as Teva International (Israel). Two caveats must be sounded here. First some generic companies like Teva have arms that deal mainly in innovative research-based products. In addition, some of the big multinational research based companies have been teaming with generic companies so as to take advantage of the post-patent term markets options. An example in this regard includes the deal struck between GSK and Ranbaxy of India. The second caveat is that research based pharmaceutical companies receive a lot of funding from public agencies. It should also be noted that such companies equally rely on the research activities of universities and other publicly funded institutes. This has been a main occurrence since the passing of the Bayh-Dole Act by the US Congress in 1981.

7 Although reference is often made to TRIPS emphasis is placed more on patents because it is the main IPRs that is used pharmaceutical companies in defending their interests. Trade marks are also important. However in the biomedical sector the importance of patents trumps that of trade marks.

8 Although used here as a generic term, developing countries are far from homogeneous and they often harbour varying IP interests. In this light see, Commission on Intellectual Property Rights, *Integrating Intellectual Property Rights and Development Policy* (2002).

protection) negotiations was that developing countries that had still not put in place the necessary protection regime be provided a transition period to adapt their legal systems to the multilateral framework.[9]

The defenders of strong intellectual property rights (IPRs) for patent owners argued – and with good reason – that patent protection for their products is not to blame for the difficulties of access faced by HIV/AIDS patients in poor countries. Attaran and Gillespie-White revealed that patents do not necessarily hamstring efforts of African countries to have access to HIV/AIDS drugs.[10] They argued that the main problems are poverty in Africa, high cost of ARVs, national regulatory requirements for medicines, tariffs, the imposition of sales taxes and above all, the lack of needed funds for ARV treatment. They concluded that 'there is no apparent correlation between access to anti-retroviral treatment, which is uniformly poor across Africa, and patent status, which varies extensively by country and drug.'[11] While highlighting the fact that the African pharmaceutical market is very small (1.1 per cent of the global market) they nevertheless proposed an equitable compromise whereby African States will adhere to clear patent rules on the one hand, and on the other the pharmaceutical companies will provide medicines to the poor without cashing in on profits.[12]

Arguments in favour of the TRIPs Agreement and its defence for patent protection for holders such as large pharmaceutical companies also relate to the fact that IPRs such as patents actually serve as a stimulus for the growth of the developing countries and Least Developed Countries (LDCs).[13] Backers of

9 WTO, India – *Patent Protection for Pharmaceutical and Agricultural Chemical Products: Report of the Panel*, WT/DS50/R, 5 September 1997, No. 5.29.

10 A. Attaran and L. Gillespie-White, 'Do Patents for Antiretroviral Drugs Constrain Access to Aids Treatment in Africa?' 286 *Journal of the American Medical Association* (2001) pp. 1886–1892, at p. 1886. See also D.W. Brock, 'Some Questions About the Moral Responsibilities of Drug Companies in Developing Countries', 1 *Developing World Bioethics* (2001) pp. 34–37, at p. 37. In the same light see L.T.C. Harms, 'Offering Cake for the South', 10 *European Intellectual Property Review* (2000) pp. 451–453, at p. 452 (discussing the very poor and low patent application levels in Ghana which was 33 in 1997 as opposed to 25000 in Korea).

11 A. Attaran and L. Gillespie-White, loc. cit. n. 10, at p. 1890.

12 *Ibid.*, p. 1891. See also WHO, UNAIDS, UNICEF, MSF, *Sources and Prices of Selected Medicines and Diagnostics for People Living with HIV/AIDS*, WHO/EDM/PAR/2004.4, at p. 3.

13 D.M. Gould and W.C. Cruben, 'The Role of Intellectual Property Rights in Economic Growth', in K. Maskus, *The WTO, Intellectual Property Rights and the Knowledge Economy* (Cheltenham/Northampton, E. Elgar 2004) pp. 594–621, at p. 616; C.M. Kalanje, 'Intellectual Property, Foreign Direct Investment and the Least-Developed Countries: A Perspective', 5 *Journal of World Intellectual Property* (2002) pp. 119–128, at p.127; I.E. Botoy, 'Potential and Substantial Benefits of the TRIPs Agreement to the Member Countries of the African Intellectual Property Organization in the Patent Field: An African Perspective', 4 *Journal of World Intellectual Property* (2001) pp. 91–102, at p. 99. For a more sceptical position regarding the benefits of the introduction of introduction of IPRs for patents as a media for facilitating FDI, innovation, efficiencies of local production, et cetera, see J.J. Nogués, 'Social Costs and Benefits of Introducing Patent Protection for Pharmaceutical Drugs in Developing Countries', in K.

stronger patent rights also note that such protective regimes are supportive of the public health system and that without effective medicines (backed by strong patents), public health policies would be compromised.[14] Other arguments in favour of IPRs relate to the fact that '[if] unauthorized use is not prevented, creative people, in the North and in the South alike, will have little incentive to invent new things.'[15] In the specific case of pharmaceutical companies, patent protection goes to the very heart of their activities. This is because once patent term expires a company loses monopoly rights over the resale of the product. Most of the companies have resorted to the use of further protective mechanisms even after the end of the term of the patent protection. Examples of such options include supplementary protection certificates. Most big companies often rely on few popular drugs or blockbusters.[16] As the patent terms for some blockbusters come to a close one can expect to witness a stronger movement by the big pharmaceutical companies for extensions and even for stronger patent protection.[17] This is not eased by the stringent patent standards that US law-makers and judges are now more than ever wont to legislate[18] and apply.[19] In addition, the recent Novartis ruling on the patenting of one of its drugs (Gleevec) in India (where a court turned down the company's request to enforce a patent

Maskus, ed., 2004, *The WTO, Intellectual Property Rights and the Knowledge Economy* (Cheltenham/Northampton, E. Elgar 2004), pp. 325–354, at p. 341. See also, M.C.E.J. Bronckers, 'The Impact of TRIPS: Intellectual Property Protection in Developing Countries', 31 *Common Market Law Review* (1994) pp. 1245–1281, at p. 1248. On the broad rationale or theories behind the introduction of patent protection (invention motivation; invention dissemination; induced commercialisation and exploitation control) see, R. Mazzoleni and R.R. Nelson, 'Economic Theories About the Benefits and Costs of Patents', in K. Maskus, ed., *The WTO, Intellectual Property Rights and the Knowledge Economy* (Cheltenham/Northampton, E. Elgar 2004), pp. 148–169, at pp. 150–157.

14 P. Vandoren, 'Médicaments sans Frontières? Clarification of the Relationship between TRIPs and Public Health Resulting from the WTO Doha Ministerial Declaration', 5 *Journal of World Intellectual Property* (2002) pp. 5–14, at p. 7.

15 G. Robbani, 'Trade-Related Aspects of Intellectual Property Rights and Least Developed Countries', 8 *Journal of World Intellectual Property* (2005) pp. 565–573, at p. 568.

16 Blockbusters are the few drugs that generate cardinal profit margins for companies. M. Chase, 'For Genentech, Success is a Balancing act: CEO Faces Pressure to Control Prices, Continue Innovation', *The Wall Street Journal*, 5 June 2007, p. 27.

17 J. von Braun and M.P. Pugatch, 'The Changing Face of the Pharmaceutical Industry and Intellectual Property Rights', 8 *Journal of World Intellectual Property* (2005) pp. 599–623, at p. 605.

18 G. Hitt, 'Patent Overhaul Heats up', *The Wall Street Journal* (6 June 2007) p. 9; S. Lohr, 'U.S. Seeks Overhaul of its Patent System', *International Herald Tribune*, 7 June 2007, p. 14. Cf. G. Hitt, 'U.S. Hits Wall on Patent Overhaul', *The Wall Street Journal*, 27 August 2007, p. 14.

19 The recent US case of *KSR International v Teleflex* (2007) highlight the fact that the Supreme Court is poised to raise the bar for patentability making it more likely that patents will be easily challenged. See 'Patently Obvious: American Supreme Court Raises the Bar for What Deserves a Patent', *The Economist*, 5 May 2007, p. 64; L. Greenhouse, 'Ruling Raises Bar for U.S. Patents', *International Herald Tribune*, 2 May 2007, p. 13.

on a minor change to the product), highlights the fact that companies will increasingly be more assertive in defending patent rights.[20]

But the introduction of a mandatory and strong, albeit minimal, international standards of intellectual property protection at the international level have raised many issues amongst which has been the rationale for such a pre-emptive regime that only makes access to intellectual property products even more difficult. The argument was first formulated in 1998 by Michael Heller. In his article on the tragedy of the anti-commons he intimated that when there is a proliferation of intellectual property protection many owners make claims to various aspects of intellectual property. This in turn leads to a situation where the right to exclusion is overstretched. When exclusive rights are inflated this leads to under-use of the available intellectual property resources – 'a tragedy of the anti-commons.'[21]

This argument encapsulates the main contention at the core of the challenges surrounding transfer of technology to developing countries. Given that there are many holders of rights to such technologies, negotiating access becomes arduous. This is not eased by the fact that most of the right owners are private individuals or institutions.[22] But the conundrum epitomised by the tragedy of the anti-commons does not only have donative implications. It also has a negative fallout for further innovation: 'A proliferation of intellectual property rights upstream may be stifling life-saving innovations further downstream in the course of research and product development.'[23] Which is to say: 'When owners have conflicting goals and each can deploy its rights to block the strategies of the others, they may not be able to reach an agreement that leaves enough private value for downstream developers to bring products to the market.'[24]

One of the main concerns that developing countries and LDCs have regarding the introduction of stricter intellectual property disciplines at the international level within the framework of the TRIPs is that it results in an increase in the prices of medicines essential for improving the health standards of their populations.[25] As Abbott has argued, for developing countries or LDCs 'the

---

20 J. Whalen, 'Novartis Loses Patent bid in Indian Court', *The Wall Street Journal*, 4 August 2007, p. 5.

21 M. Heller, 'The Tragedy of the Anticommons: Property in Transition from Marx to Markets', 11 *Harvard Law Review* (1998) pp. 621–688, at p. 622.

22 C.M. Correa, 'Review of the TRIPs Agreement: Fostering the Transfer of Technology to Developing Countries', 2 *Journal of World Intellectual Property* (1999) pp. 939–960, at p. 957.

23 M. Heller and R. Eisenberg, 'Can Patents Deter Innovation? The Anticommons in Biomedical Research', 280 *Science* (1998) pp. 698–701, at p. 698.

24 *Ibid.*, at p. 700.

25 E. Duran and C. Michalopoulos, 'Intellectual Property Rights and Developing Countries in the WTO Millennium Round', 2 *Journal of World Intellectual Property* (1999) pp. 853–874, at p. 862. See also T. Kongolo, 'The WTO Dispute Settlement Mechanism: TRIPs Rulings and the Developing Countries', 4 *Journal of World Intellectual Property* (2001) pp. 257–270, at

grant of pharmaceutical patent protection almost certainly means increasing payments to US, European or Japanese pharmaceutical companies.'[26] He further abjures the fact that most big pharmaceutical companies in the Organization for Economic Cooperation and Development (OECD) countries often invest very little in diseases that are characteristic of poor countries.[27] He notes that: 'The preponderant effect of introducing patents on pharmaceuticals in the least-developed countries will be to reduce the number of individuals who can afford to buy them.'[28] These arguments are undercut by the submission of Judge Harms of the Supreme Court of Appeal of South Africa: 'the developing world', he notes 'remains a market for surplus products of the developed world and a source of cheap raw products, the original justification for colonisation. Intellectual property rights are not exercised in order to create wealth in those countries but to create wealth from them.'[29]

Some of the cynical positions that have been adopted against the introduction of the TRIPs Agreement pertain to the fact that the Agreement and the IPRs that it intends to protect, such as patents, are a means through which wealthy multinational companies seek to dominate the world. Defenders of such views are further entrenched in their positions because they refer to the fact that TRIPs was mainly forged as a result of the actions of the Intellectual Property

p. 270 (insinuating that the broad framework of the Uruguay Rounds agreements especially the TRIPs Agreements are not sufficiently supportive of the development in developing countries and also that the agreements do not adequately recognise the characteristics, needs and aspirations of the poor countries). See also E. Henderson, 'TRIPS and the Third World: the Example of Pharmaceutical Patents in India', 11 *European Intellectual Property Review* (1997) pp. 651–663, at p. 654 (noting that the fact that IPRs benefit developed countries does not mean they will also be in the interest of developing countries); J.H. Reichman, 'Enforcing the Enforcement Procedures of the TRIPs Agreement', 37 *Virginia Journal of International Law* (1997) pp. 335–356, at p. 345 (contending that the high substantive standards of the TRIPs Agreement reflect the positions of the developed countries' most powerful industrial circles rather than the those of most entrepreneurs in developing countries); A.S. Oddi, 'TRIPS – Natural Rights and a Polite Form of Economic Imperialism', 29 *Vanderbilt Journal of Transnational Law* (1996) pp. 415–470, at p. 469 (contending that unless the TRIPS Agreement assist industrialisation in developing countries it will not be well received). Cf., J.H. Reichman, 'From Free Riders to Fair Followers: Global Competition Under the TRIPS Agreement', 29 *New York University Journal of International Law and Politics* (1997) pp. 11–93, at p. 16.

26 F.M. Abbott, 'The TRIPs Agreement, Access to Medicines, and the WTO Doha Ministerial Conference', 5 *Journal of World Intellectual Property* (2002) pp. 15–52, at p. 18; K.M. Gopakumar, 'The WTO Deal on Cheap Drugs: A Critique', 7 *Journal of World Intellectual Property* (2004) pp. 99–113, at p. 103. For a more measured appreciation of the responsibilities of pharmaceutical companies, see N. Daniels, 'Social Responsibility and Global Pharmaceutical Companies', 1 *Developing World Bioethics* (2001) pp. 38–41, at p. 41.

27 In this regard see also Susan Sell, who notes that between 1975 and 1997 only 13 out of 1233 new drugs marketed were approved for tropical diseases: S.K. Sell, 'TRIPS-Plus Free Trade Agreements and Access to Medicines', 28 *Liverpool Law Review* (2007) pp. 41–75, at p. 51.

28 F.M. Abbott, loc. cit. n. 26, at p. 21.

29 L.T.C. Harms, loc. cit. n. 10, at p. 452.

Committee which was a coalition of multinational corporations created in the 1980s with the goals of making intellectual property protection a central part of US foreign trade policy and also of capitalising on the vital role of intellectual property protection in the US domestic context as the basis of minimum standards for intellectual property protection at the international level to be enforced by the WTO.[30] Another negative stricture levelled against the TRIPs framework is that unlike the General Agreement on Tariffs and Trade (GATT), which deals with the liberalisation of trade in goods, Special and Differential Treatment (S&DT) is not applicable within the TRIPs system.[31]

The more challenging task is that of crafting exclusive rights for pharmaceutical patent owners in a manner that does not deplete access to affordable health care.[32] To engineer this fine balancing act can be difficult. The polar and diverging interests at stake can be better understood if the issue is presented in terms of human rights to one's scientific and artistic productions, on one hand, and to the right to health care on the other.

IV. BALANCING INTELLECTUAL PROPERTY RIGHTS AND RIGHT TO HEALTH

Ardent pessimists and critics of big pharmaceutical companies seldom consider that by dint of fact the firms engaged in scientific works are also entitled to the stringent protection of such entitlements as core human rights. Article 27 of the Universal Declaration of Human Rights (UDHR) provides: '(1) Everyone has the right freely to participate in the cultural life of the community, to enjoy the arts and to share in scientific advancement and its benefits. (2) Everyone has the right to the protection of the moral and material interests resulting from any scientific, literary or artistic production of which he is author.'[33]

Article 27(1) is a statement that is aimed at assisting individuals to freely participate in community life. The second paragraph to the article initially appears anodyne but is actually a very firm declaration of the commitment by States to defend the outcomes of the intellectual property of individuals. If the

---

30 J.T. Gathii, 'Contracting Intellectual Property Rights and Competition Policy Consistently with Facilitating Access to Affordable AIDS Drugs to Low-end Consumers', 53 *Florida Law Review* (2001) pp. 727–788, at p. 753, footnote 113.

31 S&DT allows developed countries to make special favours and concessions to developing and least developed countries within very strict guidelines that are endorsed by the WTO.

32 T. Kongolo and F. Shyllon, 'Panorama of the Most Controversial Intellectual Property Issues in Developing Countries', 6 *European Intellectual Property Review* (2004) pp. 258–268, at p. 261.

33 UN General Assembly, *Universal Declaration of Human Rights*, Resolution 217 A(III), 10 December 1948.

UDHR only goes so far because it is regarded a political statement devoid of forensic implications, it is important to examine the provisions of another important component of the International Bill of Rights: the International Covenant on Economic, Social and Cultural Rights (ICESCR).[34] Article 15 of the ICESCR stipulates, *inter alia*: '(1) The States Parties to the present Covenant recognize the right of everyone (a) To take part in cultural life; (b) To enjoy the benefits of scientific progress and its applications; (c) To benefit from the protection of the moral and material interests resulting from any scientific, literary or artistic production of which he is author. … (4) The States Parties to the present Covenant recognize the benefits to be derived from the encouragement and development of international contacts and cooperation in the scientific and cultural fields.'

Although there has not been an authoritative interpretation of this provision by the Committee on Economic, Social and Cultural Rights, the literal or ordinary interpretation of the wording of the provisions leaves little doubt as to the intention of the State Parties. Article 15(1)(c) in particular clearly demarcates the nature of the rights, the protection of which, constitutes the object of the entire provision. The article provides a direct protective cover for the intellectual property endowments of individuals living and doing business in the State Parties to the ICESCR. But how does this international system for the protection of IPRs as human rights compare with a similar protective cover guaranteed patients in terms of the access to affordable health care?

To begin with, the UDHR is not very clear on the issue of a human right to health. Article 25(1) is the provision that comes closest to such a right. It is to the effect that '[e]veryone has the right to a standard of living adequate for the health and well-being of himself and of his family, including food, clothing, housing and medical care and necessary social services.'[35] The ICESCR provides for a clearer appreciation of the nature of the right at issue. It stipulates, amongst others: '1. The States Parties to the present Covenant recognize the right of everyone to the enjoyment of the highest attainable standard of physical and mental health. 2. The steps to be taken by the Parties to the present Covenant to achieve the full realization of this right shall include those necessary for: … (c) The prevention, treatment and control of epidemic, endemic, occupational and other diseases; (d) The creation of conditions which would assure to all medical service and medical attention in the event of sickness.'[36]

34 UN General Assembly, *International Covenant on Economic, Social and Cultural Rights*, Resolution 2200 A(XXI), 16 December 1966.

35 UDHR, Article 25(1).

36 ICESCR, Article 12.

This provision is as expansive and ambitious in its breadth as are the European Social Charter and African (Banjul) Charter on Human and Peoples' Rights. Amongst the express commitments made by State Parties in the European Social Charter[37] are the desire to remove all causes of ill-health,[38] the provision of advisory and educational facilities for the promotion of health,[39] and the prevention of epidemic, endemic and other diseases.[40] On their part, the signatories to the African Charter on Human and Peoples' Rights are very explicit in the manner in which they couch the right to health.[41] Article 16 stipulates that: '[e]very individual shall have the right to enjoy the best attainable state of physical and mental health.'[42] It further provides that: 'States Parties to the present Charter shall take the necessary measures to protect the health of their people and to ensure that they receive medical attention when they are sick.'[43] The Committee on Economic, Social and Cultural Rights (CESCR or the Committee) has had the opportunity to provide an authoritative rendition of the Article 12 of the ICESCR.[44] It is important to analyse some of the relevant parts of the CESCR's interpretation of General Comment No. 14. The Committee started off by stating that '[h]ealth is a fundamental human right indispensable for the exercise of other human rights.'[45] It further clarified what is meant by the right to health. Such a right is not equiponderant with the right to be healthy. The right to be healthy is the higher standard of well-being that is included in the Constitution of the World Health Organization (WHO).[46] Rather, the right to health that is evoked in Article 12 of the ICESCR contains both freedoms and entitlements: 'The freedoms include the right to control one's health and body, including sexual and reproductive freedom, and the right to be free from interference, such as the right to be free from torture, non-consensual medical treatment and experimentation. By contrast, entitlements include the right to a system of health protection which provides equality of opportunity for people to enjoy the highest attainable level of health.'[47]

---

37 European Social Charter, Turin (18 October 1961) 35 *Eur. T.S.*

38 *Ibid.*, Article 11(1).

39 *Ibid.*, Article 11(2).

40 *Ibid.*, Article 11(3).

41 African (Banjul) Charter on Human and Peoples' Rights, OAU Doc. CAB/LEG/67/3 rev. 5, 21 *ILM* (1982) p. 58

42 *Ibid.*, Article 16(1).

43 *Ibid.*, Article 16(2).

44 Committee on Economic, Social and Cultural Rights (CESCR), *Substantive Issues Arising in the Implementation of the International Covenant on Economic, Social and Cultural Rights, General Comment No. 14*, E/E.12/2000/4, 22nd Session (25 April – 12 May 2000) (hereafter, General Comment No. 14)

45 General Comment No. 14, para. 1.

46 Constitution of the World Health Organization, New York, 22 July 1946, 14 *UNTS*, pp. 186 *et seq*. The very first recital to the preamble states that '[h]ealth is a state of complete physical, mental and social well-being and not merely the absence of disease or infirmity.'

47 General Comment No. 14, para. 8.

Although the Committee did not deal with the ambiguity clouding the meaning of 'attainable level of health', it nevertheless traced a fine path as to the specific interrelated and essential elements of the right. It asserted that the degree to which some of the elements are applied in different States is a function of the conditions extant therein. These essential and interrelated aspects refer mainly to availability, accessibility, acceptability and quality.[48] The most salient and relevant of these elements relates to accessibility.

'Availability' refers to the presence of functioning physical and health care facilities.[49] 'Acceptability' pertains to the respect for medical ethics and to the fact that services rendered should be culturally appropriate and correct.[50] Quality relates to the notion that services offered be of good quality; that health workers be skilled and that the medicines should be of high quality and be scientifically approved. It also refers to the importance of functioning hospital equipment, safe potable water and adequate sanitation.[51]

The CESCR noted that the element of accessibility has four components. They include: non-discrimination of access to health-related goods and services; physical accessibility of health facilities for vulnerable sections of the population including HIV/AIDS patients; economic accessibility or affordability and lastly, information accessibility.[52] The Committee leaves no room for ambiguity that the types of health concerns related to in Article 12(2)(c) include HIV/AIDS.[53]

As to the specific obligations that States are expected to honour, the Committee was unequivocal that discrimination is anathema and equality of access is a sacrosanct and hallowed entitlement. It also noted that 'states have a special obligation to provide those who do not have sufficient means with the necessary health insurance and health-care facilities.'[54] The statement of the Committee regarding the variety of obligations which States are expected to adhere to, was instructive: 'The right to health, like all human rights, imposes three types or levels of obligations on States Parties: the obligations to *respect, protect* and *fulfil*. In turn, the obligation to fulfil contains obligations to facilitate, provide and promote. The obligation to *respect* requires States to refrain from interfering directly or indirectly with the enjoyment of the right to health. The obligation to *protect* requires States to take measures that prevent third parties from interfering with Article 12 guarantees. Finally, the obligation to *fulfil* requires States to adopt

48 *Ibid.*, para. 12.
49 *Ibid.*, para. 12(a).
50 *Ibid.*, para. 12(c).
51 *Ibid.*, para. 12(d).
52 *Ibid.*, para. 12(b).
53 *Ibid.*, para. 16.
54 *Ibid.*, para. 19.

appropriate legislative, administrative, budgetary, judicial, promotional and other measures towards the full realization of the right to health.'[55]

Another obligation which States are expected to meet under Article 12 of the ICESCR is refraining from imposing embargoes or other measures of equivalent effect that impinge on the supply of adequate medicines and medical equipment to another State. It further notes that '[restrictions] on such goods should never be used as an instrument of political and economic pressure.'[56] States equally have the duty to provide essential drugs to their populations. Such essential drugs are elaborated within the framework of WHO's Action Programme on Essential Drugs.[57] In addition, signatories to the Covenant are also expected to 'take measures to prevent, treat and control epidemic and endemic diseases.'[58] Moreover, a more pointed comment is made on the need for State Parties to assist developing countries' efforts in the fulfilment of the right to health.[59] A relatively bold statement is made respecting States that have the means yet persistently fall short of meeting their obligations as stipulated in Article 12: 'A State which is unwilling to use the maximum of its available resources for the realization of the right to health is in violation of its obligations under article 12.'[60] Finally the CESCR submits that signatories should adopt a framework law at the national level to implement the obligations therein encapsulated respecting the right to health.[61]

The lack of access to affordable HIV/AIDS medicines has led some to conclude that such inadequacies raises issues of abuse of human rights.[62] The more stringent pro-rights proponents go as far as to state that the WTO-sanctioned patent rules should explicitly recognise the basic human right to health.[63] But who's rights are being abused and furthermore, who is culpable in not respecting such rights? The response often offered is that governments in richer countries

55 *Ibid.*, para. 33. Emphasis is original.

56 *Ibid.*, para. 41.

57 *Ibid.*, para. 43(d). It is revealing to note that this specific obligation is considered by the Committee to be non-derogable – meaning no possible exceptions can be contemplated: *Ibid.*, para. 47.

58 *Ibid.*, para. 44.

59 *Ibid.*, para. 45.

60 *Ibid.*, para. 47.

61 *Ibid.*, para. 56.

62 B. Pécoul, P. Chirac, P. Trouiller and J. Pinel, 'Access to Essential Drugs in Poor Countries: A Lost Battle?', 281 *Journal of the American Medical Association* (2007) pp. 361–367, at p. 361. See also C. Tuosto, 'The TRIPs Council Decision of August 30, 2003 on the Import of Pharmaceuticals Under Compulsory Licences', 12 *European Intellectual Property Review* (2004) pp. 542–547, at p. 542; L. Ferreira, 'Access to Affordable HIV/AIDS Drugs: The Human Rights Obligations of Multinational Pharmaceutical Corporations', 71 *Fordham Law Review* (2002) pp. 1133–1179, at p. 1170.

63 M. McClellan, '"Tools for Success:" The TRIPs Agreement and the Human Rights to Essential Medicines', 12 *Washington and Lee Journal of Civil Rights and Social Justice* (2005) pp. 153–175, at p. 160.

could do better in providing more money in the provision of ARVs and health care in poorer nations.[64] In this regard the arsenal of international law on human rights and development provides a rich armoury from which one can identify legal premises that necessitates prompt action by world governments to address common health problems like HIV/AIDS. One of the main objectives of the United Nations is '[t]o achieve international cooperation in solving international problems of an economic, social, cultural, or humanitarian character, and in promoting and encouraging respect for human rights and fundamental freedoms for all, without distinction as to race, sex, language, or religion ...'[65] Article 55(b)(c) of the Charter of the UN further exposes the important regard that is accorded the protection of the right to health in international law.

Apart from Article 12 of the ICESCR that makes provision for special guarantees by state parties for the right to health care, Article 12 of the Convention on the Elimination of all forms of Discrimination against Women (CEDAW)[66] allows for important safeguards in terms of the right to health care for women. Article 12(1) of CEDAW ordains that the state parties shall take all appropriate measures to eliminate discrimination against women in the field of health care. The General Recommendation 24 of the Committee charged with the implementation of CEDAW provides an important rendition of the article.[67] The Committee makes clear that the issues of HIV/AIDS care are central to the health of women and adolescent girls.[68] It also calls on States to eliminate barriers that women face in accessing health services.[69] State parties have an obligation to guarantee women acceptable health services. Acceptable health services refer to those that are delivered 'in a way that ensures that a woman gives her fully informed consent, respects her dignity, guarantees her confidentiality and is sensitive to her needs and perspectives.'[70] It also recommends that States should provide for access to information and health services for women that relate to treatment to diseases such as HIV/AIDS.[71] These statements as well as the wording of Article 12 all reflect the importance attached to the welfare of women as also provided for under Article 31(b)(iii) of the Cotonou Partnership Agreement between the European Union and countries of the African Caribbean and Pacific Group.

---

64 A. Attaran and L. Gillespie-White, loc. cit. n. 10, at p. 1891.

65 Charter of the United Nations, signed at San Francisco on 26 June 1945.

66 United Nations General Assembly, *Convention on the Elimination of all forms of Discrimination against Women* (CEDAW) Resolution 34/180 of 18 December 1979.

67 Committee on the Implementation of the Convention on the Elimination of all forms of Discrimination Against Women, General Recommendation No. 24, 20 Session, 1999 (hereafter General Recommendation No. 24).

68 *Ibid.*, para. 18.

69 *Ibid.*, para. 21.

70 *Ibid.*, para. 22.

71 *Ibid.*, para. 31(b).

Under Article 24(1) of the United Nations Convention on the Rights of the Child (CRC)[72] States are required to ensure that children enjoy 'the highest attainable standard of health and to facilities for the treatment and rehabilitation of health.' In its General Comment No. 3 on HIV/AIDS and the Rights of the Child[73], a holistic approach to the issue is proposed by the CRC Committee. This entails that other articles of the CRC such as the right to life (Article 6) and taking the best interest of the child into account (Article 3) are all vital.[74] The right also includes the prevention of mother to child transmission of HIV through the use of ARVs.[75] It also means that children have access to comprehensive treatment and care.[76] Importantly the Committee urges states that provide development cooperation to ensure that HIV/AIDS strategies are so designed as to take fully into account the rights of the child.[77]

The examples of CEDAW and the CRC indicate that there are important rules at the international level which poor countries can avail themselves of in making a better case for improved access to social health services. It is even more evocative mindful that despite a couple of exceptions (the US and Somalia) ratification of these conventions have been exemplary. The right to health is a right that is firmly embedded in the international Bill of Rights. In forging better intellectual property rights for pharmaceutical patent holders, states parties need to also be mindful of their international obligations to enhance the right to health care.

V. ACCOUNTABILITY MECHANISMS

Whilst balancing both rights is one thing, making them enforceable is another. Generally, practice has demonstrated that actors' exposure to accountability measures ensures the effectiveness of a human right. Accountability is like a chameleon as it is easily adaptable to its surroundings. This versatility engenders diverse types of the concept thereby resulting in different propositions.

The first core distinction that can be made with regard to accountability mechanisms is based upon its timing. Preventive accountability, better known as political accountability, takes place at the decision-making stage, whereas

72 United Nations General Assembly, *Convention on the Rights of the Child*, Resolution 44/25 (20 November 1989).

73 Committee on the implementation of the CRC, General Comment No. 3, HIV/AIDS and the Rights of the Child, 32 Session, CRC/GC/2003/3, 17 March 2003 (hereafter General Comment No. 3).

74 *Ibid.*, para. 5.

75 *Ibid.*, para. 26.

76 *Ibid.*, para. 28.

77 *Ibid.*, para. 41.

repressive accountability or judicial accountability is only invoked once the violation has occurred. The former is characterised by the principles of transparency, effectiveness as well as accessibility and should be sited within the broader framework of good governance and the rule of law. The latter should provide for remedies if the right to health is violated. Both mechanisms are complementary.[78]

The second distinction relates to the actors involved. The accountability of the WTO, its Member States or the multinational corporations (as being the patent holders) is very crucial. The TRIPs Agreement is the primary responsibility of the WTO. Okediji rightly concludes that the advancement of general welfare, including the challenges of global health, requires accountability on the part of institutions that manage the international intellectual property system and the processes that inform the negotiation, content, interpretation, and enforcement of intellectual property treaties. She adds that 'where domestic institutions fail, international institutions vested with such enormous responsibility including the WTO should not remain passive and indifferent to the complex and important task of developing a philosophy of law that is underpinned by the attainment of public welfare.'[79]

The responsibility imputable to international organisations was for the first time identified by the International Law Commission in 1963 in a report on the relations between States and inter-governmental organisations. Definite answers to the issue are still to be reached. The ILC Sub-Committee decided in its report on state responsibility, 'that the question of the responsibility of other subjects of international law, such as international organizations, should be left aside.'[80] Since the turn of the millennium, the truism – 'with power comes responsibility' – holds sway in relation to the responsibility of international organisations. As discussed in other contributions of this book, the International Law Association (ILA), the International Law Commission (ILC) and the Special Rapporteur, Mr. Giorgio Gaja, examined the possibilities of an accountability framework for international organisations. This analysis resulted in various conferences organised by the ILA, in draft articles proposed by the ILC and in different reports of the Special Rapporteur. However, the draft articles are yet to be adopted by the United Nations General Assembly and the accountability of international organisations are not yet already commonly accepted.

---

78 UN, High Commissioner for Human Rights and the WTO on the right to health, Fact sheet n. 31.

79 R.L. Okediji, 'Public Welfare and the Role of the WTO: Reconsidering the TRIPS Agreement', 17 *Emory International Law Review* (2003) p. 918.

80 Document A/CN.4/161, Relations between States and inter-governmental organizations, 1963, p.179.

In the Addendum 'Mission to the World Trade Organization' the Special Rapporteur, Paul Hunt, referred to the Trade Policy Review Mechanism (TPRM). As the WTO is principally driven by its Member States, the organisation established a system to review national policies. The surveillance of intellectual property rights was later embodied in its mandate with the main goal of achieving a broader transparency in this affair. Unfortunately, promoting human rights can not be found within its objectives even though the mandate of the TPRM emphasises that 'the assessment carried out under the review mechanism takes place, to the extent relevant, against the background of the wider economic and developmental needs, policies and objectives of the Member concerned.'[81] The Special Rapporteur has the opinion that such a reference includes health considerations. Moreover, he notes that 'health considerations have not been systematically included within the review.'[82]

Alternatively, there is the WTO dispute settlement. The underlying idea was to establish a control mechanism between the WTO members. When a WTO member claims that another is violating a WTO-commitment or agreement, it can file a complaint before the Dispute Settlement Body. Even though the procedure is akin to that of a tribunal or court, the focus is put on settling disputes, not rendering judgments. The process consists of several stages and starts off with a consultation of the governments concerned. Only when the alleged violating government brings human rights arguments forward as its defence, the WTO will be forced to take them into consideration.[83] Another possibility that can be put forward is a reduced, weaker version of accountability under the form of a monitoring system. This system would consist of a systematic submission of state reports to an examining Committee of Experts.[84]

With the accountability of the WTO having been discussed, we will now examine the responsibility of multinational corporations. This approach encompasses different modalities. Firstly, one can ascribe private abuses at the national level to the host state of the multinational corporation. However, this would not be very effective as the companies will probably not change their practices as the LDC's often have weaker justice systems. Accordingly, it would be better to hold the home state of the multinational corporation accountable. Social pressure following this procedure has proven to be effective. Okediji demonstrates this by

81 WTO, Annex 3 of the Marrakesh Agreement, *Trade Policy Review Mechanism*, available at www.wto.org/english/docs_e/legal_e/29-tprm.pdf.

82 Document E/CN.4/2004/49/Add.1. *The right of everyone to the enjoyment of the highest attainable standard of physical and mental health*, Report of the Special Rapporteur, Paul Hunt, Addendum 'Mission to the World Trade Organization', p. 18.

83 G.M. Zagel, 'Human Rights Accountability of the WTO', 1.2 *Human Rights And International Legal Discourse* (2007) p. 363.

84 *Ibid.*, p. 369.

taking the example of the public outcry and the ensuing embarrassment over the HIV/AIDS pandemic in South Africa that led ultimately to the US withdrawing a threat to initiate action before the WTO. Nevertheless, real redress is not achieved. Therefore, the multinational corporation should be held directly responsible for adverse human rights effects stemming from intellectual property enforcement on the basis of the 'Norms on the Responsibility of Transnational Corporations and other Business Enterprises with regard to Human Rights'.[85]

However, the only mechanism that has proven to be successful is the national enforcement of access to essential medicines before national courts, particularly, when constitutional provisions on the right to health are present. In *Minister of Health and others v. Treatment Action Campaign and others*[86] the Constitutional Court of South Africa condemned the South African government for violating the right to health by restricting the availability of the antiretroviral drug Nevirapine. To understand this case it is proper to provide a constitutional background to the issue at stake. Chapter 2 of the South African Constitution provides that: '7(2) The state must respect, protect, promote and fulfil the rights in the Bill of Rights. (...) 8(1) The Bill of Rights applies to all law, and binds the legislature, the executive, the judiciary and all organs of state. (...) 27(1a) Everyone has the right to have access to health care services, including reproductive health care.'[87] In the case, the South African government decided to make Nevirapine available only at a limited number of pilot sites in order to reduce the risk of mother-to-child transmission of HIV. Consequently and in the absence of a national programme, doctors of the public sector who were not working in those pilot sites could not prescribe the drug, even though it had been offered to the government for free. The prominent NGO Treatment Action Campaign[88] filed a motion against the government before the Pretoria High Court. The High Court decided in favour of the Treatment Action Campaign and declared that the government policy of 'prohibiting the use of Nevirapine outside the pilot sites in the public health sector is not reasonable and that it is an unjustifiable barrier to the progressive realization of the right to health care.'[89] The government lodged an appeal against this decision. Nevertheless, in 2002 the Constitutional Court reaffirmed the Pretoria ruling. An effective national

---

85 R.L. Okediji, loc. cit. n. 3, at pp. 239–241.

86 South African Constitutional Court, *Minister of Health and Others v. Treatment Action Campaign and Others* (N°2) (CCT8/02), 2002, ZACC 15; 2002 (5) SA 721; 2002 (10), BCLR 1033, 5 July 2002.

87 Chapter Two of the Constitution of the Republic of South Africa, approved by the Constitutional Court on 4 December 1996 and took effect on 4 February 1997.

88 The Treatment Action Campaign (TAC) was founded on 10 December 1998 in Cape Town, South Africa. This network consists of organisations and individuals campaigning for treatment for people with HIV and to reduce new HIV infections.

89 Pretoria High Court, *Minister of Health and Others v Treatment Action Campaign and Others*, 14 December 2001.

enforcement system is a move in the right direction. That said, one should support the establishment of an accountability system for international organisations in order to draw attention to their duty to respect human rights.

VI. CONCLUSION

International trade can affect human rights in opposite ways. Sometimes it enhances human rights. In other instances the opposite prevails. In the present case, the TRIPs Agreement has had a negative impact on the right of access to cheaper HIV/AIDS medicines. Nevertheless, intellectual property and the right to health do not need to be mutually antithetical.

The two frameworks analysed in order to provide for a better understanding of human rights and trade is arguably a good start. With availability, accessibility and good quality during the decision-making process on the one hand and obligations on Member States to respect, to protect and to fulfil on the other, the creation of a real accountability mechanism is foreseeable. Accountability is mostly a necessary incentive to achieve a given policy. Initially, advocates of a strong international trade regime sanctioned by the WTO emphasised that human rights were not relevant in the WTO context. Gradually, one can decern shifts and turns in this initial stance. However, practice demonstrates that the WTO can not (yet) be held accountable for human rights violations through the prism of the TRIPs Agreement. Instead, governments are brought before national courts in order to improve access to cheaper HIV/AIDS medicines. The latter has proven to be very effective; nevertheless an accountability mechanism for human rights violations by international organisations is desirable and worth the pursuit.

ACCOUNTABILITY OF DEVELOPMENT AGENCIES THROUGH THE USE OF HUMAN RIGHTS INDICATORS

Gauthier DE BECO*

I. INTRODUCTION

Human rights accountability of international organisations has become an important subject of discussion in recent years. As with other international organisations, development agencies should be held accountable for their human rights obligations. However, as Emilie Filmer-Wilson pointed out, mechanisms for evaluating the human rights impact of development programmes are seriously lacking.[1] Human rights indicators, such as those recently developed for monitoring compliance with human rights at the State level, could also be used for development agencies.

The aim of this contribution is to discuss the possibility of using human rights indicators to assess the consequences of development programmes on the human rights enjoyment of their beneficiaries. In this contribution, the term "development agencies" will connote UN multilateral aid agencies conducting development programmes in the field. Particular attention will be paid to UNDP and its Country Offices. This article, however, will not concern itself with the human rights violations of donor States or the misconduct of development agencies' staff members.

---

* Gauthier de Beco has a PhD in Law from the *Université catholique de Louvain* (Belgium), a Master of Laws (LL.M.) from the University of Nottingham (United Kingdom) and a Law Degree from the *Katholieke Universiteit Leuven* (Belgium). He worked as a consultant in the area of human rights indicators for both the UN and several NGOs. His publications relating to this topic include: G. de Beco, 'Measuring Human Rights: Underlying Approach', (3) *European Human Rights Law Review* (2007) p. 266; G. de Beco, 'Human Rights Indicators for Assessing State Compliance with International Human Rights', 77(1–2) *Nordic Journal of International Law* (2008) p. 23; G. de Beco, 'Human Rights Impact Assessments', 27(2) *Netherlands Quarterly of Human Rights* (2009) p. 139. The views expressed in this contribution are exclusively those of the author. Internet pages last visited on 12 August 2009.

1 E. Filmer-Wilson, 'An Introduction to the Use of Human Rights Indicators for Development Programmes', 24(1) *Netherlands Quarterly of Human Rights* (2006) pp. 156–157.

This contribution is divided into five parts. After the introduction, Part II will examine the human rights obligations of development agencies and the importance of providing them with human rights monitoring mechanisms. Part III will deal with human rights indicators and analyse their potential role for development agencies. It will discuss the development of human rights indicators and analyse the data necessary for these indicators and the existing types of human rights indicators. Part IV will examine how and with whom development agencies should establish and use human rights indicators to assess the human rights compliance of their programmes. The conclusion of this contribution is the subject of Part V.

II. THE ACCOUNTABILITY OF DEVELOPMENT AGENCIES FOR THEIR HUMAN RIGHTS OBLIGATIONS

As will be seen in this part, development agencies have human rights obligations, especially since they endeavour to integrate human rights into their programmes. A human rights-based approach to development cooperation has several advantages, including holding duty-bearers to account. Accountability requires that development agencies put in place evaluation mechanisms in which human rights indicators could play an important role.

A. THE HUMAN RIGHTS OBLIGATIONS OF DEVELOPMENT AGENCIES

International human rights create obligations not only for States, but also for individuals and international organisations. While the accountability for human rights violations of the Security Council[2] and financial international organisations, such as the World Bank, the IMF, and the WTO[3], has recently been a topic of discussion, development agencies have been virtually left out with

2 A. Reinisch, 'Developing Human Rights and Humanitarian Law Accountability of the Security Council for the Imposition of Economic Sanctions', 95(4) *American Journal of International Law* (2001) p. 855; B. Fassbender, 'Quis judicabit? The Security Council, Its Powers and its Legal Control', 11(1) *European Journal of International Law* (2000) p. 219; B. Martenczuk, 'The Security Council, the International Court and Judicial Review: What Lessons from Lockerbie?', 10(3) *European Journal of International Law* (1999) p. 545.

3 See *inter alia*: S.I. Skogly, *The Human Rights Obligations of the World Bank and the International Monetary Fund* (London, Cavendish Publishing 2001); M. Darrow, *Between Light And Shadow: The World Bank, The International Monetary Fund And International Human Rights Law* (Oxford, Hart Publishing 2003); W. Van Genugten, P. Hunt and S. Mathews, eds., *The World Bank, IMF and Human Rights* (Nijmegen, Wolf Legal Publishers 2003).

regard the evaluation of their human rights compliance. As with all international organisations, however, development agencies also have human rights obligations, since they are composed of States that have such obligations[4] and since they must at least abide by customary international law.[5] In addition, as a programme part of the UN, UNDP (which is the focus of this study) has human rights obligations under the UN Charter. Development agencies, therefore, are accountable for basic human rights violations attributable to their activities. From the 1990's, development agencies such as UNDP started to integrate human rights into their programmes, despite the fact that both human rights and development had until then been considered as two separate fields. To ensure consistency in these endeavours, the UN reached a 'Common Understanding on the Human Rights-Based Approach to Development Cooperation' among its agencies in 2003.[6] The promotion and protection of human rights has thus become one of the objectives of development agencies, an objective that must transcend all their other objectives. In view of this, it could be said that these agencies should also comply with the human rights standards they have explicitly adhered to and which they are trying to implement through their activities.

To integrate human rights into development programmes, development agencies must clearly define the human rights they want to implement. They must focus principally, albeit not exclusively, on the rights which fall within the scope of their mandates. In order to do so, some agencies are trying to develop a human rights perspective in the Millennium Development Goals (MDGs), which constitute a common agenda for the whole international community. UNIFEM, for instance, in its endeavours to implement the MDGs, is focusing on gender equality by referring to both the Convention on the Elimination of All Forms of Discrimination against Women (CEDAW) and the Beijing Fourth World Conference on Women.[7] However, implementing human rights through development cooperation is more difficult in practice than in theory, since only few human rights officers are ensuring the mainstreaming of human rights in the field and since programme managers as a rule are not acquainted with

4 S.I. Skogly, *Beyond National Borders: States' Human Rights Obligations in International Cooperation* (Antwerp/Oxford, Intersentia 2006) p. 63.

5 C.F. Amerasinghe, *Principles of the institutional law of international organizations*, 2nd rev. edn., (Cambridge, Cambridge University Press 2005) p. 400; Ph. Sands and P. Klein, *Bowett's Law of International Institutions* (London, Thomson and Sweet and Maxwell 2001) p. 459; ILA, *Report of the Seventy-First Conference, Final Report of the International Law Association Committee on the Accountability of International Organisations* (Berlin, 16–21 August 2004) p. 22.

6 UN, *The UN Common Understanding on the Human Rights-Based Approach to Development Cooperation*, Stamford Workshop (Stamford, 5–7 May 2003), available at www.unescobkk.org/fileadmin/user_upload/appeal/human_rights/UN_Common_understanding_RBA.pdf.

7 See UNIFEM, *Pathway to Gender Equality: CEDAW, Beijing and the MDGs* (New York, UN 2004), available at www.unifem.org/attachments/products/385_PathwayToGenderEquality_screen.pdf.

international human rights law. Human rights indicators would ensure better consideration for human rights not only in the headquarters of development agencies but also in their local offices. The use of such indicators would thus help development agencies meet their human rights obligations not only in theory but also in practice.

Development agencies must abide by human rights standards in two ways. First, they must aim to contribute to the promotion and protection of human rights by ensuring that their programmes have a positive impact on the local human rights situation. By so doing, integrating human rights into development provides for long-term goals and replaces a needs-based approach with a rights-based approach to development cooperation. Second, programmes must be run in a way that reflects human rights principles, including participation, non-discrimination and accountability. Development agencies must focus on vulnerable people and give them a say in the running of their programmes. With regard to accountability, a human rights-based approach to development cooperation must enable duty-bearers – *in casu* development agencies – to meet their obligations, and rights-holders – *in casu* the beneficiaries of development programmes – to make their claims.[8] The objective of this approach is also to strengthen the relationship between them.

B. MONITORING MECHANISMS FOR DEVELOPMENT AGENCIES

Development agencies have a certain power and, as the International Law Association (ILA) stated, '[p]ower entails accountability, that is the duty to account for its exercise'.[9] Accountability requires the creation of evaluation mechanisms, and this applies to any international organisation which must operate as openly and as transparently as possible.[10] Monitoring mechanisms must therefore determine whether or not development agencies have realised

8 UN, *The UN Common Understanding on the Human Rights-Based Approach to Development Cooperation*, op. cit. n. 6. The UN Common Understanding on the Human Rights-Based Approach to Development Cooperation is composed of three statements that each comprise a short explanation, the third of which stipulates that '[p]rogrammes of development cooperation contribute to the development of the capacities of 'duty-bearers' to meet their obligations and of 'rights-holders' to claim their rights'. See also: OHCHR, *Frequently Asked Questions on a Human Rights-Based Approach to Development Cooperation* (New York/Geneva, UN 2006) p. 15, available at http://un.org/Depts/dhl/humanrights/toc/toc9.pdf.

9 ILA, *Report of the Seventy-First Conference*, op. cit. n. 5, p. 2.

10 G. Hafner, 'Can International Organizations be controlled? Accountability and Responsibility', 97 *American Society of International Law Proceedings* (2003) pp. 236–240. See also: OHCHR, *Draft Guidelines: A Human Rights Approach to Poverty Reduction Strategies* (UN 2002) p. 60, available at www.fao.org/righttofood/kc/downloads/vl/docs/Human%20rights%20approach%20to%20poverty%20reduction%20strategies_draft%20guidelines.pdf.

their ambitions of integrating human rights into their work and examine the effects of their programmes on the human rights enjoyment of their beneficiaries. Development agencies could achieve this by developing human rights indicators capable of holding them to account.[11] Although monitoring human rights takes time, which delays programming, and generates costs, which reduces the budget for other activities, improving the accountability of development agencies in this way has many advantages. It increases aid efficiency, provides for transparency and encourages in-depth reflection. The use of human rights indicators in the evaluation of development programmes also enables vulnerable people to participate in the process.

Development agencies must above all be accountable to the people affected by their programmes. Accountability requires not only that these people simply be involved, but also that they be given a chance to participate in the decision-making process and feel ownership within the organisation.[12] To achieve this, vulnerable people must be identified through local NGOs or representatives of local communities and be heard when development programmes are being evaluated. Donor States could also have an interest in monitoring development programmes, since they are naturally eager to know how their funds are being used. However, there is a risk that such States evaluate programmes only in positive terms in order to justify their funding. Donor States tend to focus more on institutional performance than on participation and empowerment.[13] Finally, development agencies should evaluate their own work in order to be critical and adapt their programmes where necessary. This task should be shared between those who delegate responsibilities and those who execute them within a particular agency.[14]

III. HUMAN RIGHTS INDICATORS TO MONITOR DEVELOPMENT PROGRAMMES

Human rights indicators are a relatively recent invention.[15] For the last decade or so, human rights indicators have been developed to secure State accountability

11 E. Filmer-Wilson, loc. cit. n. 1, at pp. 155–156.

12 See N. Woods, 'Good Governance in International Organizations', 5(1) *Global Governance* (1999) p. 44.

13 H.-O. Sano, 'Good Governance, Accountability and Human Rights', in H.-O. Sano and G. Alfredsson, eds., *Human Rights and Good Governance. Building Bridges* (The Hague/London/New York, Martinus Nijhoff Publishers 2002) p. 132.

14 See G. Boyne, J. Gould-Williams, J. Law and R. Walker, 'Plans, Performance Information and Accountability. The Case of Best Value', 80(4) *Public Administration* (2002) pp. 692–693.

15 For human rights indicators in general, see G. de Beco, 'Human Rights Indicators for Assessing State Compliance with International Human Rights', 77(1–2) *Nordic Journal of International Law* (2008) p. 23.

for international human rights obligations. Treaty bodies invited States to develop indicators in order to monitor their compliance with human rights.[16] Paul Hunt, the UN Special Rapporteur on the right to health, subsequently developed right to health indicators, and also children's right to health and, in particular, child survival indicators.[17] He later provided an upgraded list of indicators relating to the right to health.[18] The Office of the High Commissioner for Human Rights (OHCHR) also proposed a framework for developing human rights indicators for monitoring State compliance with human rights.[19] Recently, it further developed this framework with the aid of a group of experts.[20] Despite their focus on States, there is no reason why these indicators could not be used to monitor the human rights compliance of development agencies.[21]

---

16 See, *inter alia*: Committee on Economic, Social and Cultural Rights, General Comment N. 15. The Right to Water (art. 11–12) (E/C.12/2002/11) para. 54 (2002); Committee on Economic, Social and Cultural Rights, General Comment N. 14. The Right to the Highest Attainable Standard of Health (art. 12) (E/C.12/2000/4) para. 57–58 (2000); Committee on Economic, Social and Cultural Rights, General Comment N. 13. The Right to Education (art. 13) (E/C.12/1999/10) para. 52 (1999); Committee on the Rights of the Child, General Comment N. 5. General Measures of Implementation of the Convention on the Rights of the Child (arts. 4, 42 and 44, para. 6) (CRC/GC/2003/5) para. 48 (2003).

17 See P. Hunt, 'Interim Report of the Special Rapporteur of the Commission on Human Rights on the Right of Everyone to the Enjoyment of the Highest Attainable Standard of Physical and Mental Health', UN Doc. A/58/427, para. 5–37 (2003); P. Hunt, 'Report of the Special Rapporteur of the Commission on Human Rights on the Right of Everyone to the Enjoyment of the Highest Attainable Standard of Physical and Mental Health', UN Doc. A/59/422, para. 59–84 (2004). Paul Hunt also developed a specific disaggregated indicator on the proportion of births attended by skilled health personnel. See P. Hunt, 'Report of the Special Rapporteur of the Commission on Human Rights on the Right of Everyone to the Enjoyment of the Highest Attainable Standard of Physical and Mental Health', E/CN.4/2006/48, paras. 39–47 (2006).

18 P. Hunt and G. MacNaughton, 'A Human Rights-Based Approach to Health Indicators', in M. Baderin and R. McCorquodale, eds., *Economic, Social and Cultural Rights in Action* (Oxford, Oxford University Press 2007) p. 303.

19 See OHCHR, *Report on Indicators for Monitoring Compliance with International Human Rights Instruments*, presented at the 18th meeting of chairpersons of the human rights treaty bodies and the fifth inter-committee of the human rights treaty bodies (HRI/MC/2006/7) (2006). In the annex of this report, the OHCHR proposed indicators relating to the right to life, the right to judicial review of detention, the right to food and the right to health.

20 See OHCHR, *Report on Indicators for Promoting and Monitoring the Implementation of Human Rights*, presented at the at the 20th meeting of chairpersons of the human rights treaty bodies and the seventh inter-committee meeting of the human rights treaty bodies (HRI/MC/2008/3) (2008). In the first annex of this report, the OHCHR proposed indicators relating to the right not to be subjected to torture and other cruel, inhuman or degrading treatment or punishment, the right to participate in public affairs, the right to education, the right to adequate housing, the right to social security, the right to work, the right to freedom of opinion and expression and the right to a fair trial. In the second annex of this report, it provided examples of meta-data sheets, to the elaboration of which the author of this contribution contributed when he was given a consultancy contract from the OHCHR.

21 E. Filmer-Wilson, loc. cit. n. 1, at pp. 155–156.

As will be seen later in this part, human rights indicators focus on discrimination and measure compliance with both human rights principles and substantive human rights. Indicators rely on four kinds of data: events-based data, socio-economic data, household perceptions and expert judgments, all of which could be more or less useful for development agencies. Three types of human rights indicators can be distinguished, namely structural, process and outcome indicators, all of which could monitor development agencies' compliance with human rights in different ways.

A. DEVELOPING HUMAN RIGHTS INDICATORS

Development agencies have not yet developed human rights indicators to evaluate their human rights achievements. To date, development agencies have been focusing mainly on quantitative results, such as the number of training courses provided and research material produced, rather than on qualitative results that measure changes in behaviour.[22] These performance indicators do not focus on the programming process in which the participation of vulnerable people and the presence of accountability mechanisms should be ensured. Development agencies are also using development indicators to investigate people's living conditions in order to define their programmes. However, such indicators only examine the state of a situation and not the right to that situation.[23] Undertaking health, housing, food and education programmes – all of which can positively influence the well-being of the population – does not mean that the rights to health, adequate housing, food and education are being properly implemented by these programmes. Development agencies might be using a top-down approach to development without consulting affected people or violating human rights that *a priori* do not fall within the scope of their mandates. Development indicators also by and large fail take into account the principle of non-discrimination. For instance, the indicators monitoring progress towards the MDGs do not focus on discrimination, and disregard gender discrimination in particular.[24] Human rights indicators are therefore necessary

---

22 CIDA, *Setting Results in Human Rights, Democratic Development and Governance at CIDA: A Needs Assessment* (CIDA, Québec 1997) p. 2, available at www.acdi-cida.gc.ca/INET/IMAGES.NSF/vLUImages/HRDG2/$file/RESULTSE.pdf.

23 T. Landman and J. Häuserman, 'Map-Making and Analysis of the Main International Initiatives on Developing Indicators on Democracy and Good Governance' (Paper presented at the Turku Expert Meeting on Human Rights Indicators, Turku/Åbo, 10–13 March 2005), available at www.abo.fi/instut/imr/research/seminars/indicators/final-report.pdf.

24 UNIFEM, *Progress of the Worlds' Women 2002. Volume 2: Gender Equality and the Millennium Goals* (New York, UNIFEM 2002) p. 60. For instance, the examination of the average literacy rate fails to provide information on the possible denial of access to education of women living in remote areas. This is why UNIFEM tried to put a gender perspective in the MDGs. See UNIFEM, *Pathway to Gender Equality: CEDAW, Beijing and the MDGs*, op. cit. note 7.

to examine whether or not programmes discriminate against the most vulnerable people whom development agencies aim to serve.

Although human rights indicators have been a recent topic of discussion, a framework for developing human rights indicators is still lacking. Human rights indicators, however, can only become a useful instrument if used consistently, otherwise they could prove ineffective and fail to make room for action. Rajeev Malhotra and Nicolas Fasel, two experts working at the OHCHR, recently tried to remedy this deficiency by dividing human rights indicators according to two interrelated human rights aspects: human rights principles and substantive human rights.[25] In order to capture human rights principles, indicators should be linked to international human rights instruments and measure the extent to which the implementation of human rights ensures participation, non-discrimination and accountability. In order to evaluate compliance with substantive human rights, on the other hand, indicators should identify the major attributes of a right by breaking down its constitutive elements. Applied to development agencies, this means that human rights indicators should not only assess the impact of a programme on the local human rights situation but also the agencies' consideration for human rights principles throughout the programming process.

Human rights indicators must fulfil several requirements in order to be effective. They must be specific, measurable, attainable, relevant, and time-framed.[26] The last requirement is essential for measuring progress in the realisation of human rights and necessitates the development of a valid time framework for data collection and data interpretation. The frequency with which human rights indicators are used should be established beforehand, and frequency intervals be neither too long nor too short. Intervals that are too long will prevent the close evaluation of the human rights compliance of development programmes, with the result that these programmes will be more difficult to adapt. Intervals, on the other hand, must not be too short, since the collection and interpretation of data as well as the resultant action to be taken on the basis of human rights indicators

---

25 R. Malhotra and N. Fasel, 'Indicators for Monitoring the Implementation of Human Rights – A Conceptual Framework' (Background paper prepared for the OHCHR expert consultation on indicators for monitoring compliance with international human rights instruments, Geneva, 29 August 2005) p. 23 [unpublished], on file with the authors.

26 These criteria are the so-called SMART-criteria. See H.-O. Sano, 'Human Rights Indicators. Purpose and Validity' (Paper presented at the Turku Expert Meeting on Human Rights Indicators, Turku/Åbo, 10–13 March 2005) p. 4, available at www.abo.fi/instut/imr/research/seminars/indicators/Human.doc. According to Hans-Otto Sano, indicators should in addition be valid, balanced, sensitive, motivating, practical, owned and clear.

take time.[27] The frequency of intervals for using human rights indicators will in fact depend on the time framework of a particular programme.

Establishing human rights indicators to hold development agencies accountable for their human rights obligations requires the participation of various actors. Although human rights indicators should be created by development agencies themselves, since they are responsible for their human rights achievements, they should ideally share this task with statisticians and human rights lawyers.[28] Regarding the latter, the UNDP Oslo Governance Centre created (with the aid of human rights experts) a User's Guide for Indicators for Human Rights Based Approaches to Development in UNDP Programming in order to help UNDP Country Offices evaluate the human rights compliance of their programmes.[29] It is currently piloting the Guide in the Offices so as to validate the framework it proposes. However, although this initiative is certainly a step in the right direction, it is more an attempt to conceptualise a human rights-based approach to development cooperation through the use of human rights indicators than an attempt to provide clear guidelines for the development of these indicators for UNDP Country Offices, something which might hamper the implementation of this Guide in the field.

B. DATA ON HUMAN RIGHTS VIOLATIONS

Human rights indicators for monitoring development programmes require human rights-related data. These can be divided into four different categories: events-based data, socio-economic data, household perceptions and expert judgments. The first category, events-based data, provides information on events. These are qualitative and objective data, due to the fact that they are expressed in numerical form and based on observable facts. These data mostly concern civil and political rights. They provide information on what has occurred, to whom it

---

27 On the timing of the evaluation of development programmes, see UNDP, *Handbook on Monitoring and Evaluating for Results* (New York, UNDP 2002), p. 46, available at www.un.org.pk/undp/prm/Rules%20&%20Guidelines/handbook-on-monitoring-and-evaluating-for-results-17april-02.pdf.

28 The importance of a multidisciplinary approach for human rights measurement was stressed at the Montreux Conference on Statistics, Development and Human Rights held in Montreux (Switzerland) in September 2001. For more information on this Conference, see www.portal-stat.admin.ch/iaos2000/index2.htm.

29 UNDP, *Indicators for Human Rights Based Approaches to Development in UNDP Programming: A Users' Guide* (Oslo, UNDP 2006), available at www.undp.org/oslocentre/docs06/HRBA%20indicators%20guide.pdf. The Swedish Agency for Development Evaluation (SADEV) also started developing human rights indicators for the evaluation of Swedish development programmes. See SADEV, *Improving Democracy and Human Rights Support. Recommendations for the Use of Indicators Based on the Case of Mozambique* (Västerås, SADEV 2006), available at www.sadev.se/Uploads/Files/61.pdf.

occurred, who carried it out, the circumstances in which it occurred and other related aspects. Events-based data can thus be disaggregated into individual violations.[30] Besides HURIDOCS, which records human rights-related events on the basis of information regarding the location, time, victims and alleged perpetrator(s) of human rights violations,[31] international NGOs such as Amnesty International, Human Rights Watch, the International Helsinki Foundation as well as national human rights institutions, local NGOs, truth commissions and foreign offices use events-based data in their reports. Since it is impossible to collect enough events-based data to achieve a complete picture of a human rights situation and since governments tend to hide this kind of information, events-based data can only reveal patterns of human rights violations, which are not that useful for monitoring development programmes.

The second category, comprising socio-economic data (also called statistical data because of their quantitative nature) provides information on the living conditions of a State which can reflect the average degree to which human rights are enjoyed in that State. Like events-based data, these are quantitative and objective data. However, in contrast to events-based data, they mainly concern economic, social and cultural rights and are as a rule readily available. The reason for this is that many international agencies, including UNDP, UNESCO, UNICEF, the ILO, FAO, UNIFEM, OECD and the Word Bank, collect socio-economic data with the cooperation of governments in order to fulfil their mandates.[32] The information collected by these agencies is mainly used to examine States' progress towards the MDGs. Since development agencies have a considerable amount of socio-economic data at their disposal or can easily obtain them from other agencies, they could use this information to monitor the human rights impact of their own programmes. The weakness of socio-economic data, however, is that they are not intended to measure human rights. Nonetheless, there are two ways in which they could be useful for monitoring development programmes. The first stems from the fact that socio-economic data help development agencies examine the political and social background of the country in which they work and thus interpret human rights indicators. The second is that these data can be supplemented by data linked to human rights

---

30 T. Landman, 'Measuring Human Rights: Principle, Practice, and Policy', 26(4) *Human Rights Quarterly* (2004) p. 918.

31 See HURIDOCS, *Events Standard Formats: A Tool for Documenting Human Rights Violations* (Versoix, HURIDOCS 2001), available at www.huridocs.org/tools/tools/esf-en-word.doc/index_html. Registration is necessary to get access to this document.

32 See R. Malhotra and N. Fasel, 'Quantitative Human Rights Indicators – A Survey of Major Initiatives', (Discussion Paper presented at the Turku Expert Meeting on Human Rights Indicators, Turku/Åbo, 10–13 March 2005) pp. 12–18, available at www.abo.fi/instut/imr/research/seminars/indicators/Background.doc.

standards and disaggregated into particular groups for use by human rights indicators.[33]

The third category of data, i.e. household perceptions, refers to information on public opinion. These are narratively-expressed data based on human perceptions which are by nature qualitative and subjective. Examples are the Gallup International Millennium Survey[34] and the METAGORA project[35] both of which are collecting worldwide opinions on governance and democracy. Barometer surveys, such as the Afrobarometer, also report on public opinion regarding the same issues. Household perceptions could help development agencies evaluate the effects of their programmes on the human rights enjoyment of their beneficiaries. They must not be regarded as a secondary source of information, since they can complete and confirm other kinds of information, and even question it. Agencies, therefore, could use questionnaires to survey the local population on whether they feel that a particular programme has had a positive impact on their human rights. Household perceptions, however, largely depend on the sensitivity of the public, whose understanding of human rights may differ from State to State.[36] This could even be the case between different groups within a single State. What needs to be established, therefore, is a clear link between the questions asked in the opinion surveys and human rights standards.

The fourth category of data, i.e. expert judgments, likewise comprises qualitative and subjective data. This kind of data, however, does not derive from the general public but from experts. Expert judgments are obtained *inter alia* from research institutes, the media and NGOs. Amnesty International and Human Rights Watch, for instance, both publish reports on widespread human rights violations, while the Cingranelli-Richards Human Rights Dataset[37] provides information on the worldwide implementation of several human rights. Other examples of expert judgments are the Political Terror Scale (based on the reports of Amnesty International and the U.S. State Department) and the Freedom House index (based on foreign reports, academic studies and NGO analyses). Expert judgments, by themselves at least, are of little use to development agencies, since most of them only provide information on civil and political rights violations in the form of composite indexes.[38] However, they could still be useful as a first

---

33 T. Landman and J. Häuserman, loc. cit. n. 23, pp. 18–19 and 35; K. Tomasevski, 'Indicators', in A. Eide, C. Krause and A. Rossas, eds., *Economic, Social and Cultural Rights* (Dordrecht/Boston/London, Martinus Nijhoff Publishers 2001) p. 391.

34 See www.gallup-international.com.

35 See www.metagora.org/html/activities/act_modules.html.

36 T. Landman, loc. cit. n. 30, at p. 924.

37 See http://ciri.binghamton.edu/faq.asp.

38 See UNDP, *Human Development Report* (2000) (New York, Oxford University Press 2000) p. 91. Composite indexes fail to take discrimination into account, with the result that they are

indication of the level of human rights promotion and protection in a particular country.

Development agencies should ideally focus on more than just one of these four kinds of data. They should use multiple information sources to make their human rights indicators reliable.[39] The most useful data for monitoring human rights compliance by development agencies are probably socio-economic data, especially since these same agencies already collect them as part of their mandates. As mentioned above, however, socio-economic data are not intended for the evaluation of human rights compliance and should therefore be supplemented by data linked to human rights standards and disaggregated into particular groups in order to be useful for human rights indicators. UNDP already made some progress in this regard. It created a Gender-Related Development Index, which refines the existing Human Development Index according to sex discrimination. It also created pro-poor and gender-sensitive indicators that can be obtained by further disaggregating data by poverty status and sex.[40] Disaggregated data should be collected by development agencies in collaboration with other agencies working in the field as well as with governments. National statistical institutes should also be asked to collect such data and have their capacities strengthened to do so by these agencies.[41] Another imperative is that development agencies identify the vulnerable groups that should benefit from their programmes and investigate the degree to which their human rights are enjoyed. As already mentioned, household perceptions on the human rights impact of development programmes could be compiled through the distribution of questionnaires. Development agencies could also try to use

---

unable to assist in designing programmes that benefit the most vulnerable groups of the population.

39 UNDP, *Indicators for Human Rights Based Approaches to Development in UNDP Programming: A Users' Guide*, op. cit. n. 29, p. 18. UN Country teams should also make use, where they already exist, of the Common Country Assessments (CCAs), which analyse the general development situation of development countries by taking into account their national priorities, and the United Nations Development Assistance Frameworks (UNDAFs), which provide for a global approach to development cooperation for such countries within the framework of the MDGs and international human rights treaties. See UN, *Common Country Assessments (CCA) and United Nations Development Framework (UNDAF): Guidelines for UN Country Teams* (Geneva, UN 2004) p. 32, available at www.undp.or.id/mdg/documents/Guidance%20for%20CCA%20and%20UNDAF.pdf. For the complete list of CCAs and UNDAFs that have been completed, see www.un.org/special-rep/ohrlls/ohrlls/cca_undaf_prsp.htm.

40 UNDP, *Measuring Democratic Governance. A Framework for Selecting Pro-poor and Gender Sensitive Indicators* (Oslo, UNDP 2006), available at www.undp.org/oslocentre/docs06/Framework%20paper%20-%20entire%20paper.pdf.

41 UNDP, *Indicators for Human Rights Based Approaches to Development in UNDP Programming: A Users' Guide*, op. cit. n. 29, p. 10. See also: E. Omar, 'Development and Human Rights: The Growing Demand for Statistics from the International Community', 18 *Statistical Journal of the United Nations Economic Commission for Europe* (2001) pp. 145–146.

data from local NGOs to supplement and, where necessary, critically review data obtained from public institutions.

C. STRUCTURAL, PROCESS AND OUTCOME INDICATORS

According to Paul Hunt, human rights indicators can be divided into structural, process and outcome indicators.[42] This division has subsequently been taken over by the OHCHR.[43] Structural indicators measure intention to abide by international human rights law. At State level, structural indicators examine the ratification of human rights treaties and their incorporation into domestic legislation. With regard to development agencies, these indicators are at first sight unnecessary, since they are not parties to these instruments. Development agencies, however, may examine whether their activities have encouraged the State in which they work to become a party to human rights treaties and adapt its domestic legislation accordingly. UNDP, for instance, has developed in this way specific, mostly structural, indicators for evaluating the impact of its right to information programmes.[44] Overuse of structural indicators, however, should be avoided, since human rights compliance depends by and large on other factors that cannot be evaluated by them.

Process indicators measure efforts undertaken to implement human rights. They examine de facto compliance with human rights treaties. While at State level these indicators focus on the conduct of States, they can evaluate the consideration of development agencies for human rights principles (which, as mentioned earlier, represent one of the two human rights aspects to be addressed by human rights indicators) when carrying out their programmes.[45] As already mentioned, these principles are participation, non-discrimination and accountability, which must be integrated into any human rights based-approach to development cooperation. This means that process indicators should evaluate

---

42 P. Hunt, 'Interim Report of the Special Rapporteur of the Commission on Human Rights on the Right of Everyone to the Enjoyment of the Highest Attainable Standard of Physical and Mental Health', op. cit. n. 17, paras. 22–29; P. Hunt, 'Report of the Special Rapporteur of the Commission on Human Rights on the Right of Everyone to the Enjoyment of the Highest Attainable Standard of Physical and Mental Health', op. cit. n. 17, paras. 59–72.

43 OHCHR, *Report on Indicators for Monitoring Compliance with International Human Rights Instruments*, op. cit. n. 19, at paras. 16–20; OHCHR, *Report on Indicators for Promoting and Monitoring the Implementation of Human Rights*, op. cit. n. 20, at paras. 18–22. For an analysis of structural, process and outcome indicators, see also: R. Malhotra and N. Fasel, loc. cit. n. 25, p. 15; R. Malhotra and N. Fasel, loc. cit. n. 32, p. 28.

44 UNDP, *A Guide to Measuring the Impact of Right to Information Programmes. Practical Guidance Note* (Oslo, UNDP 2006), available at www.undp.org/governance/docs/A2I_guides_righttoinfoimpact.pdf.

45 UNDP, *Indicators for Human Rights Based Approaches to Development in UNDP Programming: A Users' Guide*, op. cit. n. 29, pp. 14 and 17.

existing evaluation mechanisms, including the scope these mechanisms give for redress and changes in programmes where necessary. These indicators should also evaluate the level of participation of vulnerable people and consideration by development agencies for the principle of non-discrimination in their activities. This would include examination of the endeavours by development agencies to reach the most vulnerable people and ways to include them in the evaluation of their programmes. Besides monitoring compliance with human rights principles, process indicators could measure how development agencies contribute to the realisation of human rights in the countries in which they work. The latter would then assess the agencies' activities aiming at enhancing the promotion and protection of human rights at local level.[46] Lastly, process indicators could also measure whether development programmes have resulted in more endeavours by the State to implement human rights.

Outcome indicators, just like process indicators, also evaluate de facto compliance with human rights treaties. However, in contrast to process indicators, they focus more on the outcome of efforts than on the efforts themselves.[47] With respect to development agencies, these indicators could be used to measure the human rights situation of the State in which these agencies are active before, while and after running a programme. Since development agencies cannot aim to realise all human rights at once and since they must prioritise their action, outcome indicators may partly be limited according to the objectives of a particular programme. As a result, some outcome indicators will vary according to the agency's mission, while others will embody the common basic human rights standards that the agency must consistently try to achieve through its programmes. Outcome indicators could be inspired by the MDG indicators. However, as mentioned earlier, the latter should be further disaggregated into particular groups if they are to serve as human rights indicators.

Two considerations should be made in relation to the three types of human rights indicators that could be used by development agencies. Firstly, human rights indicators are only useful in combination with each other. Outcome indicators alone are informative, since they do not pay attention to the way development programmes are conducted. Similarly, process indicators need outcome indicators in order to evaluate the concrete results of development programmes. Secondly, additional information is necessary for interpreting the selected human rights indicators. As already mentioned, this could be provided by development agencies drawing upon the (socio-economic) data they already have on the social and political environment in which they operate.

---

46 Such process indicators could assess trainings, information programmes and care provided by development agencies to improve the human rights enjoyment of their beneficiaries.

47 R. Malhotra and N. Fasel, loc. cit. n. 25, p. 15; R. Malhotra and N. Fasel, loc. cit. n. 32, p. 28.

IV. THE USE OF HUMAN RIGHTS INDICATORS IN DEVELOPMENT PROGRAMMING

As will be seen in this part, establishing human rights indicators that monitor human rights compliance by development agencies is a continuing process. Human rights indicators can measure both the agencies' consideration for human rights principles and the impact of development programmes on the local human rights situation. Human rights indicators should also be used by a variety of actors, particularly by those that should benefit from these programmes.

A. ESTABLISHING HUMAN RIGHTS INDICATORS FOR DEVELOPMENT PROGRAMMES

Human right indicators must be established *prior* to starting development programmes. Before selecting the indicators to monitor development agencies' compliance with human rights, however, two preliminary steps are required. Firstly, in order to assess the potential impact of development programmes on people's lives, development agencies must clarify their objectives and examine their capacities to implement human rights.[48] They should do so by referring to human rights standards. This allows development agencies to establish benchmarks against which their activities will be measured and to be held accountable for their human rights obligations. Secondly, before starting a programme, development agencies should analyse the local human rights situation by using different types of human rights indicators mentioned above.[49] This will not only help development agencies define their priorities but also enable them to measure the changes in the human rights situation once their programmes are completed. Because of their limited capacities, however, agencies should limit themselves to examining those human rights that directly relate to their mandates, although such a limitation exercise might sometimes prove difficult to carry out. The overall assessment of the human rights situation of a country is a task for the State. This requires that it develops its own human rights indicators, as recommended by treaty bodies. Ideally, therefore, development agencies should cooperate with States when assessing local human rights situations.

Two different kinds of indicators should be created for measuring the effect of development programmes on the human rights enjoyment of their beneficiaries.

48 See F. Raine, 'The Measurement Challenge in Human Rights', 3(4) *International Journal on Human Rights* (2006) pp. 21–23.

49 UNDP, *Indicators for Human Rights Based Approaches to Development in UNDP Programming: A Users' Guide*, op. cit. n. 29, pp. 12–13.

The first kind of indicators should be selected by development agencies to determine whether they are giving sufficient consideration to human rights principles throughout their programmes. These are process indicators which, as mentioned earlier, should examine the level of participation, non-discrimination and the presence of accountability mechanisms. These human rights indicators must therefore measure the extent to which vulnerable people have been given an equal chance in expressing their views from the start (and even before) until the end of a programme. They must also evaluate whether the same people have been given a chance to make their claims heard should they think that the agency has violated their human rights. The second kind of indicators, which can be of any type, should analyse the impact of the programme on the local human rights situation. These are the same as the above-mentioned indicators for assessing the human rights situation before devising a programme. These indicators should measure the direct and, where possible, indirect as well as the positive and negative impact of the programme on the situation. They must be able to detect whether development programmes have discriminated against particular groups or flagrantly violated the human rights of the local population. However, it might sometimes be difficult to attribute a change in human rights terms to a particular intervention, since such a change can have multiple causes.[50] External factors, such as civil strife or natural disasters, might eliminate the positive impact of development programmes. Similarly, the consequences of a particular action on human rights are indefinite and can therefore not be completely measured, especially since human rights are interrelated and interdependent.

Once established, human rights indicators should be used to assess development agencies' human rights compliance. As mentioned previously, this could be done at regular intervals, both during and after development programmes. In order to hold development agencies accountable for their human rights obligations, the result of human rights indicators should be made public in a way that is understandable to the public concerned. This supposes not only the translation of the information into local languages but also the use of a format adapted to the targeted public. In addition, whatever human rights indicators might reveal must lead to real consequences, an aspect which the UNDP Oslo Governance Centre's User's Guide seems to miss. Failure by development agencies to comply with human rights obligations must be sanctioned in a way that needs to be defined in the programme itself. Without such consequences, human rights indicators might become a mere formality. Should human rights indicators reveal that an agency has breached its human rights obligations, programmes must be adapted or abandoned and guarantees given that mistakes will not be

50 B. Andreassen and H.-O. Sano, 'What's the Goal? What's the Purpose? Observations on Human Rights Impact Assessment' (Oslo, Norwegian Centre for Human Rights 2004) p. 12, available at www.humanrights.uio.no/forskning/publikasjoner/arkiv/rn/2004/0204.pdf.

repeated. In the case of violation of basic human rights, compensation should be provided to the victims, and programme managers made to apologise.

B. ACTORS USING HUMAN RIGHTS INDICATORS FOR DEVELOPMENT PROGRAMMES

A variety of actors could be involved in the use of human rights indicators for development programmes: development agencies themselves – programme managers in particular – NGOs, donor States as well as those benefiting from development programmes. Although development agencies are themselves responsible for establishing human rights indicators, they should seek the cooperation of those benefiting from their programmes and the aid of human rights lawyers and statisticians. They should also pool human rights-related data that they already have or can collect easily from the other actors involved. Programme managers should then evaluate their programmes at regular intervals using the established human rights indicators, something that external actors should also be involved in.[51] Another party that could independently monitor development agencies' compliance with human rights on the basis of the information provided by these indicators is NGOs. Donor States could also refer to human right indicators in directing aid, although this is often a politically loaded operation.

Programme beneficiaries, in particular, should be given a chance to have a say in the evaluation of development programmes, since they are entitled to somehow take part in the running of these programmes. As mentioned earlier, they should be involved from the beginning to the very end of a programme. Before starting a programme, development agencies should endeavour to reach those vulnerable people usually excluded from public affairs and inform them of the agencies' intentions. Human rights indicators could then be established by development agencies, taking people's expectations into account. Those benefiting from development programmes should be further consulted both during and after a programme through opinion surveys. Once the programme is over, they should be given the opportunity to make their claims on the basis of the information provided by the human rights indicators. Even though the participation of as large a number of people as possible in the evaluation of development programmes is to be recommended, it is not feasible to have all those benefiting from a programme participate in its evaluation. NGOs and representatives of

[51] The UNDP suggests that the evaluation of its programmes should be carried out by external agents such as evaluation firms or individual evaluators as well as staff members of other UNDP Country Offices. The participation of governmental civil servants in the evaluation teams, however, is not recommended by UNDP. See UNDP, *Handbook on Monitoring and Evaluating for Results*, op. cit. n. 27, p. 55.

local communities will have to represent the local population and be given the opportunity to determine in their name whether development agencies are contributing towards the realisation of their human rights. Defining who will represent the recipients of aid, however, is a delicate task.[52] It is not always those in a strong position in society that speak in the name of vulnerable people. Development agencies should therefore use maximum transparency as well as the most objective criteria when selecting those taking part in the evaluation of their programmes. Notwithstanding this constraint, all parties concerned should be given the opportunity to hold an agency accountable for ignoring their right to participate in the evaluation should they regard their participation as having been unduly refused or undermined by the agency.

V. CONCLUSION

Development agencies should be accountable for their human rights obligations, especially since they endeavour to integrate human rights into their programmes. To abide by these obligations, they must not only ensure that development programmes improve the local human rights situation, but also that human rights principles are taken into consideration throughout their programmes. Accountability requires that development agencies put in place evaluation mechanisms in which, as suggested in this contribution, human rights indicators can play an important role. In this way indicators could give a concrete meaning to the human rights based-approach to development and cooperation opted for by UN agencies, including the UNDP. Although the UNDP Oslo Governance Centre's User's Guide provides a general framework for this purpose, it does not offer practical guidelines for the development of human rights indicators by UNDP Country Offices.

Of the four kinds of data on which human rights indicators are based, socio-economic data and household perceptions are of greatest interest to development agencies. The former, which development agencies already have at their disposal, are best supplemented with disaggregated data obtained from governments and statistical institutes, whereas the latter can be obtained from the beneficiaries of their programmes through the distribution of questionnaires. Of the three types of human rights indicators that can be used, process indicators might be particularly useful to development agencies, since they can assess the extent to which these agencies observe the principles of participation, non-discrimination and accountability when running their programmes. These indicators are therefore beneficial in that they can help agencies enhance the qualitative aspect

52 See H.-O. Sano, loc. cit. n. 13, at p. 138.

of their activities and ensure that vulnerable people achieve maximum empowerment.

The two kinds of indicators that should be established by development agencies are ones that measure their compliance with human rights principles and ones that measure the impact of their programmes on the local human rights situation. Measurement of the latter, however, is complicated by the fact that changes are not readily attributable to an agency's interventions. The results of human rights indicators should be made public and lead to redress in case of basic human rights violations. Different actors, especially programme beneficiaries despite their representatives being difficult to identify, should be involved in assessing development programmes.

To conclude, human rights indicators for assessing the human rights compliance of development agencies could create a culture of accountability that might increase the transparency and sustainability of development programmes. They could foster a community of learning in which programme beneficiaries can have a say.

PART V.

STAFF OF INTERNATIONAL ORGANISATIONS

ACCOUNTABILITY OF INTERNATIONAL ORGANISATIONS FOR VIOLATIONS OF THE HUMAN RIGHTS OF STAFF

Chittharanjan Felix AMERASINGHE*

I. INTERNATIONAL ORGANISATIONS AND THE SUBSTANTIVE LAW OF HUMAN RIGHTS

Is human rights law binding on international organisations? They are not parties to any conventions, although some of them, viz., the UN and the Council of Europe, have drafted human rights conventions which are in force now.

Let us start from the beginning to see whether international organisations are bound by a law of human rights, particularly in their relations with staff. To determine whether or not international organisations are bound to human rights law, we must first establish whether human rights law is customary or is rooted in general principles of law that is binding on all international actors. With this in mind, we begin then by considering the UN Charter of 1945 in which the requirement of respect for human rights is scattered over several Articles. In this text, references to human rights appear in the Preamble and Article 1 dealing with the purposes of the UN. Article 55 requires that the UN shall promote 'respect for and observance of human rights'. Article 62 states that the ECOSOC is to make recommendations in order to secure respect for human rights. A Human Rights Commission was created and expanded in 1967, eventually becoming a rigorous and effective council of forty-seven members. The Universal Declaration of Human Rights was introduced in 1948. It impressively set a high standard in its drafting of nearly 29 Articles. However, despite such accomplishments there were serious disagreements as to the Declaration's effect, exemplified by the work of Professor Hersch Lauterpacht, who in the 1950s argued that there is no such human rights law as such. By contrast, Canadian Professor Humphrey, who, as head of the Human Rights Division in the UN

* B.A., LL.B., Ph.D., LL.D. (Cambridge, UK), LL.M. (Harvard, USA); Former Judge, UN Administrative Tribunal, Registrar, World Bank Administrative Tribunal, Full Professor of Law, University of Ceylon, Sri Lanka.

Secretariat, opposed such views. This debate continued well on into the 1960s. Then in 1966 the UN drafted the International Covenant on Civil and Political Rights with an Optional Protocol. It came into force on 23 March 1976. And with its inception well over half of the world community had become parties to this convention. The International Covenant on Economic, Social and Cultural Rights was drafted in 1966 and came into force on 3 January 1976. Again, more than 100 States are parties to this Covenant. The European Convention on Human Rights, drafted in 1950, came into force on 3 September 1953 (the recent wholesale amendment of the Convention in the 1990s mainly dealt with secondary rules and left substantive human rights unaffected). Later, the American Convention on Human Rights of 1969, which came into force on 18 July 1978, also enacted substantive human rights.

From this historical survey we can thus conclude that, due to the work of the UN and the Human Rights Commission (now Council), human rights are recognised as part of customary international law or as general principles of law. Such is supported by the fact that States avoid admitting violations on the assumption that human rights are indeed law.

By our conclusion, it is evident that non-State-entities, such as international organisations, are now bound by human rights law as *ius cogens*. Without commenting as such on the reach of human rights law, international organisations are essentially bound not merely as international persons with States as members, but as international persons *per se*. They must submit to *ius cogens*. That there are specific conventions (UN sponsored) on specific human rights, such as freedom from torture and slavery, does not dilute the general principles of law.

An interesting case decided by the Council of Europe Appeals Board as early as 1973 well illustrates that respect for the human rights of staff has been recognised as founded on general principles of law.

In *Artzet*[1] the applicant claimed payment, in pursuance of Article 13 of the Staff Regulations of the Council of Europe[2], on the allowance for heads of families as well as in respect to dependant children. The respondent refused her request to be treated as a head of a family because a resolution passed subsequently by the

1 Council of Europe Appeals Board, Appeal No. 8 *Artzet* (1973), *Case-Law Digest* (1985) p. 42. Reference should also be made on the subject of this contribution to C.F. Amerasinghe, *The Law of International Civil Service*, 2nd edn. (Oxford, Clarendon Press 1994) 2 Volumes. Much reliance has been placed on that work for the substance of this contribution.

2 See C.F. Amerasinghe, ed., *Staff Regulations and Staff Rules of Selected International Organizations* (Washington D.C., Office of the Executive Secretary, World Bank Administrative Tribunal 1983) at p. 209.

Council of Ministers of the Council of Europe had provided that, whereas all male staff members who were married would be treated as heads of families, female staff members would be so treated only in three exceptional cases. The result was that, even though the applicant was earning more than her husband, she was not accorded the rights as head of family. The Appeals Board of the Council of Europe referred to the principle that there should be no discrimination based on sex as a general principle of law and as deriving also from the written law governing the Council of Europe, stated: '[t]he Board finds that the distinction of which the appellant complains constitutes a discrimination contrary to the principles set forth above. It follows that the Board cannot approve the disputed decision based on Resolution (69)38, since that decision is compatible neither with the Statute of the Council of Europe nor with the general principles of law, whose legal weight is greater than that of the resolution in question.'[3]

We must now consider what relationship human rights principles – hold as general principles of law – to other sources of international administrative law, particularly to legislative acts of organisations. First, it is unclear what place general principles of law occupy, and in turn human rights principles, in the overall hierarchy of sources of law. No conflict of sources arises where general principles are applied as a supplement to written law or as being implied in the interpretation of written law. Likewise, there is no problem where the written law reflects a general principle of law.[4] But a conflict may arise where, for example, a general principle of law requires the administrative authority not to take a certain course of action which the written law expressly permits in taking such action. This is the case where, for example, written law expressly permits discriminatory treatment as between the sexes, whereas general principles of law prohibit such discrimination.

In my book *International Civil Service Law* a pertinent analysis accords to such a dilemma: '[t]here is not much authority on the point and there is an apparent conflict among the authorities that do exist. In a few cases the view taken has apparently been that the written law takes precedence over general principle of law. Thus, in *di Palma Castiglione* the LNT stated clearly that it was only in the absence of rules of positive law that the tribunal could consider general principles of law.'[5] In *Mullan*[6] the UNAT refused to apply the general principle of law

---

3 Council of Europe Appeals Board, op. cit. n. 1, p. 47.

4 ILOAT, *Bustos*, Judgment No. 701, 14 November 1985 (1985) (PAHO); ILOAT, *de Padirac* (*No. 2*), Judgment No. 911, 30 June 1988 (UNESCO).

5 LNT, *di Palma Castiglione* Judgment No. 1 (1929) p. 3. See also ILOAT, *Ronault*, Judgment No. 856, 10 December 1987 (UNESCO); ILOAT, *Vikmanovic*, Judgment No. 896, 30 June 1988 (CIPEC).

6 UNAT, *Mullan*, Judgment No. 162, 10 October 1972, JUNAT Nos. 114–166 p. 387.

against discrimination between sexes in the face of an explicit Staff Regulation which permitted such discrimination.[7]

However, there is some authority for the view that general principles of law can be superior hierarchically to the written law of an international organisation. First, there are some general principles of law, such as the rule against an amendment which violates acquired or essential rights, which are in fact applied even in the face of written rules to the contrary.[8] Secondly, the ILOAT said clearly in *Ferrechia* that the rule that a staff member must be given the right to be heard before a disciplinary sanction is imposed on him, deriving as it does from a general principle of law, must be respected 'even where contrary provisions exist'.[9] This approach was followed by the Appeals Board of ELDO in *Decision No. 6*[10], where the tribunal held that an express term in the applicant's contract of employment which resulted in the violation of principles against non-discrimination could not be enforced. Thirdly, it is clear from the jurisprudence of tribunals that they do try to interpret the written law so as to conform to general principles of law.[11]

It would seem, thus, that considerable importance is attached to general principles of law in the hierarchy of sources of law, even if there are statements to the contrary. The decision in *Mullan* is suspect and apart from this decision no decision has actually disregarded a general principle of law in the face of a conflicting written law. On the other hand, there is considerable evidence that general principles of law are superior to the written sources of law. The fact particularly that tribunals tend to interpret written rules so as to conform to general principles of law and not conflict with them is proof that tribunals do regard such principles as of special importance even in relation to the written law. *The reasonable conclusion seems to be that as regards the general principles of law of a fundamental nature* they are superior hierarchically to the written law in particular and could, indeed, be the supreme source of law relating to the international civil service.[12]

---

7 For other cases in which a similar approach is implied in general statements, see ILOAT, *Sharma*, Judgment No. 30, 13 January 1957 (ILO) at p. 3; UNAT, *Sletten*, Judgment No. 274, 2 October 1981, JUNAT Nos. 231–300 at p. 456.

8 See, in particular, WBAT, *de Merode*, Decision No. 1, 5 June 1981, *WBAT Reports* (1981).

9 ILOAT, *Ferrechia*, Judgment No. 203, 14 May 1973 (ILO). In some cases the ILOAT has been at pains to point out that the written law was not in conflict with a general principle of law and could, therefore, be enforced: see, e.g., ILOAT, *Verdrager*, Judgment No. 325, 21 November 1977 (WHO); ILOAT, *Haas*, Judgment No. 473, 28 January 1982 (Eurocontrol).

10 ELDO Appeals Board *Decision No. 6* (1971).

11 See cases cited *supra* n. 9. See also NATO Appeals Board *Decision No. 203(a)* (1985); ECJ, Cases 75 and 117/82, *Razzouk and Beydoun* [1984] *ECR* p. 1530; ECJ, Case 262/80, *Andersen and Others* [1984] *ECR* p. 203; ECJ, Case 266/83, *Samara*, [1985] *ECR* p. 189.

12 C.F. Amerasinghe, op. cit. n. 1, pp. 156–7. Italics added for emphasis and footnote numbers changed.

The rule against discrimination, or for equality of treatment, and the principle that a staff member generally has a right to be heard before the imposition of a disciplinary sanction is imposed on him, are examples fundamental human rights principles of a general nature. We may conclude that human rights law governs the actions of international organisations both generally (see Kosovo and East Timor) and in relations with its staff.

In *Artzet* a legislative act was considered subject to the general principles of law so that an administrative decision pursuant to such an act was considered null and void. The administration was thus compelled to recognise the rule against discrimination based on sex.

Clearly, legislative acts of international organisations in regard to the rights of staff which international organisations possess the power to perform are subject to general principles of law that are fundamental and the equivalent of *ius cogens*, such as those recognising the human rights of persons – that includes the staff of international organisations.

II. ACCOUNTABILITY

If it is accepted that human rights principles are a *ius cogens*, which govern, even by implication, the treatment of staff by international organisations, what about accountability? Is judicial machinery necessary and can it be provided?

A. DESIRABILITY OF JUDICIAL MACHINERY[13]

Administrative settlement, with or without the help of an advisory body, may well be a practical way of settling employment disputes within an international organisation. The history of the World Bank's approach to such disputes is, however, instructive in that it shows settlements solely by administrative procedures may not be an acceptable solution.

Until the 1970s the World Bank had been a comparatively small and simple organisation with few employees (less than 1,000 in 1960), mainly with high professional qualifications. Such persons were assured of employment conditions of exceptionally high standards because their services had to be retained. At this time, Staff Rules and Regulations simply did not exist, let alone an independent judicial tribunal to look after disputes in staff matters.

13 This subsection is based on and taken from, in large measure, C.F. Amerasinghe, op. cit. n. 1, pp. 38–41.

By 1980, the World Bank had nearly six thousand staff members from over one hundred countries and given such increases, the staff also desired for change for several reasons. First, there was, and remains considerable cultural diversity and complexity in the organisation. In addition, the activities of the World Bank had spread into a variety of fields and its operations had greatly increased. Naturally, the World Bank's organisational and managerial structure had also increased in complexity. Within this environment, staff members could be subjected to administrative decisions relating to a variety of matters involving rights and duties, particularly with regard to careers, salaries, allowances, benefits, and pension rights. Such decisions could sometimes, whether through error of judgment, inadvertence, negligence, or even bad faith, violate the rights of a staff member or staff members. Conversely, a staff member could feel that a decision taken by management violated his rights as derived from his contract of employment, whether such rights were believed to emanate from his terms of appointment or from the policy or regulations of the World Bank. Such situations frequently occur in national administrations and there is no reason why they could not occur in an international organisation.

In the 1970s an internal appeals procedure had been established within the World Bank which gave the staff members the right to recourse to an Appeals Committee. This appeals procedure, however, did not have the characteristics of judicial proceedings. Moreover, the Committee was composed of members chosen from amongst the staff and its competence was limited to making recommendations to the Vice President for Personnel and Administration or to the President, who had the unfettered right to make the final decision. The jurisdiction of the Appeals Committee was also circumscribed. This Appeals Committee, therefore, was never seriously regarded as being able to handle disputes between staff members and the institution. Consequently there was considerable discontent among the staff as a consequence. Staff members were eager to have available to them a judicial means of settlement and, indeed, a few of them even took their complaints to national courts. It was thus in the interest of both the staff and the administration of the organisation that there be some method of judicial settlement provided for employment disputes, as otherwise staff morale could have been seriously affected.

The League of Nations had provided for a right of appeal for members of its staff to a deliberative organ, the Council of the League. This right of appeal was limited to complaints against termination of employment by dismissal but was believed to be a necessary safeguard from the very outset. Indeed, at the first meeting of the Fourth Committee, which considered the staff and organisation of the Secretariat, the Committee decided that the right of appeal should be expressly made available.[14] Appeal, therefore, was directed to the Council of the League. It could be brought only against a decision of dismissal and only by staff members appointed for a period of five years or more. The resolution granting the right of appeal adopted by the League Assembly at its First Session on 17 December 1920 provided '[t]hat all members of the Secretariat and of the International Labour Office appointed for a period of five years or more by the Secretary-General or the Director of the International Labour Office shall, in the case of dismissal, have the right of appeal to the Council or to the Governing Body of the International Labour Office as the case may be.'[15]

There was little discussion in the Assembly about the matter. In introducing the report of the Fourth Committee to the Assembly, the Rapporteur merely stated that the reason for it was obvious. While members of the staff had this right of appeal, it was used only in one instance. In 1925 Mr. Monod, a former official of the Secretariat of the League, filed a complaint against the Administration. The Council, faced with the question of the procedure to be followed in dealing with the appeal, first requested the Supervisory Commission to undertake an enquiry. On the basis of its report the question was submitted to a body of three persons possessing judicial experience to be designated by the acting President of the Council after consultation with the Chairman of the Supervisory Commission. The Council resolution provided that the Council 'declares in advance that it will adopt the conclusions of this body as its own decision in the case'.[16] By this action the Council recognised that the guarantee to staff members of due process in contractual matters should take the form of quasi-judicial consideration rather than decision by governmental representatives. The quasi-judicial body found for the complainant and made an award of £750. The Council adopted the conclusions of the Committee's report and instructed the Secretary General to take the necessary action.

The fact that the deliberative organ invested with the power of settling the employment dispute did not investigate the matter and take a decision on its own must show that by its very nature as a non-judicial body it was unsuited to this task. Indeed, the fact that it sought the opinion of a quasi judicial body whose conclusions it decided in advance to adopt proves that the Council itself felt that the matter should be dealt with in a judicial manner rather than by an organ of a political nature. From this episode it may be deduced that settlement other than by judicial means was an unsuitable alternative. In any case, decision by a

14 League of Nations, Records of the 1st Assembly, Meetings of Committees, II, at pp. 7, 90, 91
15 League of Nations, Records of the 1st Assembly, Plenary Meetings, at pp. 663–4.
16 League of Nations, Council Resolution (8 June 1925) *Official Journal*, 6th year, No. 7, Minutes of the Thirty-Fourth Session of the Council, at p. 858.

political organ, even though it was not the administrative organ, would still mean that the organisation was judge in its own cause.

The method of settlement adopted in the *Monod Case* – namely in reference to a body of jurists – would not have generated the confidence among the staff that would naturally have been placed in a judicial body of a permanent or quasi-permanent nature.

That settlement by the administrative organ, a deliberative organ, or even an *ad hoc* body of jurists, was an inadequate procedure was realised even by the League of Nations at a very early stage. As early as 1921, soon after the League was created and long before the *Monod Case*, the desirability of having some method of permanent judicial settlement for employment disputes was discussed by the Assembly of the League. The question was raised in the Assembly, for example, whether the Council of the League, in spite of its high authority, was a sufficiently independent body to settle disputes of this kind[17], and the need was emphasised for establishing a judicial body comparable to the French Conseil d'État.[18] After the *Monod Case*, it is significant that the Rapporteur of the Supervisory Commission[19], who was entrusted with the task of examining the question of an administrative tribunal, firstly (in a negative sense)discarded the concept of an advisory body because such a body, even if independent, could never give final decisions; and secondly (in a positive sense) found in favour of judicial settlement of employment disputes, particularly because of the advantages of impartiality and the need for binding decisions. He was of the view that judicial settlement would enhance rather than diminish the authority and position of the administration because it would mean that it was ready, in case of doubt, to submit to an independent judge.

In deliberations at the first session of the UN General Assembly, at which the establishment of an administrative tribunal was discussed, one delegation presented a proposal that an Administrative Council, composed of representatives of the staff and the administration, should be created by the Secretary General as an alternative to a tribunal.[20] This proposal was not accepted. Instead, the General Assembly opted for judicial settlement of employment disputes for the obvious reason that judicial machinery was the most desirable. Clearly, judicial machinery would ensure accountability, granted that tribunals would give binding decisions.

17 League of Nations, Records of the 2nd Assembly, Meetings of Committees, II, at p. 71.
18 *Ibid.*, at pp. 71–72.
19 League of Nations Document C.C. 196.
20 UN Doc. 45, A/C.5/56.

B. JUDICIAL MACHINERY: A HUMAN RIGHT[21]

Let me point out that the establishment of or reference to judicial machinery is now recognised not only as desirable, but as a human right itself. When the WBAT was being established, one of the reasons given by the President of the Bank for establishing a tribunal was one of principle.[22] It was a principle accepted in many national legal systems and reaffirmed in the Universal Declaration of Human Rights. This principle required that where administrative power was exercised, there should be available machinery, in the event of disputes, to accord a fair hearing and due process to the aggrieved party. The procedure of the Appeals Committee of the Bank was, in fact, as already pointed out, incapable of fulfilling this function. Hence, there was a need for an independent judicial body to decide complaints relating to the exercise of administrative power.

The fundamental principle that the exercise of administrative power should be subject to judicial control is implied in Article 6 of the European Convention on Human Rights, which provides: 'In the determination of his civil rights and obligations ..., everyone is entitled to a fair and public hearing ... by an independent and impartial tribunal established by law.' The European Court of Human Rights favoured a broad approach to the interpretation of this Article. In *Delcourt* the European Court said: 'In a democratic society within the meaning of the Convention the right to a fair administration of justice holds such a prominent place that a restrictive interpretation of Article 6(1) would not correspond to the aim and purpose of that provision.'[23] Subsequently, this issue of administrative power was adverted to in *Application 4523/70, X* v. *Federal Republic of Germany*[24], where the application of the principle that the exercise of administrative power should be subject to judicial control was not rejected. Now one should also look at *Waite and Kennedy* decided by the ECHR in 1999 where the Court regarded the existence of the availability of judicial settlement by an administrative tribunal as a reason for not insisting on the exercise of the power of judicial settlement by a national court (German).[25] Judicial restraint was not regarded as a violation of Article 6 of the European Convention.

---

21 See also for this subsection, C.F. Amerasinghe, op. cit. n. 1, pp. 41–42.

22 See Memorandum to the Executive Directors, dated 14 January 1980, from the President of the World Bank, Documents R80–8, IDA/R80–8, and IFC/R80–6, at pp. 1–2.

23 ECtHR, *Delcourt*, 11 *Publ. ECHR*, Series A (1970) p. 15.

24 ECtHR, *X v. Federal Republic of Germany*, Application 4523/70, 14 *Yearbook of the ECHR* (1971) at p. 630.

25 ECtHR, *Waite and Kennedy v. Germany*, Application No. 26083/94, 30 *EHRR* (1999) p. 261, especially at paras. 50–73. See also ECtHR, *Beer and Regan v. Germany*, Application No. 28934/95, 33 *EHRR* (1999), at p. 6; A. Reinisch and U. Weber, 'In the Shadow of Waite and Kennedy', 1 *International Organizations Law Review* (2004) p. 59.

C. AUTHORITY TO ESTABLISH COURTS

Do international organisations have the authority to establish courts to settle staff disputes and are the judgments of such courts final and binding on the organisations themselves? Since many international organisations have either their own internal courts or use the internal courts of other organisations to settle employment disputes judicially, a prior question is whether they can have such internal courts, i.e., international administrative tribunals, to judicially settle such disputes. Few organisations have provisions in their constitutions expressly authorising the establishment of such tribunals. The existence of such a power has depended on implication in the interpretation of constitutional texts.

In the view of the ICJ the General Assembly of the United Nations had the power to establish international administrative tribunals. In the *Effect of Awards Case* the Court explained the reasons for its conclusion:

> 'When the Secretariat was organized, a situation arose in which the relations between the staff members and the Organization were governed by a complex code of law [...]. It was inevitable that there would be disputes between the Organization and staff members as to their rights and duties. The Charter contains no provision which authorizes any of the principal organs of the United Nations to adjudicate upon these disputes and Article 105 secures for the United Nations jurisdictional immunities in national courts. It would, in the opinion of the Court, hardly be consistent with the expressed aim of the Charter to promote freedom and justice for individuals and with the constant preoccupation of the United Nations to promote this aim that it should afford no judicial or arbitral remedy to its own staff for the settlement of any disputes which may arise between it and them.'[26]

The Court based its conclusion on the principle that the organisation must be deemed to have those powers which, though not expressly provided in the constituent instrument, were conferred upon it by necessary implication as being essential to the performance of its duties.[27] It referred to the necessity of giving effect to the paramount consideration of 'securing the highest standards of efficiency, competence and integrity', which is mentioned in Article 101 of the Charter. The ICJ in the *Effect of Awards Case* took the view that the UN had the authority to establish a true judicial organ with independence and the capacity to give binding decisions like any court of a national State. The IAT set up by the UN was not a subordinate organ of the General Assembly exercising

26 ICJ, *Effect of Awards of compensation made by the United Nations Administrative Tribunal*, Advisory Opinion, *ICJ Rep.* (1954) at p. 57.

27 *Ibid.*, pp. 56–57, citing the *Reparation Case*, ICJ, *Reparation for Injuries Suffered in the Service of the United Nations*, Advisory Opinion, *ICJ Rep.* (1949) p. 182.

delegated powers and without power to bind the General Assembly by its judgments:

> 'It has been argued that an authority exercising power to make regulations is inherently incapable of creating a subordinate body competent to make decisions binding its creator. [...] The contention that the General Assembly is inherently incapable of creating a tribunal competent to make decisions binding on itself cannot be accepted. [...] The question cannot be determined on the basis of the description of the relationship between the General Assembly and the Tribunal, that is, by considering whether the Tribunal is to be regarded as a subsidiary, a subordinate, or a secondary organ, or on the basis of the fact that it was established by the General Assembly. It depends on the intention of the General Assembly in establishing the Tribunal, and on the nature of the functions conferred upon it by its Statute. An examination of the language of the Statute of the Administrative Tribunal has shown that the General Assembly intended to establish a judicial body; moreover, it has the legal capacity under the Charter to do so.'[28]

The judicial organ created could decide disputes relating to employment and bind the organisation, including the principal organ of the organisation which created it, namely the General Assembly.

The Court also said that the General Assembly itself, in view of its composition and functions, could hardly act as a judicial organ – considering the arguments of the parties, appraising the evidence produced, establishing the facts and declaring the law applicable to them – and all the more so because one party to the disputes was the UN itself.[29] This confirms the position that the administrative tribunal was a judicial organ whose judgments could only be reviewed, if at all, by another body of a judicial nature.

The ICJ did refer to Article 101 of the Charter yet concluded that the provisions of that Article were not necessary to give the UN the authority to establish an administrative tribunal. The notion of 'essentiality' for the performance of its duties or functions was the basis of its reasoning. It may also be noted that, though the League of Nations and the ILO did not have provisions in their constitutions like Article 101 of the UN Charter, they both established international administrative tribunals without their authority to do so ever being questioned.[30]

28 ICJ, *Effect of Awards of compensation made by the United Nations Administrative Tribunal*, op. cit. n. 26 p. 61.
29 *Ibid.*, p. 56.
30 For the above analysis of the *Effect of Awards Case*, see C.F. Amerasinghe, op. cit. n. 1, pp. 34 *et seq.*

While some international organisations have specific provisions in their constituent instruments giving the organisations power to conduct their personnel relations, other organisations do not. In the case of the World Bank Group, for example, the Articles of Agreement of all the institutions give the President responsibility for the organisation, appointment and dismissal of the staff, subject to the general control of the Executive Directors or Board of Directors.[31] It is implied in this responsibility and control given to the President and Executive Directors or Board of Directors that the setting up of a judicial entity to settle disputes in staff matters would be reasonable and functionally justifiable. The situation is comparable to that in the UN, where Chapter XV of the Charter is less explicit than the Articles of the World Bank Group on the functions of the Secretary-General and General Assembly *vis-à-vis* the staff. In both cases, however, it is clear that functionally the chief executive and a legislative or quasi-legislative organ together have responsibility in staff matters. Deriving a power vested in the organisation to set up an administrative tribunal is not difficult. On the other hand, the absence of express provisions dealing with the staff and personnel relations in the constituent instrument of an organisation does not detract from such a power, because it is within the accepted purpose and function of all international organisations to employ staff and conduct smooth and effective personnel relations. Hence, an international organisation would have the necessary authority to set up or submit to the jurisdiction of an administrative tribunal with the power to give, in the matter of a true judicial organ, decisions binding on the organisation concerned, including its deliberative or legislative organ which decided to establish or submit to the jurisdiction of the tribunal.

International administrative tribunals are not subordinate organs in fact – they are plainly meant to be independent judicial organs – just organs.

III. INDEPENDENCE OF JUDICIAL ORGANS

However, these judicial organs must be independent if they are to be a viable means of ensuring accountability. There is a paradox here. They are created by, in effect, one party to a dispute (the organisation) but they must act as an independent and impartial organ. While so far international administrative tribunals have generally been regarded as acting as independent and impartial organs, the Statutes must ensure that the organs must not only dispense impartial justice, but that in their creation and operation they give the appearance of dispensing such justice and are not tempted to be partial or biased. It is not my

[31] Article V(5)(g) of the IBRD's Articles of Agreement; Article IV(5)(b) of the IFC's Articles; and Article VI(5)(b) of the IDA's Articles. See also Article 33(a) of the MIGA Articles.

purpose here to dissect the existing Statutes of international administrative tribunals. However, I may be allowed to point out three important areas where Statutes have failed to provide necessary safeguards against partiality and bias. It must be noted that following what was said in *Waite and Kennedy*, as previously mentioned by the ECHR, the absence of impartial judicial settlement by a proper judicial organ may be justification for a national court to refuse to recognise the jurisdictional immunity of the relevant international organisation, because the staff member would otherwise be subjected to non-recognition of a human right.

A. QUALIFICATIONS

Let us first consider the important question of the qualifications of international administrative tribunals. Statutes of tribunals differ widely. In the case of the ECJ, the judges who sit on the Court of First Instance on cases concerning employment disputes are judges of the Court and must, consequently, possess the qualifications as judges of the Court. The treaties[32] require that the judges be persons whose independence is beyond doubt and who possess the qualifications required for appointment to the highest judicial office in their respective countries or who are jurisconsults of recognised competence. The Statute of the UNAT as well as the Statutes of the ILOAT are silent on the professional qualifications of judges, as was the Statute of the LNT.[33] Theoretically, even non-lawyers could be appointed as judges, and in the case of the UNAT this sometimes happened. The provisions of the UNAT Statute are, in my opinion, not very appropriate. Now a Panel of Experts appointed by the SG has recommended that only national administrative judges should qualify to be judges of the UNAT, which is better but too narrow.

The Statutes of the WBAT and of the IDBAT are significantly different and are recommended. The former provides that the judges, although referred to as 'members', shall be persons of 'high moral character and must possess the qualifications required for appointment to high judicial office or be jurisconsults of recognized competence'.[34] This provision is based partially, as can be seen, on Article 2 of the Statute of the ICJ. The Statute of the IDBAT has a similar provision.

Shockingly enough, most statutes do not prevent former staff members of the particular organisation from being judges! And if this were not egregious

32 See Article 183 TFEU, Article 139 of the EURATOM Treaty, and Article 32b of the former ECSC Treaty.

33 Respectively, Article 3 of the UNAT Statute; Article III of the ILOAT Statute; and Article III of the LNT Statute.

34 Article IV.1 of the Statute.

enough, the fact that there are instances of this being the case is even more so. In the UNAT one of the judges is a former staff member of the UN. When statutes of international administrative tribunals do not have appropriate provisions relating to qualifications, the bench may be composed of unqualified or disqualified persons who have no idea of impartial justice or who could appear not to have such an idea.

B. EMOLUMENTS

The judges of many international administrative tribunals are not paid fees but are given honoraria; UNAT had given an honorarium, but now even that has been taken away. Does this practice attract qualified jurists or judges? WBAT and the Asian Development Bank Administrative Tribunal judges are paid a respectable and appropriate fee per each day of work completed. For a tribunal to be effective as a sentinel of accountability judges must be appropriately rewarded, not only to avoid corruption but to attract the best-quality judges or jurists. Now the UN Panel of Experts has recommended treating judges, for the purposes of emoluments, as being at the Assistant Secretary General level. Such are good signs of progress.

C. RENEWALS OF TERMS OF APPOINTMENT

Many Statutes expressly provide for the reappointment of judges at the end of their term, sometimes limited only to a second term. Thus, the UN Statute in Article 3.2 and the WBAT Statute in Article IV.3 provided for unlimited reappointment, while the IDBAT Statute in Article III.3 and the OASAT Statute in Article III.3 provided for appointment of only one additional term. Now the UNAT and WBAT have limited reappointment by election to one term. Some Statutes, such as the Statute of the Appeals Board of OECD, are silent on the matter. In the absence of a specific provision relating to reappointment, it is likely that the appointing authority will have an implied power to reappoint a judge without limit. The terms of judges may be two (see Article 51(b) of the Statute of the WEU Appeals Board) or three (see Article IV.3 of the WBAT Statute) years or, sometimes, yet seldom longer (see Article III.3 of the OASAT Statute). It will be readily appreciated that judges could be influenced to give biased decisions in favour of the organisation concerned in the hope of being reappointed, considering particularly that their terms are generally short. Hence, the possibility of reappointment may not be entirely conducive to independence and impartiality. For this reason, a limitation on the power to reappoint to one additional term may work to some extent in favour of independence and impartiality, at least during the second term; but even this is undesirable, because the temptation to favour the international organisation in the first term remains. I proposed to the UN and the World Bank after retiring from the judiciary of international administrative tribunals, having only one long term – e.g., seven years rather than two terms of, e.g., four years. The question of re-election or reappointment is a serious one impinging on the objectivity and impartiality of the system of accountability.

IV. HUMAN RIGHTS RECOGNISED BY INTERNATIONAL ADMINISTRATIVE TRIBUNALS

International administrative tribunals have recognised human rights (impliedly without reference to them as human rights) in settling disputes concerning employment between staff and organisation, by scrutinising the process of administrative decisions. The right to non-discrimination of every kind may be regarded as an example of a human right, although it goes beyond conventional law. We have already considered *Artzet* decided by the COEAB, which considered discrimination based on sex. The conventional law usually forbids discrimination in regard to the recognition of the human rights entrenched in the conventions. But international administrative tribunals will sanction discrimination based on sex, race, etc. per se. There are numerous cases dealing with such discrimination in which staff members as applicants have had success in securing a remedy.

A. DISCRIMINATION BASED ON SEX[35]

Cases in which the principle of non-discrimination was held to affect the exercise of legislative power have been decided by different tribunals. It will suffice to examine one more of them here, apart from the *Artzet Case,* to which reference has already been made. In *Callewaert-Haezebrouck* (*No. 2*)[36] the applicant contested a Staff Regulation (Article 28 of Appendix IV) which opened membership of the sickness insurance scheme of the IPI to 'wives' and made provision for a contribution of 25 per cent from IPI in these circumstances. The applicant, a staff member of IPI, had applied to have her husband made a member of the insurance scheme, but ultimately was compelled to pay the full costs of the insurance for her husband without a 25 per cent contribution from IPI. The respondent contended that the text of the Staff Regulation which had been adopted by IPI's Administrative Council applied only to wives of male staff members and not to husbands of female staff members and that, therefore, the applicant could not claim the benefit of the provision for her husband who was

---

35 On this subject, see particularly, my 1 op. cit. n. 1, pp. 319 *et seq.*

36 ILOAT, *Callewaert-Haezebrouck* (*No. 2*), Judgment No. 344, 8 May 1978 (IPI).

not a staff member of IPI. This provision, it was held, discriminated between male and female staff members, only the wives of male staff members being entitled to benefit from the insurance of their husbands. Such discrimination, the tribunal said, were against the general principles of law, and particularly of the international civil service, in an administrative decision, the application of a text which so discriminated could not be permitted.

B. DUE PROCESS OF LAW

The strict requirement of due process of law for administrative decisions relating to disciplinary measures is another reflection of accountability of organisations for the violation of human rights.

The ILOAT has held that the applicant must be informed in clear and precise terms of the grave charges against him and must be allowed to defend himself before the competent authority before the latter takes its decision.[37] The UNAT has also emphasised the need to respect the right of defence[38] and has held that there was a tainting procedural irregularity where formal charges have never been made and the applicant had not been given an opportunity to rebut the charges.[39]

Further, a proper inquiry must be held. Thus, in a case where the applicant was disciplined for attempted theft from a shop, only the shop manager and three of his employees were heard in evidence. Only one of them had witnessed the alleged theft. This was held to be an inadequate inquiry.[40] On the other hand, the ILOAT has not committed itself to the view that an oral hearing is always necessary, in so far as it assumed in *Schofield* (*No. 3*) that the case could have

---

37 ILOAT, *Hickel*, Judgment No. 5, 27 February 1947 (IIIC). See also ECJ, Cases 18 and 35/65 *Gutmann*, [1966] *ECR* p. 103, where the need of the precise indication of the charges was emphasised. See also ILOAT, *Contaifer*, Judgment No. 888, 30 June 1988 (PAHO) and ECJ, Case 141/84, *de Compte* [1985] *ECR* p. 1951, where it was held that a right to a fair hearing had been denied on the facts of the cases.

38 UNAT, *Zang-Atangana*, Judgment No. 130, 23 May 1969, JUNAT Nos. 114–166 p. 155. The Appeals Board of the Council of Europe and NATO have also emphasised the right of defence: Council of Europe Appeals Board, Appeal No. 78 *Pagani* (1982), *Case-Law Digest* (1985) p. 113; NATO Appeals Board, Decision No. 58 (1975) *Collection of the Decisions 46 to 73* (1976).

39 UNAT, *Lindblad*, Judgment No. 183, 23 April 1974, JUNAT Nos. 167–230 p. 126. See also OECD Appeals Board, *d'Espinay-Saint-Luc*, Decision No. 44 (1974), *Recueil des décisions 1 à 62* (1979) p. 124. In WBAT, *Gyamfi*, Decision No. 28, 22 April 1986, *WBAT Reports* (1986), at p. 24, it was held that the right of defence had not been respected, because of repeated failures to inform the applicant of the accusation against him and to hear his side of the case.

40 ILOAT, *Flad*, Judgment No. 172, 3 May 1971 (WHO). See also UNAT, *Roy*, Judgment No. 123, 31 October 1968 (ICAO), JUNAT Nos.114–166 p. 89.

been decided on the written record alone.[41] It is also clear that, in any case, the written record must be complete. The position seems to be that in appropriate circumstances the administration may be required to hold an oral inquiry, if this is necessary for the completeness of the record.

In *Larcher*[42] the Appeals Board of OECD held that, even if the Staff Regulations were silent, the applicant was entitled to the right to defend himself. In that case, a supervisor's report of a specific incident was sent to the Personnel Department and the applicant was informed that the supervisor would have to let the Chief of Personnel know that the applicant had committed a fault, but the applicant was not informed that disciplinary sanctions would be imposed, nor was any attempt made to make him aware of the charges. It was held that this was a tainting procedural irregularity. From this case it also emerged that the fact that the applicant was given a hearing by the Advisory Committee after the decision to terminate his employment had been taken did not cure the defect that existed. Further, where the written law contains provisions concerning submissions and replies and the right of defence, these must be followed.[43]

V. CONCLUSION

We may now draw some conclusions about the accountability of international organisations for the violations of the human rights of their staff.

Human rights law is *ius cogens* which binds international organisations in their employment relations with staff. There can be no question about this.

Accountability for human rights violations of staff by organisations is made possible by the creation by such organisations of international administrative tribunals, which organisations have the power and imperative to create. Moreover, the provision of recourse to judicial machinery for staff is in satisfaction of a human right of staff, even though the manner in which human rights are protected is through the questioning of administrative decisions.

While judicial machinery is provided for the enforcement of human rights, there is something to be desired in the provisions of current statutes of international administrative tribunals insofar as they do not provide adequate safeguards for the independence and impartiality of such tribunals. A good look must be taken

41 ILOAT, *Schofield* (*No. 3*), Judgment No. 410, 24 April 1980 (WHO) at p. 6.

42 OECD Appeals Board, Decision No. 53 (1975), *Recueil des décisions 1 à 62* (1979) p. 145. On the right of defence see also Council of Europe Appeals Board, *Pagani*, op. cit. n. 38, p. 113.

43 See ECJ, Case 35/67, *van Eick* [1968] *ECR* p. 329, where it was held that the written law had been followed.

at providing for such matters as the proper qualifications for judges, emoluments of judges, and the possibility of bias because renewal of appointment terms, even if only for a second term, is permitted. Administrative justice through judicial organs of international organisation has come of age and requires a complete overhaul. Failing that, accountability can only be ensured by recourse to national courts.

That having been said, it cannot be gainsaid, as some examples of decisions rejecting discrimination and the absence of due process of law in disciplinary cases show, that international administrative tribunals can be equipped to protect the human rights of staff and are intended to do so.[44]

44 On both non-discrimination and due process of law see C.F. Amerasinghe, op. cit. n. 1, vol. 1, chap. 22, and vol. 2, chap. 6.

HUMAN RIGHTS ACCOUNTABILITY OF INTERNATIONAL ORGANISATIONS *VIS-À-VIS* THEIR STAFF: THE UNITED NATIONS

Sarah Hunt*

INTRODUCTION

At a time of increasing international integration and the growth of the UN and its international system of organisations, functional and effective safeguards of individual rights are gaining importance in the field of public international law. Problems are also emerging, due to lack of understanding of the full implications of international organisational immunity. Although a significant proportion of these problems occur in the field, many of them are generated by lack of accountability, lack of responsiveness and lack of competence in UN Headquarters offices. This contribution only examines the lack of accountability of international organisations towards their staff. Improving accountability will improve performance.

---

* The author is a Solicitor of the Supreme Court of New South Wales and a member of the Register of Foreign Attorneys within the *Ordre des Avocats* in the Canton of Geneva. She worked extensively in the law of the international civil service at Schwab, Flaherty, Hassberger and Crausaz, a Swiss Law firm practising Swiss civil, criminal and commercial law, trusts and international law and now practices in international trade and shipping law as an Associate at Davies, Johnson and Company. She co-founded the CAIO, the Centre for Accountability of International Organisations, www.caio-ch.org in 2003 with Edward Flaherty. CAIO is a NGO which has been instrumental in drafting, presenting and promoting solutions for violations of human rights by international organisations, including submissions to the UN Redesign Panel. Statement of acknowledgment: the author is grateful to the local Geneva legal community for their support and recognition for the need for a local solution to a problem of international dimensions. She acknowledges the assistance of the Directors of CAIO, who include senior members of the Australian and English judiciary, academics and students, with gratitude. Particularly in order are thanks to the British Governor of Human Rights, Françoise Hampson, the Honourable Geoffrey Robertson QC, Dr David Lawson, President of the Foreign Section of the Geneva Bar Association, the Honourable Justice Robyn Layton QC, Justice of the Supreme Court of South Australia and Edward Flaherty of Schwab, Flaherty and Associates. Without them, CAIO would not have been able to make a substantive contribution to recent reforms to the United Nations internal legal system; see www.caio-ch.org/Current_Projects.html and www.caio-ch.org/about_us.html.

Since its inception in 1945, the UN has sustained huge growth and, with its Funds and Programs, now employs over 55,000 people worldwide. The UN possesses its own independent rule-making powers and has unique authority over all workers falling within its jurisdiction.[1]

The International Court of Justice has stated that international organisations, as subjects of international law, 'are bound by any obligations incumbent upon them under general rules of international law, under their constitutions or under international agreements to which they are parties.'[2]

The UN enjoys international immunity from suit in national courts, and has significant administrative control over its own internal justice system, making it critical that it respect minimum independence standards in international law. Senior staff of international organisations enjoy immunity similar to that of national diplomats.[3]

This contribution examines problems with the United Nation's internal legal system and difficulties faced by litigants within the system, when measured against public international law standards. It traces the history of diplomatic immunity, examines Headquarters agreements with states that confer that immunity on International Organisations and relates this to failings within the UN's internal legal system. This is particularly relevant in light of the recent UN Redesign Panel Report, a report into the failings of the UN's internal legal system, a quasi-judicial peer review system. The contribution concludes looking forward to the new legal system, the United Nations Dispute Tribunal, a professionalised judicial system implemented as of July 2007 and anticipates consequences of the reforms.

I. THE HISTORY OF DIPLOMATIC IMMUNITY: HOW DID IT BECOME PROFESSIONALISED?

Professional diplomats have long been the subject of local community suspicion and intrigue, often considered trouble-makers who were not properly part of the local community.

---

1 K. O'Fathartaigh, 'The United Nations internal legal system: Problems when analysed in light of classic administrative law principles', available at www.caio-ch.org/reforms/Intern_Paper_II.pdf. Kate O'Fathartaigh, Solicitor, Supreme Court of South Australia during her internship with the Centre for Accountability of International Organisations, July 2006 (www.caio-ch.org).

2 ICJ, *Interpretation of the Agreement of 25 March 1951 Between the WHO and Egypt*, Advisory Opinion, *ICJ Rep.* (1980) pp. 89–90, para. 37.

3 Full diplomatic immunity is reserved for international organisation staff at Professional Level Professional 5 or 'P5' and above.

The French Revolutionaries of 1789 were suspicious of the diplomatic service, as were the emancipatory thinkers of the Enlightenment. Drawing on critiques of the *philosophes*, revolutionaries attacked the secrecy, luxury, privileges and the 'mysteries' of diplomatic relations.[4] The revolutionary Jerome Petion, a lawyer and former Mayor of Paris, opposed giving power to diplomats[5] who were 'driven' by 'their ambition, their passion, their immoderate desire for vainglory; they attacked their neighbours; they believed themselves just when they were strong; they troubled the peace of all Europe and poured out the gold and the blood of the French in great waves.'[6]

Others went further, arguing that 'based on reason, foreign policy and diplomacy would become unnecessary [...] the new world would be a world without diplomats.'[7] The revolutionaries were particularly critical of permanent ambassadors, who were regarded as dangerous because they were spies and 'ambitious intriguers who revelled in outward luxury and show.'[8] The French were not alone. Thomas Jefferson shared the same view of the diplomatic service. He regarded the diplomats as the 'pest of the peace of the world, as the workshop in which nearly all the wars of Europe are manufactured.'[9]

Yet, the benefits of international immunity are much commentated on, acknowledged as generally useful and helpful – and for the most part, complied with both in the modern international diplomatic community and in law.[10] To date, little attention has been paid to the effect of violations of human rights, which are caused, created, or contributed to by the practical effect of the UN's immunity, which leads to lack of accountability.

---

4 For example Jacques Benigne Bossuet and Louis de Rouvroy. Other writers considered international affairs a system of anarchy, unscrupulous and rife with corruption. See L. Frey and M. Frey, *The History of Diplomatic Immunity* (Columbus, Ohio State University Press 1999) p. 714.

5 Citing CAIO intern N. Hanrahan, 'A History of Diplomatic Immunity and the Development of International Organisation Immunity', available at www.caio-ch.org.

6 See L. Frey and M. Frey, op. cit. n. 4, p. 714.

7 Felix Gilbert, quoted in L. Frey and M. Frey, op. cit. n. 4, p. 716.

8 The sentiments of the journalist L. M. Prudhomme, *Revolutions de Paris*, No. 92 (Paris, 16 April 1791), paraphrased by L. Frey and M. Frey, op. cit. n. 4, at p716.

9 Thomas Jefferson quoted in L. Frey and M. Frey, op. cit. n. 4, p717.

10 International immunity is now a working part of the practice of many civil or international lawyers; the author's practice has regularly requested the lifting of international immunity through the Swiss Mission to the United Nations to enable a divorce or to enforce an order for maintenance against a non-compliant diplomat spouse.

II. AN INTERNAL RECOGNITION OF FAILINGS OF THE UN LEGAL SYSTEM

The UN, in recognition of the failings of its internal justice system launched an Expert Panel to Redesign the UN's internal legal system during the first part of 2006, the findings of which were handed down on 27 July 2006.

Subsequent to submissions made to this Panel on behalf of CAIO, the author analyses the internal justice system of international organisations, particularly in light of recent public criticisms by senior international jurists such as Geoffrey Robertson QC and those by CAIO, the Centre of Accountability of International Organisations – www.caio-ch.org[11] – and the International Commission of Jurists – www.icj-org.

Research into this area has developed through the work of the network "CAIO", the Centre for Accountability of International Organisations[12], a not-for-profit network supported by international organisation staff associations and staff unions.

It is the author's view that the minimum set of standards, defined by international and regional human rights treaties, are not met by the internal justice systems of the UN and its international organisations, particularly in relation to the right to a fair trial. This is based on practical experience in the law of international civil service and analysis of the practical and procedural defects of the UN's internal legal system[13] with the Honourable Justice Robyn Layton QC of the Supreme Court of Adelaide, former Murray Wilcox QC, former Justice of the Federal

---

11 The Centre for Accountability of International Organisations has the following goals:
a. To promote means to ensure international organisations are held properly accountable for their actions, and to prevent the abuse of privileges and immunities;
b. To promote the development of criteria necessary to ensure the accountability of international organisations;
c. To promote transparent and effective means to ensure the rights of those having dealings with international organisations (including employees) are properly respected;
d. To promote the implementation of measures to ensure international organisations conform to their obligations under international and national law;
e. To support initiatives aiming to improve the standard of legal protection provided for those having dealings with international organisations. [For a full overview of CAIO's activities, please consult www.caio-ch.org].

12 The Centre is supported by the Geneva *Ordre des Avocats*, or Order of Lawyers and was launched with the assistance of the International Commission of Jurists, Geneva, a NGO which promotes the rule of law throughout national legal systems through its many National Chapters.

13 The law of the international civil service is not only procedurally difficult for Applicants [in the sense of no document discovery, no public hearings, and so no cross-examination], but jurisprudentially unique; the absence of *stare decisis* means that the Tribunal can on occasion reverse its own jurisprudence – see, for example, ILOAT, *Re Rees-Gildea et al v IFRC*,

Court of Australia, Justice Robert Nicholson QC of the Federal Court of Australia and British Governor of Human Rights, Professor Françoise Hampson.[14] The development of a body of work, through academic papers commissioned through the Centre of Accountability of international organisations has considerably furthered understanding of the legal issues.

A consistent and agreed feature of the debate around minimum standards is that the UN's internal legal system falls short of those standards laid out in regional and human rights treaties, particularly in regard to the failure of the UN's primary internal courts, the UNAT and ILOAT, the United Nations and International Labour Organization Administrative Tribunals, to hold public hearings. This is a major omission in that it is a failure to accord procedural fairness in the determination of the civil rights of international organisation staff or international civil servants over the past 19 years.

III. APPLICABILITY OF HUMAN RIGHTS PRINCIPLES AND INTERNATIONAL LAW: GENERAL UNDERSTANDING *VS* PRACTICE IN THE FIELD OF THE LAW OF THE INTERNATIONAL CIVIL SERVICE

International organisations, as subjects of international law are often considered to be subject to international law; though in fact, the opposite is the case.[15] The laws which apply to them are their own internal rules, regulations and internal circulars and a jurisprudence known as 'the law of the international civil service', created by two UN Tribunals, the International Labour Organization and the United Nations Administrative Tribunals, or the ILOAT and UNAT.[16] Each Tribunal refers to its own jurisprudence, although neither conforms to *stare decisis* and neither provide for the right of appeal to any higher court.

Judgment No 2450, 6 July 2005, when the Tribunal overturned its own jurisprudence in relation to the nature of the tax-free status of international civil servants.

14 Board Members and President of the Board of CAIO, www.caio-ch.org [the Centre for Accountability of Human Rights], respectively.

15 See Keith J. Webb and Arthur van Neck, supervised by J.P.J. van Wielink LL.M, Amsterdam International Law Clinic 'The Non-compliance of the International Labour Organisation with Administrative Tribunal with the Requirements of Article 6 of the European Convention for the Protection of Human Rights the EHCR', available at www.caio-ch.org/reforms/Non_compl_ILOAT_wrt_Art6_EHCR.pdf; see also www.caio-ch.org "Current projects" under "Home" – *Submissions to the UN Redesign Panel by the Centre for Accountability of Intentional Organizations.*

16 www.ilo.org/dyn/triblex/triblex_browse.home and http://untreaty.un.org/UNAT/main_page.htm.

Aside from treaty law which, due to its non-ratification, is not applicable to international organisations, general principles of law and due process, as fundamental norms within any legal system, should theoretically be applicable.

In practice, the lack of public court hearings over the previous 16 years, the absence of any form of document discovery and the absence of independent or professional legal staff separate from the international organisations within first-instance tribunals [sometimes resulting in quite overt witness intimidation] have all resulted in a down-grading of due process. This is manifested in occasionally prolonged delays,[17] in individuals with a clear conflict of interest sitting on first-tier review boards, only to later on refuse to disqualify themselves despite adroit request for same as well as several other predictable procedural anomalies. The result is a net system which fails the minimum adequate standard test laid out by the European Court in the seminal case of *Waite and Kennedy v Germany.*[18]

In the face of such problems, CAIO President and Board Members Professor Françoise Hampson[19] and President Professor Reinisch[20] have turned their attention to the application of minimum standards derived from human rights law, within the UN.

In addition to international, national and EC law, employment relevant legal rules may be derived from human rights law as an entitlement of all individuals, even international organisation staff; so are potentially enforceable by individuals.

As postulated by Professor Reinsich, it can be argued that these rights must be applied as a minimum standard test against any international organisations. Given their status as effectively small, separate and sovereign areas that exercise a unique set of practices: sometimes relatively lawless; sometimes parochial; while at other times a reasonable, interpretation of staff rights,[21] it must be argued that a minimum test must apply, when externally measured by international and regional treaty bodies, wherein the host State has ratified the

---

17 As an example: a case filed against the World Health Organization or WHO, with the AFRO Regional African WHO Board, took over 12 months to fail to issue any judgment, despite a series of reminders. The first-instance quasi-judicial board failed to take any action. This is not uncommon; indeed, Applicants have been known to wait over 5 years for a final judgment from the UN internal system.

18 ECtHR, *Waite and Kennedy v. Germany*, Application No. 26083/94, 30 *EHRR* (1999) p. 261.

19 President of CAIO and British Governor of Human Rights and Professor of Human Rights and International Law at the University of Essex.

20 Professor of Public Law at the University of Vienna, Austria and author, Board Member of CAIO.

21 Which almost invariably falls below minimum due process rights in civil hearings; see www.caio-ch.org.

treaty or convention. If not, there would be no effective remedy for the victim, rending them *otiose*.

What is the 'reasonable alternative means' standard for enforcement of civil rights, meeting standards equivalent to human rights accountability measures?[22] Given the absence of enforceable human rights, a means for enforcing such rights must be sought after. One practical mechanism for those seeking redress for violations of international civil servant rights within the 'dysfunctional'[23] internal UN legal system is to seek redress from the European Court of Human Rights.[24] To understand why an Applicant would file with the European Court, we turn now to the Court's jurisprudence involving international civil servants, of which two primary issues present themselves.

In *Waite and Kennedy v. Germany*[25], the European Court of Human Rights described the basic test applicable in deciding whether or not the applicants and employees of the European Space Agency, had suffered a violation of their rights under the Convention, through being deprived of access to local or State courts. The test: whether the UN internal legal system constitutes a '*reasonable alternative legal forum*': 'a material factor in determining whether granting ESA immunity from German jurisdiction is permissible under the Convention is whether the applicants had available to them *reasonable alternative means* to protect effectively their rights under the Convention.'[26]

The European Court has indicated that it will interpret and apply the Convention in a manner which renders those rights by Applicants before it 'practical and effective, not theoretical and illusory'.[27]

---

22 ECtHR, *Waite and Kennedy*, op. cit. n. 18, para. 68.

23 UN General Assembly, 'Administration of Justice at the United Nations: Report of the Redesign Panel on the United Nations System of Administration of Justice', A/61/205, by members of the Redesign Panel, Mary Gaudron QC, Justice Louise Otis, Ahmed El-Kosheri, Diego Garcia-Sayan and Kingsley C. Moghalu, submitted to the UN Secretary-General on 20 July 2006 for transmission to the General Assembly (hereafter UN Redesign Panel Report), describes the UN's internal legal system as 'dysfunctional' at para. 150.

24 Another potential is the filing of test litigation in the United States, either under the ACTA [Alien Tort Claims Act] or original jurisdiction of the US Supreme Court [28 U.S.C. 1251(b)(1); Article III of the US Constitution alleging proceedings involve actions or proceedings to which ambassadors, other public ministers, consuls, or vice consuls of foreign states are parties…"].

25 ECtHR, *Waite and Kennedy*, op. cit. n. 18.

26 *Ibid.*, para. 68 (emphasis added). A substantially identical and simultaneously decided case was ECtHR, *Beer and Regan v. Germany*, Application No. 28934/95, 33 *EHRR* (1999) p. 3.

27 See ECtHR, *Christine Goodwin v. United Kingdom*, Application No. 28957/95, *ECHR* (2002), p. 583, at para. 74. See also e.g. ECtHR, *Matthews v. the United Kingdom*, Application No. 24833/94, 28 EHRR (1999) p. 364, at para. 34; ECtHR, *Soering v. UK*, Application No. 14038/88, 11 *EHRR* (1989) p. 439, at para. 87; ECtHR, *Artico v. Italy*, Application No. 6694/74,

In applying that test to the legal system within the European Space Agency (ESA) the Court assessed whether or not that international organisation had exceeded a "margin of appreciation", which was granted in light of the organisation's immunity from jurisdiction. The European Court did not conduct a significant analysis of the ESA internal Appeal Board's practice, procedure or level of function, *vis-à-vis* the civil rights of international civil servants. 'In the Court's view, the German courts had not exceeded their margin of appreciation in giving effect to ESA's[28] immunity from jurisdiction, as the applicants could and should have had recourse to the ESA Appeals Board[29] as a 'reasonable alternative means' of redress.[30] Furthermore, the Court argued (like the Commission[31] that the test of proportionality could not be applied so as to compel an international organisation to submit itself to national litigation in relation to employment conditions prescribed under national labour law.'[32]

The Court ruled on the jurisprudential question of whether or not the margin of appreciation was exceeded, but failed to conduct any further, detailed, analysis. If that analysis were correctly performed and presented to the European Court, one wonders whether it would find that the practice fails to meet minimum requirements for a fair trial.

IV. THE POTENTIAL APPLICATION OF PUBLIC INTERNATIONAL LAW TO INTERNATIONAL ORGANISATIONS

Professor August Reinisch, Professor of Public Law of the University of Vienna, a respected commentator and the author of *International Organizations Before National Courts*[33] – in taking a practical approach to the application of the principles of public international law and good governance, has produced an insightful commentary.

---

3 *EHRR* (1980) p. 1, at para. 33; ECtHR, *Airey v. Ireland*, Application No. 6289/73, 2 *EHRR* (1979) p. 305, at para. 24.

28 European Space Agency.

29 See ESA Staff Regulations, Chapter VIII, Regulations 33 to 41; ESA Convention, Annex I art XXVII [ESA was established under the Convention for the Establishment of a European Space Agency (adopted 30 May 1975, entered into force 30 October 1980) 14 ILM 864].

30 ECtHR, *Waite and Kennedy*, op. cit. n. 18, para. 69.

31 The European Commission of Human Rights.

32 Cf Commission Report *c.q.* 'Opinion' of 2 December 1997, Application No. 26083/94, included in ECtHR, *Waite and Kennedy*, op. cit. n. 18, paras. 43–84 and paras. 79–80.

33 A. Reinisch, *International Organizations before National Courts* (Cambridge, Cambridge University Press 2000).

Professor Reinisch's work for CAIO[34] and its sponsors has focused on a series of analytical questions, which may be summarised as follows:

A. WHAT SUBSTANTIVE LEGAL STANDARDS APPLY TO THE RIGHTS AND ENTITLEMENTS OF INTERNATIONAL ORGANISATION STAFF MEMBERS?

Employment or labour laws typically include protections such as:

- a safe working environment meeting minimum Occupational Health and Safety standards;
- regulations on the hours, salary and evaluation or appraisal for employees;
- just remuneration, retirement pay and sick leave/maternity/disability benefits;
- protection against arbitrary or unfair dismissal;
- the right to be free from sexual and psychological harassment 'mobbing' by supervisors and co-workers;
- effective redress mechanisms enabling enforcement of the above.

B. THESE AND MANY OTHER EMPLOYEES RIGHTS ARE GUARANTEED IN VARIOUS ILO CONVENTIONS, IN MOST NATIONAL LEGAL SYSTEMS AND IN EUROPEAN UNION LAWS

The difficult and largely unexplored legal issue is whether and to what extent they are also binding upon international organisations. A more complete answer to this question than what is permitted in this short contribution may be found in the series of research papers by the Amsterdam International Law Clinic focusing on these issues, found at www.caio-ch.org.

C. A RELEVANT AND RELATED QUESTION IS THE EXTENT TO WHICH INTERNATIONAL LAW OR FUNDAMENTAL CONCEPTS SUCH AS DUE PROCESS, ARE APPLICABLE

Currently, the standards regularly tolerated by both Tribunals, in failing to order public hearings, permit document discovery or otherwise provide an adequate alternative forum, fall far below the minimum standard described by the

[34] The Centre has enjoyed the support of a number of academic institutions in formal study and analysis of the legal issues that present; see www.caio-ch.org for details.

European Court in *Waite and Kennedy v Germany.*[35] A full analysis with reference to public law principles and jurisprudence is set out in the series of Amsterdam International Law Clinic Papers under "Rule of law," on the CAIO website.[36]

The question that naturally arises: 'Is there a legal responsibility under human rights treaties on the part of the host State to properly supervise small areas of expressly granted immunity from the jurisdiction of the host State local courts once these violations are drawn to the attention of the host State?' And furthermore: 'What parameters then apply?' Several subsequent questions follow along this inquiry.

Are there a core set of labour rights as defined in both ILO conventions and in human rights treaty obligations, which States are legally bound to secure, enforce, monitor and regulate? And by extension, do such labour rights apply, even though such States have individually signed Headquarters Agreements with those international organisations guaranteeing them immunity; or does a State have no further responsibility for breaches of minimum convention standards by organisations, once it has signed an International Organisation Headquarters Agreement?[37]

Headquarters Agreements describe the international immunity and the privileges enjoyed by international organisations located physically on the territory of host States, where they are 'headquartered'. These Agreements provide for an exchange of rights and responsibilities between the Organisation and the State; the State deferring its sovereign powers, including ordinary application of local laws, to the international organisation, which in turn acknowledges its responsibility to comply with the host State local laws. The Agreements, modelled on the 1946 Agreement between the International Labour Organization and Switzerland[38], set out basic responsibilities for international organisations. In theory, the organisations should provide social security or

35 See ECtHR, *Waite and Kennedy*, op. cit. n. 18; necessary reading for a full understanding of this topic.

36 See V.A. Böhre, S.E. von Dewall, LL.M., I.J. Middel and C.E. Steer, supervised by E. de Wet and J.P.J. van Wielink LL.M, Amsterdam International Law Clinic, 'The (Non-) Application of International Law by the ILO Administrative tribunal: Possible legal avenues for establishing responsibility', July 2004, www.caio-ch.org; and N.E. Kuijer, S.L. Park M.I.A., Amsterdam International Law Clinic, 'Judicial Independence of the ILO Administrative Tribunal: The potential for reform', April 2005, www.caio-ch.org.

37 Headquarters Agreements between international organisations and Switzerland are available at the Swiss Federal Department of Foreign Affairs at www.eda.admin.ch/eda/en/home/topics/intord/intorg/html.

38 Agreement between the Swiss Federal Council and the International Labour Organization concerning the legal status of the International Labour Organization in Switzerland (entered into force 27 May 1946) 15 *UNTS* 377.

pension payments, respect local laws and provide adequate alternative dispute resolution systems.[39]

States should not be allowed to escape their legal responsibility to all citizens on their sovereign territory in respect of longstanding, ratified conventions by providing privileges and immunities to international organisations.[40] It would render such ratification meaningless, and afford impunity to Convention violations.

In analysing whether or not the substantive standards set out in the European Convention are met by international organisations, recalling the test of "practical and effective, not theoretical and illusory" a key task for the European Court is to examine the practice and procedure of the internal quasi-judicial UN legal system. A significant amount of information on this topic has been generated by CAIO, and more recently, by the UN itself in the UN's Redesign Panel report.[41] Accountability in government eventually translates to good government. Why should this identical principle not follow, by logical induction, for international governance?

It is important to recall that the UN itself is a creature of not only international, but public international law. It has a duty to respect these principles internally in order to uphold the standards it espouses to the international community. In so doing, not only does it set a good example to those nation States with less developed legal systems, but, given the sprawling nature of its bureaucracy and the tendrils of each organisation's national branch, better internal management and improved internal governance will result.[42]

The obligation to provide a fair trial

The obligation to provide a fair trial before an independent and impartial court, as prescribed by human rights treaties[43], is breached by the UN's irregular and

---

39 In practice, not all of these conditions are fulfilled, for example, there is no social security and the alternative legal system is far from an adequate alternative to the Swiss Justice system a highly functional civil justice model – see www.caio-ch.org 'Rule of Law' and 'Current Projects'.

40 For a series of detailed legal arguments exploring this proposition, see V.A. Böhre, S.E. von Dewall, LL.M., I.J. Middel and C.E. Steer, loc. cit. n. 36.

41 www.caio-ch.org; see 'Current projects' under 'Home' and 'Rule of law' under 'Contact us', and the UN Redesign Panel Report, op. cit. n. 23.

42 Unfortunately, the UN has been wracked with internal scandals ranging from 'Oil-for-Food' to 'Sex-For-Food' and refugee girl rape by UN Blue Helmets. Law reform is part of the solution to these problems.

43 Including Article 10 of the *Universal Declaration of Human Rights* and Article 6 of the *Universal Declaration of Human Rights.*

ongoing failure to grant a single public hearing over the past 16 years within the ILOAT, the Tribunal with jurisdiction over most international organisations.[44]

The Tribunal's current practice violates the right to a fair trial and other fundamental employment rights prescribed in human rights law.[45] Specific failings include absence of due process, lack of transparency and violation of minimum independence standards for courts and internal quasi-judicial boards. For an overview of these breaches, see the Honourable Justice Robertson Q.C.'s legal opinion, wherein he opines that the internal system fails to fully conform to the "universally applicable" human rights standards in two fundamental respects; first, in that the judges appointed to the Tribunal are not independent but "contract judges" reappointed every three years by the ILO. Second, he points out that the Tribunal's failure to hold public hearings since 1995 is unlawful and *ultra vires.*[46]

V. INTERNAL CLAIMS INVOLVE APPEALS AGAINST ADMINISTRATIVE DECISIONS RELATING TO DISCIPLINE OF STAFF OR GRIEVANCES, INVOLVING OTHER STAFF OR MANAGEMENT

How are such proceedings characterised?

Review of Administrative decisions

Administrative decisions giving rise to issues which adversely affect staff fall into two major categories[47]:

---

44 See 'jurisdiction', under www.ilo.org/public/english/tribunal/guidefj.htm.

45 Including the *Universal Declaration of Human Rights* (Articles 10 & 23), and regional treaties such as the *European Convention on Human Rights* (Article 6).

46 Honourable Justice Geoffrey Robertson QC's legal opinion, available at www.caio-ch.org, 'Legal Links' under 'Contact us'. '11. I was astonished to be informed that ILOAT routinely and invariably denies all applications for oral hearings, since such a practice would contravene its Statute and Rules. But I have examined its recent decisions, and have found no case in which a hearing application has been granted. Instead, in the Preamble to every judgment in cases where such application has been made, there is the routine recital: "Having examined the matter submission and decided not to allow the complainants' application for hearings'. By this formula, it appears on the face of these judgments, the Tribunal invariably decides that it shall not afford oral hearings. I am told that between 1995 and 2001, oral hearings were requested in over two hundred cases, and refused in every instance. This practice in effect renders otiose Article V of the Statute and Article 12 of its Rules. It is not, in my view, a practice that is permitted by the Statute: it is ultra vires and unlawful'.

47 See www.caio-ch.org; 'Current Projects' under 'Home': 'Submissions to the UN Redesign Panel' by the British Governor of Human Rights Professor Françoise Hampson, the Honorable Justice Robyn Layton Q.C, Justice of Supreme Court of South Australia and the author, Sarah

a. Grievance complaints – namely administrative decisions made by persons in authority within an organisation in respect of complaints made by staff. Such administrative decisions may be made in relation to complaints made on topics such as conduct of other staff, job requirements, job specifications and particular conditions under which employment is undertaken. They may also include serious complaints by staff in relation to the conduct of managers where allegations of misconduct, intimidation or harassment are made.
b. Disciplinary Issues – namely administrative decisions concerning matters such as demotion, transfer, suspension, termination or other forms of disciplinary action against staff.

Usually, in national law, these terms are subject to different processes depending on the relative seriousness of the complaint or disciplinary decision. Under international law, there is human rights case law which suggests that, depending on circumstances, such proceedings may be in character civil or criminal. In order to ensure that internal UN procedures conform to the requirements of due process; the procedures must provide an effective remedy as it is defined in human rights law, not merely due process.[48]

Failings by the UN internal legal system

The list of failings, both procedural and jurisprudential, endured by Complainants filing with the UN's internal legal system are significant. Despite good will, untrained members of quasi-judicial internal boards rarely produce good law. The presence of one trained lawyer on a board can make a noticeable difference.

Procedural failings by the UN internal legal system may be summarised as follows:[49]

- Reluctance or inability to call witnesses, significant levels of witness intimidation [particularly noticeable in individual charges of misconduct, criminal behaviour, sexual harassment and instances of internal fraud];
- Failure or inability to use any available mechanism to call reluctant witnesses;
- Reluctance or inability to create summaries of fact and to draw conclusions of fact, a basic skill in evidence-based judgment-writing;

Hunt, Coordinator, CAIO, on behalf of the Centre for Accountability of International Organisations.

48 See CAIO submissions to UN Redesign Panel, op. cit. n. 17, also the Honourable Justice Geoffrey Robertson QC's legal opinion, op. cit. n. 46 and Amsterdam International Clinic Reports, loc. cit. n. 36.

49 CAIO Submissions to UN Redesign Panel, op. cit. n. 47, updated from original.

- Excessive dependence on experts, particularly experts chosen and hired by the Respondent Organisation, often leading to biased conclusions of fact;
- Difficulty in understanding and so ruling on points of law, for example burden of proof; inability to remain impartial in making judgment calls involving balancing of a variety of conflicting evidence;
- Failure to address issues of law as pleaded, instead electing merely to rule on procedural or administrative issues – often rendering such 'decisions', despite months or even years of delay, *otiose* or useless;
- Inability to understand issues of liability, particularly where subtleties are involved, often creating a bias towards the Respondent Organisation;
- Inability to write reasoned judgments, taking into account all relevant facts and not disregarding relevant facts;
- Lack of understanding of the principle of the need for the members of the internal board to be independent from any matters relating to the issues before them[50];
- Lack of experience or understanding of issues of quantum, leading to failure to actually make recommendations on quantum of damages.[51]

The right to a fair trial and public hearing is the key to all of the shortcomings of the UN's internal legal system.

Of all of these shortcomings, from the perspective of the legal practitioner, the most severe is the failure of the UN's main internal Tribunal, the ILOAT[52], to provide a single public hearing over the past 19 years. This situation is significantly aggravated by the seriousness of various cases brought before it, including summary dismissal over alleged fraud and in light of the concurrent UN immunity, which deprives Complainants of ordinary access to the Swiss [or local/national] justice system. These cases range from summary dismissal for due investigation of major fraud, allegations of homicide, allegations of suicide allegedly due to mobbing, to a number of very severe cases of psychiatric illness due to workplace mobbing or field injuries. Most are compensated by an internal compensation or pension system controlled by the employer, thus raising serious concerns.

---

50 The author's personal favourite is a harassment case brought by one international civil servant against another, who happened to be the in-house lawyer. The gentleman in question did not see fit to disqualify himself from defending the case on the part of the international organisation concerned [as this matter is current, the names of the parties are not mentioned, to avoid causing prejudice to the Applicant].

51 Approximately 2% of internal quasi-judicial Boards dare to make any recommendations at all, generally falling significantly short of what even the conservative Tribunals themselves recommend.

52 www.ilo.org/dyn/triblex/triblex_browse.home.

As opined by former Secretary-General on behalf of the NGO, the International Commission of Jurists, Louise Doswald-Beck[53], in Geneva, 2002, on the right to a public hearing: 'This right consists of both the right of the parties to be present at the hearing and the right of the public to have access to the hearing. The aim is to ensure that justice is done and is seen to be done, and this cannot be verified if hearings are held in secret. This was underlined by the European Court of Human Rights in a defamation case: Helmers v Sweden[54]: 'the public character of proceedings before the judicial bodies...protects litigants against the administration of justice in secret with no public scrutiny'. It added that a person bringing proceedings must be sure 'that his case was being determined by a tribunal, the independence and impartiality of which he could verify.'[55]

VI. THE UN REDESIGN PANEL REPORT

The release in 2006 of the UN Redesign Panel Report[56], admitting to multiple failings within the UN's internal legal system, marks the first formal recognition of an internal set of standards that are increasingly seen as unacceptable when measured against human rights treaties. Or more bluntly, the UN's internal legal system is itself 'dysfunctional'[57]:

> '72. The decisions of UNAT are not always consistent and its jurisprudence is not well developed. In particular, it does not have a coherent jurisprudence as to the duties owed by an international organisation to its staff. Thus, there is a widespread view, which is largely correct, that the formal justice system affords little, if any protection of individual rights, such as the right to a safe and secure workplace or the right to be treated fairly and without discrimination.
> 73. In summary, the structure of the formal justice system is both fragmented and over-centralised. It is slow, expensive and inefficient. It does not provide proper or adequate remedies and fails to guarantee individual rights. It neither promotes managerial efficiency nor accountability. It generally lacks transparency, and fails to satisfy minimum requirements of the rule of law. It enjoys neither the confidence nor the respect of staff, management or Member States.'[58]

53 Louise Doswald-Beck is Professor of International Law, Graduate Institute of International studies (HEI) and Director of the University Centre for International Humanitarian Law (UCIHL); see her opinion at www.caio-ch.org, on the question of the right to a public hearing, see 'legal links' under 'contact us', www.caio-ch.org.

54 ECtHR, *Helmers v. Sweden*, Application No. 11826/86 *EHCR* (1991) p. 44.

55 L. Doswald-Beck and R. Kolb, *Judicial Process and Human Rights: United Nations, European, American and African systems: texts and summaries of international case-law* (Kehl, Engel 2004)

56 UN Redesign Panel Report, op. cit. n. 23.

57 *Ibid.*, para. 150.

58 *Ibid.*, at paras. 72–73. Emphasis added.

What triggered the UN to constitute a Redesign Panel for its internal legal system?

It seems the UN's recognition of its dysfunctional internal legal system was triggered by at least three factors. The first, and most important, was the lobbying by the African States through the UN General Assembly for much-needed reform. The second was the agitation of the NGO CAIO through both public seminars and discussion panels, complemented by the strategic filing of test litigation in both the European Court of Human Rights and, more recently, the US Supreme Court.[59]

The less obvious factor was the gradual dissemination of academic papers setting out the problems associated with UN mismanagement; absence of accountability and a series of significant breaches *vis-à-vis* conventional concepts of due process, including *stare decisis*; the concept of an independent appeal court; and most importantly, the need for a professionalised, independent, first-tier decision-making tribunal.[60]

A few words on the practical implications of the UN's immunity are called for in any contribution discussing human rights accountability of international organisations *vis-à-vis* their staff.

Lifting of the Immunity: Theory vs Practice:

In theory, when a criminal act is committed, even a relatively minor one, the international immunity ordinarily applicable over those involved should be lifted.[61] The discretion to lift or to 'waive' the international immunity lies with the Secretary-General or Director-General of the organisation itself. The equivalent in private industry would be to have the Managing Director decide whether or not to allow a criminal inquiry or prosecution involving its workers to take place.

---

59 US Supreme Court case of *Cythia Brzac et al v. United Nations, Kofi Annan, Ruud Lubbers, Wendy Chamberlin, Werner Blatter, Kofi Asomani, Raymond Hall, A.-W. Bijleveld, Daisy Buruku, Defendants*, [Supreme Court case no 136, application for original jurisdiction, case also filed with New York State Discrimination Tribunal for breach of US Discrimination Laws].

60 As recommended by the UN Redesign Panel Report chaired by Mary Gaudron Q.C. in its Recommendations.

61 Provision for this lifting is generally found in the Headquarters Agreement with the Host State.

The waiver of the UN's Immunity: a rarity for criminal prosecutions

In fact, it is rare that criminal or potential criminal acts committed in Headquarters [as opposed to field][62] operations are, in practice, successfully prosecuted.[63] Rather, we see a situation as typified by current matter in the author's legal practice. In this instance, an investigation by the local Swiss magistrate has not able to take place due to the international organisation's immunity. The lifting of the immunity in relation to the prosecutorial power was only permitted against the chief fraudster. This is despite fraudulent activities, which the Complainant alleges were widespread. Whether or not the fraud was widespread, as the Complainant alleges, there is no reason why any international organisation officials should enjoy immunity from the power of both investigation and prosecution, due to the unilateral discretion of the Secretary-General to waive the immunity of the organisation as a whole.

It is easy to see why the immunity is rarely lifted to enable prosecutions in practice; not many managing directors of multinational companies would permit themselves to be prosecuted if they had the unilateral choice to simply refuse to be subject to the jurisdiction of the court. Reform of the discretionary power of the Secretary-General of international organisations is required. The solution proposed by the author would be to commission an independent judicial panel composed of senior independent judges and legal practitioners in making judicial determinations on a biannual basis. The key to success in such an initiative would be the *complete independence* of such a committee from the UN and its international organisations, thus ensuring independence in decision-making.

Currently, international organisations have no internal FOI [Freedom of Information] procedures. Instead, many internal UN documents are classified as "secret", "confidential" or most commonly "Internal Confidential Memoranda". The UN internal legal system, notoriously, does not even have a procedure for document discovery for its own staff, let alone an FOI or equivalent. This leads to

---

62 For a thorough overview of this topic, often involving sexual abuse of young refugees or local inhabitants, see F. Hampson, *Working Paper on the Accountability of International Personnel taking part in Peace Support Operations* (E/CN.4/Sub.2/2005/42), by Professor Françoise Hampson, [CAIO President] in her capacity as a member of the UN Sub-Commission on the Promotion and Protection of Human Rights.

63 In the case in *re Qin*, the widower of a victim of alleged suicide due to workplace mobbing [psychological mobbing], Mr Qin [ILOAT, *Qin*, Judgment No. 1752, 9 July 1998 (ILO)], made a criminal complaint to the Geneva Prosecutor. Despite a request for the lifting of the international organisation's immunity by the Chief Prosecutor in order to enable an independent investigation to take place, the immunity was never lifted. Instead, the ILO Administrative Tribunal refused to re-examine medical questions at the first tier level, instead permitting a first-instance internal board, advised only by an in-house medical panel, to provide the definitive analysis.

regular failure to achieve document discovery, even when the document can be very precisely identified. A registry, with ordinary discovery procedures, is the obvious solution.

The UN and its international organisations themselves are far from being an ideal employer. Unspoken pressures whisper through troubled corridors. Women suffer from such conditions in particular. Not only is the reality of psychological harassment ever-present, the constant threat of non-renewal of contract can sometimes take a nasty turn. Women are sometimes subjected to the age-old threat of 'put out, or get out'. Those 'lonely nights in the office', or 'conference opportunity' can lead to inappropriate suggestions which in most modern corporations would see an executive walk the plank, or worse, result in a damaging public lawsuit. Yet in the UN internal system, it is difficult to prove sexual harassment.[64]

An obligation not only to comply with international standards, but to strive for best practice as an example to nations with developing legal systems

As subjects of international law, international organisations should follow basic principles of international law. Yet staff members of international organisations are unable to enforce legal rights enjoyed by nationals resident in member States having ratified the conventions.[65] The United Nations immunity prevents the application of national laws directly, which directly affords impunity and fails to guarantee accountability. The present system is far from ideal in administrative and employment law and sets a poor example for those states which are in the process of developing their legal systems.

While the UNAT statute is currently under review and redesign, no parallel movement has yet been taken regarding the much-needed review of the statute of the closely related ILOAT and its rules and procedures. CAIO will continue to lobby for such reform, in accordance with its mandate, until appropriate reforms are implemented.

64 E. Flaherty and S. Hunt, 'Rule without Law? Injustice at the United Nations', *Geneva Post Quarterly* (April 2006) Inaugural Launch edition, p. 8.

65 See the legal opinion of G. Robertson QC, op. cit. n. 46; also refer to Vincent A. Böhre, Sophia E. von Dewall, LL.M., Ingeborg J. Middel, Cassandra E. Steer, loc. cit. n. 36 and N. E. Kuijer, S. L. Park M.I.A., loc. cit. n. 36.

Whistleblowers – a consistent lack of protection, rather than a consistent practice of following due process

A. The unfortunate truth of whistleblowing within the UN

Unfortunately, summary dismissal of an internal auditor is but one of many practical examples of just how whistleblowers are treated in the UN international system of organisations by senior mangers. While one can note the undeniable fact that whistleblowers are treated in a like manner all around the world, the unique feature of UN is that so often, whistleblowers are not only disgraced but permanently ostracised, to the point where they find it hard to find other employment.[66]

B. Whistleblowers require a public hearing, rapidly – for vindication

Unless whistleblowers are delivered the immediate and relieving balm of vindication through justice, particularly those uncovering fraud, or victims of mobbing – both of which are difficult to prove without a public hearing – they often collapse, both psychologically and physically.[67] It is also difficult to sustain a major legal battle after the personal deflation that naturally accompanies any sudden demission or sacking.

C. Psychological harassment – a common workplace phenomenon in international organisations

Psychological harassment or "mobbing" has been described by the World Health Organization as "*repeated, unreasonable behaviour directed towards an employee, or group of employees, that creates a risk to health and safety.*"[68] Bullying is subtle, involving a misuse of power and authority against a powerless victim.

---

66 The author's practice has seen several of these cases, with at times, horrendous outcomes and lives destroyed, see www.ilo.org/public/english/tribunal; Judgment No. 2861.

67 The author's legal practice sees a number of severely psychiatrically unwell individuals, who become victims of 'mobbing' or psychological harassment, ranging from depression, to post-traumatic stress disorder, some with suicidal symptoms. Working for an international organisation is not always the diplomatic perk-laden job it is notoriously characterised as, particularly not for the bottom half of the employee hierarchy, most of whom lack any job security. [Approximately 60% of international organisation staff are on some form of short-term contract].

68 World Health booklet 'Protecting Worker's Health – Raising Awareness of Psychological Harassment at Work' states at page 29 in relation to the proper prevention of mobbing: in general the law should address the following points, taking into account local cultures when devising strategies.

1. encourage preventative measures to reduce occurrences of workplace bullying;
2. protect workers to engage in self-help to address bullying and provide incentives to employers who respond promptly, fairly and effectively;

A recent survey commissioned by the World Health Organization Staff Association, externally performed by independent expert Professor Dieter Zapf of the Johann Wolfgang Goethe University of Frankfurt, measured the rate of mobbing, or psychological harassment, within the World Health Organization at a ***minimum prevalence of 6.9%***. That is, of total WHO employees, a minimum of 6.9% are subject to harassment or mobbing lasting for six months or more, a rate twice the national average throughout Europe. Professor Zapf concluded that the problem was poor management; his suggestion was to call for the improvement of internal dispute resolution procedures.[69]

The question frequently asked is: 'What causes psychological harassment?' Does the UN attract people who have a tendency towards harassing their colleagues, or is it the competitive environment which causes such unfortunate behaviour? Is it due to the effect of the UN's immunity or rather of its privileges? The answer is 'both' – sadly, the absence of internal regulation has lead to the abuse of internal privileges. Immunity has played a crucial role in the development of international diplomatic relations.[70] It is now time to take a closer look at what immunity really entails, with a sharp focus on the human rights accountability of international organisations, towards both staff and third parties.

Partial implementation of the reforms including hiring of an independent judiciary

On 1 July 2009 a truly extraordinary development in the history of UN immunity and rule of law within the UN occurred: for the first time, independent judges were appointed to rule upon UN internal decision-making.[71]

A list of outstanding issues in UN General Resolution 63/253 suggests that chief among General Assembly concerns included delays, transitional measures, financial arrangements and cost-sharing measures. For the moment, it must be celebrated that after five years of lobbying for reform, the UN has finally adopted a new system of justice, incorporating real judges, independently examined and selected. However, a few key criticisms of the new legal system passed rapidly into reality on 24 December 2008 should not be forgotten; despite a serious lobby

---

3. provide proper relief to targets of severe bullying, including compensatory damages and, where applicable, reinstatement to his or her position;
4. punish bullying and the employers who allow them to abuse their co-workers." from D. Yamada 2003.

69 D. Zapf, 'The Geneva Staff Association Survey of Harassment in the Workplace', by Professor D. Zapf of the Johann Wolfgang Göethe University of Frankfurt. Professor Zapf drew the conclusion that "*the results indicate a high base rate of mobbing in the workplace at WHO*".

70 See L. Frey and M. Frey, op. cit. n. 4, and CAIO intern N. Hanrahan, loc. cit. n. 5.

71 See UN General Assembly, 'Resolution 64/253 on the Report of the Fifth Committee', A/63/642, 63rd session, agenda item 129, 74th plenary meeting, 24 December 2008.

for greater judicial powers, the UN internal legal service did all it could to curtail and restrict the powers of the nascent judiciary.

CONCLUSION

The UN and its international organisations are in frequent violation of human rights standards, and of the more ordinary standards of accountability such as due process. This will persist until the UN takes solid moves towards reform. At least the UN has finally recognised that reform is called for and is reluctantly underway. It will be interesting to chart the development and progress of the implementation of the proposed reforms recommended by the UN Redesign Panel. It is predictable that as the UN gradually conforms to the rule of law, it will attract better quality candidates and become a more effective organisation, so becoming gradually more accountable.[72]

However, the international community would do well to take into account before next embarking on major international project such as Oil-For-Food, or national building projects such as UNTAET (the United Nations Transitional Administration in East Timor), the effect of proper rule-of-law bodies and regulation. In absence of a proper framework for independent regulation of international organisation decision-making, corruption, conflict of interest and consequent waste of resources tend to be the rule, rather than the exception. The United Nations and its international organisations would be better off regulated far more strictly by proper, law-making bodies.

Whilst it is debatable whether this role can ever be adequately performed by internal bodies, the author strongly recommends for further reading an elegant essay examining why international immunity for international organisations should, in most cases, be waived in favour of justice: see Dr Matthew Parish's discussion in "On International Organisations", presented at the American Branch of the International Law Association (ABILA) annual International Law Weekend in New York, 22–24 October 2009, "Panel – Challenges to transnational governance"[73], which presents the case for doing away with International Organisation immunity to reduce lack of accountability and impunity.

---

[72] For a discussion of the United Nations Dispute Tribunal reforms which explains how the judges were selected and how the reforms were finally implemented, listen to an interview with the author and senior international jurist and author, Geoffrey Robertson QC, on World Radio Switzerland, available at http://worldradio.ch/wrs/programmes/yourspace/yourspace-un-law-reforms.shtml.

[73] The final version of this paper available on the CAIO website by the end of 2009, available at www.caio-ch.org, "Papers".

The "immunity-impunity" is one which is sorely in need of proper debate and consequent law reform. The issue is important not only for the working conditions within international organisations, but more importantly, for the "flow-on" effects of accountability in such organisations, which include improved services to victims of human rights abuses around the world and eventually, a world improved through better international monitoring.

WORKPLACE EQUALITY IN INTERNATIONAL ORGANISATIONS: WHY IS IT AN ILLUSORY CONCEPT?

Osmat Azzam JEFFERSON*

I. INTRODUCTION

International organisations claim control over their workplace. Under a functionalist approach, they are entitled to independent governance of staff members.[1] Each organisation implements provisions of its own constitutive instruments, develops its own internal administrative law, often with administrative courts, makes its own rules, and establishes and enforces regulations and staff procedures. Legally, these instruments have supremacy in law over any other source of law and are binding on all members of the organisation, including the staff.[2] International organisations are also granted immunity from suit in national courts.[3] Whereas scholars and international lawyers may agree that international organisations should be afforded immunity from national courts based only on their 'functional necessity' (a qualified immunity needed by the organisation to achieve its objectives),[4] there are

---

* Professor of Science, Technology, and Law, Queensland University of Technology (QUT). MIntLaw 2008, Australian National University, Ph.D. 1990, Cornell University. The author owes a debt of gratitude to Kim Rubenstein, Margaret Thornton, and Hilary Charlesworth for their encouragement and comments on earlier versions of this work. The author also thanks August Reinisch, Eva Rathgeber, Leslie Ewart (FICSA), Neale Hooper, and Laurence C. Fauth for their constructive feedback on earlier drafts of this contribution and the sharing of background materials. Internet pages were last visited on 9 December 2009.

1 C.F. Amerasinghe, *Principles of the Institutional Law of International Organizations*, 2nd edn. (Cambridge, Cambridge University Press 2005) p. 272.

2 C.F. Amerasinghe, op. cit. n. 1, at p. 274.

3 A. Reinisch, *International Organizations before National Courts* (Cambridge, Cambridge University Press 2000) p. 35.

4 S. Herz, 'International Organizations in US Courts: Reconsidering the Anachronism of Absolute Immunity', 31 *Suffolk Transnational Law Review* (2008) p. 471, at p. 527 (discussing the qualification statutory basis of international organizations' immunity in the USA and how initially congressional authorisation came about after the ratification of United Nations Charter, to grant certain international organisations legal and practical independence from territorial authority and to afford privileges, which are normally reserved for diplomatic

enduring debates as to whether this functional necessity trumps the constitutional rights of staff, under international law, to gain access to equality guarantees in employment disputes.[5]

Since national courts tend to accept a broad scope of the 'functional necessity' immunity of international organisations, in particular in employment disputes, and all attempts to make that functional immunity work in a way that does not lead to absolute immunity have not been successful, alternative solutions are sought to balance the right of international organisations to protect their independent internal laws against the equally important right of staff members to pursue their employment claims against their employers, the international organisations, within a governance structure that is built on principles of equality and the rule of law.[6] To achieve such a balance, international organisations offer their staff a judicial or quasi-judicial recourse to justice. Briefly, each organisation has some informal and formal mechanisms for managing the workplace and settling disputes with staff. The exhaustion of the informal procedures precedes the right of a staff member to present their case before an internal administrative court.[7] Owing to breaches in accountability standards and abuse of discretionary power, the internal justice system in many of the international organisations has been subject to many reviews and revisions.[8]

Judge Amerasinghe argues that the lack of access to national courts does not mean that the employment relationship between international civil servants and

---

officers, to their officials. However, since the nature and scope of these immunities were ambiguous, in 1976, Congress established new statutory guidelines that clarified and restricted foreign sovereign immunity.).

5 A. Reinisch, 'The Immunity of International Organizations and the Jurisdiction of Their Administrative Tribunals', 11 *Institute for International Law and Justice Working Paper* (2007) pp. 7–8 (Global Administrative Law Series), available at http://iilj.org/publications/documents/2007-11.GAL.Reinisch.web.pdf (discussing developments in some European court cases that restricted absolute immunity for international organisations to support concepts of equality).

6 A. Reinisch and U.A. Weber, 'In the Shadow of Waite and Kennedy – The Jurisdictional Immunity of International Organizations, the Individual's Right of Access to Courts and Administrative Tribunals as Alternative Means of Dispute Settlement', 1 *International Organizations Law Review* (2004) pp. 64–66.

7 H. Dean, 'Due Process: The Rights of World Bank Staff in Misconduct Investigations', in C. de Cooker, ed., *Accountability, Investigation and Due Process In International Organizations* (Boston/Leiden, Martinus Nijhoff Publishers 2005) pp. 98–100.

8 UN General Assembly, 'Report of the Redesign Panel on the United Nations System of Administration of Justice', A/61/205 (2006), available at www.un.org/ga/president/62/issues/resolutions/a-61-205.pdf. See also Opinion on ILOAT reform, by G. Robertson, para. 15 (London, Doughty Street Chambers 2002), available at www.ilo.org/public/english/staffun/info/iloat/robertson.htm.

international organisations is 'outside the pale of law'.[9] The constitution of any organisation empowers it to establish an impartial and independent administrative court to safeguard equality and access to justice, even in the absence of express provision, and a judgment rendered by such a court is *res judicata* and binding on the parties to the dispute.[10] So in this contribution I look into the internal administration of international organisations from a slightly different perspective. I consider international organisations as first and foremost political actors rather than agents of public goods and using a constitutional approach, I pose the following questions: how are the concepts of equality understood, used, and valued within international organisations? What are the checks and balances in the internal governance structure? Are there relevant differences between the formal and the substantive laws? How do they impact on the realisation of equality? Can any of the legal discrepancies be challenged or changed to achieve equality?

Because equality is an ambiguous term, I refer to equality as a comprehensive system of rules for the protection of human rights that is based on the nature of the treatment and the result of the treatment. In Vierdag's terms, 'quest for equality implies both equality as "equal treatment of equals" (…) and equality as "unequal treatment for unequals" (…)'.[11] In this sense, equality in law precludes all forms of discrimination and besides being a legal concept, is also a moral concept. Therefore, in part II I review the concepts of equality and discrimination, as understood and applied through specific judgments of the administrative tribunals in international organisations. In part III I dissect the ensemble of employment relations between international organisations and their staff members and map the power in that relationship to identify core elements that clarify the nature of their internal governance as well as the checks and balances in its structure. In part IV I discuss how international organisations manoeuvre and operate in practice within this structure. Recognizing the dichotomy between an intention to build a rules-based approach to internal governance and a political will to maintain autonomy, in part V I identify the strategic rules and procedures that impact on the realisation of equality concepts in international organisations and affect the loyalty and commitment of staff to the mission of the organisation. In part VI I survey actions taken by these organisations in

9 C.F. Amerasinghe, op. cit. n. 1, at p. 278.

10 C.F. Amerasinghe, 'And What About International Civil Servants? – UN Administrative Tribunal', *UN Chronicle* (Winter 1998) p. 1 (discussing the criteria for an impartial and independent administrative tribunal), available at http://findarticles.com/p/articles/mi_m1309/is_4_35/ai_54823727.

11 E.W. Vierdag, *The Concept Of Discrimination In International Law* 7–18 (The Hague, Martinus Nijhoff Publishers 1973). See also C. Tobler, *Indirect Discrimination: A Case Study into the Development of the Legal Concept of Indirect Discrimination under EC Law* (Antwerp/Oxford, Intersentia 2005) pp. 17–34.

response to various reports, scandals, and public outbursts and outline the proposed redesign of internal justice systems and how these changes are still being debated. I end with a personal view.

By considering the practices of primarily the United Nations (UN), the World Bank, and the Consultative Group on International Agricultural Research (CGIAR), my legal analysis shows that the internal governing structure has more rules and procedures to govern employees and few, if any, rules to control the discretionary power of executives. While the rules and regulations, the existence of administrative courts, and current procedures for anti-discrimination rules may give the semblance of a balanced justice system in international organisations, the procedural guarantees of 'due process', the accountability standards, and the enforcement rules are not in place to safeguard the equality rights of staff. I argue, based on the practice of these organisations, that until there is a major commitment to establish a rules-based approach to the governing structure, enforcement procedures to safeguard individual rights, and the inclusion of an established line of authority to the executive branch of international organisations, anti-discrimination rules will continue to be applied disproportionately among staff members and discriminatory practices will remain very difficult to legally prove or challenge.

II. EQUALITY AND DISCRIMINATION CONCEPTS IN INTERNATIONAL ORGANISATIONS

Under international law, there is a mainstream belief that international organisations are bound by the general principle of equality.[12] However, very few international organisations acknowledge the principle of equality in their constitutive treaties (Articles 1 and 8 of the UN Charter).[13] The administrative tribunals of international organisations, through their specific judgments, hold that the principle of equality is applicable in employment relations and consistently invoked under general legal principles to control the exercise of administrative powers and discretions.[14]

The concept is recognised as being that 'those in like case[s] should be treated alike, and that those who are not in like case[s] should not be treated alike'.[15]

12 A. Reinisch, loc. cit. n. 5, at p. 6.

13 UN Charter, Art. 1 and 8, available at www.un.org/aboutun/charter/.

14 C.F. Amerasinghe, op. cit. n. 1, at p. 288.

15 B.D. Patterson, 'The Jurisprudence of Discrimination as Opposed to Simple Inequality in the International Civil Service', 36 *Georgia Journal of International and Comparative Law* (2007) p. 2 (discussing the principles of employment discrimination law as adopted by administrative tribunals).

The similarly situated argument, however, does not take into account the result of the treatment, an important part of the Aristotelian view of equality. The view encompasses a dichotomy because the first part implies equal treatment or equality 'before' the law whereas the second part implies 'the notion of proportionality', which underlies the principle of granting each person her/his due or equality 'in' the law.[16] Equality 'before' the law, as a legal and technical principle, thus requires equal treatment within a group, any group that can be made, whatever its character may be, whereas equality 'in' the law is more of a political principle. It involves the notion of *suum cirque tribuere*, that equal treatment prevails as long as there are no relevant inequalities to consider and the character of the legal differentiations themselves matter.[17] If our aim is to prohibit discrimination and achieve equality, then the requirement for equal treatment needs to be always supplemented with the requirement for unequal treatment.[18] Based on this understanding, specific judgments of the World Bank Administrative Tribunal (WBAT)[19] invoked legal concepts that share similar moral characteristics, such as principles of 'due process' of law and fair treatment or 'integrity and fairness', whereas the United Nations Administrative Tribunal (UNAT) invoked principles of 'contract or conflict of laws', the contractual 'force majeure', 'good faith', 'unjust enrichment', and estoppel.[20]

In his analysis of discrimination cases by various international organisations' administrative tribunals for the last thirty years or so, Patterson summarised his findings thus: 'the tribunals have comparatively few opportunities to develop this jurisprudence [equality], and they have not always seized those chances to elaborate a coherent framework. This, coupled with the fact that the tribunals are not bound by each other's precedents, has resulted in divergent approaches to this general principle of law, with no tribunal consistently applying either a formalist or a substantive framework. The result is a lack of predictability in the

16 E.W. Vierdag, op. cit. n. 11.

17 *Ibid.*, pp. 17–18.

18 *Ibid.*, p. 8. See also *Mr. R.A.-O. v. UNESCO*, ILOAT Judgment, No. 2193 (2003) para. 27 (J. Hugessen dissenting), available at www.ilo.org/public/english/tribunal/fulltext/2193.htm.

19 P.C. Hansen, 'The World Bank Administrative Tribunal's External Sources of Law: A Retrospective of the Tribunal's First Quarter-Century (1981–2005)', 6 *The Law and Practice of International Courts and Tribunals* (2007) p. 36 (discussing *Gyamfi*, WBAT Decision, No. 28 (1986) para. 45 and the procedural flaws that are considered violations of due process as '(i) the harshness of the applicant's suspension and his exclusion from the Bank's premises; (ii) the Bank's repeated failure to inform the applicant properly as to the accusations laid against him, and to allow him an opportunity to present his side of the case; (iii) the Bank's failure to reveal the names of the applicant's accusers; (iv) the Bank's denial of the applicant's right to confront or cross-examine his accusers, or to call supportive witnesses) (v) the inclusion in the *ad hoc* reviewing committee of persons previously involved in the investigation of the applicant; and (vi) the Bank's assembling of witnesses prior to a later Appeals Committee's hearing').

20 C.F. Amerasinghe, op. cit. n. 1, at p. 290.

application of the principle of equality in the international civil service.'[21] In other words, Patterson's findings suggest that rules applied in dispute resolutions for discrimination cases remain lacking consistency and uniformity within and across international organisations. Patterson acknowledges that these concepts remain broad and lacking in procedural standards, substantive laws, or clear anti- discrimination policies similar to Title VII of the U.S. Civil Rights Act of 1964, the UK Race Relations Act of 1968, or the Canadian Human Rights Act of 1976.[22]

III. MAPPING THE CORE RULES IN THE ENSEMBLE OF EMPLOYMENT CONDITIONS

With the recognition of broad provisions for non-discrimination rules at international organisations, the lack of enforceability mechanisms to guard the legal character of equality in law, and in the search for alternative solutions that balance the right of staff to equality while respecting the immunity of international organisations based on their 'functional necessity', I dissect the ensemble of employment relations and attempt to identify the core elements and rules that diverge from or converge with the even-handed balance in the legal relationship between staff and international organisations.

A. THE CONTRACT WITH THE ORGANISATION

The employment relationship usually oscillates between being contractual or statutory, and with the exception of the European Union (EU) and the Organisation for Economic Co-operation and Development (OECD), almost all other organisations claim a contractual relationship with their staff.[23] In the case of the UN, a provision is made in the Staff Regulations and Staff Rules for a letter of appointment that is based on an offer and an acceptance without a clear reference to a contract of employment, but in several cases UNAT has assumed that the relationship is not solely contractual.[24]

In practice, though, the nature of the relationship may extend beyond the contract. Once an appointment is made, an employee receives an offer or a letter and by signing that letter, the employee accepts not only the terms of the contract

21 B.D. Patterson, loc. cit. n. 15, at p. 32.

22 *Ibid.*, p. 5.

23 C.F. Amerasinghe, n. 1, at p. 281.

24 UNAT, *Kaplan*, Judgment No. 19 (1953) para. 3, available at http://untreaty.un.org/unat/UNAT_Judgements/Judgements_E/UNAT_00019_E.pdf.

but also all the other bits (explicit and implicit) of what makes up the internal law of the institution. In *de Merode*, WBAT stated: 'the fact that the Bank's employees enter its service on the basis of an exchange of letters does not mean that these contractual instruments contain an exhaustive statement of all relevant rights and duties. The two sides are agreed on this point. The contract may be the *sine qua non* of the relationships, but it remains no more than one of a number of elements which collectively establish the *ensemble* of conditions of employment operative between the Bank and its staff members.'[25] In *Kaplan*, in establishing the legal position of staff members UNAT distinguished between contractual elements and statutory elements, the personal status of each staff member being contractual (nature of contract, salary, and position within the institute) and all other matters that affect the organisation in general and its proper functioning being statutory. The tribunal went on to add that while the contractual elements cannot be changed without the agreement of the two parties (private contract law), the statutory elements may change without further notice and the changes are binding on staff members.[26]

B. WHAT ARE THE STATUTORY ELEMENTS?

In *de Merode*, WBAT stated that statutory elements can be found in the constituent instrument of the organisation, Staff Rules and Regulations, and depending on their content, certain manuals, circulars, notes and statements issued by the various hierarchical management teams.[27]

1° Constituent instruments

The constituent instrument is regarded as the basic statute or constitution of the organisation and it prevails on the basis of the hierarchical priority of the tribunal, as was addressed and confirmed in *Howrani* judgment No. 4 by UNAT and in *de Merode* by WBAT.[28] So, for example, the UN Charter and the Articles of Agreement of the Bank are the constituent instruments for these organisations. Article 1 of the Charter provides broad equal rights 'promoting and encouraging respect for human rights and for fundamental freedoms for all without distinction as to race, sex, language, or religion', while Article 8 acknowledges the principle of equality and particular antidiscrimination norms and rules about sex discrimination in employment at the UN.[29]

25 WBAT, *de Merode*, Decision, No. 1 (1981) paras 16–18.
26 UNAT, *Kaplan*, op. cit. n. 24, at para. 3.
27 WBAT, *de Merode*, op. cit. n. 25, at para. 18.
28 *Howrani*, UNAT Judgment, No. 4 (1951) p. 21 para. 1; WBAT, *de Merode*, op. cit. n. 25, at paras 27–28; C.F. Amerasinghe, n. 1, at p. 285–286.
29 UN Charter, *supra* note 13.

2° *Internal rules and policies*

The rules and policies are decisions taken in the exercise of power accorded to the executive branch to conduct the functions and purposes of the organisation.[30] Formally, they are the by-laws that the staff member needs to refer to. In addition, the administration of the organisation, in the exercise of powers derived from the constitution or delegated by the executive organ, establishes staff rules and even some manuals, circulars, notes, and public statements of the organisation are also considered sources of law.[31] Some tribunals have held that the rules need to conform with and not contradict staff policies.[32] As for public statements, there is no clear rule to confirm them as *opinio juris*, or even more critically, a 'codicil' to the contract; in *de Merode*, the tribunal stated that it would determine on a case-by-case basis whether these statements were binding on the staff, based mainly on their consistent practice within the organisation.[33]

3° *Practice of the organisation*

The organisation's own administrative practice is considered an unwritten source of law and may give rise to legal rights or to 'general principles' of international administrative law.[34] There is a strict requirement by the tribunals that the practice of the institution is consistent and not arbitrary because of the conviction that it represents a legal obligation on the part of the organisation towards its staff, as was recognised by the International Court of Justice in its Advisory Opinion on Judgments of the Administrative Tribunal of the International Labour Organization (ILO).[35] In the practice of the organisation, the constant and uniform usage element is critical for rules to be accepted as law.[36]

C. THE RIGHT OF RECOURSE TO AN ADMINISTRATIVE COURT

Court due procedures for resolving disputes between employees and employers are clear. Once a case is brought to court, a public record is produced. Evidence is given under oath and each party can present legal arguments in their own defense and in response to the other. Once these arguments are submitted, a binding decision is made by a judge and can be enforceable. In international

---

30 C.F. Amerasinghe, n. 1, at p. 286.
31 *Ibid.*
32 *Ibid.*
33 P.C. Hansen, loc. cit. n. 19, at p. 6–7.
34 B.D. Patterson, loc. cit. n. 15, at p. 5.
35 WBAT, *de Merode*, op. cit. n. 25, at para. 23; *ICJ Rep.* 1956, p. 91.
36 C.F. Amerasinghe, n. 1, at p. 291 (discussing the 1950 ICJ Reports).

organisations, however, settling employment disputes is a more complex process wherein 90 percent of disputes are resolved through an internal and informal process and 10 percent through an administrative court or tribunal, if the organisation has established or subscribed to one.[37] The internal adjudication process varies between the different organisations.

In the UN, the right of recourse to an administrative court was granted to staff in 1949 after the organisation established an independent court with binding power[38] and the decision was recognised and approved by the ICJ in the *Effect of Awards of Compensation* case.[39] To confirm its independence and impartiality as a court, the Statute of UNAT was not part of the Staff Regulations and was not meant establish it as an advisory organ or subordinate branch of the Assembly. Instead, it was enacted as a distinct instrument by the General Assembly to constitute an independent and truly judicial body capable of making final judgments without appeal and based on a well-established and recognised principle of law in the field of employment relations.[40] The tribunal became qualified to deal with any matter relating to employment relations with present and past UN employees after they had exhausted other means of internal dispute resolution.[41] Similarly the World Bank, being a financial institution carrying out its purposes through financial activities rather than through consultation or policy recommendation, recognised the legal vacuum in which the Bank operated within the US and elsewhere around the globe; and wanting to be independent from political organisations such as the UN, it established WBAT voluntarily in 1980.[42] There is a claim that the Bank also wanted to resolve employment disputes and hold supervisors and officials legally accountable for the decisions they made in managing the Bank's workforce, and therefore accorded its staff the right of recourse to a judicial court.[43]

The tribunal is empowered to 'hear and pass judgment upon any application by which an individual member of the staff alleges non-observance of the contract

37 R.A. Gorman, 'The Development of International Employment Law: My Experience on International Administrative Tribunals at the World Bank and The Asian Development Bank' 25 *Comparative Labor Law & Policy Journal* (2004) p. 428.

38 UN General Assembly, 'Establishment of a United Nations Tribunal', GA/RES 351 A(IV), 24 November 1949, available at www.un.org/ga/search/view_doc.asp?symbol=A/RES/351 (IV)&Lang=E.

39 C.F. Amerasinghe, *Documents on International Administrative Tribunals*, Introduction (Oxford, Clarendon Press 1989).

40 C.F. Amerasinghe, loc. cit. n. 10.

41 United Nations Administrative Tribunal Statute, Art. 2 & 7 (last amendment was on 13 April 2005 by resolution 59/283), available at http://untreaty.un.org/UNAT/Statute.htm.

42 C.F. Amerasinghe, op. cit. n. 39.

43 R.A. Gorman, loc. cit. n. 37, at p. 424.

of employment or terms of appointment of such staff member'.[44] Its decisions are based on sources of law such as staff employment contracts, statutory elements of the relevant organisation and of the specific tribunal, and a somewhat open-ended range of general principles of law.[45] The procedural details regarding the operation of the Bank are contained in the Bank's Articles of Agreement. The 'contract of employment' and 'terms of appointment' are defined under Article II (1) of the Statute to 'include all pertinent regulations and rules in force at the time of alleged non-observance'.[46] Under Article II (2), the Statute imposes two jurisdictional prerequisites: the exhaustion of internal remedies that allow the aggrieved staff member or their representative to present their case first to the Appeals Committee; and if the staff member remains dissatisfied, their submission of an application to the tribunal within 120 days of the final management decision.[47] Under Article II (3), the Statute also imposes an additional limitation. Only an individual complaint may be considered by the tribunal, implying no allowance for collective bargaining or representation by a union or association on behalf of the employee, and that the governing staff rules are usually made unilaterally by the Bank.[48] It is important to note here as well that the jurisprudence developed by WBAT or any other tribunal is a prime source for the general principles of international administrative law with self-limiting power to replace the Bank's decisions with its own.[49] This restriction implies that the decision-making power remains within the internal rules of the organisations.

In summary, these core elements ensure the control and compliance of the governed staff without any checks or clear provisions on how the international organisations are themselves accountable to their staff or the public. In fact, at present there are heated debates on whether administrative tribunals actually meet the standards of an independent and impartial judicial review due to a lack of complete independence from the executive branches of their organisations, the jurisdictions being restricted to the internal laws of the organisation, the nature, qualifications, and duration of judges' tenure, as well as, in some tribunals, a lack of enforcement procedures against the organisations (UNAT).[50] I shall discuss later more of these limitations and their impact.

---

44 World Bank Administrative Tribunal Statute, Art. II (1980), available at http://lnweb90.worldbank.org/crn/wbt/wbtwebsite.nsf/(resultsweb)/42053A8AD4A5300585256AD8004ABA13.
45 WBAT, *de Merode*, op. cit. n. 25, at paras 18–30.
46 World Bank Administrative Tribunal Statute, op. cit. n. 44, Art. II para. 1.
47 *Ibid.*, Art. II para. 2.
48 R.A. Gorman, loc. cit. n. 37, at p. 3.
49 P.C. Hansen, loc. cit. n. 19, at p. 7.
50 Opinions are available at www.ilo.org/public/english/staffun/info/iloat/index.htm.

IV. HOW ARE THE CORE RULES USED AND WHAT IS THEIR IMPACT ON STAFF?

As a public forum for all states' political leaders to debate and advance their concerns, the UN has grown to 14,000 employees this year.[51] The World Bank, which started as a financial organisation promoting economic development, mainly in developing countries, has grown from a few hundred employees in 1940 to 10,000 today with an expanded development agenda.[52] In the CGIAR, the Bank's oldest and largest global public program, with a mandate to harness the best in science to produce more and better food, reduce poverty and sustain the environment, there are almost 8,000 scientists and staff after a similar modest start with a few hundred in 1971.[53] What do these organisations have in common? Amongst a widely varying staff from all walks of life, some are committed and determined to make a difference and some are in for the ride. Over the years, the workplace has expanded with newcomers, contracts implying long-term job security have been initiated, modified, or terminated and most importantly, the hierarchical bureaucracy has been strengthened with a legitimate claim to immunity from suit in national courts. While the introduction of rules and regulations and of informal and formal adjudication processes were helpful in creating the semblance of a justice system, the legal relationship between international organisations and their staff, as we have seen from the previous section, remains broad in equality provisions and unbalanced in accountability enforcement. Moreover, staff in many organisations observed that 'the real guardians of the rules, norms, and values of [these] organisations' seem to apply the rules 'differently when it concerns senior staff or when it concerns junior staff'.[54] In this section, I survey some of the discriminatory practices used internally and discuss their effects on junior and selected staff groups.

A. EFFECT ON JUNIOR STAFF

In 2004, a series of events shook the UN. In the words of the retired head of legal services at the UN, François Loriot, 'never in its history has the credibility and relevance of the UN been so heavily damaged by a series of corruption,

51 United Nations, Human Resources Management, https://jobs.un.org/elearn/production/home.html.

52 World Bank, available at http://web.worldbank.org/WBSITE/EXTERNAL/EXTABOUTUS/0,,contentMDK:20101240~menuPK:1697052~pagePK:51123644~piPK:329829~theSitePK:29708,00.html.

53 CGIAR, available at www.cgiar.org/who/index.html.

54 C. de Cooker, 'Ethics and Accountability in the International Civil Service', in C. de Cooker, ed., *Accountability, Investigation and Due Process in International Organizations* (Boston/Leiden, Martinus Nijhoff Publishers 2005) p. 51.

mismanagement and sexual harassment scandals, reaching the highest levels of authority'.[55] An independent survey carried out throughout the UN system revealed that the staff had no trust in senior UN officials, the UN staff unions protested a lack of compliance by the senior management with its own *Nine Global Compact Principles*, and in 2005, an independent investigation the Oil-for-Food Programme uncovered 'major procurement irregularities, gross negligence in contract administration and misconduct by top UN officials'.[56]

Loriot's report revealed how a skewed legal relationship between international organisations and their staff could destabilise trust in the integrity, objectivity, and impartiality of the governing body and, potentially, introduce new policy tools into the internal laws of international organisations that are based on impunity. While avoiding any public or legal exposure, these tools enforce old discriminatory biases and enable subtle and varied forms of discrimination. At the UN, for example, when impunity at the senior level was used as a policy tool, a discriminatory bias persisted between staff members at various levels of authority and the bias was accepted as a legitimate practice of the organisation.[57] The more discretion a staff member possessed, the more options were available for them 'to turn around the situation, manipulate the evidence and get off the hook'.[58]

In the UNAT case *Levy*, the tribunal found Mr. Levy, a 16-year-old staff member, negligent in maintaining inaccurate and misleading records. When he claimed that he was following strict orders from his supervisors, the tribunal still found him guilty for his failure to ask his supervisors for written instructions and to document his reservations. Is this a practice that staff will need to adhere to? The tribunal was aware that 'should staff members in such situations record their views or ask for written instructions, they would do so at their hazard; the climate in the organisation is not hospitable to such behavior and a staff member who would overtly challenge a supervisor in this manner would suffer the consequences. In this regard, the Standards of Conduct call for a level of independence, professionalism and courage that is, unfortunately, at present, more apt to be punished than rewarded.'[59] Recognising the substantive harm of certain practices for the staff within the workplace, the tribunal did not address the legitimacy of impunity over the promotion of good administration of justice at international organisations and owing to his serious misconduct and violations

---

55 F. Loriot, 'Accountability at the United Nations – in Need of a Genuine External Enforcement Body', in C. de Cooker, ed., *Accountability, Investigation and Due Process In International Organizations* (Boston/Leiden, Martinus Nijhoff Publishers 2005) p. 66.

56 *Ibid.*

57 *Ibid.*, p. 67.

58 *Ibid.*, p. 68.

59 UNAT, *Levy*, Judgment, No. 1034 (2002).

of United Nations Development Program policies, Mr. Levy was, rightly so, dismissed. According to Loriot, however, none of his supervisors were approached. Indeed, the case raises arguments about the presumed legality of the instructions received from supervisors and about the obligations of international organisations to provide claimants with 'reasonable alternative means to protect effectively their rights'.[60]

Whom should the staff trust in a hostile workplace environment that prevents people from expressing reservations or from reporting supervisors' improper acts?[61]

The potential and substantive harm to the individual, financial and emotional, caused by a lack of procedural guarantees of due process and by abuse of power can be even more pronounced. In January 1997, a Washington Post article reported that Mr. Bangoura, a staff member fighting drug traffic operations in Africa, embezzled UN funds and committed sexual harassment of a female colleague in Africa.[62] Within four days, the Secretary General issued a statement to the press indicating that such misconduct would not be tolerated and that the employee would be severed from service. In April 1997, Mr. Bangoura filed an appeal with the Joint Appeals Board claiming his innocence.[63] In July 1998, the Board recognised the improper use of discretion, the arbitrary decisions, and the denial of due process for the appellant by the office of the Secretary General and submitted its recommendations to the Secretary General's Office; however, it took another seven months (to February 1999) for the Secretary General to decide on the Board's report by rejecting a public apology to Mr. Bangoura and paying him compensation of only $20,000.[64] By that time, Mr. Bangoura had not only been without a job for almost two years, but was also a refugee and with a ruined reputation. In late February 1999, he filed an appeal with UNAT and eventually, almost five years after the 1997 event, he was granted judgment: the tribunal endorsed the Appeal Board findings of a major breach of due process by the administration and a violation of the rule of presumption of innocence.[65] Although the tribunal awarded him two years' base salary (the maximum under the tribunal's Statute), Mr. Bangoura has incurred a loss of five years' employment and a psychological burden for the rest of his life. Unfortunately, such an experience also discourages staff from seeking remedies from judicial courts in

60 ECtHR, *Waite and Kennedy v. Germany*, Application No. 26083/94, 30 *EHRR* (1999) p. 13.
61 F. Loriot, loc. cit. n. 55, at p. 70 (discussing current bottlenecks in the internal justice system within the UN).
62 *Ibid.*, p. 71.
63 *Ibid.*, p. 72.
64 *Ibid.*
65 *Ibid.*

their employment disputes and legitimises alternative practices based on power play among staff.

B. EFFECT ON SELECTED GROUPS OF STAFF

Recently, the office of the World Bank president and its established Department of Institutional Integrity (INT) were implicated in breaching established due process procedures and confidentiality, conflicting imperatives, and biases towards US nationals for higher ranking positions and remuneration of INT staff.[66] The report by the Government Accountability Project (GAP) is available online (www.whistleblower.org) and discusses these events in more detail. For the purpose of this contribution I will focus on the CGIAR, which is a US-based enterprise and which, although lacking a legal personality, the World Bank's sponsorship and provision of the chairmanship give an international legitimacy.[67] The CGIAR and its 15 centers provide a clear example on how a central, tightly-knit and power-based governance structure can nurture and sustain discriminatory biases in the workplace.

Until recently, the CGIAR had no charter or constitution, by-laws, or written rules of procedure and relied on informal procedural guidelines.[68] The World Bank has been the largest donor in the CGIAR system and contributes to its management and the research programs of its individual centres.[69] The internal structure of the system remains fragile due to 1) a funding situation that is ad hoc (voluntary donations rather than entitlements)[70] and restrictive (donors tie their funding to their own research, personnel, or institution), 2) consensus-based decision-making (or no decision-making because of the wide constituency of member States, private sector actors, and NGOs) that leaves the Chairperson, the World Bank vice-president, with the ultimate responsibility to 'declare and articulate' a consensus position, 3) the fragmentation of and competition for

66 B. Edwards and T. Morrison, 'Review of the Department on Institution Integrity at the World Bank (Government Accountability Project, Washington D.C., 5 & 6 September 2007)', available at www.whistleblower.org/doc/2007/INT%20review%209.05.07.pdf pp. 3–5 (based on interviews with World Bank staff, the report reveals management patterns for the abuse of authority within the INT department of the World Bank).

67 C. Farrar, 'The Consultative Group For International Agricultural Research – Case study for the UN Vision Project on Global Public Policy Networks' (1999), p. 5, available at *www.gppi.net/general/indexed_search/*. For an example of a specific agreement, see http://untreaty.un.org/unts/60001_120000/21/14/00040655.pdf.

68 J.R. Anderson and D.G. Dalrymple, 'The World Bank, the Grant Program, and the CGIAR: A Retrospective Review', p. 3 (World Bank Operations Evaluation Department, Working Paper Series No 1, 1999), available at www.worldbank.org/html/cgiar/publications/cgiaroed.pdf.

69 *Ibid.*

70 *Ibid.*, p. 62.

resources amongst the 15 centres it manages, and 4) its perceived political bias.[71] The fragility of the system's structure impacts on employment relations in individual centres at various levels. Owing to the restricted and project-based funding, individual centres undergo various hiring and retrenchment cycles at all levels but substantively at the level of junior employees. Short-term instead of long-term contracts are the norm, and to ensure the continuity and flexibility of research programs, substantive resources remain consolidated under the discretion of the senior managers of individual centres.

Each of the individual 15 centres is autonomous, possesses a legal personality based on their functions and purposes, and is self-governed by a board of trustees.[72] Eleven out of the 15 centres are located in developing countries where strong class, gender, and race differences intersect in employment relationships. The centres have internationally and nationally recruited staff. Whereas rules and policies for nationally and internationally recruited staff may vary between individual centres, employment relations with nationally recruited staff are generally covered by national employment laws or as agreed upon in individual treaties signed between the centre and the host state.[73] The rights and obligations of the staff are subject to the specific terms of the treaties. Such agreements may also guarantee that the governance of the employment relations with internationally recruited staff is solely the responsibility of the organisation and that its internal laws are subject to the accorded immunities and privileges of international organisations.[74] None of the individual centres has its own administrative tribunal to settle employment disputes with its staff; however, some centres subscribe to the ILO's administrative tribunal.[75]

Under the current system and in practice, the only available remedy for employment disputes for internationally recruited staff at the centres is an informal internal Appeals Committee.[76] While staff rules and regulations

---

71 World Bank Independent Evaluation Group, The CGIAR at 31: Celebrating Its Achievements, Facing Its Challenges 4 (World Bank Operations Evaluation Department, Précis number 232, 2003), available at www.worldbank.org/oed/cgiar/.

72 World Bank Independent Evaluation Group, The CGIAR at 31: An Independent Meta-Evaluation of the Consultative Group on International Agricultural Research 31 (World Bank Operations Evaluation Department, Volume 1: Overview Report, 2003), available at www.worldbank.org/oed/cgiar/.

73 Colombia and International Center for Tropical Agriculture, Agreement on the Headquarters of the International Centre for Tropical Agriculture (CIAT), signed on 5 May 1987 and registered by Colombia on 20 October 1988, No. 2649, Art. 4.9.b.

74 *Ibid.*, Art. 4.9.a.

75 Italian Court of Cassation, *Drago A. v. International Plant Genetic Resources Institute (IPGRI)*, No. 3718 (unpublished), 19 February 2007, *ILDC* 827 para. H4 (IT 2007) (on file with author).

76 International Institute of Tropical Agriculture, Personnel Policy Manual for Internationally Recruited Staff (IITA, November 2004), available at http://intranet.iita.org/resources/IRS%20policy%20manual.pdf.

guarantee the right of the staff to bring their grievances to a committee, they are silent on the procedural guarantees for 'fair treatment'. As Amerasinghe has pointed out, the Appeals Committee does not rely on judicial processes and the decisions taken are not based on legal rules or principles.[77] Members of the international staff then often have no explicit recourse to judicial procedures. Considering the stressful dynamics of these workplaces, the constant movement of senior executives between states, the pressure to deliver, the ambition and prejudices of senior managers, and their discretionary power privileges, arbitrary procedures and hasty decisions are not uncommon and discriminatory biases, intentional or unintentional, are often encountered among internal groups and between groups.[78]

Nationally recruited staff account for 85% of the workforce (6,800) in a wide range of employment categories, covering mainly the basic managerial and technical services needed for the day-to-day operation of the organisation.[79] At least until recently, almost all internationally recruited staff held higher positions than nationally recruited staff and were better paid due to their international status and granted privileges and immunity. Beside the highly visible and strained differences between the two categories of staff, gender is salient in these organisations. Because of the gender performative character and its parallelism to the performative and discursive nature of race as well, individuals act according to certain prescribed notions of what it means to be a 'man' or a 'woman', reflecting norms of behaviour in the external society.[80] Similar to the stereotypes and inflexible racial labelling of a sustained white supremacy, rules of conduct, implicit and explicit, and other organisational enforcement mechanisms regulate gender performance and ensure conformity with mainstream norms.[81] Surveys conducted at these centers confirm that 73% of the staff members in the CGIAR are male and all key senior positions are still male-dominated, whereas women's positions dominate the secretarial, administrative, and scientific support services.[82] Half of the internationally recruited women in

---

77 C.F. Amerasinghe, op. cit. n. 1, at pp. 489–494.

78 G. Debebe and The Center for Gender in Organizations, Inspiring Transformation... Lessons from the CGIAR Women's Leadership Series 9–11 (The Gender and Diversity Program of the Consultative Group on International Agricultural Research, Working Paper 47, 2007), available at www.genderdiversity.cgiar.org/publications/WorkingPaper47.pdf.

79 CGIAR, Review of Total Structures for Nationally Recruited Staff 2 (Summary of Results for Phase 3 of the CGIAR Review of Total Compensation, 2003), available at www.cgiar.org/who/structure/executive/exco9/PDF/exco9_comp_study_phase3.pdf.

80 J. Bond, International Intersectionality: A Theoretical and Pragmatic Exploration of Women's International Human Rights Violations', 52 *Emory Law Journal* (2003) p. 71, at p. 98.

81 *Ibid.*

82 G. Jayasinghe and B. Moore, 'First the Good News...Staffing in the CGIAR 2003' (The Gender and Diversity Program of the Consultative Group on International Agricultural Research, Working Paper 40, 2003), available at www.genderdiversity.cgiar.org/resource/default.asp, para. 5.

senior positions leave the institute within 3–5 years of their employment[83] and the latest figure on women's participation in centre management shows that only 9% are actively involved.[84] Moreover, on a closer scrutiny of this figure women's role is more one of support rather than of real decision-making.[85]

With the availability of only broad provisions for 'fair treatment' and a closed internal administrative structure, Vicki Schultz, a Ford Foundation Professor of Law and the Social Sciences at Yale Law School, offers some insights into the dynamics that occur internally within traditional male-dominated workplaces (such the CGIAR). When women are denied the information, training, and assignments necessary to succeed, they can easily appear (or actually become) less than fully proficient at their jobs. This then becomes the justification that makes their firing or other differential treatment look gender-neutral. 'She got fired because she wasn't performing', or, 'we didn't give her the good assignments because she couldn't handle them' is usually the justification, when the truth is that harassment and discrimination prevented her successful performance.'[86] Similarly, in the absence of accountability standards within an organisation many staff would leave voluntarily and the few stubborn ones who try to resist are eased out by careful planning, an established paper trail documenting their alleged incompetence, and the semblance of 'fair' treatment dismissal procedures.[87] The male domination of the workplace can then be reinforced and the traditional gender segregation reassured for more years to come. As also suggested in the UNAT judgment *Levy*, a repressive and vicious workplace environment, which is based on power rather than rules of law, may lead to coercive internal relationships among staff.

---

83 *Ibid.*, para. 7. See also E. Rathgeber, 'Female and Male CGIAR Scientists in Comparative Perspective' (The Gender and Diversity Program of the Consultative Group on International Agricultural Research, Working Paper 37, 2002), pp. 11–52, available at www.genderdiversity.cgiar.org/publications/genderdiversity_WP37.pdf.

84 G. Jayasinghe and B. Moore, loc. cit. n. 82, at para. 5.5.

85 N. Allen, 'Executive Selection in the CGIAR: Implications for Gender and Diversity' (The Gender and Diversity Program of the Consultative Group on International Agricultural Research, Working Paper 30, 2001) p. 4, available at www.genderdiversity.cgiar.org/publications/genderdiversity_WP30.pdf.

86 V. Schultz, 'Understanding Sexual Harassment Law in Action: What Has Gone Wrong and What Can Be Done About It', 29 *Thomas Jefferson Law Review* (2006) p. 119, available at www.law.yale.edu/documents/pdf/Faculty/SchultzUnderstandingSexualHarassmentLawinAction.pdf.

87 G. Jayasinghe and B. Moore, loc. cit. n. 82, at paras 7.11–7.23 (discussing voluntary departures and some of their causes with the unknown reason being a dominant cause). E. Rathgeber, loc. cit. n. 83, at p. 58 (discussing short contracts for women and their implications).

V. WHAT CORE ELEMENTS ARE NEEDED TO REALISE EQUALITY?

Schultz argues that a hostile workplace environment does as much harm as sexual discrimination and contributes to or even sustains a discriminatory workplace wherein employees are always constrained by their sex, race, religion, or national origin to do their work.[88] The subtlety of these discriminatory practices, the lack of explicit policies for nonsexual forms of discrimination, and the tightly knit secretive management structure make it very difficult to legally challenge or even prove the discriminatory act. If, however, in this section we reject the claim that international organisations, as political players, are expanding only their executive power, and presume instead that they have a quest to realise equality amongst their staff and to establish a rules- rather than power-based governance structure, then the premise entails the question as to the nature of the discrepancies that exist in the internal laws and how these can be changed.

A. THE UNILATERAL RIGHT OF THE ORGANISATION TO AMEND STATUTORY ELEMENTS

Amerasinghe clarifies that although statutory elements are not part of the contract of employment, they may govern the employment relationship, and therefore 'the power to alter the terms of conditions of employment' may be different in the two employment relations (contractual relation only or contractual and statutory relation).[89] Based on the view that the legal position is generally recognised by most international organisations, one can argue here that the position (the right to use various statutory elements in the conditions of employment) may extract any basis of equality between the employer, in this case the organisation, and the employee and diminish the latter's ability to bargain with the management. In other words, the relationship between an individual and the organisation extends beyond just a contractual agreement between two equal parties (private contract law) to a relationship that is dependent on written and unwritten sources of law within the specific boundaries of the internal structure of one of the parties, the employer. This *de facto* inequality of bargaining power for staff members in a workplace wherein 90% of the employment disputes are settled internally and without recourse to a judicial court has an implicit or explicit impact on the power relationships between and among various staff groups at different levels of authority.

---

88 V. Schultz, loc. cit. n. 86, at p. 119.

89 C.F. Amerasinghe, op. cit. n. 1, at p. 282.

B. AMBIGUOUS AND UNCLEAR BROAD PROVISIONS OF ANTI-DISCRIMINATION LAWS

Broad constitutional provisions and general principles remain the primary protections against employment discrimination in international organisations.[90] Apart from referring to 'the general principles of law', tribunals have not considered specific claims that rely on international human rights conventions or other conventions.[91] Some contend that human rights conventions are persuasive law but non-binding,[92] including Article 26 of the International Covenant on Civil and Political Rights (1966),[93] Article 2 of the Universal Declaration of Human Rights,[94] and Article 14 of the European Convention on Human Rights.[95] Because broad pronouncements leave many procedural and substantive aspects of discrimination law unaddressed, one may question why international organisations have not developed a comprehensive legislation governing claims of employment discrimination, such as Title VII of the U.S. Civil Rights Act of 1964. Was it a strategy intended to maintain discriminatory practices internally? In international organisations, discriminatory acts in all their forms, both sexual and nonsexual, are, unfortunately, still perceived as individual pathological behaviour based on a sexual content in the workplace, rather than about sexism. The position of women in these organisations, for example, allows many forms of sex-based discrimination, as briefly described above. Women can also face discrimination from supervisors because they are not sufficiently docile and compliant or bullying because they are too vulnerable. The discriminatory practice could be simple interpersonal hostility, a 'ganging up' on a co-worker, or emotional abuse. The subtlety of these actions is part of the normal day-to-day operation of the workplace and it is very difficult to challenge them legally unless there are strict scrutiny from tribunals and enforceable procedural standards.[96] Employing widely varying nationalities and working at geographically dispersed and sometimes isolated locations around the world, international organisations cannot afford a culture with permissive discriminatory norms.

---

90 B.D. Patterson, loc. cit. n. 15, at p. 4.

91 P.C. Hansen, loc. cit. n. 19, pp. 7–8 n. 21 and 24–27 (discussing *Agodo*, WBAT Decision, No. 76, (1989) and *Sharpston*, WBAT Decision, No. 251 (2001).

92 B.D. Patterson, loc. cit. n. 15, at p. 5.

93 International Covenant on Civil and Political Rights, Art. 26, UNGA Res. 2200A(XXI), UN GAOR, Supp. No. 16, UN Doc. A/6316 (16 December 1966), 999 UNTS 171, entered into force 23 March 1976, available at www1.umn.edu/humanrts/instree/b3ccpr.htm.

94 Universal Declaration of Human Rights, Art. 2, UNGA Res. 217A (III), UN GAOR, Supp. No. 16, UN Doc. A/810 (10 December 1948) available at www.un.org/Overview/rights.html.

95 European Convention on Human Rights and Fundamental Freedoms, Art. 14 (Rome, 4 November 1950). Text completed by Protocol No. 2 (ETS No. 44) of 6 May 1963 and amended by Protocol No. 3 (ETS No. 45) of 6 May 1963, Protocol No. 5 (ETS No. 55) of 20 January 1966 and Protocol No. 8 (ETS No. 118) of 19 March 1985) available at www.pfc.org.uk/node/328.

96 *Ibid.*, pp. 449–450.

VI. INFORMAL REMEDIES AND ADMINISTRATIVE COURTS

Staff members of the UN and the World Bank are obligated under the organisation's constitutive instruments to exhaust the available informal and internal remedies before accessing a judicial or quasi-judicial administrative court.[97] While these procedures may represent an informal, inexpensive, and expeditious mechanism for resolving disputes according to the organisation's best interests and avoid any major adverse exposure, they need to meet some general legal principles for judicial hearings.[98] An internal appeals committee, which, under its own rules, is not entitled to make a judgment but may simply provide advice to the head of the organisation, cannot be regarded as an adequate alternative remedial mechanism. Based on the broad principles of fair treatment and due process, there are many drawbacks. The partiality of an internal committee can be represented by a simple conflict of interest in 1) its membership, which may include persons directly involved in the complaint (or their representatives), persons within the organisation but who are not competent in the subject matter, or others who cannot voice their true opinions due to internal pressures and/or fear for their own careers, and 2) its purpose, which is simply to provide advice to the executives based on the organisation's administrative perspective. Such shortcomings not only deny equality in the international workplace but also sustain an administrative perspective that uses a variety of strategies, orthodox and unorthodox, to achieve its goals. An internal committee that lacks independent or external review processes conducts its own investigation of the issues raised by a complainant and decides for itself on the basis of its own findings, without any accountability or transparency, whether an interim order should be made.

Based on the early experiences of the UN and the failure of these informal remedies to resolve employment disputes, the UN established UNAT in 1949.[99] In 1980, President Robert McNamara voluntarily established WBAT, mainly 'to bring the rule of law to the Bank's internal operations, to regulate the behaviour of management so as to assure fair treatment of staff members, and as a result to enhance the morale of the staff and to make the Bank a desirable and efficient place to work'.[100] While it is a mainstream belief that administrative courts are entrusted with the duty of administering justice in employment relations and that their judgments are *res judicata* and binding on both the individual

97 UNAT Statute, op. cit. n. 41, Art. 2 & 7; World Bank Administrative Tribunal Statute, op. cit. n. 44, Art. II (1980).
98 A. Reinisch und U.A. Weber, loc. cit. n. 6, at p. 101.
99 C.F. Amerasinghe, loc. cit. n. 10, at p. 2.
100 R.A. Gorman, loc. cit. n. 37, at p. 2.

complainant and the organisation, the procedural guarantees of the impartiality and independence of the court are not yet in place[101] nor, as a matter of fact, are they available for the informal dispute settlement mechanisms.[102] Article 3 of UNAT's Statute implies a strong link with the executive branch of the administration and with the provision of Article 10; one could argue that the enforcement of a tribunal's decision rests not with the tribunal but with the Secretary General, who 'in the interests of the UN' will approve the final decision.[103] The ICJ confirmed a deficiency in the enforcement procedures for UNAT judgments.[104] As a matter of principle, there is a conflict of interest. In addition, nowhere in the Statute is there an explicit and established line of authority to the Secretary General and the executive branch of management.[105] If a tribunal's jurisprudence is limited to the internal laws of the organisation and one administrative tribunal is not bound to follow the same approach taken by another tribunal, let alone the final decision of another tribunal,[106] the consistency and uniformity of equality rules will not develop into rules of law. It is reasonable then to claim that the tribunals exist merely as a veneer that expands rather than restricts the power-based governance structure at international organisations.

A. ACCOUNTABILITY STANDARDS AND THEIR ENFORCEMENT

When analyzing questions of accountability and ethics in international organisations, Chris de Cooker observed that they operate in response mode. Very few organisations initiate their own codes of conduct without any apparent internal or external pressure and the codes are often a reaction to particular incidents.[107] In doing so, the organisations tend to develop and introduce these codes without prior genuine role models or engaging with staff on such principles as efficiency, transparency and accountability. Because the codes are based on international legal standards, which may be in conflict with the local norms and laws of certain staff groups, they may require a legal framework to render them obligatory standards and principles of behaviour for all the staff concerned.[108] Unfortunately, studies have shown a lack in the consistency and uniformity of usage of codes as legal documents at international organisations. For example,

101 C.F. Amerasinghe, loc. cit. n. 10, at p. 2.
102 *Ibid.*
103 UNAT Statute, op. cit. n. 41, Art. 3 & 10.1.
104 C.F. Amerasinghe, loc. cit. n. 10, at p. 3.
105 J. Klabbers, 'The Bustani Case before the ILOAT: Constitutionalism in Disguise?', 53 *The International and Comparative Law Quarterly* (2004) p. 458.
106 B.D. Patterson, loc. cit. n. 15, at p. 6.
107 C. de Cooker, loc. cit. n. 54, at p. 5.
108 *Ibid.*, pp. 20–21.

the following code reflects the basic anti-gender discrimination rules of public administration. 'I will not engage in or tolerate any form of harassment in the workplace, including sexual harassment and abuse of power. As a manager/supervisor, I will not solicit favours, loans or gifts from staff, nor will I accept unsolicited ones that are more than token value. I recognise that there is an inherent conflict of interest and potential abuse of power in having sexual relations with staff under my supervision. Should I find myself in such a relationship, I will resolve this conflict of interest without delay.'[109] The senior management of the UN High Commissioner for Refugees and their staff signed it, however, it remains no more than a moral code without any binding effect.

B. CAN THESE LEGAL DISCREPANCIES BE CHALLENGED AND CHANGED?

In 1999, the internal justice system or the conflict resolution system, as referred to in the World Bank, was changed and expanded into five distinct components: the Office of Ombudsman, the Mediation Office, the Office of Ethics and Business Conduct, the Appeals Committee, and WBAT. For further information I refer the reader to a recent article detailing the due process rights of staff at the Bank.[110] I focus here on the UN's reform of its justice system since it is the most recent and is still being debated.

In 2006, pursuant to UN resolution 59/283,[111] a panel of external and independent experts was established to review and possibly redesign the system of administration of justice at the UN. To demonstrate accountability and transparency in the review, the panel's findings were reported during the 61st session of the General Assembly.[112] The panel found that the internal administration of justice 'fails to meet many basic standards of due process established in international human rights instruments'.[113] Moreover, the panel found that '[n]either the Joint Appeals Board (JAB) nor the Joint Disciplinary Committee (JDC), the main bodies in which the formal processes of the internal justice system are initiated, has power to take binding decisions. They can only make recommendations and thus cannot determine the rights or obligations of the persons concerned. This leaves UNAT as a one-tier justice system with no right of appeal. At the same time, JAB and JDC are composed of staff members

---

109 *Ibid.*

110 H. Dean, loc. cit. n. 7, p. 98 at para. 4.

111 UN General Assembly, Res. 59/283, para. IV, UN Doc. A/RES/59/583, 2 June 2005.

112 UN General Assembly, 'Report of the Redesign Panel on the United Nations system of administration of justice', A/61/205, (2006), available at www.un.org/ga/president/62/issues/resolutions/a-61-205.pdf.

113 *Ibid.*, para. 5.

acting in an advisory capacity to the Secretary-General and, thus, do not meet the basic standards required to guarantee their independence. That the administration of justice in the United Nations lags so far behind international human rights standards is a matter of urgent concern requiring immediate, adequate and effective remedial action.'[114] The panel went on to propose 'a new, decentralised, independent and streamlined system by strengthening the informal system of internal justice, by providing for a strong mediation mechanism in the Office of the Ombudsman and by merging the offices of the Ombudsman of the United Nations and its funds and programmes; by establishing a new, formal system of justice that replaces advisory boards with a professional and decentralised first-instance adjudicatory body that issues binding decisions that either party can appeal to UNAT; and by guaranteeing "equality of arms", thus ensuring for all staff members access to professionalised and decentralised legal representation.'[115]

In February and April 2008, the General Assembly, through resolution 62/228 and the report of the Secretary General 62/782, reaffirmed its previous decisions and established a revised framework for a new internal justice system that is to be implemented by January 2009.[116] Reviewing the various comments received from the UN Staff Union[117] and the Bar Association for International Governmental Organisations,[118] it seems that the work of translating the promises into reality at the UN is going to be a hard and long journey.

VII. PERSONAL VIEW

In this contribution, I examined how workplace equality is understood, applied, and valued through the practice of international organisations, mainly the UN and the World Bank. It appears that administrative courts have invoked many general principles of equality that share a similar moral character; however, their application lacks consistency and uniformity and thus cannot be interpreted as implying specific provisions. They are, therefore, of limited value when it comes to defining the law applicable to disputes between the staff of international

114 *Ibid.*, para. 11.

115 *Ibid.*, para. 14.

116 UN General Assembly, Resolution 62/228, para. III.B, UN Doc. A/RES/62/228, 6 February 2008; UN Secretary-General, 'Report on Administration of Justice', UN Doc. A/62/782, 3 April 2008, chapter VII.

117 United Nations Staff Union Staff Council, *Preliminary Proposals on the Internal Justice System* (New York, 5 June 2008) available at www.whistleblower.org/doc/StaffCouncilAOJproposal.pdf, p. 1 para. 2.

118 Bar Association For International Governmental Organizations. Petition to the UN Member States and to the 5th & 6th Committee Members on UNSG Report A/62/782 Relating to the Draft Statute of the United Nations Dispute Tribunal (8 May 2008).

organisations and the organisations themselves. Mapping the power structure in the employment relationship and reviewing the practice of the international organisations revealed a skewed governance structure that has a deep and disparate effect on the individual rights of staff, mainly junior and minority staff groups. All legislative, executive, and judicial powers are controlled by one hand without appropriate checks in the system. As one of the US founding fathers wrote, '[i]n framing a government which is to be administered by men over men, the great difficulty lies in this: you must first enable the government to control the governed; and in the next place oblige it to control itself'.[119]

Whereas one can argue that international organisations have managed to orchestrate enough balances in the internal laws controlling their staff, they have failed to put in place checks to control their executives. At this juncture in time, when international organisations are under public pressure to improve their accountability and transparency mechanisms, when they are being challenged and even denied immunity in national courts because they lack adequate internal mechanisms for addressing complaints or assuring procedural guarantees of 'due process',[120] it is in their best interests to redesign and implement effective equality-based rules and to examine rules-based governance structures. The legal entitlement to bind staff with unclear statutory elements during their employment, the entitlement to maintain broad provisions for discrimination without detailed and clear procedural guarantees for due process, the ability to process 90 percent of employment complaints through informal and internal mechanisms that do not adhere to any judicial procedures, and last but not least the ability to avoid enforcement of accountability standards on executives, have and will continue to have a disparate impact on staff, allow arbitrary decisions, and perpetuate discriminatory practices that are difficult to prove or challenge legally.

I fear that simply establishing more bureaucratic internal justice structures without first creating and enforcing internal norms based on social justice may well prove to be yet another failed attempt to realise our ideals of equality and of fostering peace, development, and prosperity in diverse societies.

---

119 A. Hamilton or J. Madison, 'The Structure of the Government Must Furnish the Proper Checks and Balances between the Different Departments', Federalist No 51, *New York Packet, February 8, 1788* available at www.foundingfathers.info/federalistpapers/fedindex.htm.

120 Brussels Labour Court of Appeal (4th chamber), *Siedler v. Western European Union*, 17 September 2003.

AN INTERNATIONAL ORGANISATION'S POINT OF VIEW

Edward Kwakwa*

I. INTRODUCTION

This contribution presents an international organisation's point of view regarding the theme of 'Accountability for Human Rights Violations by International Organisations'. I will suggest that human rights *are* important to international organisations.

However, some preliminary caveats are called for before further proceeding. First, not all international organisations are the same. They vary due to differing mandates, visions and activities. Secondly, my contribution is informed by my experience as Legal Counsel at my international organisation in particular. Such particular experience does not necessarily equate with or reflect the experience of other Legal Counsels from other international organisations. Thirdly, I will be concentrating on the human rights obligations of international organisations *vis-à-vis* their staff members. In doing so, I will certainly avoid specific international organisations such as the IBRD, WTO and the UN in respect of peacekeeping, as they are all topics for separate contributions by other authors.

This contribution is also based on some assumptions. Namely, accountability has several different aspects, including financial, legal, political and administrative. In discussing accountability, I should make clear that I am not referring to liability. Nor am I referring to responsibility. In this sense, accountability ought to be distinguished from legal liability under domestic law, and international responsibility under general international law.

---

* Legal Counsel, World Intellectual Property Organization (WIPO), Geneva; Extraordinary Professor of Law, Centre for Human Rights, University of Pretoria, South Africa. This is a written form of a speech delivered in the Plenary Session at the International Conference on Accountability for Human Rights Violations by International Organisations, Brussels, 16–17 March 2007. The views expressed are those of the author, and do not necessarily reflect the views of WIPO or the United Nations.

II. HUMAN RIGHTS OBLIGATIONS OF INTERNATIONAL ORGANISATIONS

Key questions to keep in mind during our analysis are: what are international organisations accountable for and to whom are they accountable? A fundamental question against this background: how can an international organisation be bound, for example, by treaties to which it is not a party? Does an international organisation have any obligations to non-staff members? I only raise these questions without intending to answer them, in the hope that someone else will adequately address them within this book.

It is common knowledge that under traditional approaches to human rights, non-state actors were deemed to be beyond the direct reach of international human rights law. They were not capable of being parties to relevant treaties, so they were only bound to the extent obligations accepted by States could be applied to international organisations by Governments. In short, international organisations were generally considered not to be bound directly by human rights law.

As more public functions were placed into the hands of international organisations, it became clear that the traditional paradigms needed revising. Some degree of accountability on the part of international organisations was thus needed. I would suggest that this is a good development for various reasons. First, accountability of international organisations is not new. It is in fact inherent in the whole nature of international organisations and has become even more so as the scope of activity of international organisations has grown dramatically. Secondly, the issue of human rights is central to good governance. It is a key performance indicator for international organisations. As a result, international organisations now find strength in their human rights records. Thirdly, international organisations suffer the consequences of ignoring this vital part of public international law. The likelihood that compliance will be recognised and rewarded acts as an incentive for international organisations to ensure that their human rights records are laudable.

The promotion of human rights is now of common concern at least in UN system organisations. A few examples that demonstrate this point: the World Bank's mission is the alleviation of poverty. This includes the fulfilment of basic human needs for nutrition, safe water, education, health and housing, amongst others. So the work of the Bank is at the core of human rights.[1]

---

1 See, e.g., R. Dañino, 'The Legal Aspects of the World Bank's Work on Human Rights: Some Preliminary Thoughts', in The World Bank, *The World Bank Legal Review: Law, Equity and Development*, vol. 2 (The Hague, Martinus Nijhoff Publishers 2006) pp. 295–324; R. Dañino,

The Food and Agriculture Organization of the United Nations' (FAO) involvement in making sure people have regular access to enough high-quality food to lead active, healthy lives is grounded in human rights.[2] The International Labour Organization (ILO) is devoted to reducing poverty, achieving fair globalisation and advancing opportunities for women and men to obtain decent and productive work in conditions of freedom, equity, security and human dignity.[3] The United Nations Educational, Scientific and Cultural Organization (UNESCO) has a constitutional mandate to contribute to the promotion of human rights through, among others, its programs on multilingualism and cultural diversity.[4] The World Health Organization's (WHO) constitution in 1946 (that is, two years before the venerable Universal Declaration of Human Rights), declared that the highest attainable standard of health is a human right.[5] And this does not even take into account the Organization which I am affiliated with, WIPO.[6]

In effect, each international organisation plays a role or delivers a public good, and thus lays the groundwork for the realisation of human rights.

'The Legal Aspects of the World Bank's Work on Human Rights', 41 (1) *The International Lawyer* (2007) pp. 21–25 (arguing his personal conviction that 'work in this area is a moral imperative and also because of [his] sense that human rights are progressively becoming an explicit and integral part of the World Bank's work.'); D. Kinley, 'Human Rights and the World Bank: Practice, Politics, and Law', in The World Bank, *The World Bank Legal Review: Law, Equity and Development*, vol. 2 (The Hague, Martinus Nijhoff 2006) (article discussing the place of human rights in the strategic thinking and operational practices of the World Bank).

2 The right to food guidelines and other areas of FAO's work are also in the human rights arena. On the mandate, activities and structure and finance of FAO, see generally *www.fao.org/UNFAO/about/mandate_en.html.*

3 See generally, *www.ilo.org.*

4 See generally *www.unesco.org.*

5 See generally *www.who.int.*

6 WIPO can also claim to be engaged in several activities that affect human rights. It is recalled that the principle of national treatment in intellectual property (IP) and trade is anchored on the principle of non-discrimination. Even the Universal Declaration of Human Rights (UDHR) makes reference to IP rights. Article 27 of the UDHR states that everyone has the right to freely participate in the cultural life of the community, to enjoy the arts and to share in scientific advancement and its benefits; everyone has the right to the protection of the moral and material interests resulting from any scientific, literary or artistic production of which he is the author. Article 51 of the International Covenant on Economic, Social & Cultural Rights stipulates that everyone has the right to benefit from the protection of the moral and material interests resulting from any scientific, literary or artistic protection of which he is the author. See generally E. Kwakwa, 'Intellectual Property Law Comes of Age as a Human Rights Concept', *Africa Legal Aid Quarterly* (Jan-Mar 2000) pp. 5–11.

III. HUMAN RIGHTS OBLIGATIONS OF INTERNATIONAL ORGANISATIONS *VIS-À-VIS* THEIR STAFF MEMBERS

What, then, is the situation as it exists today? International organisations enjoy on the territory of their Member States, in conformity with the laws of those States, such legal capacity as may be necessary for the fulfilment of their objectives and for the exercise of their functions. As a consequence, international organisations are generally immune from legal or judicial process in domestic legal systems. Attributing privileges and immunities to international organisations is an essential means of ensuring the proper functioning of such organisations. But the corollary to immunity of international organisations is that, as affirmed by the International Court of Justice in the *Cumaraswamy* Advisory Opinion[7], they are responsible for their actions under international law, which includes the duty to compensate in cases of violations. This was in effect affirmed by the ICJ in relation to the United Nations Administrative Tribunal (UNAT). As the United Nations enjoyed immunity before national courts, it would be incompatible with the purposes of that Organisation, especially with the aim to 'promote freedom and justice for individuals', if it provided no alternative forum for deciding on disputes between the organisation and its staff. International civil servants are deprived of the right of access to domestic employment law guaranteed to other workers. They must therefore be afforded comparable rights by international organisation administrative and other tribunals if unjust discrimination is to be avoided. Individuals should have access to a remedy, in case of a breach of their human rights.

The situation today is that means *do* exist for staff with grievances. Most international organisations in fact have internal administrative boards ("Internal Appeal Boards") to which staff members can first make an appeal. Prior to making that appeal, staff members normally are allowed to make a direct appeal to the executive head of the international organisation asking him or her to review an administrative decision which, in the staff member's view, fails to observe their terms of appointment or the provisions of the staff regulations. If the staff member is satisfied with the response or reaction of the executive head, that should normally be the end of the story. If, however, the staff member is not satisfied with the response of the executive head, they can then appeal internally

---

7 ICJ, *Difference Relating to Immunity from Legal Process of a Special Rapporteur of the Commission on Human Rights*, Advisory Opinion, *ICJ Rep.* (1999) p. 62. The ICJ also affirmed in the *WHO/Egypt Opinion* of 1980 that 'International Organisations are subjects of international law and, as such, are bound by any obligations incumbent upon them under general rules of international law, under their constitutions or under international agreements to which they are parties.' ICJ, *Interpretation of the Agreement of 25 March 1991 between the WHO and Egypt*, Advisory Opinion, *ICJ Rep.* (1980) pp. 89–90.

to what is normally referred to as an Internal Appeal Board.[8] The procedures from this stage on are almost uniform in all international organisations. The staff member writes a Brief setting out their arguments and the relief sought; the Administration of the international organisation then responds with a Reply Brief, which in turn elicits a Rejoinder from the staff member, followed by a Surrejoinder by the Administration. The Internal Appeal Board then issues its recommendations which are addressed to the executive head. This is the equivalent of the exhaustion of local remedies in public international law.

The decision of the Internal Appeal Board, it should be stressed, is merely advisory or recommendatory in character. It is not automatically binding.

If the staff member is not satisfied with the decision or recommendation of the Internal Appeal Board or with the response of the executive head to the recommendation, they can then appeal as a final step to an administrative tribunal.

Certain guarantees are provided from a human rights perspective. In general, international organisations either recognise the jurisdiction of existing administrative tribunals or establish their own.[9] Those tribunals organise and function under conditions that guarantee their independence. It is important to mention, for example, that a staff member is entitled to the assistance of any person whom he or she may choose. Staff members also have the right (often exercised in practice), to have the time limits within which they can file briefs or rejoinders extended. While oral hearings are hardly ever provided, the Statutes of most international organisation Tribunals provide for oral hearings.[10]

---

8 The Internal Appeal Board is an important body within the scheme of the administration of justice in international organisations. Although it is not necessarily a judicial or legal body, it performs important functions and, in effect, settles or prevents some 60% of cases from escalating to the higher-level administrative tribunals. Internal Appeal Boards are also cheaper for staff, who often resort to them without lawyers.

9 Some 44 international organisations (including most of the specialised agencies of the UN system) recognise the jurisdiction of, and use the International Labour Organization Administrative Tribunal (ILOAT) as an administrative tribunal to which appeals can be made, and some 11 (including the UN itself, as well as UNDP, UNICEF and UNHCR) recognise the jurisdiction of, and use the United Nations Administrative Tribunal (UNAT). For details on the United Nations' new system of administration of justice which became operational on 1 July 2009, see generally www.un.org/en/oaj/unjs. Other organisations, such as the World Bank and the IMF, have their own stand-alone administrative tribunals.

10 Article V of the Statute of the ILOAT provides that '[t]he Tribunal shall decide in each case whether the oral proceedings before it or any part of them shall be public or *in camera*', and Article 12 of the Rules of the ILOAT states, *inter alia*, that the ILOAT shall determine the conduct of any hearings, and hearings shall include 'oral submissions by the parties and may, with leave from the Tribunal, include oral testimony by any witness.'

Under the procedures of the ILOAT, Article 13.1 of the Rules allows anyone to intervene in a complaint on the grounds that a ruling by the Tribunal may affect them.

There is a clear set of applicable law: the Staff Regulations and Staff Rules of the organisation; the contractual terms of appointment; and general principles of law.[11]

The composition of the Internal Appeal Boards also guarantees some, though not all, rights to staff members. For example, the Chairman of the WIPO Appeal Board is appointed by the Director General of WIPO. But the staff regulations and staff rules of WIPO provide that the Chairman must be 'designated by the Coordination Committee [an executive Committee of Member States], on a proposal made by the Director General after consultation of the Staff Council, from among persons having experience in international staff matters, who is not a staff member, or former staff member,' of WIPO. Thus, the Director General can only appoint the Chairman of the Internal Appeal Board in consultation with the Staff Council of WIPO, the representatives of all staff members. And finally, the Director General's choice of Chairman of the Appeal Board *must* be approved by the Member States of WIPO. The other members of the Appeal Board are member designated by the Director General – a member elected by all the staff members – as well as a secretary of the Board, who has no vote or no participation in the deliberations of the Board. Surely the aforementioned body does not get much more independent than this?

It is trite knowledge that Internal Appeal Board decisions are advisory or recommendatory, not judicially binding. But where the executive head does not accept the recommendations of the Board, he or she must provide reasons.[12] The

11 ILOAT case law takes into account general principles of law, such as the principle of estoppel, the principle of unjust enrichment, and the principle of equality of treatment. To be sure, several ILO cases specifically mention human rights. See, e.g., ILOAT, 31 January 1994, Judgment No. 1333 (1994) (EPO) ('The law that the Tribunal applies in entertaining claims that are put to it includes not just the written rules of the defendant organisation but the general principles of law and basic human rights'); ILOAT, 4 April 2004, Judgment No. 2292 (2004) (EPO)('In fact, the EPO as such is not a member of the Council of Europe and is not bound by the Convention (European Convention on Human Rights) in the same way as signatory states. Nevertheless, the general principles enshrined in the Convention, particularly the principles of non-discrimination and the protection of property rights, are part of human rights, which, as declared by both the President of the Office and its Administrative Council in 1994, in compliance with the Tribunal's case law, apply to relations with staff'); ILOAT, 2 February 2005, Judgment No. 2391 (2005) (ITU), at paragraph 6 ('consistent principle has it (see Judgment 1445, under 7) that there cannot be breach of equal treatment unless there is different treatment of officials who are in like position in fact and in law').

12 A long line of ILOAT cases has established this principle. See, eg., ILOAT, 14 July 2004, Judgment No. 2355 (2004) (EPO) (appeal in respect of the European Patent Organisation

executive head is in fact required by the staff regulations and staff rules to give full consideration to the advisory opinion of the Internal Appeal Board when taking his or her decision on cases where an appeal has been made.

It is also recalled that in addition to Internal Appeal Boards, there are several other administrative means and mechanisms used by international organisations to enhance the human rights of their staff members. These include formal as well as less formal mechanisms, such as mediation, grievance panels, Ombudsman offices and the like.[13]

Most international organisations also have what is referred to as a Joint Advisory Committee (JAC).[14] Such committees have staff representation, and disciplinary sanctions normally can be given to staff members only after consultation with such joint consultative bodies. The JAC is composed of the Director General's representative, plus two staff representatives and a secretary to the JAC.

Certain critics allege, in the specific area of staff disputes, that there are too many loopholes that result in denying the human rights obligations of international organisations where their staff members are concerned. I will briefly respond to some of these allegations.

(EPO), in which the ILOAT held that the EPO had 'failed to show that the President [of the EPO] had any valid reason for rejecting the recommendations of the Appeals Committee [the internal appeal board of the EPO], which had heard the witnesses and made specific findings of fact', and that an international organisation had the obligation 'to give reasons when the executive head decides not to follow the recommendation of its internal appeal body.' See also ILOAT Judgment No. 2391, op. cit. n. 11 (appeal in respect of the International Telecommunication Union (ITU), in which the ILOAT held that 'the Secretary-General [of the ITU] did not follow the recommendation of the Appeal Board [the internal appeal board], which had precisely indicated that the disputed decision 'appear[ed] to breach the principle of proportionality in the application of disciplinary sanctions'. He was therefore under an obligation to state the reasons why he was disregarding that recommendation and instead maintaining the initial sanction, which is the second most serious, particularly so as to enable the Tribunal to check whether the principle of proportionality had been observed … As the Secretary-General has not satisfied that obligation, his decision of 6 November 2003 must be set aside on the grounds that no reason has been given for the chosen sanction and the case must be referred back to him for a new decision').

13 The World Bank Inspection Panel, for example, was established in 1993 to increase the accountability of World Bank lending and to respond to private individuals who believe their interests could be harmed by World Bank financed projects. For a description of the historical, legal and operational procedures of the World Bank Inspection Panel, see generally G. Alfredson and R. Ring, eds., *The Inspection Panel of the World Bank; A Different Complaints Procedure* (The Hague, Martinus Nijhoff Publishers 2001).

14 Under the WIPO Staff Regulations and Staff Rules for example, there is a Joint Advisory Committee that advises the Director General on principles of personnel administration and general questions of staff welfare or any administrative matter which he or she may refer to it, and has the competence to submit to the Director General proposals for such amendments as it may wish to have made to the Staff Regulations or Staff Rules.

First, it is alleged that the staff member or complainant who brings a case against the Administration does not know the names of judges who will decide a case until the judgment is announced, thus denying the staff member the right to object in advance to any real or perceived appearance of bias or conflict of interest. I would say this is nothing exceptional. It is recalled that even in domestic systems, complainants do not get to choose their own judges.

Secondly, it is alleged that judges are appointed or reappointed at the sole discretion of international organisations. This is not true. To use the ILOAT as an example, judges are appointed by the ILO Conference (of Member States), even if on the recommendation of the Director General. There is no direct input by Complainants, and nor is there by Respondents (i.e. the international organisations). UNAT judges are also appointed by the UN General Assembly (on the proposal of countries from which the judges originate).

Thirdly, it is alleged that staff members are deprived of fundamental legal guarantees because there are no oral hearings. But it is no doubt the same disadvantage for an international organisation. The fact that the ILOAT, for example, may not have had any oral hearings in the last decade or so does not by any means imply that staff members are thus deprived of certain fundamental human rights. The ILOAT relies, without further investigations, on facts as established by Internal Appeal Boards. Human rights treaties require a "fair and public hearing" for disputes concerning civil obligations. The adversary system, as we know, presupposes that oral testimony and argument can transform or critically affect the judicial approach to both facts and law. This is not a universally accepted presupposition. Oral hearings can, in any case, have a positive or a negative outcome for staff members. In factoring in the need for such oral hearings, considerations to keep in mind include the associated costs for such hearings, the likely impact of the hearings,[15] and indeed the need for the hearings at all, considering that the Internal Appeal Board would likely have had its own oral hearings anyway. Under these circumstances, the decision by administrative tribunals to hold oral hearings only in the most compelling of circumstances would seem to be a very reasonable one.

Fourthly, it is alleged that there must be some avenue of appeal, and that the present system where there is no further right of appeal after the Tribunal's decision denies staff members the inherent right of appeal which is needed for an effective judicial mechanism. To this criticism, I respond that there is no

15 There have been several instances in which staff members have been known to ask for oral hearings which would require mandatory attendance by executive heads and other members of senior management, even in situations where such high officials did not need to appear for such hearings.

guarantee that yet another layer of appeal would produce any other results. The ILOAT and other administrative tribunals are already an appellate jurisdiction in the sense that, taking into account the different internal review procedures, their decisions mark the third and final hearing of an individual case. If yet another level of jurisdiction were to be introduced, there would be a risk of unreasonably delaying the judicial settlement of staff disputes. The desirability in principle of an appellate mechanism would seem to be outweighed by the need to avoid additional delays and increasing costs that any such mechanism would entail. Another level of appeal would not *a priori* constitute an improvement. It would simply add another instance to an already lengthy process, further delaying the settlement of staff disputes. Attention should perhaps be focused on improving the quality, reasoning and consistency of the administrative tribunals' case law.

Finally, it is recalled that a number of domestic, mostly European cases have held that courts are not obliged to give effect to privileges and immunities of international organisations unless the international organisations provide impartial and effective alternative dispute settlement mechanisms. In effect, that the privileges and immunities of international organisations will not be given effect unless the requirement of Article 6(1) of the European Convention on Human Rights to guarantee a 'right to a fair and public hearing' is met. The European Court of Human Rights has thus actually confirmed the privileges and immunities of international organisations while noting the need to ensure that the international organisations are not above the law.[16]

For the sake of completeness, it is recalled that international organisations also have complaints about the administration of justice and the extent to which international organisations are sometimes exploited by staff members under the pretext of seeking human rights. For example, international organisations sometimes ask the ILOAT to award nominal costs against complainants for wasting the time, energy and resources of the international organisation, and for pursuing a frivolous claim against the international organisation. And yet, as far as can be recalled, the ILOAT has never acceded to this request, although it is abundantly clear that staff members sometimes bring frivolous complaints deliberately. The fact that complaints against international organisations are always virtually free of charge for the staff members, and the absence of the risk of financial sanctions evidently tends to encourage unfounded, or even vexatious

16 *See* A. Reinisch, 'Waite and Kennedy v. Germany, and Beer and Regan v. Germany, European Court of Human Rights', 93 (4) *American Journal of International Law* (1999) pp. 933–938. The case law of the European Court of Human Rights makes clear that international organisations have to provide "reasonable alternative means" in order to enjoy immunity. The alternative means should provide staff members with the same or similar guarantees as those embodied in the European Convention on Human Rights.

and often frivolous complaints. The frequent frivolous and repetitive complaints to the ILOAT and other administrative tribunals absorb the international organisations' resources, and impede the ability of the international organisations to deal more appropriately and expeditiously with the many meritorious complaints which are brought by other staff members. More importantly, the costs and waste of time in the international organisations that have to respond to such meritless claims are substantial. At a minimum, it might be a good idea if administrative tribunals could consider imposing cost penalties in the most exceptional situations where it is called for. The dissuasive and chilling effects of possible adverse award of costs could go a long way in curbing the tendency of bringing frivolous complaints.

IV. CONCLUSION

It should be recognised that international organisations have indeed come a long way in terms of their respect for the human rights of staff members.[17] The human rights obligations of international organisations also continue to be on the radar screen of the world community. For example, the International Law Commission is currently discussing the issue in the context of its agenda item on the responsibility of international organisations.[18] Furthermore, the compilation of this book is also a testimony to the attention being paid to the subject.

---

17 Noteworthy and recent examples include, for example, the fact that most international organisations now grant recognition and entitlements to the same sex partners of staff members. In respect of international organisation behaviour in other areas, standard arbitration clauses are inserted in all commercial contracts and purchase agreements between international organisations and private parties. This is done by the international organisations as a way of meeting their obligations and avoiding the criticism that international organisations hide behind their privileges and immunities. This is also in line with the requirements of the 1946 Convention on the Privileges and Immunities of the United Nations and the 1947 Convention on the Privileges and Immunities of the Specialised Agencies, both of which provide an obligation for the international organisations to make provision for appropriate modes of settlement of disputes arising out of contracts or other disputes of a private character to which the international organisation is a party. In addition, in respect of their privileges and immunities, it is trite knowledge that those privileges and immunities are provided not for the personal benefit and convenience of officials of the international organisation *per se*, but in order to ensure the freedom of action of the international organisation and the complete independence of its agents. In that respect, the international organisation's executive head normally has the right and indeed the duty to waive the immunity of any official (or of the organisation itself) when he or she considers that such immunity is hindering the normal course of justice, and that it is possible to take such action without prejudicing the interests of the international organisation.

18 As matters stand at present, see International Law Commission, *Report of the Sixty-first session (4 May to 5 June and 6 July to 7 August 2009)*, UN Doc. A/64/10, chapter IV, paras. 31–51.

LIST OF CONTRIBUTORS

Chittharanjan Felix Amerasinghe

Chittharanjan Felix Amerasinghe has been Judge of the UN Administrative Tribunal, Registrar at the World Bank Administrative Tribunal and Full Professor of Law, University of Ceylon, Sri Lanka. He holds the degrees of Bachelor of Arts, Bachelor of Laws, Ph.D. and is Doctor of Laws of the University of Cambridge. He also holds an LL.M. from Harvard.

Peter R. Baehr

Peter R. Baehr has been Professor of International Relations at the University of Amsterdam and Professor of Human Rights at the Universities of Leiden and Utrecht. He has served as Executive Secretary (later member) of the Scientific Council for Government Policy (WRR), The Hague, and as Director of the Netherlands Institute of Human Rights (SIM), Utrecht.

Niels M. Blokker

Niels M. Blokker holds a Ph.D. from Leiden University, where he has been Lecturer since 1984 and subsequently Senior Lecturer on Law of International Organisations. In 2003, he was appointed Professor of International Institutional Law (Schermers Chair). He is also Deputy Head of the International Law division at the Netherlands Ministry of Foreign Affairs. His research concentrates on the law of international organisations.

Eva Brems

Professor Eva Brems is at Ghent University since October 2000. She holds an LL.M. from Harvard (1995) and a Ph.D. in Law from the University of Leuven (1999) with a dissertation on *Human Rights: Universality and Diversity* (Nijhoff, 2001). She is author of numerous publications on human rights and a member of the editorial board of several law journals.

Gauthier de Beco

Gauthier de Beco holds an LL.M. from the University of Nottingham and a Ph.D. in Law from the University of Louvain. He is author of several publications, including *Non-Judicial Mechanisms for the Implementation of Human Rights in European States* (Bruylant, 2010). He is currently working as Legal Adviser at the Human Rights Unit of the Belgian Ministry of Justice.

Eric De Brabandere
Eric De Brabandere is Lecturer in international law at Leiden University and Visiting Professor at the Université Catholique de Lille. He holds an LL.M. from the University of Geneva and a Ph.D. from Ghent University. His areas of expertise include dispute settlement, arbitration, general international law, human rights and the law of peace and security.

Olivier De Schutter
Olivier De Schutter is Professor at the University of Louvain and at the College of Europe, Natolin, member of the Global Law School, New York University, and Visiting Professor at Columbia University. He is the UN Special Rapporteur on the right to food since May 2008. Between 2002 and 2007, he was coordinator of the EU network of independent experts on fundamental rights.

Ige F. Dekker
Ige F. Dekker is Professor of International Institutional Law at Utrecht University. His research focuses on constitutional aspects of the law in relation to international and European organisations, the law in relation to international financial and economic organisations, the theory of international law and the relationship between national and international law.

Jeroen Denkers
Jeroen Denkers completed his Ph.D. at Tilburg University, The Netherlands, published as *The World Trade Organization and Import Bans in Response to Violations of Fundamental Labour Rights* (Intersentia, 2008). He now works as a Legal Adviser at the Legislation Department of the Dutch Ministry of Justice.

Ulf Häußler
Ulf Häußler is Assistant Legal Advisor Operational Law, NATO ACT, Norfolk/VA, USA. He acted as Legal Advisor in the German Armed Forces and was Legal Advisor in SFOR in Bosnia and Herzegovina and in KFOR. He worked as Research Fellow and Lecturer in international, constitutional and administrative law at the Universities of Regensburg, Würzburg and Konstanz.

Sarah Hunt
Sarah Hunt is Solicitor of the Supreme Court of New South Wales and member of the Register of Foreign Attorneys in Geneva. She worked at Schwab, Flaherty, Hassberger and Crausaz, where she co-founded the CAIO with Edward Flaherty. Since 2007 she has specialised in international trade, shipping and contract disputes at Davies, Johnson and Company SA.

Remzije Istrefi

Remzije Istrefi holds an LL.M. from the University of Notre Dame and a Ph.D. in international human rights law and international organisations from the University of Prishtina, Kosovo, where she is Lecturer at the Department of Political Science. She worked as Human Rights Advisor with the OSCE Mission in Kosovo and as consultant for international and national institutions.

Nicola Jägers

Nicola Jägers is Associate Professor at the Department of European and International Law, Tilburg University, The Netherlands. She holds a master's degree both in history and law and obtained her Ph.D. at the Netherlands Institute of Human Rights (SIM) in 2002. Her dissertation was published as *Corporate Human Rights Obligations: In Search of Accountability* (Intersentia, 2002). Her research interests mainly concern corporate responsibility and the position of NGOs in international (human rights) law.

Christine Janssens

Christine Janssens is Ph.D. candidate at the Faculty of Law and Criminology of Vrije Universiteit Brussels, where she works in the context of the inter-university research project on accountability for human rights violations by international organisations conducted by Prof. Jan Wouters, Prof. Eva Brems and Prof. Stefaan Smis and funded by the Flemish Research Fund (FWO). She is also a member of the Centre of International Law and of the research group Fundamental Rights and Constitutionalism (FRC).

Osmat Azzam Jefferson

Osmat Azzam Jefferson is a chief scientist at Cambia, a non-profit organisation and a Professor of Science, Technology, and Law at Queensland University of Technology. She obtained her Ph.D. from Cornell University. She worked in USAID sponsored projects with Puerto Rico, the Dominican Republic, and University of Wisconsin-Madison and at International Agricultural Centers in the Philippines and Syria. In 2008, Dr. Jefferson was qualified with a Masters in International Law from the Australian University in Canberra, Australia.

Stephen Sevidzem Kingah

Stephen Sevidzem Kingah graduated from the Vrije Universiteit Brussels in October 2008. He holds a Ph.D. on "Access to Affordable HIV/AIDS Medicines in the Southern African Development Community (SADC): Coherence of EC Rules and Policies" and works as a Researcher at the Institute for European Studies of the Vrije Universiteit Brussels.

Edward Kwakwa
Edward Kwakwa is Legal Counsel at the World Intellectual Property Organization (WIPO), is Visiting Professor of Law at the Graduate Institute of International and Development Studies in Geneva and Extraordinary Professor of Law at the Centre for Human Rights of the University of Pretoria. He holds an LL.B. degree from the University of Ghana, an LL.M. from Queen's University in Canada and an LL.M. and J.S.D. from Yale University.

Gjylbehare Bella Murati
Gjylbehare Bella Murati is Ph.D. candidate at Ghent University, where she works in the context of the inter-university research project on accountability for human rights violations by international organisations conducted by Prof. Jan Wouters, Prof. Eva Brems and Prof. Stefaan Smis and funded by the Flemish Research Fund (FWO). She holds an LL.M. degree in international human rights law from the University of Essex. She worked for the International Committee of the Red Cross and the Ombudsperson in Kosovo, and was legal consultant to various international organisations.

Frederik Naert
Frederik Naert is a member of the Legal Service of the Council of the EU and associate fellow of the Leuven Centre for Global Governance Studies and visiting lecturer at the Institute for International Law, University of Leuven. He completed his Ph.D. at the University of Leuven, published as *International Law Aspects of the EU's Security and Defence Policy, with a Particular Focus on the Law of Armed Conflict and Human Rights* (Intersentia, 2009).

Rekha Oleschak-Pillai
Rekha Oleschak-Pillai is Senior Research Fellow at the Institute of Federalism of the University of Fribourg.

Kristin Bergtora Sandvik
Kristin Bergtora Sandvik is Senior Researcher at the Peace Research Institute Oslo (PRIO). She holds an S.J.D. from Harvard Law School. She has published legal and ethnographic work on humanitarianism, refugee studies, women's rights and international institutions. Her work currently focuses on human security, international law and the expanding role of international humanitarian organisations in the "global emergency zone".

Pierre Schmitt
Pierre Schmitt is Research Fellow at the Institute for International Law and the Leuven Centre for Global Governance Studies at the University of Leuven, where he works in the context of the inter-university research project on accountability for human rights violations by international organisations conducted by Prof.

Jan Wouters, Prof. Eva Brems and Prof. Stefaan Smis and funded by the Flemish Research Fund (FWO). He obtained an LL.M. in International and Comparative Law from the Vrije Universiteit Brussels in 2005, worked as Attorney at the Bar of Liège and as Assistant at the University of Liège.

Stefaan Smis
Stefaan Smis is Professor of International Law at the Vrije Universiteit Brussels, Belgium, Reader at the School of Law of the University of Westminster and Guest Lecturer at Ghent University and at the Catholic University of Bukavu, Democratic Republic of Congo. He holds a Ph.D. in international human rights law from the VUB, is member of the ILA Committee on the rights of indigenous peoples and regularly publishes articles and book contributions in the domain of international and human rights law.

Matteo Tondini
Matteo Tondini currently works as Post-Doctoral Researcher at the Vrije Universiteit Amsterdam, Faculty of Social Sciences, Department of Governance Studies. He has been military legal officer (IT Navy) and project advisor to the Italian Development Cooperation Office in Kabul, Afghanistan. He is an associate member of the San Remo International Institute of Humanitarian Law.

Ralph Wilde
Ralph Wilde has been a member of the Law Faculty at University College London, University of London, since July 2002. He is also an Adjunct Professor at Georgetown University Law Center. He was formerly Supervisor in International Law at Trinity, Corpus Christi and St. Edmund's Colleges, Cambridge, Guest Lecturer at Cambridge University's Faculty of Law and the Henry Fellow and Visiting Scholar at Yale Law School.

Jan Wouters
Jan Wouters is Professor of International Law and International Organisations, Jean Monnet Chair *Ad Personam* 'EU and Global Governance' and Director of the Leuven Centre for Global Governance Studies and Institute for International Law at the University of Leuven, Belgium. He is Visiting Professor at the College of Europe, President of the Flemish Foreign Affairs Council and *Of Counsel* at Linklaters. He holds an LL.M. from Yale University, a Ph.D. from the University of Leuven and was Visiting Researcher at Harvard Law School.

TABLE OF CASES

I. INTERNATIONAL JURISDICTIONS

European Court of Justice

European Court of Human Rights

Inter-American Commission on Human Rights

Inter-American Court of Human Rights

International Court of Justice

International Criminal Tribunal for the Former Yugoslavia

International Labour Organization Administrative Tribunal

North Atlantic Treaty Organization Appeals Board

Organization for Economic Co-operation and Development Appeals Board

United Nations Administrative Tribunal

Italy

South Africa

Switzerland

The Netherlands

United Kingdom

United States

INDEX

E

F

G

H

I

V

W

Y

www.ingramcontent.com/pod-product-compliance
Ingram Content Group UK Ltd.
Pitfield, Milton Keynes, MK11 3LW, UK
UKHW051917100926
8556IPUK00021B/1231

9 781780 68066

ACCOUNTABILITY FOR HUMAN RIGHTS VIOLATIONS BY INTERNATIONAL ORGANISATIONS